165-572-6

D0138775

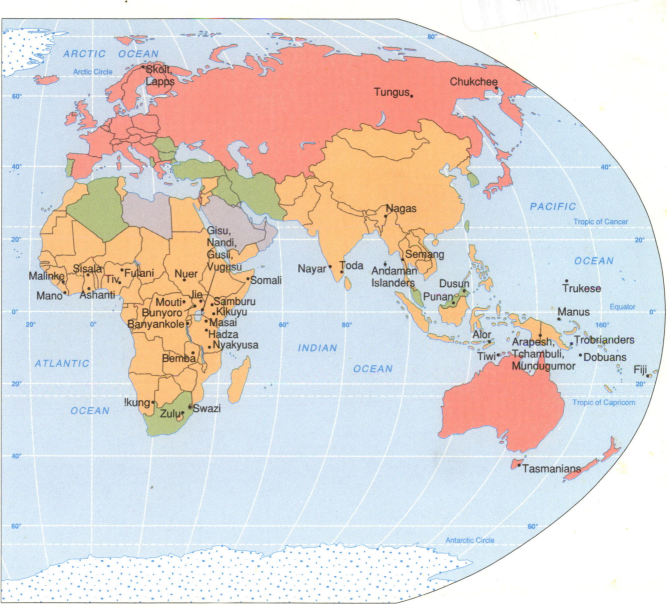

ARCTIC OCEAN

Arctic Circle

Skolt,
Lapps

Chukchee

Tungus

60°

80°

40°

60°

PACIFIC

Tropic of Cancer

40°

20°

Nagas

OCEAN

20°

Gisu,
Nandi,
Gusii,
Vugusu

Semang

Malinke

Sisala

Nuer

Nayar   Toda

Andaman
Islanders

Dusun

Trukese

Fulani

Tiv

Punan

Equator

Mano

Ashanti

Somali

Manus

20°

0°

Mouti

Jie

Samburu

Alor

Arapesh,

Trobrianders

160°

Bunyoro

Kikuyu

Tiwi

Tchambuli,

Dobuans

Banyankole

Masai

INDIAN

Mundugumor

Fiji

Hadza

20°

Bemba

Nyakyusa

OCEAN

ATLANTIC

!kung

Zulu   Swazi

Tropic of Capricorn

OCEAN

20°

40°

Tasmanians

60°

60°

Antarctic Circle

# Anthropology

## AN APPLIED PERSPECTIVE

# Anthropology

## AN APPLIED PERSPECTIVE

### Gary Ferraro

THE UNIVERSITY OF
NORTH CAROLINA
AT CHARLOTTE

### Wenda Trevathan

NEW MEXICO
STATE
UNIVERSITY

### Janet Levy

THE UNIVERSITY OF
NORTH CAROLINA
AT CHARLOTTE

**WEST PUBLISHING COMPANY**

Minneapolis/St. Paul

New York

Los Angeles

San Francisco

Copyedit:            Julie Bach
Composition:         G & S Typesetters, Inc.
Cover Image:         Robert Estall photographs
                     © Angela Fisher & Carol Beckwith
Index:               E. Virginia Hobbs
Text Design:         K. M. Weber
Front Endsheets:     Adapted by permission from pages 12–13 of
                     *World Regional Geography: A Global Approach*
                     by George F. Hepner and Jesse O. McKee.
                     Copyright © 1992 by West Publishing Company.
                     All rights reserved.

**West's Commitment to the Environment**

In 1906, West Publishing Company began recycling materials left over from the production of books. This began a tradition of efficient and responsible use of resources. Today, up to 95 percent of our legal books and 70 percent of our college and school texts are printed on recycled, acid-free stock. West also recycles nearly 22 million pounds of scrap paper annually—the equivalent of 181,717 trees. Since the 1960s, West has devised ways to capture and recycle waste inks, solvents, oils, and vapors created in the printing process. We also recycle plastics of all kinds, wood, glass, corrugated cardboard, and batteries, and have eliminated the use of Styrofoam book packaging. We at West are proud of the longevity and the scope of our commitment to the environment.

Production, Prepress, Printing and Binding
by West Publishing Company.

Copyright © 1994 by WEST PUBLISHING COMPANY
610 Opperman Drive
P. O. Box 64526
St. Paul, MN 55164-0526

All rights reserved.

Printed in the United States of America

01  00  99  98  97  96  95  94  8  7  6  5  4  3  2  1  0

**Library of Congress Cataloging-in-Publication Data**

Ferraro, Gary
    Anthropology : an applied perspective / Gary Ferraro, Wenda
Trevathan, Janet Levy.
        p.    cm.
    Includes bibliographical references and index.
    ISBN 0-314-02879-X (alk. paper)
    1. Ethnology.   2. Applied anthropology.   I. Trevathan,
Wenda.   II. Levy, Janet.   III. Title.
[GN316.F46   1994]
306—dc20                                             93-23619
                                                     CIP

◆ ◆ ◆       PHOTO CREDITS       ◆ ◆ ◆

## Chapter 1

1 © Joe Viesti/Viesti Associates; 5 © Karen Kasmauski/Woodfin Camp and Associates, Inc.; 5 Gary Ferraro; 6 UPI/Bettmann; 8 Mike Mazzaschi/Stock Boston; 9 Crosier Fathers and Brothers, Minneapolis, MN; 12 © Eva Momatiuk and John Eastcott, 1978/Woodfin Camp and Associates, Inc.; 14 © Mike Maple, All Rights Reserved/Woodfin Camp and Associates, Inc.

## Chapter 2

17 Kamal Sahai from *Crafts of Jammu, Kashmir, and Ladakh* published by Grantha Corporation, 80 Cliffedgeway, Middletown, NJ 07701, USA in association with Mapin Publishing Pvt. Ltd., Ahmedabad. Copyright © Grantha Corporation; 18 left Patrice Flesch/Stock Boston, right Irven DeVore/Anthro-Photo File #0011; 19 Zefa/H. Armstrong Roberts; 21 Gary Ferraro; 22 © P. de Wilde/Viesti and Associates; 23 John Coletti/Stock Boston; 25 H. Armstrong Roberts; 27 top H. Armstrong Roberts, bottom H. Armstrong Roberts; 30 Robert Caputo/Stock Boston

## Chapter 3

35 © Blumebild/H. Armstrong Roberts; 37 Greg Laden/Anthro-Photo; 38 Owen Franken/Stock Boston; 40 Comstock, Inc.; 41 © Brown Brothers; 43 Gary Ferraro; 44 John Elk/Stock Boston; 45 Daemmrich/Stock Boston; 48 David Austen/Stock Boston

## Chapter 4

57 Gary Ferraro; 59 Bettmann; 60 Bettmann; 60 Precision Graphics, Inc; 61 Reprinted by permission from p. 95 of *Introduction to Physical Anthropology* 5/e by Harry Nelson and Robert Jurmain. © 1991 West Publishing Company. All Rights Reserved; 66 © William H. Allen, Jr.; 68 © M. W. Tweedie/Photo Researchers, Inc; 70 Precision Graphics, Inc.

## Chapter 5

75 © Tom McHugh/Photo Researchers, Inc.; 77 Bettmann; 78 Reprinted by permission from p. 211 of *Introduction to Physical Anthropology* 5/e by Harry Nelson and Robert Jurmain. © 1991 West Publishing Company. All Rights Reserved; 79 Reprinted by permission from p. 211 of *Introduction to Physical Anthropology* 5/e by Harry Nelson and Robert Jurmain. © 1991 West Publishing Company. All Rights Reserved; 80 Reprinted by permission from p. 211 of *Introduction to Physical Anthropology* 5/e by Harry Nelson and Robert Jurmain. © 1991 West Publishing Company. All Rights Reserved; 81 Precision Graphics, Inc.; 82 © M. Loup/Jacana/Photo Researchers, Inc.; 82 © J. P. Ferrero/Jacana/Photo Researchers, Inc.; 83 After Napier, J. R. and A. C. Walker. 1967 Vertical Clinging and Leaping. *Folia Primatologica* 6:204–219, and Napier, J. R. and P. H. Napier. 1985 *The Natural History of Primates.* Cambridge: The MIT Press/Precision Graphics, Inc.; 83 left © Ron Austing/Photo Researchers, Inc., right © Tom McHugh/Photo Researchers, Inc.; 84 S. R. Maglione/Photo Researchers, Inc.; 84 © Tom McHugh/Photo Researchers, Inc.; 85 left © Tom McHugh/Photo Researchers, Inc., right Wenda Trevathan; 85 After Fleagle, J. G. 1977 Brachiation and Biomechanics: The Siamang as an Example. Malay Nature Journal 30:45–51. and Napier, J. R. and P. H. Napier, 1985 *The Natural History of Primates.* Cambridge: The MIT Press/Precision Graphics, Inc.; 88 top Steve Ferrari/Anthro-Photo, bottom © Edmund Appel/Photo Researchers, Inc.; 89 top © S. Cordier/Jacana/Photo Researchers, Inc., bottom © Ranka Sekulic/Anthro-Photo; 90 top Wenda Trevathan, bottom Irv Devore/Anthro-Photo; 93 Irv Devore/Anthro-Photo; 95 Richard Wrangam/Anthro-Photo; 96 After Goodall, J. 1986 *The Chimpanzees of Gombe.* The Belknap Press of Harvard University Press/Precision Graphics, Inc.

continues following Index

# About the Authors

**Gary Ferraro**

has been a professor of anthropology at UNC-Charlotte since 1971. He received his BA from Hamilton College and his MA and Ph.D. from Syracuse University. With primary research interests in African kinship and marriage systems, he has conducted research in Kenya and Swaziland and has served as a consultant for USAID, the Peace Corps, and the World Bank. He has been a Fulbright scholar at the University of Swaziland and has taught with the University of Pittsburgh's Semester at Sea Program. He is the author of *The Two Worlds of Kamau* (1978), *The Cultural Dimension of International Business* (1990 and 1994), *Cultural Anthropology: An Applied Perspective* (1992) and a number of journal articles.

**Wenda Trevathan**

is a biological anthropologist whose major research interests are human birth, sexuality, and reproductive behavior. In addition to a Ph.D. in anthropology from the University of Colorado, Wenda has also received midwifery training which enabled her to pursue research on childbirth. She is the 1990 recipient of the Margaret Mead Award, presented jointly by the American Anthropological Association and the Society for Applied Anthropology. In addition to this text, Wenda is the author of *Human Birth: An Evolutionary Perspective* and a textbook on physical anthropology, co-authored with A. J. Kelso. She is currently an Associate Professor of Anthropology at New Mexico State University.

**Janet Levy**

received an A.B. in anthropology from Brown University and a Ph.D. in anthropology from Washington University. She has taught anthropology and archaeology at UNC-Charlotte for fourteen years and has been a visiting professor at the University of Leeds, England, and at the University of Oregon.

Dr. Levy has conducted archaeological research in both western Europe and North America, and is interested in prehistoric social and religious systems. She is currently working on an excavation of an archaeological site related to the historic Catawba Indian Nation in South Carolina. She is also interested in ethics in anthropology and has served as the chairperson of the Committee on Ethics of the American Anthropological Association.

# Brief Contents

# Contents

# Preface

Most undergraduates enter college having studied humans in a chronological or historical perspective. In high school they study some ancient history, a fair amount of European history, perhaps some non-Western history, and a lot of U.S. history. The study of anthropology as presented in this text provides college students with different ways of viewing the human condition. It provides a much deeper time frame than the past several thousand years by looking at human biological and cultural development over the past several *million* years. Moreover, university undergraduates are often curious to learn how people from different cultural settings use different solutions to solve universal human problems. Recognizing this curiosity—and building upon it—this text provides students with a readable and comprehensive introduction to how humans have developed, both biologically and culturally, over time and how the many contemporary cultures of the world compare with one another.

This text is designed to reflect and reinforce the holistic and integrated nature of the discipline of anthropology. Since the turn of the century, anthropology has taken a four-field approach to the study of humans. Since its beginnings as an academic discipline, anthropology has included the subfields of cultural anthropology, physical anthropology, archaeology, and anthropological linguistics. Although like other disciplines anthropology has become increasingly specialized in recent years, it has never abandoned its four-field approach. Many anthropologists—the three authors of this text included—feel strongly that the four-field approach provides anthropology with its unique perspective. Indeed, the three authors represent three of the four fields (cultural anthropology, physical anthropology, and archaeology), providing a broader representation than in any other general anthropology textbook currently available. Every effort has been made in this text to show interrelationships among the subfields and how they collaborate to answer questions about the human condition.

While aiming at a comprehensive and readable introduction to the field of anthropology, this text is designed to do more. It demonstrates how an understanding of anthropology can help solve societal problems. Most students enrolled in introductory anthropology courses never take another course in cultural anthropology. The introductory course may provide the only opportunity to show them the relevance of the discipline to themselves and to society.

This applied perspective—the most distinctive feature of the book—is seen in two formats. First, at the ends of chapters 2 through 23, case studies illustrate how the data and concepts from each chapter have been used to help solve specific societal problems. For example, readers will learn how the skeletal remains of a murder victim were identified with the help of the human skeletal collection at the Smithsonian Institution in Washington, D.C.; how an understanding of Amish religious beliefs enabled a cultural anthropologist (serving as an expert witness) to influence the final decision in a federal court case; and how archaeological knowledge of prehistoric obsidian tools has contributed to significant improvements in present-day eye surgery. The second applied feature of the text is the Cross-Cultural Miscues found throughout the chapters dealing with cultural anthropology. These short boxed scenarios provide readers with real-life examples of the price paid for *not* understanding cultural differences. (These Cross Cultural

Miscues should be distinguished from the boxed-in sections called Setting the Record Straight, found in chapters 4 through 11, which correct various popular misconceptions about physical anthropology and archaeology.) Together these two applied features provide students with a wide range of applications of anthropology affecting people and professions around the world. These case materials serve as important reminders that the study of anthropology involves more than mere exposure to stones, bones, and exotic lifestyles but rather has relevance for our everyday lives.

This text—intended for use in a one-semester course in general anthropology—draws upon insights gained from a number of different approaches to the discipline, including evolutionism, diffusionism, functionalism, and structuralism, among others discussed in chapter 3. Since the study of cultural anthropology involves such vast subject matter, important insights have emerged from many different theoretical perspectives. This inclusive approach has been adopted because it would be too limiting to write an introductory text from a single theoretical perspective.

◆  ◆  ◆

## Acknowledgments

The authors are deeply thankful to many people who have contributed to the writing and production of this book. We are indebted to Lynne Goldstein, Gregg Henry, Jim McKenna, Naomi Miller, William Ringle, Scott Rushforth, Ed Staski, and Vincas Stepnaitis, all of whom willingly provided valuable feedback. We want to particularly thank the following reviewers who provided insightful criticisms on various drafts of the manuscript: Caroline Banks, University of Wisconsin–River Falls; Donna Birdwell-Pheasant, Lamar University; Donald Blakeslee, Wichita State University; Donald Brockington, University of North Carolina–Chapel Hill; James Green, University of Washington; Gilbert Kushner, University of South Florida; Ronald McIrvin, University of North Carolina–Greensboro; James Mielke, University of Kansas; Laura Putsche, University of Idaho; Mark Tromans, Broward Community College; and Marilyn Wells, Middle Tennessee State University.

From its inception this book has been handled in a professional and competent manner by the editorial staff at West Publishing Company. Special thanks are due to executive editor Peter Marshall, who nurtured into reality the original vision of an introductory anthropology textbook with an applied focus. The authors also wish to express their thanks to Emily Autumn for her careful attention to detail in the production of the book and to Jane Bass for her quick and thorough responses to a large number of administrative details.

And, finally, the authors would like to thank their many students of introductory anthropology over the years (a combined total of fifty-three years), who have helped shape and refine the ideas and interpretations found in this book.

## CHAPTER 1

# What is Anthropology?

How does anthropology differ from other social and behavioral sciences?

What is the four-field approach to the discipline of anthropology?

What contributions can anthropology make to the solution of social problems?

When most North Americans hear the word "anthropologist," a number of images come to mind. They picture, for example,

◆ Dian Fossey devoting years of her life making systematic observations of mountain gorillas in their natural environment in Rwanda
◆ the field anthropologist wearing natural-fibered clothing and Birkenstocks, interviewing an exotic tribesman about the nature of his kinship system
◆ the excavation of a jawbone that will be used to demonstrate the evolutionary link between early and modern humans
◆ a linguist meticulously recording the sounds of various words from a native informant who speaks a language that has never before been written down
◆ a team of archaeologists in pith helmets unearthing an ancient temple from a rain forest in Guatamala

Each of these impressions—to one degree or another—accurately represents the concerns of scientists who call themselves anthropologists. Anthropologists do in fact travel to the far corners of the world to study little-known cultures (cultural anthropologists) and languages (anthropological linguists). There are also anthropologists who unearth fossil remains (physical anthropologists) and various artifacts (archaeologists) of people who lived thousands, and in some cases, millions of years ago. Despite the fact that these anthropological subspecialties engage in substantially different types of activities and generate different types of data, they are all directed toward a single purpose, that is, the scientific study of humans, both biologically and culturally, in whatever form, time period, or region of the world they might be found.

Anthropology has long been viewed as an interesting and legitimate scientific enterprise because it helps us understand human evolution and contemporary populations both culturally and biologically. While this is certainly sufficient reason to include anthropology in any college curriculum, many people fail to see what relevance the study of anthropology has for their everyday lives. But, as this text is designed to demonstrate, the study of anthropology has had, and continues to have, very real significance for the solution of societal problems. For example, did you know that

◆ anthropologists serve as consultants to help western businesspeople better understand the cultures of their international business partners?
◆ experimental stone-flaking techniques used by archaeologists have led directly to the improvement of modern-day chest and eye surgery?

◆ anthropologists routinely apply their traditional techniques of skeletal analysis to help law enforcement officials identify missing persons and homicide victims?
◆ an anthropological linguist who had conducted research in Black English Vernacular served as an expert witness in a federal district court hearing, the outcome of which led to curriculum reform for teaching Standard English to Black Americans in Michigan?
◆ archaeological research on prehistoric agricultural adaptation has directly contributed to the improvement of agricultural systems in the modern world?
◆ recently, American archaeologists have used their techniques for analyzing prehistoric garbage dumps to better understand the problems of solid waste disposal facing modern American cities?
◆ anthropological research on food consumption patterns among the Zulu of South Africa was directly responsible for the creation of a successful health delivery system for these people?
◆ testimony by an anthropologist about the culture of the Amish people of Wisconsin served as the basis for a major ruling by the U.S. Supreme Court?
◆ the anthropological study of nonhuman primates (chimpanzees) in their natural environment has led to some potentially useful drugs for humans?
◆ the collection of sociocultural data among gay males in New York City has contributed to the continuing search for a solution to the AIDS epidemic?

These are just a few examples of the relevance of anthropological insights, methods, and theories to our everyday lives. As you read further in this text, you will discover a number of other ways in which the study of anthropology has made direct contributions to solving practical societal problems. To be certain, the study of anthropology looks at the human condition in both an evolutionary and contemporary perspective. It examines how humans have changed physically and culturally over the course of the past several million years, and it studies the various similarities and differences among the thousands of linguistic and cultural groups that inhabit today's world. And while this remains the core of anthropology, it is important to bear in mind that anthropology is not an esoteric subject that serves little purpose other than making university students slightly more interesting cocktail conversationalists. Rather—and this is the major thrust of this text—the study of anthropology does impact our personal and professional lives in very significant ways.

Anthropology—derived from the Greek words *anthropos* for "human" and *logos* for "study"—is, if we take it literally, the study of humans. This is an accurate description to the extent that anthropology raises many questions about the human condition. And yet this literal definition is not particularly illuminating, for a number of other academic disciplines also study humans. For example, sociologists, biologists, psychologists, political scientists, economists, philosophers, and historians all study human beings. What gives the discipline of anthropology the right to refer to itself as the study of humans? What is it that distinguishes anthropology from all of these other disciplines?

Anthropology is the study of people—their origins, development, and contemporary variations, wherever and whenever they have been found on the earth. Of all the disciplines that study humans, anthropology is by far the broadest in scope. The subject matter of anthropology includes fossilized skeletal remains of early humans, artifacts and other material remains from archaeological sites, and all of the contemporary and historical cultures of the world. The task that anthropology has set for itself is an enormous one. Anthropologists strive for an understanding of the biological and cultural origins and evolutionary development of the species. They are concerned with all humans, both past and present, as well as humans' behavior patterns, thought systems, physiological variations, and material possessions. In short, anthropology aims to describe, in the broadest sense, what it means to be human.

In their search to understand the human condition, anthropologists, drawing on a wide variety of data and methods, have created a diverse field of study. Many specialists within the field of anthropology frequently engage in research that is directly relevant to other fields. It has been suggested (Wolf, 1964:13) that anthropology spans the gap among the humanities, the social sciences, and the natural sciences. To illustrate, anthropological investigations of native art, folklore, values, and supernatural belief systems are primarily humanistic in nature; studies of social stratification, comparative political systems, and means of distribution have a good deal in common with the social science investigations of sociology, political science, and economics respectively; and studies of comparative anatomy and radiocarbon dating are related to the natural sciences of biology, chemistry, and physics.

The breadth of anthropology becomes apparent when one looks at the considerable range of topics discussed in papers published in the *American Anthropologist* (one of the primary professional journals in the field). For example, the following topics have recently appeared in the *American Anthropologist* during the 1990s:

- recovery of American Indian populations following smallpox epidemics
- the origins of agriculture in the Near East
- migration, education, and the status of women in southern Nigeria
- explaining differences in overseas experiences among employees of the General Motors Corporation
- sexual behavior among Bonobo chimpanzees
- status and power in classical Mayan society
- men's and women's speech patterns among the Creek Indians of Oklahoma
- theories of modern human origins
- comparison of social interaction among old women and old female Japanese monkeys
- the role of maize in bringing about political changes in Peru between 500 and 1500 A.D.

The global scope of anthropological studies has actually increased in recent years. In the early 1900s, anthropologists concentrated on the non-Western, nonliterate, and technologically simple societies of the world, content to leave the study of industrial societies to other disciplines. In the past several decades, however, anthropologists have been studying cultural and subcultural groups in industrialized areas while continuing their studies of more exotic peoples of the world. It is not at all uncommon today for anthropologists to apply their field methods to the study of hard-core unemployed men in our nation's cities, the corporate culture of a multinational business, rural communes in California, or urban street gangs. Only when the whole range of human cultural variation is examined will we be in a position to test the accuracy of theories about human behavior.

Traditionally, anthropology, as practiced in the United States during the present century, is divided into four distinct branches or subfields: (1) physical anthropology, which deals with humans as biological organisms; (2) archaeology, which attempts to reconstruct the cultures of the past, most of which have left no written records; (3) anthropological linguistics, which focuses on the study of language in historical, structural, and social contexts; and (4) cultural anthropology, which examines similarities and differences among contemporary cultures of the world (Table 1-1).

Despite this fourfold division of anthropology and the considerable specialization among the practitioners, there has been a long-standing tradition in the discipline that emphasizes the interrelations among these four subfields. Moreover, in recent years there has been considerable blurring of the boundaries among the four branches. For example, the relatively new area of

TABLE 1-1 ◆ Branches of Anthropology

| Physical | Archaeology | Linguistics | Cultural Anthropology |
|---|---|---|---|
| Paleontology | Historical Archaeology | Historical Linguistics | Economic Anthropology |
| Primatology | Prehistorical Archaeology | Descriptive Linguistics | Psychological Anthropology |
| Human Variation | Contract Archaeology | Ethnolinguistics | Educational Anthropology |
| | | Sociolinguistics | Medical Anthropology |
| | | | Urban Anthropology |
| | | | Political Anthropology |

specialization known as medical anthropology draws heavily from both physical and cultural anthropology; educational anthropology bridges the gap between cultural anthropology and linguistics; and sociobiology looks at the interaction between culture and biology.

# Physical Anthropology

**Physical anthropology** is the study of the human condition from a biological perspective. Essentially, physical anthropologists are concerned with two broad areas of investigation. First, they are interested in reconstructing the evolutionary record of the human species. That is, they ask questions about the emergence of humans and how humans have evolved up to the present time. This area of physical anthropology is known as human **paleontology** or **paleoanthropology**. The second area of concern to physical anthropologists deals with how and why the physical traits of contemporary human populations vary across the world. This area of investigation is referred to as **human variation.** Physical anthropologists differ from comparative biologists in that they study how culture and environment have influenced these two areas of biological evolution and contemporary variations.

## EVOLUTIONARY RECORD OF HUMANS

In their attempt to reconstruct human evolution, paleoanthropologists have drawn heavily upon fossil remains (hardened organic matter such as bones and teeth) of humans, protohumans, and other primates. Once these fossil remains have been unearthed, the difficult job of comparison, analysis, and interpretation begins. To which species do the remains belong? Are the remains human or those of our prehuman ancestors? If not human, how do the remains relate to our own spe-

cies? When did these primates live? How did they adapt to their environment? To answer these questions, paleoanthropologists use the techniques of comparative anatomy. They compare such physical features as cranial capacity, teeth, hands, and the shape of the head of the fossil remains with those of humans or other nonhuman primates. In addition to comparing physical features, paleoanthropologists look for signs of culture, such as tools, to help determine the humanity of the fossil remains. If, for example, fossil remains are found in association with tools, and if it can be determined that the tools were in fact made by these creatures, it is likely that the fossils will be considered human.

The work of paleoanthropologists must be conducted with meticulous attention to detail. Even though the quantity of fossilized materials is growing each year, the paleoanthropologist's data set is limited. Much of the evolutionary record remains under the ground. Of the fossils that have been found, many are partial or fragmentary, and frequently they are not found in association with tools or other cultural artifacts. Consequently, to fill in the human evolutionary record, physical anthropologists draw upon the work of a number of other specialists: paleontologists (who specialize in prehistoric plant and animal life), archaeologists (who study prehistoric material culture), and geologists (who provide data on local physical and climatic conditions).

Physical anthropologists have since the 1950s developed an area of specialization of their own that helps shed light on human evolution and adaptation over time and space. This is the relatively new field of study known as **primatology**—the study of our nearest living relatives (apes, monkeys, and prosimians) in their natural habitat. Primatologists study the social behavior of such nonhuman primate species as gorillas, baboons, and chimpanzees in an effort to gain clues concerning our own evolution as a species. Since physical anthropologists do not have the luxury of observing the behavior of our human ancestors several million years ago, they can learn how early humans mights have responded to certain environmental conditions and changes in their developmental past by studying contemporary nonhuman primates in similar environments. For example, the simple yet very real division of labor among baboon troops can shed light on role specialization and social stratification in early human societies.

## PHYSICAL VARIATIONS AMONG HUMANS

Although all humans are members of the same species and therefore are capable of interbreeding and producing viable, fertile offspring, considerable biological variations exist among human populations. Some of these differences are based on visible physical traits such as the shape of the nose, the thickness of the lips, and the color of the skin. Other variations are based on less immediately observable biochemical factors such as blood type or susceptibility to diseases. For decades physical anthropologists attempted to document the human physical variations throughout the world by dividing the world's populations into various racial groups

(**race** refers to a group of people who share a greater statistical frequency of genes and physical traits with one another than they do with people outside the group). Today the physical anthropologist's attention is more focused on trying to explain *why* the variations exist by asking such questions as "Are Inuits better endowed physically to survive in colder climates?" Why do some populations have darker skin than others? Why are most Chinese adults unable to digest milk? Why is the blood type B nonexistent among Australian aborigines? How have certain human populations adapted biologically to their local environments? To help answer these and other questions involving human biological variation, physical anthropologists draw upon the work of three allied disciplines: (1) **genetics** (the study of inherited physical traits), (2) **population biology** (the study of the interrelationship between population characteristics and environment), and (3) **epidemiology** (the study of differential effects of disease on populations).

Physical anthropologists also realize that there is a close relationship between human culture and biology. One of the primary features of the human environment

A paleontologist unearths a prehistoric burial.

Primatologists study such nonhuman primates as this mountain gorilla of Ruanda.

is culture, which provides many challenges to past and current biological adaptations. For example, if a physical anthropologist wants to explore the effects of a disease on a population, he or she must consider not only the genetics of the population, but also hygiene, diet, housing types, kinship structure, and economic factors. The impact of the disease on the people is more likely to be influenced by cultural factors than by the biological characteristics of the people.

## Archaeology

**Archaeology** is the study of the lifeways of people from the past, accomplished by excavating and analyzing the things they leave behind, including, in some cases, written records. The purpose of archaeology is not to fill up museums by collecting exotic relics from prehistoric so-

cieties. Rather it is to reconstruct the cultures of people who are no longer living. Since archaeology concentrates on societies of the past, archaeologists are limited to working directly with only one of the three basic components of culture—material culture. The other two components (ideas and behavior patterns) are not preserved after people have been absent for thousands, and in some cases millions, of years.

The data that archaeologists have at their disposal are incomplete. Not only are archaeologists limited to material remains, but most material possessions that may have been part of a culture do not survive thousands of years under the ground. As a result, archaeologists search for fragments of material evidence—such as arrowheads, hearths, beads, postholes, and burial stones—that will enable them to piece together as much of the culture as possible. A prehistoric garbage dump is particularly revealing, for the archaeologist can learn a great deal about how people live from what they throw

An excavation of a prehistoric culture at Twin Ditch in Eldred, Illinois

away. These material remains are then used to make inferences about the nonmaterial aspects of the culture being studied. For example, finding that different skeletal remains in the same grave site are found with varying amounts of personal possessions could lead to the explanation that some type of social stratification based on material wealth existed.

Once the archaeologist has collected the physical evident, the difficult work of analysis and interpretation begins. By studying the bits and pieces of material culture left behind (within the context of both environmental data and anatomical remains), the archaeologist seeks to determine, among other things, how these people supported themselves, whether or not they had a notion of an afterlife, how roles were allocated between men and women, whether some individuals were more prominent than others, and whether the people engaged in trade with neighboring peoples.

Present-day archaeologists work with both historic and prehistoric cultures. Historical archaeologists help to reconstruct the cultures of people both who used writing and about whom historical documents have been written. For example, historical archaeologists have contributed significantly to our understanding of colonial American cultures by analyzing material remains that can supplement such historical documents as books, letters, graffiti, and government reports. Prehistoric archaeology, on the other hand, deals with that vast segment of the human record prior to the invention of writing. Given the several million years of human existence, writing is a very recent development, first appearing about 5,500 years ago. Prehistoric archaeologists attempt, then, to reconstruct cultures that existed prior to the development of writing. Archaeology remains the one scientific enterprise that systematically focuses on prehistoric cultures, and consequently has provided us with a much fuller time frame for understanding the record of human development.

## Anthropological Linguistics

**Anthropological linguistics** is that branch of the discipline that studies human speech and language. Although humans are not the only species that have systems of symbolic communication, we have by far the most complex form. In fact, some would argue that language is the most distinctive feature of being human, for without language we could not acquire and transmit our culture from one generation to the next.

Linguistic anthropology, which studies contemporary human languages as well as those of the past, is divided into four distinct branches: historical linguistics, descriptive linguistics, ethnolinguistics, and sociolinguistics.

**Historical linguistics** deals with the emergence of language in general and how specific languages have diverged over time. Some of the earliest anthropological interest in language was focused on the historical connections among languages. For example, nineteenth-century linguists working with European languages demonstrated similarities in the sound systems between a particular language and an earlier parent language from which the language was derived. In other words, by comparing contemporary languages, linguists have been able to identify certain language families. More recently, through the technique known as glottochronology, linguists can now determine when two related languages began to diverge from one another.

**Descriptive linguistics** is the study of sound systems, grammatical systems, and the meanings attached to words in specific languages. Every culture has a distinctive language with its own logical structure and set of rules for putting words and sounds together for the purpose of communicating. In its simplest form, the task of the descriptive linguist is to compile dictionaries and grammars for previously unwritten languages.

**Ethnolinguistics** is that branch of anthropological linguistics that examines the relationship between language and culture. Aspects that are emphasized in any given culture (for example, types of snow among the Inuits, cows among the pastoral Masai, or automobiles in our own culture) are reflected in the vocabulary of that culture's language. Moreover, ethnolinguists explore how different linguistic categories can affect how people categorize their experiences, how they think, and how they perceive the world around them.

The fourth branch of anthropological linguistics, known as **sociolinguistics**, examines the relationship between language and social relations. For example, sociolinguists are interested in investigating how social class influences the particular dialect a person speaks. They also study the situational use of language—that is, how people use different forms of a language depending on the social situation they may find themselves in. To illustrate, the words and grammatical structures most U.S. college students choose when conversing with a roommate or close personal friend are significantly different from the linguistic style they use when talking to a grandparent, a priest, or a personnel director during a job interview.

For the sociocultural linguist, this type of public graffiti (found in Maracaibo, Venezuela) is an important source of data on language usage.

## Cultural Anthropology

**Cultural anthropology** is that branch of the discipline that deals with (a) the study of specific contemporary cultures (**ethnography**) and (b) more general underlying patterns of human culture derived through cultural comparisons (**ethnology**). Before cultural anthropologists can examine cultural differences and similarities throughout the world, they must first describe in as much detail as possible the features of specific cultures. These detailed descriptions (ethnographies) are the result of extensive field studies (usually a year or two in duration) in which anthropologists observe, talk to, and live with the people they are studying. The writing of relatively large numbers of ethnographies over the course of the present century has provided an empirical basis for the comparative study of cultures. In the process of developing these descriptive accounts, cultural anthropologists may provide insights into such questions as "How are the marriage customs of a group of people related to the group's economy?" What effect does urban migration have on the kinship system? In what ways have supernatural beliefs helped a group of people adapt more effectively to its environment? Thus, while describing the essential features of a culture, the cultural anthropologist may also explain why certain cultural patterns exist and how they may be related to one another.

Ethnology refers to the comparative study of contemporary cultures wherever they may be found. Ethnologists seeks to understand why people today and in the recent past differ in terms of ideas and behavior patterns and what all cultures in the world have in common with one another. The primary objective of ethnology is to uncover general cultural principles, "rules" that govern human behavior. Since all humans have culture and live in collectivities called societies, there are no populations in the world today that are not viable subjects for the ethnologist. The lifeways of Inuits living in the Arctic tundra, Greek peasants, !Kung hunters of the Kalahari desert, and the residents of a retirement home in Southern California have all been studied by cultural anthropologists.

The description and comparison of the many peoples of the world during the twentieth century have demonstrated the magnitude of the task facing ethnographers and ethnologists. The relatively small number of cultural anthropologists are faced with enormous cultural diversity (thousands of distinct cultures whose members speak mutually unintelligible languages), numerous features of culture that could be compared, and a wide range of theoretical frameworks for comparing them. To describe even one small aspect of a culture requires many months of interviewing people and observing their behavior. Even with this large expenditure of time, rarely do contemporary ethnographers describe total cultures. Instead, they usually describe only the more outstanding features of a culture and then investigate a particular aspect or problem in greater depth.

## AREAS OF SPECIALIZATION

Since the description of an entire culture is usually beyond the scope of a single ethnographer, there has been a tendency in recent decades for cultural anthropologists to specialize. They have frequently identified themselves with one or more of the following areas of specialization:

1. *Psychological anthropology* Concerned with studying the individual within a cultural context, psychological anthropology examines such topics as emotional functioning, motivation, personal well-being, mental models, comparative human development, and the acquisition of culture.

2. *Economic anthropology* Dealing with how goods and services are produced, distributed, and consumed cross-culturally, this area of specialization focuses on such topics as division of labor, patterns of work, systems of exchange, and control of property.

3. *Urban anthropology* By concentrating on how such demographic factors as size, density, and heterogeneity affect customary ways of behaving, urban anthropologists examine a number of important issues, including urban poverty and homelessness, the role of women in cities, problems of labor migration, and the impact of multinational corporations on traditional cultures.

Cultural anthropologists gather information about the contemporary peoples of the world through the conduct of direct field studies. Here a cultural anthropologist talks with an Asmat man from Irian Jaya.

EXHIBIT 1-1

**Ethnicity in the United States**

Despite our reputation as the great "melting pot," there remains a considerable amount of ethnic diversity in the United States.

Source: Reprinted by permission from page 110 of *World Regional Geography: A Global Approach* by George F. Hepner and Jesse O. McKee. Copyright © 1992 by West Publishing Company. All rights reserved.

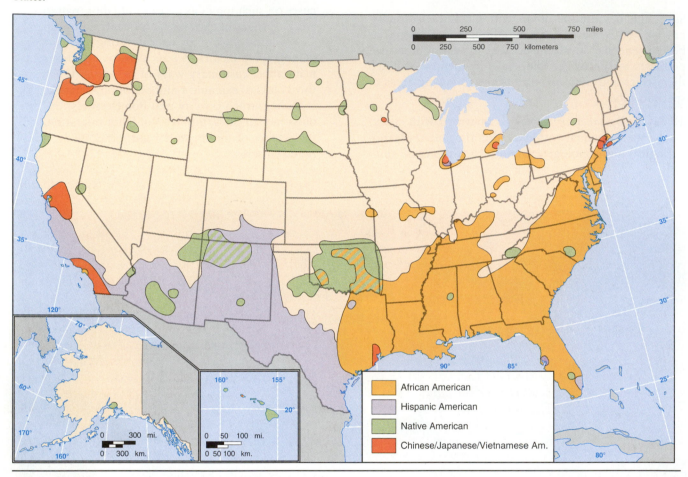

African American

Hispanic American

Native American

Chinese/Japanese/Vietnamese Am.

4. *Educational anthropology* This specialized branch of cultural anthropology explores the relationship between anthropological theories, methods, and insights on the one hand and educational practices, problems, and institutions on the other. Among the concerns of the educational anthropologist are bilingual education, comparative forms of education, and the ethnography of the classroom.

5. *Medical anthropology* Practitioners of this specialized area study the biological and cultural factors that affect health, disease, and sickness. By incorpo-

rating cultural, biological, historical, and linguistic data within its domain, medical anthropology has contacts with a number of other disciplines and draws upon a wide variety of approaches.

6. *Applied anthropology* Cutting across most of the other five areas, this specialized branch conducts research aimed at solving specific societal problems.

These six areas of specialization within cultural anthropology make up only a partial listing. Other specialties include agricultural anthropology, legal anthropology, ecological anthropology, political anthropology, the anthropology of work, and nutritional anthropology, among others.

## HOLISM

A distinguishing feature of the discipline of anthropology is its holistic (comprehensive) approach to the study of humanity. Indeed, it is this notion of **holism** that most dramatically distinguishes anthropology from the discipline of sociology. The study of anthropology is holistic in a number of important respects. First, the anthropological approach involves both biological and sociocultural aspects of humanity. That is, anthropologists are interested in people's genetic endowment as well as what people acquire from their sociocultural environment after birth. By and large, sociologists do not study the biological component of human behavior. Second, anthropology has the deepest possible time frame, starting with the earliest beginnings of humans several million years ago right up to the present. With few exceptions, sociologists concentrate their studies on contemporary populations. Third, anthropology is holistic to the extent that it studies all varieties of people wherever they may be found. That is, anthropology's global perspective considers the lifeways of East African pastoralists, Polynesian fishermen, and Japanese businesspeople as equally legitimate subjects of study. Generally sociologists, particularly those in the United States, have tended to focus on Western, industrialized populations, although this is less true today than it has been in the past. And, finally, anthropologists study many different aspects of human experience. To illustrate, an anthropologist who is conducting direct, observational fieldwork may be collecting data on a wide variety of topics, including family structure, marital regulations, house construction, methods of conflict resolution, diet, means of livelihood, religious beliefs, language, space usage, and art. For the anthropologist, the term holism has also been used to recognize the interrelations of different aspects of culture to each other.

In the past, cultural anthropologists have made every effort to be holistic by covering as many aspects of a culture as possible. In more recent decades, however, the accumulated information from all over the world has become so vast that most anthropologists have become more specialized or focused. To illustrate, one anthropologist may concentrate on marital patterns while another may focus on farming and land-use patterns.

Despite the recent trend toward specialization, anthropologists continue to analyze their findings within their proper cultural context. Moreover, when all of the various specialties within the discipline are viewed together, they represent a comprehensive or holistic view of the human condition.

## ◆ ◆ ◆ Cultural Relativism

A perspective closely allied with anthropology since the turn of this century is **cultural relativism**—the belief that any part of a culture (e.g., an idea, a thing, or a behavior pattern) must be viewed from within its proper cultural context rather than from the viewpoint of the observer's culture. The cultural relativist asks "How does a cultural item (such as a belief or a behavior pattern) fit into the cultural system of which it is a part?" rather than "How does it fit into my own culture?" If we view a foreign cultural item from the point of view of our own culture, it is not likely to make much sense. Nothing in our culture will support the existence of this cultural item. But if we view the foreign cultural item as a cultural relativist—i.e., from within its original cultural context—a number of other parts of that culture will tend to support it. First formulated by Franz Boas and later developed by one of his students, Melville Herskovits (1972), cultural relativism rejects the notion that any culture, including our own, possesses a set of absolute standards by which all other cultures can be judged. Cultural relativity is a cognitive tool that helps us understand why people think and act the way they do.

Perhaps a specific example of cultural relativity will help to clarify the concept. Anthropologists over the years have described a number of cultural practices from around the world that appear morally reprehensible to most Westerners. For example, the Dani of western New Guinea customarily cut off a finger from the hand of any close female relative of a man who dies; the kikuyu of Kenya routinely remove part of the genitalia of teenage girls for the purpose of suppressing their maleness; and the Dodoth of Uganda extract the lower front teeth of young girls in an attempt to make them more attractive. Some arctic cultures practice a custom that would strike typical Westerners as inhumane at best: When aging parents become too old to contribute their share of the work load, they are left out in the cold to die. If we view such a practice by the standards of our own Western culture, we would have to conclude that it is cruel and

When trying to understand the behavior of culturally different people (such as the Inuits of Alaska), it is important to view their behavior within their own cultural and environmental contexts.

heartless, hardly a way to treat those who brought you into the world. But the cultural relativist would look at this form of homicide within the context of the culture of which it is a part. Anthropologists John Friedl and John Pfeiffer (1977:331) provide a culturally relativistic explanation of this Eskimo custom:

It is important to know . . . that this . . . (custom is not practiced) against the will of the old person. It is also necessary to recognize that this is an accepted practice for which people are adequately prepared throughout their lives, and not some kind of treachery sprung upon an individual as a result of a criminal conspiracy. Finally, it should be considered in light of the ecological situation in which the Eskimos live. Making a living in the Arctic is difficult at best, and the necessity of feeding an extra mouth, especially when there is little hope that the individual will again become productive in the food-procurement process, would mean that the whole group would suffer. It is not a question of Eskimos not liking old people, but rather a question of what is best for the entire group. We would not expect—and indeed we do not find—this practice to exist where there was adequate food to support those who were not able to contribute to the hunting effort.

## Contributions of Anthropology

One of the major contributions of anthropology to the understanding of the human condition stems from the very broad task that it has set for itself. Whereas such disciplines as economics, political science, and psychology are considerably more narrow in scope, anthropology has carved out for itself the task of examining *all* aspects of humanity for *all* periods of time and for *all* parts of the globe. Owing to the magnitude of the task, anthropologists must draw upon the theories and data from a number of other disciplines in the humanities, the social sciences, and the physical sciences. As such, anthropology has been in a good position to integrate the various disciplines dealing with human physiology and culture.

Because of its holistic approach, the data and theories of anthropology have served as a powerful corrective to deterministic thinking. That is, this broad, comparative perspective serves as a check against oversimplified explanations concerning all of humanity based on evidence obtained from the Western world. A case in point is the revision of the notion of what a city is. Based largely on the study of American and European cities in the first several decades of the twentieth century, Western social scientists defined a city as a social system in which kinship ties were less elaborate than in rural communities. While this was an accurate picture of cities in the industrialized areas of Europe and the United States, it was hardly accurate as a universal definition of urbanism. Since the 1950s, urban anthropologists studying cities in the non-Western world have called into question this "universal" characteristic of the city. For example, Horace Miner (1953) found substantial kinship interaction—which took the form of joint activities, mutual assistance, and friendship ties—in the West African city of Timbuktu; Oscar Lewis (1952), in an article aptly entitled "Urbanization without Breakdown," found that extended kinship networks were every bit as real in Mexico City as they were in rural Tepoztlan; and more recent studies (Moock, 1978–79; Keefe, 1988) have found equally significant kinship ties in urban areas. Thus, urban anthropology, with its broad cross-cultural approach, has revised our thinking about the theory of urbanism.

One of the four fields of anthropology, cultural anthropology, examines cultural differences and similarities among the contemporary peoples of the world. Although some people view cultural anthropology as devoted to documenting the exotic customs of people in far-off places, only by learning about cultural variations and similarities will we be able to avoid generalizing about "human nature" solely on the basis of observations from our own culture. It is not unusual for people to believe that their beliefs and behaviors are natural, reasonable, and therefore human while believing that those who think and act differently are somewhat less than human. This strong comparative tradition in cultural anthropology helps to reduce the possibility that our theories about human nature will be culture-bound. For example, studies from all subfields of anthropology have revealed that great works of art are found in all parts of the world; that social order can be maintained without having centralized, bureaucratic governments; that prehistoric peoples developed very sophisticated cultural solutions to problems; that reason, logic, and rationality did not originate solely in ancient Greece; and that all morality does not stem from Judeo-Christian ethics. Anthropology, in other words, prevents us from taking our own cultural perspective too seriously. As Clifford Geertz (1984:275) reminds us, one of the tasks of anthropology is to ". . . keep the world off balance; pulling out rugs, upsetting tea tables, setting off fire crackers. It has been the office of others to reassure; ours to unsettle."

Still another contribution of anthropology is that it helps us better understand ourselves. The early Greeks claimed that the educated person was the person with self-knowledge ("know thyself"). One of the best ways to gain self-knowledge is to know as much as possible about one's own culture, how that culture developed, and how it relates to our biological evolution—that is, to understand the forces that make us who we are. And the very best way of learning about our cultural and biological development is to learn something about other peoples of the world. The anthropological perspective, with its emphasis on the comparative study of cultures, should lead us to the conclusion that our culture is just one way of life among many found in the world, and that it represents one way (among many) to adapt to a particular set of environmental conditions. Through the process of contrasting and comparing, we gain a fuller understanding of both other peoples and ourselves.

Thus anthropology, with its holistic, cross-cultural perspective, has contributed in a number of important ways to the scientific understanding of humanity. Moreover, the study of anthropology is important because it enables individuals to better comprehend and appreciate their own cultures. But, we may ask, does anthropology have any relevance to our everyday lives? Students of biochemistry can apply their skills to the discovery of new wonder drugs; creative arts students can produce lasting works of art; and students of architecture can design buildings that are both beautiful and functional. According to popular perceptions, the study of anthropology has little to offer other than a chance to dabble in exotic cultures of the world. As we hope to demonstrate in this text, nothing could be further from the truth. Anthropology has relevance for all of our lives, both personally and professionally. Since anthropology is primarily concerned with the scientific study of culture, and since our lives and our jobs are conducted within a cultural context, anthropologists have some practical things to say to us.

## RESEARCH

Anthropologists, like other social scientists, engage in both basic and applied research. Basic research in anthropology is directed at gaining scientific understanding for its own sake rather than for any practical ends.

Applied research in anthropology, on the other hand, seeks scientific knowledge for the sake of solving particular social problems. For much of the twentieth century, anthropologists have devoted most of their energy to basic research—that is, testing hypotheses concerning such issues as the rise of civilization, the functions of religious institutions, and the evolution of bipedalism in our early ancestors. Anthropologists from all four subdisciplines have also applied many of the methods, theories, and insights gained from basic research to the solution of societal problems. For example, practitioners of forensic anthropology, an applied branch of physical anthropology, work closely with medical examiners and coroners, using their expertise on bones to help identify human skeletal remains for legal purposes (Stewart, 1979). Archaeologists in recent decades have applied their unique skills to the area of cultural resource management, which evaluates and helps preserve our nation's cultural heritage (Hill and Dickens, 1978). An-thropological linguistics has been applied in a wide range of settings, including the improvement of language instruction (Cowan, 1979), the development of intercultural training programs (Samovar and Porter, 1991), and public decision making for language use in specific language communities (Eastman, 1983). Cultural anthropologists have applied their trade to the evaluation of various social programs both here and abroad, market research, classroom management, and the improvement of health delivery systems, to mention but a few.

## APPLICATIONS

In the past decade there has been an increased interest in applying anthropology. Graduate and undergraduate courses in applied anthropology, as well as doctoral dissertations on applied topics, have been on the rise. Moreover, there has been a noticeable increase in the

This group of snake handling fundamentalists would be a possible subject of study for present day cultural anthropologists.

number of anthropologists working outside of universities and museums in such capacities as administrators, cultural resource managers, evaluators, planners, forensic specialists, and research analysts. In fact, within the past several years there has been a movement within the American Anthropological Association to recognize applied anthropology as the fifth major subdivision of anthropology.

Acknowledging this increasing interest in making anthropology practical, this text has developed a particular focus on applying anthropology. To demonstrate how widely anthropology has been applied to the solution of practical societal problems, each of the remaining chapters in the book concludes with applied case studies. Each case study has been selected to show how the information from the particular chapter has been applied to the understanding and solution of practical problems.

## ◆ Summary

1. The academic discipline of anthropology involves the study of both the biological and cultural origins of humans. The subject matter of anthropology is wide-ranging and includes fossil remains, nonhuman primate behavior, artifacts from past cultures, past and present languages, and all of the prehistoric, historic, and contemporary cultures of the world.
2. As practiced in the United States, the discipline of anthropology follows an integrated four-field approach comprising (a) physical anthropology, (b) archaeology, (c) anthropological linguistics, and (d) cultural anthropology.
3. The subdiscipline of physical anthropology focuses on three primary concerns: (a) paleoanthropology (constructing the biological record of human evolution through the study of fossil remains), (b) primatology (the study of nonhuman primate behavior for the purpose of gaining insights into human adaptation to the environment), and (c) studies in human physical variation (race) among the contemporary peoples of the world.
4. The subfield of archaeology has as its primary objective the reconstruction of past cultures, both historical and prehistorical, from the material objects cultures leave behind.
5. Anthropological linguistics, which studies both present and past languages, is divided into four major subdivisions: historical linguistics (the study of the emergence and divergence of languages over time); descriptive linguistics (the structural analysis of phonetic and grammar systems in contemporary languages); ethnolinguistics (the explanation of the relationship between language and culture); and sociolinguistics (how social relations affect language).
6. Cultural anthropology has as its aim the study of contemporary cultures wherever they are found in the world. Part of the task of cultural anthropology involves describing particular cultures (ethnography), while the other part involves comparing two or more cultures (ethnology).
7. A long-standing tradition in anthropology is the holistic approach. The discipline is holistic (or comprehensive) in four important respects: it looks at both the biological and the cultural aspects of human behavior; it has the broadest possible time frame by looking at contemporary, historical, and prehistorical societies; it is global in that it examines human cultures in every part of the world; and it studies many different aspects of human cultures.
8. In order to give themselves the best possible chance of understanding other cultures, anthropologists practice cultural relativity, the notion that when viewing any part of another culture, observers must view the culture from within its original cultural context rather than from their own cultural context.
9. The study of anthropology is valuable from a number of different viewpoints. From the perspective of the social and behavioral sciences, cultural anthropology is particularly valuable for testing theories about human behavior within the widest possible cross-cultural context. For the individual, the study of different cultures provides a much better understanding of one's own culture. From a societal point of view, the understanding of different cultures can contribute to the solution of pressing societal problems.

## ◆ Key Terms

| | |
|---|---|
| anthropological linguistics | historical linguistics |
| archaeology | holism |
| cultural anthropology | paleontology |
| cultural relativism | (paleoanthropology) |
| descriptive linguistics | physical anthropology |
| epidemiology | population biology |
| ethnography | primatology |
| ethnolinguistics | race |
| ethnology | sociolinguistics |
| genetics | |

# ◆ Suggested Readings

Angeloni, Elvio (Ed.). *Anthropology 1991–92*. Guilford, Conn.: Dushkin Publishing, 1991. This annual edition of readings put out by Dushkin contains a new selection of articles each year that covers the fields of social and cultural anthropology. As a useful supplement to the "broad brush" approach taken by most textbooks, this collection of readings provides the student with forty in-depth articles by anthropologists writing on their own research.

Barrett, Richard. *Culture and Conduct: An Excursion in Anthropology* (2nd ed.). Belmont, Calif.: Wadsworth, 1991. By examining some of the questions, ideas, and issues facing modern anthropology, Barrett provides an interesting introduction to how cultural anthropologists investigate unfamiliar cultures.

Campbell, Bernard G. *Humankind Emerging* (5th ed.). Boston: Little-Brown, 1988. Up-to-date, encyclopedic, and handsomely illustrated, this is perhaps the best single introduction to the field of human biological evolution.

Fagan, Brian M. *People of the Earth* (6th ed.). Glenview, Ill.: Scott, Foresman, 1989. A readable and straightforward presentation of the human record from the origins of humankind up to the rise of civilization.

Fromkin, Victoria, and Robert Rodman. *An Introduction to Language* (4th ed.). New York: CBS College Publishing, 1988. A spritely written introduction to the field of anthropological linguistics.

Kluckhohn, Clyde. *Mirror for Man: Anthropology and Modern Life*. New York: McGraw-Hill, 1949. Although written in 1949, this classic study remains one of the best introductions to the discipline because it demonstrates in a number of concrete ways how the study of different cultures—both past and present—can contribute to the solution of contemporary world problems.

Liebow, Elliot. *Tally's Corner*. Boston: Little-Brown, 1967. This ethnographic study of hard-core unemployed street men in Washington, D.C., serves as a reminder that anthropologists, despite their emphasis on non-Western societies, use participant observation as a method of study in their own society.

Oliver, Douglas L. *Invitation to Anthropology*. Garden City, N.Y.: The Natural History Press, 1964. This slim volume, neither a text nor a definitive introduction to the discipline, was written as a brief overview of things the author thought every high school graduate should know about cultural anthropology.

# The Concept of Culture

What do anthropologists mean by the term *culture?*

How do we acquire our culture?

Despite the enormous variation among different cultures, are there some common features found in all cultures of the world?

Despite the fact that the term "culture" is used today as a scientific concept by most of the social sciences, it has received its most precise and thorough definition over the years from the discipline of anthropology. Whereas sociology has concentrated on the notion of society, economics on the concepts of production and distribution, and political science on the concept of power, anthropology has focused on the culture concept. From anthropology's nineteenth-century beginnings, culture has been central to both ethnology and archaeology and has been an important, if not major, concern of physical anthropology. Anthropology, by constantly examining different lifeways throughout space and time, has done more than any other scientific discipline to refine our understanding of the concept of culture.

## Culture Defined

In its ordinary, nonscientific usage, the term "culture" refers to such personal refinements as classical music, the fine arts, world philosophy, and gourmet cuisine. For example, according to this popular use of the term, the "cultured" person is one who listens to Bach rather than the Beatles, orders escargot rather than barbecued ribs, can distinguish between the artistic styles of Monet and Toulouse-Lautrec, prefers Grand Marnier to Kool-Aid, and attends the ballet instead of a hockey game. For the anthropologist, however, the term, used in a much broader sense, includes far more than just the "finer things in life." The anthropologist does not distinguish between "cultured" people and "uncultured" people.

All people have culture, according to the anthropological definition. The Australian aborigines, living as they do with a bare minimum of technology, are as much cultural animals as are Pavarotti or Baryshnikov. Thus, for the anthropologist, arrowheads, creation myths, and grass huts are as legitimate items of culture as is a Beethoven symphony, a Warhol painting, or a Sondheim musical.

Over the past century, anthropologists have formulated a number of definitions of the concept of culture. In fact, in the often-cited work by Kroeber and Kluckhohn (1952), over 160 different definitions of culture were identified. This proliferation of definitions should not, however, be seen as a chaotic battleground where no consensus exists among practicing anthropologists. In actual fact, many of these definitions say essentially the same thing. One early definition, and one that has been widely quoted up to the present time, is the one suggested by nineteenth-century British anthropologist Edward Tylor. According to Tylor (1871:1), culture refers to "that complex whole which includes knowledge, belief, art, morals, law, custom, and any other capabilities and habits acquired by man as a member of society." More recently, culture has been defined as "a mental map which guides us in our relations to our surroundings and to other people" (Downs, 1971:35), and perhaps more succinctly as "the way of life of a people" (Hatch, 1985:178).

Adding to the already sizeable number of definitions, for our purposes we will define the concept of culture as *everything that people have, think, and do as members of a society*. This definition can be instructive because the three verbs correspond to the three major compo-

According to the anthropological perspective, this San hunter has as much culture as does the world class tenor Pavarotti.

CHAPTER 2 ◆ THE CONCEPT OF CULTURE

EXHIBIT 2-1
**The Three Components of Culture**

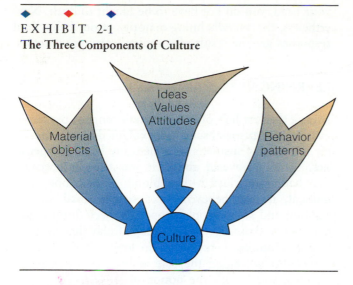

nents of culture. That is, everything that people *have* refers to material possessions; everything that people *think* refers to ideas, values, and attitudes; and everything that people *do* refers to behavior patterns. Thus, all cultures comprise (a) material objects, (b) ideas, values, and attitudes, and (c) patterned ways of behaving.

## Culture Is Shared

The last phrase in our working definition—"as members of a society"—should remind us that culture is a shared phenomenon. For a thing, idea, or behavior pattern to qualify as "cultural," it must have a meaning shared by two or more people within a society. It is this shared nature of culture that makes our lives relatively uncomplicated. Since people *share* a common culture, they are able to predict, within limits, how others will think and behave. For example, when you meet someone for the first time in the United States, it is customary to shake the person's hand. If both you and the person you are meeting are from the United States, neither of you will wonder what is meant by an outstretched hand. Both of you will know, with near absolute certainty, that the extended hand is a nonverbal gesture signifying friendship rather than, for example, a sexual advance, a hostile attack, or an attempt to steal your wallet. Outside our familiar cultural setting—where meanings are not shared with other people—misunderstandings and breakdowns in communication occur.

People from the same culture are able to predict one another's behavior because they all have been exposed to the same cultural conditioning. Yet a word of caution is necessary. To say that culture *conditions* our thoughts, values, and behaviors is hardly to imply that culture *determines* them. People are influenced by their cultures, but we should not think of them as unthinking robots who live out their lives exactly according to cultural dictates. If this were the case, we would expect total conformity to the cultural norms in all societies. But the study of anthropology informs us that despite the fact that most of the people conform to most of the cultural norms most of the time, there is always some segment of the culture's population that, for a number of reasons, deviates from those norms. Some people may deviate from expected norms for purely biological reasons such as hormonal imbalances, hyperactivity, or physiologically based mental disorders. Or an individual's personal history can lead to a culturally unorthodox way of thinking or acting (for example, a person who as a child was traumatized by a hurricane expresses unreasonable reactions to inclement weather). Another explanation is that in all societies one can expect to find a certain amount of differentiation based on gender, age, class, or-

Such large, complex cultures as exist in the United Kingdom comprise a number of distinct subcultural groups that set them apart from the mainstream.

ethnicity. That is, the son of a wealthy physician in Athens will likely have a different set of values and behavioral expectations than the son of a rural Greek peasant farmer. And, finally, societal rules are never adhered to strictly. Despite the fact that culture exerts a powerful influence, people continue to express their "free will" by either reinterpreting the rules, downplaying their consequences, or disregarding them altogether (as with the case of the Catholic who practices birth control or the conscientious objector who flees to Canada rather than serving in a war).

## Culture Is Learned

Culture is not transmitted genetically. Rather, it is acquired through learning or interacting with one's environment. This process of acquiring culture after we are born is called enculturation. We acquire our culture (ideas, values, behavior patterns) by growing up in it. When an infant is born, he or she enters a cultural environment in which many solutions to the universal problems facing all human populations already exist. The child merely needs to learn or internalize those solutions in order to make a reasonable adjustment to his or her surroundings. A male child born in Kansas will probably watch a good deal of television, attend schools with books, desks, and teachers, eventually learn to drive a car, and marry one wife at a time. A male child born among the Jie of Uganda is likely to grow up playing with cows, learn most of what he knows from peers and elders rather than teachers, undergo an initiation ceremony into adulthood that involves being anointed with the undigested stomach contents of an ox slaughtered for the occasion, and have at least three or four wives. Even though these children were born into two radically different cultures, they share one important thing in common—that is, both children were born into an already existing culture, and they have only to *learn* the ways of thinking and acting set down by the cultures.

If we stop to think about it, a great deal of what we do during our waking hours is learned. Brushing our teeth, eating three meals a day, sweeping the floor, attending school, wearing a wristwatch, stopping at a red light, sleeping on a mattress, and waving goodbye are all learned responses to our cultural environment. To be certain, some aspects of our behavior are not learned but are genetically or biologically based. For example, a newborn infant does not need to be given a workshop on the art of sucking; or, if someone throws a brick at your head, you do not have to be taught to duck. Nevertheless, the overwhelming majority of our behavioral responses are the result of complex learning processes.

### LEARNING VERSUS BIOLOGY

During the first half of the twentieth century, psychologists and other social scientists explained human behavior in terms of instincts or genetically based propensities. Gypsies traveled about, it was thought, because they had wanderlust in their blood; black people were musical, it was believed, because they had natural rhythm; and some people supposedly were born criminals owing to their genetic makeup. Today this interpretation of human behavior is no longer held. Instead, while acknowledging the role of biology, most social scientists agree with the notion of tabula rasa, which means that humans are born with little predetermined behavior. If humans are to survive, they must learn most of their coping skills from others in their culture. This learning process usually takes a number of years. As early as 1917, anthropologist A. L. Kroeber recognized the importance of learning for human adaptation to the environment.

Take a couple of ant eggs of the right sex—unhatched eggs, freshly laid. Blot out every individual and every other egg of the species. Give the pair a little attention as regards warmth, moisture, protection and food. The whole of ant "society," every one of the abilities, powers, accomplishments, and activities of the species . . . will be reproduced, and reproduced without diminution, in one generation. But place on a desert island . . . two or three hundred human infants of the best stock from the highest class of the most civilized nation; furnish them the necessary incubation and nourishment; leave them in total isolation from their kind; and what shall we have? . . . only a pair or a troop of mutes, without arts, knowledge, fire, without order or religion. Civilization would be blotted out within these confines—not disintegrated, not cut to the quick, but obliterated in one sweep. (1917:177–78)

### LEARNING STYLES

Even though there is an enormous range of variation in cultural behavior throughout the world, the process by which all people acquire their culture is the same. Westerners frequently make the erroneous assumption that if a Hadza tribesman of Tanzania does not know how to solve an algebraic equation, he must be less intelligent than someone who does know how to solve it. Yet no evidence suggests that members of some cultures are fast

Although these children growing up outside of Bombay, India learn different cultural content than do U.S. children, the process of acquiring culture through learning is common to all cultures.

learners while members of other cultures are slow learners. The study of comparative cultures has taught us that people in different cultures learn different cultural content (attitudes, values, ideas, and behavioral patterns), and they learn with similar efficiency. The Hadza tribesman has not learned algebra because such knowledge would not enhance his adaptation to life in the East African grasslands. He does know, however, how to track a wounded bush buck that he has not seen for three days, where to find groundwater, and how to build a house out of locally found materials. In short, people learn (with relatively equal efficiency) what it is they need to know to best adapt to their environments.

Some degree of learning is nearly universal among all animals. But no other animal has as great a capacity for learning or relies as heavily on learning for its very survival as humans do. This is an extraordinarily important notion, particularly for people who are directly involved in the solution of human problems. That is, if human behavior was largely instinctive (genetic), there would be little reason for developing programs aimed at changing people's behavior, such as programs in agricultural development, family planning, or community health.

## Culture Channels Biological Processes

All animals, including humans, have certain biologically determined needs that must be met in order to stay alive and well. We all need to ingest a minimal number of calories of food each day, protect ourselves from the elements, sleep, and eliminate wastes from the body, among other things. It is vital for us to distinguish between these needs and the ways by which we satisfy them. For example, all people need to eliminate wastes from the body through defecation, but how often, where, in what physical position, and under what social circumstances we defecate are questions answered by our individual cultures.

A dramatic example of how culture can influence or channel our biological processes was provided by anthropologist Clyde Kluckhohn (1949:19), who spent much of his career in the American Southwest studying the Navajo culture. Kluckhohn tells of a non-Navajo woman he knew in Arizona who took a somewhat perverse pleasure in causing a cultural response to food. At luncheon parties she frequently served sandwiches filled with a light meat that looked and tasted similar to tuna salad or chicken salad but had a distinctive taste. Only after all the guests had finished lunch would the hostess inform them that they had just eaten rattlesnake meat salad. Invariably, someone would vomit upon learning what she had eaten. Here is an excellent example of how the biological process of digestion was influenced by a cultural idea. Not only was the process influenced, it was reversed! The culturally based idea that rattlesnake meat is a despicable thing to eat triggered a violent reversal of the normal digestive process.

## OUR BODIES AND CULTURE

The nonmaterial aspects of our culture such as ideas, values, and attitudes can have an appreciable effect on the human body. Culturally defined attitudes concerning male and female attractiveness, for example, have resulted in some dramatic effects on the body. Burmese women stretch out their necks with neck rings; Chinese used to bind the feet of girls; men in New Guinea put bones through their noses; and scarification and tattooing are practiced in various parts of the world for the same reasons that women and men in the United States pierce their ear lobes, that is, because their cultures tell them that it looks good. People intolerant of such cultural practices fail to realize that, had they been raised in those other cultures, they would be practicing those very customs.

Even our body shape is related to a large extent to our cultural ideas. In the Western world, people go to considerable lengths to be as slender as possible. We spend millions of dollars each year on running shoes, diet plans, appetite suppressants, and health spa memberships to help us lose weight or stay thin. However, our notion of slimness as beautiful is hardly universally accepted. In parts of Africa, for example, Western women are perceived as emaciated and are considered to be singularly unattractive. This point was made obvious to one of the authors of this text when he was conducting fieldwork in Kenya during the 1970s. After months of living in Kenya, he learned that he was pitied by many of his male Kikuyu friends for having such an unattractive wife (5'5" and 114 pounds). Kikuyu friends would often come by his house with a bowl of food or a

This Burmese woman is stretching out her neck with neck rings because her culture considers this to be attractive. This form of bodily mutilation illustrates the principle that cultural ideas or values can affect the form and/or function of the physical body.

CHAPTER 2    THE CONCEPT OF CULTURE

chicken and discreetly whisper, "This is for your wife." He considered his wife to be beautifully proportioned, but his African friends thought she needed to be fattened up in order to be beautiful.

## Culture Change

Thus far culture has been presented as a body of things, ideas, and behavior patterns transmitted from generation to generation through the process of learning. Such a view of culture, focusing as it does on continuity among the generations, tends to emphasize its static rather than dynamic aspects. And yet a fundamental principle underlying all cultures is that nothing is as constant as change. Some cultures, particularly those small-scale, non-Western societies that are so often the object of anthropological study, change quite slowly, while others change more rapidly. Despite the variation found in the speed by which cultures change, one thing is certain: no cultures remain completely static year after year.

### THE PROCESSES OF CHANGE

Cultures change according to two basic processes: internal changes (innovations) and external changes (cultural diffusion). Innovations—the ultimate source of all culture change—can be spread to other cultures. Those same innovations can also occur at different times and in different cultures independently. But it is important to bear in mind that not all innovations lead to culture change. An individual can come up with a wonderfully novel thing or idea, but unless it is accepted and used by the wider society, it will not lead to a change in the culture.

Some internal changes involve only slight variations of already existing cultural patterns. In some cases, the changes involve the fairly complex combination of a number of existing cultural features to form a totally new cultural feature. To be certain, internal culture changes involve creativity, ingenuity, and in some cases genius. To a large extent, however, the internal changes possible in any given culture are usually limited to what already exists in a culture. The automobile was invented in the United States because it was part of a cultural tradition that included previous innovations such as the internal combustion engine, the horseless carriage, and the wheel, to mention but three. Since innovations depend on the recombination of already existing elements in a culture, the greatest likelihood is that inno-

The Western ideal of equating physical attractiveness with thinness is not shared by all cultures of the world.

vations will occur in societies with the greatest number of cultural elements. This is another way of saying that internal culture change occurs more frequently in technologically complex societies than it does in less developed ones.

The other source of culture change, which comes from outside of the culture, is known as cultural diffusion—the spreading of a cultural element from one culture to another. As important as innovations are to the process of culture change, cultural diffusion is actually responsible for the greatest amount of change that occurs in any society. In fact, it has been estimated that the overwhelming majority of cultural elements found in any society at any time got there through the process of cultural diffusion rather than innovation. The reason for this is that it is easier to borrow a thing, idea, or behavior pattern than it is to invent it. This is not to suggest that people are essentially uninventive, but only that cultural items can be acquired with much less effort by borrowing them rather than inventing them.

## CAUSES OF CULTURAL CHANGE

Most anthropologists acknowledge that cultures change by means of both internal and external mechanisms, but there is no such agreement on the primary causes of culture change. Do cultures change in response to changing technologies and economies, or do these changes originate in values and ideologies? Some people argue that the "prime mover" of change is technology. They cite, for example, the invention of the automobile and its many effects on all aspects of the American way of life. Others assert that ideas and values lead to culture change to the extent that they can motivate people to explore new ways of interacting with the environment, thereby inventing new items of technology. Still others suggest that cultures change in response to changes in the physical and social environment. For example, changes in U.S. attitudes concerning mothers working outside of the home have occurred because of changing economic conditions and the need for two salaries. The discipline of anthropology has not been able to make definitive statements about the actual causes of culture change; no doubt the truth is a combination of these views. The forces of culture change are so complex, particularly in more technologically advanced societies, that it is difficult, if not impossible, to identify any single factor as most important. The most reasonable way of viewing culture change, then, is as a phenomenon brought about by the interaction of a number of different factors, such as ecology, technology, ideology, and social relationships. The topic of culture change will be discussed in greater depth in Chapter 23.

◆   ◆   ◆

# Evaluating Cultural Differences

While waiting to cross the street in Bombay, India, an American tourist stood next to a local resident who proceeded to blow his nose in the street. The tourist's reaction was instantaneous and unequivocal: "How disgusting!" she thought. Her response to this cross-cultural encounter was to evaluate the Indian man's behavior on the basis of standards of etiquette established by her own culture. According to those standards, it would be considered proper to use a handkerchief in such a situation. But if the man from Bombay were to see the American tourist blowing her nose into a handkerchief, he would be equally repulsed, thinking it strange indeed for the woman to blow her nose into a handkerchief and then put the handkerchief back into her pocket and carry it around for the rest of the day.

## ETHNOCENTRISM

Both the American and the Indian evaluated each other's behavior according to their own cultural assumptions and practices. This way of responding to culturally different behavior is known as ethnocentrism—the belief that one's own culture is most desirable and superior to all others. It is, in other words, viewing the rest of the world through the narrow lens of one's own culture.

Incidents of ethnocentrism are extensive. For example, we can see ethnocentrism operating in the historical accounts of the American Revolutionary War by both British and American historians. According to U.S. historians, George Washington was a folk hero of gargantuan proportions. He led his underdog Continental Army successfully against the larger, better equipped Red Coats; he threw a coin across the Potomac River; and he was so incredibly honest that he turned himself in for chopping down a cherry tree. What a guy! But according to many British historians, George Washington was a thug and a hooligan. Many of Washington's troops were the descendants of debtors and prisoners who could not make a living in England. Moreover, Washington did not fight fairly. Whereas the British were most gentlemanly about warfare (i.e., standing in open fields in their bright red coats shooting at the enemy), George Washington sneaked around ambushing them. A number of British military historians have described Washington in much the same way that recent American historians have described the leaders of the Viet Cong during the Vietnam conflict. U.S. and British historians were describing the same set of historical events, but their own biased cultural perspectives led to two radically different interpretations.

No society has a monopoly on ethnocentrism; it is a deeply ingrained attitude found in all known societies. It should be obvious why ethnocentrism is so pervasive throughout the world. Since most people are raised in a single culture and never leave that culture during their lifetime, it is only logical that their own way of life—their values, attitudes, ideas, and ways of behaving—appear to them to be the most natural. Indeed, unless

Although most people in the U.S. view their bathing habits as being very hygienic, most Japanese would disagree. The Japanese—who clean themselves before soaking in a tub with clean water—feel that North Americans can't get really clean if they step out of a bath filled with dirty soapy water.

members of a society believe that their culture is the best for them (i.e., unless they are ethnocentric), they will be insufficiently motivated to pass their culture on to the next generation. Even though ethnocentrism is present to some degree in all peoples and all cultures, it nevertheless serves as a major obstacle to understanding other cultures. Even people who think of themselves as openminded will have difficulty controlling the impulse to evaluate the ideas or actions of culturally different people. And when one does make a valuative judgment, it will in all likelihood be based on one's own cultural standards. Because it is so difficult to suppress our ethnocentrism, we frequently find ourselves expressing surprise, horror, outrage, disgust, disapproval, or amuse-

ment when encountering a life-style different from our own. Although we cannot eliminate ethnocentrism totally, by becoming aware of our own ethnocentrism, we will be able to set aside our value judgments long enough to learn how other cultures operate.

Nineteenth-century anthropology was plagued with ethnocentrism. Some of the early contributors to the discipline described culturally different peoples in the most bigoted of terms. William McGee, for example, the first president of the American Anthropological Association, was frequently guilty of the most obnoxious forms of ethnocentrism. Here, for example, McGee manages to debase the non-Western societies of his time by confusing the concepts of race, language, and culture.

Possibly the Anglo-Saxon blood is more potent than that of other races; but it is to be remembered that the Anglo-Saxon language is the simplest, the most perfectly and simply symbolic that the world has ever seen; and that by means of it the Anglo-Saxon saves his vitality for conquest instead of wasting it under the Juggernaut of a cumbrous mechanism for conveyance of thought. (McGee, 1895:281)

## CULTURAL RELATIVISM

Anthropologists since the turn of the century have led a vigorous reaction against the perils of ethnocentrism. As cultural anthropologists began to conduct empirical fieldwork among different cultures of the world, they recognized a need to provide dispassionate and objective descriptions of the people they were studying. Following the lead of Franz Boas in the United States and Bronislaw Malinowski in Britain, twentieth-century anthropologists have been part of a tradition that calls upon the fieldworker to prevent his or her own cultural values from coloring the descriptive accounts of the people under study. According to Franz Boas, the father of modern anthropology in the United States, the way in which anthropologists are to strive for that level of detachment is through the practice of cultural relativism. This is the notion that other cultures can be evaluated and understood only in accordance with their own standards, not from the cultural perspective of the observer. For Boas, cultural relativism involved maintaining strict neutrality when describing and contrasting culturally different populations. The anthropologist was to avoid making value judgments about the relative merits of one culture over another. Since each culture was thought to have its own integrity, the anthropologist was expected to resist all temptations to see how other cultures measure up to his or her own.

For Boas, cultural relativism was an ethical mandate as well as a strategic methodology for understanding other cultures. In his attempt to counter the methodological abuses of people like McGee and set anthropology on a more scientific footing, Boas perhaps overemphasized the importance of cultural relativism. If cultural relativism is taken to its logical extreme, we arrive at two indefensible positions. First, from a methodological perspective, if every society is a unique entity that can be evaluated only in terms of its own standards, then any type of cross-cultural comparison would be virtually impossible. Clearly, however, if cultural anthropology is to accomplish its major objective—that is, scientifically describing and comparing the world's cultures—it needs some basis for comparison.

A second difficulty with taking the notion of cultural relativism too literally is that, from an ethical standpoint, we would have to conclude that absolutely no behavior found in the world would be immoral provided the people who practice it concur that it is morally acceptable or that it performs a function for the well-being of the society. To practice cultural relativity, however, does not require that we view all cultures as morally equivalent. That is, not all cultural practices are equally worthy of tolerance and respect. To be certain, some cultural practices (such as the genocide perpetrated by Stalin, Hitler, or the Serbs in Bosnia) are morally indefensible within any cultural context. And, as Bagash (1981) reminds us, if we refuse to acknowledge our own values and compare, evaluate, and judge other cultures, we may be paralyzed in coping with the everyday world. Yet, if our goal is to *understand* human behavior in its myriad forms, then cultural relativism can help us identify the inherent logic behind certain ideas and customs. Sometimes cultural anthropologists have been criticized for being overly nonjudgmental about the customs they study, but as Barrett (1984 : 8) has suggested,

. . . the occasional tendency for anthropologists to treat other cultures with excessive approbation to the extent that they sometimes idealize them, is less cause for concern than the possibility that they will misrepresent other societies by viewing them through the prism of their own culture.

## ◆ ◆ ◆ Cultural Universals

A major contribution of cultural anthropology during the twentieth century has been its descriptive documentation of the thousands of cultures that inhabit the face of the earth. Again, following the Boasian tradition of empirical descriptive ethnography, hundreds of cultural anthropologists have set out since the turn of the century to describe the wide variety of cultures found in the contemporary world. As a result, the discipline of anthropology has been far more effective at documenting cultural differences than showing similarities among cultures. This preoccupation with different forms of behavior and different ways of meeting human needs was the result, at least in part, of wanting to move away from the premature generalizing about "human nature" that was so prevalent around the turn of the century.

This vast documentation of culturally different ways of behaving has been extraordinarily important for our understanding of the human condition. The significant number of cultural differences illustrates how flexible and adaptable humans are compared to other animals: each culture has developed a different set of solutions to the universal human problems facing all societies. For example, every society, if it is to survive as an entity, needs a system of communication enabling its members to send and receive messages. That there are thousands of mutually unintelligible languages in the world today certainly attests to human flexibility. When viewed from a somewhat higher level of abstraction, however, all of these different linguistic communities display an important common denominator, i.e., they all have developed some form of language. This example reminds us that, despite the many differences, all cultures of the world share a number of common features, called cultural universals, in that they have all worked out solutions to the problems facing all human societies. We can gain a clearer picture of cultural universals by looking in greater detail at the universal needs that give rise to them.

## BASIC NEEDS

One of the most fundamental requirements of all societies is to see to it that the basic physiological needs of its people are met. Clearly, people cannot live unless they receive a minimum amount of food, water, and protection from the elements. Since a society will not last without living people, every society needs to work out systematic ways of producing (or procuring from the environment) those absolutely essential commodities and then distributing what it sees as necessary to its members. In the United States, goods and services are distributed according to the capitalistic principle of "each according to his or her own capacity to pay." In socialist countries such as Cuba or China, distribution takes place according to the principle of "each according to his or her need." The Hadza of Tanzania distribute

Although many features of this U.S. school and this Koranic school in Africa are different, both schools represent a response to the universal need shared by all societies to transmit their cultures to future generations.

meat according to how an individual is related to the person who killed the animal. The Pygmies of Central Africa engage in a system of distribution called "silent barter," whereby they avoid face-to-face interaction with their trading partners. Many societies distribute valuable commodities as part of the marriage system, sending considerable quantities of livestock from the family of the groom to the family of the bride. Even though the details of each of these systems of distribution varies greatly, every society has worked out a patterned way of ensuring that people get what they need for survival. As a result, we can say that every society has an *economic system.*

In addition to the need to produce and distribute vital commodities to its members, all societies face a number of other universal needs. For example, all societies need to make provisions for orderly mating and child rearing; this need gives rise to patterned *systems of marriage and family.* If a society is to endure, it will need to develop a systematic way of passing on its culture from one generation to the next. This universal societal need for cultural transmission leads to some form of *educational system* in all societies. A prerequisite for the longevity of any society is the maintenance of social order. That is, most of the people must obey most of the rules most of the time. This universal societal need to avoid destruction through anarchy leads to a set of mechanisms that coerce people to obey the social norms, which we refer to as a *social control system.* Since people in all societies are faced with life occurrences that defy explanation or prediction, all societies have developed systems for explaining the unexplainable, most of which rely on some form of supernatural beliefs such as religion, witchcraft, magic, or sorcery. Thus, all societies have developed a *system of supernatural beliefs* that serve to explain otherwise inexplicable phenomena. And since all societies, if they are to function, need for their members to be able to send and receive messages with relative efficiency, they all have developed *systems of communication,* both verbal and nonverbal.

Despite what may appear to be an overwhelming amount of cultural variety found in the world today, all cultures, owing to the fact that they must meet certain universal needs, share a number of traits in common. Those mentioned above represent some of the more obvious cultural universals, but many more could be cited. Anthropologist George Peter Murdock (1945: 124) compiled a list of cultural universals that can provide us with a look at what our species has in common (see table 2-1):

For much of the present century, cultural anthropologists have been focusing their efforts on explaining cultural differences. In an attempt to reestablish the discipline's focus, which petered out with Murdock's list of cultural universals in the 1940s, Donald Brown (1991: 130–40) has explored in considerable detail what is common to all cultures and societies. Of particular interest is Brown's description of "The Universal People," a composite culture of all peoples known to anthropologists. While drawing heavily from Murdock's (1945) listing, as well as from Tiger and Fox (1971) and Hockett (1973), Brown makes a convincing case that cultural universals exist, are numerous, and are theoretically significant for carrying out the work of anthropology.

## Culture Is Adaptive

Culture represents the major way by which human populations adapt to or relate to their environments so that they can continue to reproduce and survive. Most living organisms other than humans adapt to their environments by developing physiological features that

equip them to maximize their chances for survival. For example, certain predators, such as wolves, lions, and leopards, have developed powerful jaws and canine teeth used for killing and ripping the flesh of animals. Humans, on the other hand, have relied more on cultural rather than biological features for adapting to their environments. Through the invention and use of such cultural tools as spears, arrows, guns, and knives, humans are able to kill and butcher animals even more efficiently than an animal could with its massive jaws and teeth. The discovery of such chemical substances as penicillin, quinine, and the polio vaccine has provided the human species a measure of protection against disease and death. The proliferation of agricultural technology over the past century has dramatically increased humans' capacity to feed themselves. Since humans rely much more heavily upon cultural than upon biological adaptation, they are enormously flexible in their ability to survive and thrive in a wide variety of natural environments. Because of the **adaptive nature of culture,** people are now able to live more successfully in places that previously were only marginally inhabitable (such as the Kalahari Desert and the Arctic region) or uninhabitable (such as under the sea or in outer space).

The notion that culture is adaptive should not lead us to conclude that every aspect of a culture is adaptive. It is possible for some features to be adaptively neutral, that is, neither enhancing nor diminishing the capacity of a people to survive. Moreover, it is even possible for some features of a culture to be maladaptive or dysfunctional. For example, the large-scale use of automobiles, coupled with industrial pollutants, is presently destroying the quality of the air in our environment. If these cultural behaviors continue much longer, they will destroy our environment to such an extent that it will be unfit for human habitation. It is not likely that such a maladaptive practice will persist indefinitely. Either the practice will disappear when the people become extinct or the culture will change so that the people will survive. Whichever occurs, the maladaptive cultural feature will eventually disappear.

An understanding of the adaptive nature of culture is further complicated by its relativity. What is adaptive in one culture may be maladaptive or adaptively neutral in another culture. For example, the mastery of such skills as algebra, word analogies, and reading comprehension are all necessary for a successful adaptation to life in the United States, for they all contribute to academic success, landing a good job, and living in material comfort. Such skills, however, are of little value in helping the Nuer herdsman adapt to his environment in the Sudan. Also, the adaptability of a cultural item will vary over

**TABLE 2-1** ◆ **Murdock's Cultural Universals**

| Are there any additional universals you would add to the following list? | | | |
|---|---|---|---|
| age grading | etiquette | joking | postnatal care |
| athletics | faith healing | kin groups | pregnancy usages |
| bodily adornment | family | kin terminology | property rights |
| calendar | feasting | language | propitiation of |
| cleanliness training | fire making | law | supernatural beings |
| community organization | folklore | luck superstitions | puberty customs |
| cooking | food taboos | magic | religious ritual |
| cooperative labor | funeral rites | marriage | residence rules |
| cosmology | games | mealtimes | sexual restrictions |
| courtship | gestures | medicine | soul concepts |
| dancing | gift giving | modesty | status differentiation |
| decorative art | government | mourning | surgery |
| divination | greetings | music | tool making |
| division of labor | hair styles | mythology | trade |
| dream interpretation | hospitality | numerals | visiting |
| education | housing | obstetrics | weaning |
| eschatology | hygiene | penal sanctions | weather control |
| ethics | incest taboos | personal names | |
| ethnobotany | inheritance rules | population policy | |

SOURCE: George Peter Murdock, "The Common Denominator of Cultures," in Ralph Linton (Ed.), *The Science of Man in the World Crisis*. New York: Columbia University Press, 1945, p. 124.

time within any particular culture. For example, the survival capacity of traditional Eskimo hunters living on the Alaskan tundra would, no doubt, be enhanced appreciably by the introduction of guns and snowmobiles. Initially, such innovations would be adaptive because they would enable the Eskimo hunters to obtain caribou more easily, thereby enabling people to eat better, be more resistant to disease, and generally live longer. After several generations, however, the use of guns and snowmobiles could, in all likelihood, become maladaptive, for the newly acquired capacity to kill caribou more efficiently would eventually lead to the depletion of a primary food supply.

## Cultures Are Integrated

To suggest that all cultures share a certain number of universal characteristics is not to imply that cultures are comprised of a laundry list of norms, values, and material objects. Instead, cultures should be thought of as integrated wholes, the parts of which, to some degree, are interconnected. When we view cultures as integrated systems, we can begin to see how particular culture traits fit into the whole system and, consequently, how they make sense within that context. Equipped with

such a perspective, we can begin to better understand those "strange" customs found throughout the world.

One way of describing this integrated nature of cultures is by using the organic analogy first employed by some of the early functionalist anthropologists. This approach compares any culture to a living organism such as the human body. The human body contains a number of systems all functioning to maintain the overall health of the organism. These include the respiratory system, digestive system, skeletal system, excretory system, reproductive system, muscular system, circulatory system, endocrine system, and lymphatic system. Any anatomist or surgeon knows (a) where these systems are located in the body, (b) what function each plays, and (c) how the various parts of the body are interconnected. Surely no sane person would choose a surgeon to remove a malignant lung unless that surgeon knew how that organ was related to the rest of the body.

### CULTURAL INTERCONNECTIONS

In the same way that human organisms have various parts that are both functional and interrelated, so too do cultures. When conducting empirical field research, the task of the cultural anthropologist is to describe the various parts of the culture, show how they function, and determine how the parts are interconnected. When describing cultures, anthropologists frequently identify such parts or "systems" as the economic system, kinship system, social control system, marriage system, military system, religious system, aesthetic system, technological system, and linguistic system, among others. These various parts of a culture are more than a random assortment of customs. Even though more often than not anthropologists fail to clearly spell out the nature and dimensions of these relationships, it is believed that most of the parts of a culture are to some degree interconnected. Thus, we can speak of cultures as being logical and coherent systems. It is this interconnectedness that allows archaeologists to reconstruct past behavioral patterns by examining material remains.

The notion of the interconnectedness of the parts of a culture can be illustrated with examples from any culture. The Samburu of East Africa are seminomadic pastoralists who keep relatively large numbers of cows. An anthropologist studying the Samburu and their herds would no doubt describe the cow as part of the economic system. The cow's blood and milk are routinely consumed as a source of food; skins are used to make clothing, shoes, and jewelry; the cow's urine is used as an antiseptic; and cow dung is a principle material for house construction. These are all economic functions. Cows play an important role in other systems as well. Since cattle are exchanged in order for a legal marriage to take place, cows are part of the marriage system; since they are sacrificed for the ancestor gods, they play a significant role in the religious system; and as cows are frequently the subject of songs, poems, epics, and folktales, they are also an integral part of the aesthetic system. Thus, to the extent that cattle function in a number of systems in the Samburu culture, we can see how the culture is integrated.

For this East African pastoralist, cows are more than just an economic commodity. Since these cows also play roles in legitimizing marriages, allocating social status, and making religious sacrifices, we say that the various parts of a culture tend to be interconnected.

## "Primitive" Cultures

A fundamental feature of the discipline of cultural anthropology is that it is comparative in approach. Whether studying religions, economic systems, ways of resolving conflicts, or art forms, cultural anthropologists look at these aspects of human behavior in the widest possible context, ranging from the most technologically simple foraging societies at one end of the continuum to the most highly industrialized societies at the other. Societies with simple technologies, once referred to as "primitive," are described by contemporary cultural anthropologists by other terms such as "preliterate," "small-scale," "egalitarian," or "technologically simple." Owing to the misleading implications that something "primitive" is both inferior and earlier in a chronological sense, the term primitive will not be used in this text. Instead we will use the term "small-scale," which refers to societies that (a) have relatively small populations, (b) are technologically simple, (c) are usually preliterate (i.e., not having a written form of language), (d) have little labor specialization, and (e) are unstratified. To make such a distinction between small-scale and complex societies should not imply that all societies can be pigeonholed into one or the other category. Rather, it would be more fruitful to view all of the societies of the world along a continuum from most small-scale to most complex.

## Culture and the Individual

Throughout this chapter we have used the term "culture" to refer to everything that people have, think, and do as members of a society. Whether we are talking about the Chinese, Yanamamo, or Samoans, all peoples have a shared set of meanings that serve as a collective guide to their behavior. Since people from the same culture learn essentially the same set of values, rules, norms, and expected behaviors, their lives are made somewhat less complicated because they know, within broad limits, what to expect from one another. For example, when people are walking through a crowded hallway in the United States, there is a general understanding that everyone will keep to his or her right. Since most Americans share that common cultural understanding, the traffic usually flows without serious interruption. Should someone walk down the lefthand side of the hallway, traffic will likely slow down because

many people will be unsure how to cope with the oncoming person. Such an incident is disruptive and produces anxiety for the simple reason that normal, expected, and predictable behavior did not occur.

## Summary

1. For purposes of this book, we have defined culture as everything that people have, think, and do as members of a society.

2. Culture is shared by members of the same society. This shared nature of culture enables people to predict—within broad limits—the behavior of others in the society. Conversely, people become disoriented when attempting to interact with others from a culturally different society because they do not share the same culture.

3. Culture is acquired not genetically but through a process of learning that anthropologists call enculturation. People in different cultures learn different things, but no evidence suggests that people in some cultures learn more efficiently than people in other cultures.

4. Certain aspects of culture—such as ideas, beliefs, and values—can affect our bodies and our biological processes. More specifically, certain culturally produced ideas concerning beauty can influence how people alter their bodies.

5. Cultures—and their three basic components of things, ideas, and behavior patterns—are constantly experiencing change. While the pace of culture change varies from society to society, no cultures are totally static. Cultures change internally (innovations) and by borrowing from other cultures (diffusion).

6. There are essentially two ways of responding to unfamiliar cultures. One way is ethnocentrically—looking at another culture, or a part of that culture, from your own cultural perspective. The other way is from the perspective of a cultural relativist—from within the context of the other culture. Cultural anthropologists strongly recommend the second mode.

7. In spite of considerable variations in cultures found throughout the world, certain common features (cultural universals) are found in all cultures. Cultural anthropology, the scientific study of cultures, looks at both similarities and differences in human cultures wherever they may be found.

8. Cultures help people adjust to their environments and consequently increase their chances for survival.

9. A culture is more than the sum of its parts. Rather, a culture should be seen as an integrated system in which all parts are interrelated to some degree. This cultural

integration has important implications for the process of culture change, for a change in one part of the system is likely to bring about changes in other parts.

## ◆ Key Terms

| | |
|---|---|
| adaptive nature of culture | ethnocentrism |
| cultural diffusion | innovation |
| cultural relativism | organic analogy |
| cultural universals | tabula rasa |
| enculturation | |

## ◆ Suggested Readings

Gamst, Frederick C., and Edward Norbeck (Eds.). *Ideas of Culture: Sources and Uses*. New York: Holt, Rinehart & Winston. 1976. This is a collection of writings over the past hundred years on the notion of culture, the concept that is central to the discipline of anthropology.

Hall, Edward T. *The Hidden Dimension*. Garden City, N.Y.: Doubleday, 1969. Hall introduces the science of proxemics to show how a very subtle aspect of culture—how people use space—can have a powerful impact on international business relations, cross-cultural encounters, and the fields of architecture and urban planning.

Linton, Ralph. *The Study of Man*. New York: Appleton-Century, 1936. Written more than half a century ago to provide beginners with the basics of anthropology, Linton's classic work remains one of the best introductions to the field of cultural anthropology.

White, Leslie A., with Beth Dillingham. *The Concept of Culture*. Minneapolis, Minn.: Burgess Publishing, 1973. The written version of a series of lectures White gave on the concept of culture in which he defines culture essentially as a symbolic system.

As this chapter has attempted to demonstrate, culture exerts a powerful force on the lives of individuals. Within broad limits, our culture influences our values, beliefs, behaviors, perceptions, and view of the world. The degree to which this is true becomes particularly apparent to us when we step outside our own culture or when we interact with people from different cultural backgrounds. Our own culture tends to shape our thinking to such a degree that we often fail to realize that people from other cultures do not share our assumptions or perceptions of reality.

# Culture

### ◆ Different worldviews can lead to cross-cultural miscommunication.

Stearns (1986:21–22) provides us with a poignant example of how a Western-trained physician failed to communicate some important medical information to his patient in rural Yucatan because of their very different views of the world. A ninety-year-old Mayan woman from Yucatan attended a regional health clinic for the treatment of a digestive tract problem. After examining the woman, the Western-trained physician gave her some pills with the instructions to take "one pill three times per day." Unfortunately, the woman never took the pills because she did not understand the directions. The directions were understandable to most Westerners, but they had no meaning for the Mayan woman. The doctor failed to understand that the woman did not own a clock; in fact, she could not tell time. Her culture had afforded her little practice in abstract visualization. Consequently, the concept of "three times per day" made no sense to her. In this situation the lack of cultural understanding resulted in the doctor's failure to accomplish his professional task, i.e., cure the woman's digestive track ailment. Stearns (1986:22) reminds us that the outcome could have been quite different if the physician was more culturally sensitive.

Had the doctor observed routine activities of a wife in the Maya home, he would have seen women preparing tortillas three times a day for their families. After synthesizing this data collected while interacting in the village, the rural doctor might have employed a culturally appropriate solution: giving the woman instructions to take a pill each time she prepared tortillas for her husband.

### ◆ Cultural anthropologists can assist in the design of appropriate housing for culturally different people.

When architects design buildings, they need to have a thorough understanding of the laws of physics and the nature of building materials if the structure is not to fall down. Architecture, however, involves more than bricks and mortar. Since buildings are used by people to serve certain functions, the architect must also pay attention to the culture of the people who will use the building. Because people of different cultures have different values, attitudes, and behavior patterns, it is likely that they will use their physical spaces differently. In other words, low-income housing in Djakarta, Indonesia, if it is designed with the users in mind, will look substantially different from low-income housing in Philadelphia.

To ensure that buildings are designed in culturally appropriate ways, architects in recent years have worked with cultural anthropologists. One such effort was the Payson Project, a U.S. government project aimed at building a community of homes for Apache Indians in central Arizona during the late 1970s. Much to the credit of the project, anthropologist George Esber was invited to be part of the planning team to serve as a cultural adviser. His role involved (a) conducting anthropological research on the space needs of the local Apache people and (b) translating these needs into appropriate design features for the architects.

Esber's research (1987) was an interesting mixture of traditional methods and a creative technique designed specially to elicit data relevant for this housing project. The initial data gathering involved ethnographic mapping of the location of houses in the existing community and the interior use of space in these houses. Interviewing was also used to determine the social networks of relationships that existed in the community. And finally, Esber gave each family a model house kit comprised of moveable wall segments and pieces of furniture so they could design their own housing preference. He then photographed and analyzed these model plans before sharing this information with the architects.

This anthropological research revealed some important features of contemporary Apache life that had important design implications for the housing project. Most Apaches preferred an internal house design that divided the space into sleeping areas on the one hand and a large living area on the other. Esber found that his informants preferred an open design with a minimum of partitions in the general living space. Such a floor plan (combining cooking, eating, and general living in a single room) is very much in keeping with traditional Apache houses and the Apaches' patterns of social interaction. Through participant-observation Esber learned that Apaches enter social situations in a slow, gradual manner. This step-by-step approach permits the somewhat reticent Apaches to determine whether they want to continue the interaction after having assessed the social situation. Esber (1987:192) goes on to say,

Apaches prefer large rooms and open spaces so they can have a full view of the social setting but can maintain enough distance from others so that verbal interaction is not necessary. From this vantage point, the behavior of others comes to be known, and further social intercourse may follow from the judgements made.

This is just one example of how anthropological insights about the cultural needs of the Apaches were accommodated through architectural design. The anthropological contribution involved an understanding of patterns of social interaction and space usage among the Apaches. Unlike houses built for other Apache communities without anthropological input, the houses designed for the Payson Project were used with a high degree of satisfaction. On other reservations many Apaches were unwilling to move into new houses built on an Anglo model that were not designed in collaboration with anthropologists. Those who did found the houses unsatisfying, and many moved back into their old homes. Esber (1987:194) concludes:

Government officials were unable to understand why new houses were being scorned because they assumed that anyone would like a new house. However, the issue was not one of having new quarters but rather of experiencing the comfort of home in culturally appropriate housing.

## CHAPTER 3

# Applied Anthropology

How have anthropologists applied their theories, methods, and insights to the solution of practical problems during the course of the present century?

What special contributions can anthropology make as an applied science?

In what ways are applied anthropologists faced with ethical dilemmas when conducting fieldwork?

Even though anthropologists, to one degree or another, have always applied their findings, theories, and methods to the solution of human problems, an increasing number of anthropologists at various times during the past half century have become involved in research aimed very explicitly at practical applications. These practitioners represent a relatively new and growing subdiscipline known as *applied anthropology*. Characterized by their problem-oriented research among the world's contemporary populations, these pragmatic anthropologists attempt to apply anthropological data, concepts, and strategies to the solution of social, economic, and technological problems, both at home and abroad. Over the past decades a number of terms have been given to these attempts to use anthropological research for the improvement of human conditions. They include *action anthropology, development anthropology, practical anthropology,* and *advocacy anthropology.* For purposes of this chapter, however, we will use the more widely accepted and generic term, applied anthropology.

A distinguishing feature of cultural anthropology is its direct, experiential approach to research through the technique known as participant-observation. While in recent years cultural anthropologists have increasingly worked in industrialized societies, for the most part they have conducted field research in parts of the world experiencing serious societal problems, such as poor health, inadequate food production, high infant mortality, and rampant population growth, to mention but a few. The very nature of anthropological research—involving as it does living with people and frequently befriending them—makes it difficult for cultural anthropologists to ignore the enormity of the problems they face every day. It should, therefore, come as no surprise that many cultural anthropologists feel a sense of responsibility for helping to solve, or at least alleviate, some of these pressing social problems.

Although much of what has been called applied anthropology has focused on cultural anthropology, all of the subfields of anthropology engage in various types of applied activities. Indeed, the central theme of this text is that the application of anthropological theory, data, and methods cuts across all of the subfields.

Archaeologists who might be called *applied archaeologists* focus mainly on research aimed at conserving archaeological sites and resources threatened by construction and development. This kind of archaeology has been called **public archaeology, salvage archaeology,** or **contract archaeology** but is most commonly known as *cultural resource management (CRM).* CRM archae-

ologists work for federal, state, and local governments, for museums and Native American tribes, and for private firms that contract with public agencies. The U.S. Corps of Engineers and the U.S. Forest Service employ many CRM archaeologists, as do historic preservation offices in different states. Although this kind of applied archaeology occurred earlier, the major impetus for the development of CRM was a series of historic preservation laws passed during the 1960s and 1970s that mandated government concern for preserving historical and archaeological remains in the United States.

While CRM archaeologists might be called "full-time" applied archaeologists, other archaeologists take part in various applied projects. Archaeological expertise has been used in science education, materials conservation, museum reconstructions, planning for solid waste disposal, and the revival of ancient agricultural techniques.

The two major areas in which physical anthropologists conduct applied work are forensic anthropology and biomedical anthropology. Forensic anthropologists help law enforcement agencies identify skeletal remains of unknown individuals killed by homicide, warfare, or natural or technological disasters. Through years of research on human skeletal biology, forensic anthropologists have developed techniques for assessing the age, sex, stature, and ethnic affiliation of skeletal remains. These techniques can be used to provide details about a skeleton's biological traits, which can then be matched with cultural artifacts such as dental work, clothing, and jewelry to aid in the identification process. Occasionally, the cause of death can be determined from the study of the skeletal remains. Most physical anthropologists who conduct forensic investigations are members of the American Academy of Forensic Sciences, which provides opportunities for board certification and advanced training in newly developed techniques.

Biomedical anthropologists are concerned with such issues as human health, disease, growth, aging, nutrition, and fertility. Many conduct their research in medical schools or in clinical settings. Biomedical anthropologists receive training in fields such as anthropometry (measurement of the human body), statistics, population genetics, human evolution, and epidemiology. They recognize that cultural factors may play as great a role in determining who gets ill as do biological factors. An example of a biomedical approach to a disorder is the examination of the interaction of genetics, diet, age, sex, stress, and environment in the development of hypertension (high blood pressure). AIDS is another example of a disorder that is clearly related to cultural factors (see the Applied Perspective in Chapter 13).

These cultural resource managers are conducting salvage archaeology by excavating a prehistoric site prior to highway construction

## Applied Versus Pure Anthropology

For much of the present century, many anthropologists have distinguished applied anthropology from "pure" or "academic" anthropology. So-called pure anthropology was seen as being concerned only with the advancement of the discipline in terms of refining its methods and theories and providing increasingly more valid and reliable anthropological data. Applied anthropology, on the other hand, was characterized as being primarily aimed at changing human behavior for the sake of ameliorating contemporary problems. However, both types of anthropology are hardly mutually exclusive enterprises. Applied anthropology, if it is to be done effectively, must take into account all of the theories, methods, and data that have been developed by the discipline as a whole. More academically or theoretically oriented anthropologists are indebted to applied anthropologists for stimulating their interests in new areas of research.

Applied anthropology has, in other words, contributed significantly to scholarly and research activities, for as Goldschmidt (1979:5) reminds us, "the more a field is engaged in practical affairs, the greater the intellectual ferment; for programmatic activities raise issues and often new approaches which would otherwise escape the attention of the discipline." The distinction between pure and applied anthropology is a false dichotomy, for the two have experienced a parallel development and have been mutually supportive.

### APPLIED ANTHROPOLOGY'S IMAGE

To claim that applied and academic anthropology grew up together is not to suggest that they have enjoyed equal status within the profession. For much of this century, applied anthropology has had a relatively negative image due to its early association with colonialism. Most of the colonial powers, the British in particular, employed anthropologists to help facilitate the administration of local populations. The findings from their anthropological studies were used to meet the needs of the colonial administrators, which were rarely the same as the needs of the people themselves. Because of this association with colonial administrations, applied anthropology was stigmatized as an enterprise with a dubious set of ethical standards. In a more general sense, some anthropologists have rejected applied anthropology because they feel it would require them to compromise their cultural relativity. How can one be a cultural relativist, they would argue, when making suggestions on how people should change their cultures? Until recently, applied anthropology was seen by many anthropologists as something less than fully legitimate. As one commentator (Angrosino, 1976:3) has put it, "like an aristocratic family going into trade to keep up payments, applied anthropologists were felt to be simplifying the complex wisdom of their craft and getting their hands dirty in service."

## Organizations Supporting Applied Anthropology

Much of the applied anthropology carried out in recent decades has been supported by large public and private organizations seeking to better understand the cultural dimension of their sponsored programs. These include such international agencies as the U.S. Agency for International Development (USAID), the World Bank, the World Health Organization (WHO), the Ford Foundation, and the Population Council; certain national organizations such as the National Institutes of Health, the Bureau of Indian Affairs, and the U.S. Department of Agriculture; and on a local level, various hospitals, private corporations, school systems, urban planning departments, state offices of historic preservation, substance abuse programs, facilities for the aged, and family planning clinics.

Applied anthropologists study such social problems as rural poverty, illustrated by this Kentucky coal-mining family.

## RECENT LITERATURE

Perhaps the best way to illustrate how anthropological data have been applied to the solution of human problems is by listing a selection of case studies that have appeared in the recent literature. Although the range of applied anthropology is far wider than can be surveyed here, the following case studies should serve to illustrate the diversity of uses to which anthropological data have been put.

◆ The use of cultural data concerning African pastoralists to develop a more workable livestock development program (M. Horowitz, 1986).

◆ An analysis of housing policy implications of anthropological data gathered in a soup kitchen in a Connecticut town (Glasser, 1989).

◆ The detailed analysis of a child's skeletal remains by a physical anthropologist in order to determine the proper identity of a murder victim (Snow and Luke, 1989).

◆ The cultural resource investigation of historic and prehistoric remains along the Savannah River prior to the construction of a major dam (Anderson and Joseph, 1988).

◆ The application of ethnographic data on Apache Indians to a clinical nursing program on the San Carlos Apache Indian Reservation in San Carlos, Arizona (Gronseth, 1988).

◆ The introduction of an anthropological approach to the training of U.S. Peace Corps volunteers (Nolan, 1986).

◆ The analysis of cultural differences between Japanese and U.S. businesspersons involved in a joint venture contract (Hamada, 1988).

◆ The assessment of the social feasibility of a settlement project in northern Cameroon (Hoben, 1986).

◆ The study of local communities whose environments are affected by contaminated groundwater by an anthropologist who served on an interdisciplinary groundwater research project (Fitchen, 1988).

# The Anthropologist's Involvement in Applied Projects

The extent to which an applied anthropologist becomes involved in any given project can vary considerably. At the least interventionist extreme are those who provide information for planners and decision makers. This information can range from very concrete observational data to low- and intermediate-level concepts and propositions to the most abstract level of general theory. At another level, applied anthropologists, working alone or as members of an interdisciplinary team, may use the collected data to construct a plan for bringing about a desired change in a particular population. At the most interventionist extreme, applied anthropologists become involved in actually implementing and evaluating particular projects. Although relatively rare, these "action anthropologists" feel a professional responsibility not only to make their research findings available but also to propose, advocate, and carry out policy positions.

## SPECIALIZED ROLES OF APPLIED ANTHROPOLOGISTS

Applied anthropologists play a number of specialized roles, which are more thoroughly described by Van Willigen (1986:3–6).

**Policy researcher.** This role, perhaps the most common role for applied anthropologists, involves providing cultural data to policy makers so they can make the most informed policy decisions.

**Evaluator.** Also quite common, evaluators use their research skills to determine how well a program or policy has succeeded in its objectives.

**Impact assessor.** This role entails measuring or assessing the effect that a particular project, program, or policy has on local peoples. For example, the anthropologist serving in the role of impact assessor might determine the consequences, both intended and unintended, that a federal highway construction project may have on the community through which it runs.

**Planner.** In this fairly common role, applied anthropologists actively participate in the design of various programs, policies, and projects.

**Research analyst.** In this role, the applied anthropologist interprets research findings so that policy makers, planners, and administrators can make more culturally sensitive decisions.

**Needs assessor.** This role involves conducting a fairly specialized type of research designed to determine ahead of time the need for a proposed program or project.

**Trainer.** This is essentially a teaching role in which the applied anthropologist imparts cultural knowledge about certain populations to groups that are expected to work in cross-cultural situations (e.g., training a group of U.S. engineers to be better aware of the cultural environment of Saudi Arabia where they will work for two years building a U.S. embassy).

**Advocate.** This relatively rare role involves becoming an active supporter of a particular group of people. Usually involving at least some political action, this role is most frequently combined with other roles.

**Expert witness.** This role, usually played on a short-term basis, involves the presentation of culturally relevant research findings as part of judicial proceedings through legal briefs, depositions, or direct testimony.

**Forensic specialist.** In this role, experts use physical anthropological techniques to develop evidence in the identification of human remains.

**Cultural resource manager.** This role involves carrying out studies and excavations at construction sites for the purpose of determining how best to preserve culturally and historically significant sites.

**Administrator/manager.** When applied anthropologists assume direct administrative responsibility for a particular project, they are working in this specialized role.

**Cultural broker.** This role involves serving as a liaison between the program planner and administrators on the one hand and local ethnic communities on the other.

These specialized roles are not mutually exclusive. Applied anthropologists will sometimes play two or more of these roles as part of the same job. For example, as part of one's role as a policy researcher, an applied anthropologist may also conduct research as a needs assessor before a program is initiated and as an impact assessor and evaluator after the program has concluded.

## ◆ ◆ ◆
# Special Features of Anthropology

What does the discipline of anthropology have to offer as an applied science? The answer to this question lies largely in the unique approach to the study of humans that anthropology has taken from its earliest beginnings. Some of the special features of anthropology that contribute to its potential as a policy science are (1) participant-observation, (2) the holistic perspective, (3) the development of a regional expertise, (4) the emic view, and (5) the basic value orientation of cultural relativism.

**Participant-observation.** Direct field observation, a hallmark of twentieth-century anthropology, can lead to a fuller understanding of the sociocultural realities than might be possible by relying on secondary sources of information. Also, the rapport developed while conducting participant-observation research can be drawn upon in the implementation stage of the applied project.

**The holistic perspective.** This distinctive feature of anthropology forces us to look at multiple variables and see human problems in their historical, economic, and cultural contexts. This conceptual orientation reminds us that the various parts of a sociocultural system are interconnected to the extent that a change in one part of the system is likely to cause changes in other parts. The holistic approach also encourages us to look at the problem in terms of both the short run and the long run.

Applied anthropologists can serve as consultants, or "cultural brokers," to help businesspersons better understand the cultures of their international business partners.

**Regional expertise.** Many anthropologists, despite recent trends toward specialization, continue to function as "culture area specialists" (e.g., Africanists, Micronesianists). The cultural anthropologist who has conducted doctoral research in Zambia, for example, will frequently return to that country for subsequent field studies. Thus, long-term association with a cultural region provides a depth of geographic coverage that most policy makers lack.

**The emic view.** A major insight of anthropology in general—and applied anthropology specifically—is that linguistic and cultural differences invariably exist between project bureaucrats and the local client populations. Whatever the setting of a particular project—be it an agricultural development scheme in Zimbabwe, an inner-city hospital in Detroit, or a classroom in rural Peru—the applied anthropologist brings to the project the perspective of the local people, what anthropologists call the **emic view.** By describing the emic view (using the mental categories and assumptions of the local people rather than their own), anthropologists can provide program planners and administrators with strategic information that can seriously affect the outcome of programs of planned change.

**Cultural relativism.** The basic principle of cultural relativism (see Chapter 2), a vital part of every cultural anthropologist's training, tends to foster tolerance, which can be particularly relevant for applied anthropologists working in complex organizations. For example, tolerance can help anthropologists cross "class" lines and relate to a wide range of people in the complex organization (e.g., hospital, school system) in which they are working.

The five features of anthropology just discussed can very definitely enhance the discipline's effectiveness as a policy science. Nevertheless, when compared to other disciplines, anthropology has some drawbacks that limit its effectiveness in solving societal problems. First, anthropologists have not, by and large, developed any time-effective research methods; the widely used anthropological data-gathering technique of participant-observation, which usually requires up to a year or more, is not particularly well suited to the more accelerated time schedules of applied programs of change. Second, in an attempt to protect "their people," anthropologists frequently assume an "underdog bias" that prevents them from balancing the interests of the local people with those of the project administrators. Finally, with their strong tradition of qualitative research methods, anthropologists have been relatively unsophisticated in their use of quantitative data, although recently a number of anthropologists have begun to use more quantitative approaches.

## The Rise of Applied Anthropology

Although it is possible to trace the roots of applied anthropology back to Herodotus in the fifth century B.C. (Van Willigen, 1986:18), World War II marked a significant acceleration of interest in applying the insights of anthropology to the solution of contemporary societal problems. The decade of the 1930s witnessed an appreciable increase in the number of anthropologists being hired in nonacademic settings. As previously mentioned, anthropologists outside the United States were hired by colonial governments to conduct research on native populations for the purpose of administering these dependent peoples more effectively. Close to home, anthropologist John Collier, President Franklin Roosevelt's commissioner of Indian affairs, created the

John Collier, an applied anthropologist who became the Commissioner of Indian Affairs during Franklin Roosevelt's administration.

Applied Anthropology Unit of Indian Affairs in the early 1930s for the purpose of studying the prospects of certain Indian groups that were developing self-governing organizations, as required by the 1934 Indian Reorganization Act; anthropologists hired by the U.S. Department of Agriculture conducted research on economic development at certain Indian reservations; and such anthropologists as W. Lloyd Warner and Burleigh Gardner, working as part of the interdisciplinary Committee on Human Relations in Industry at the University of Chicago, engaged in applied anthropological research on issues related to industrial management, working conditions, and productivity.

## APPLIED ANTHROPOLOGY DURING WWII

Even though applied anthropologists were becoming increasingly active during the years of the Great Depression, the real stimulus came in the 1940s. According to Partridge and Eddy (1978:27), " . . . the crisis of war provided unprecedented opportunities for anthropologists to participate in efforts related to war activity."

The practical contributions anthropologists made during the war years were wide-ranging. A sizeable number of U.S. anthropologists, after years of working among contemporary "primitive" cultures, returned to the United States to apply their skills to their own society. The war had generated so much interest in the practical uses of anthropology that in 1941 the Society for Applied Anthropology was founded at Harvard University, along with the new scholarly journal called *Applied Anthropology,* which was subsequently renamed *Human Organization.* In fact, the entire profession of anthropology in the United States was so committed to contributing to the war effort that the American Anthropological Association passed a resolution in 1941 pledging the skills and knowledge of its membership to the successful completion of the war. While too extensive to describe completely, the following were among some of the more notable contributions made by anthropologists during the war years:

1. In 1939 the National Research Council established the Committee for National Morale to consider how insights from anthropology and psychology could be applied to the improvement of morale during wartime.
2. In 1942, Randall and Damon, two physical anthropologists, used their expertise in human anatomy to redesign British gun turrets on aircraft for use by U.S. gunners.
3. The National Research Council in 1940 set up the Committee on Food Habits to provide scientific research on nutritional levels and food preferences, which helped establish the government's policy on wartime food rationing.
4. After the United States officially entered the war in late 1941, an appreciable number of distinguished anthropologists joined the war effort by providing cultural data for the Office of War Information. The national character studies conducted by Geoffrey Gorer, Margaret Mead, and Ruth Benedict among others were used to help the federal government make important decisions on the conduct of relations with our allies as well as our adversaries.
5. Perhaps the best-known (and most controversial) involvement of anthropologists during the war years centered on their work with the relocation of Japanese-American interns on the West Coast. Such anthropologists as Conrad Arensberg, Alexander Leighton, and Edward Spicer conducted research in the internment camps and served as liaisons between the Japanese-Americans interns and the government administrators. Even though the professional ethics of the anthropologists involved came under question (some colleagues considered them to be supporting an illegal, immoral, and inhumane process), the anthropologists themselves viewed their participation as helping to alleviate a potentially more inhumane process.

## APPLIED ANTHROPOLOGY DURING THE 1950S AND 1960S

In the several decades after the war, applied anthropology continued its development but in a different fashion and without the fervor of the war years. While most leading U.S. anthropologists had contributed their skills to government service during the war, during the 1950s and 1960s a chasm developed between applied anthropology and academic anthropology. This was largely the result of the unprecedented growth of higher education during these decades. The personnel shortages in academia caused by the sudden growth in higher education led many graduates to take teaching and research positions in departments of anthropology rather than work as applied anthropologists. In addition to the postwar availability of academic positions, the general exodus from government employment was accelerated by an increasing disenchantment with national policy surrounding the politics of McCarthyism, the cold war, and the Vietnamese conflict. Thus, once again, many anthropologists turned their attention to theoretical, rather than applied, problems.

The accelerated growth of academic anthropology during the 1950s and 1960s by no means put an end to applied anthropology. Several significant changes did emerge, however, in the way that applied anthropology was practiced in the decades following the war. First, the relatively limited role of researcher/consultant that applied anthropologists played during the 1930s and 1940s was expanded considerably to include more implementation and intervention. According to Van Willigen (1986:28–29), "instead of merely providing information and an occasional recommendation, the anthropologists begin [*sic*] to take increasing responsibility for problem solution." A second change, closely related to the first, involved the question of how applied anthropologists dealt with their own values. Prior to the 1950s, most anthropologists adhered to a **value-free philosophy,** whereby they studiously avoided interjecting their own values into their work. The earlier applied anthropologists, in an attempt to maintain their scientific objectivity, avoided making any recommendations as to what policy they thought should be followed. During the postwar years, however, some applied anthropologists argued that, since it was impossible to separate personal values from one's own work, applied anthropologists should feel free to set goals and objectives for their clients, provided they made explicit their own value positions.

This greatly expanded role of applied anthropologists during the fifties is perhaps best illustrated by two projects, one involving a Native American group in Iowa

After World War II, many anthropologists left government service and returned to positions in colleges and universities. This trend, which continued through the 50s and 60s, witnessed a return to more theoretical concerns.

The understandings that emerge from applied anthropological studies of peasant farming communities can be helpful in agricultural development programs.

and the other involving Peruvian peasants. In the first, under the direction of Sol Tax, six graduate students from the University of Chicago participated in the **Fox Project,** a program involving both research on and intervention in the culture of the Fox Indians. Viewing many of the problems faced by the Fox Indians as stemming from their relationship to the non-Indian community, the project participants introduced several innovations, such as adult education programs, crafts projects, and scholarships, designed to instill self-confidence and enable the Indians to take greater control over their lives. (For a good description of some of the consequences of this early attempt at "action anthropology," see Gearing, Netting, and Peattie, 1960).

The other example of anthropological intervention during the 1950s was the **Vicos Project** headed by Allan Holmberg and his colleagues at Cornell University (Holmberg, 1971). This experimental five-year project, administered jointly with the Peruvian Institute of In-

digenous Affairs, focused on transforming a nonproductive and dependent hacienda (a large farm worked by serflike peasants) into an economically productive and self-governing community. Under the careful supervision of both anthropologists and technicians, a number of innovations were introduced, including new farming technology (seeds, fertilizers, insecticides, etc.), educational programs, a school lunch program, and sewing lessons for women. Long-held suspicions among the peasant farmers gradually decreased to the point where the farmers became so empowered that they began to seek communal solutions to their problems. By the end of the project there were significant improvements in levels of family income, health standards, and education. Perhaps the most dramatic consequence of the Vicos Project was that the families living on the hacienda came to own the land themselves rather than working on it as sharecroppers. The Vicos Project, then, serves as a model development project whereby planned social and

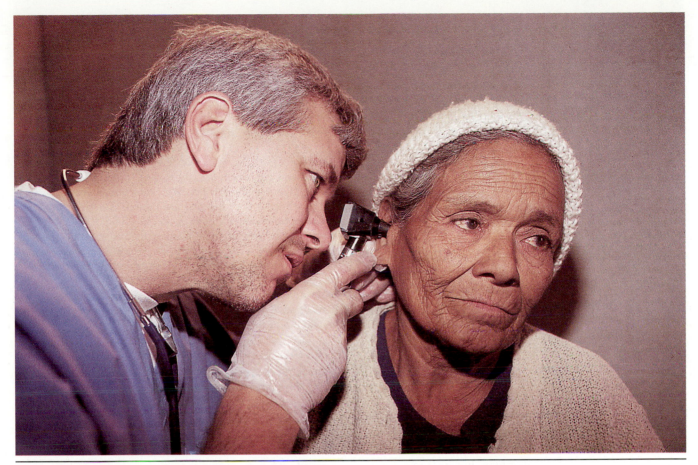

Applied anthropological research helps medical personnel provide more efficient services to Third World peoples. Here a Western doctor provides medical assistance in rural Honduras.

economic changes are brought about by cooperative efforts between applied anthropologists, local administrators, and the indigenous people.

## APPLIED ANTHROPOLOGY DURING THE 1970S AND 1980S

The 1970s and 1980s have witnessed what Angrosino (1976) refers to as the **new applied anthropology,** characterized by contract work for public service agencies done away from academic campuses. Whereas many of the applied anthropologists of the 1950s and 1960s were essentially academics who were engaged in short-term applied projects, many of the new applied anthropologists are not academics but are full-time employees of the hiring agencies. This developmental stage is largely the result of two important trends essentially external to the discipline of anthropology. First, for the past two decades there has been a dramatically declining market for academic jobs. The abundance of jobs that marked the fifties and sixties became a shortage of jobs during the seventies and eighties. A second factor contributing to the new applied anthropology is the increase in federal legislation mandating policy research that can be accomplished effectively by anthropologists. For example, the National Historic Preservation Act (1966), the National Environmental Policy Act (1969), the Foreign Assistance Act (1973), and the Community Development Act (1974) all provide for policy research of a cultural nature. Some of these laws call for cultural anthropologists to conduct environmental impact studies on those communities affected by federally funded projects. Others create employment opportunities for applied anthropologists (cultural resource managers) who are expected to preserve our historical/prehistorical heritage that could be destroyed by building projects.

The consequence of these two factors (fewer academic jobs coupled with greater research opportunities) was an increase in anthropology Ph.D.s finding employment outside of academia. This trend has been marked by the development of various master's programs in applied anthropology as well as by the rise in professional organizations of applied or practicing anthropologists, such as the Washington Area Association of Professional Anthropologists (WAPA), and a proliferation of state and regional organizations.

◆  ◆  ◆
## The Ethics of Applied Anthropology

All field anthropologists—whether applied or theoretical—find themselves in social situations that are both varied and complex because they work with people in different role relationships. They are involved with, and have responsibilities to, their subjects, their discipline, colleagues both in and outside of anthropology, their host governments, their own governments, and their sponsoring agencies.

Applied anthropologists must operate in an even more complex situation, for their work frequently is aimed at facilitating some type of change in the culture or social structure of the local population. Under such socially complex conditions it is likely that the anthropologist, having to choose between conflicting values, will be faced with ethical dilemmas. For example, how do you make your findings public without jeopardizing the anonymity of your informants? Can you ever be certain that the data your informants gave you will not eventually be used to harm them? How can you be certain that the project you are working on will in fact be beneficial for the target population? To what extent should you become personally involved in the lives of the people you are studying? Should you intervene to stop illegal activity? These are just a few of the ethical questions that arise when doing anthropological research. (For case materials on a wider range of ethical issues, see Appell, 1978.)

Like all applied anthropologists, archaeologists may face difficult ethical questions (see Green, 1984). They have obligations to their employers, but they also have obligations to the public at large to preserve as much as possible of our historical and prehistorical heritage. Moreover, they bear a responsibility to their colleagues in archaeology to acquire the best quality data possible from sites that are about to be destroyed. Some people would say that CRM archaeologists also have an ethical obligation to the "data base," the actual archaeological

remains, comparable to the obligation that cultural anthropologists have to their living informants.

While recognizing that anthropologists continually have to face such ethical decisions, the profession makes it clear that each member ultimately is responsible for his or her own ethical conduct. According to the Principles of Professional Responsibility of the American Anthropological Association (as revised through 1990),

Anthropologists' relations with their discipline, with the individuals and groups among whom they conduct research or to whom they provide services, with their employers and with their own host governments, are varied, complex, sensitive, and sometimes difficult to reconcile. In a field of such complex involvements, misunderstandings, conflicts and the need to make choices among apparently incompatible values are constantly generated. The most fundamental responsibility of anthropologists is to anticipate such difficulties and to resolve them in ways that are compatible with the principles stated here. If such resolution is impossible, anthropological work should not be undertaken or continued.

A concern for professional ethics is hardly a recent phenomenon among anthropologists. As early as 1919, Franz Boas, the guru of the first generation of anthropologists in the United States, spoke out vociferously against the practice of anthropologists engaging in spying activities while allegedly conducting scientific research. Writing in *The Nation,* Boas (1919:797) commented, "A person who uses science as a cover for political spying . . . prostitutes science in an unpardonable way and forfeits the right to be classed as a scientist." While anthropologists since the beginning have been aware of the ethical dilemmas they face, the profession did not adopt a comprehensive code of behavioral standards until the 1970s. In 1971 the American Anthropological Association adopted the Principles of Professional Responsibility and established its Committee on Ethics, while the Society for Applied Anthropology published its Statement on Professional and Ethical Responsibilities in 1975.

### PROJECT CAMELOT

The publication of these professional codes of ethics in the 1970s was, to a large degree, precipitated by a controversial event that occurred in the preceding decade—**Project Camelot,** a six-million-dollar research project funded by the U.S. Army to study the causes of civil violence in a number of countries in Asia, Latin America, Africa, and Europe. More specifically, Project

Camelot was designed to gather data on counterinsurgency that would enable the U.S. Army to cope more effectively with internal revolutions in foreign countries.

The research project, which had hired the services of a number of prominent anthropologists and social scientists, was scheduled to begin its work in Latin America. Six months after the project director was hired, however, Project Camelot was canceled by the secretary of defense. Word about this clandestine operation in Chile was brought to the attention of the Chilean senate, which reacted with outrage over the apparent U.S. interference in its internal affairs.

Although the project never got under way, it had enormous repercussions on the social sciences in general and the discipline of anthropology in particular. The heated debate among anthropologists that followed revolved around two important questions. First, was Project Camelot a legitimately objective attempt to gather social science data, or was it a cover for the U.S. Army to intervene in the internal political affairs of a sovereign nation? And second, were the participating anthropologists misled into thinking that scientific research was the project's sole objective while in fact they were really (and perhaps unwittingly) serving as undercover spies?

One of the very practical and immediate consequences of the Project Camelot controversy was the cloud of suspicion that fell over all legitimate anthropological research. For years afterward many U.S. anthropologists experienced difficulties trying to prove that they were not engaged in secret research sponsored by the CIA or the Department of Defense. On a personal note, five years after the demise of Project Camelot in Chile, one of the authors of this text was questioned on several occasions by his Kikuyu informants in Kenya (who were aware of Project Camelot) about his possible links with the United States government.

The discipline of anthropology learned in important—albeit costly—lesson from the Project Camelot affair. That is, anthropologists have a responsibility to their subjects, their profession, their colleagues, and themselves to be aware of the motives, objectives, and assumptions of the organizations sponsoring their research. In other words, all anthropologists have an ethical responsibility to avoid employment or the receipt of funds from any organization that would use their research findings to support policies that are inhumane, potentially harmful to the research subjects, or in any way morally questionable. Given the nature of applied anthropology, such ethical questions are particularly relevant for the simple reason that they are more likely to present themselves.

## ANTHROPOLOGISTS' MAJOR AREAS OF RESPONSIBILITY

The codes of professional ethic adopted by the American Anthropological Association (AAA) and later by the Society for Applied Anthropology are not appreciably different. Both codes cover the major areas of responsibilities for practicing anthropologists, including the following:

*Responsibility to the people studied.* According to the AAA, the anthropologist's paramount responsibility is to the people he or she studies. Every effort must be made to protect the physical, psychological, and social well-being of the people under study. The aims and anticipated consequences of the research must be clearly communicated to the research subjects so they can be in the best position to decide for themselves whether or not they wish to participate in the research. Participation is to be voluntary and should be based on the principle of informed consent. Informants should not be exploited, and their right to remain anonymous must be protected.

*Responsibility to the public.* Anthropologists have a fundamental responsibility to respect the dignity, integrity, and worth of the communities that will be directly affected by the research findings. In a more general sense, anthropologists have a responsibility to the general public to disseminate their findings truthfully and openly. They are also expected to make their findings available to the public for use in policy formation.

*Responsibility to the discipline.* Anthropologists bear responsibility for maintaining the reputation of the discipline and their colleagues. They must avoid engaging in any research that cannot be freely and openly reported. Anthropologists must refrain from any behavior that will jeopardize future research for other members of the profession.

*Responsibility to students.* Anthropologists should be fair, candid, and nonexploitative when dealing with their students. They should alert students to the ethical problems of research and should acknowledge in print the contributions that students make to their professional activities, including both research and publication.

*Responsibility to sponsors.* Anthropologists have a professional responsibility to be honest about their qualifications, capabilities, and purposes. Before accepting employment or research funding, an anthropologists is obligated to reflect sincerely upon the purposes of the sponsoring organizations and the potential uses to which the findings will be put. Anthropologists must re-

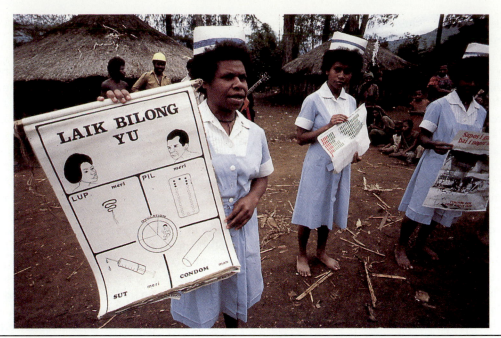

Since programs designed to reduce rapid population growth must be sensitive to local cultural patterns, applied anthropology is playing an increasingly important role in family planning efforts throughout the world. Here, nurses provide contraceptive information to local people at a family planning clinic in Papua New Guinea.

tain the right to make all ethical decisions in their research and must report the research findings accurately, openly, and completely.

*Responsibility to one's own government and the host government(s).* Anthropologists should be honest and candid in their relationships with both their own and the host governments. They should demand assurances that they will not be asked to compromise their professional standards or ethics as a precondition for research clearance. They should conduct no clandestine research, write no secret reports, and engage in no debriefings.

## ◆ Summary

1. Traditionally, many anthropologists have distinguished between pure anthropology (aimed at refining the discipline's theory, method, and data) and applied anthropology (focusing on using anthropological insights for the solution of practical social problems). For much of this century, applied anthropology has occupied a lower status within the discipline, although in recent years it has gained increasing respectability within the profession.
2. Applied anthropologists work in a wide range of settings, both at home and abroad. Moreover, they play a number of specialized roles, including policy researcher, impact assessor, expert witness, trainer, forensic specialist, and cultural resource manager.
3. Compared to other social sciences, anthropology can make a number of unique contributions as a policy science. For example, anthropologists bring to a research setting their skills as participant-observers, the capacity to view human phenomena from a holistic perspective, their regional expertise, a willingness to see the world from the perspective of the local people (emic view), and the value orientation of cultural relativism.
4. Applied anthropology grew in activity during the 1930s. At the beginning of the following decade, WWII provided vast opportunities for anthropologists to turn their efforts to applied projects relating to the war. The postwar boom in higher education lured many anthropologists back into academic positions during the 1950s and 1960s, but the subsequent decline in academic positions for anthropologists during the 1970s and 1980s resulted in an increase in applied types of employment outside of colleges and museums.
5. Anthropologists in general—but particularly applied anthropologists—face a number of ethical problems when conducting their research. One very important ethical issue to which applied anthropologists must be sensitive is whether the people being studied will benefit

from the proposed changes. Both the American Anthropological Association and the Society for Applied Anthropology have identified areas of ethical responsibility for practicing anthropologists, including responsibilities to the people under study, the local communities, the host governments as well as their own government, other members of the scholarly community, organizations that sponsor research, and their own students.

## ◆ Key Terms

| | |
|---|---|
| administrator/manager | impact assessor |
| advocate | needs assessor |
| cultural broker | new applied anthropology |
| contract archaeology | planner |
| cultural relativism | policy researcher |
| cultural resource manager | Project Camelot |
| emic view | public archaeology |
| evaluator | research analyst |
| expert witness | salvage archaeologist |
| forensic specialist | trainer |
| Fox Project | value-free philosophy |
| holistic perspective | Vicos Project |

## ◆ Suggested Readings

Appell, G. N. *Ethical Dilemmas in Anthropological Inquiry: A Case Book.* Waltham, Mass.: Crossroads Press, 1978. This case book presents scenarios dealing with a broad range of ethical situations faced by anthropologists in the field. Over ninety different cases are presented, explaining the relations of the anthropologist to informants, the host community, the host government, funding agencies, and other scholars.

Bodley, John H. *Anthropology and Contemporary Human Problems.* Palo Alto, Calif.: Mayfield Publishing, 1984. Bodley argues that many of the problems facing the world today—such as overconsumption, resource depletion, hunger and starvation, overpopulation, violence, and war—are inherent in the basic cultural patterns of modern, industrial civilization.

Chambers, Erve. *Applied Anthropology: A Practical Guide.* Englewood Cliffs, N.J.: Prentice-Hall, 1985. A synthesis of the field of applied anthropology focusing on (a) how the profession has responded to changing career opportunities during the present century, (b) types of applied anthropology being conducted, and (c) the ethical issues involved in applied anthropology.

Eddy, Elizabeth, and W. Partridge (Eds.). *Applied Anthropology in America* (2nd ed.). New York: Columbia University Press, 1987. A collection of essays by noted applied anthropologists on various aspects of applying anthropology to American society. The introductory essay by the editors provides a particularly good discussion of the development of applied anthropology in the United States.

Podolefsky, Aaron, and Peter J. Brown (Eds.). *Applying Anthropology: An Introductory Reader.* Mountain View, Calif.: Mayfield Publishing, 1989. A collection of essays designed to help students better understand how anthropological insights and methods can contribute to the solution of human problems. While the majority of the volume is devoted to applied cultural anthropology, eighteen segments deal with applied biological anthropology and applied archaeology.

Van Willigen, John. *Applied Anthropology: An Introduction.* South Hadley, Mass.: Bergin and Garvey, 1986. Along with Chambers (1985), an excellent introduction to the growing field of applied anthropology for students contemplating a nonacademic career in anthropology. Topics covered include the history of applied anthropology, various intervention strategies, ethical issues, and the role of applied anthropologists in evaluation research.

Van Willigen, John, Barbara Rylko-Bauer, and Ann McElroy (Eds.). Making Our Research Useful. Boulder, Colo.: Westview Press, 1989. A recent collection of firsthand reports by applied anthropologists that tends to focus on strategies for increasing the use of anthropological research findings by policy makers.

Wulff, Robert, and Shirley Fiske (Eds.). *Anthropological Praxis: Translating Knowledge into Action.* Boulder, Colo.: Westview Press, 1987. A collection of essays by applied anthropologists written especially for this volume on how they applied their trade to the solution of specific societal problems. Dealing with cases from both home and abroad, all of the case studies, written in the same format, discuss (a) client and problem, (b) process and players, (c) results and evaluation, and (d) the anthropological difference.

## Some Detailed Examples

Anthropologists have applied their theories, methods, and insights to a wide range of practical social problems throughout much of the present century. They have played a number of different roles as they have brought their unique anthropological skills to bear on the solution of social problems. Here we examine in some depth three specific instances of how anthropology can be useful in our everyday lives. These cases show how applied anthropologists have (1) served as cultural mediators in a dispute between local Trukese villagers and the government, (2) suggested practical measures for improving a family planning clinic in Ecuador, and (3) evaluated the cultural dimension of a nationwide educational program in the United States.

◆ **Applied anthropologists serve as mediators in a dispute between Trukese villagers and the local government over a government-sponsored construction project.**

Whenever central governments institute programs of planned change—be it in agriculture, medicine, family planning, or education—more likely than not problems will emerge with the local target population. This is because governments and local populations frequently have different cultural values and interests and starts from a different set of cultural assumptions. In some situations, the policies and plans of the central government are so much at odds with the needs of the local population that an impasse emerges. Demonstrations, petitions, and other forms of popular protest may arise in opposition to the government's plans, hostilities and mistrust may be generated in both camps, and in some serious cases, the progress of the proposed project may come to a virtual standstill. In such situations, cultural anthropologists have been recruited to serve as intercultural mediators between the government and the local people whose lives are being affected by the government programs. In the words of Richard Salisbury (1976:255), anthropologists serve in the role of "societal ombudsmen."

In the late 1970s, the government of the Trust Territories for the Island of Truk (administered by the United States) made plans to expand the airport. The plans were drawn up and the environmental impact study (required by U.S. law) was completed without consulting the local villagers. The airport expansion, as proposed, would have created a number of problems for the local people. For example, certain local fishing areas would be destroyed by proposed dredging operations; the expanded runway would prevent the villagers from mooring their boats near their homes; construction would destroy several cultural and historical landmarks; and during construction the project would generate high levels of noise and dust. Naturally, the people objected. Protest demonstrations and the threat of a legal injunction to stop construction convinced the government that it had a serious problem.

In an attempt to address some of the complaints of the local people, the government appointed Thomas King, an archaeological consultant in historic preservation, to mediate officially between the government and the local villagers on all matters pertaining to construction impact. While having no official status in the mediation process, King's wife, Patricia Parker, a cultural anthropologist who was conducting ethnographic research on Trukese land law, played an important role translating the villager's concerns into language the government officials could understand (see Parker and King, 1987).

The first order of business facing this wife and husband negotiating team was to work with the villagers to develop a list of specific grievances that could serve as the basis for negotiations. Meetings were held in the various villages to allow the local people themselves to reach some consensus on the nature of their complaints against the proposed airport expansion. Parker, fluent in the local language, attended these meetings and provided detailed outlines of the villagers' concerns to King, who, in turn, brought the concerns up with the government officials. This team of "cultural negotiators" worked successfully, for they supplemented each other's strengths.

Parker and King thus served as cultural mediators or cultural brokers between the government and the local Trukese villagers. Since they came to understand the constraints and interests of both sides of the controversy, they were able to mediate from a fairly strong knowledge base, thereby avoiding a hardening of positions on either side. As a result of the efforts of these anthropological intermediaries, the following modifications were made. First, dredging operations were changed to the extent that local fishing areas were only minimally affected, and where they were affected, the villagers received block grant compensation for the potential loss of food. Second, the government agreed to construct a new anchorage for local fishing boats. And, third, construction plans were altered so that the cultural and historic landmarks were not destroyed. In the final analysis, the use of two anthropologists to mediate between the interests of the government and the local Trukese villagers worked out satisfactorily for all parties concerned. The villagers were pleased with most of the modifications made in the original plans and the compensation they received. The government, although its costs were increased, now has an expanded airport, the building of which was not delayed due to litigation.

◆ **Applied physical anthropologists use their understandings and measurement of human anatomy to redesign gun turrets on Allied aircraft during WWII.**

Prior to World War II the sub-discipline of physical anthropology—with its focus on the study of human biological evolution and contemporary human variations—was almost exclusively a "pure" or academic scientific endeavor. In other words, physical anthropologists were pursuing knowledge for its own sake and were not particularly concerned with using their insights or methods for the solution of societal problems. Wars, however, often bring about some strange and surprising events. Who would have imagined that military needs during World War II would have served as the catalyst that initiated a field of applied physical anthropology which has since come to be known as "Engineering Anthropology?"

Before entering the war in 1941, the United States had supplied Britain with bombing aircraft equipped with gun-turrets (movable enclosures which

51

housed the gunner and two machine guns). The size and structure of the gun turrets were built by U.S. aircraft manufacturers to accommodate British gunners. Upon entering the War after the bombing of Pearl Harbor, U.S. military commanders expected their own flight crews to use these same aircraft. Much to their dismay, however, they found that only a small percentage of American crewmen could fit into the gun turrets designed according to British specifications. At the suggestion of Harvard physical anthropologist Dr. E. A. Hooton, The Aero Medical Laboratory hired a team of physical anthropologists to conduct an anthropometric survey of U.S. aircrewmen. Within months these applied physical anthropologists had collected sufficient data on the body sizes of U.S. aircrew members to redesign the gun turrets. According to Hertzberg (1975:456), himself an engineering anthropologist, these redesigned gun turrets

. . . increased every American gunner's efficiency in defense, greatly reduced the discomfort of long occupancy in a cramped enclosure, and insured effective means of rapid escape from an aircraft in emergency, or the removal of a casualty. In a life-or-death struggle, even a small advantage in combat effectiveness enhances survival. As these turrets reached the combat zone, a full stream of gunners became available to man (sic) them, compared to the previous trickle; gunner efficiency in defense rose and the rate of aircraft loss declined; so that finally American airpower could destroy Axis manufacturing and supply capability, forcing an end to the war.

◆ **An anthropological study of womens' attitudes and behaviors in Ecuador results in practical recommendations for maximizing the use of family planning clinics.**

For the past several decades, many development experts have identified high birth rates as the major obstacle to economic development among the lesser developed nations of the world. No matter how successful programs in health, education, and agriculture may be, any gains will be offset if the society is experiencing high annual population growth. Consequently, many international development organizations have given top priority to family planning programs designed to slow population growth. Since any attempt to reduce rapid population growth must be sensitive to local cultural patterns, applied anthropologists have played an increasingly significant role in family planning programs throughout the world.

A common way to evaluate the success of family planning programs is to measure the extent to which people actually participate in them. A family planning clinic, for example, is only as successful as the number of people who use its services. A number of significant factors may affect whether women initially attend, or return to, family planning clinics, including womens' attitudes toward contraception, the quality of the interaction with staff members, and the length of time they wait to see a doctor. Susan Scrimshaw (1976), an applied anthropologist studying family planning clinics in Ecuador, identified another significant factor—womens' modesty—that had important implications for how women felt about attending family planning clinics.

Using traditional anthropological methods, Scrimshaw collected data on sixty-five families living in Guayaquil, Ecuador, a tropical port city of approximately 1 million people. Scrimshaw found that small girls in Guayaquil, as in South America generally, are taught the virtues of modesty at a very early age. Though boys are frequently seen without pants up until the age of four or five, little girls always have their genitals covered. Since girls usually reach puberty without any prior knowledge of menstruation, their first menstruation is both frightening and embarrassing. In general, Scrimshaw found that girls and women in Guayaquil do not have very positive attitudes about their bodies, their sexuality, or such natural bodily processes as menstruation, all of which are associated with the word *verguenza* (literally "shame" or "embarrassment"). Given this strong sense of modesty that women have about their bodies, their sexuality, and reproduction, it is not surprising that these Ecuadorian women feel uncomfortable even talking about contraceptives, let alone submitted to gynecological examinations.

Scrimshaw also conducted a survey on the use of family planning clinics among 2,936 women. She found that even though 74 percent of the women questioned wanted more information on birth control methods, only 20 percent of them had actually ever taken the initiative to find the information, and less than 5 percent of the women surveyed had ever been to a family planning clinic. When those women who had attended were asked why they never returned, nearly half (48 percent) indicated they had been influenced by shame and embarrassment (*verguenza*). Information gained through participant-observation at a number of these family planning clinics helped explain why women were so reluctant to return to the clinics. Screening questions were asked by an intake worker usually in earshot of other patients. Doctors gave patients very little explanatory information while requesting a large amount of information from them, much of which was never used. The clinics provided no place for women to undress in private and did not supply the women with gowns, nor were the women properly draped during their physical exams. Even for women in the United States who were usually afforded these courtesies, gynecological exams are often uncomfortable and embarrassing. Submitting to a physical examination under conditions of minimal privacy was even more difficult for these Ecuadorian women because of their strong cultural emphasis on feminine modesty.

On the basis of these findings on womens' modesty, Scrimshaw (1976: 177–78) made the following practical recommendations for maximizing the use of family planning clinics in Guayaquil:

1. Discreetness: Interviews with women in clinics should not be held within the hearing of anyone but the parties directly involved. Questions should be kept to a minimum.
2. Privacy: Wherever possible, a woman should be given privacy to undress (even a screen or curtain would help). The examining room should insure security and privacy.
3. Awareness of modesty: A drape should be provided for a woman's legs.

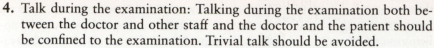

4. Talk during the examination: Talking during the examination both between the doctor and other staff and the doctor and the patient should be confined to the examination. Trivial talk should be avoided.

5. Frequency of visits to the clinic and examination: Many clinics require monthly visits for examinations and supplies. In most cases such frequent examinations are unnecessary, and supplies can be picked up every three months.

6. Male versus female physicians: All women questioned said they preferred female physicians. Women should be actively recruited and employed wherever possible.

These are the types of recommendations that can be useful to those administering family planning clinics in Ecuador. While none of these proposed changes by themselves will make or break a family planning program, this case study does point up the need for the clinical staff to understand and acknowledge the feelings of modesty of Ecuadorian women. It also demonstrates the role that cultural anthropologists can play in bringing this important social value to the attention of the clinical staff.

◆ **An applied educational anthropologist, working as part of an interdisciplinary team, contributes a unique perspective to the evaluation of a nationwide program to educate high school dropouts.**

David Fetterman, a Ph.D. in educational/medical anthropology from Stanford University, provides an excellent example of how cultural anthropology can be applied to the evaluation of a national educational program (see Fetterman, 1987 and 1988). Working for a private research corporation specializing in evaluation research, Fetterman was the anthropologist on a multidisciplinary team responsible for evaluating the Career Intern Program, an alternative high school program designed to enable dropouts and potential dropouts to earn a high school degree while working at their own pace. This nationwide program, funded by the Department of Labor and monitored by the National Institute of Education, allowed most students to complete their high school education on an accelerated basis, usually in two years rather than the traditional three. The Career Intern Program represents one of the few exemplary educational programs for economically disadvantaged minority youth.

Being in charge of the ethnographic portion of the evaluation, Fetterman was responsible for producing case studies of each of the four program sites: Bushwick, New York; Poughkeepsie, New York; East Detroit, Michigan; and Seattle, Washington. More specifically, Fetterman's task involved analyzing all of the components in the program—the students, teachers, counselors, directors, disseminators, monitors, funders, and even the evaluators themselves—in order to identify the relationship between student outcomes and various program components. Fetterman used traditional anthropological data-gathering techniques such as participant-observation, nonparticipant-observation, and structured and unstructured interviews. Fetterman's ethnographic research differed from more traditional anthropological research in that less fieldwork time was available for this evaluation project. Rather than spending six or eight months in each site, he made intensive two-week visits to each site every three months for a total period of three years.

Fetterman's findings—some of which were couched in anthropological terminology—can be summarized as follows:

1. For each of the program sites the "ethos" or cultural component of the programs was documented. For example, Fetterman showed that while maintaining high expectations, teachers, counselors, and administrators created a supportive environment for students. He also showed that the long list of rules and regulations gave students both behavioral guidelines as well as a feeling that people cared about them.

2. Fetterman described the role that certain rituals played in developing group loyalty and identity. These rituals included basketball games, bake sales, student council elections, and perhaps most importantly, the periodic appreciation days during which students were recognized for their achievements in a number of areas. These rituals bonded students and staff and brought a sense of social solidarity to the entire school.

3. The ethnographic evaluation also identified the importance of certain rites of passage (ceremonies acknowledging one's change of status) for students' self-esteem. In addition to the final graduation ceremony, the programs were divided into "new groups" and "old groups" of students. Fetterman found that passing from the new group to the old group served as an important milestone for students, letting them know that they could in fact finish the program.

4. And finally, the ethnographic evaluation was able to document some significant student outcomes, such as positive attitudinal changes, increased attention spans, improved communication skills, enhanced cognitive skills, and greater ability to cope with authority.

The use of anthropology in evaluating a nationwide educational program provided the multidisciplinary team with a perspective it was not likely to get from other disciplines. One such contribution was conceptual. The problem that Fetterman was presented with originally was to determine the extent to which a prototype program was being replicated in these four sites under evaluation. But from an anthropological perspective, Fetterman rejected the notion of four sites replicating a prototype. While perhaps a reasonable evaluation design for a program in the physical sciences, it was not particularly relevant for the social sciences. In his evaluation Fetterman was interested in how well the programs adapted to local circumstances rather than how precisely they conformed to past programs. By focusing the evaluation on *adaptation* rather than replication, Fetterman was able to describe more accurately the success of each program.

A second contribution of the ethnographic approach was that it provided a picture of the sociocultural context in which the program was operating.

Ethnographic descriptions of inner-city neighborhoods—where theft, drug abuse, prostitution, and murder are common occurrences—provided insights into the types of influences bearing on the students in the programs.

Fetterman's study represents one more instance of how anthropology can be applied to the solution of human problems. It differs from most other applied educational research projects in several important respects. Whereas most anthropological research applied to education is frequently conducted in a single location, Fetterman was looking at a large national educational program with multiple sites. Moreover, Fetterman's project was somewhat unusual in that it was multidimensional to the extent that it analyzed not only classrooms but other related program components such as community environments, government agencies, and even the outside evaluators. Fetterman's study illustrates how cultural anthropology is carving out a role for itself in evaluating educational programs.

## CHAPTER 4

# Biology, Genes, and Evolutionary Theory

What are the fundamentals of evolutionary theory that are necessary for an understanding of human evolution?

How are biological traits transmitted from one generation to the next?

How do humans and other animals respond genetically to environmental changes?

As noted at the beginning of Chapter 3, among the most serious problems we face as a species are poor health, food shortages, high infant mortality, and a high rate of population growth. Many of these challenges result from imbalances between the biological needs we have as human beings and the social and technological means we have of meeting those needs. To understand these imbalances and to develop ways of meeting human needs in socially responsible and humane ways, we need to consider how millions of years of evolution have shaped our current biological existence and how culture has become our primary way of adapting to challenges in our environments.

Virtually everything we do as human beings is a result of learning. Although we recognize the biological bases of many of our learned behaviors, we have come to believe that culture will enable us to transcend any limitations that our biology places on us. For example, if we depended only on our biological adaptations to move around, we would be restricted to walking, running, and swimming on the surface of the water. Our cultural adaptations have enabled us to transcend the limits imposed on movement by our biology so that now we can fly thousands of miles into space and travel deep beneath the sea.

Our biology also requires that human females deliver their infants though a birth canal that is relatively narrow. The narrow configuration of the birth canal resulted from changes that occurred as we adapted to **bipedal** (two-legged) walking. If the baby is too large to pass through the birth canal, both mother and child could die. Culture again, however, has enabled us to transcend this restraint, since large babies can be born through cesarean section. Modern medicine has also allowed thousands of people with potentially lethal diseases or disorders to live far longer and in far better health than they would have even a hundred years ago. Not only are they surviving, but many people are able to reproduce who would not have been able to do so in the past. There is some concern, in fact, that this may perpetuate genes that otherwise have negative value for the human species.

While we welcome these advancements, do they come to us entirely without costs? Are there limits or constraints placed on cultural behavior that will eventually catch up with us? In order to answer this question, we must take a look at human biological history and adaptations. This and the following four chapters will review our adaptations as mammals, as primates, and as members of the human family. Against this background we will later explore the many ways in which different cultures of the world build upon that biological baseline. Only by understanding the interaction of cultural and biological forces affecting human lives and livelihoods will we be able to think about ways of approaching the major problems we face today as individuals, as populations, and as a species.

First we need to understand what kinds of traits are genetically based, how they are inherited, and why they vary in modern human populations. This requires an introduction to human genetics and evolutionary theory.

♦　♦　♦

# History of Evolutionary Theory

Many of the fundamental ideas of how evolution occurs were developed in the last century by Charles Darwin (1809–1882). In the scientific communities of the nineteenth century, the fact of evolution or change in species through time was generally accepted, although there were few adequate explanations of why change occurs, where new traits come from, or how they are passed along through time. Darwin answered the first question by proposing that change occurs by a process known as **natural selection**. His argument went something like this:

1. Many more animals in a species are born than live to reproduce a new generation;
2. There is a great deal of variation within a single species in the natural world;
3. There is a connection between this variation and the process by which some members of a species die and some live to reproduce;
4. "Nature" selects for reproducing the next generation those individuals that have characteristics best suited for survival in a given environment;
5. Through many generations of this process, characteristics of species change or evolve.

In his writings about natural selection, Darwin focused extensively on survival. This was a misplaced emphasis, however, and resulted in a short time frame for evolution. We now know that evolution is a process that proceeds over many generations, so it is reproduction that is important, not simply survival. In order to be an evolutionary success, an individual not only must have characteristics that enable survival to an age at which reproduction can occur but also must reproduce and transmit those characteristics to offspring. Certainly reproduction does not occur without survival, but survival alone is not sufficient for an individual trait to be

Charles Darwin (1809–1882), who introduced the concept of evolution by natural selection, is sometimes called the "father" of evolutionary theory.

human bipedalism (walking on two legs) as an example, proposing that **quadrupedal** (four-legged) individuals who practiced upright posture could make anatomical changes in their lifetimes that could be passed on to future generations. Each generation could then further perfect the anatomy for efficient bipedalism. Lamarck's theory did not withstand the test of evidence, however, and was gradually superseded by Darwin's theory of change through natural selection. The important distinction between the two is that Lamarck saw the living organism as the active agent (the cause) of evolutionary change, whereas Darwin saw the environment as the active agent.

One common theory during Darwin's time for the way in which traits were passed along from one generation to the next was that characteristics of the parents were "blended" in the offspring. Consider, for example, that a child with a tall mother and a short father may grow to a medium height, an apparent blending of the stature characteristics of the parents. Or a man with blond hair and a woman with dark brown hair may produce a child with light brown hair, again, the appearance of blending. Commonly, however, a child may have traits possessed by only one of the parents. The most obvious example of this is that a man and woman virtually always produce a child that is either male like the father or female like the mother—never a child that is a blend of the two. Obviously, then, characteristics of parents are handed down separately to offspring so that a child may express a characteristic that only one of the parents has.

naturally selected if it is not passed on to succeeding generations through reproduction. Thus, natural selection involves both survival and reproductive success.

Two major problems threatened Darwin's theory of evolution by natural selection: he could not explain how new characteristics arose, nor could he explain how the favored characteristics were passed along from one generation to the next. One of Darwin's predecessors, the Frenchman Jean Baptiste Lamarck (1744–1829), had advanced the theory of acquired characteristics. This theory proposed that organisms could modify their physical characteristics through use and disuse, according to what was needed to survive in a given environment. Furthermore, they could pass these changes along to their offspring. Thus, Lamarck argued that the origin of new characteristics was within the organism. He used

## MENDEL AND EARLY THEORIES ABOUT GENETICS

Gregor Mendel (1822–1884), working in the late nineteenth century, answered the questions about transmission of traits by demonstrating several fundamental principles of genetic inheritance. First, experimenting with ordinary garden peas, he showed that characteristics were transmitted from one generation to the next through discrete particles. The offspring of two different pea plants were always like one parent or the other, never a blending of the two. For example, when a plant that produced yellow peas was crossed with a plant that produced green peas, the offspring produced yellow peas, never yellow-green peas. Mendel called the traits that appeared in the hybrid or crossed forms the **dominant** traits; those that did not appear were called the **recessive** traits. If Mendel had stopped with his first

Gregor Mendel (1822–1884), working with garden peas, demonstrated the fundamental principles of genetics.

was dominant over green, all of them produced yellow peas. When these hybrids reproduced, some of their offspring possessed two particles for green, so the recessive trait finally appeared in the third generation (Exhibit 4-1).

We now call these particles **genes**; we call the various forms of each particle (here green and yellow peas) **alleles**. If a plant has identical alleles for a particular gene pair (both green or both yellow), we say it is **homozygous** for that characteristic. If a plant has one of each, we say it is **heterozygous**. We call the physical manifestation of the characteristic (here green or yellow peas) the **phenotype** and the actual genetic combination (homozygous or heterozygous) the **genotype**.

Mendel's experiments with garden peas involved a number of traits, including shape of the peas (round or

◆ ◆ ◆

EXHIBIT 4-1a

**Result of crossing a plant with green peas and a plant with yellow peas.**

Male gametes
(Yellow gametes only)

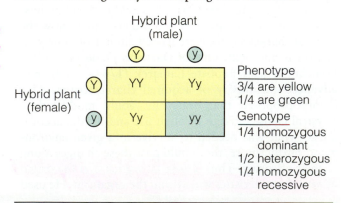

Female gametes
(Green gametes only)

| | Y | Y |
|---|---|---|
| y | Yy | Yy |
| y | Yy | Yy |

Phenotype
all yellow peas

Genotype
all heterozygous

**All offspring are yellow, because yellow is dominant over green. But all are heterozygous, bearing one allele for yellow and one for green.**

◆ ◆ ◆

EXHIBIT 4-1b

**Result of crossing the hybrid offspring with each other.**

Hybrid plant
(male)

Hybrid plant
(female)

| | Y | y |
|---|---|---|
| Y | YY | Yy |
| y | Yy | yy |

Phenotype
3/4 are yellow
1/4 are green

Genotype
1/4 homozygous dominant
1/2 heterozygous
1/4 homozygous recessive

crossing, he might have concluded that the trait that did not appear was no longer present. But he went one step further and crossed his hybrid peas. In the next generation, some of the plants produced green peas, demonstrating that the recessive characteristic had been retained, even when it was not expressed a generation earlier.

This experiment resulted in the conclusion that we now refer to as Mendel's **particulate theory of inheritance**: characteristics are passed from one generation to the next through discrete particles that retain their ability to be expressed, even though they may not be apparent in every generation. Further, these particles are inherited in pairs, one from each parent. This is known as the **law of segregation**. In the garden pea example, the green-pea parent passed along one particle for "green" and the yellow-pea parent passed along one particle for "yellow." The hybrid offspring thus inherited one particle for each characteristic, but since yellow wrinkled), color of the unripe pods (green or yellow), position of the flowers (terminal or axial), and length of the stem (tall or short). Examination of how these various traits were passed from one generation to the next revealed that they were passed along independently. For example, a plant with round green peas could cross with a plant with wrinkled yellow peas, producing among the offspring plants with round yellow peas, a combination not seen in either of the parents. This is referred to as Mendel's **law of independent assortment**: genes responsible for one trait are carried to the next generation independently of genes responsible for other traits (Exhibit 4-2).

To illustrate these laws of inheritance, consider some observable human characteristics. If you can roll your tongue longitudinally, then you possess at least one allele for "tongue rolling," which is inherited as a dominant. The expression of the trait (here the ability to roll the tongue) is your phenotype. Your genotype (the actual alleles you inherited) may be homozygous (two alleles for tongue rolling) or it may be heterozygous (one allele for tongue rolling, one for the recessive trait of not

**EXHIBIT 4-2**

**The law of independent assortment: the alleles for shape (smooth and yellow) are inherited independently of the alleles for color (yellow and green).**

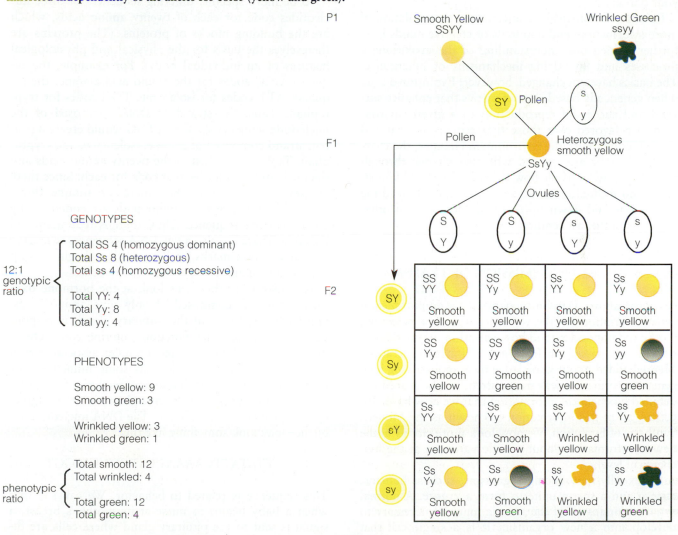

GENOTYPES

Total SS 4 (homozygous dominant)
Total Ss 8 (heterozygous)
Total ss 4 (homozygous recessive)

12:1 genotypic ratio

Total YY: 4
Total Yy: 8
Total yy: 4

PHENOTYPES

Smooth yellow: 9
Smooth green: 3

Wrinkled yellow: 3
Wrinkled green: 1

Total smooth: 12
Total wrinkled: 4

phenotypic ratio

Total green: 12
Total green: 4

being able to roll your tongue). If you cannot roll your tongue, you know you are homozygous recessive for that characteristic. A second trait to consider is the type of earlobe you have. If the lower part of your earlobe is attached directly to your head, you are said to have the phenotypic trait "attached earlobes." This is inherited as a recessive, so your genotype is homozygous. If your earlobe hangs free, you have the dominant characteristic, so your genotype may be homozygous dominant or heterozygous.

For each of these two traits (tongue rolling and earlobes), you inherited one allele from your biological mother and one from your biological father. They were inherited independently of each other, so you may express one trait that is observed in your mother, and the other may be the one your father exhibits. Or, you may express a combination observed in neither or both of your parents.

Recent technological advancements, accumulation of more information, and hundreds of creative minds have further refined our understanding of the evolutionary processes and underlying mechanisms of inheritance. The basics have not changed, however: Evolution occurs when genetically based characteristics that enhance survival and successful reproduction in a given environment are favored over those that reduce survival and reproduction. Since the environment changes, the characteristics that are favored will also change through time. But now let us see how time, accumulated knowledge, and technological advancements have refined the basic ideas laid down by Darwin, Mendel, and other scientists of the last century.

## DNA AND THE TRANSMISSION OF TRAITS

As noted above, Darwin recognized the importance of genetic variation for the working of natural selection, but he did not understand how variation originated nor how it was passed on from generation to generation. Mendel added to our knowledge by demonstrating how genetic information was transmitted, but he lacked the detailed biochemical information that we now have. Together, all of this information is known as the Modern Synthesis of Evolution. We now look more closely at the newest information about genetic variation at the biochemical level.

In sexually reproducing organisms, such as humans, an egg and a sperm unite to form a **zygote**. A normal zygote contains all of the genetic material necessary to develop into a new organism. It is a single cell that

grows through a process of cell division called **mitosis**, which produces daughter cells with the same genetic material contained in the original zygote. Cells are composed of several structures, including the nucleus. The genetic material is actually contained in long strands of an organic compound called **deoxyribonucleic acid** or **DNA**, located on **chromosomes** in each cell nucleus. Chromosomes look like threads under an electron microscope and carry the genetic information coded in the DNA. DNA is composed of four organic compounds known as **nucleotides**: Guanine, cytosine, adenine, and thymine, usually abbreviated as G, C, A, and T. These nucleotides are arranged on the DNA strand in a sequence that determines which gene is expressed. The sequence of nucleotides is similar to an alphabet of four letters. These letters combine to form "words" that give instructions to a cell about which gene to manufacture.

To be more specific, differing sequences of three nucleotides code for each of twenty **amino acids**, which are the building blocks of proteins. (The proteins are themselves the basis for the physical and physiological features of an individual body). For example, the sequence GCC codes for the amino acid alanine; the sequence ATT codes for isoleucine; TGG codes for tryptophan. Thus, the strand of DNA composed of the nucleotide sequence GCCATTTGG would create a protein strand composed of alanine, isoleucine, and tryptophan. Table 4-1 is a list of the twenty amino acids and the nucleotide sequences that code for each. Since there are fewer amino acids than there are unique three-nucleotide units, several amino acids are coded for by more than one sequence. Thus, there is redundancy in the code. There are also a few DNA sequences that serve as "punctuation marks," telling a cell to begin or stop making a protein.

To illustrate further, let's look at the hormone **oxytocin**, which is composed of only nine amino acids. Oxytocin, produced in the pituitary gland, is responsible for, among other functions, uterine contractions during labor and the milk ejection reflex associated with nursing in mammals. It also has some influence over maternal behavior. The amino acid sequence for oxytocin is cystine-tyrosine-isoleucine-glutamine-asparagine-cystine-proline-leucine-glycine. The DNA nucleotide sequence may look something like this:

TGTTATATTCAAAATTGTCCTTTAGGT

This sequence is related to behavior. We can say that when a baby begins to nurse at its mother's breast, a signal is sent to the pituitary gland where cells are directed to produce the series of amino acids that synthesize the hormone oxytocin. And it is this hormone that causes the milk to flow into the baby's mouth.

nursing → signal to pituitary gland → amino acid sequence for oxytocin assembled →
milk flow into baby's mouth

**Mutation** As noted above, one of Darwin's problems was explaining the source of new characteristics in an organism. One source is now known to be **mutation**. A mutation is a change in a gene that results in the production of a different allele, often resulting in a different genotype. This mutation can happen at the level of the DNA nucleotides. Note from Table 4-1, for example, that a mutation in the nucleotide sequence AAT to AAG

would result in a change in the amino acid from asparagine to lysine. Usually when this type of mutation occurs it results in a nonviable organism, but occasionally the new amino acid sequence does not mean a lethal gene; instead it codes for a different kind of protein, and perhaps a different phenotype.

When a mutation is the result of a change in a single nucleotide, it is called a "point mutation." Such a point mutation may have occurred with the origin of the allele for sickle-cell hemoglobin. Normal hemoglobin has glutamic acid as the sixth amino acid in the protein sequence (Exhibit 4-3). It is coded for by CTC. A point mutation changed the nucleotide thymine to adenine, resulting in the code CAC, which codes for the amino acid valine. That simple one-nucleotide substitution (out of a total of several hundred nucleotides in the hemoglobin molecule) resulted in a new allele at some time in human

**TABLE 4-1 ◆ The Genetic Code**

| First Letter | \| Second Letter \| | | | | Third Letter |
|---|---|---|---|---|---|
| | **T** | **C** | **A** | **G** | |
| **T** | TTT TTC } Phe<br>TTA TTG } Leu | TCT TCC TCA TCG } Ser | TAT TAC } Tyr<br>TAA OCHRE<br>TAG AMBER | TGT TGC } Cys<br>TGA ?<br>TGG Tryp | T C A G |
| **C** | CTT CTC CTA CTG } Leu | CCT CCC CCA CCG } Pro | CAT CAC } His<br>CAA CAG } GluN | CGT CGC CGA CGG } Arg | T C A G |
| **A** | ATT ATC ATA } Ileu<br>ATG Met | ACT ACC ACA ACG } Thr | AAT AAC } AspN<br>AAA AAG } Lys | AGT AGC } Ser<br>AGA AGG } Arg | T C A G |
| **G** | GTT GTC GTA GTG } Val | GCT GCC GCA GCG } Ala | GAT GAC } Asp<br>GAA GAG } Glu | GGT GGC GGA GGG } Gly | T C A G |

NOTE:

| Amino Acid | Abbreviation | Amino Acid | Abbreviation | Amino Acid | Abbreviation |
|---|---|---|---|---|---|
| Alanine | Ala | Glycine | Gly | Proline | Pro |
| Arginine | Arg | Histidine | His | Serine | Ser |
| Asparagine | AspN | Isoleucine | Ileu | Threonine | Thr |
| Aspartic Acid | Asp | Leucine | Leu | Tryptophan | Tryp |
| Cysteine | Cys | Lysine | Lys | Tyrosine | Tyr |
| Glutamic Acid | Glu | Methionine | Met | Valine | Val |
| Glutamine | GluN | Phenylalanine | Phe | | |

SOURCE: F.H.C. Crick. The Genetic Code: III. *Scientific American.* San Francisco: W. H. Freeman, 1966.

EXHIBIT 4-3

**Substitution of one base at position #6 produces a sickling hemoglobin.**

Point Mutation

| Normal Hemoglobin | | Sickling Hemoglobin | |
|---|---|---|---|
| DNA sequence | Amino acid | Amino acid | DNA sequence |
| • | | | • |
| • | #1 | #1 | • |
| • | | | • |
| • | | | • |
| • | | | • |
| T | | | T |
| G | #4 threonine | #4 threonine | G |
| A | | | A |
| G | | | G |
| G | #5 proline | #5 proline | G |
| A | | | A |
| C | | | C |
| T | #6 glutamic acid | #6 valine | A |
| C | | | C |
| C | | | C |
| T | #7 glutamic acid | #7 glutamic acid | T |
| C | | | C |
| T | | | T |
| T | #8 lysine | #8 lysine | T |
| T | | | T |
| • | • | • | • |
| • | • | • | • |
| • | • | • | • |
| • | • | • | • |
| • | • | • | • |
| • | #146 | #146 | • |
| | #1652 (including introns) | | #1652 |

SOURCE: Courtesy of West Publishing Company / *Introduction to Physical Anthropology* 5/e by Harry Nelson and Robert Jurmain.

---

evolutionary history. The significance of this mutation and the explanation for its being favorably selected will be discussed further in Chapter 7.

**Recombination** Another source of genetic change in a population results from the ways in which the genes are replicated during reproduction. As noted above, the genes (strands of DNA) are located on chromosomes. The number of chromosomes varies from species to species. Humans, for example, have 46 chromosomes; butterflies have 62, dogs have 78, and horseshoe crabs have 254. This number represents the **diploid**, or full chromosome complement of each cell in the body. The sex cells, or **gametes**, are an exception, in that sperm and eggs have only half (**haploid**) the number of chromosomes. This is necessary so that when each sex cell combines with one from the other sex, the resulting zygote will have the normal full complement. Unlike other body cells, sex cells reproduce themselves through the process of **meiosis**. This process involves a reduction in the number of chromosomes to half the full complement.

During meiosis, genes are reshuffled so that all of the gametes contain unique combinations. Then the gametes from the mother and father are combined at fertilization. This reshuffling of the genes from the parents is referred to as **recombination** and is the primary source of new variation on which natural selection can act. The number of gene combinations that result from this process is so vast that it is virtually impossible for two identical gametes to ever be produced this way. One estimate is that the number of unique individuals that could result from a single human mating is about 70 trillion (Nelson and Jurmain, 1991).

## THE MODERN UNDERSTANDING OF EVOLUTION

These are the essential components of what we now understand about the evolutionary process. This understanding results from adding three major sets of ideas: (1) Darwin's ideas about natural selection (natural selection operates on variability in a population); (2) Mendelian genetics (variability comes from genetic recombination during meiosis); and (3) knowledge that the variable traits are transmitted through DNA. We can now look at evolutionary change on several levels. Our original definition of evolution as "change through time" can now be modified to "changes in gene frequencies through time." An important thing to remember is that we now know that the processes that account for new variation are completely independent of the processes that rearrange the variability. In other words, natural selection cannot "create" new variation; it can only act upon that which occurs by chance through changes in biochemical compounds.

We have seen that evolutionary change can be brought about by mutation, recombination, and natural selection. Two additional processes by which changes in gene frequencies occur are **genetic drift** and **gene flow** or **migration**. In the first, chance factors may produce gene frequency changes in a small population.

**Genetic Drift** Imagine a population of one hundred people, half of whom can roll their tongues, half of whom cannot. Now imagine that all of the tongue-rollers are lost at sea during a hurricane due to causes completely unrelated to tongue-rolling. The non-tongue-rollers would be the only ones left to produce the next generation. Since there are no tongue-rolling alleles left in the population, all of the subsequent generations would be unable to roll their tongues. But the disappearance of the allele was due not to selection against it but rather to chance factors (i.e., the hurricane). Small populations are simply at greater risk for changes (drift) in gene frequencies due to chance.

More commonly, genetic drift occurs in circumstances far less obvious than a natural disaster. In a small population, some people may not marry or produce offspring for reasons entirely unrelated to factors usually associated with natural selection. Rather, the failure to reproduce may be due entirely to chance factors. But because the population is small, the chance factors have a more pronounced effect on gene frequencies in future generations. If the population were larger, the effect of chance factors might not be so obvious.

A simple illustration of this can be seen in the tossing of a coin. If you toss it ten times, you expect it to come up heads half of the time, tails the other half. But with only ten tosses, it would not be unusual to come up with six heads and four tails, or even nine heads and one tail. If you increase the number of tosses, it becomes more likely that the 1:1 ratio will be achieved. With one hundred tosses, you would likely conclude the coin was not fair if it came up heads ninety times and tails ten times. In other words, chance would not likely be the explanation for such a deviation from expectation in the larger sample, whereas it was acceptable in the small sample. In a similar way, we expect that males and females will be born at approximately equal rates in a population. This expectation is not necessarily challenged when five sisters give birth only to boys, but if all women in Birmingham gave birth to boys in one year, we would assume that some force other than chance was operating on the sex ratio of boys and girls in that city.

**Migration** The effects of in- or out-migration on gene frequencies in a population are fairly obvious. If an anthropologist conducts a genetic survey of a population in one decade and returns several decades later to find a very different set of gene frequencies, the first question would be whether there has been a recent addition or subtraction of members of the population. A genetic survey of Miami, for example, would have yielded very different gene frequencies in 1940 from what would be found today, in part because of recent waves of immigration from the Caribbean and Central America.

**Evolutionary Fitness** We noted above that evolutionary success is measured by both survival and reproductive success. Individuals are the entities that survive and reproduce, but genes are the entities that are passed along from one generation to the next. Thus, "fitness" of an individual is measured by survival and reproduction, but **fitness** in the evolutionary sense is measured by the number of genes passed on to the next generations. Since evolutionary fitness is measured by the number of genes in succeeding generations, it is possible to be "fit" without actually having children of your own, since your genes are represented in all of your biological relatives.

This is the concept of **inclusive fitness**. The richest, most powerful man and woman in the world may be regarded as successful or fit on one level, but if they fail to pass on their genes in large numbers to subsequent generations by having children, they are not regarded as fit in an evolutionary sense. Their servant, with dozens of children and grandchildren, may be far more successful in that measure. Fitness is, of course, a relative concept, so we can conclude from the above that the servant is *relatively* more fit, in an evolutionary sense, than the rich man and woman.

◆　◆　◆

# Patterns of Evolutionary Change

So far we have been taking a close-up view of evolutionary change. A. J. Kelso (Kelso and Trevathan, 1984) has likened this to looking at an oil painting of a landscape from very close range where individual brush strokes are clear. This is what we see when we discuss evolution as changes in gene frequencies. When we step back from the painting, the brush strokes fade, and the landscape comes into view. When we step back from evolution, the genes fade and species and populations come into view.

## THE SPECIES CONCEPT

What is a **species**? Organisms are in the same species if they are capable of interbreeding and producing fertile offspring. For example, horses and donkeys are able to mate and produce the hybrid offspring known as a mule. We still consider horses and donkeys members of different species, however, because the hybrid mule is infertile, incapable of reproducing itself. Domestication (including laboratory experimentation and zoo practices) has resulted in occasional breeding of two species that results in fertile offspring. Since this type of contact would not be expected under natural conditions, it is still appropriate to regard the parents as members of two separate species.

## RESPONSES TO ENVIRONMENTAL CHANGE

Whereas natural selection acts upon individuals or genes, it is the species (or population) that is the unit of evolutionary change, the entity that responds to environmental change. Let's consider what might happen to a species or population that experiences a major environmental change. There are two simple outcomes: change or no change. An inability to adapt to an environmental change may result in extinction of the species or population.

**Extinction** It is estimated that more than 99 percent of all species that have ever lived are now extinct (Raup, 1986), suggesting that this is the most common response of species to environmental change. In fact, it is mass extinctions that serve as major paleontological markers. Extinctions mark the ends of the Ordovician, Devonian, Permian, Triassic, and Cretaceous periods (Exhibit 4-4). Perhaps as many as 96 percent of species became extinct at the end of the Permian period.

The extinction episode that has recently received the greatest attention is that which occurred at the end of the Cretaceous (approximately 65 million years ago), marked by the disappearance of the dinosaurs. The disappearance of these large reptiles probably enabled the mammals to evolve the complexity we see today, a complexity that includes ourselves. The event thought to have caused the extinction of the dinosaurs is the impact of an asteroid, which caused global environmental changes, including dramatic cooling of the earth (Kerr, 1992). The lowered temperatures were incompatible

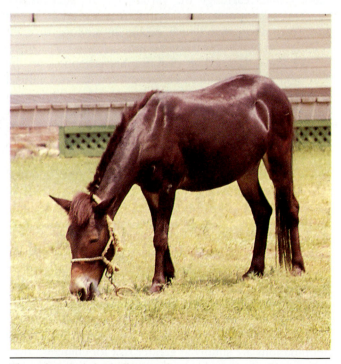

The mule is the hybrid offspring of two separate species (horse and donkey), so it is not capable of reproducing itself.

EXHIBIT 4-4
**The Periods of the Paleozoic and Mesozoic Eras.** The boundaries between periods are often marked by mass extinctions.

| Era | Period Systems | Time M.Y.A.* | Events |
|---|---|---|---|
| **Mesozoic (Middle Life)** | Cretaceous (chalk) | 65 — 136 | Appearance of placental and marsupial mammals. Dinosaurs peak and become extinct. First modern birds. |
| | Jurassic (Jura Mts., France) | 190 | Great age of dinosaurs—flying and swimming dinosaurs. First toothed birds. |
| | Triassic (from tripartite division of strata of Germany) | 225 | Reptiles dominant. First dinosaurs. Egg-laying mammals. |
| **Paleozoic (Ancient Life)** | Permian | 280 | Reptilian radiation. Mammal-like reptiles. Many forms die out. |
| | Carboniferous (abundance of coal) | 345 | First reptiles. Radiation of amphibia. Modern insects evolve. |
| | Devonian (Devonshire in England) | 395 | Age of fish. Amphibians—first air-breathing vertebrates. First forests. |
| | Silurian (the Silures, an ancient British tribe) | 430 | Jawed fishes appear. First air-breathing animal—scorpion-like aurypterid. Definite land plants. |
| | Ordovician (the Ordovices, an ancient British tribe) | 500 | First fishes. Trilobites still abundant. Graptolites and corals becoming plentiful. Possible land plants. |
| | Cambrian (Roman name for Wales) | 570 | Trilobites abundant, also brachiopods, jellyfish, worms, and other invertebrates. |
| **Precambrian** | | | |

NOTE: *Million years ago

SOURCE: Courtesy of West Publishing Company / *Introduction to Physical Anthropology* 5/e by Harry Nelson and Robert Jurmain.

---

with life for dinosaurs. Dinosaurs were too **specialized** to respond to the major environmental changes brought about by the asteroid's impact.

Specialization has advantages under certain circumstances, but it places limits on the ability of an organism to respond to changes. The koala bear, for example, is a specialized leaf-eater whose diet is extremely limited. It may be better than any other animal at eating eucalyptus leaves, but the koala would be in trouble if the eucalyptus species were to become extinct.

In contrast to the specialized dinosaurs, the mammals were apparently fairly **generalized** and could adapt to the climatic changes. Their ability to maintain a constant body temperature, independent of air temperature, was an important component of their generalized adaptability that enabled them to survive the colder temperatures. Thus, a second type of "no change" response to environmental change is seen in organisms that can adjust to changes without becoming **extinct** or changing genetically.

**Adaptation through Genetic Change** It is the ability to respond to environmental change by changing genetically that is of primary interest to those who study evolution. First, it is important to note that individuals do not change or evolve. That is, unlike Lamarck's speculations, individuals cannot bring about changes in their anatomy or physiology in order to better adapt to environmental challenges. Rather, selection occurs due to the variability that is already present in the species or population. Consider the classic example of the peppered moth, *Biston betularia*. Like many insects that are preyed upon by birds, the peppered moth of England has protective coloration that helps to camouflage it against the light, lichen-covered trees on which it rests. Most of the peppered moths in the past were the light-colored forms that blended with the lichen, thus providing better camouflage. Dark-colored forms were also present, but since they did not have sufficient protective coloration, they were most often preyed upon by birds. Thus, the birds served as the agent of natural selection, keeping the frequencies of the genes for dark coloration lower than those for light coloration. With industrialization, however, many of the lichens darkened from air pollution so that the dark-colored moth was better pro-

tected than the light-colored variety. Birds then preferentially preyed upon the light-colored form, with the result that the gene frequencies in succeeding generations changed in favor of the dark coloration. It is important to note that the two color forms were already present in the population and that selection acted differentially on them depending on the environmental circumstances. The light-colored moths were not able to change their coloration in response to the change in the environment, as Lamarck might have predicted.

Another example is melanism in rattlesnakes of the Southwestern United States deserts. Most desert rattlesnakes are sand-colored to provide them camouflage protection from hawks, owls, and eagles, which prey upon them. In areas of recent volcanic activity, however, dark-colored forms that blend in with the black lava flows are more common than the light-colored forms. As with the peppered moths, the dark form of the rattlesnake has greater survival and reproductive success on the lava, whereas the light-colored forms are the successful ones on the desert soil. The frequencies of the genes for dark coloration are higher in the populations of snakes that live on the lava flows and the genes for light coloration are higher in populations that live in sandy soils.

The light-colored moth is more easily preyed upon against the dark barked trees so the gene frequencies for light coloration are lower than the frequencies for dark coloration.

**Speciation** In most of these examples, we have been talking about survival. It is important to remember, however, that it is differential reproductive success that defines evolutionary success. That is, the different colored moths and rattlesnakes did not just out-survive the alternatives; they out-reproduced them. Thus, evolutionary change involves two processes: differential survival *and* differential reproduction. These yield changes in the genetic structure of a population, as in the frequencies of the dark- and light-colored moths and rattlesnakes. But is genetic change the same as speciation? The two forms of the moth and rattlesnake are not reproductively isolated, so they are not separate species. How much genetic change does it take to bring about reproductive isolation? This is fairly easy to determine in living forms, but how do we judge this in fossil forms? Looking at physical differences, we may conclude that a fossil from 2 million years ago is genetically different from an organism living today, but how can we know if they are different species? In fact, when we attempt to picture evolutionary relationships, we often draw a line from a species in the past to one in the present, like so:

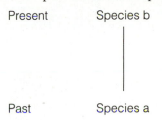

This depicts a continuous relationship, and yet species, by definition, are discontinuous. This process is called **anagenesis,** and it is common to refer to the two forms as separate species, but there is no known time or event in the past that pinpoints reproductive isolation. Some scholars argue that we cannot refer to these as two separate species unless we can demonstrate reproductive isolation at a specific time. Others argue that when two forms, widely separated in time, look very different from each other, it is appropriate to call them separate species.

The effect of separation in time on speciation may not be known, but the effect of geographical separation is a bit clearer. In fact, geographic isolation is probably the most common cause of speciation. When members of a species become separated by a body of water, a mountain range, or a desert, for example, the populations are effectively reproductively isolated from each other. After sufficient time has passed, and if different environmental and selective forces operate on the two populations, it is likely that reproductive isolation between them would be maintained, even if the barrier were removed. When

there is an identifiable separation, we refer to the process as **cladogenesis,** depicted as

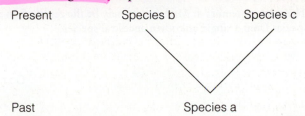

Occasionally in the history of life on earth, a number of species have apparently evolved from one or two ancestral species in a process known as an **adaptive radiation.** This most commonly occurs when a new environment is occupied or when widespread extinctions leave open a number of empty ecological **niches.** For example, when the dinosaurs became extinct at the end of the Cretaceous, mammals experienced an adaptive radiation as populations occupied the vacated niches. Similarly, when the first lemurs reached the island of Madagascar during the Eocene, an adaptive radiation in this family occurred, resulting in several descendant new species within a relatively short time (Exhibit 4-5).

**Phyletic Gradualism and Punctuated Equilibrium** Much of our discussion of evolutionary processes so far has assumed that speciation is brought about by gradual accumulation of enough genetic changes that reproductive isolation eventually occurs. This is referred to as **phyletic gradualism** and probably accounts for many speciation events. The fossil record, however, does not offer much support for this view of speciation. More typically observed in fossils are long periods of relative stability or equilibrium, followed or "punctuated" by brief periods of rapid change after which new species are apparent. This process, **punctuated equilibrium**, solves the problem of continuous versus discontinuous evolutionary change. Rapid speciation, as depicted in the punctuation model, would produce reproductive isolation in a relatively short time, thus maintaining the definition of species as discontinuous entities.

Genetic drift is a key to understanding how evolution by punctuated equilibrium could occur. For example, if a small population were temporarily separated from the rest of the species, rapid genetic change due to chance factors could occur in the isolated group, resulting in reproductive isolation and thus, speciation, in a relatively short period of time. If the changes due to chance factors also conveyed selective value on members of the new species, the population would increase to a point where it replaced the original, ancestral species (Gould and Eldredge, 1977). Thus, the fossil record

EXHIBIT 4-5
**The modern lemurs at Madagascar may be the result of an adaptive radiation of species from a single unknown ancestral species.**

would depict a period of stability in the ancestral species followed by rapid appearance of and replacement by the descendent species.

## ◆ Summary

1. Almost every aspect of human behavior is based on learning, but there are biological underpinnings to our behavior that are inherited from mammalian and primate ancestors.

2. Charles Darwin's major contribution to the development of evolutionary theory was his demonstration that evolutionary change occurs through natural selection, the process by which characteristics that enhance survival and reproductive success are preserved in succeeding generations.

3. Gregor Mendel developed the fundamental principles of genetic inheritance. They are (a) characteristics are passed from one generation to the next through discrete particles known as genes; (b) genes are inherited in pairs, one from each parent; and (c) genes are inherited independently of each other.

4. A gene is actually a segment of deoxyribonucleic acid or DNA, located on chromosomes in the cell nucleus. DNA determines the sequence of amino acids that are linked together to form a protein. This protein, in turn, determines a physical characteristic or phenotype of an individual.

5. There are five sources of genetic change in populations. The most common, by far, is the shuffling or recombination of genes that occurs through mating. Other sources of change include mutation, genetic drift, migration, and natural selection.

**6.** A species is composed of organisms that can breed with each other and produce fertile offspring.

**7.** Three potential outcomes can result from a change in an organism's environment. The most common response is extinction. Other possible outcomes are genetic change through natural selection and, perhaps, evolution of a new species. In some cases an organism is so generalized in its characteristics that it can adjust to an environmental change without being affected genetically.

## ◆ Key Terms

| | |
|---|---|
| adaptive radiation | law of independent |
| alleles | assortment |
| amino acids | law of segregation |
| anagenesis | meiosis |
| bipedal | migration |
| chromosomes | mitosis |
| cladogenesis | natural selection |
| deoxyribonucleic acid | niche |
| (DNA) | nucleotides |
| diploid | oxytocin |
| dominant | particulate theory of |
| fitness | inheritance |
| gametes | phenotype |
| gene flow | phyletic gradualism |
| generalized | punctuated equilibrium |
| genes | quadrupedal |
| genetic drift | recessive |
| genotype | recombination |
| haploid | specialized |
| heterozygous | species |
| homozygous | zygote |
| inclusive fitness | |

## ◆ Suggested Readings

Darwin, Charles *On the Origin of Species*, New York: Mentor Books, 1958 (1859). The book that historians of science mark as beginning the shift in scientific thinking about life on earth. Packed with details and poetic in places, it is a pleasure to read.

Dawkins, Richard. *The Blind Watchmaker*, New York: W. W. Norton, 1986. Recognizing that many people have difficulty accepting the idea that all of life's grandeur could have evolved by natural selection, Dawkins carefully documents the processes that underlie evolution in a convincing and readable way.

Eiseley, Loren. *The Immense Journey*, New York: Random House, 1958. Known as much as an essayist as a physical anthropologist, Eiseley provides personal perspectives on evolution in a thoughtful and readable style. He conveys a sense of the wonder inspired by the process of evolution.

Gould, Stephen Jay. *Ever Since Darwin*, New York: W. W. Norton, 1977. This and several other of Gould's books are collections of his monthly essays on evolution written for *Natural History* magazine. His writing is excellent and the reader can probably find in these collections an essay on just about any subject dealing with evolution, from historical and contemporary perspectives. Gould is also one of the architects of the concept of punctuated equilibrium and several of his essays provide detail on that theory.

Greene, John C. *The Death of Adam*, New York: Mentor Books, 1961. Despite popular association of Darwin's name with evolution, evolutionary thinking did not begin with him. Greene documents the contributions of Darwin's predecessors and contemporaries from Newton to Einstein in a readable history of ideas that formed the bases of modern science.

Watson, James D. *The Double Helix,* New York: Atheneum, 1968. An exciting adventure story about the discovery by James Watson and Francis Crick of the structure of DNA. Fun insights into the human side of laboratory science and of some of the best-known personalities in genetics and molecular biology.

# Evolution and Genetics

## ◆ Ethnobotanists demonstrate the value of biodiversity

As noted in the previous chapter, the most commonly occurring pattern in the history of life on earth is extinction. Extinction usually comes about when a species cannot adapt to the changing conditions of its environment. Sometimes these environmental changes are catastrophic and many species become extinct in a very short time. At other times, the process is gradual, and changes in the environment may not be apparent. When we think about humans becoming extinct, we usually think of potential catastrophes, like nuclear winter, showers of asteroids and comets, or mass starvation. But as anthropologist Barry Bogin (1985) points out, we are much more likely to become extinct due to a gradual decrease in ecological diversity. This is because we are part of that diversity, and we are dependent on other animal and plant species for our food, medicine, raw materials, fuel, and livelihoods. We may not notice when one species becomes extinct, but as the numbers of extinctions increase, the effects will also become more obvious. As we have noted, our lack of specialization is one of the keys to our success as a species. But our generalized adaptations require a generalized and diversified environment.

Many people consider conservation of resources and biodiversity concerns that only wealthy nations can afford. They believe species are saved from extinction at the expense of saving people and nations from poverty. But in his influential writings, E. O. Wilson argues that plant and animal species that are now close to extinction offer potentially thousands of unrealized economic benefits. He suggests that we should pursue new ways of exploiting ecosystems and species for their economic value in pharmaceuticals, foods, fuel sources, and ecotourism. A common argument for preserving species is that a cure for cancer or AIDS may be contained in the chemical makeup of a seemingly otherwise insignificant plant or insect on the verge of extinction.

Anthropologists known as ethnobotanists or ethnobiologists have contributed to our understanding of the potential economic benefits of many species based on their observations of the uses made by traditional people. For example, secretions from the skin of a frog species used by Peruvian Indians to boost their hunting success have been found to contain powerful psychopharmacologic properties that may be useful in treating depression and Alzheimer's disease (Amato, 1992).

Other wild species have the potential for increasing the genetic resistance of common crops. For example, a species of wild maize from near Guadalajara, Mexico, is resistant to most diseases common to commercial corn crops. If its genes were transferred into other varieties, it could substantially boost domestic production of corn in all parts of the world. This wild species was discovered only a week before the entire known gene pool would have been destroyed in the clearing of new land for agricultural fields (Wilson, 1992).

In addition to preserving plants and animals that may have unknown economic value, we must preserve the knowledge of how these species are used. This knowledge is possessed by healers, artisans, hunters, horticulturalists, and other traditional people who best know the values of the species in their natural environments. That means that preserving human biocultural diversity must be added to the list of environmental concerns. And equally important to some is that the traditional people who possess the knowledge reap some of the economic benefits that the world has gained from them (Posey, 1990).

### ◆ DNA Fingerprinting may aid law enforcement.

We noted in the previous chapter that genetic material for all living things is contained in strands of DNA. The nucleotides cytosine, guanine, adenine, and thymine are the same in every living species, but what makes species differ from each other is the sequence of these nucleotides. In the same way, individual human beings differ from each other in the sequences of some sections of DNA. No person will have a DNA sequence that is identical to that of another unless he or she happens to have an identical twin. In this way, DNA sequences are similar to fingerprints, which also are unique for every person. Law enforcement specialists have thus turned to molecular biologists in their attempts to identify criminals and victims of crimes.

If biological material such as blood, semen, bone, or hair is available at a crime scene, samples can be analyzed biochemically for their DNA sequence, which can then be compared to samples from persons suspected of having committed the crime. For example, if semen can be collected from a rape victim, the DNA sequence derived from it may be useful in convicting the rapist if it matches the sequence collected from a suspect. The method is most useful for excluding a falsely accused person, but it can also provide evidence that a suspect is guilty with some degree of probability. As in all forensic work, it is difficult, if not impossible, to *prove* that someone is guilty with this method. This is true for science in general: It is far easier to disprove something than to prove it.

Though most scientists and law enforcement specialists regard DNA fingerprinting as a potentially highly useful tool, it is still a long way from uncritical acceptance in the courtroom. One reason is that there are not yet well-established standards for quality assurance in the laboratories that provide the DNA sequences. There are also problems with the statistical methods used to interpret a match. The odds of two samples matching by chance are not yet clear, although they appear to be, at the very minimum, one in several hundred thousand when the human species is considered as a whole (Roberts, 1992). For certain subpopulations, however, where more genetic (and thus DNA) homogeneity exists, the odds of finding a match by chance may be higher.

Although acceptance of DNA fingerprinting is far from universal, most people, supporters and critics alike, agree that once the kinks have been worked out, this is "possibly the most powerful innovation in forensics since the development of fingerprinting" (Lewontin and Hartl, 1991:1,745).

73

## CHAPTER 5

# Our Place in Nature

What is the place of human beings in the system used to classify plants and animals?

What are the characteristics that distinguish primates from other orders of mammals?

What types of social organization are found among primates?

What are the characteristics that distinguish humans from other primates?

In the previous chapter we discussed the ways in which evolutionary processes have produced the vast array of living forms we see around us. Part of that array includes the other **primates**, the animal group that includes ourselves and our closest living relatives, monkeys and apes. We know that humans are closely related to chimpanzees and monkeys and that we have many things in common with these animals. But we also sense that we are different from other animals. In this chapter we will discuss the characteristics that make us like other mammals and like other primates. Then we will discuss the ways in which humans are different from all other animals. We begin with an overview of ways in which scientists organize the living world.

## Classification

Classification is basic to the way we organize our world. Almost everything we come in contact with can be described in classificatory terms: hot, warm, cool, cold; hard, soft; short, medium, tall; yellow, black, purple, green; animal, vegetable, mineral; Muslim, Christian, Jew, Buddhist. The way we classify things has a lot to do with our experience of the world and with the "things" in our world. For example, if your experience with carpentry tools is limited to household chores, you may classify tools as wrenches, hammers, screwdrivers, and pliers. A professional carpenter or mechanic would likely divide tools into far more categories, however. The category "wrenches" might be divided into allen wrenches, crescent wrenches, pipe wrenches, open-end wrenches, closed-end wrenches, and socket wrenches.

The worldview of scientific classification as discussed in this chapter is that living things can be organized on the basis of evolutionary relationships. And since evolutionary relationships are stated as hypotheses to be tested with data, our system of classification is a series of hypotheses that may be confirmed or supported with new scientific developments. Thus, it is a fluctuating structure that can be revised at any time. When we say that two individuals are members of the same species, we are saying that they are able to breed with each other. If further data were to reveal that some populations of what were assumed to be the same species were actually unable to interbreed, then we would have to revise our classification.

This kind of revision is fairly common. Bird-watchers who develop life lists of birds they have seen are often disgruntled when the classification of birds is revised so that what were once regarded as two or three separate species are now regarded as a single species. This happened, for example, when the yellow-shafted flicker of the East Coast, the red-shafted flicker of the West, and the gilded flicker in between were collapsed into a single species, now know as the common flicker. The birds had been interbreeding all along; the ornithologists just didn't recognize that for a long time.

If we think of a **taxonomy** (another word for a classification system) as a series of hypotheses to be tested, then we will understand why anthropology textbooks written in the 1960s will present different taxonomies than those written today. They were not wrong in the 1960s; rather, new data and new ways of analyzing old data have forced a number of revisions of that taxonomy.

Before discussing the current set of hypotheses that we use to describe the relationships among primates, it is important to discuss general guidelines for developing scientific taxonomies. First of all, a classification of living things must consider entire groups or populations of organisms. In other words, the variability found in a population is as important as any characteristic that can be used to describe a single individual in that group. Individuals are not classified; groups are.

Consider, for example, the variability that exists in the species *Canis familiaris,* the domesticated dog. If we used the German shepherd to describe that species (the "type" specimen), what would we do with the Chihuahua? If we were committed to the characteristics used to describe the German shepherd, we might be inclined at first to put the Chihuahua in a different species. But the two are not reproductively isolated (they may not be able to breed directly with each other because of size limitations, but they can mate with intermediary breeds), so they are members of the same species.

For many species, physical differences between males and females are so great that at first consideration they may be placed in separate species. Sex differences in size, coloration, or other nongenital characteristics are examples of **sexual dimorphism** (*di* = two; *morph* = form). In one species of anglerfish, for example, females are about ten times larger than the males, which attach themselves permanently in what is essentially a parasitic relationship. It would be easy, but mistaken, to conclude that the sexes were two species living as parasite and host. Among the primates there are a number of species, including gorillas and some baboons, that show a great deal of sexual dimorphism, especially in body size.

This need to consider the variability inherent in a population is especially problematic when trying to classify or identify fossil material. Careers in paleoanthropology rise and fall as debates rage over whether two different forms are members of the same species or represent two separate species. When there are size differences, for example, some taxonomists will argue that they represent two different species; others argue that they represent large and small populations (like African Efe pygmies and Swedes today); still others suggest that they may represent the two sexes of the same species.

## HISTORY OF SCIENTIFIC CLASSIFICATION

Since classification of living things is fundamental to being human, the first attempt to order the natural world is probably too ancient to identify. Carolus Linnaeus (1707–1778) is sometimes called the "father" of scientific taxonomy, because the classification system he developed provides the basis for the one we use today. He did not view his taxonomy as a set of hypotheses, however, since he assumed that the varieties of life were created by God and remain today just as they were at the time of creation. We call his system of classification a **phenetic** system since it is based on physical similarities among organisms. In this system, organisms are placed in the same species because they look alike. The system we use today, based on evolutionary relationships, is a **phyletic** system: organisms look alike because they are in the same species. This is not a trivial difference in meaning, so consider these two sentences carefully. The results of phenetic and phyletic systems are likely to be the same in most cases, but the underlying philosophies are different.

Modern phyletic taxonomy is based on **homologies,** similarities among organisms that represent descent from a common ancestor (Exhibit 5-1). Similarities that are not based on common descent are called **analogies** (Exhibit 5-2). The challenge to taxonomists is to distinguish between homologies and analogies, and this is not always easy. Detailed examination of the bones of a bird's wing and those of our arm, for example, reveals that these are homologous structures, even though they function in very different ways. The radius, ulna, humerus, carpals, metacarpals, and phalanges are all inherited from the last common ancestor of birds and primates. The wings of birds and butterflies, however, are analogous structures. Even though they function in much the same way (to propel the animal through the air), they are not structures inherited from a common ancestor.

Ideally, a taxonomy reconstructs the phylogeny or evolutionary history of a group of organisms. But, as

Carolus Linnaeus (1707–1778) is sometimes called the "father" of scientific taxonomy.

noted above, this is, in reality, a set of hypotheses to be tested. For example, in Exhibit 5-3 are two commonly used but slightly different taxonomies for the primates. They are competing hypotheses about relationships. We assume that a *real* taxonomy exists and it is our job to find it.

A number of recently developed techniques help test the hypotheses about relationships. First, computers and the ability to process massive volumes of data help us analyze hundreds of characteristics at a time. We assume that if enough characters are evaluated, evolutionary relationships will be revealed.

A second technique relies on biochemical similarities among organisms at the level of proteins, amino acids, and DNA. The physical similarities we observe in organisms, if they are homologies, are usually indicative of

**Homologies. Frogs, lizards, birds, and humans all have similar forearm bones because of descent from a common ancestor.**

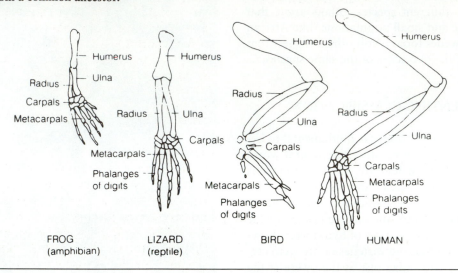

FROG
(amphibian)          LIZARD
(reptile)          BIRD          HUMAN

genetic similarities. Thus, by comparing the DNA of two organisms we can get direct information about the genes and determine how close the relationship is. We now know, for example, that chimpanzees and humans have almost identical DNA. This tells us that we are much more closely related to chimpanzees than we are to orangutans, with whom we share a lower percentage of DNA. Another way of saying this is that we shared a common ancestor with chimpanzees much more recently than we did with orangutans. We will try to put a time frame on these relationships in Chapter 6.

Biochemical similarities among organisms help determine the relationships among organisms at levels higher than the species. The Linnaean system arranges organisms in a hierarchy, beginning at the species level and ending at the kingdom level (Exhibit 5-4). Each higher level is ever more inclusive and reflects greater time depth than the one beneath it. Theoretically, members of one genus should be more closely related to each other and should share a more recent common ancestor than they do with members of another genus. Members of a family should be more closely related to each other than they are to members of another family, and so on through the various taxonomic levels.

Traditional taxonomy (see Exhibit 5-3a) places chimpanzees, gorillas, and orangutans in the family Pongidae and humans in the family Hominidae. Since a taxonomy should reflect evolutionary relationships, the evidence of

the DNA similarities calls into question the placing of chimpanzees and gorillas into a genus and family separate from the one in which humans are placed. An alternative taxonomy (see Exhibit 5-3b) based on the biochemical evidence, places chimpanzees, gorillas, and humans in the family Hominidae, leaving only the orangutan in the family Pongidae.

## CLASSIFICATION OF HUMAN BEINGS

Exhibit 5-4 outlines the taxonomic position of our species. Humans are in the kingdom Animalia because they, unlike plants, are mobile and depend on energy from sources other than the sun. We are in the phylum Chordata because we share with all other members of that phylum the homologous characteristics of notocord and gill slits. During prenatal life, we and other mammals exhibit the slits; these disappear in later life, whereas they are retained throughout life in other chordates such as fish and amphibians.

We are in the subphylum Vertebrata because we possess a vertebral column, a bony one in the case of mammals. (Sharks, with their cartilaginous skeletons, are also vertebrates.) We are in the class Mammalia because we share with others in that class the following homologous characteristics: (1) **homoiothermy** (ability to maintain a constant body temperature); (2) **viviparity** (live

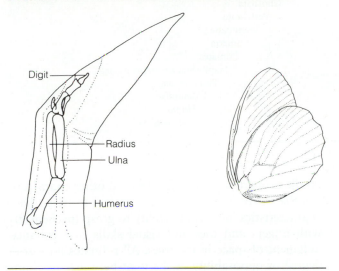

EXHIBIT 5-2

**Analogies.** The wings of birds and butterflies function in similar ways but they are not alike in structure. Their wing structures were not inherited from a common ancestor.

Labels on figure: Digit, Radius, Ulna, Humerus

birth); (3) mammary glands; (4) hair; (5) **heterodontism** (different kinds of teeth; Exhibit 5-5); (6) one bone in the lower jaw; and (7) three bones in the middle ear. When considering living forms, the first four characteristics would be sufficient for placing a specimen in the class Mammalia, but none of these would be preserved in fossil forms. Thus, the last three characteristics are important for paleontologists who must decide if a fossil is a mammal or a reptile.

## CHARACTERISTICS OF PRIMATES

Humans are in the order Primates, distinct from other orders of mammals such as Insectivora (shrews, moles, hedgehogs), Carnivora (cats, dogs, bears, raccoons, weasels, civets, and hyenas), Rodentia (beavers, squirrels, mice, rats, porcupines), Lagomorpha (pikas, rabbits, hares), and Pinnipedia (seals, walrus). With the exception of the middle ear structure, there is no single characteristic that distinguishes primates from all other orders of mammals. Rather, a complex of characteristics

EXHIBIT 5-3(a)

**Taxonomy of the Primate Order: Alternative A**

| | |
|---|---|
| Order | Primates |
| Suborder | Prosimii |
| Superfamily | Lemuroidea |
| Family | Lemuridae |
| Family | Indriidae |
| Family | Daubentoniidae |
| Superfamily | Lorisoidea |
| Family | Lorisidae |
| Superfamily | Tarsioidea |
| Family | Tarsiidae |
| | |
| Suborder | Anthropoidea |
| Superfamily | Ceboidea |
| Family | Callitrichidae |
| Family | Cebidae |
| Superfamily | Cercopithecoidea |
| Family | Cercopithecidae |
| Superfamily | Hominoidea |
| Family | Hylobatidae |
| Family | Pongidae |
| Genus | *Pongo* |
| Genus | *Pan* |
| Genus | *Gorilla* |
| Family | Hominidae |
| Genus | *Homo* |

Fleagle, J. *Primate Adaptation and Evolution.* N.Y.: Academic Press, 1988.

EXHIBIT 5-3(b)

**Taxonomy of the Primate Order: Alternative B**

| | |
|---|---|
| Order | Primates |
| Suborder | Strepsirhini |
| Superfamily | Lemuroidea |
| Family | Lemuridae |
| Family | Indriidae |
| Family | Daubentoniidae |
| Superfamily | Lorisoidea |
| Family | Lorisidae |
| | |
| Suborder | Haplorhini |
| Superfamily | Tarsioidea |
| Family | Tarsiidae |
| Superfamily | Ceboidea |
| Family | Callitrichidae |
| Family | Cebidae |
| Superfamily | Cercopithecoidea |
| Family | Cercopithecidae |
| Superfamily | Hominoidea |
| Family | Hylobatidae |
| Family | Pongidae |
| Genus | *Pongo* |
| Family | Hominidae |
| Genus | *Pan* |
| Genus | *Gorilla* |
| Genus | *Homo* |

Richard, A. *Primates in Nature.* N.Y.: W. H. Freeman, 1985.

EXHIBIT 5-4

**The Position of Humans in the Linnaean System.**

| Kingdom | Animalia |
|---|---|
| Phylum | Chordata |
| Subphylum | Vertebrata |
| Class | Mammalia |
| Subclass | Eutheria |
| Order | Primates |
| Suborder | Haplorhini or Anthropoidea |
| Superfamily | Hominoidea |
| Family | Hominidae |
| Genus | *Homo* |
| species | *sapiens* |

must be considered. This complex reflects two adaptations: (1) to an **arboreal** (tree-living) niche and (2) to visually oriented food-getting.

Adaptation to life in the trees requires grasping ability. Two ancestral characteristics, five fingers on each hand and the collarbone, have been retained in primates because they contributed to success in trees. In many modern mammals, those characteristics have disappeared as selection favored, for example, rapid speed

◆ ◆ ◆

EXHIBIT 5-5

**Reptilian and mammalian teeth.**

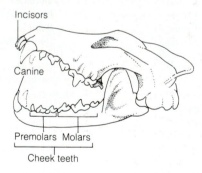

Incisors

Canine

Premolars Molars

Cheek teeth

MAMMALIAN
(heterondont)

REPTILIAN (alligator)
(homodont: no differentiation of teeth)

on the ground. Selection also favored other characteristics that further contributed to survival in trees. These characteristics include the ability to grasp (**prehensility**) with fingers and toes and visual skills that enhanced judgment of space in the trees. All primates have some degree of opposability at the joint between the thumb and fingers, and all except humans have this flexibility in the joint between the big and little toes. Primates also have nails instead of claws on their digits and more sensitive fingertips than most other mammals have. Opposability, nails, and sensitive fingertips all contribute to enhanced speed and skill in movement through the trees.

Moreover, two visual characteristics, **binocular** and **stereoscopic** vision, have enhanced both travel in the trees and food-getting among primates (Exhibit 5-6). The term "binocular" refers to the placement of the eyes at the front of the head so that the visual fields overlap, thus increasing three-dimensional vision. Binocular vision, not unique to primates, is found in most animals that depend on sight to find their food, such as cats and predatory birds (raptors) such as hawks and owls. Stereoscopic vision describes the way in which visual images are received by the brain, a further aid to seeing in three dimensions. In most mammals, fibers from the left eye cross over to the right hemisphere of the brain where the information is interpreted, and vice versa for the right eye fibers. In stereoscopic vision, fibers from both eyes are received by both hemispheres of the brain. Selection for increased visual keenness was apparently accompanied by decreasing smell (**olfactory**) acuity. Although some primates depend heavily on smell, particularly in social interaction, the order as a whole can be described as more vision-dependent than smell-dependent.

Primates have fewer teeth than many other mammals (thirty-six in most prosimians and New World mon-

**Comparison of binocular and stereoscopic vision.**

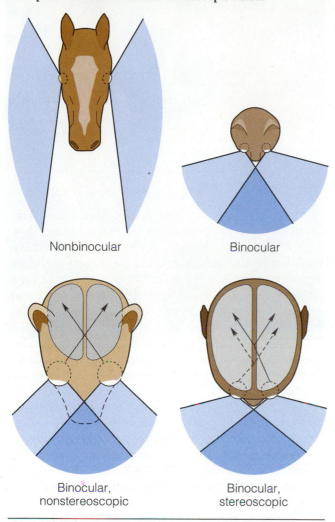

Nonbinocular  Binocular

Binocular, nonstereoscopic  Binocular, stereoscopic

keys; thirty-two in Old World monkeys, apes, and humans). The middle ear is contained entirely in a single bone in primates rather than surrounded by two or three separate bones as in other mammals. Paleontologists can use this unique characteristic of the middle ear to determine whether or not a fossilized specimen is a primate.

Overall brain expansion has also been used to describe primates. In general, we can say that primates have greater **encephalization quotients** (brain size relative to body size) than most other mammals. Higher encephalization quotients suggest greater intelligence, another characteristic used to portray primates.

A number of characteristics related to reproduction have been used to describe primates, including the tendency to give birth to one young at a time. Primates also have relatively slow maturation rates, affording more time for the young to learn about complex environments and social systems.

## PRIMATE SUBORDERS

The taxonomic category known as the suborder has recently come under close scrutiny by those who work on classification of the primates. There are presently two separate taxonomies, representing two hypotheses. The older one (Exhibit 5-3a) divides the order Primates into the suborders Prosimii (lemurs, lorises, and tarsiers) and Anthropoidea (monkeys, apes, and humans). Recent biochemical evidence, however, challenges the hypothesis that tarsiers are more closely related to lemurs and lorises than they are to the other primates. Proponents of this challenge suggest that the suborder divisions should be as follows (Exhibit 5-3b): Strepsirhini (lemurs and lorises) and Haplorhini (tarsiers, monkeys, apes, and humans).

There are six superfamilies in the order Primates, and about this there is not much controversy. This chapter will focus, therefore, on this level. These six superfamilies are the Lemuroidea (lemurs), Lorisoidea (lorises), Tarsioidea (tarsiers), Ceboidea (New World monkeys), Cercopithecoidea (Old World monkeys), and Hominoidea (apes and humans).

1. *Lemuroidea.* Lemurs are found only on the island of Madagascar, off the east coast of Africa. They are a classic example of an adaptive radiation, the likely descendants of a small ancestral population that arrived on the island 50 to 60 million years ago. Today, there are approximately twenty-two species representing a great deal of diversity in a single superfamily. In the group are nocturnal and diurnal forms, arboreal and semiterrestrial forms, **insectivores** (insect-eaters) and **omnivores** (animals that eat a wide variety of foods), and mouse-sized and baboon-sized forms. Unfortunately, the origin of their name, which means "ghost," is too apt: many have recently become extinct and several are endangered because of human activity on the island in the last two thousand years.

2. *Lorisoidea.* Lorises are the mainland equivalents of Madagascar's lemurs. They include the lorises and pottos of South and Southeast Asia and the bushbabies or galagos of equatorial Africa. All are nocturnal, insectivorous, and solitary in their social behavior.

The sifaka is one of the lemurs of Madagascar.

The slow loris is a nocturnal primate from Asia.

3. *Tarsioidea.* This pivotal superfamily overlaps the "lower primates" (lemurs and lorises) and the "higher primates" (monkeys, apes, and humans). Tarsiers are like the higher primates in their brain and nose structure and in their visual and reproductive systems. They are like the lower primates in that they are insectivorous, nocturnal, and solitary. The biochemical evidence indicates that they are more closely related to the higher primates. There are three species distributed in the islands of Southeast Asia.

An unusual pattern of **locomotion** (way of moving) is found among some lemurs, lorises, and tarsiers, known as **vertical clinging and leaping** (Exhibit 5-7). Vertical clingers and leapers have powerful, elongated hind limbs which they use to propel themselves from one vertical tree trunk to another. The forelimbs are used to support themselves at rest and are not involved in locomotion except in a limited way.

4. *Ceboidea.* All of the monkeys of the New World (the Americas) are in the superfamily Ceboidea, which includes two families, Callitrichidae and Cebidae. The small tamarins and marmosets are callitrichids,

found in the tropical rain forests of Brazil, Colombia, and Bolivia. They are entirely arboreal and diurnal, feed on insects and tree gums, typically give birth to twins, and have nails that look like claws. Like the rain forest that is their home, many are threatened or endangered.

Ceboids include capuchins, howlers, spider monkeys, and squirrel monkeys. All are arboreal quadrupeds and all but the night monkey are diurnal. They are found in both Central and South America. All have three premolars, some have prehensile tails, and they have adapted to a variety of food sources, including insects, fruits, leaves, seeds, and flowers.

5. *Cercopithecoidea.* The guenons, colobines, mangabeys, vervets, and baboons of Africa and the macaques and langurs of Asia comprise the superfamily Cercopithecoidea, the Old World monkeys. The variety in the superfamily includes terrestrial and arboreal forms. They have the same number and type of teeth that we do. Although some (the colobines and langurs) are specialized leaf-eaters, most are omnivores, consuming a variety of foods, as we do.

**Vertical clinging and leaping.**

Redrawn from Napier & Walker 1967, and Napier and Napier 1985.

The tarsier, found in Southeast Asia, is an example of a vertical clinger and leaper.

The spider monkey is a New World monkey with a prehensile tail.

African vervets, like most Old World monkeys, live in social groups.

The orangutan is found in Indonesia and is one of the most endangered primate species.

**6.** *Hominoidea.* Finally, the superfamily Hominoidea includes the apes and humans. The gibbons and siamangs of Southeast Asian rain forests are in the family Hylobatidae. They are relatively small apes (sometimes called the "lesser apes") and are exclusively arboreal. Their mode of locomotion, **brachiation,** is characterized by swinging arm over arm through the trees (Exhibit 5-8). All apes have the ability to brachiate and the related characteristic of longer forelimbs than hind limbs, but only the gibbon depends primarily on brachiation as a way of moving around. Their diet consists mostly of fruits. Although several species are threatened or endangered, the gibbons are far more successful today than the great apes (orangutans, chimpanzees, gorillas) in diversity and abundance.

In discussing the other hominoid families, we stand on shaky taxonomic ground again. As mentioned earlier, the traditional classification describes the family Pongidae as including the chimpanzee, orangutan, and gorilla. The family Hominidae includes only humans. Certainly, from our perspective, the three great apes look more like each other than any of them look like us. The biochemical evidence suggests, however, that humans, chimpanzees, and perhaps gorillas, should be in one family and the orangutan should be in another. As with the suborder distinctions, we will not try to resolve this controversy here; rather, we will discuss each group separately.

The orangutan is found in Indonesia and is among the most endangered species on earth. Despite their large body size (males reach statures of five feet and weights of 165 pounds), they spend most of their time in the trees because of the swampy habitat in which they live most of the year. Females are almost half the size of males, illustrating extreme sexual dimorphism. They feed primarily on fruit and leaves.

Gorillas, also threatened, are found in equatorial Africa. There is only one species but two distinct populations or subspecies: the mountain gorilla and the lowland gorilla. They are almost exclusively vegetarian and spend most of their time on the ground. Males are as tall as six feet and weigh as much as four hundred pounds; females are about half the size of males.

Gorillas are found in the lowland and highland rainforests of central Africa.

Chimpanzees are believed to be our closest living relatives.

◆ ◆ ◆
EXHIBIT 5-8
**The Siamang and gibbon are true brachiators.**

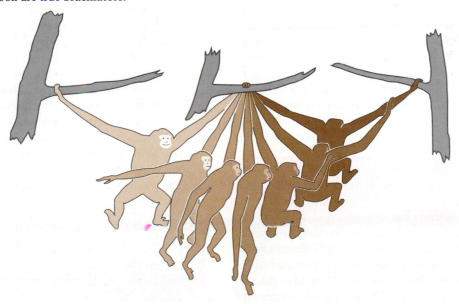

Redrawn from Fleagle, 1977 and Napier and Napier, 1985.

Chimpanzees are also found in equatorial Africa and, like the other great apes, are in danger of extinction. Two species are recognized: the common chimpanzee and the pygmy chimpanzee, or bonobo. They occupy a greater variety of habitats, consume a greater array of foods, and seem to have a wider social and behavioral repertoire than the other apes, but this perception may be due to the fact that there have been more long-term studies of chimpanzees than of any of the other apes.

Humans, *Homo sapiens,* can be easily distinguished from the other apes today by their large brains, language capabilities, and complex material culture. These characteristics, however, are not particularly useful when dealing with fossils, so the one attribute that we can say distinguishes humans from all other primates is bipedalism or two-legged locomotion. Humans are far from endangered, occupy a wider variety of habitats than any other single species on earth, and have a behavioral repertoire that will require the rest of this book to describe. But again, perhaps it just seems that way because the species has been studied so extensively.

## Primate Social Systems

Until the 1960s, most information we had on the behavior of nonhuman primates was based on observations of captive populations in zoos or research laboratories. Since that time, however, hundreds of studies have been carried out in wild populations, and our understanding of primate behavior has increased enormously. In many cases, the behaviors that were observed in captive populations turned out to be quite different from the behaviors observed in the wild. The differences may be somewhat similar to descriptions that would emerge of human behavior in prisons compared to those based on "normal" conditions.

Nonhuman primates have been studied for at least two reasons: (a) to understand them as members of the living world, and (b) to gain a better understanding of past and contemporary human behavior. We are primates, after all, and even though we consider ourselves very different from other animals, we still share a number of fundamental similarities. Among these similarities is the fact that most primates are social animals. All animal young must *learn* how to find food and mates and must avoid being killed. Most primates must learn how to do these things in the context of a social group. The

exceptions are the nocturnal primates, which are solitary for most of their lives. Nocturnal primate males and females come together for mating, and the young spend a portion of their lives with their mothers, but otherwise, nocturnal lemurs, lorises, and tarsiers can be described as solitary primates. The only habitually solitary diurnal primate is the orangutan.

A small family social system that is composed, typically, of a monogamous (one-mate) pair and their offspring is relatively rare in mammals but fairly common in primates. It has been estimated (Hrdy, 1981) that of the approximately two hundred species of primates, thirty-seven (18 percent) are monogamous in some or all cases (Kinzey, 1987, believes that figure is too high). Best known are marmosets and tamarins, some lemurs and tarsiers, the night monkey, all gibbons and siamangs, and most humans. Recent field studies have provided evidence that some marmosets and tamarins may actually breed in **polyandrous** groups, where a single female mates with two or more males, all of whom provide care for her offspring.

Probably the most common form of social organization found in primates is the small group composed of one or two adult males, two or three adult females, and their young of various ages. Species that organize themselves this way include many lemurs, most New World monkeys, langurs, colobines, and the gorilla. These are primarily forest-dwelling species.

Large multimale, multifemale groups are common in the more terrestrial primates such as macaques, baboons, vervets, and chimpanzees. For most of these animals, large groups provide the advantage of safety in numbers in an environment of relatively abundant but widely spaced resources. The large group size is also associated with a complex social structure, including dominance hierarchies among both males and females.

We will now review selected species of primates that illustrate the diversity of habitats, behavior, and social organization found in the order. We will organize this section as in the review above: solitary species, small monogamous family groups, small polygynous groups, and large multimale–multifemale groups.

EXAMPLES OF SOLITARY SPECIES:
NOCTURNAL PROSIMIANS AND ORANGUTANS

**Nocturnal Prosimians.** As noted above, most of the solitary species of primates are nocturnal; therefore, since primatologists are diurnal, we have far less information on these species than we do on the diurnal primates. Additionally, they are usually small, move either very

SETTING THE
RECORD STRAIGHT

◆    ◆    ◆

◆    ◆    ◆

When zoo animals are housed in settings inappropriate for their species, most of them suffer poor growth, illness, and even death. For example, when a colony of hamadryas baboons was originally established at the London Zoo, adult males and females were housed together in close quarters. In the wild, hamadryas arrange themselves in one-male harem groups, and adult males have little tolerance for the close presence of other adult males. Forced to live in close proximity in the zoo setting, the adult males fought for access to the breeding females until most of the females were killed or had to be removed for their safety. Today zoo keepers are very careful to match social groups in zoos as closely as possible to the form found in wild populations.

slowly or very quickly, and, since they do not live in groups, are generally difficult to locate and follow.

To say that a species is solitary is not to suggest that their social lives are simple. A close investigation of social systems in prosimians reveals a great deal of variation (Bearder, 1987). In general, male home ranges do not usually overlap those of other males, but male ranges overlap female ranges for breeding purposes.

Nocturnal primates consume a wide variety of foods, with insects predominating in the diets of tarsiers and tree gums predominating for many lorises. Twin and triplet births are more common in the prosimians than they are in the anthropoid primates. As young males mature, they forage on their own, covering large distances until they ultimately set up their own territories, which they defend from other adult males. Maturing females also establish ranges that either overlap those of their mothers or are entirely separate, depending on the species.

**Orangutans.** Unlike the other great apes, orangutans spend most of their time in the trees, feeding primarily on fruits and leaves. Adult females and their dependent offspring cover small home ranges, overlapped by one or more larger adult male ranges. Female ranges are apparently fairly stable, whereas male ranges are more likely to change. Birth intervals are long (five to seven years), and juveniles begin ranging independently of their mothers, gradually setting up home ranges near their mothers, in the case of daughters, or ranging more widely, in the case of males. Subadult males appear to mate as frequently with females as do adult males (Rodman and Mitani, 1987).

## EXAMPLES OF SMALL FAMILY GROUPS: MARMOSETS AND GIBBONS

Most field researchers believe that the tendency to live in small, often monogamous, family groups is due to ecological circumstances. Most of the species that do organize themselves this way live in arboreal environments where resources are distributed evenly, although not necessarily abundantly, throughout the species' ranges. The resources cannot support large groups and are often defended against other members of the groups' species.

**Marmosets and Tamarins.** Marmosets and tamarins have often been described as monogamous, but recent long-term field studies suggest that their social systems are more complex and more flexible than is usually associated with true monogamy (Kinzey, 1987). Groups with two or more pair-bonded adults, groups with one female mated with two or more males, and groups with one male and two or more adult females have all been reported. Even solitary marmosets and tamarins have been observed (Goldizen, 1987). One common characteristic of these primates, however, is that care of infants is often provided by members of the family other than the mother. The mother nurses her young, of course, but carrying and other aspects of caretaking are often performed by the juveniles, subadults, and adult males. When there are two or more adult males in a family group, all may participate in care of the infants.

**Gibbons.** Gibbons have long been described as monogamous primates, and there has been no recent field study to challenge that description. Thus, their social system

Marmosets often form monogamous pair bonds and males typically participate in care of the offspring.

Gibbons are found in South and Southeast Asia. They usually mate for life and defend their territories from other mated pairs.

may be less flexible than that observed in the marmosets and tamarins. Gibbons are also highly territorial and actively defend their home ranges from other territorial monogamous pairs with adjacent ranges. Gibbons have infants approximately once every two years, and young are dependent on their parents until they are about six. Thus, a typical family group may include as many as six, although the average is about four (Leighton, 1987). Adult males and females are about the same size (they are **monomorphic**, as opposed to dimorphic) and appear to be **codominant** (one sex is not dominant over the other).

## EXAMPLES OF SMALL GROUPS: DIURNAL LEMURS, HOWLER MONKEYS, HAMADRYAS BABOONS, AND GORILLAS

Ecological factors also have an effect on group size for primates that do not form permanent pair bonds. Where resources are abundant, groups of lemurs and monkeys tend to be large; where they are scarce, they tend to be small, perhaps consisting of a single adult male and two or more adult females and their young. The latter is often referred to as a "harem" system and is common in some baboon species, gorillas, and some species of langurs. Male harem leaders tend to actively prevent other males from having access to breeding females in their groups. Otherwise, in groups with more than one adult male, mating opportunities tend to be correlated with dominance among the males, although many exceptions have been observed.

**Diurnal Lemurs.** Sifakas and ring-tailed lemurs have been studied more extensively than any other species of Madagascan primates. They live in groups that range in size from two to twelve (sifakas) and five to twenty-two (ring-tailed lemurs). As discussed above, the size of the group appears to be related to resource abundance. Where populations are dense, home ranges are often defended against other members of the species. Unlike most other primate species described, females are usually dominant over males in access to resources. Males are often peripheral and may wander from group to group, especially during the mating season. The mating season is apparently a chaotic time for these lemurs, and the order observed for the social group during most of the year appears to dissolve. Fighting among males at this time is often intense and may be more important in determining access to reproductive females than dominance position in the group during the rest of the year (Richard, 1985).

**Howler Monkeys.** The six species of howler monkeys occupy the widest distribution of any New World monkey. They range from southern Mexico to northern Argentina, occupying a wide variety of habitats (Crockett and Eisenberg, 1987). With such variety of habitats, it is not surprising that their social organization is also variable and flexible. Most species, however, organize themselves in small groups of from five to fifteen animals, typically with more adult females than adult males. Their diet consists primarily of leaves, and they travel only short distances each day. Social rank within groups is not easily observed, suggesting that it is not a very strong determinant of social interaction. In fact, howler monkeys apparently engage in less social interaction in their groups than has been reported for most other primates. Also unlike most other primates, both males and females of some howler species leave their natal troops when they become mature. Often, the emigration is preceded by severe fights in the group (Crockett, 1984). In most other primate species, either males or females emigrate, but not both.

**Hamadryas Baboons.** As with most of the primate species discussed, environment and resource distribution have great impact on social organization and group size of hamadryas baboons. Perhaps few primates live in environments as harsh as theirs: a desert environment, devoid of trees and with few predictable water sources. Home ranges are typically very large for these herbivorous primates. At night, groups of as many as two hundred animals can be found seeking refuge on rocky ledges. But the primary foraging and breeding unit is small, consisting of one adult male and two or more adult females with their young. This unit is described as a harem. New harem units are formed as adult males "kidnap" adult females of an aging or injured male, or "adopt" juvenile females. Other adult males without a harem usually form peripheral associations with an intact harem unit, eventually taking over when the older male dies or is no longer able to maintain leadership and control of his group (Richard, 1987). When resources are more abundant, as in the rainy season, several harem units may forage together in bands, although sexual activity is still usually confined to the harem.

**Gorillas.** Gorillas occupy dense rain forests of central Africa. Although the adults are too large to be considered arboreal, their behavior and social organization is a lot more like those of other arboreal primates than it is like the other great apes. Their vegetarian foods are relatively abundant, and home ranges are somewhat

Diurnal ring-tailed lemurs are found in Madagascar where they live in small to medium-sized social groups.

Howler monkeys range from Mexico to Argentina. They use their prehensile tails as fifth arms. Their diet is primarily vegetarian and they live in small to medium-sized social groups.

Hamadryas baboons live in arid parts of north Africa where they organize themselves socially in one-male harem units.

large and overlapping. Gorillas live in small groups of one dominant "silverback" male, one or more subordinate "blackback" males, several adult females, juveniles, and infants. The females are usually unrelated to each other. Adult males appear to tolerate the continued presence of their adult sons in their groups, although the sons become peripheral as they become sexually mature. Females usually emigrate when they reach sexual maturity. The silverback male is clearly dominant over all other members of the group. Gorilla diet is primarily leaves, and they spend most of their day eating and resting. Interaction among group members is somewhat infrequent in comparison to other primate species.

## EXAMPLES OF LARGE GROUPS:
## SAVANNAH BABOONS AND CHIMPANZEES

Savannah baboons, macaques, and chimpanzees are usually found in large groups, averaging about fifty animals. Their diets are variable, and they can best be described as omnivorous. They are more terrestrial than most primates, which probably accounts for their larger groups: terrestrial primates, particularly young ones, are generally more vulnerable to predation, and there is safety in numbers. Because of the large groups and the

Savannah baboons live in large multimale-multifemale troops. Because they are so common in Africa, they have been extensively studied by primatologists.

fact that primatologists are also terrestrial, we know more about these animals than we do about any of the more arboreal species. Essential resources such as food, water, and sleeping trees are typically widely dispersed, so home ranges are larger than those of other primates. As with any large social group, some form of internal structure helps to maintain group cohesion. For the large troops of baboons, macaques, and chimpanzees, a dominance hierarchy among males and females helps to determine who has access to resources. Thus, when competition over food or reproductive females becomes acute, the dominance hierarchy, rather than a fight, usually determines priority.

**Savannah Baboons.** Savannah baboons are distributed widely throughout central Africa and are so variable in body shape, size, and coloration that they were once thought to represent as many as five separate species. Subsequent research has determined that the populations are not reproductively isolated, however, so all are now placed in a single species. Troops forage together over large areas each day, depending on the distribution of resources, grasses being their primary food source. Since in some parts of Africa there is little overlap of troop home ranges, encounters between troops are rare. In other areas, particularly where waterholes are few and far between, home range overlap and troop encounters are frequent. Females typically remain in their natal troops, and males almost always emigrate when they become sexually mature.

**Common Chimpanzees.** Almost everyone who has access to a television or *National Geographic* knows something about chimpanzees because of the long-term studies of Jane Goodall. We discuss them here in the context of large troops, but their social organization is highly fluid. Chimpanzees live in communities that have within them any number of groups, highly variable in size and structure. Community size ranges from fifteen to eighty, and there is almost no overlap of community ranges. In fact, communities may occasionally exhibit hostility toward each other to the extent that it has been called "warfare." Within a community can be found solitary chimpanzees, mother and infant groups, groups of several females and dependent young, male–female temporary pair bonds, groups of males, and multimale–multifemale groups.

One of the most cohesive units within the community is a group of related males. Adult males tend to range over the entire community home range, whereas females tend to have much smaller ranges, overlapped by that of the males. Males usually remain in their birth communities for their entire lives, and females most often leave to join other communities. As with migration patterns reported for other primates, this pattern tends to reduce the incidence of inbreeding.

The dominance hierarchy among males is fairly well defined, and adult males are dominant over all females. The highest ranking males ("alpha males") tend to be those in their physical prime. Females spend most of their time alone or with their offspring, so dominance among adult females is not clear-cut. Mother–offspring relationships appear to last a lifetime.

Chimpanzees are omnivorous, like humans, and consume fruits, leaves, insects, and small animals. Other aspects of their behavior will be described below.

## ARE HUMANS "JUST ANOTHER PRIMATE"?

When we were describing physical characteristics, geographic distribution, and taxonomic status of primate species, we discussed humans right along with the other members of the order. Behavior, however, seems to require a different approach. Whereas we have devoted a paragraph or two to the behavior and social organization of the other species, we will devote the majority of chapters of this text to the same aspects of humans. That is partly because this is an **anthropology** rather than a **primatology** text, but we also believe that humans are different enough from other primates to deserve considerably more detail. But before we discuss the differences, let's explore some of the behaviors that are similar to those of other primates.

**Diet and Food-getting Behavior.** The primate order includes species that specialize in insects (insectivores like the tarsier), fruits (**frugivores** like the gibbon), leaves (**folivores** like the colobines), and tree saps and gums (**gummivores** like the marmosets). Giving a species a diet label implies that at least 50 percent of its diet comes from the named source. Species that have highly variable diets and cannot be so labeled may be called generalized herbivores or omnivores. Although some humans may consider themselves vegetarians, the species can best be described as omnivorous. Our generalized dentition and physiology also confirm that we are omnivores.

Like other primates, we depend primarily on vision to locate and identify foods, with our senses of touch, taste, and smell also contributing information. Also like other primates, we use our hands to gather and process foods. But our food-getting pattern has one important difference: all humans process at least some of their foods with heat, either by boiling, roasting, baking, or grilling. This important discovery dramatically increased the range of foods that humans could eat and, thus, the variety of habitats they could live in.

Humans also consume a greater percentage of animal protein than do other monkeys and apes (the insectivorous prosimians obviously consume more than humans do). Omnivorous primates are capable of metabolizing animal protein and will usually consume it when opportunities arise. In general, however, the caloric expenditure for obtaining animal protein exceeds the caloric return, so chasing live animals for food is not the wisest foraging strategy, as long as other protein is more readily available. Baboons and chimpanzees have been described as "opportunistic hunters" in that they will kill and consume small animals on occasion. More systematic hunting of game may have been a critical adaptive step early in human evolutionary history.

**Sex and Reproduction.** Female monkeys, apes, and humans have similar ovarian cycles. If the egg is not fertilized or the zygote not implanted, menstruation occurs and the cycle begins again. Cycle lengths vary from species to species: eleven to twenty-seven days in New World monkeys, twenty-one to forty days in Old World monkeys, twenty-nine to thirty-seven days in apes, and twenty-five to thirty-two days in humans (Richard, 1985). Human cycles differ from those of other primates in at least three ways: (1) the amount of blood shed at menstruation is greater; (2) human sexual activity is not concentrated at the time of ovulation; (3) most contemporary humans have far more menstrual cycles in their lifetimes than their predecessors or other primate females. It should also be noted that some primate species are seasonal breeders; that is, their cycles occur only at restricted times of the year, usually tied to cycles of resource availability. Squirrel monkeys are examples of seasonal breeders.

New World monkeys, gorillas, and orangutans show no evidence of bleeding at the beginning of a new cycle. Chimpanzees and some Old World monkeys have an obvious menstruation, although it does not last the three or four days that is typical of humans (Richard, 1985). The function of this relatively heavy menstrual flow is still unknown. Perhaps it evolved as a "signaling device" to indicate that a female is not pregnant.

Female mammals are generally most receptive to sexual advances of males when they are ovulating. This period of sexual receptivity is referred to as **estrus**, and unambiguous signs, signals, or behaviors are associated with it. For example, when a female baboon or chim-

panzee is in estrus, she exhibits a swollen **perineal** area (the area between the anus and the vulva), emits chemical signals (**pheromones**), and acts like she is interested in copulation, often by inviting males to mount her. At other times she is not as interested in sex or may refuse to be mounted by males, although copulations at times other than ovulation are not unusual in these species.

Human females do not show clear signs that they are ovulating; in fact, determining the time of ovulation requires careful monitoring for most women. It is neither obvious to them nor to the males in their vicinity. Furthermore, their interest in sex, while it may rise slightly at the time of ovulation, is independent of it. Human females have been called "continuously sexually receptive" because they are interested in sex at almost all times during their menstrual cycles. Furthermore, human females engage in sexual activity when they are pregnant and when they are nursing, behaviors that are rare in other primate species. Helen Fisher (1982) calls humans "sex athletes," noting that we spend more time and energy on aspects of sexuality than any other animal species known. Speculations on the evolution of these differences in sexuality are offered in Chapter 6.

Too often when we compare humans to other primates, we use humans who live in industrialized societies as our models. But we live in a cultural and technological environment very different from that of our ancestors or that of many humans today who live in less industrialized parts of the world. Using ourselves as a model leads us to draw conclusions about human differences that may not be warranted. For example, we note that some women may have as many as 450 menstrual cycles in their lifetimes (twelve to thirteen cycles per year for thirty-five years from age 15 to 50). Thus, we assume that the normal state for a female is cycling. This is not true for any other primate, nor is it true for many contemporary or ancestral women. For them, the normal state of an adult female is or was pregnant or lactating. Constant cycling, therefore, is unique for modern women practicing birth control. Otherwise, human females are similar to other primates in their reproductive cycles.

Other aspects of the reproductive life cycle include length of gestation, period of nursing, birth intervals, and total number of offspring born in a lifetime. For each of these, the human length or number is typically greater than that of other primates, but otherwise the components are similar. Gestation is approximately 163 days for macaques, 175 days for baboons, 228 days for chimpanzees, 256 days for gorillas, and 267 days for humans (Harvey and Clutton-Brock, 1985). Macaques and baboons nurse their infants for about fifteen

When she is in estrus, the savannah baboon female will exhibit a pink to bright red swollen perineal area. This is a signal that she is sexually receptive and most males find her attractive during this time. Here, the male is grooming the female as she invites his attention by "presenting" her perineal area to him.

months; chimps and gorillas for about four years. The usual nursing length cited for humans is about two years, and even that seems too long by Western standards. Many hunting-and-gathering populations nurse their infants as long as chimpanzees do, however, suggesting that the ancestral pattern for humans may be more in line with that for the apes.

The interval between births is roughly the length of nursing added to the length of gestation. Thus, gorillas and chimpanzees have birth intervals as long as five years, longer than for most human populations. It is likely, however, that the birth interval for human populations before the development of agriculture was longer.

The total number of offspring born to a female primate is a function of her reproductive life span, her health, the interval between births, and infant mortality. Wild populations of monkeys and apes appear to average about five offspring per female.

**Parental Care.** A characteristic of primates is a long period of infant dependency. Thus, in terms of time and energy expended, parental effort is relatively high in these species. Mother–infant bonds can be strong and may last a lifetime. Female macaques and baboons, spe-cies in which the females tend to remain in their natal troops, spend most of their time in clusters of maternal descent groups known as **matrilines**. Care of older infants is often shared in these groups, and members of matrilines tend to groom each other more frequently than they do unrelated individuals. Chimpanzee females also tend to spend most of their time with mothers and daughters, although, since female emigration is common in this species, adult females may live in different communities from those of their mothers. Female transfer is also common in gorillas.

Paternal care is rare in mammals because, for most species, mating is promiscuous and the biological father is usually unknown. Since natural selection tends to favor investment of time and energy only in one's own offspring, we find adult males routinely caring for young only in those species in which paternity is assured. These are the pair-bonded species such as marmosets, harem-breeding monkeys, and gibbons. Human mating systems also provide some assurance that a woman's mate is the father of her child; paternal care reaches its greatest levels for mammals in some human populations (Hewlett, 1992). As we shall see in Chapter 6, many believe that the human tendency to form pair bonds is related to the selective advantage favoring care by both mothers and fathers.

**Kinship, Friendship, and Society.** Our discussions of matrilines and paternal care remind us that relationships with kin are important in primate societies. Many individuals, particularly females in **matrifocal** groups, spend their entire lives in the company of kindred. Social grooming, one of the most important behaviors for both hygiene and social cohesion, is found widely among female kin. Many primates spend hours of every day engaged in quiet, mutual grooming, using their hands and teeth to gently search the fur for insects. It is through this mechanism that friendship bonds are formed and defined.

Dominance hierarchies among both males and females are often kinship based (Gouzoules and Gouzoules, 1987). Just as high-status human families tend to produce high-status children, dominant females tend to produce dominant offspring in many monkey and chimpanzee populations. It should be noted that breeding tends to take place between unrelated individuals, and many have argued that avoidance of incest is a characteristic common to human and nonhuman primates. Although sexual activity has been reported between mothers and sons and brothers and sisters, its frequency is much lower than would be expected if some avoidance were not taking place.

Primatologists have long been aware that kinship was an important component of primate society, but only recently have they begun to turn their attention to friendship (Smuts, 1985). Friendship seems to be especially important in male–female relationships. To say that most primates mate promiscuously is not to say that females mate with just anyone. Females of most species appear to be highly selective in soliciting and allowing copulations. Barbara Smuts, for example, found that in the baboon troops she has studied, females tend to mate preferentially with the males with whom they spend the most feeding, sleeping, and grooming ("social") time. She calls these relationships friendships and suggests that they are formed on the same basis as human friendships. Personality seems to have a lot to do with it, and the male with the most female friends is not necessarily the dominant male in the social group. Smuts believes that a male friend is often the father of a female's offspring, and indeed, these friends often act paternally toward the young, providing protection and a playground. She reports several instances in which infants used the male's body as a "trampoline" (Smuts, 1987).

**Intelligence, Curiosity, and Self-awareness.** We have noted that primates have large brains relative to body size. Does this larger brain mean a higher IQ (intelli-gence quotient)? It probably does, but unfortunately the measurement of IQ in nonhuman primates is plagued with the same difficulties as the measurement of IQ in humans. We have not come up with a good definition of intelligence, nor with an objective way of measuring it. Monkeys and apes perform well on most human intelligence tests designed for human infants and young children, so we assume that their reasoning skills are similar to ours. In laboratory situations they have been trained to understand abstract concepts, and chimpanzees appear to recognize themselves in mirrors. We can also conclude that species that live in complex societies like those of most primates are heavily dependent on intelligent learning for their survival and reproductive success (Essock-Vitale and Seyfarth, 1987).

**Tool-using and Local Traditions.** Several primate species have demonstrated the ability to make and use tools to solve problems related to foraging. These skills have also been used to argue for high intelligence and reasoning in primates. Chimpanzees, for example, have frequently been observed modifying twigs and sticks to use in foraging for insects. Typically the process involves stripping leaves from a sturdy twig, sticking the "tool" into a hole in a termite mound, twisting it around until termites latch onto it, and pulling the twig out filled with termites, which are then licked off. Another example of tools in the context of foraging is the use of rocks to crack open hard nuts (Essock-Vitale and Seyfarth, 1987). Often a tool may be collected or prepared far from the food source, suggesting that the animal has an image in his or her mind of what it will be used for. This is a level of intelligence above what would be required in picking up a nearby rock or twig when the food is found.

Tools are also used to threaten or attack intruders and to clean the body. Some form of tool use has been reported for eighteen species of monkeys and apes, far more than for any other mammalian order. There appears to be a great deal of variation in tool use from population to population, suggesting the development of local traditions (Nishida, 1987).

Other examples of local traditions have been observed in Japanese macaque populations, a species that has probably been studied longer than any other primate. One famous Japanese macaque female, Imo, has been called a monkey "genius." She invented several behaviors that were rapidly transmitted to other members of her troop so that all animals in the troop today exhibit these behaviors. These included washing the sand off of the sweet potatoes they were given and separating sand from wheat by dropping a handful of both into the water so that the wheat floated to the top where it was easily picked up. These practices enabled Imo and the troop members who followed her example to consume more food in less time and to avoid chewing sand, which quickly wears down the teeth.

Some primatologists have referred to these patterns as results of cultural learning. Look back at the definition we gave for culture in Chapter 2: culture comprises (a) material objects; (b) ideas, values, attitudes; and (c) patterned ways of behaving. Do the modified termite "fishing poles" and the rocks used to open nuts constitute material culture? Does the idea of the tool that chimpanzees appear to carry around in their heads constitute culture? Clearly, there are patterned ways of behaving in monkey and chimpanzee groups that are the result of learning. Some anthropologists prefer to restrict the use of the term "culture" to humans. Others argue that many animals have culture, and that what we see in humans is a matter of degree, not of kind. Certainly human culture is far more complex than that observed in any other animal, and its transmission is largely dependent on language. That alone may warrant using a different term for the way in which humans interact with the world.

**Communication and Language.** Primates, like many mammals, have complex communication systems. Goodall, for example, has documented dozens of specific calls for chimpanzees that she refers to as their "vocabulary." These include grunts, squeaks, screams, barks, pants, laughs, and hoots. Similar lists of calls that appear to have specific meanings have been generated for other primate species as well. Primates also communicate through touch and vision. Facial grimaces are frequently used for communication by chimpanzees (Exhibit 5-9). These are all modalities that are used by humans for communicating, but we depend primarily on a form of communication we call "language."

We used to argue that tool using was unique to humans, but there is too much evidence of tool-use in other animals to maintain that claim. There is debate about whether we can claim culture as uniquely ours. Perhaps the final bastion of humanness is language. But that also is not unchallenged. If language is defined as communication through abstract symbols (see Chapter 14), then we have examples of chimpanzees communicating with colored plastic blocks and computer symbols to demonstrate that it is not unique to humans. Many apes have been taught to use American Sign Language. Perhaps, like culture, language in humans is a matter of

A female chimpanzee is using a tool to fish for termites in the Gombe Stream Reserve.

**Facial expressions of chimpanzees. (After D. Bygott in Goodall, 1986.)**

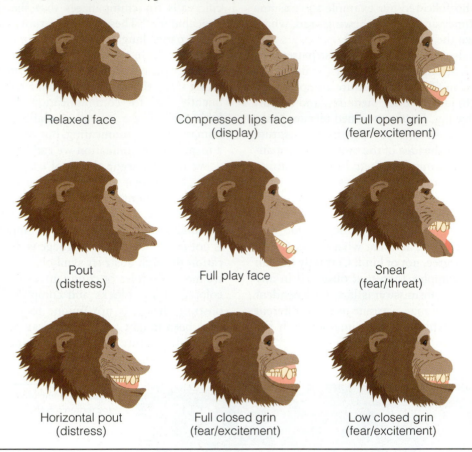

Relaxed face

Compressed lips face
(display)

Full open grin
(fear/excitement)

Pout
(distress)

Full play face

Snear
(fear/threat)

Horizontal pout
(distress)

Full closed grin
(fear/excitement)

Low closed grin
(fear/excitement)

degree, not of kind. But although primates clearly have the intelligence to communicate with each other and with us using abstract symbols that they did not invent, they will never be able to speak a human language because of limitations in their vocal anatomy (see Chapter 6).

### ◆ Summary

1. Scientific classification of plants and animals is based on evolutionary relationships. The assumption is that species in one group (e.g., a genus) are more closely related to each other and share a more recent common ancestor than they do with species in another group.
2. The classification of human beings includes the following levels: kingdom Animalia; phylum Chordata; class Mammalia; order Primates; superfamily Hominoidea; family Hominidae; genus *Homo*; species *sapiens*.
3. Humans share seven fundamental characteristics with other mammals: (a) homoiothermy; (b) viviparity; (c) mammary glands; (d) hair; (e) heterodontism; (f) one bone in the lower jaw; and (g) three bones in the middle ear.
4. Primate characteristics reflect adaptation to tree-living and visually-oriented food-getting. These characteristics include (a) five fingers on each hand and foot; (b) a collarbone; (c) grasping (prehensile) hands and feet; (d) binocular and stereoscopic vision; (e) nails instead of claws; (f) large brain size relative to body size.
5. The six primate superfamilies include Lemuroidea (lemurs), Lorisoidea (lorises), Tarsioidea (tarsiers), Ceboidea (New World monkeys), Cercopithecoidea (Old World monkeys), and Hominoidea (apes and humans).

**6.** Primates live in a variety of social systems, including monogamous pair bonds (e.g., gibbons), small single-male groups (e.g., some baboons and gorillas), and large multimale and multifemale groups (other baboons and chimpanzees). Some primates, including nocturnal lemurs and orangutans, are solitary for most of their lives.

**7.** Humans differ from other primates in the following characteristics: (a) habitual two-legged walking; (b) greater dependence on animal foods and on heat-altered (cooked) foods; (c) lack of clear signs of ovulation in females and greater degree of sexual activity at times other than ovulation; (d) greater degree of paternal care; (e) more emphasis on tools and other material culture; and (f) use of a symbolic spoken language for communication.

## ◆ Key Terms

| | |
|---|---|
| analogies | matrilines |
| anthropology | monomorphic |
| apneas | olfactory |
| arboreal | omnivores |
| binocular | perineal |
| brachiation | phenetic |
| codominant | pheromones |
| encephalization quotients | phyletic |
| estrus | polyandrous |
| folivores | prehensility |
| frugivores | primates |
| gummivores | primatology |
| heterodontism | sexual dimorphism |
| homoiothermy | stereoscopic |
| homologies | taxonomy |
| insectivores | vertical clinging and |
| locomotion | leaping |
| matrifocal | viviparity |

## ◆ Suggested Readings

Cheney, Dorothy L. and Robert M. Seyfarth. *How Monkeys See the World,* Chicago: University of Chicago Press, 1990. Cheney and Seyfarth have spent many years observing the vervets of Amboseli National Park, Kenya. In this book, they attempt to get into the minds of these animals and present their best guess of how these animals understand themselves and their world. It is also an excellent summary of good fieldwork in primatology.

Fossey, Dian. *Gorillas in the Mist,* Boston: Houghton Mifflin, 1983. A detailed and in-depth look at the gorillas that Fossey studied in Rwanda. This is also an emotional adventure story that will heighten awareness of the perils that these magnificent animals face in their war-torn habitat.

Goodall, Jane. *In the Shadow of Man,* Boston: Houghton Mifflin Co., 1971. Delightful and personal story of Goodall's early years observing chimpanzees in the Gombe Stream Reserve of Tanzania. The chimps she describes have distinct personalities and the stories of their lives bring tears and laughter.

Goodall, Jane. *The Chimpanzees of Gombe,* Cambridge: The Belknap Press of Harvard University Press, 1986. A more detailed and scientific analysis of Goodall's long-term studies of the chimpanzees. This is still very readable and serves as a good sequel to her 1971 book. There are hundreds of illustrations.

Jolly, Alison. *The Evolution of Primate Behavior,* New York: Macmillan, 1985. This is one of the leading textbooks in primate behavior. It covers such topics as ecology, social structure, communication, demography, socialization, sex, competition, cognition, and intelligence.

Smuts, Barbara, Dorothy L. Cheney, Robert M. Seyfarth, Richard W. Wrangham, and Thomas T. Struhsaker. *Primate Societies,* Chicago: University of Chicago Press, 1987. A collection of 40 articles about primates in the wild written by some of the foremost primatologists working in the field today. Just about every species you would want to know about is described in this book.

# Learning From Nonhuman Primates

In this chapter we have reviewed the characteristics that humans share with other primates and have emphasized how closely related we are to the great apes, especially the chimpanzee. This close biological similarity is one of the reasons chimpanzees and several monkey species are commonly used for testing new drugs and other products of human technology, but the similarities are also among the reasons for objections to the use of primates or any animals in biomedical research.

Proponents of using primates as models argue that this is the best way we can test drugs and techniques that will alleviate human suffering. For example, the chimpanzee is one of the few species that can be infected with the human immunodeficiency virus (HIV), which causes AIDS. For this reason, it is argued, the chimpanzee is an appropriate animal on which AIDS vaccines and treatments can be tested before they are administered to human beings. Opponents of using chimpanzees and monkeys in biomedical research argue that it is unethical for one species (human beings) to experiment on another, just as it is unethical for one population of humans to experiment on another. Their view is that a hierarchical arrangement of species ("speciesism") is as abhorrent and unacceptable as racism. This is a complex and controversial subject. In this book, we want to emphasize how much we can learn about ourselves from merely observing the behavior of other species in their natural settings. The following applied perspectives show us two ways that primate species in their natural settings help us understand human health.

### ◆ Self-medication by chimpanzees suggests potential useful drug for humans.

While studying chimpanzee behavior in Tanzania, Harvard anthropologist Richard Wrangham noted that on occasion chimps would seek out young leaves of a plant that was not typically in their daily diet. Furthermore, they would carefully swallow the leaves whole, making faces indicating distastefulness as they did so. This behavior and the fact that the leaves were found undigested in the dung, suggested that they were not being consumed for their nutritional value.

Wrangham collected samples of the plant and sent them to University of California at Irvine pharmacologist Eloy Rodriguez. Rodriguez identified the plant as aspilia and found that it contained the chemical compound thiarubrine-A, which has strong antibiotic properties. The chimps are apparently using the plant for its medicinal properties, perhaps to help them control internal parasites.

Further observations of their behavior in association with this plant indicate that it is usually consumed at dawn when the compound is most active. Similar examples of self-medication have been reported by other primatologists studying chimpanzees. Hoping that thiarubrine-A may be useful in treating certain human illnesses, Wrangham and Rodriguez have filed for a patent, planning to use some of the proceeds to help preserve chimpanzee habitat in Africa. "I like the idea of chimps showing us the medicine and then helping to pay for their own conservation," Wrangham says (Howard, 1991).

Another example of "self-medication" has been observed by Karen Strier (1993) in howler and muriqui monkeys of South America. These monkeys keep themselves free of intestinal parasites by eating the plants that are consumed by Amazonian people for the same purpose. Perhaps further observations of primate consumption patterns will reveal as yet unknown medicinal properties of many plant species.

### ◆ Are human infants "designed" for solitary sleep?

Sudden infant death syndrome (SIDS) is the leading cause of nonaccidental death of children between one month and one year of age in the United States (2 in 1,000 births). It is defined as the sudden death of an infant or young child when no known causes are apparent. Deaths occur while the infant is sleeping. Is there something about the environment of a sleeping infant that makes him or her more vulnerable to unexplained causes of death? One way to pursue this is to look at infant sleeping patterns in other human cultures and in nonhuman primates.

Anthropologist Jim McKenna (1986; 1990) notes that SIDS occurs less frequently in some human populations than in others and has never been reported in nonhuman primates. In both these groups, infants and mothers virtually always sleep together. McKenna studied how separation from their caregivers would affect infant monkeys' physiology. He suggests that mother–infant sleeping patterns may help explain some of the variation in SIDS rates cross-culturally. SIDS rates peak between ages two and four months. This suggests that some SIDS cases may be related to complex changes taking place in human brain development at this age that help prepare the infant for language.

For the first few months of an infant's life, breathing is under reflexive or automatic control. Eventually the brain develops to the point that breathing comes under the control of higher brain functioning. It appears that environmental signals, such as parental breathing sounds, may be important in the early development of voluntary breathing. Thus, proximity to auditory breathing cues from sleeping partners (e.g., the parents) may contribute to an infant learning to breathe more efficiently.

Some infants who die from SIDS were suffering slight colds, experiencing prolonged breathing pauses (**apneas**), or sleeping for longer periods of time. (Most babies who die from SIDS experience no symptoms at all.) None of these that are known to occur can be assumed to be the primary cause of death, since the vast majority of infants experiencing similar challenges to breathing do not die. McKenna suggests that infants who are sleeping with their mothers, breathing in rhythm with them, may respond more efficiently (for example, by waking) when internal challenges like stuffy noses or apneas interfere with their breathing than infants who are not sleeping with their mothers.

To determine if a relationship between sleep environment and infant breathing patterns exists, McKenna and his colleague, Sarah Mosko, monitored the breathing of several mother–infant pairs in a specially designed "sleep lab." They found that when the infants were sleeping with their mothers, they experienced much greater variation in waking and sleeping patterns and breathing than when they were sleeping alone, and many of

these arousals overlapped. This variation may enable infants to "practice" returning to regular breathing after interruptions. McKenna believes that this practice may be particularly important during the period when the infant brain is undergoing so much reorganization, between four and six months of age. Without this practice, infants may occasionally "forget" to breathe, and death may result.

McKenna argues that human infants are designed by evolution to sleep in close proximity with their caregivers, particularly during the time when the brain is undergoing rapid reorganization and growth. During this time, infants may respond in important ways to their mothers' sensory cues or signals until the transition is complete. This worked fine in the human evolutionary past when mothers and infants routinely slept together (as they do in most cultures of the world today), but it is not always possible today in our society where infants are expected to sleep alone. McKenna suggests that we may be encouraging physiological independence too soon, but he also adds that this hypothesis will likely explain only a fraction of the SIDS cases that are reported each year. Infant–parent co-sleeping will not by itself solve the puzzle of SIDS deaths. He concludes his studies by suggesting that modern medical researchers should accord human infants their evolutionary past. If they do so, they can ask new questions about medical tragedies such as SIDS, which thus far have resisted explanation and prevention.

## CHAPTER 6

# The Early Evolutionary History of Primates and Hominids

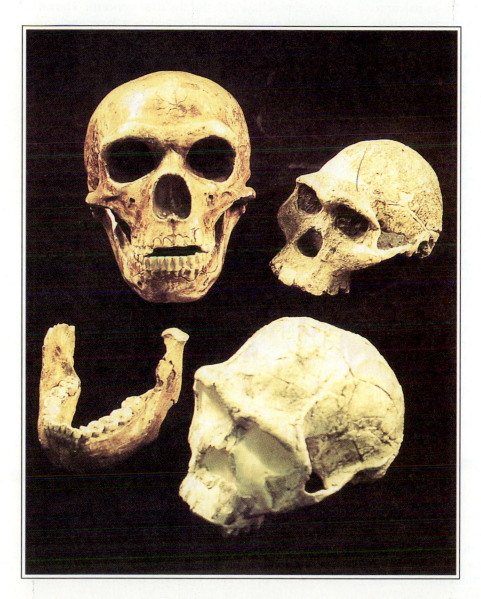

What is the evolutionary history of the primates?

When, where, and why did the hominid family appear with its characteristic mode of locomotion, bipedalism?

Who are our ancestors, the australopithecines, *Homo habilis*, and *Homo erectus*? What did they look like? When and where did they live?

As noted in the previous section, understanding something about the evolutionary history of human infants may help us solve an unusual health problem, Sudden Infant Death Syndrome. We believe that an understanding of the evolutionary history of our entire species may reveal further avenues to solving several other current health challenges. The material presented in this chapter will help us begin that search.

In the last chapter it was emphasized several times that a taxonomy or classification is actually a hypothesis that is constantly subjected to change in light of new data and methods. In this chapter we will review the current hypotheses concerning the evolutionary history of primates, with emphasis on human ancestry. The scientific disciplines that focus on the fossil record of primates and humans are known, respectively, as **paleoprimatology** and **paleoanthropology**. The terms primate paleontology and human paleontology are also used.

There are three dimensions to the discipline of paleontology: time, space, and form (Kelso and Trevathan, 1984). The age of a fossil, its geographic location, and its physical characteristics are all necessary to understand its relationship to living forms. If any one of these key pieces of information is missing, it is extremely difficult, if not impossible, to make a claim about where the fossil fits in the evolutionary scheme of things.

It must be emphasized that fossilization is an extremely rare event. A number of conditions must be met in order for remains to be fossilized: (a) they must be buried quickly; (b) they must be deposited in an area with few bacteria or other contributors to decomposition; (c) they must remain undisturbed; (d) certain soil and water conditions must exist; and finally, (e) in order for the rare fossils to be of any use to paleontologists, they must be discovered. What does a map of fossil locations reveal (Exhibit 6-1)? More than anything else, it tells us that physical conditions for preservation were met and that current demographic and political conditions were such that fossils were discovered. In other words, a map of fossil localities may tell us more about the distribution of the paleontologists than about the distribution of the species when it was alive.

## Dating Fossils

One of the biggest challenges to interpreting a fossil is determining when the organism lived. A variety of dating methods have been used. Some of these dating methods simply tell whether a fossil is older or younger than another. These are **relative dating** methods in that an age

can be stated only relative to another form. Perhaps the most simple, and oldest, method is based on the stratigraphic layer in which the fossil is found. Thus, a fossil found in a lower layer is assumed to be older than a fossil found above it. Rather than dating the fossil itself, this method requires certainty that the fossil is in its original context. Paleontologists know that many forces cause fossils to be moved from their original context, including water movement, soil erosion, burrowing animals, and human activities. An assessment of the effects of these forces must first be done before it can be assumed that a dating method based on context is warranted.

A related technique, known as **biostratigraphy**, relies on the other plant and animal species found in the same stratigraphic layer as the fossil of concern. Thus, if a fossilized primate skull is found in a layer with other mammals known to be of a certain age, and it is concluded that the fossil is in its original context, then it can usually be assumed that the primate lived at the same time. Analysis of pollen, known as **palynology**, can provide similar information, with the added advantage that it can help to determine what the climate was like at the time the species lived.

If a fossil is imbedded in volcanic rock, it is possible to date the surrounding material using the known decay rate of radioactive isotopes of the element potassium. This type of dating method provides **chronometric** dates, those that are given in years before present. Many fossil finds from East Africa and Southeast Asia, both areas of known volcanic activity, have been dated using the **potassium-argon** method. The radioactive isotope of potassium, K40, is transformed ("decays") through a series of complicated steps into the rare gas argon, at the rate of half per 1.3 billion years. In other words, half of the K40 that was present when the volcanic material originally cooled will have decayed to argon in 1.3 billion years, the **half life** of K40. Such a large half life means that this technique is useful for dating the oldest rocks on earth and material older than 100,000 years. It has been particularly important for paleoprimatologists, who are interested in material from 65 million years ago to recent times. We shall see in Chapter 9 that a similar method relying on the radioactive isotopes of carbon can be used to date organic material younger than 50,000 years.

Another radioactive element that has been used to date volcanic material is uranium 238. When U238 decays, tiny **fission tracks** are left behind in the rock, most easily observed in obsidian. Counting the number of tracks, using a scanning electron microscope, can give an estimate of the time since the obsidian was formed.

EXHIBIT 6-1
**Map of East African fossil site locations.**

HADAR

OMO · *Ethiopia*

*Lake Turkana* KOOBI FORA

*Lake Victoria* · *Kenya*

OLDUVAI GORGE

LAETOLI
*Tanzania*

MAKAPANSGAT
KROMDRAAI · STERKFONTEIN
SWARTKRANS
TAUNG
*South Africa*

**Paleomagnetism** is a dating technique based on the reversals of the magnetic poles. Today we are in a period of "normal polarity" in which the north pole is positive and the south pole is negative. There have been frequent periods in the past when this situation has been reversed, however, and the planet was in a state of "reversed polarity" (Exhibit 6-2). Magnetic rocks preserve the record of polarity, so it is possible to determine whether a rock layer was deposited during a period of reversed or normal polarity. We now know that the period from about 700,000 years ago to the present has been one of normal polarity, as was the period from 1.6 to 1.8 million years ago. The time in between, except for a brief time from 890,000 to 950,000 years ago, was a period of reversed polarity. Assuming a fossil is in its original context, researchers can determine whether it was deposited during a normal or reversed period.

Ideally, several of these dating methods will be used when trying to determine the time frame for a fossil find. For example, dating the fossil known as "Lucy" (found in Ethiopia) required using potassium-argon, fission track, paleomagnetism, and biostratigraphy. Since each of these methods is subject to error, only when all four methods came up with similar estimates was the date for Lucy as 3.3 million years accepted by most paleoanthropologists. Be reminded, however, that all four methods date the context rather than the fossil itself.

**Paleomagnetic sequences correlated for major East African sites—Olduvai, East Turkana, Omo. (After Issac, 1975.)**

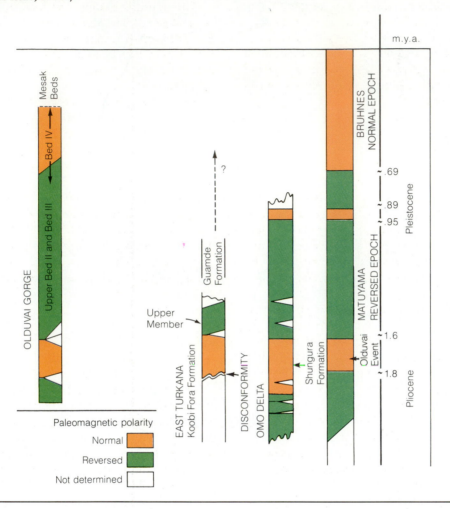

## MOLECULAR DATING

In the previous chapter we discussed how taxonomies often use similarities in proteins, amino acids, and DNA to assess relationships among living organisms. These similarities have also been useful in estimating the time since a species evolved and the ages of fossils representing ancestral species. There have been attempts to estimate the rate of change in DNA so that a molecular "clock" can be developed. These attempts are not without their problems, however. It is uncertain whether different segments of DNA change at different rates, and whether rates vary between lineages and over time. Another problem is that the clock has to be set from a

"known" time. Typically that "known" time has been the estimated date of divergence, based on the fossil record, of Old World monkeys from the ape–human line. That estimate is 30 million years but is subject to challenge. Accepting that date for setting the clock leads many scientists to argue that the degree of similarity between chimpanzee and human DNA requires a very recent time of separation or divergence of the lineages, on the order of 5 million years ago.

Few paleontologists are ready to rely solely on the molecular data for dating species, but similarities in DNA can serve as independent checks on dates arrived at by more traditional methods. For example, in the early 1970s, the estimate of a 5-million-year divergence date for chimpanzees and humans was far more recent than the paleontological estimate of 20 million years. The conflicting dates sparked a flurry of studies of the fossil material and eventually forced a revision of the human family tree, accepting an origin date for hominids as closer to the 5-million-year mark than the previously believed date of 20 million. We will discuss this later in the chapter, but the point to be made here is that the more techniques one can use to assess dates for fossil material and for lineage divergence, the closer one is likely to get to the true dates.

## The Fossil Record

The story of primate evolution logically begins with the origin of mammals during the Mesozoic era, approximately 220 million years ago. The first mammals are recognized by the marker characteristics of (a) heterodontic teeth anchored in the jaw, (b) a single bone in the lower jaw, and (c) three bones in the middle ear. Other mammalian characteristics such as homoiothermy (maintenance of constant body temperature), viviparity (giving birth to live young), and hair are not observable in the fossil record. These were small animals, and it is likely that most were nocturnal and insectivorous. With the extinction of the dinosaurs at the end of the Mesozoic (65 million years ago), an increase in mammalian species occurred, and most modern orders of mammals originated during the early Cenozoic era (Exhibit 6-3). Because the rate of evolutionary change was so great during the early Cenozoic, there is much confusion in the fossil record of this time period (the Paleocene), and it is difficult to identify species that can be unarguably placed in one taxonomic order or another. Paleoprimatologists are certain that the earliest primates appeared during this time, but there is a great deal of disagreement about individual species.

### PALEOCENE PRIMATES

The earth was a very different place during the Paleocene epoch (65 to 53 million years ago) than what it is today. Most of the world had been tropical during the Mesozoic, but temperatures began to fall in the Northern and Southern hemispheres during the Paleocene. These climatic changes contributed to the instability of the evolving mammalian orders. Primates, for example, are tropical animals, but were evolving into a world in which the tropics were shrinking toward the equator.

Because environmental change is often followed by extinction or genetic change in species, it is not surprising that the fossil record during this time is hard to understand.

The configuration of the land masses on earth also looked very different during the Paleocene. North America and Eurasia were connected in a single northern continent, and South America was closer to Africa than it was to North America. India was an island continent (Exhibit 6-4).

Contributing to the confusion of primate evolution are Paleocene animals known today as plesiadapiforms. These are sometimes referred to as archaic primates since it has been difficult to determine their relationship to the later primates of the Eocene; some claim they are not primates at all but are more closely related to a group known as "flying lemurs." Suffice it to say here that at least some of these plesiadapiforms may represent the first primates and thus may include our ancestors. One reason we feel certain that primates evolved during the Paleocene is that by the time of the Eocene, animals with clear primate characteristics were common.

### EOCENE PRIMATES

The prosimians (or strepsirhines) had their heyday during the Eocene epoch (53 to 35 million years ago). Two families have been identified, the Adapidae and Omomyidae, comprising perhaps fifty-two genera, by one estimate (Conroy, 1990). Almost all of these are found in what is today Europe and North America. There is no Eocene primate known from Africa or South America. They were a diverse group and looked somewhat like modern lemurs, lorises, and tarsiers. The ancestors of modern lemurs and lorises were probably in the family Adapidae, whereas the ancestor of modern tarsiers was probably an omomyid. Since tarsiers are closely related to the monkeys and apes, it has been suggested that they also have ancestors in the family Omomyidae. Other paleontologists argue that the anthropoids (monkeys and apes) are so different from omomyids and adapids that their ancestors must belong to an as yet unidentified group (Culotta, 1992).

### OLIGOCENE PRIMATES

In contrast to their distribution in the Eocene, there are very few primate fossils in the Northern hemisphere from the Oligocene epoch (35 to 25 million years ago).

| Era | Period | Epoch | Time | Glacial Sequence |
|-----|--------|-------|------|------------------|
| | | | Years ago | Alpine |
| Cenozoic | Quaternary | Holocene | | |
| | | Upper Pleistocene | 10,000 | |
| | | | 40,000 | Würm |
| | | | 75,000 | Riss |
| | | | 100,000 | Würm |
| | | | 125,000 | |
| | | Middle Pleistocene | 175,000 | Riss |
| | | | 225,000 | |
| | | | 265,000 | Mindel Riss |
| | | | 300,000 | |
| | | | | Mindel |
| | | | 380,000 | |
| | | | 400,000 | |
| | | | 430,000 | Gunz-Mindel |
| | | | 500,000 | Günz |
| | | | 750,000 | |
| | | Lower Pleistocene | | Uncertain Geological Sequences |
| | | | 1.8 million | |
| | Tertiary | Pliocene | 5 million | Hominids (Australopithecines) present |
| | | Miocene | 25 million | Hominoidea (apelike creatures) Dryopithecines flourish Probable appearance of hominids |
| | | Oligocene | 35 million | Anthropoidea and appearance of Hominoidea |
| | | Eocene | 53 million | Prosimians flourish; possible appearance of Anthropoidea |
| | | Paleocene | 65 million | Appearance of Prosimii |

Because of continued cooling in the Northern hemisphere, it is likely that most primates became extinct there. Almost all of our evidence of Oligocene primates comes from a single location, the Fayum area of Egypt. Twelve genera have been identified from the Fayum deposits, representing at least three families, the **Parapithecidae**, the **Propliopithecidae**, and the **Tarsiidae**. A few rare forms have been identified from South America, indicating the earliest evidence of primates on that continent.

Some of these Oligocene primates were monkeylike in many ways. They were diurnal, and fruit was probably a major component of their diets. Some of their dental and skeletal characteristics show similarities with prosimians, but in most features they are clearly aligned with the anthropoids. Thus, we can conclude that they are in the suborder with monkeys and apes, but probably belong in families separate from either of these groups. We can also conclude that the ancestors of modern monkeys and apes are among the fossils known from the Oligocene, but we cannot say for certain which species or genus gave rise to Ceboids, Cercopithecoids, and Hominoids.

The New World monkeys most likely first evolved in Africa and migrated to South America by some unknown route. An alternative, but less likely, hypothesis is that the New World monkeys are descended from New World omomyids and that their similarities to Old World monkeys are analogies rather than homologies.

## MIOCENE PRIMATES

The Miocene (25 to 5 million years ago) fossil record includes the first unambiguous Old World monkeys and apes and, perhaps, the first hominids. At the beginning of the Miocene, ape species far outnumbered monkey species, but by the end of the epoch the ratio had reversed itself to the situation we find today, where monkeys far outnumber apes.

As many as sixteen genera of hominoids have been identified from Miocene deposits of Africa, Asia, and Europe (Conroy, 1990). The taxonomy is controversial,

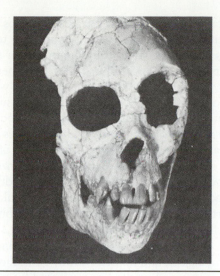

*Proconsul africanus* is an example of an African Miocene hominoid.

but among the genera that have been described from the Miocene are *Ramapithecus, Sivapithecus, Gigantopithecus, Dryopithecus, Proconsul,* and *Kenyapithecus.* They are distinguished by a number of features, including the thickness of the tooth enamel, suggesting differences in diet. All were quadrupedal, forest-living animals whose diets were probably composed of leaves, seeds, nuts, and fruits. There is no evidence of true brachiation, a characteristic that today defines the hominoids.

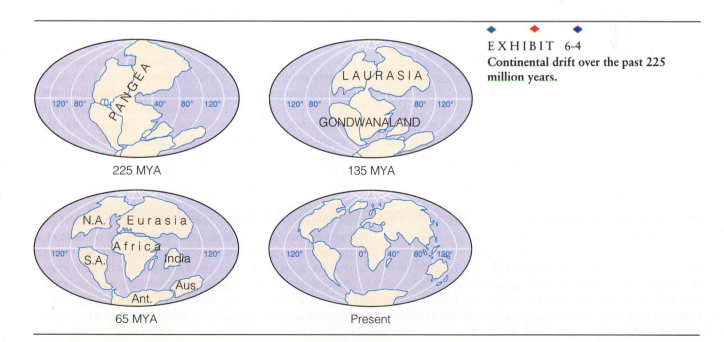

225 MYA

135 MYA

65 MYA

Present

EXHIBIT 6-4
**Continental drift over the past 225 million years.**

Understanding the phylogenetic relationships among the Miocene hominoids and their relationship to living hominoids has been enhanced by biomolecular studies. For example, it was once argued that specimens now known as ramapithecines (or sivapithecines) were the ancestors of humans and were, in fact, the first members of the family Hominidae. This would have required a date of 20 million for the divergence of the lines leading to the great apes and to humans. The finding of only a 1 percent difference in DNA between chimpanzees and humans, however, would not support the hypothesis of a divergence date so long ago. The biomolecular studies support the following divergence dates: gibbon line separated from other apes and humans about 12 million years ago; orangutan line separated from the line to gorillas, chimpanzees, and humans about 10 million years ago; chimpanzee and gorilla line separated from human line about 5 million years ago (Conroy, 1990).

Given these divergence times, there are two competing hypotheses concerning the phylogenetic relationships of the ramapithecines and modern apes: (1) the ramapithecines are the last common ancestors of all great apes; and (2) the ramapithecines are related only to orangutans and are not ancestral to gorillas, chimpanzees, and humans. The biomolecular data favor the first hypothesis, but the physical features of ramapithecines are most like those of orangutans, favoring the second hypothesis.

One thing for certain is that the Miocene epoch was characterized by major climatic changes that led to the extinction of many of the ape species and favored the evolution of many monkey species in Africa and South America. Apes that survived these changes have descendants that live in isolated pockets in central Africa and Southeast Asia. Monkeys are found in a variety of ecological settings on five continents, as reviewed in the previous chapter. One exception to the demise of the apes is the line that ultimately led to humans. We are not sure which Miocene species gave rise to that line, but somewhere in that collection of fossils, or perhaps a form not yet discovered, is our own ancestor, perhaps the first true hominid.

## THE ORIGIN OF HOMINIDS AND BIPEDALISM

The first unquestioned hominids appear in East Africa between 4 and 5 million years ago. Unfortunately, the fossils from this time period are scarce and fragmentary, so we cannot be more specific than that. Most hominids from the origin to about 2 million years ago have been assigned to the genus *Australopithecus*. Four species have been recognized: *Australopithecus afarensis, A. africanus, A. robustus,* and *A. boisei.* The first members of the genus *Homo* appear between 2 and 2.5 million years ago. Three species are recognized to have lived since that time: *Homo habilis, H. erectus,* and *H. sapiens.* Australopithecines and *Homo* species were contemporaneous for about a million years, but no australopithecine fossil has been found to have lived more recently than 1 million years ago.

Before continuing to discuss the hominid fossils, however, it is necessary to define the hominids more precisely. In the previous chapter it was noted that the only characteristic of hominids that leaves an unambiguous clue in the fossil record is bipedal (two-legged) locomotion. But the process of evolution from a quadrupedal (four-legged) form of locomotion to bipedalism is a complex one, and we have no fossil that represents an intermediate stage. Some have suggested that the origin of bipedalism and, by definition, the hominids, was an example of a "punctuational" event (see Chapter 4 for a review of the theory of punctuated equilibrium).

For efficient bipedalism to have evolved from quadrupedalism, changes had to take place in (a) the skull, (b) the pelvis, (c) the vertebral column, and (d) the lower limbs. To balance the skull on top of the spine, for example, the **foramen magnum** (the hole in the skull through which the spinal cord passes to the brain) must be positioned further forward in bipeds than in quadrupeds. The muscles of the neck region are smaller and positioned to contribute to balancing the head in an upright position rather than lifting it up as in quadrupedalism. The vertebral column of bipeds is S-shaped so that the center of gravity is over the hips, again contributing to upright balance and stability.

The pelvic areas of quadrupeds and bipeds are very different in structure and orientation (Exhibit 6-5). The **ilium** (hip bone) of a biped is shorter, broader, and expanded front to back in comparison to the ilium of a quadruped. The **ischium** (bone you sit on) is also shorter and broader, and the **pubic bone** (bone above the genitals) is directly opposite the **sacrum** (the bone at the base of the spine at the back of the pelvis). All of the muscle attachments are also positioned differently. The hind limbs of bipeds are longer and more massive than the forelimbs. Moreover, the feet of the biped, unlike that of a quadruped, lack an opposable big toe. All of these changes enhance stability, upright balance, and power in forward movement, which we call walking. Since these are not simple changes, bipedalism must have pro-

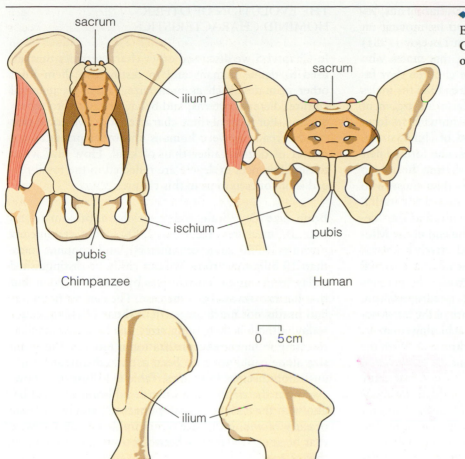

EXHIBIT 6-5
Comparison of the pelvis of a biped and of a quadruped.

sacrum

ilium

sacrum

ischium

pubis

pubis

Chimpanzee

Human

0    5 cm

ilium

ilium

pubis

pubis

ischium

Chimpanzee

Human

vided numerous advantages in order for it to be favorably selected in our ancestors.

Why did bipedalism evolve? Various theories have been offered, including those that relate bipedalism to (a) having the hands free for manipulating the environment, (b) energy efficiency, (c) dietary adaptations, and (d) reproductive success. There are obvious advantages in having the hands free for a tool-using animal, but evidence for the routine use of stone tools appears at least 2 million years after bipedalism in the fossil record, so it does not appear to be the "cause" of bipedalism.

Clifford Jolly (1970) has argued that the ability to move around on the hind limbs provided advantages for ancestral hominids as they moved into a savannah environment where they relied more heavily on small seeds of savannah grasses. His theory, often called the "seed-eating hypothesis," has been used to account not only for bipedalism but also for changes in teeth that occurred at about the same time.

Nancy Tanner and Adrianne Zihlman (1976) suggested that bipedalism was favored because it improved the ability of hominid females to gather food and carry it to safe places to share with their children. Thus, females who could efficiently carry food by moving on two legs had healthier children. Owen Lovejoy (1981) added males to this scenario, arguing that males who carried food to their mates and to the children they fathered would also have healthier children than the males who provided no resources. This is also an argument for the evolution of the tendency of humans to form male–female bonds during the period of childbearing. Lovejoy argued that males and females who formed pair bonds would, by cooperating in food-getting, be able to have more offspring in their lifetimes than those who continued the ape pattern of "every animal for itself."

It is also possible that bipedalism evolved as the "default" mode of locomotion. Toward the end of the Miocene, hominoids began to feed more selectively on fruits. Brachiation, the ability to hang beneath the terminal branches on which fruits typically grow, was perhaps selectively favored over generalized quadrupedalism. The shoulder structure and musculature of the late Miocene apes, while not that of fully brachiating animals, had been selectively modified in that direction. With the drying trend at the end of the Miocene, at least one of these ape species, our ancestor, began to spend more and more time foraging in the savannah grasslands that began to appear over much of Africa. Selection for full brachiation did not continue in our ancestor, but perhaps it had gone far enough that quadrupedal movement was no longer very efficient, just as it is not efficient in modern great apes. The most efficient locomotion in the savannahs where great distances must be covered to secure adequate resources may have been in the direction of bipedalism. Certainly bipedal walking today is more efficient for covering great distances than the quadrupedal walking of apes (Rodman and McHenry, 1980).

## THE EVOLUTION OF OTHER HOMINID CHARACTERISTICS

In Chapter 5 we discussed other characteristics that are used to define humans and to distinguish them from other primates, such as brain size, language, material culture, dietary patterns, and behavior related to reproduction. For most of these characteristics, we noted that the difference between humans and other primates is a matter of degree rather than of kind. How and when these differences in degree are reflected in the fossil record is of concern to us in this chapter.

**Brain Size** Our brain today weighs approximately 3 pounds, measures 1,200 to 2,000 cubic centimeters (mean is 1,350 cubic centimeters), and contains more than 10 billion neurons. We can easily be distinguished today from our closest relatives by this trait alone, but that has not always been the case. The earliest hominids had brains not much larger than those of chimpanzees today, although their body sizes were slightly smaller, resulting in higher encephalization quotients. But brain size alone could not have been used to distinguish early australopithecines from apes. Table 6-1 illustrates, however, that the trend toward increased brain size had begun with the earliest australopithecines, and by the time of early *Homo*, brain size of hominids was about twice that of apes. Today it is between three and four times that of apes.

**Language** In Chapter 5 we discussed the fact that apes probably have the mental ability to communicate with abstract symbols, but they do not have the vocal tract anatomy to use a complex spoken language. They also do not appear to have the specialized brain structures related to language. These include **Wernicke's area** and

TABLE 6-1 ◆ Mean endocranial capacity, estimated body mass, and encephalization quotients for a series of hominoids.

| | Mean Endocranial Capacity (cc) | Estimated Body Mass (kg) | EQ (Actual Value) | EQ (as % of *H. sapiens* Value) |
|---|---|---|---|---|
| *P. troglodytes* | 395.0 | 45.0 | 2.6 | 34 |
| *A. afarensis* | 413.5 | 37.1 | 3.1 | 41 |
| *A. africanus* | 441.2 | 35.3 | 3.4 | 45 |
| *A. robustus* | 530.0 | 44.4 | 3.5 | 46 |
| *H. habilis* | 640.2 | 48.0 | 4.0 | 53 |
| *H. erectus* (Asia and Africa) | 937.2 | 53.0 | 5.5 | 72 |
| *H. e. pekinensis* | 1,043.0 | 53.0 | 6.1 | 80 |
| *H. sapiens* | 1,350.0 | 57.0 | 7.6 | 100 |

SOURCE: From Conroy (1990) after Tobias (1987).

EXHIBIT 6-6

**A map of the human brain showing features and associated functions.**

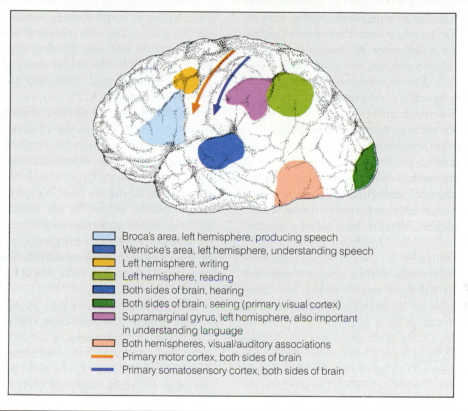

- Broca's area, left hemisphere, producing speech
- Wernicke's area, left hemisphere, understanding speech
- Left hemisphere, writing
- Left hemisphere, reading
- Both sides of brain, hearing
- Both sides of brain, seeing (primary visual cortex)
- Supramarginal gyrus, left hemisphere, also important in understanding language
- Both hemispheres, visual/auditory associations
- Primary motor cortex, both sides of brain
- Primary somatosensory cortex, both sides of brain

**Broca's area,** both located in the left hemisphere for most humans (Exhibit 6-6). Wernicke's area is related to content and comprehension of speech, and Broca's area directs motor actions for speech. When these specialized regions first appeared in human evolution is debatable because of the limited information available from fossilized brain cases. The general consensus, however, is that the australopithecines do not show evidence of fully developed Wernicke's and Broca's areas, but members of the genus *Homo* do (Lewin, 1989).

Speech involves other anatomical features, including the larynx, pharynx, tongue, and lips. The larynx (air passageway) of most mammals is located high in the neck so that air goes directly from the nose to the lungs. Breathing and swallowing are therefore separate functions. Humans beyond the age of two years have a different configuration: the larynx and pharynx (food passageway) are located low in the throat so that the two passageways converge. This means that breathing and swallowing cannot occur at the same time. This can be a dangerous situation in that food and water can go "down the wrong tube" and indeed, many people die of choking every year. The advantage, however, is that the converging larynx and pharynx provide an expanded chamber over the vocal chords, enabling a great deal of variation in the sounds that can be made (Laitman, 1984).

Human infants have maintained the general mammalian pattern of being able to swallow and breathe at the same time. This is necessary in order for nursing to occur. But by approximately age two, when the infant becomes a fully bipedal animal, the larynx has descended in the throat, providing the large chamber for the vocal patterns of language. Parents should realize that no matter how smart their infants appear to be, they will never be able to use a human language until the vocal tract anatomy reaches the near-adult configuration. Just as with chimpanzees, human infants probably have the brain power to begin speaking at an earlier age, but they lack the vocal apparatus to do so.

When in human evolution did the modern vocal tract appear? Of course the larynx and pharynx do not fossilize, but the base of the skull preserves a record of the positions of these two tracts. In the australopithecines, it appears that the configuration is like that of most mammals. The conclusion is that australopithecines could not use a language as complex as ours. *Homo habilis* and *Homo erectus,* however, show a larynx lower in the neck than that of other mammals, although not as low as seen in modern humans. They could probably use a wider array of sounds, but some scholars conclude that it may not have been until modern *Homo sapiens* that full-blown human language appeared (Laitman, 1984). Others argue that features of Neandertal anatomy such as the **hyoid bone** (a small U-shaped bone in the neck region to which tongue and larynx muscles are attached) suggest that these people had language capabilities as extensive as ours (Arensburg et al., 1990).

**Culture** We have seen from earlier chapters that the concept of culture is a difficult one to define. We chose to define it (Chapter 3) as "everything that people have, think, and do as members of a society." It should be obvious that finding evidence of culture according to this definition would be extremely difficult, if not impossible, when depending on the fossil record. Thus, when we talk about the development of culture in the past, we usually concern ourselves with only material culture, that is, "things" that people make and use. Furthermore, when looking for the earliest evidence of culture, we must focus on "things" that are preserved in the fossil record. That means that termite "fishing poles," net bags, wooden digging sticks, and leather straps would not be present in layers associated with early hominids, even if they were used, as they undoubtedly were. Stone tools, however, are preserved, and they provide unambiguous evidence of modification of natural objects. So the best we can do to approximate the origin of material culture is to locate the earliest stone tools. These are always found in association with *Homo;* there is no clear evidence that australopithecines used stone tools. The earliest date derived so far is 2.5 million years (Conroy, 1990). Certainly we can assume that australopithecines, and even some of the hominoids of the Miocene, used natural objects as tools, or even modified twigs and sticks to use as tools. But we can only infer this from our knowledge of tool manufacture and use by chimpanzees; we have no direct evidence.

**Diet and Food-Getting** Human eating habits differ from those of other primates in at least two ways: (a) humans hunt and consume animal protein more frequently, and (b) all modern humans use heat to alter foods. Fortunately, evidence of fire is preserved in the fossil record. The earliest known use of fire by hominids comes from Swartkrans, in South Africa, dated about 1 million years ago in association with *Homo erectus* (Conroy, 1990). The fact that this was the first hominid species to expand its range to the colder areas of the world is independent evidence that controlled use of fire did not precede *Homo erectus*.

For a long time paleoanthropologists believed that hunting was the key to the success of hominids in that most human characteristics resulted from selection for hunting skills. This interpretation, however, focusing on only male contributions and behaviors, is a limited perspective to use in describing human evolution. Recently, careful fieldwork has resulted in a revised scenario in which gathering of plant material, particularly by women, became as important as hunting of animals in the story of human evolution. But to ignore the importance of animal protein would be an oversight in telling the story.

There are two reasons why increased consumption of animal protein may have been important to early human adaptation: (1) since meat is the most easily carried food substance, it would have been important in providing food for others; and (2) the plant products that provide the most nutrients in human diets today were not available to humans before the controlled use of fire. Specifically, the grains, legumes, and many of the tubers that form the staples of world diets cannot be consumed in anything but very small quantities unless they are cooked (Stahl, 1984).

Thus it can be argued that hominid populations before fire that were able to efficiently take advantage of available animal protein had an advantage over those that relied solely on plant products. The key word here is "efficiently." As noted in Chapter 5, most primates do not hunt, because the effort expended in obtaining animal protein usually far outweighs the benefits. As hominids moved into the savannahs of Africa, however, more opportunities for capturing animals arose, and meat may have become a more important component of the diet at that time. Opportunistic hunting (i.e., hunting only when game presented itself) was probably the norm for the australopithecines. Beginning perhaps with *Homo erectus,* the human pattern was one of **persistence hunting**, in which a key to capturing game was not usually speed but the ability to follow animals over long distances. As noted above, bipedal walking over long distances by humans is a more efficient use of energy than the quadrupedal walking of most of their prey.

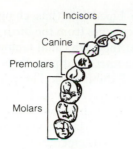

Incisors

Canine

Premolars

Molars

Modern Human

In Miocene hominoids the front teeth (incisors and canines) are larger than the back teeth (premolars and molars). Pictured here are the teeth of a modern hominid, *Homo sapiens*. Like other hominids, we have relatively large back teeth and small front teeth.

Simply by "walking their prey to death," early hominids may have been able to compete successfully with other hunting species on the savannahs of Africa. Later, with more sophisticated tools, hunting efficiency improved even further.

It is also likely that scavenging played a role in early human adaptation. Hominids with stone tools could take advantage of nutritious substances located in the skulls (the brain) and long bones (the marrow) of abandoned carnivore kills. Indeed, there is evidence of hominid stone tool cut marks located on top of carnivore teeth marks on fossil bones at Olduvai Gorge in Tanzania (Shipman, 1986).

We have skipped over some fundamental dietary changes that occurred in hominids prior to the beginnings of systematic hunting. These are reflected in changes in the teeth. Since the teeth are the most likely parts of an animal to be preserved, they are important in interpreting much of the material we have available on early hominid groups. The dental traits of Miocene hominoids included large incisors and canines (front teeth) and small molars and premolars (back teeth). The reverse pattern describes our teeth: we have small incisors and canines and relatively large molars and premolars. The trend has been toward reduction in size of the front teeth and increase in size of the back teeth. This is undoubtedly related to changes in diet away from fruits and toward small seeds and nuts. Small seeds are highly nutritious, but only if they are ground up so that the nutrients are available. Broad, flat molars probably enabled early hominids to obtain more food value from the seeds that were available on the savannahs. The later australopithecines (*A. robustus* and *A. boisei*) exhibit the extreme in molar size, suggesting that the ability to process food by grinding with the molars was a key to their survival.

Efficient grinding requires that the jaw be able to move in a rotary fashion, a difficult, if not impossible, process for apes with large interlocking canines. Thus, as selection favored grinding surfaces on molars, it also favored reduction of the canines to the size of the other teeth. In contrast to humans, apes and monkeys have large canines that extend beyond the level of the other teeth. Males generally have larger canines than females. Another characteristic associated with small front teeth is a less projecting jaw and flatter face, which also contribute to balancing the head more effectively on the spine of a biped.

**Reproduction** As noted in Chapter 5, human sexuality and reproduction differ from what has been reported for nonhuman primates. Human females, for example, lack the physical or behavioral signs of ovulation and display high frequency of sexual activity when not ovulating. But again, these behaviors do not fossilize, so we are limited in our ability to determine when these differences first appeared in the hominid line.

Why might they have been selected in the first place? Several propositions have been offered for the lack of external signs of ovulation. One is that at some point in human evolution, females became aware that ovulation, intercourse, and pregnancy were linked. Desire to have fewer offspring led some females to avoid intercourse at the time they were ovulating; those who did so successfully avoided pregnancy and had fewer offspring to whom to pass the clear signs of ovulation. Those whose signs of ovulation were somewhat ambiguous could not accurately determine when they were fertile and had more offspring to whom to pass along those ambiguous signs. Eventually the earth became populated with hominid females who lacked signs of ovulation (Burley, 1979).

When a female chimpanzee is in estrus (i.e., is sexually receptive), there is a great deal of excitement in the social group as males hover around waiting for opportunities to mate with her (Goodall, 1971). Overt fighting over estrus females is rare, but distractions during this time are frequent. It has been suggested that the frenzy associated with estrus may have been maladaptive in early hominid social groups where peaceful cooperation and sharing would have been important for survival. Thus, one argument for the loss of visible signs of estrus is that they were selected against in human females because those who did not exhibit the signs had more and healthier children raised in environments of cooperation rather than competition (Daniels, 1983).

Another set of arguments is that a female who engages in sexual activity when she is not ovulating can use this behavior as capital to exchange for resources, protection, and care for her offspring (Fisher, 1982; Lovejoy, 1981; Symons, 1979). If she mates with several males, and no one is sure when ovulation and conception occur, then all of these males may be willing to provide resources for her young whose paternity is uncertain (Hrdy, 1981). These young will, therefore, be more likely to survive and pass on their genes for concealed ovulation.

Many of the scenarios for the evolution of concealed ovulation and frequent sexual activity focus on the advantages of monogamous pair bonds in human evolution. The argument runs something like this: (1) Humans give birth to very dependent offspring; (2) the more help a female can get in providing care and resources for her offspring, the more likely her offspring are to survive; (3) males are logical candidates for providing assistance, but they are not likely to do so for young that are not their own; (4) the only way to ensure paternity is for males to spend most of their time with one or two females and make certain that no other males have access to them when they are ovulating; (5) males are not likely to form semipermanent bonds with females who are sexually receptive only once or twice every four years; (6) therefore, females who engaged in sexual activity at times other than ovulation were more successful in keeping the males around (Alexander and Noonan, 1979; Lovejoy, 1981).

Despite the relative merits of the above scenario, establishing a time for appearance of the human pattern of sexuality is not possible. One clue can give indirect evidence of monogamy, however. In species that mate monogamously, size dimorphism in the adults is low, meaning that males and females are approximately the same size. In species where mating is promiscuous or polygynous (i.e., a male with two or more mates), size dimorphism is great, with males typically 50 to 100 percent larger than females. The larger size apparently gives males an advantage in competition with other males for access to sexually receptive or estrus females. Size dimorphism appears to have been great in australopithecines, suggesting that they were polygynous. Only with modern *Homo sapiens* do we begin to see convergence of size in males and females. We are still size dimorphic, however, which is consistent with the evidence that most human societies exhibit polygynous marriage. Thus, it seems unlikely that humans were monogamous early in their evolutionary history as some have suggested (Lovejoy, 1981).

Another aspect of reproduction, the process of birth, is also different for humans. Reorientation of the pelvis in adaptation to bipedalism has changed the way in which the infant emerges from the birth canal. Most primate infants enter the birth canal facing in the same direction as their mothers and pass through it to emerge without turning (Exhibit 6-7). The pelvis of a bipedal human female, however, is twisted. This means that the infant must enter the birth canal facing side-to-side, turn in the middle, and exit facing front-to-back. Furthermore, the human infant emerges facing away from the

◆　　　◆　　　◆

EXHIBIT 6-7

**Emergence of the neonatal head in bipedal and quadrupedal species.**

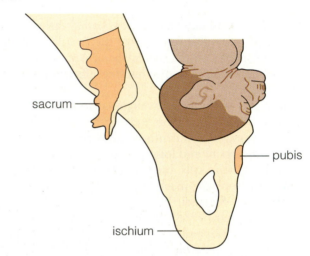

(a) Passage of the monkey fetal head through the pelvis, lateral view.

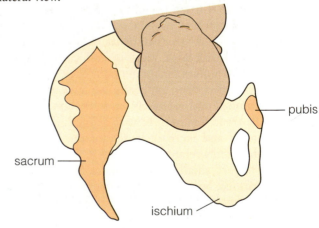

(b) Passage of the human fetal head through the pelvis, lateral view.

There is a great deal of variation across cultures in how childbirth is experienced, but one aspect is almost universal: women usually give birth in the presence of close friends and relatives. This practice has many benefits; among them is that having supportive people around tends to reduce anxiety, thus easing the birth process. In the United States and Canada, until recently, women gave birth in unfamiliar hospital settings with unfamiliar people. Anxiety and fear were common experiences of women in these settings, contributing to prolonged labor, greater dependence on pain-relieving medication, and more cesarean sections. Recognition that birth is as much an emotional as a physical event, and providing for a laboring woman's emotional needs by allowing the presence of family members at delivery, would have decreased the incidence of many birth complications. Fortunately, many hospitals and birth centers have responded to the requests of women for more emotional support, and birth is once again becoming a social event. Certainly the evidence that women have sought assistance at delivery for almost 5 million years lends credence to the suggestion that the emotional aspects of birth are deeply rooted in our evolutionary history.

mother rather than toward her, as in nonhuman primates. This provides a challenge to the mother, who must reach behind her to pull the infant from the birth canal. This might explain why humans routinely seek assistance at the time of birth rather than seek isolation as do almost all other mammals. Simply having someone else there to guide the baby out, to wipe its face so that it can begin breathing, and to keep the umbilical cord from choking it would have significantly reduced mortality associated with birth (Trevathan, 1987).

Fortunately we have several examples of fossilized hominid birth canals. The series of rotations and the emergence of the infant in a direction away from the mother probably began with the origin of bipedalism, and thus with the origin of hominids. Assistance at birth may not have become critical, however, until the beginnings of *Homo*, which had considerably larger brains. It was also at this time that the pattern of giving birth to infants with very undeveloped brains began. Up until *Homo*, hominid females probably gave birth to infants with about half of their brain growth completed. This is the typical mammalian pattern; australopithecine birth canals would have easily accommodated infants with a brain size of 225 cubic centimeters, about half the adult size. *Homo habilis* may have been the last hominid to follow this mammalian pattern, however. The human

pelvis can deliver an infant with about 350 cubic centimeters, only about 25 percent of the size of adult *Homo sapiens*. Since the origin of *Homo,* brain development at birth has decreased, so that today we give birth to infants that are far more helpless than our closest primate relatives, or than the infants of our ancestors were likely to have been (Trevathan, 1987).

## THE FOSSIL RECORD OF THE AUSTRALOPITHECINES

Four species of australopithecines are generally accepted by paleoanthropologists, although there is by no means unanimity of agreement on this. One of the major areas of disagreement about taxonomy of this group is how much variability there is in each of the species described. Paleoanthropologists have been described as "lumpers" (those who are willing to accept a great deal of variability in a species) and "splitters" (those who argue that even small differences indicate separate species). At one time or another, there have been as many as eleven different scientific names given to the fossils that we now consider to belong to one of four species of a single genus (Day, 1986).

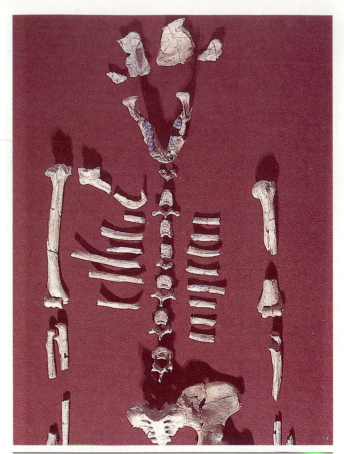

"Lucy" (*Australopithecus afarensis*) is one of the most complete skeletons of an australopithecine ever found. She was discovered in 1974 in Ethiopia by Donald Johanson.

A few general characteristics can be described for the genus as a whole. Australopithecines were fully bipedal, although they may not have walked as efficiently as we do today. They had brains not much larger than those of modern chimpanzees and gorillas. Their front teeth (canines and incisors) were small, although more apelike than ours are; their back teeth (molars and premolars) were flattened grinding surfaces, much like ours, although larger. Size dimorphism between the sexes appears to have been great. No australopithecine fossils have been found outside of Africa, nor has any australopithecine been found in unambiguous association with stone tools or fire. As mentioned above, without fire it is not likely that hominids could survive winters of temperate regions, so the absence of non-fire-using hominids from the rest of the Old World is not surprising.

We will now review each of the four species of *Australopithecus,* beginning with the oldest known form, *Australopithecus afarensis.* The other three are *Australopithecus africanus, Australopithecus robustus,* and *Australopithecus boisei.*

**Australopithecus afarensis** Perhaps one of the best-known fossil discoveries in recent years is the specimen known as "Lucy" from the Afar area of Ethiopia. Lucy is notable in that more of her skeleton has been recovered than from any other australopithecine. It has been estimated that she lived between 3 and 3.4 million years ago, which makes her one of the earliest fossil hominids known. Donald Johanson, who has recovered remains of an estimated thirty-five individuals from this local-

The footprints of two bipedal hominids were found by Mary Leakey in Tanzania in 1978. They walked through volcanic ash in East Africa approximately 3.5 million years ago.

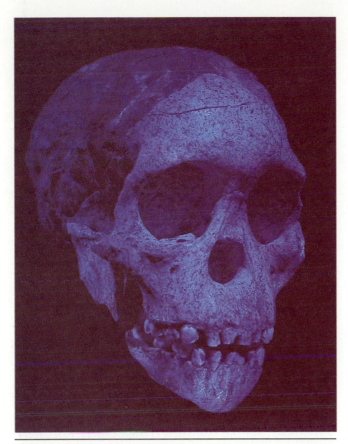

The Taung child was discovered in South Africa in 1924. Raymond Dart identified it as a hominid and called it *Australopithecus africanus*.

between apes and humans. But he decided that the human features predominated, and called it *Australopithecus africanus*. Among other features, the Taung child appeared to have been fully bipedal.

Not surprisingly, his conclusions were met with a great deal of controversy. One of the problems facing its acceptance by the scientific community was the fact that the new taxon was based on the fossil of a child. A few years later, however, several adult forms of this species were found in other locations in South Africa, so Dart's original claims for the Taung fossil have been supported. To date, all specimens that can be confidently assigned to *Australopithecus africanus* have been found in South Africa. All have come from limestone deposits, which has made dating them difficult. The time frame for *Australopithecus africanus* appears to be between 2 and 2.5 million years ago.

**Australopithecus robustus** Several other fossils were discovered in the limestone deposits of South Africa in the first half of this century. These are much more robust than the forms that had been assigned to *A. africanus*, so a new taxon, *Australopithecus robustus*, was designated. One of the major distinctions is that the robust forms have large, flat molars and premolars, clearly designed for crushing and grinding. Some have argued that this is evidence that *Australopithecus robustus* was a vegetarian. The dentition of *Australopithecus africanus* is more generalized, suggesting that it was omnivorous. Bones from the hip and leg regions of *A. robustus* fossils indicate that it was bipedal. Fossils of this species have also been found in East Africa where volcanic material makes dating easier; the range for *A. robustus* appears to be from 2.5 to 1 million years ago.

**Australopithecus boisei** This form has sometimes been described as "hyperrobust" in that the robust features of *Australopithecus robustus* have been taken to the extreme: the molars, premolars, and facial features are even larger. Another obvious feature of *A. boisei*, as well as *A. robustus*, is a pronounced sagittal crest along the top of the skull, unlike that observed in any other hominid species. This crest is related to the size of the chewing apparatus, which indicates that powerful muscles operated when the animals were chewing their foods. The best-known examples of this species are the fossils known as "Zinjanthropus" discovered by Mary Leakey in 1959, and the one known as WT17000, discovered in 1985. All *Australopithecus boisei* fossils discovered so far come from East Africa. The time frame is 2.5 to 1 million years ago. overlapping both *Australopithecus africanus* and *Australopithecus robustus*.

ity, claims that all are from the same species (Johanson et al., 1982). Others, however, argue that more than one australopithecine species is represented in this collection (Conroy, 1990). This is an example of differences of opinion between lumpers and splitters.

*Australopithecus afarensis* is also known from a site in Tanzania known as Laetoli. This is the location of the famous footprints that were discovered by Mary Leakey in 1976. A trail of prints was left in volcanic ash by at least three individuals walking there approximately 3.6 million years ago. The footprints are clearly those of bipedal hominids.

**Australopithecus africanus** The first fossil to be described as an australopithecine was found in 1924 in the mining area of Taung in South Africa. It was the skull of a child and consisted of the face region, the mandible, and a natural cast of the brain. The man who analyzed the fossil, anatomist Raymond Dart, concluded that it was a previously unknown form intermediate in features

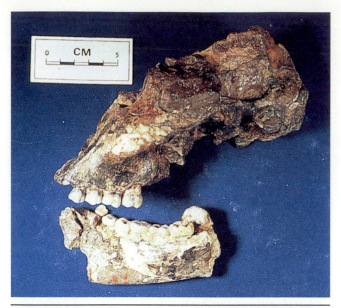

A fossil of *Australopithecus robustus* from Kromdraai, South Africa.

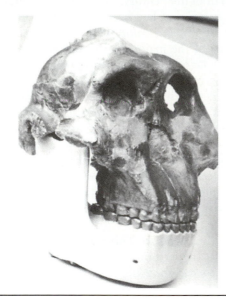

A skull of "Zinjanthropus" found by Mary Leakey in Olduvai Gorge in 1959. It is now considered an example of *Australopithecus boisei*.

## PHYLOGENY OF THE AUSTRALOPITHECINES

How do the australopithecines relate to each other and to more recent hominids of the genus *Homo*? There is not an easy answer to this question, and there are many interpretations. Three currently popular hypotheses are: (1) *Australopithecus afarensis* is the first hominid and it is ancestral to all other hominids, directly to *Australo-*

*pithecus africanus* and *Homo habilis* (Exhibit 6-8a); (2) *A. afarensis* and *A. africanus* are just regional variants of the same species (by the taxonomic rules this would mean that both should be called by the oldest of the two names, *Australopithecus africanus*), which is ancestral to the robust australopithecines and *Homo habilis* (Exhibit 6-8b); (3) *Australopithecus afarensis* is ancestral to *Australopithecus africanus*, which is in turn ancestral to the robust forms and *Homo habilis* (Exhibit 6-8c). There are numbers of other proposed hypotheses, but these three seem to represent the opinions of most paleoanthropologists. Remember that these are hypotheses, and they are constantly subject to revision or rejection as new fossils are discovered, new dates are determined, or new interpretations are provided for the currently available material.

## THE FOSSIL RECORD OF EARLY *HOMO*

The taxonomy of *Homo* is slightly less confusing, but not without problems. When the first specimens that we now know as *Homo habilis* were discovered by Louis and Mary Leakey in 1960, many paleoanthropologists argued that they were East African examples of *Australopithecus africanus*. There are still proponents of this hypothesis, but the estimated cranial capacity of *Homo habilis* is so much greater than that of any of the australopithecines that most are willing to accept that the fossils warrant designation as members of the genus *Homo*. Two generalizations that can be made about this genus are that cranial capacity for all *Homo* species is above 600 cubic centimeters and that stone tools are associated with all three recognized species, *Homo habilis*, *Homo erectus*, and *Homo sapiens*. As noted previously, it is also the only genus believed to have used a form of spoken, symbolic language similar to what humans use today. In general, members of the genus *Homo* are taller than the australopithecines, and size dimorphism between the sexes appears to decrease from *Homo habilis* to modern *Homo sapiens*.

**Homo habilis** This species first apears in Africa between 2.5 and 2 million years ago. It is similar to *Australopithecus africanus* in having less robust facial features and smaller teeth than seen in the other australopithecines. But its average cranial capacity is between 650 and 700 cubic centimeters, a clear distinction from any australopithecine. Fossils have been found primarily at East African sites, including Olduvai Gorge, Koobi Fora, and East Lake Turkana.

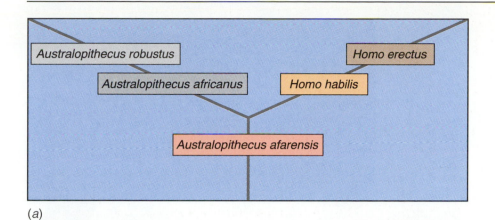

(a)

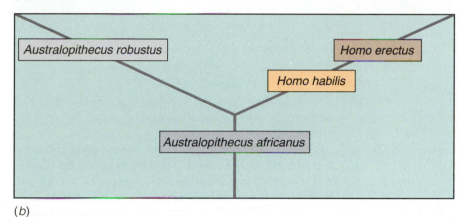

(b)

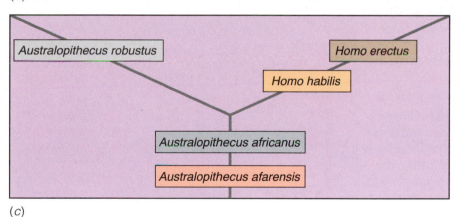

(c)

Stone artifacts found in association with *Homo habilis* have been called the "Oldowan" technology after the fossil-rich site at Olduvai Gorge. In fact, Louis Leakey, who discovered and named the first *Homo habilis* fossil, selected the name, which means "handyman," because of the association with so many stone tools. The artifacts include manufactured items that could have been used as scrapers, picks, anvils, hammers, axes, and cleavers (Exhibit 6-9). Most were made by striking a small rock at an angle, removing a flake, and leaving a sharp edge behind. There is debate about whether the remaining core or the flakes were the primary tool (Toth, 1987), although it is likely that both were used. Though simple, these tools were efficient at

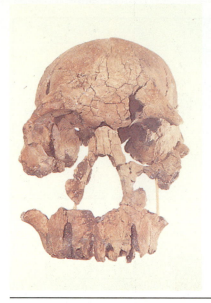

A *Homo habilis* skull found by Richard Leakey in Kenya in 1973. It is often referred to by its museum specimen number, "1470."

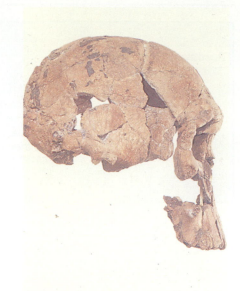

slicing through material as tough as the hides of elephants and rhinoceroses, a fact demonstrated by Louis Leakey, who butchered an entire elephant using only Oldowan tools. Most interpretations of the Oldowan tools conclude that they were made opportunistically and used at the site and time of manufacture.

It should be noted that australopithecines have also been found at these sites in association with both early *Homo* and stone tools, but the tendency has been to claim that the tools were manufactured by *Homo*. *Homo habilis* remains have not been identified from deposits less than 1.75 million years old.

**Homo erectus** In parts of East Africa, sites yielding fossils of *Homo erectus* have overlapped in time with those of *Homo habilis*, leading some to argue that there is no justification for the taxonomic division of early *Homo* into two species. The overlap in time and in morphology suggests that the forms may not have been reproductively isolated, and that *Homo habilis* is simply an older form of the species *Homo erectus*. Others argue that *Homo erectus* made such significant cultural advancements that it is justifiable to treat it as a separate species. *Homo erectus* was the first hominid species to migrate out of Africa, the first to control and use fire, the first to establish home bases to which individuals returned after a day of foraging for food, and the first to give birth to very helpless infants with extended childhoods. Their tools were also much more complex than those of earlier hominids, and their brain size increased to the point of

overlapping what is occasionally observed in modern human beings.

Remains of *Homo erectus* have been found in Africa, Asia (mainland and islands), and Europe. The first fossil of this species was found in 1891 in Java by the Dutch physician Eugene Dubois. Others were found near Beijing, China, in the late 1920s and 1930s. The Chinese

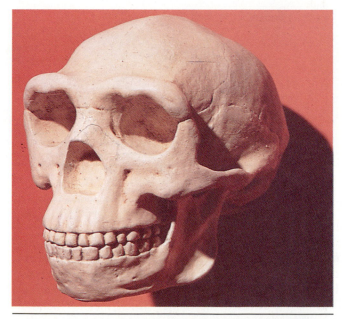

A reconstructed skull of the Chinese form of *Homo erectus*. The original fossil material was lost during World War II.

EXHIBIT 6-9
**Examples of Oldowan Tools**

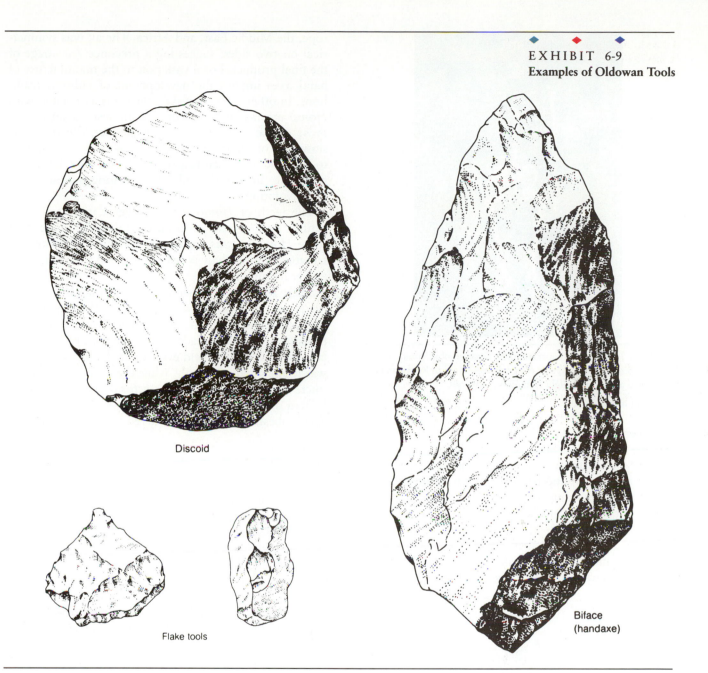

Discoid

Flake tools

Biface
(handaxe)

material disappeared during World War II, but excellent drawings and casts are available of the fossils. African sites of *Homo erectus* include several familiar to us from the review of australopithecine sites: Swartkrans in South Africa; Olduvai Gorge and Laetoli in Tanzania; Koobi Fora in Kenya; and the Hadar region of Ethiopia. A particularly remarkable find was made at West Lake Turkana in 1985 of an almost complete skeleton of a child, whose estimated age at death was twelve years. He lived about 1.6 million years ago and has skeletal features that reflect a mixture of australopithecine and modern human anatomy.

It appears that *Homo erectus* evolved in Africa between 1.6 and 1.8 million years ago and began to migrate to other parts of the Old World about 1 million years ago. Its cranial capacity ranges from 750 to 1,150

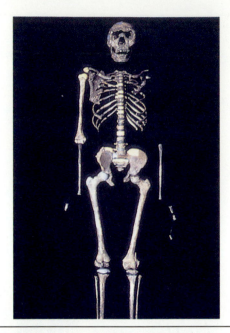

KNM-WT 15000 is an almost complete skeleton of a *Homo erectus* boy of approximately 12 years of age. It was found in Kenya and has been dated at approximately 1.6 million years old.

cubic centimeters. Many of its facial features are more massive than described for either *Homo habilis* or *Homo sapiens*. Its teeth are larger than ours, the nuchal (back of the head) and brow regions were pronounced, and it had a receding forehead. It was also very tall, probably taller than most modern human populations (Eaton et al., 1988).

A tool industry described for *Homo erectus* is the Acheulian, named after the distinctive hand ax that is found in association with *Homo erectus* fossils in Eu-

This distinctive Acheulian biface is often called a "hand axe," although it was probably used for a variety of purposes. These tools are associated with *Homo erectus* sites in Europe, the Middle East, and Africa.

rope, the Middle East, and Africa. The ax was symmetrical on two sides, suggesting a preconceived image of the final product. Local variation in the manufacture of hand axes implies the development of cultural traditions. In other ways, however, the tools associated with *Homo erectus* represent only a modest advance over those of the Oldowan industry. In fact, the relatively slow pace of change in tool technology from 2.5 million to 250,000 years ago is associated with worldwide homogeneity in material culture for a long period of human evolution.

The teeth of *Homo erectus* suggest increased meat eating, and several paleoanthropologists argue that some *Homo erectus* populations engaged in more systematic hunting than is believed to have been true of earlier hominids.

There seems to be general consensus that *Homo erectus* is ancestral to *Homo sapiens,* but there is a great deal of disagreement about how, when, and where that transformation took place. Did all *Homo erectus* populations all over the world evolve into *Homo sapiens,* or was it one population only, while the others became extinct? And if only one *Homo erectus* population was the human ancestor, which one was it: African or Asian? These questions will be considered in the next chapter.

## ◆ Summary

1. The context in which a fossil is found is extremely important in determining its date and relationship to other life forms. Dating techniques commonly used for primate and hominid fossils include biostratigraphy (using other fossils with known dates), potassium-argon (measuring the rate of radioactive decay in volcanic rock), and paleomagnetism (using known periods of magnetic pole reversals). All of these methods date the context of the fossil rather than the fossil itself.

2. The earliest primates evolved during the Paleocene epoch, approximately 65 million years ago. Lemurlike primates were common in North America and Europe during the Eocene epoch (53 to 35 million years ago). The first monkeys, and perhaps the first apes, appeared during the Oligocene epoch (35 to 25 million years ago). Ape species were abundant during the Miocene epoch (25 to 5 million years ago), and the first humans may have evolved during this time, although we do not yet have fossil evidence for this important (to us) event.

3. The first unquestioned hominids, with the unique characteristic of bipedal walking, appeared in East Africa between 4 and 5 million years ago. These earliest forms, lasting until about 1 million years ago, have been

placed in the genus *Australopithecus,* with four species recognized: *A. afarensis, A. africanus, A. robustus,* and *A. boisei.*

4. Bipedalism resulted from major anatomical changes in the skull, vertebral column, pelvis, and lower limbs. Only humans exhibit these changes, and only humans walk habitually on two legs. Proposed explanations for why bipedalism evolved include those related to (a) having the hands free for manipulating the environment, (b) energy efficiency, (c) dietary adaptations, and (d) reproductive success.

5. Other major anatomical changes associated with the evolution of humans include increasing brain size and changes in vocal tract anatomy, the birth canal, and teeth. Dependence on material culture and systematic hunting of animal prey are also characteristics of humans.

6. Anatomical changes in adaptation to bipedal walking resulted in changes in the birth canal so that humans are now somewhat dependent on assistance at the time of delivery and give birth to relatively helpless infants.

7. Although they can be classified into four different species, all australopithecines exhibit the following characteristics: (a) they were bipedal animals; (b) their brains were smaller than ours; (c) their fossils are found only in Africa; (d) there is no evidence that they used fire or manufactured stone tools.

8. *Homo habilis,* the earliest member of the genus *Homo,* evolved in Africa approximately 2 million years ago. It is associated with stone artifacts known as Oldowan tools. The oldest remains of *Homo erectus,* the next to evolve (1.8 million years ago), are also from Africa. *Homo erectus* was apparently the first to use fire and migrate out of Africa to Asia and Europe. A distinctive tool known as the Acheulian hand ax is associated with many populations of *Homo erectus.* Brain size increased in this species to the point that at the higher end it overlaps that of modern humans.

## ◆ Key Terms

| | |
|---|---|
| Adapidae | ischium |
| archaic primates | Omomyidae |
| biostratigraphy | paleoanthropology |
| Broca's area | paleomagnetism |
| chronometric | paleoprimatology |
| fission tracks | palynology |
| foramen magnum | Parapithecidae |
| half life | persistence hunting |
| hyoid bone | plesiadapiforms |
| ilium | potassium-argon |
| Propliopithecidae | sacrum |
| pubic bone | Tarsiidae |
| relative dating | Wernicke's area |

## ◆ Suggesting Readings

Conroy, Glen C. *Primate Evolution,* New York: Norton, 1990. A useful textbook with comprehensive review of primate fossils from the Paleocene, Eocene, Oligocene, and Miocene. The last chapter is an overview of hominid paleontology.

Ciochon, Russell L. and John G. Fleagle. *The Human Evolution Source Book,* Englewood Cliffs, NJ: Prentice Hall, 1993. A collection of 60 of the most important papers in human evolution to have been published in the last three decades. All retain their original illustrations and text. This book is essential to any student interested in the history of thinking about human evolution and in the foundations of contemporary theory.

Falk, Dean. *Braindance: New Discoveries about Human Origins and Brain Evolution,* New York: Henry Holt, 1992. Falk is one of the leading scholars of human brain evolution. In this book she discusses the relationship of the human brain to bipedalism, why the human brain is so large, and what studies of the brain can reveal about early hominid taxonomy. She argues convincingly that the brains of australopithecines and members of the genus *Homo* are significantly different.

Johanson, Donald C. and Maitland Edey. *Lucy: The Beginnings of Humankind,* New York: Simon and Schuster, 1981. A personal recounting of the discovery of the *Australopithecus afarensis* fossil known as Lucy. Many of the controversies surrounding her discovery and interpretation are described as are the personalities who play leading roles in hominid paleontology today. This book provides a glimpse into the human drama of paleontological research.

Landau, Misia. *Narratives of Human Evolution,* New Haven: Yale, 1991. Landau reminds us that much of our speculation about human evolution resembles storytelling, specifically the hero myth of Western tradition. Our stories of early hominid behavior change with our perspectives of ourselves and the world in which we live.

Lewin, Roger. *Human Evolution: An Illustrated Introduction (3rd Edition),* Cambridge: Blackwell Scientific, 1993. A brief overview of the current theories and controversies in human evolution with numerous illustrations. This is a good companion book for an introductory course in human evolution for students who want more detail than provided in most textbooks.

Nelson, Harry and Robert Jurmain. *Introduction to Physical Anthropology,* St. Paul: West, 1991. This is a popular textbook focusing entirely on physical anthropology. It provides more detail on the subjects we have covered in this chapter.

# Why Study Human Skeletal Remains?

Perhaps few topics in physical anthropology are more controversial today than the collection and study of human skeletal remains, particularly those from the ancestors of Native Americans. A great deal of our current understanding of variation in the human skeleton and the effects of malnutrition and disease on the skeleton come from past and current studies of skeletons collected during the nineteenth and twentieth centuries as part of archaeological investigations in North America. A great deal of information on past cultures and life-styles also is known from study of skeletons.

Huge collections of Native American remains have been housed in institutions such as the Smithsonian and university museums. Not surprisingly, a number of Indian tribes have expressed concern over the treatment of these remains and have requested that they be returned to the tribes for reburial. This is a very sensitive issue in which scientific and humanistic goals have come into conflict. The discipline of anthropology, particularly physical anthropology and archaeology, has been sharply divided on the issue. At one extreme are those who support reburial of all remains currently housed in museum collections; at the other extreme are those who argue against reburial of any skeletons. A resolution somewhere in between these two extremes is most likely.

The challenge posed by the nonscientific community includes the questions of why so many skeletons are needed for study and what can be gained from the study of skeletons in the first place. We will not attempt to present all sides of the controversy here, but we will describe two examples of how skeletal remains were used by modern researchers.

## ◆ The relationship of growth of human vertebrae to adult health and mortality.

It has long been known that early childhood nutrition affects not only growth but also adult health and life expectancy. There is evidence, however, that if nutrition is improved during childhood, "catch-up" growth can occur so that the early effects are hidden. The question remains whether the early malnutrition still has lifelong effects. A team of six physical anthropologists and medical researchers examined the sizes of the holes in vertebrae through which the spinal cord passes (Clark et al., 1986). The size of the spinal canal is apparently determined by four years of age, so if malnutrition occurs before that time, the hole will be small, no matter how much growth occurs later in cases where nutritional status is improved. Thus, a child who was malnourished in infancy but who later had a much improved diet might appear to be normal in overall body size and stature but would still have small spinal canals in his or her vertebral column.

The researchers examined more than 2,000 vertebrae from ninety individuals to test the association between early growth and nutritional status and adult health, stature, and life span. They found that the size of the vertebral canal was a better predictor of life span and adult health than was completed skeletal stature. The only way that association could have been established was with a large enough sample to know that it was a common pattern occurring in many individuals, rather than an unusual genetic phenomenon restricted perhaps to a few families. The fact that it was common and occurred to many people over a long period of time (the skeletal remains covered 350 years) suggested that it might be common in current populations. This was later confirmed with X-ray analysis of vertebral canals of living people.

The researchers suggest that small vertebral canals might be related to altered immune function, which may explain why people who were malnourished in infancy appear to experience more illnesses than those who were better nourished. Their studies of vertebral canals of living people indicated that those with smaller canals also had more psychological problems, poorer school performance, and higher job absenteeism. This study, based initially on a large sample of skeletal remains, emphasizes the importance of poor nutrition and slowed growth on lifelong health. It suggests that increased emphasis on improving prenatal and infant nutrition is warranted, considering the costs in later life.

### ◆ Skeletal identification aided by Smithsonian collections.

In 1984, a human skeleton was found near Rapid City, South Dakota. Clothing and other evidence suggested a local man who had been missing for several months, but since homicide was suspected, positive identification was necessary. X-rays were available for the missing man, and those, along with the skeletal remains, were sent to Douglas Ubelaker, a physical anthropologist at the Smithsonian Institution in Washington, D.C. Ubelaker was able to confirm that the skeleton was that of a man between ages 30 and 46 (Ubelaker, 1990). Skeletal characteristics indicated Mongoloid affiliation, suggesting that the person was an American Indian. The X rays showed healed fractures of the leg and elbow, confirmed in the skeletal remains. Fractures to the skull suggested that the cause of death had been blunt force trauma to the face and head.

All of the analysis that Ubelaker had performed so far suggested that the skeleton was indeed that of the missing man. But to strengthen the case, he went further in his investigation. A small notch on the right shoulder blade matched perfectly with a notch observed in the X rays. But the question remained whether this notch was unique to the missing man or was characteristic of many other Indian people.

Ubelaker compared the right shoulder blade from the skeleton to those of two hundred other skeletons in the Smithsonian collections. The notch was not found in any of the other skeletons, confirming his belief that it was a unique feature characteristic of the missing man. With this final piece of evidence, he was able to present his assessments to the court, and a conviction of second-degree murder was obtained. According to the prosecuting attorney, the case could not have been prosecuted without the positive identification of the victim. Ubelaker suggests that this case demonstrates the importance of museum collections of human skeletal material (Ubelaker, 1990).

## CHAPTER 7

# Origin, Spread, and Variation of *Homo Sapiens*

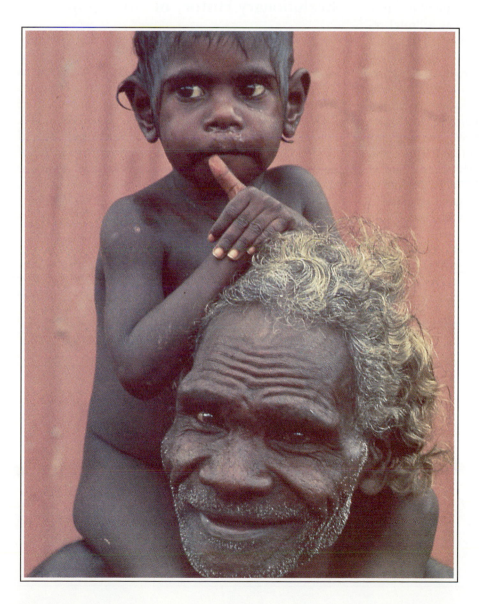

Who were the first members of our species, *Homo sapiens,* and when and where did they evolve?

Who were the Neanderthals and what is their relationship with us?

How have human populations adapted to heat, cold, solar radiation, and high altitude?

What are human races?

Whether *Homo sapiens* evolved once or several times has been a controversial topic since the beginnings of paleoanthropology. The two competing hypotheses are referred to as the continuity or multiregional model and the replacement or single-origin model. The multiregional model (Exhibit 7-1a) proposes that all of the modern populations of *Homo sapiens* evolved from regional populations of *Homo erectus*. For example, it has been suggested that the Chinese *Homo erectus* evolved into the populations that were ancestral to modern Asians, the *Homo erectus* populations from Africa evolved into modern African populations, and so on.

Supporters of the single-origin model (Exhibit 7-1b) argue that *Homo sapiens* evolved from one geographic population of *Homo erectus* and then spread throughout the world as *Homo erectus* populations in other places became extinct. In its extreme it is a "total replacement model" because it argues that all hominid populations other than the one at the place of origin (usually argued to be Africa) became extinct. An alternative to the total extinction of *Homo erectus* populations is that if reproductive isolation had not occurred between the worldwide *Homo* populations, then interbreeding could have taken place between the migrants and the local populations they encountered. This could be called a "replacement with interbreeding" model (Exhibit 7-1c), implying that, although modern humans have descended primarily from the original population of *Homo sapiens,* we do have within us genes from other populations as well.

The multiregional model argues for very ancient roots for modern populations of Asia, Africa, and Europe, whereas the replacement or single-origin model argues for more recent origins of those regional variants.

In Chapter 4 we noted that the transition from *Homo erectus* to *Homo sapiens* is an evolutionary pattern known as anagenesis in that the two species are continuous, representing evolution in a lineage in which there is no discrete event marking reproductive isolation. Thus, it might be more appropriate to refer to all members of the genus *Homo* as simply "early *Homo*" and "modern *Homo.*" But the same debate over where to draw the line between *Homo erectus* and *Homo sapiens* would continue as we decide where to draw the line between "early" and "modern," so few of the problems would be solved.

## Evolutionary History of *Homo sapiens*

We have several candidates for time lines between early and modern forms of *Homo sapiens*. One relies on fossil evidence and would be at approximately 350,000 to 300,000 years ago, when we first see "sapiens" features in the fossil record. A second candidate would be about 180,000 to 200,000 years ago, the time that DNA analysis suggests modern humans arose. A third would be 35,000 to 40,000 years ago, when modern material cultural traditions (those of the period known as the Upper Paleolithic) arose.

### FOSSIL EVIDENCE

One question that must be resolved in trying to find the time line is "How much like us must these ancestors have been in order for us to call them 'modern *Homo*

EXHIBIT 7-1

**Alternative models for the origin of *Homo sapiens*.**

SOURCE: Adapted from Aiello, 1993.

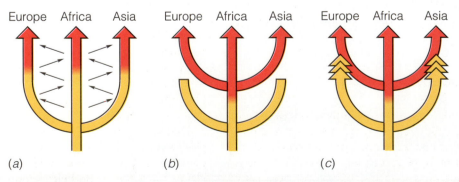

*sapiens*'?" If the answer is "virtually indistinguishable from us," then the line would have to be drawn about 35,000 to 40,000 years ago. If the answer is "when *Homo sapiens* features first appear in the fossil record," then the 300,000 year date would be appropriate. Glenn Conroy summarizes the anatomical features that distinguish *Homo sapiens* from other members of the genus. These include (1) a less robust skeleton; (2) a high, rounded brain case; (3) small or absent brow ridges; (4) small teeth and jaw regions; (5) flatter face; and (6) a chin (Conroy, 1990:330). Not all of the fossils currently called *Homo sapiens* meet all of these criteria. In fact, only beginning about 35,000 years ago do we see evidence of all six criteria in all fossils recovered.

Fossils with some features characteristic of *Homo sapiens* have been found in deposits dating as far back as 350,000 years ago in China (Yunxian in Hubei province), 300,000 years in Africa (the Bodo fossil from the Awash valley, Ethiopia), and 250,000 years in Europe (Arago, France) and north Africa (Jebel Ighoud, Morocco). Not surprisingly, these skulls also show features that some would associate with *Homo erectus*. Examples of more recent sites, dating at around 100,000 years ago, are Border Cave, Klasies River Mouth, and Broken Hill in southern Africa; Omo and Koobi Fora in east Africa; and Mount Qafzeh in Israel. A specialized *Homo* population, collectively called "Neanderthals," was distributed throughout Europe between 100,000 and 32,000 years ago. This controversial group will be discussed further in a separate section of this chapter.

In support of the multiregional model for the origin of modern *Homo sapiens,* many of the early fossils show features that are found in modern people inhabiting the same geographical region today. For example, early Asian fossils have dental features such as shovel-shaped incisors, which are found in modern Asian populations but are rare in European and African fossil and modern populations. Fossils from Java show physical features still found in modern Indonesian people, representing a time span of approximately 700,000 years (Frayer et al., 1993). If total replacement had occurred in the past, we would not expect to see evidence of this continuity in physical features.

## THE MOLECULAR EVIDENCE

In Chapter 5 we indicated how comparisons of DNA among organisms can help to confirm hypotheses about taxonomic relationships and times since divergence of lineages. Analysis of DNA can also increase our understanding of relationships *within* lineages and may help determine the time of origin of *Homo sapiens*. There are two types of DNA available for analysis within lineages: that located in the nucleus (nuclear DNA) and that located in the mitochondria (mitochondrial DNA). An individual inherits half of its nuclear DNA from its father and half from its mother. Mitochondrial DNA is inherited differently, however: it all comes from the mother. This is because the only mitochondria an individual inherits is that which was located in the egg at fertilization; the sperm carries no mitochondria and, thus, no mitochondrial DNA. Thus, it is possible to trace maternal ancestry through comparisons of mitochondrial DNA, just as it is possible in the United States and Europe to trace paternal ancestry through comparisons of surnames.

Genes come from both mother and father, but surnames in Western cultures traditionally come only from the father and mitochondrial DNA comes only from the mother. And, just as a surname can be "lost" in a generation in which only daughters are produced, mitochondrial DNA can be "lost" in a generation in which only sons are produced (Avise, 1983). Both of these phenomena have probably occurred hundreds of thousands of times in human history.

Mitochondrial DNA accumulates mutations more rapidly than nuclear DNA, and it appears to do so at a somewhat constant rate. In comparing two strands of mitochondrial DNA, a molecular anthropologist can ascertain how different they are and how long it has taken to accumulate those differences. This, in turn, can be translated into an estimated time when the individuals last shared a common ancestor. Three molecular biologists/anthropologists at the University of California at Berkeley—Rebecca Cann, Mark Stoneking, and Allan Wilson—followed this strategy when they compared mitochondrial DNA of 147 women from various populations around the world. Their analysis revealed that the last common ancestor for all of these women lived approximately 200,000 years ago. Furthermore, since the women in their sample of African origin showed more variation in their mitochondrial DNA than any other cluster, they concluded that this last common ancestor lived in Africa. This hypothesized female ancestor has been called the "mitochondrial Eve," because Cann, Stoneking, and Wilson (1987) believe that all of our mitochondrial DNA can be traced back to one woman. Our nuclear DNA, of course, comes from thousands of other ancestors.

There is a great deal of controversy surrounding this relatively new technique and its somewhat surprising conclusions (Templeton, 1993). Those who accept the claims made by the Berkeley group argue that this helps to pinpoint the origin of *Homo sapiens*. But among the criticisms are the following: (1) One cannot assume a constant rate of change for mitochondrial DNA, so the estimated date may be wrong; (2) there are other ways of interpreting the data so that the Asian groups show the most variability, suggesting an Asian origin for our species; (3) the original sample used by Cann and her colleagues was not a good one, and a better sampling strategy would yield very different results; and (4) the computer program used to calculate the differences was used inappropriately (Barinaga, 1992). These are serious considerations, and they require that we critically evaluate the conclusions. There is little doubt, however, that the technique, once some of the "kinks" have been worked out, will be useful in assessing relationships among populations.

One of the reasons that the conclusions of Cann have been challenged is that they do not fit well with the fossil record as some interpret it (Frayer et al., 1993). Others, however, claim that the mitochondrial evidence that *Homo sapiens* arose in Africa approximately 200,000 years ago is quite consistent with the fossil evidence (Stringer and Andrews, 1988). Since it is most consistent with the single-origin hypothesis of modern human origins, it is not surprising that the paleontologists who have embraced Cann's claims are those who support this model. Frayer and his colleagues (1993) note that if the "clock" for the origin of all modern mitochondrial DNA were to be pushed back as far as 800,000 years ago, then both the molecular and fossil data could be accommodated in a single model. This would be a single-origin model with roots more ancient than those currently claimed. Since that time populations have adapted to challenges and changes in the local and regional environments, and thus some traits tend to cluster in certain geographic areas. But, clearly, interbreeding must have taken place among hominid populations all over the world since that time or we would not be so similar today (Templeton, 1993).

## THE CULTURAL EVIDENCE

The stone tools associated with *Homo habilis* and *Homo erectus*, discussed in the previous chapter, are referred to as Lower Paleolithic, meaning the beginning of the Stone Age. Tools such as those of the Oldowan industry were crude, probably often made as they were needed using available materials in a fashion described as "opportunistic." The Acheulian industry exhibits more refinements and local variation, suggesting more systematic manufacture. Both traditions produced mainly core tools where the chunk of rock is shaped into the primary tool. The tools are generally multipurpose, used for chopping, grubbing, digging, cutting, etc.

The technology of the Middle Paleolithic is typically associated with Neanderthal populations of Europe, the Middle East, and North Africa. Referred to as the Mousterian industry, it is primarily a flake tool tradition. A special method, called the Levallois technique, was used in the manufacture of Mousterian tools. In this technique, a core was carefully prepared from which were struck large flakes that were then further chipped to make the primary tools. This technique yielded far more cutting edge per weight of stone, representing much greater efficiency in tool manufacture. Most of these flakes were carefully worked to produce a great variety of tool types used for a variety of specialized functions. One archaeologist estimates that as many as sixty different tool types are associated with Middle Paleolithic technologies (Lewin, 1989). Clusters of these tool types may represent local traditions. It should be noted that populations not otherwise identified as Neanderthal also used the Levallois technique and manufactured tools that can be called Mousterian.

Approximately 40,000 years ago, stone tool technology reached a complexity that is now referred to as the Upper Paleolithic. An estimated one hundred different types of tools have been identified (Lewin, 1989). Many were made from substances other than stone, such as ivory, shell, and bone. Some archaeologists have been so impressed with the tools of the Upper Paleolithic that they have argued that a different kind of hominid must have made them. Thus, they suggest that the Upper Paleolithic signals the appearance of modern *Homo sapiens*. Others argue that the tool cultures of the Upper Paleolithic are simply logical developments of the previous cultures and that no abrupt break is evident.

The first tool traditions of the Upper Paleolithic, called the Aurignacian and Chatelperronian, have many technological similarities to the preceding Mousterian. To complicate matters further, recently a skeleton of Neanderthal type associated with Chatelperronian tools has been excavated in France, and skeletons of Neanderthal and modern type have been discovered in Israel, both associated with classic Mousterian tools. These finds confuse the widely assumed association of Neanderthals with Mousterian tools on the one hand and modern *Homo sapiens* with other technologies on the other. Thus, as with the fossil and molecular evidence, the cultural evidence does not help to resolve the question of when modern human beings arose.

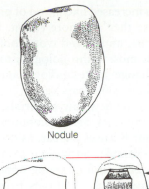

Nodule

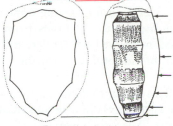

The nodule is chipped
on the parameter.

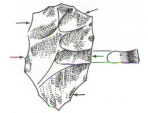

Flakes are radially removed
from top surface.

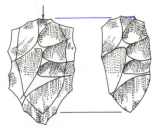

A final blow at one end
removes a large flake.

A Mousterian tool made by the Levallois technique.

## THE NEANDERTHALS

One reason that there is so much controversy over the origin of modern humans is that there is debate over a specialized European population of *Homo sapiens* known as Neanderthals. As noted above, this group dates from 125,000 to 32,000 years ago (Lewin, 1989) and shows mixed features of *Homo erectus* and *Homo sapiens*. They have very pronounced brow ridges and forward-jutting jaws, for example, which are characteristic of *Homo erectus*. But their brains may have been larger than those of modern humans. They were very muscular, stocky people, and the Neanderthal pelvis is unlike that of either *Homo erectus* or *Homo sapiens* in that the pubic bone is much longer than that seen in any other hominid. Some scholars have argued that the features of classic Neanderthals are so unusual and specialized that they represent an evolutionary dead end and are, therefore, not in our ancestry. Others suggest that the Neanderthals can be easily accommodated by the multiregional model. They are seen as representing the local transformation from European populations of *Homo erectus* to modern European populations.

Another problem presented by the Neanderthals is that there is evidence outside of Europe of populations that are much more modern in appearance than the Neanderthals. Large brains, high foreheads, flatter faces, and smaller teeth are all characteristics described for these populations, which precede and overlap in time the Neanderthals. The supporters of the single-origin model suggest that these are descendants of that "mitochondrial Eve," who migrated out of Africa into areas inhabited by the Neanderthals, living along with them for a few thousand years. If the populations were reproductively isolated, then interbreeding between the two did not occur, and the simplest conclusion is that the Neanderthals became extinct while the more modern-looking populations evolved into modern *Homo sapiens*. It is more likely, however, that the populations

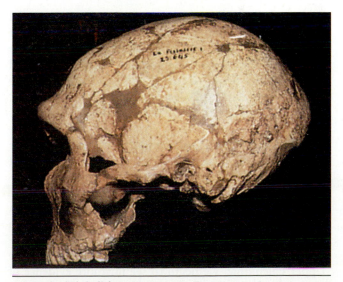

A Neanderthal skull from La Ferrassie, France.

were not reproductively isolated, that interbreeding between the two did occur, and that modern human beings carry the genes (i.e., the nuclear DNA) of both the African "Eve" and the European Neanderthal populations. But, perhaps by quirk of fate, we only carry the mitochondria of the African branch.

Whatever their taxonomic status, Neanderthals show some of the first solid evidence of cultural characteristics that we consider uniquely human. The most interesting of these is the evidence that Neanderthals buried their dead, perhaps with some sort of ritual. This suggests a more human attitude toward death than is suspected of other primates or previous hominid populations. It is this practice that has resulted in the large sample of Neanderthal remains that is available for analysis: more than three hundred individuals have been discovered and identified as Neanderthal.

Some of the skeletons show evidence of pathologies and disabilities that suggest some form of special care for incapacitated individuals. They also appear to have been successful hunters of large game, further evidence of cooperative ventures. Ornamentation and other nonutilitarian use of materials also appears for the first time in association with Neanderthal fossils. Despite the arguments over the physical form of Neanderthals, there is general acceptance that they were very "humanlike" culturally. Perhaps this alone warrants their inclusion in our ancestry.

## CULTURAL ADVANCEMENTS IN THE UPPER PALEOLITHIC

We noted above that the stone tool technology of the Upper Paleolithic (40,000) shows marked advancement in complexity over those of previous traditions. Upper Paleolithic stone tools are manufactured in a blade tool tradition from prepared cores. This technique has some similarities to the Levallois technique but produces long, slender, often parallel-sided blades that are then further chipped into a broad diversity of tools. A blade tool tradition produces more cutting edge per weight of stone than a flake tool technique, thus increasing efficiency of raw material use. As noted above, the number of different tools, with specialized functions, increases from the Middle to the Upper Paleolithic. Stone tools have been the indicators of culture change for the first 2 million years of evolution in the genus *Homo* because other material was not often preserved. But, by the time of the Upper Paleolithic, we begin to see far more evidence of material culture than just stone tools. This change may be partly due to increased likelihood of preservation and recovery because they are more recent, but the virtual explosion of bone, antler, and ivory tools in the Upper Paleolithic leads most anthropologists to conclude that a significant change in technology and culture took place after about 40,000 years ago.

In addition to the new raw materials, other changes occurred at this time as well. Compound tools such as the atlatl or spear-thrower appear, as do tools for making tools. For example, **burins** are stone tools with a special chisel edge used for carving bone tools. Barbed harpoons indicate the use of foods from rivers, lakes, and oceans. Many of the bone, antler, and ivory objects are engraved or sculptured, showing an interest in aesthetics.

Hunting skills seem to have improved during this time, at least in terms of the size and numbers of game captured. Upper Paleolithic peoples in Europe are often referred to as "Big Game Hunters" in recognition of their emphasis on the hunting of large animals such as wooly rhinoceros, mastodon, and bison. Hunting methods included driving large herds of animals such as bison and horses over cliffs. In fact, in some areas of the world, the hunting success of Upper Paleolithic peoples may have led to the extinction of some large game species.

Many Paleolithic sites, from at least the time of *Homo erectus*, are found in caves. During the Upper Paleolithic, however, there is more evidence of habitations in

Carved Venus figurines exhibit exaggerated feminine characteristics, leading some to suggest that they may have been fertility symbols.

the open air. By 60,000 years ago, people were occupying Siberia, which must have required significant skills at building shelters. Among the bone tools found in Upper Paleolithic sites are the first needles, suggesting the development of tailored clothing, almost certainly made from prepared animal skins.

The spectacular cave art of southwestern Europe appears to have begun about 18,000 years ago, but examples of small, portable art objects precede that by several thousand years. Among the portable objects, known as **mobiliary art,** are a series of sculptures of female figures known as "Venuses." These carved or modeled figures represent women whose feminine characteristics such as breasts, buttocks, and pregnant abdomens are emphasized. Unlike the later cave paintings, the Venus figures are found all over Europe, and even in Eastern Siberia. They are often thought to be associated with some kind of fertility ritual, but this is very difficult to determine.

The amazing thing about the cave paintings in France, Spain, and North Africa is their magnitude, surpassing in size and grandeur anything seen before that time or elsewhere in the world. The cave art is mostly paintings made with mineral pigments mixed with animal fat, but also includes engravings and bas-relief in clay on the cave walls. Most commonly depicted are lifelike animal figures, abstract shapes, and outlines of human hands. Human figures are rare and, when present, are often far more crude than the animal figures. The animals represented include many species that were hunted by Paleolithic people, including mammoth, boar, reindeer, and wild horse. Many different parts of the caves have been painted, including both large accessible chambers near the front of the caves and tiny cramped spaces far inside. Although sometimes the groupings of animals seem to be purposeful scenes, in other cases, animals seem to be painted over and next to previous drawings with no concern for the earlier pattern.

Many of the painted caves, as well as other sites, also contain rich collections of carved and engraved bone and ivory objects. These may also be engraved with lifelike animal figures or with geometric forms.

There have been various attempts to interpret the meaning and significance of the forms of artistic expression, but, not surprisingly, there has been no consensus. The cave paintings are often interpreted as parts of hunting rituals because they represent animals whose butchered bones show up in archaeological sites. Others suggest that the cave art represents coming-of-age rituals or markers of ethnic affiliation or even "art for art's sake" (although most anthropologists would reject this last). Some of the portable objects have rows of marks that some think are a primitive lunar calendar. All of these interpretations are possible. One important thing to note is the regional diversity in art, suggesting diversity of cultural traditions. We can no longer talk about a generalized *Homo sapiens*. Certainly by 18,000 years ago we encounter people with so much variation in local cultural traditions that we can only rarely make statements that apply to the species as a whole. We now have to talk about regional traditions, local cultures, and possibly individual ethnic groups. Our shift of focus is now away from the species toward specific subpopulations.

## THE SPREAD OF HUMANS THROUGHOUT THE WORLD

Beginning about 40,000 years ago, human populations began to migrate to parts of the world that had not previously been inhabited by hominids. Although Southeast Asia was occupied by *Homo erectus* perhaps a million years ago, the first date of occupation of Australia and New Guinea is 40,000 years ago. Although no direct evidence of boats has been found, we know from geological evidence that the occupation of Australia must have required crossing of water and, thus, human skills in boat building. The other migration of interest was the one to the Americas. This will be discussed further in Chapter 11.

## POST-PALEOLITHIC DEVELOPMENTS

Much of the Middle and Upper Paleolithic periods were times of colder-than-present climate in the northern hemispheres with glaciers covering parts of the earth. Anthropologists date the end of the Paleolithic to approximately 10,000 years ago, at which time glaciers were melting and worldwide climate was approaching modern conditions. By this time, all major land masses in the world were occupied by *Homo sapiens*. The climate changes, and perhaps to some extent, human hunting practices, resulted in the extinction of many of the game species on which several human populations were dependent. This meant that a broader base of food resources had to be exploited and, in general, the diversity of foods consumed by humans increased. The period during which diversification of resources and lifestyles occurred is often called the **Mesolithic** in the Old World; in North America it is referred to as the **Archaic** cultural period.

In much of Europe, Africa, and the Near East, the major change in stone tools is the development of **mi**-

**croliths.** These are small, delicately chipped stone flakes, often formed in careful geometric shapes of triangles, rhomboids, and half-circles, that are inset into handles of bone, antler, and wood. In some parts of the world, tools made by grinding and pecking stone are added to the technology in addition to chipped-stone tools. The extraordinary cave art and the elaborately engraved bone and antler objects disappear in Europe, although bone tools are still widely used. The most important cultural changes occur in subsistence and settlement patterns. We will discuss post-Paleolithic developments in more detail in Chapters 10 and 11.

◆　◆　◆
# Variation in Modern Human Populations

What did these hominids of 40,000 years ago look like, other than being "anatomically modern"? What color was their skin, their eyes, their hair? What was the texture of their hair and how much body hair did they have? Were they tall and thin, or short and stocky? Were they more or less variable than human populations today? Were they all of one blood type, or does the variation we see today in ABO, Rh, and other blood types go back that far? One way to explore these questions is to review the various environments in which human populations are found today and to examine the physical traits that reflect adaptations to these environments. Based on current fossil evidence, it appears that our hominid ancestors evolved in the savannahs of East Africa, and we can assume that the challenges imposed by heat stress, intense sunlight, and seasonal dryness were probably among the earliest faced. It also appears that the earliest hominid migrations out of Africa occurred approximately 1 million years ago, so physical changes reflecting adaptation to temperate and cold climates have occurred since that time.

## ADAPTATIONS TO HEAT

Crucial to a species' adaptation to hot environments is an efficient mechanism for cooling the body. Perhaps one of the first changes that occurred in the course of human evolution was selection for the ability to cool the body through sweating and evaporation. Associated with this genetic adaptation was selection for decreased amounts and thickness of hair, since thick body hair interferes with evaporative cooling.

Many mammals have sweat glands, but none can match humans for the amount of sweat produced. An average human working in normal, dry heat will sweat about one liter per hour; up to three liters per hour will be lost by a person performing heavy work in high heat. People whose ancestors have lived in hot, dry areas for thousands of years produce less sweat per unit of work (Frisancho, 1985), suggesting adaptation to heat stress on the genetic or developmental level.

Obviously, maintaining adequate levels of water is one of the biggest problems for an animal that cools through evaporation in arid environments. One liter of water lost is equivalent to 1.5 percent body weight loss. Loss of as much as 10 percent of body weight is life-threatening for the average person. Unfortunately, the human thirst mechanism has not kept pace with the evolution of sweating in humans. Often a person does not feel thirsty until too much water has been lost. Attempts to drink enough to replace the amount lost often results in nausea and abdominal cramps. Clearly one important adaptation for sweating hominids was the technological ability to carry water in savannah areas. Salt loss with sweating is also a problem. Populations that have long adapted to desert heat do not appear to lose as much salt as recent migrants.

## ADAPTATION TO SOLAR RADIATION

Intense solar radiation is another environmental stress our ancestors faced in adapting to savannah environments of Africa. The skin color pigment melanin (present in varying degrees in the skin of all people except albinos) serves as a screen against excessive ultraviolet radiation, which can damage internal organs and cause potentially lethal skin cancers. The more melanin present in the skin, the darker the color will be and the more effective the screen. Within certain limits, the amount of melanin varies throughout life and with exposure to the sun. For all people (except albinos), the amount increases with exposure to the sun, a phenomenon most easily seen in the tanning of light-skinned people. This pattern also works on the population level. Natural selection has favored genes for greater melanin production, and thus greater protection, in populations that live in areas of intense sunlight, such as those found in most equatorial regions of the world (Exhibit 7-2). Thus, people who trace their ancestry to populations from equatorial areas are darker-skinned than people who trace their ancestry to populations from temperate,

---

### EXHIBIT 7-2
**Distribution of skin color**

SOURCE: After C. S. Coon and E. E. Hunt, *The Living Races of Man* © 1965 Alfred A. Knopf, Inc.

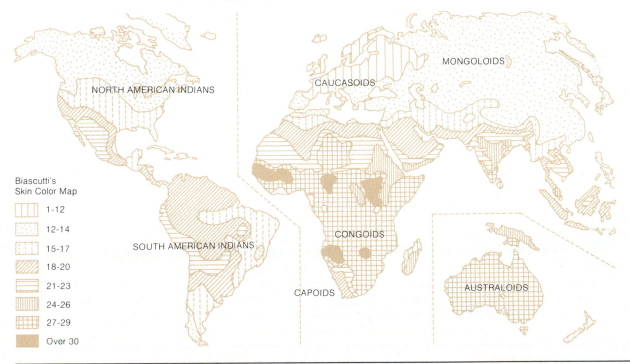

northern regions. Most of the exceptions can be ascribed to recent migrations.

How pigmented was the skin of early hominids? It is likely that the populations that first migrated out of Africa one million years ago were dark-skinned, just as the populations who remained in Africa are today. Over hundreds of generations of adapting to colder climates and less intense sunlight, however, gradually lessening of pigmentation would have occurred. This suggests that the lighter skin color of present-day temperate peoples is simply the result of "relaxed selection," a process whereby genes for lighter pigmentation were simply not eliminated at the expense of genes for dark pigmentation. But is there any evidence that genes for lighter pigmentation would have been favorably selected?

One possible selective advantage of lighter skin color in areas of low sunlight is that vitamin D is more easily manufactured by those with less melanin in their skin.

Vitamin D, synthesized in the body with sufficient exposure to sunlight, is responsible for maintaining calcium in bones and teeth. Without sufficient exposure to sunlight, children often develop **rickets,** a disorder that leads to malformation of bones and teeth. For women who had rickets as children, delivering a baby through a malformed pelvis was usually impossible before caesarean section, so it is a problem that directly inhibits reproductive success. Moreover, there is also evidence that darkly pigmented skin is more susceptible to frostbite, suggesting another reason dark skin may have been selected against as populations moved into cold regions (Exhibit 7-3).

Melanin also plays a role in the color of hair and eyes, although other pigments are involved as well. Hair with a large amount of melanin is darker than hair with very little melanin, and, in general, the pattern is the same as observed for the skin. Thus, populations living in areas

◆ ◆ ◆

EXHIBIT 7-3

**The effect of environmental factors on skin color**

SOURCE: from Frisancho, 1981.

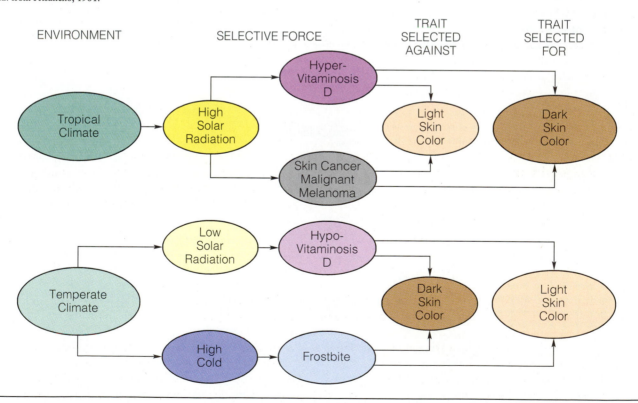

of intense sunlight tend to have darker hair than populations living in northern latitudes. Actually, light hair is rare, found only in northern European populations, suggesting a rather recent and restricted selection for low melanin production. Since dark hair is the norm for contemporary humans, we can conclude that the vast majority of human populations in the past had dark brown or black hair, just as they do today.

The color of the iris of the eye is also related to the amount of melanin present. As with skin, melanin provides protection for the eyes from ultraviolet light. Thus, it would be expected that darkly pigmented eyes would be common in tropical regions. Light-colored (blue) eyes occur in northern Europeans, often in association with light skin and blonde hair. Today, brown eyes are the species norm and probably predominated in early human populations.

## ADAPTATIONS TO COLD

Challenges provided by extreme cold temperatures are probably more recent than those of extreme heat. As noted, *Homo erectus* was the first hominid to inhabit cold, or even temperate, areas of the world. Thus, whereas our adaptations to heat can probably be traced to the earliest primates, our adaptations to cold are relatively recent, perhaps less than 1 million years. Most of the responses we have to cold stress are cultural: we build fires, cover ourselves in blankets or animal skins, and seek shelter in caves or houses. Short-term physiological responses include vasoconstriction of the blood capillaries, increase in basal metabolic rate, and shivering. It has been estimated that shivering alone can increase heat production to almost three times the basal level (Frisancho, 1985). We also tend to eat more food, particularly fats and carbohydrates, move around to increase internal heat generation, and curl up to reduce the surface area exposed.

Adaptations to cold climates have also resulted in changes in body shape. The ideal body shape for conserving heat is short and stocky, whereas the ideal shape for dissipating heat is tall and thin. These shapes reflect the amount of body surface area for evaporative cooling. Thus, one would expect animals (including humans) living in arctic regions to be stockier than those living in tropical regions.

For mammals, the length of the extremities is also important for heat conservation or dissipation. In cold areas, short extremities would be favored because they conserve heat, whereas long extremities, which increase

These short and stocky Inuits (Eskimos) have the ideal body shape for conserving heat.

surface area for dissipation of heat, would be favored in hot areas. Indeed, arctic peoples like the Inuit and Lapps are short and somewhat stocky, with short extremities, and many central African people are typically tall and thin with long arms and legs. Small body size appears to serve well in the hot and humid tropical rain forests of Africa and Asia where many pygmoid peoples live. There are exceptions to these patterns of body size and shape, but in general, human body weight increases in populations of the world as mean annual temperature decreases (Harrison, 1988).

Fat layers of people living in cold climates tend to be thicker, providing more insulation. Metabolic rates of people exposed to chronic cold, such as the Inuit and Northern Athabascans, tend to be higher than populations not living in cold climates. Populations such as the Australian aborigines and the Kalahari San who experience great daily variation in temperature, appear to have lower basal metabolic rates, a characteristic that reduces skin temperature and enhances their ability to adapt to cold nighttime temperatures. These people are not subjected to frostbite, however, so lowering skin temperature does not cause them the problems it would if arctic populations experienced the same response.

## ADAPTATION TO HIGH ALTITUDE

Of the various stressful environments reviewed in this section, humans have occupied high elevations most recently, and thus there has been less time to adapt to the stresses posed. Occupation of the high plains and mountains of Ethiopia, Turkey, Iran, the Himalayas and Tibetan Plateau, and the Altiplano of the central Andes probably began in the last 10,000 years (Molnar, 1983).

High altitude environments pose a number of challenges to humans, including aridity, cold, high winds, higher ultraviolet radiation, short growing season (and, therefore, inadequate nutrition), and low oxygen, or **hypoxia.** Since most of these stresses are also experienced by some populations at lower elevations, the primary stress of concern when investigating populations at high altitude is hypoxia.

People who are born and grow up at high altitudes have larger lung volumes and larger hearts (especially the right ventricle, which sends blood to the lungs) than their relatives who grow up at lower elevations (Frisancho, 1985). They also mature later and many show no evidence of the typical adolescent growth spurt. Skeletal growth may not be completed until the early twenties. Growth retardation may be as much due to nutritional stress as to lack of oxygen, however. Respiratory diseases at high altitudes are common and often cause death in young children.

Living at high elevations can have negative impact on reproduction, especially for recent migrants. In fact, when the Spanish conquered the Incas, they had to locate their centers of government in lowland areas, because the first-generation Spanish women had difficulty reproducing in the Incan cities, all of which were above 10,000 feet. The primary effect of high altitude on reproduction seen today is in the higher incidence of low birth weight resulting from growth retardation in utero (Moore and Regensteiner, 1983). This reflects lowered maternal oxygen transport during pregnancy. Rates of miscarriage, prematurity, and infant mortality are all higher in recent migrants to high altitudes. Populations that have been at high elevations for generations do not show this negative effect on reproduction.

## ACCLIMATIZATION

As we have used the term "adaptation" in the above paragraphs we have assumed that populations have undergone some sort of genetic change in adapting to various environmental stresses. This may be true for those who have lived in the same area for thousands of years, but most humans are also able to make short-term adjustments to environmental challenges through a process known as **acclimatization.** For example, when exposed to high heat, most humans have the ability to cool themselves through dilation of the blood vessels, lowered basal metabolic rate, and sweating. We also tend to seek shade, work less, and eat less of some nutrients and more of others (e.g., salt). Of course, cultural mechanisms for response to heat stress are also available.

Temporary forays to high altitudes by lowlanders usually result in increased breathing and heart rate in response to lowered oxygen. If they stay at high altitudes for a few days, their red blood cell production will also be stepped up. Red blood cells are the carriers of oxygen to the rest of the body tissues, so an increase in their production results in more cells to carry the less available oxygen.

## OTHER GENETIC TRAITS

The genetically determined characteristics described above are known as **polygenic** traits because they are determined by several pairs of genes. It is estimated, for example, that three or four genes determine skin pigmentation (Harrison, 1988). Body shape and form is determined as much by environmental conditions, including diet, as it is by genes. The inheritance of eye color and hair color is somewhat confusing, but it is evident that several genes are involved for each. Since polygenic traits are difficult to study, many anthropologists specializing in human genetic variation have chosen instead to study traits that are better understood. These include the genes that determine blood types and variation of hemoglobin. Most are determined by single gene pairs, so their distribution in human populations is more easily understood.

**ABO Blood Types.** Genes determining blood types are especially interesting to anthropologists because they are easy to measure, are determined at birth, and do not change throughout life. Because of the dangers associated with blood transfusion, hundreds of thousands of people have been typed, so there is a large database to

| Individual's Genotype | Phenotype (Blood Group) | Antibodies in Serum | Reaction will occur with the following kinds of blood: |
|---|---|---|---|
| OO | O | anti-A and anti-B | A, B, AB |
| AA AO | A | anti-B | B, AB |
| BB BO | B | anti-A | A, AB |
| AB | AB | neither | none |

**T A B L E  7-1 ◆  The ABO Blood Group System**

study. There are at least a dozen different systems involved in the concept of "blood type." The ones we are most familiar with are the ABO system and the Rh system. A single gene pair appears to determine ABO blood type. There are three alleles: A, B, and O. A and B are **codominant,** meaning that both are expressed in a person who inherits both. O is recessive and will be expressed only if a person inherits two O alleles. A person's phenotype (i.e., the blood type) is based on the antigen that is expressed. Thus, a person who inherits at least one allele for A and the other for A or O is blood type A. This person also manufactures the antibody known as "anti-B," and the person who is blood type B manufactures the antibody "anti-A." People with blood type O produce both anti-A and anti-B. People with blood type AB produce neither antibody. Table 7-1 summarizes the ABO genotypes, phenotypes, antigens, and antibodies.

Since its discovery in 1900, great numbers of people from many different areas of the world have been sampled for ABO blood type. Table 7-2 illustrates some of the variation in the frequencies of the alleles from population to population. In general, the B allele reaches its highest frequencies in Asia, the O allele in the Americas, and the A allele in Australia. What accounts for the pattern of distribution? Is it simply a random phenomenon, or are the evolutionary forces of natural selection, genetic drift, and migration operating on the ABO system?

Certainly migration can explain some of the patterns seen. For example, blood type B is absent from Australia except for small pockets along the northern coast, suggesting contact with Malay and Chinese fishermen. Genetic drift, and a related phenomenon called **founder effect,** can explain some of the patterns. For example, blood type A reaches its highest frequencies among the

North American Blood and Blackfeet Indians. Perhaps the effect of small sample size can explain this distribution. If the small founding groups of island areas by chance happened to have no person carrying one of the alleles, the descendants will also lack the allele, even if the population from which the founders emigrated had high frequencies of the allele.

Perhaps the most interesting evolutionary force to consider when examining the distribution of ABO alleles is natural selection. Is there any evidence that natural selection is operating differentially on the blood types? Two likely sources of natural selection have been proposed. One is due to maternal–fetal incompatibility. Just as there are incompatible transfusions, it is also possible for a mother and fetus to be incompatible at the ABO locus. For example, a woman who is blood type O cannot receive transfusions from a person who is blood type A. In the same way, mothers who are blood type O may have a difficult time carrying a fetus that has blood type A. In most cases, these incompatible fetuses are rejected so early in pregnancy that the women are not even aware they have conceived.

The other source of natural selection is infectious diseases, which more frequently affect people of one blood type over another. People who are blood type O, for example, appear to be more susceptible to viral diseases (Harrison, 1989), which were major killers in the past and may be partially responsible for the distribution we see today of the ABO alleles.

One of the patterns observed that has not been explained is that in the native populations of the Americas, blood type O reaches its highest frequencies and type B appears to have been absent before European migrations. Considering the evidence that the Americas came from Asia, where blood type B reaches its highest frequencies, its apparent absence in the Western hemisphere is problematic. Three possible explanations have been offered. Perhaps the B allele is the result of a recent mutation that occurred in Asia less than 10,000 years ago, meaning it was not present in the populations of 20,000 or more years ago from which the Americans derived. Or perhaps its absence in the Americas is due to genetic drift or founder effect. Finally, in the absence of infectious diseases, maternal–fetal incompatibility may explain why the O allele is so high and the A and B alleles are rare or absent. According to this theory, many A and B fetuses were lost during the 10,000 years before European contact, but the counter-selective forces of infectious diseases were not operating against type O individuals before those diseases came to the Americas with the Europeans.

| Place | Population | Number Tested | O | A | B | AB |
|-------|-----------|--------------|------|------|------|------|
| Lebanon | Armenian | 3,080 | 867(28.15) | 1,423(46.20) | 389(12.63) | 401(13.02) |
| France | Basques | 516 | 299(57.95) | 198(38.37) | 14( 2.71) | 5( .97) |
| Hungary | Gypsies | 975 | 278(28.51) | 259(26.56) | 344(35.28) | 94( 9.64) |
| Israel | Jews | 633 | 237(37.44) | 237(37.44) | 113(17.85) | 46( 7.27) |
| Austria | Steiermark | 1,927 | 696(36.12) | 890(46.19) | 237(12.30) | 104( 5.40) |
| Belgium | Brussels | 1,419 | 644(45.38) | 614(43.27) | 113( 7.96) | 48( 3.38) |
| Czechoslovakia | Czechs | 2,085 | 455(21.82) | 1,006(48.25) | 450(21.58) | 174( 8.35) |
| Denmark | Copenhagen | 9,538 | 4,010(42.04) | 4,151(43.52) | 932( 9.77) | 455( 4.67) |
| Ireland | Dublin | 9,388 | 5,050(53.79) | 3,079(32.80) | 1,019(10.85) | 240( 2.56) |
| Finland | Helsinki | 1,600 | 810(50.62) | 510(31.87) | 193(12.06) | 87( 5.44) |
| France | Paris | 14,303 | 6,112(42.73) | 6,528(45.64) | 1,188( 8.31) | 475( 3.32) |
| Greece | Athens | 21,635 | 9,408(43.48) | 8,361(38.64) | 2,826(13.06) | 1,040( 4.81) |
| Iceland | Reykjavik | 878 | 478(54.44) | 281(32.00) | 96(10.93) | 23( 2.62) |
| Sweden | Lund | 3,363 | 1,361(40.47) | 1,518(45.14) | 330( 9.81) | 154( 4.58) |
| England | London | 10,000 | 4,578(45.78) | 4,219(42.19) | 890( 8.90) | 313( 3.13) |
| Scotland | Glasgow | 6,011 | 3,036(50.96) | 2,115(35.18) | 654(10.88) | 179( 2.98) |
| India | U.P. Hindus | 2,357 | 712(30.21) | 577(24.48) | 877(37.21) | 191( 8.10) |
| Indo-China | Vietnam | 1,069 | 430(40.22) | 289(27.03) | 297(27.78) | 53( 4.96) |
| Thailand | Bangkok | 6,267 | 2,336(37.27) | 1,369(21.84) | 2,071(33.05) | 491( 7.83) |
| Philippines | Filipinos | 69,148 | 31,049(44.90) | 17,751(25.67) | 16,839(24.35) | 3,509( 5.07) |
| Indonesia | Java | 7,129 | 2,795(39.21) | 1,907(26.75) | 1,948(27.32) | 479( 6.72) |
| China | Peking | 1,000 | 307(30.70) | 251(25.10) | 342(34.20) | 100(10.00) |
| Japan | Kyoto | 6,205 | 1,812(29.20) | 2,359(38.02) | 1,377(22.19) | 657(10.59) |
| Japan | Ainu | 1,198 | 308(25.71) | 337(28.13) | 412(34.39) | 141(11.77) |
| Egypt | | 10,045 | 3,279(32.65) | 3,570(35.65) | 2,448(24.37) | 748( 7.45) |
| Ghana | Accra | 1,540 | 851(55.26) | 338(21.95) | 316(20.52) | 35( 2.27) |
| Nigeria | Yoruba | 365 | 186(50.96) | 83(22.74) | 80(21.92) | 16( 4.38) |
| Kenya | Kikuyu | 449 | 271(60.36) | 84(18.71) | 89(19.82) | 5( 1.11) |
| Madagascar | Imerina | 572 | 205(35.84) | 78(13.64) | 213(37.24) | 76(13.29) |
| North America | Blackfeet, Blood | 270 | 47(17.41) | 221(81.85) | 9( 0.00) | 2( 0.74) |
| U.S.A. | Navajo | 457 | 332(72.65) | 123(26.91) | 1( 0.22) | 1( 0.22) |
| U.S.A. | Pueblo | 353 | 311(88.10) | 41(11.61) | 0( 0.00) | 1( 0.28) |
| U.S.A. | Boston | 120,281 | 55,089(45.80) | 47,752(39.70) | 12,990(10.80) | 4,450( 3.70) |
| Peru | Mestizos | 6,634 | 4,612(69.52) | 1,338(20.17) | 607( 9.15) | 77( 1.16) |
| Peru | Indians | 500 | 480(96.00) | 15( 3.00) | 5( 1.00) | 0( 0.00) |
| Tierra del Fuego | Ona | 21 | 21(100.00) | 0( 0.00) | 0( 0.00) | 0( 0.00) |
| Australia | Aborigines | 102 | 44(43.14) | 58(56.86) | 0( 0.00) | 0( 0.00) |
| New Zealand | Maori | 1,335 | 591(44.27) | 707(52.96) | 21( 1.57) | 16( 1.20) |

SOURCE: Mourant et al. *The ABO Blood Groups*, Chas. C. Thomas, 1954, and Kelso and Trevathan, 1984.

**Hemoglobin Genes.** Hemoglobin is a protein that is responsible for the transport of oxygen in the blood. There is a great deal of variation in the gene that controls hemoglobin production, and hundreds of alleles have been described, most of which have very low frequencies. The most common and dominant allele, which most people possess, is HbA. When rare alleles are inherited in the homozygous form (i.e., a person gets a rare allele from each parent), they can cause problems, often leading to death. One allele that reaches high frequencies in some parts of the world is the sickle-cell form, HbS. In Chapter 4 it was noted that this allele probably resulted from a single mutation in the DNA.

The HbS allele and some of the other variants reach their highest frequencies in populations of equatorial Africa, the Mediterranean, India, and parts of Southeast Asia (Exhibit 7-4). Not coincidentally, they are associated with the infectious disease malaria (Exhibit 7-5).

EXHIBIT 7-4

**Distribution of the sickle cell allele in the Old World.**

SOURCE: Courtesy of D. E. Schreiber, IBM Research Laboratory, San Jose.

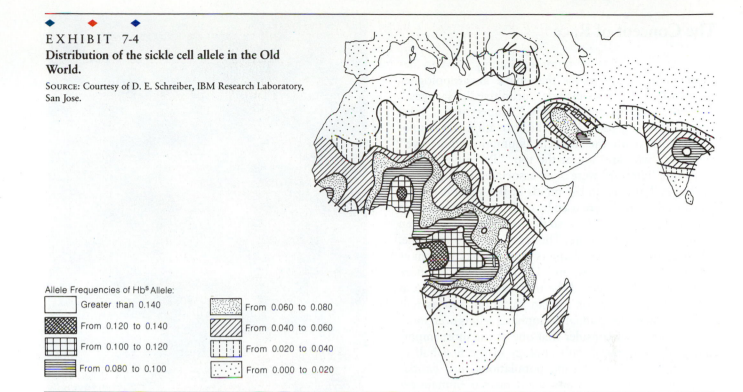

Allele Frequencies of Hb$^S$ Allele:

| | |
|---|---|
| ☐ Greater than 0.140 | ▦ From 0.060 to 0.080 |
| ▨ From 0.120 to 0.140 | ▧ From 0.040 to 0.060 |
| ▦ From 0.100 to 0.120 | ▥ From 0.020 to 0.040 |
| ▤ From 0.080 to 0.100 | ⠿ From 0.000 to 0.020 |

People who inherit two HbS alleles have a reduced ability to carry oxygen in their blood, and they usually die before adulthood from the disease known as sickle-cell anemia. Since most people who carry this allele in homozygous form die before reproducing, it seems that the allele would never reach very high frequencies, yet it has in some populations. The only way this could happen would be if there were some selective advantage to the heterozygote who carries one allele for HbS and one for HbA. A number of studies have indicated that people who have this combination are protected against the deadly effects of malaria, which explains the high frequency of HbS in the areas of the globe where malaria is common.

◆ ◆ ◆

EXHIBIT 7-5

**Malaria distribution in the Old World.**

SOURCE: A. E. Mourant, et al., *The Distribution of the Human Blood Groups and Other Polymorphisms,* Oxford University Press, © 1976. By permission of publisher.

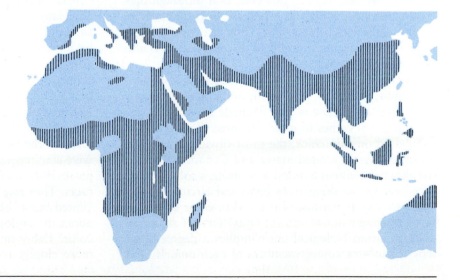

## The Concept of Race

There are a number of terms commonly used to describe human populations that make anthropologists uncomfortable. These include "primitive," "savages," "inferior," "barbarians," "pagans," "superstitious," and "race." Most suggest a hierarchical relationship among populations, with the implicit assumption that "we" (whoever "we" are) are at the top. "Primitive," "savage," and "inferior" were often associated with particular "races," at least in the minds of the general public. Many of the terms were used by early anthropologists in their professional writings, so they have not always been regarded as inappropriate. The term *race,* for example, was used to title entire chapters in textbooks written as recently as 1977 (Brues) and 1985 (Molnar). In more recent textbooks, we find the term in a brief section at the end of a chapter on human variation, just as it is appearing here. Its gradual deemphasis seems even more unusual when we consider that one of the most important goals of physical anthropology in the first half of this century was organizing populations into entities called races, determining how many races of humans existed on earth, and ascertaining origins and migrations of human races.

So, what happened to human races? Have they ceased to exist, or is it simply no longer fashionable or acceptable to discuss races? To some extent, both answers are true. The notion that races no longer exist should be modified to suggest that races probably never existed at all, at least in the forms most of us imagine them. When described by biological anthropologists in the first part of this century, races were considered to be real biological units. We now realize, however, that although they remain pervasive social concepts, they no longer have validity as biological concepts. Thus, we would argue that it is not only unacceptable to discuss races, it is also scientifically incorrect.

To understand the demise of the race concept, we need to examine the history of scientific and popular thinking about race. First, how is race defined? Most likely, the first thing that comes to mind for most of us is a category based on skin color, the most obvious marker in countries like the United States and Canada. (The fact that skin color comes to mind is, in itself, a sociocultural phenomenon, resulting from historical circumstances.) What are the limitations of using skin color as a basis for organizing humans into subunits? First of all, an organization into biological units implies a degree of genetic relatedness among members of each unit. If races

An Australian aborigine man whose dark skin is well-adapted to the desert environment in which he lives.

exist as biological units, members of one race must be more closely related to each other than they are to members of any other race.

Because skin color is caused by several genes, there are many limitations to its usefulness. It is quite possible, for example, for three people who are siblings to be placed in three different races, if skin color is the criterion used. If a dark-skinned man marries a light-skinned woman, their genes may recombine in a number of ways: they may produce one child with dark skin like the father, one child with light skin like the mother, and one child with a skin color that appears to be a blend of the two. In South Africa, before the Pass Laws were eliminated, these three children might have carried passes indicating that they "belonged" to three separate races. They might have attended separate schools in the United States before desegregation. What does this say about the biological reality of race when based on skin color? Other than identical twins, no human beings are more closely related to each other than siblings (and

A woman from southern India, where dark skin is also an advantage because of heat and sun exposure.

A dark-skinned African woman.

parents and children). The three children in this example are related to each other by 50 percent of their genes, and yet they could be placed in three separate racial categories. As a contrasting example, three people from three continents whose skin color was almost the same, such as an Australian aborigine, a person from Southern India, and a person from central Africa, might all be placed in the same race if skin color alone were used as the criterion for classification.

When used to describe populations of other animals, race would be equivalent to the concept of the subspecies, by which some degree of reproductive isolation is implied. Whereas some populations of humans in the past may have been geographically isolated, clearly there are no truly isolated human populations today.

The concept of race implies a fixed boundary, a demarcation of some sort, that can be used to organize human variation. But it is difficult to determine what that boundary is. If we define a race as a population with a set of genetic traits that differ from other populations,

that may provide us with a definition of a boundary, but then the challenge is deciding which traits should be used to make up this population. Are skin color and head shape better bases on which to organize populations than ABO and rh blood type? Does the fact that we can see the former make them better markers? Or does the fact that we can use laboratory tests to measure the latter make them better? And if we could decide which characteristics to use, we then have difficulty with people who have a mixture of the traits. These are just a few of the problems one faces in trying to organize human populations on the basis of biological traits.

Another problem of racial categorizing has been determining how many races of humans existed on earth. Estimates have ranged from three (Negroid, Caucasoid, Mongoloid) to hundreds, depending on the criteria chosen for classification. To illustrate the sociocultural aspects of assessing numbers, consider the cases of the United States and Brazil, countries with similar demographic histories. Both were originally inhabited by

Indians and were settled voluntarily by European colonists and involuntarily by African slaves. The popular concepts of races are very different in the two countries, however. In the United States, traditionally three major races (European-derived, African-derived, and Native) have been recognized. In Brazil, with almost the same genes recombining, more than fifteen races have been recognized.

Once a number was estimated, labeling the races was a challenge. By considering the terms often used for races in everyday talk, we can see that the way most of us think about race is as a cultural category, not a biological one. Geopolitical terms include African-American, European, Native American, Malaysian, Hispanic, Mexican-American, and Scandinavian. Linguistic terms include Aryan, Anglo-Saxon, and "Anglo." Religious terms include Jewish, Hindu, and Muslim. These terms tell us little about biological characteristics.

One way to determine how we can go about defining race and delineating races is to decide why we need to organize human variability in the first place and what the goal of the classification is. Clearly there have been political reasons to be concerned about this issue in the past (e.g., Nazi Germany, South Africa under apartheid, the United States before segregation was outlawed, and dozens of contemporary conflicts over "ethnic purity"). But are there good reasons for delineating races today? Many universities, professional schools, federal agencies, and private corporations are concerned about having on their rosters members of "under-represented minorities." These groups are identified with such terms as African-American, Hispanic-American, and American Indian. But are these races, ethnic groups, or social entities? No matter what we call them, the fact that they are under-represented or minority groups (at least in the United States and Canada) has nothing at all to do with biological factors. People fall into these categories for social, political, historical, and economic reasons.

There has been a renewed interest in human biological variation because of the Human Genome Project. The goal of this project is to identify the chromosomal location and DNA sequence of every one of the 100,000 or so genes in the human genome or gene pool. Recently there has been criticism that the project has sampled primarily "white" populations in industrialized nations, and thus is not representative of the entire human genome. In response to this concern, several anthropologists and geneticists have formed the Human Genome Diversity project, designed to collect data from as many populations around the world as possible. A particular goal is to sample populations that are on the verge of disappearing. It is believed that this database will aid in understanding evolutionary processes, surveying human diversity, and, perhaps, preventing diseases in vulnerable populations.

But, how does one determine what a population is and how many distinct populations exist? One suggestion is to simply collect samples every one hundred miles or so, and not be concerned about relationships among and within these samples. Other scientists, however, prefer to sample from "well-defined" populations, although there is much disagreement on how to define these. Suggestions include linguistically defined populations, geographically isolated populations, and genetically distinct populations. Another concern is how many populations should be sampled. Anthropologists involved in the project agree that 400 is a reasonable number (considering logistics and finances, primarily), but there is almost no agreement on what those 400 populations should be (Roberts, 1992). Although the effort and intent may be admirable, the challenges are reminiscent of those faced in the first part of this century by anthropologists who were trying to determine how many "races" of humans there were in the world.

To say that anthropologists are no longer concerned with organizing human variability into discrete units known as races is not to say that they are no longer interested in variation in the traits that characterize human beings. In fact, studying human variation is still one of the primary goals of biological anthropologists today. This variation can tell us a great deal about past and current evolutionary forces operating on human populations and about past migrations. It is also true that traits tend to be distributed differentially in different populations, so it is often useful to consider geographically based groups of people when describing traits such as we have done above with ABO genes and degrees of pigmentation. Often anthropologists find it easy to use some of the old racial terminology in describing these traits, as in a statement like "shovel-shaped incisors tend to occur in higher frequencies in Asian or Mongoloid populations than in African or Negroid populations." It is also not inappropriate for genetic counselors to be alerted to the fact that genetically determined diseases such as Tay Sachs and sickle-cell anemia may be higher in some populations than in others. But, in most cases, the concept of race as used by biological anthropologists today is not the same as that used earlier in this century.

In Chapter 5 we argued that any classification system is actually a set of hypotheses about relationships that must be tested with actual data. In the first part of this century, there were many scientific hypotheses about racial classification. The hypotheses were based on a belief that there were distinct clusters of people that were genetically homogeneous and different from any other group. The challenge was to identify, name, and describe those clusters. The fundamental hypothesis has been disproved, however, with data demonstrating that these units are not now discrete, never will be, and may never have been, because of interbreeding, migration, and shifting criteria for classification. Since the fundamental assumptions have been changed, the resulting classifications or racial "taxonomies" are no longer valid.

Does that mean that races do not exist? Certainly they exist in the minds of most people, and there is no question that human beings differ from one another. But most of the ways in which we differ are due to sociocultural rather than biological phenomena. There is absolutely no sound biological evidence that such characteristics as intelligence, moral behavior, piety, gullibility, altruism, militarism, nurturance, athletic prowess, musical ability, running speed, or physical strength vary along population or racial lines. Many of these characteristics have biological roots that are then shaped by learning. Whereas there is no question that there is a great deal of biological variation between individual humans in these traits, there is no evidence that one population, as a group, has more or less of any of these characteristics than another.

## ◆ Summary

1. Two hypotheses about the origin of modern humans are that (a) *Homo sapiens* evolved several times from regional populations of *Homo erectus* (the multiregional model), and (b) *Homo sapiens* evolved once from a single *Homo erectus* population and spread to the rest of the world (the single-origin model). The fossil evidence seems to support the multiregional model, whereas the molecular analysis of DNA seems to support the single-origin model. The time for the origin of modern *Homo sapiens* is also controversial, with estimates ranging from 40,000 to 350,000 years ago.
2. The Neanderthals are a specialized European population of early *Homo sapiens* that have long been difficult to place in the human evolutionary tree because of their unusual physical characteristics. Their cultural behavior suggests, however, that they were very similar to modern human beings.
3. The Upper Paleolithic, the time from 40,000 years to approximately 10,000 years ago, is marked by numerous advances in stone tool technology and other aspects of human material culture. A greater variety of finished tool types and a greater variety of raw materials used characterize this period. Spectacular cave art was produced in southwestern Europe beginning about 18,000 years ago. There is continuing debate about what this art meant to the people who made it, but among the proposals are (a) hunting magic, (b) religious expression, (c) and calendarlike record keeping.
4. Fully modern human beings were common on earth beginning about 40,000 years ago. As they adapted to colder regions of the world, selection favored stocky body shape with short arms and legs or large overall body size, the ideal form for conserving heat. Living in colder regions probably also favored a gradual lightening of skin color to enhance production of vitamin D in areas of less intense sunlight. Human populations living in tropical areas benefit from darker skin, which protects them from the harmful effects of both ultraviolet light and excess vitamin D, and either small or long and linear body shape, an adaptation to heat.
5. The distribution of other genetic traits in populations of the world results from the interaction of natural selection, cultural practices, and migration patterns. For example, populations are highly variable in the frequencies of the genes for ABO blood types. The variation may result from the selective effects of maternal–fetal incompatibilities and infectious diseases. Another example is the gene for sickle-cell anemia, which appears to be related to the distribution of malaria.
6. The concept of race as a discrete group of people is not useful in describing biological variation in modern human populations. Most of the ways in which human beings differ are due to sociocultural rather than biological phenomena.

## ◆ Key Terms

| | |
|---|---|
| acclimatization | mesolithic |
| archaic | microliths |
| burins | mobiliary art |
| codominant | polygenic |
| founder effect | rickets |
| hypoxia | |

## Suggested Readings

Auel, Jean M. *Clan of the Cave Bear,* New York: Crown, 1980. This and three other novels form a series of pure fiction about an Upper Paleolithic heroine (Ayla) who has numerous adventures in ice-age Europe. The stories are loosely based on archaeological information but the author's imagination is clearly evident. The novel may inspire further inquiry into what archaeologists think might have really been going on at this time and, for this reason, it is recommended here.

Gould, Stephen Jay. *The Mismeasure of Man,* New York: Norton, 1981. A thorough and devastating critique of the scientific search for a relationship between intelligence and race. Gould also provides a historical overview of IQ measurement in general, including a debunking of the twin studies of Cyril Burt.

Jones, S., R. Martin, and D. Pilbeam (eds). *The Cambridge Encyclopedia of Human Evolution,* New York: Cambridge University Press, 1992. Everything you ever wanted to know about current thinking on human evolution.

Leakey, Richard and Roger Lewin. *Origins Reconsidered: In Search of What Makes Us Human,* New York: Doubleday, 1992. This is a well-written book by two people who have spent a lot of time writing, reading, and researching the subject of human evolution. Leakey has also contributed an inordinate amount of fossil discoveries to the record of human evolution.

Trinkaus, Eric (ed.). *The Emergence of Modern Humans: Biocultural Adaptations in the Late Pleistocene,* Cambridge, England: Cambridge University Press, 1989. A collection of nine papers that discuss the origin of modern humans from the perspective of the multiregional model. The relationship between modern humans and Neanderthals is also a feature.

#### ◆ New genetic techniques help reunite families torn apart by war

In the previous chapter, we discussed how the search for the "grandmother" of us all has been aided by analysis of mitochondrial DNA. Recently this same technology has been used to help reunite grandmothers with their grandchildren in Argentina. In the late 1970s, thousands of university students and young professionals who opposed the military regime that overthrew Isabel Peron's government were "disappeared," their young children often kidnapped and adopted by members of the military elite. Once the atrocities were exposed, the grandmothers of these children organized themselves into the Abuelas de Plaza de Mayo (Grandmothers of the Plaza of May) with the goal of determining the fate of their children and grandchildren. Massive efforts on the part of these determined women located many of the missing grandchildren, but most of the evidence was circumstantial and was not sufficient to establish their identities in court.

In 1984, geneticist Mary Claire King, who had been involved in mitochondrial DNA research, was invited by the American Association for the Advancement of Science to help find stronger evidence that the children are who the grandmothers claim they are. By comparing the mitochondrial DNA in a hypothesized maternal grandmother with that of an alleged missing grandchild, King can estimate the likelihood of biological relatedness, with the probability of a mistake being only one in a thousand. Since the technique is so new, it has not yet met with full acceptance by the Argentine courts, but the potential to identify missing relatives using this method is great. The Abuelas de Plaza de Mayo may never know the fate of their own children, but they may someday be reunited with their grandchildren as the children reach the age at which they themselves will begin to search for their families.

#### ◆ The issue of race is used in identification of human skeletal remains

Forensic anthropology is the application of anthropological techniques of skeletal analysis to law enforcement issues (Sauer, 1992). It is most commonly used in missing persons and homicide cases and in mass disasters, including war. No matter what the reason for investigation, when a forensic anthropologist is presented with a collection of bones for identification, she or he wants to provide the law enforcement agency with as much information as possible that can be used to identify the person.

Typically, a report will include such characteristics as sex, age, stature, evidence of pathology or unusual skeletal features, and race. But as we have noted in this chapter, most physical anthropologists reject the concept of race as a useful way of considering human biological diversity. Does this mean that forensic anthropologists see race as a valid category while other physical anthropologists reject it? According to Norman Sauer (1992) in an article subtitled "If Races Don't Exist, Why Are Forensic Anthropologists So Good at Identifying Them?", the two practices are not necessarily in conflict.

# Understanding Human Variation

147

Sauer argues that the continued practice of routinely assigning skeletons to racial categories is not inconsistent with the goal of many physical anthropologists to educate the public about the meaningless of racial categories. The object of a forensic anthropology study is an individual, whereas the object of physical anthropology in general is populations. As we have noted, it is meaningless to talk about racial categories at the level of the population, but it may not be inconsistent to use biological variables to construct an individual profile that may be useful in matching a missing person's report or otherwise identifying the unknown skeletal remains. In constructing the final report, a forensic anthropologist seeks to determine how the individual whose skeleton is being analyzed would have been described in life. In other words, how would individuals in society have perceived this individual? In the United States and Canada, at least, any such description of a living person would include race or ethnic affiliation. If the goal is to identify the person, using socially constructed biological variables may be an important key to that search.

Despite the claims in the title of Sauer's article, forensic anthropologists are not always "good at" predicting the socially perceived race of an individual skeleton. Because there has been so much population mixture, almost all inherited features, including those expressed in the skeleton, are mixtures of characteristics once assumed to apply to one race or another. For example, shovel-shaped incisors, most commonly found in Asian and Asian-derived populations, have often been used to assign a skull to the category "American Indian" in the United States. But many people who express characteristics that would otherwise lead to their being labeled as "white" or "black" have shovel-shaped incisors, often due to American Indian ancestry. It is impressive and perhaps surprising that forensic anthropologists' predictions of socially perceived assignments of race are so often consistent with what society would have labeled the individual when he or she was alive.

## ◆ Populations differ in their response to medical treatments

Theresa Overfield, a nurse-anthropologist, has noted that many medical practitioners in the United States and Canada assume that disease processes and responses to medication that have been observed in one population are the same in other populations. But, she notes, just as populations have different physical characteristics because they have adapted to different environments, they also often have different physiological characteristics. This means that populations may differ in their ability to metabolize chemicals, including nutrients and drugs (Overfield, 1985).

One example is the effects of isoniazid, a drug used to treat tuberculosis. Some people metabolize this drug very rapidly, whereas others process it much more slowly. Those who metabolize it slowly are at risk for developing temporary disorders of the nervous system during the treatment period, especially if high doses are given. If the doses are spread out over a longer period, the negative reactions are less likely to occur. But for those who metabolize it rapidly, lower doses over longer periods of time are not effective. Overfield suggests that it is important to consider treatment options when working with patients from different ethnic backgrounds. More than half of European-derived populations in the United States are slow processors of isoniazid, whereas 90 percent of Asians are rapid processors.

Psychiatrists have long observed that patients from European-derived populations often require far greater doses of psychiatric medication than those from Asian-derived populations. For example, Asians require far lower doses of tranquilizers to achieve the same therapeutic effects that larger doses have on European-derived populations. The opposite pattern exists with reaction to Benadryl: Asians require about twice the dose, per body weight, to achieve the same effect as Europeans do. Barbiturates also have different effects on Europeans and Asians. Recognition of these potential differences could avert mistakes of overdosing some people or prescribing for others doses so low that the drugs have no effect.

Gillian Bentley (1993) has been studying variation in levels of the reproductive hormone progesterone in several populations in the world and has noticed that, in general, women in more industrialized nations of the world have significantly higher levels of progesterone than women in traditional populations. There are also population differences in metabolism of exogenous hormones such as those found in many oral contraceptives. She thus cautions that oral contraceptives designed for women in industrialized nations may be inappropriate for women in traditional populations and advises that careful attention be given to variations in hormone metabolism before oral contraceptives are recommended.

## CHAPTER 8

# Biocultural Adaptations

What is the relationship between culture and biology?

What effect does our evolutionary history have on our lives today?

What were the causes of illness and death in the evolutionary past?

How did our nutritional needs evolve?

Are humans still evolving?

In the previous chapter, we discussed how human populations have adapted to the stresses of heat, cold, and high altitudes. This adaptation process must have been somewhat successful, because only occasionally do people die from heat, cold, and high altitude stresses. Thus, we cannot conclude that these are major climatic forces of natural selection acting on modern human populations. What is killing modern people? Pick up today's paper and the chances are you will find stories about the three big killers: war, disease, and starvation. (As we write this chapter, hundreds of people are dying every day in Bosnia and Sarajevo, thousands are dying of starvation in Somalia and Ethiopia, and AIDS is striking down hundreds of people every day.) If we think of war as a form of predation, then we can see that the three factors that have always controlled populations of living things (predation, starvation, and disease) are still having powerful effects on our own species. We tend to think that culture and technology have made us independent of evolutionary forces. But clearly that is no more true now than it was 10,000 years ago. To some extent, it may seem that these forces are having an even greater impact because of the sheer numbers of people affected.

Our biology is a result of millions of years of evolutionary history: 225 million years of mammalian evolution, 65 million years of primate evolution, 5 million years of hominid evolution, 2 million years of evolution of the genus *Homo*. The first populations to live in settled villages dependent on agriculture appeared about 10,000 years ago (see Chapter 10). Thus, we can conservatively say that more than 99 percent of our evolutionary history as hominids occurred when we lived as nomadic gatherers of wild foods, in small social groups, and with simple technology. Our biology reflects adaptation to that type of environment. Our dietary, health, emotional, and psychological needs were shaped during that time, and the last 10,000 years have not been long enough for humans to adapt fully to the contemporary environment that has largely been created by humans.

Understanding something about the environment in which human biology evolved may help us understand many of the problems we face as individuals and as a species today. But how do we determine what the environment of human evolution was? Certainly information from the fossil and archaeological records can help us with this reconstruction, as can information gained from observing modern monkeys and apes. In their attempts to understand the life-styles of early humans, anthropologists also turn to studies of twentieth-century hunter-gatherer populations who have, until recently, lived under circumstances roughly similar to those of our Paleolithic ancestors. The groups most extensively studied include the San of South Africa, the Australian

Many scholars believe that studies of contemporary hunters and gatherers, such as these Kalahari San men, can provide information useful for understanding what our ancestors' lives were like.

aborigines, and South American Indian groups. Clearly these are not our ancestors, but they provide for us a "window" into our past.

Many of our biological and behavioral characteristics evolved because in the past they contributed to adaptation, but they may be maladaptive today. An example is our ability to store fat. This was an advantage when food availability often altered between abundance and scarcity. Those who could store fat during the times of abundance could draw upon those stores during times of scarcity and remain healthy, resist disease and, for women, maintain the ability to reproduce. Today people with adequate economic resources spend much of their lives with relative abundance of foods. That formerly positive ability to store extra fat has now turned into a liability, considering the number of disorders associated with obesity. Our "feast or famine" biology is now incompatible with the constant "feast" many of us face today.

Similarly, our genetically based "sweet tooth" was once a positive adaptation because it led our ancestors to seek out fruits and other foods that provided needed nutrients, especially carbohydrates. There was rarely an excess of sweet foods (honey was the only pure sugar consumed in the evolutionary past), so overconsumption was not likely a problem. Today, in the presence of great abundance of refined sugars in the form of candy, pastries, and soft drinks, the natural quest for sweets leads to tooth decay and other maladies that were rare in the past.

In the past 10,000 years, the primary challenges to human adaptation have been those generated by human cultural changes. We can thus say that our biology today results from the interaction of both cultural and physical forces. To illustrate this we will discuss in the following sections the interaction of culture and biology in shaping human food needs and the effects of disease on human health. Keep in mind that most of the biological features associated with our adaptations were shaped during the time before agriculture.

◆  ◆  ◆
# Culture, Biology, and Disease

When an individual is exposed to a disease-causing organism (a **pathogen**), what determines whether or not he or she will experience illness or disability? What makes one person become ill with a disease while another person appears to be unaffected? The extent to which one's ancestors have been exposed to the disease

is an important factor. For example, people in isolated areas of the world whose ancestors were never exposed to the measles virus can become seriously ill and die from a disease that seems relatively mild to Westerners. A large percentage of the original Native Americans died from the physical and social consequences of European-introduced diseases within a few years of contact in the fifteenth century. Diseases such as measles, malaria, smallpox, and influenza had unusually lethal consequences in this previously unexposed population. One of the reasons each of us is here today is that our ancestors survived the great epidemics of Europe, Asia, Africa, and the Americas. Those who had genotypes that were unable to resist or recover from those diseases were eliminated during the epidemics and leave few or no descendants today.

Our own individual biology and life experiences also affect whether or not we suffer from a disease. Some people have genotypes that make them less susceptible to some pathogens. Immunities we have built up during our lives also determine whether or not we will get sick when exposed to a pathogen. Clearly, social and economic circumstances affect our health. If we are living in unsanitary conditions or have inadequate diets, we may suffer from diseases that others, living under better circumstances, can resist. If we have the economic and educational resources to receive immunizations and regular medical care, we may be less likely to become ill than those who are unable to afford such care. It is no surprise that, in general, those who are relatively poor and powerless are in worse health than those who have economic and political power. Thus, we can see that both cultural and biological factors determine whether or not we get sick when exposed to a pathogen.

## CAUSES OF DEATH IN THE EVOLUTIONARY PAST

What factors were responsible for most human illness and death in the evolutionary past? Today the big killers of humans throughout the world are respiratory infections (4.3 million deaths in 1991), diarrheal diseases (3.5 million deaths), tuberculosis (2.9 million), AIDS (1.5 million), malaria (1 million), and measles (.88 million) (Bloom and Murray, 1992). Since chimpanzees suffer and often die from respiratory diseases, we can conclude that such diseases also caused problems for the last common ancestor of chimpanzees and humans. Since malaria also affects nonhuman primates, we can conclude that this and some other parasitic diseases

Air and water pollution resulting from industrialization provide challenges to human health today.

would have suffered and perhaps died, but then the infection would have died out as no further contacts were made. Overall mortality was thus low, never coming close to the numbers killed by epidemics of these diseases in the past several centuries.

Another way in which diseases are spread in modern populations is through unsanitary water and exposure to human wastes. This is also a recent innovation in human evolutionary history. Humans in the evolutionary past were generally nomadic, so wastes rarely accumulated to levels that caused sanitation problems. Thus, diseases such as typhoid, cholera, and hepatitis were probably rare or nonexistent in the past. Once people began living in settled communities, human and animal waste products accumulated, creating conditions for the rapid spread of infectious organisms. Awareness that unsanitary living conditions and contaminated water contributed to the spread of disease did not come about until the nineteenth century. In the intervening 10,000 years, millions of people have died from diseases to which the human organism has only recently been exposed. Infectious diseases were probably the major source of natural selection on human populations during that time, as they are today.

Clearly cultural practices related to hygiene and living conditions have a great impact on the origin and spread of human diseases. There are other ways in which cultural traditions affect disease patterns. For example, building houses above the flight ceiling of mosquitoes can prevent or slow the spread of malaria in areas of the world where the disease is present. Market visiting patterns may have contributed to the spread of the bubonic plague in thirteenth-century Europe. Child-rearing practices, such as whether or not children are allowed to play on the ground, affect disease distribution. And, of course, medical systems are cultural traditions that affect the spread and impact of disease.

There is no question that people today are living longer and healthier lives than their ancestors did. Improved living conditions and medical advancements are, in part, responsible for current patterns of illness and death. As noted above, the major causes of death are still the infectious diseases. But people in technologically advanced societies are dying from "diseases of civilization" that occur as a result of two factors: (1) incompatibility of our current life-styles with the environments in which we evolved; and (2) diseases of aging that are now appearing, having been "uncovered by preventing earlier causes of mortality" (Williams and Nesse, 1991:14). We will discuss these diseases of civilization further at the end of this chapter.

affected humans in the evolutionary past. Many other contagious diseases, however, such as measles, tuberculosis, smallpox, bubonic plague, and various influenza strains, originally were diseases of now-domesticated animals, so we can conclude that they have been problems for humans only in the last 10,000 years. Only when people began living in settled villages did they come in frequent contact with the animals that were responsible for the spread of many contagious diseases.

Most contagious diseases, by their very nature, also require a certain number of people in order to survive. Humans in the evolutionary past most likely lived in small bands, similar in size to those observed by anthropologists in hunter-gatherer communities today and in chimpanzee and monkey troops. If an infectious agent appeared in one of those bands, the people in that group

## Nutritional Adaptation

Our nutritional needs have co-evolved with the types of food that were available to our ancestors throughout our evolutionary history. Since the earliest mammals and the first primates were probably insect eaters, we inherited our ability to digest or **metabolize** animal protein from them. The Eocene primates evolved the ability to metabolize most vegetable material. Our ape-like ancestors of the Miocene were fruit eaters, so we are able to metabolize fruits. Furthermore, our needs for specific vitamins and minerals reflect those ancestral nutritional adaptations. A good example is vitamin C or **ascorbic acid.**

Vitamin C plays an important role in the metabolism of all food and the production of the energy that we use to stay alive. It is a crucial organic compound for all animals, so crucial that most animals are able to manufacture or **synthesize** it internally and are not dependent on dietary sources. It is likely that most of the early primates (Paleocene and Eocene forms) were able to make their own vitamin C. As the monkeys evolved, however, they began to eat more leaves and fruits and less animal protein so that they were getting plenty of vitamin C in their diets. At some point in early monkey evolution, it is hypothesized that some individuals "lost" the ability to synthesize the vitamin through, perhaps, a genetic mutation. This loss would not have been disadvantageous as long as dietary sources of vitamin C were regularly available. In fact, it may have been selectively advantageous to conserve the energy required for the manufacture of vitamin C, so that natural selection favored those individuals in a species that were unable to synthesize it. Eventually all descendants of these early monkeys (i.e., modern monkeys, apes, and humans) were unable to synthesize vitamin C and became entirely dependent on food sources.

In the human evolutionary past, the inability to manufacture vitamin C was never a problem because of the abundance of the vitamin in the human diet. It has been estimated that the average daily intake of vitamin C during the evolutionary past was 440 mg, compared to an approximate 90 mg in the current American diet (Eaton and Konner, 1985). It was so unlikely that a person in the evolutionary past would consume no sources of vitamin C that we are fairly certain that **scurvy** (the disease that results from a vitamin C deficiency) was an unknown disorder until recently. In fact, it may not have been very common until humans developed the technological ability to remain at sea for several weeks until all fresh food reserves were exhausted. Today it is most common in infants who are fed exclusively on powdered or canned milk that does not have vitamin C added.

Humans also lack the ability to synthesize some of the amino acids that are necessary for growth and maintenance of the body. As noted in Chapter 4, twenty amino acids make up the proteins of all living things. Plants synthesize all of the amino acids, but animals must get some or all from the foods they consume. **Lactobacillus,** for example, is a bacterium that lives in milk; since it can get all twenty amino acids from the milk it consumes, it is unable to synthesize any of them. Humans cannot synthesize nine of the amino acids in the amounts necessary to run our bodies, and we must get those from the foods we eat. Interestingly, the amounts of each of the amino acids we need parallel the amounts present in animal protein (Table 8-1), suggesting that animal proteins may have formed a significant component of ancestral hominid diets when our specific nutrient needs were evolving. The parallel between our amino acid needs and that present in animal protein is another source of evidence that meat consumption may have been important in early hominid evolution, as noted in Chapter 6.

Biologically, most humans can best meet their needs for protein from animal sources, but meat consumption is expensive, in both ecological and economic terms. By combining vegetables such as legumes and grains, we also obtain the nine essential amino acids in the correct

| TABLE 8-1 ◆ Biological Values of Common Foods | | |
| --- | --- | --- |
| | Complete | Biological Value |
| Human milk | yes | 100 |
| Egg | yes | 94 |
| Cow's milk | yes | 84 |
| Fish | yes | 83 |
| Meat | yes | 74 |
| Soybeans | yes | 73 |
| Brown rice | no | 73 |
| Whole wheat | no | 65 |
| Green leafy vegetables | no | 64 |
| White rice | no | 63 |
| Potato | no | 60 |
| Corn | no | 60 |
| Kidney beans | no | 58 |
| White bread | no | 52 |

SOURCE: From Eaton, Shostak, and Konner, 1988.

**Complementarity of beans and wheat**

Adapted from Scientific American

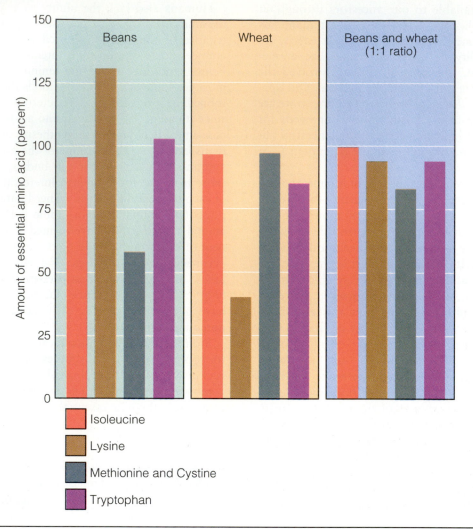

proportions (Exhibit 8-1). (You will remember from Chapter 6, however, that most of the important sources of vegetable protein were not edible by humans until the discovery of fire.) Thus, most populations meet their needs for protein by eating enough variety of vegetable foods that an adequate proportion of amino acids is achieved. Examples of familiar cuisines that reflect these combinations include beans and corn in Mexico, beans and rice in Caribbean cultures, rice and lentils in India, and black-eyed peas and cornbread in the southern United States. These are all examples of how cultural processes interact with biological processes to produce successful adaptations.

Another example of biological and cultural interaction in meeting nutritional needs is seen in the traditional methods for processing corn into tortillas. Wherever corn is a major part of the diet, it is associated with a high incidence of the disease **pellagra,** which results from a deficiency of the vitamin niacin. The exception to this pattern is the Americas, where corn was originally domesticated and where pellagra is not common. The reason for this appears to be the practice of adding lime or ashes to the cornmeal when making tortillas. The additives increase the availability of niacin in the corn so that it can be absorbed by the body. Unfortunately, when corn was exported to the rest of the world

SETTING THE
RECORD STRAIGHT

Cow milk has been described as a "perfect food" by nutritionists and dairy producers. Indeed, its amino acid content matches almost perfectly the proportions needed by humans. For this reason, milk has often been among the foods sent to populations experiencing famine or war-induced starvation. Unfortunately, many adults and children beyond the age of weaning cannot metabolize milk sugar (lactose), with the result that they have severe diarrhea and stomach cramps when they consume milk products that contain lactose. In fact, when the human species is examined as a whole, there are more people who are unable to process milk sugar than those who can consume milk as adults. Using the United States perspective of what is a good food may have resulted in increased misery and even death for some people in regions and times of severe food stress.

after the "Columbian Exchange," the cultural technology was not exported with it.

This example is useful for illustrating the analogy between cultural and biological evolutionary processes. We noted in Chapter 4 that biological traits evolve as natural selection operates on the variability that exists in a species or population. By a similar process, cultural changes often occur as populations invent or adopt new practices that enhance survival. After corn was introduced into the early Mexican diet, it is possible that two traditions existed: one of processing tortillas with lime or ashes, one without. Perhaps those who used lime or ashes were healthier and had more children than those who did not, so that the practice was "selected" and eventually became the dominant tradition. As the people who ate corn without lime or ashes died out, so too did that tradition.

In Chapter 4 we asked whether culture has enabled us to transcend the limitations placed upon us by our biology. At this stage of human history, it seems that we are still constrained by our evolved nutritional needs. These needs reflect adaptation to a food base that included a great deal of variety. Not only did we evolve against a background of variety, we are now "stuck with" requirements for variety. As agriculture has evolved, the human food base has become narrower, leading to the appearance of nutritional deficiency diseases that, like scurvy and pellagra cited above, probably did not exist in the evolutionary past.

The ancestral diet, while perhaps high in animal protein, was low in fats, particularly in saturated fats (Table 8-2). This is because the fat of wild animals is primarily

### TABLE 8-2 ◆ Selected Meats: Protein and Fat Content

| 100 Gram Portion | | Grams of Protein | Grams of Fat |
|---|---|---|---|
| *Domestic Meat* | Prime lamb loin | 14.7 | 32.0 |
| | Ham | 15.2 | 29.1 |
| | Regular hamburger | 17.9 | 21.2 |
| | Choice sirloin steak | 16.9 | 26.7 |
| | Pork loin | 16.4 | 28.0 |
| *Wild Game* | Goat | 20.6 | 3.8 |
| | Cape buffalo | — | 2.8 |
| | Warthog | — | 4.2 |
| | Horse | 20.5 | 3.7 |
| | Wild boar | 16.8 | 8.3 |
| | Antelope | — | 3.0 |
| | Beaver | 30.0 | 5.1 |
| | Muskrat | 27.2 | 4.1 |
| | Caribou | — | 2.4 |
| | Moose | — | 1.5 |
| | Kangaroo | — | 1.2 |
| | Turtle | 26.8 | 3.9 |
| | Opossum | 33.6 | 4.5 |
| | Wildebeest | — | 5.4 |
| | Thomson's gazelle | — | 1.6 |
| | Kob (waterbuck) | — | 3.1 |
| | Pheasant | 24.3 | 5.2 |
| | Rabbit | 21.0 | 5.0 |
| | Impala | — | 2.6 |
| | Topi | — | 2.2 |
| | Deer | 21.0 | 4.0 |
| | Bison | 25.0 | 3.8 |

SOURCE: From Eaton, Shostak and Konner, 1988.

NOTE: Dashes indicate that figures are not available.

| TABLE 8-3 ◆ Percentage of Polyunsaturated Fats in Selected Meats | | Polyunsaturated Fatty Acids as % of all Fatty Acids |
|---|---|---|
| Domestic Meat | Beef | 2.0 |
| | Pork | 9.6 |
| | Lamb | 2.7 |
| | Veal | 4.2 |
| | Chicken | 17.0 |
| Wild Game | Cape buffalo | 30.0 |
| | Eland | 35.0 |
| | Hartebeest | 32.0 |
| | Giraffe | 39.0 |
| | Kangaroo | 36.0 |
| | Warthog | 43.0 |
| | Caribou | 22.0 |
| | Grouse | 60.0 |

SOURCES: Domestic Meat section of Table XII from Watt, B. K., Merrill, A. L., *Composition of Foods.* Agriculture Handbook No. 8, U.S. Dept. of Agriculture, Washington, D.C., 1975. From Eaton, Shostak, and Konner, 1988.

unsaturated (Table 8-3). The diet was also high in complex carbohydrates, including fiber, low in salt, and high in calcium. We do not need to be reminded that the contemporary American diet has the opposite configuration of the one just described. It is high in saturated fats and salt and low in complex carbohydrates, fiber, and calcium (Table 8-4). There is very good evidence that many of today's diseases in the industrialized countries are related to the lack of fit between our diet today and the one with which we evolved (Eaton, Shostak, and Konner, 1988).

The dietary problems faced by people in the developing countries are often quite different from the ones described above. Certainly many people in all parts of the world, both industrialized and developing, suffer from inadequate supplies of foods of any quality. We read daily of thousands dying from starvation due to drought, warfare, or political instability. Some people may be able to obtain adequate calories but do not get sufficient protein to maintain optimal health. It is estimated that in the developing world 25 percent of the population gets insufficient protein.

Deficiencies of specific nutrients are common in some parts of the world. **Beriberi,** caused by a deficiency of the vitamin thiamine, is the fourth-leading cause of death in the Philippines. It is associated with the refined rice diet common in the Philippines. Ironically, unrefined rice is an excellent source of thiamine, but the thiamine is removed with processing. This is an example of how cultural values may undermine biological adaptations. That is, refined white rice is seen as more pure and of higher social value than the more nutritious unrefined rice. Similarly, refined white bread was once more valued in the United States than unrefined whole wheat bread.

Mineral deficiencies are also common today. Iron-deficiency anemia, for example, is a leading cause of pregnancy complications in many parts of the world, including the United States. Insufficient iodine causes **goiter** in adults and **cretinism** (a form of mental retardation) in infants whose mothers were deprived during pregnancy.

| TABLE 8-4 ◆ Late Paleolithic, Contemporary American, and Recently Recommended Dietary Composition | Late Paleolithic Diet | Contemporary Diet | Recent Recommendations |
|---|---|---|---|
| Total dietary energy (%) | | | |
| Protein | 33 | 12 | 12 |
| Carbohydrate | 46 | 46 | 58 |
| Fat | 21 | 42 | 30 |
| Alcohol | ~0 | (7–10) | — |
| P:S ratio | 1.41 | 0.44 | 1 |
| Cholesterol (mg) | 520 | 300–500 | 300 |
| Fiber (gm) | 100–150 | 19.7 | 30–60 |
| Sodium (mg) | 690 | 2,300–6,900 | 1,000–3,300 |
| Calcium (mg) | 1500–2000 | 740 | 800–1,500 |
| Ascorbic acid (mg) | 440 | 90 | 60 |

SOURCE: From Eaton, Shostak, and Konner, 1988.

In summary, our nutritional needs were shaped in an environment that included times of scarcity alternating with times of abundance. The variety of foods consumed was so great that nutritional deficiency diseases were rare. Meat was probably an important part of the diet in many parts of the world, but, because the meat was low in fats, the negative effects of high meat intake that we see today did not occur. Our diet today is often incompatible with the needs that evolved in the millions of years preceding the development of agriculture. The consequences of that incompatibility include both starvation and obesity.

## ASSESSING THE HEALTH OF PAST POPULATIONS

So far we have been discussing nutritional needs and disease patterns that can be inferred from knowledge of how pathogens act and what we assume about past human environments. Do we have any direct evidence of health and disease in past populations? A number of diseases and disorders leave a record in the skeleton. Nutritional stress, for example, can be observed in skeletal remains (Ortner and Putschar, 1981). Cases of scurvy, resulting from deficiency of vitamin C, and rickets, resulting from deficiency of vitamin D, both leave records in skeletal remains. **Osteoporosis,** caused by calcium deficiency, and anemia, resulting from iron deficiency, also leave traces in the skeleton.

Recent techniques for assessing trace minerals in the skeleton are also useful in determining diet adequacy in the past. **Harris lines,** observable in arm and leg bones, are evidence of arrested growth, which often results from malnutrition or disease. Several infectious diseases manifest themselves in the skeleton, including tuberculosis, syphilis, and leprosy. Malignant and benign tumors leave records in bone. Evidence of cavities and gum disease can be seen in teeth. As expected, there is very little evidence of stresses from nutritional deficiencies and contagious diseases in remains of people who lived as hunter-gatherers.

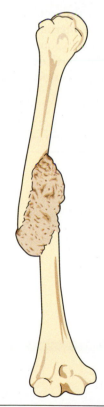

Many diseases and disorders leave their mark in the human skeleton. This is an example of a poorly healed upper arm (humerus) fracture.

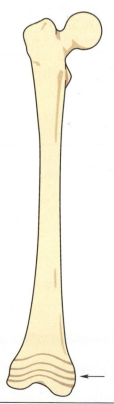

The arrow points to Harris lines on this upper leg bone (femur). These indicate periods of growth interruption, resulting from malnutrition or disease.

# Anthropology of the Life Cycle

Examination of the human life cycle is a good way to look at the interaction of culture and biology. Life cycle stages are often determined by biological events, but each is played out in a cultural context that defines and characterizes it. For example, puberty is marked in girls by the first menstruation. But what that means to an individual girl is greatly influenced by the cultural context in which she lives. For some it may mean going into seclusion for several weeks or months; for others it may mean that they can now marry. Whatever new restrictions or new freedoms are associated with the first menstruation, they are entirely culturally determined.

Anthropologists have coined the phrase "life crisis event" to describe biocultural transitions in the life cycle that typically have social significance. The "universal" life crisis events (those that are recognized in almost every culture studied) are birth, puberty, marriage, and death. Often these are marked or celebrated with rites of passage (see Chapter 21) that mark changes in social position. An example is the rite of passage typically celebrated in association with puberty, which marks the transition from child to adult.

Not all animals have life cycle stages, and humans have more stages than most other mammals (Exhibit 8-2). Protozoa, for example, have only one stage: they come into being, reproduce, and die without any change recognized as a stage. Many invertebrates have two stages: larval and adult. Almost all mammals have the stages of gestation, infancy (the period of nursing), and adulthood. Many, including all primates, add a juvenile stage in between infancy and adulthood. Monkeys and apes have a stage that can be defined as "subadult" or adolescence, during which many adult features are present but they are not able to reproduce or are not socially recognized as adults. Humans have all of these five stages (gestation, infancy, childhood, adolescence, and adulthood) and add a sixth, the postreproductive stage, which is somewhat well marked in women, less so in men. The biological marker of this stage for women is the cessation of menstruation, or **menopause.**

## CONCEPTION AND GESTATION

The biological aspects of conception and gestation can be discussed in a fairly straightforward way, drawing information from what is known about reproductive biology at the present time. A sperm fertilizes an egg, the resulting zygote travels through the fallopian tubes to become implanted in the uterine lining, and the embryo develops until it is mature enough to survive outside of the womb, at which time birth occurs. But this is clearly not all there is to human pregnancy and birth. Female

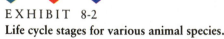

EXHIBIT 8-2

**Life cycle stages for various animal species.**

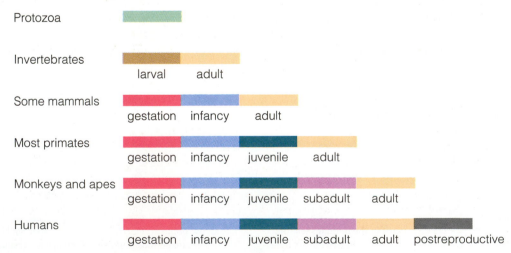

biology may be somewhat similar the world over, but cultural rules and practices primarily determine who will get pregnant, when, where, how, and by whom.

Almost every culture in the world has an explanation for conception, many of which are very different from what is understood scientifically about this event. Most recognize an association between intercourse and conception, although the father's contribution is perceived in a variety of ways. Sexual intercourse may be the mechanism by which the womb is opened up for the spirit of the child to enter. Or the father may provide the entire "seed" of the child, the mother serving only as a receptacle in which the seed matures. There is also variation in the understanding of the best time to conceive. A few cultures believe that it is the mixture of menstrual blood and semen that causes pregnancy. More common, however, is a belief that sexual intercourse during menstruation is dangerous or simply ill advised.

Once pregnancy has occurred, there is much variation in how the woman should behave, what she should eat, where she should and should not go, and how she should interact with other people. The interruption of menstruation is recognized by almost all people as evidence of pregnancy. Once that is recognized, women in almost every culture experience a change in their lifestyles. Relationships with husbands during pregnancy may be changed. In some cultures it is believed that sexual intercourse is necessary for the fetus to grow; in others sexual intercourse may be forbidden throughout pregnancy.

Almost every culture known, including our own, imposes dietary restrictions on pregnant women. Many of these appear to serve an important biological function, particularly that of keeping the woman from ingesting toxins that would be dangerous for the fetus. A good example of a potential toxin whose consumption in pregnancy is discouraged in the United States is alcohol.

Food aversions to such things as coffee, alcohol, and other bitter substances that many women experience during pregnancy may be evolved adaptations to protect the embryo from toxins. Nausea of early pregnancy may also function to limit intake of foods potentially harmful to the embryo at a critical stage of development (Profet, 1988; Williams and Nesse, 1991).

Thus, it appears that our biological heritage includes adaptations that improve pregnancy outcome, but we reinforce these with cultural restrictions that improve it even more (or, in some rare cases, make it worse). This is not to say that every food restriction of pregnancy is adaptive, but it is to suggest that many are likely to be advantageous if they are evaluated carefully. For example, many of the foods forbidden to women during pregnancy are proteins. Common examples are eggs and chicken. These may, at first, seem maladaptive in that proteins are important for growth and development. But they also cause stress on the kidneys, which are already under great strain during pregnancy; physicians in the United States often advise against consumption of excess protein.

Limiting food intake may also seem maladaptive to us, but if the fetus grows too large for safe delivery, death of both mother and child may occur (where it is not possible to have a cesarean section). An infant who is underweight at birth may be at a disadvantage, but perhaps not as great as one who is too large. Even the seemingly odd restrictions, such as not eating a fruit of a certain color (for example, a yellow fruit such as a banana may be associated with a child appearing yellow at birth), may function, at the very least, to focus the woman's attention on her diet, surely a good concern to have during pregnancy.

As noted in Chapter 5, gestation lengths in chimpanzees, gorillas, and humans are very similar, although for other life cycle stages, human lengths are almost twice those of chimpanzees and gorillas. Ashley Montagu (1961), Stephen Jay Gould (1977), and others have suggested that the human gestation period may actually be about 15 to 18 months, but we are delivered "early" in order to be born at all, because of the large size of the human fetal head compared to the relatively narrow maternal pelvis. Extending the gestation period by 6 to 9 months would bring it more into line with what would be expected from looking at other life cycle stages (Exhibit 8-3). Montagu suggested the term *exterogestation* for the period following birth when human infants are particularly helpless, much more so than any other primate. During this time, the human infant shares the growth pattern of other primate fetuses, not of other primate infants. Bone development, for example, looks like that of a monkey fetus, as do digestive enzymes.

Perhaps the most obvious difference between the human and other primate infants at birth is the degree of brain development (Table 8-5). As noted in Chapter 6, the human brain at birth is about 25 percent of what it will be in adulthood, measuring approximately 350 cubic centimeters. By one year, it will have more than doubled in size, tripling by age three. In contrast, nonhuman primate infants are born with brains averaging one-half the sizes of adults of their species.

An undeveloped brain seems necessary in order for birth to occur through a narrow pelvis, but it may also

EXHIBIT 8-3
**Primate age spans.**
Figures from Harvey and Clutton-Brock, 1985, and Jolly, 1985.

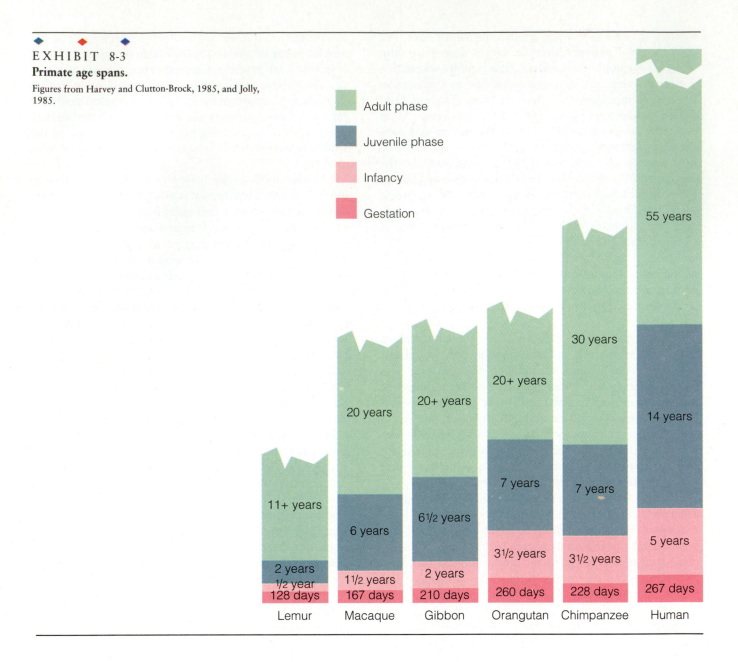

Adult phase

Juvenile phase

Infancy

Gestation

| | | | | | |
|---|---|---|---|---|---|
| | | | | | 55 years |
| | | | | 30 years | |
| | 20 years | 20+ years | 20+ years | | 14 years |
| 11+ years | | | 7 years | 7 years | |
| | 6 years | 6½ years | | | 5 years |
| 2 years | | 2 years | 3½ years | 3½ years | |
| ½ year | 1½ years | | | | |
| 128 days | 167 days | 210 days | 260 days | 228 days | 267 days |
| Lemur | Macaque | Gibbon | Orangutan | Chimpanzee | Human |

be advantageous for other reasons. For a species as dependent on learning for survival as we are, it may be adaptive for most of our brain growth to take place in the presence of environmental stimuli rather than in the relatively unstimulating uterus. This may be particularly true for a species dependent on language. The language centers of the brain develop in the first three years of life when the brain is undergoing its rapid expansion; these three years have been called critical ones for the development of language in the child.

## BIRTH

Birth is one of the "universal" life crisis events that is celebrated with ritual in almost every culture studied. In fact, the relatively little fanfare associated with childbirth in the United States is unusual by world standards. Because risk of death for both mother and child is so great at birth, it is not surprising that it is surrounded with ritual significance. Perhaps because of this high risk of death we tend to think that birth is far more difficult

| | |
|---|---|
| Harbor porpoise | 38% |
| California seal | 50% |
| Horse | 52% |
| Llama | 76% |
| Cow | 44% |
| Galago | 40% |
| Howler monkey | 57% |
| Spider monkey | 58% |
| Rhesus macaque | 68% |
| Hamadryas baboon | 40% |
| Common chimpanzee | 36% |
| Gorilla | 56% |
| Human being | 26% |

◆  ◆  ◆

EXHIBIT 8-4

**The relation between the average diameters of the birth canal of adult females and average head length and breadth of newborns of the same species.**

After Jolly, 1985.

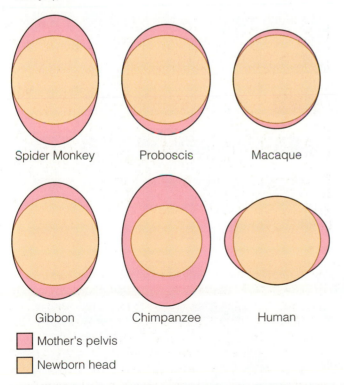

Spider Monkey   Proboscis   Macaque

Gibbon   Chimpanzee   Human

■ Mother's pelvis
■ Newborn head

in humans than it is in other mammals. But, since almost all primate infants have large heads relative to body size, birth is challenging to many primates (Exhibit 8-4).

As discussed in Chapter 6, with the origin of bipedalism, the pelvis was reoriented so that the infant was born facing away from the mother. Other primates are born facing the mother, which facilitates her ability to reach down and guide the infant out of the birth canal. Thus, humans have solved the challenge of difficult birth with the cultural solution of birth attendants (Trevathan, 1987). A survey of world cultures reveals that it is very unusual to give birth alone, particularly to a first child. Even in cultures where the ideal may be to give birth alone, it rarely happens that way (Eaton, Shostak, and Konner, 1988).

Much of the ritual surrounding birth is designed to ensure the health of the mother and infant. Depending on size and complexity of the community, all members may be involved in ritual activities at the time of a birth; or perhaps only relatives will be involved. Unlike the trend in the United States, fathers in other world cultures are rarely present at birth, although they usually have some specific assignment or duty at this time.

Once the birth is over, there is a great deal of variability in what is regarded as proper treatment of the new mother and child. Commonly the two are isolated from contact with the wider community, and the mother is encouraged to spend most of her time with her newborn infant. Certainly this is adaptive in providing her time to recover from the strain of delivery and establish successful breast-feeding. Restricting contact with other community members undoubtedly decreases dangers of infection at a vulnerable time for mother and child.

Where infant mortality is particularly high, it is common to delay naming the child until a particularly stressful time has passed. Often the child is then presented to the community after this time of high risk, and much ceremony surrounds the naming. It is, in fact, very unusual to name a child before birth, the common practice in the United States. This is evidence of our relatively low rates of infant mortality. In many cultures, it is as much expected that a child will die as that it will live.

## INFANCY

Infancy is defined as the period during which nursing takes place, typically four years for humans. When we consider how unusual it is for a mother to nurse her child for even a year in the United States or Canada, this figure may surprise us. But, considering that four years of nursing is the norm for chimpanzees, gorillas, orangutans, and for women in foraging societies, most anthropologists conclude that four years was the norm for most humans in the evolutionary past (Eaton, Shostak, and Konner, 1988). Other lines of evidence confirm this, including the lack of other foods that infants could consume until the origin of agriculture and the domestication of milk-producing animals. In fact, if the mother died during childbirth in the evolutionary past, it is very likely that the child died also, unless another woman was available to nurse the child.

Human milk, like that of other primates, is extremely low in fats and protein (Exhibit 8-5). This nutrient content is found in animals that are never separated from their infants and that nurse in short, frequent bouts. Not coincidentally, prolonged, highly frequent nursing suppresses ovulation (Konner and Worthman, 1980); this helps to maintain a four-year birth interval during which infants have no nutritional competition from siblings. Thus, nursing served as a natural birth control mechanism in the evolutionary past, as it does in some populations today.

EXHIBIT 8-5

**Carbohydrate, protein, and fat composition of milk of selected mammals.**

From Ben Shaul, 1962.

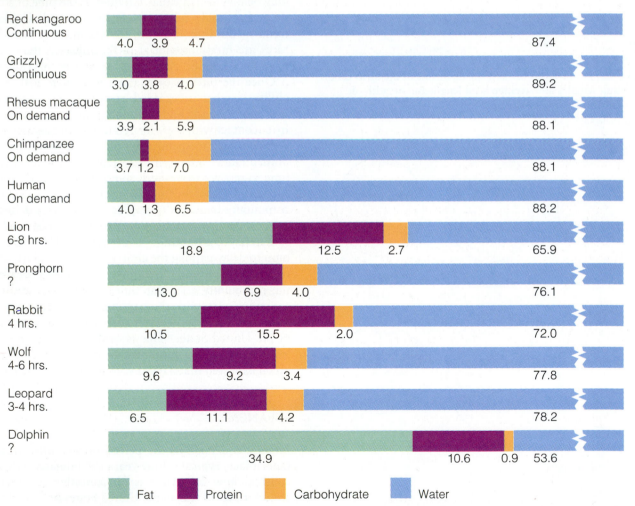

Breast milk also provides important antibodies that contribute to infant survival. Throughout the world, breast-fed infants survive at far greater rates than those who are not breast-fed or are weaned too early. The only exception to this is in societies where scientifically developed milk substitutes are readily available and appropriately used. The importance of adequate nutrients during the period of rapid brain growth cannot be underestimated. Thus, it is not surprising that there are many cultural practices designed to ensure successful nursing.

## CHILDHOOD

Humans have unusually long childhoods, reflecting the importance of learning for our species. Childhood is that time between weaning and puberty, when the brain is completing its growth and acquisition of technical and social skills is taking place. For most other mammals, once weaning has occurred, getting food is left to individual effort. Humans may be unique in the practice of providing food for children or juveniles (Lancaster and Lancaster, 1983). This requires much extra effort by parents, but the survival rate of offspring is much higher than in other primates (Table 8-6). During childhood, the roles of fathers and older siblings become very significant. While mothers are often involved with caring for new infants, the jobs of socialization and childcare often fall upon other family or community members.

Play is a mechanism by which social and technological skills are acquired in many mammalian species. But again, the importance of play for learning and survival may reach its zenith in humans. In small communities, play groups may not be segregated by gender, and appropriate sex roles may not be learned until puberty. In larger communities, play groups are often composed only of boys or only of girls, so gender-appropriate behavior may be learned very early. There is much variation across cultures in what is regarded as appropriate behavior for boys and girls. In general, however, girls are socialized for behaviors and activities that are compatible with childcare. In most societies, there is little segregation by age, as is so typical in the United States, where the institutionalized school system determines who spends time with whom. Anthropologists think that multi-age play groups were the norm in the evolutionary past (Eaton, Shostak, and Konner, 1988).

## ADOLESCENCE

A number of biological events mark the transition to adulthood for both males and females. These include increase in body size and change in body shape, and the development of testes and penises in boys and breasts in girls. Hormonal changes are the driving forces behind these changes; they are marked by increased testosterone production in boys and increased estrogen production in girls. As noted above, **menarche** (the onset of menstruation) is a clear sign of puberty in girls and is usually the marker of this transition in cultures where the event is ritually celebrated.

In humans and other primates, females reach maturity before males do, although they are not usually capable of becoming pregnant until several years after the first menstruation. A number of factors affect the onset of puberty in humans, including genetic patterns (parents and children tend to become mature at about the same ages), nutrition, disease, and stress.

For girls, it appears that a certain amount of body fat is necessary for menarche and the maintenance of ovulation (Frisch, 1988). Both diet and activity levels affect the accumulation of body fat. This may explain the trend toward decreased age of menarche that has been noted in human populations in the last several hundred years, and the tendency for girls who are very active and thin to mature later than those who are heavier and less active. High activity and low body fat also characterize many ballet dancers and marathon runners who often cease to menstruate during periods of intense training.

Since pregnancy and nursing require an increase in caloric consumption, body fat may serve as a signal to the body that there is enough caloric reserve to support a pregnancy. When the levels of body fat fall too low, ovulation may cease temporarily to prevent initiation of

---

TABLE 8-6 ◆ Providing for Juveniles

| | Percent of those who survive: | |
| --- | --- | --- |
| | *Weaning* | *Adolescence* |
| Lion | 28 | 15 |
| Baboon | 45 | 33 |
| Macaque | 42 | 13 |
| Chimpanzee | 48 | 38 |
| Provisioned macaques | 82 | 58 |
| !Kung | 80 | 58 |
| Yanomamo | 73 | 50 |
| Paleoindian | 86 | 50 |

Adapted from Lancaster and Lancaster, 1983.

In many cultures menarche is marked with celebration. These girls of the Ituri forest of central Africa are celebrating having reached puberty.

not ovulatory and define the period of adolescence for them. Adulthood comes with the first pregnancy.

Many human societies celebrate the rite of passage to adulthood with great ritual (see Chapter 21). Often physical marks, such as circumcision, scarification, or change in dress or hairstyle, will define a person's new status. New restrictions or new freedoms come with the new status. Most other members of society recognize the transition and accept the person as an adult. In our society, however, there is great ambiguity about when adulthood is reached. In the United States, for example, we can drive (in most states) at age 16, vote and join the military at 18, and drink alcoholic beverages at 21. Many of us remain dependent on our parents until we graduate from college; others become economically independent at far earlier ages. Some have even argued that one way to decrease the turmoil and uncertainty of the teen years is to have some sort of celebration of the transition from child or adolescent to adult, complete with rights, obligations, and privileges that are clearly defined.

## AGING

It may seem like we have skipped over the most significant part of the life cycle, adulthood. That is, after all, the longest stage of life. But, to some extent, that is what the rest of this book is about. Adults are the ones most involved in and responsible for getting food (Chapter 15), preserving ritual (Chapter 21) and art (Chapter 22), and maintaining the economic (Chapter 16), social (Chapters 17, 18, 20), and political (Chapter 19) systems. Pregnancy and child care occupy at least thirty years of most women's lives in most cultures, as they likely did in the evolutionary past. During adulthood the status of an individual may change as new skills are acquired or new achievements are made. Where such records are kept, status may be defined by chronological age, such as the common pattern of retirement at age 65 or 70 in the United States.

For women, menopause, or the end of menstruation, is a somewhat clear sign of entry into a new phase of the life cycle. This occurs at approximately age 50 in all parts of the world. Perhaps this was only a decade or two from the end of the life span in the evolutionary past, but today, this event occurs when women have as much as one third of their active and healthy lives ahead of them. As noted above, a long period of postreproductive time is not found in other primates. Female chimpanzees and monkeys experience decreased fertility

a pregnancy that is likely to fail. A girl in the evolutionary past probably reached puberty at about age 16 and had her first child at about age 20 after a few years of menstrual cycles in which ovulation does not occur.

Adolescence is that period of time between puberty and the completion of physical growth or social recognition of adulthood. This social recognition may result from marriage, bearing a child, or a particular accomplishment. In primates, the equivalent stage is defined in males as the time from when they are capable of fertilization to completion of physical growth. At this point they have male-specific features and size and are recognized as adults by other members of the social group. Females begin to engage in sexual behavior, exhibiting signs of estrus (sexual receptivity) before they are capable of bearing young. These early cycles are usually in their later years, but most continue to have monthly cycles until their deaths. Occasional reports of menopause in apes and monkeys have been noted, but it is far from a routine and expected event.

Why do human females have such a long period when they can no longer reproduce? One theory relates to parenting. In the evolutionary past of humans, it took about twelve to fifteen years before a child became independent. The argument is that females are biologically "programmed" to live twelve to fifteen years beyond the birth of their last children (Mayer, 1982). This suggests that the human life span in the evolutionary past was about sixty-five years, a figure in line with what is known for contemporary hunter-gatherers and for prehistoric populations.

Postreproductive years are somewhat well defined for women, but "old age" is a very ambiguous concept. In the United States we tend to associate it with physical changes and decreased activity. Thus, a person who is vigorous and active at age 70 might not be regarded as "old," whereas another who is frail and debilitated at age 55 may be considered old.

One reason we are concerned with the definition of old age is that it is generally regarded negatively and is typically unwelcomed in the United States, a culture noted for its emphasis on youthfulness. This is quite different from many other societies where old age brings with it wealth, higher status, and new freedoms, particularly for women. This is because high status is often correlated with knowledge, experience, and wisdom, which are themselves associated with greater age in most societies. Such has been the case throughout most of history, but today, in technologically developed countries, knowledge is changing so rapidly that the old may not control any relevant knowledge.

By and large, people today are living longer than they did in the past because, in part, they are not dying from the infectious diseases. The top five killers in the United States, for example, are heart diseases, cancer, stroke, accidents, and chronic obstructive lung disease. Together these account for 75 percent of deaths (Eaton, Shostak, and Konner, 1988). All of these are considered "diseases of civilization" in that most can be accounted for by conditions in the modern environment that were not present in the past. Examples include cigarette smoke, air and water pollution, alcohol, automobiles, high fat diets, and environmental carcinogens. As noted above, their high incidence is also due to the fact that people are living to older ages because of other factors associated with technological advancement, such as improved hygiene, regular medical care, and new medical technologies.

The final phase of the life cycle, if we can call it that, is death. Humans all over the world celebrate this transition, often with great fanfare and expense. Some people interpret evidence from Neandertal remains to mean that ritual treatment of the dead may go back as far as 100,000 years in human history. Death is a less ambiguous transition than any of the others previously described, although there is great variation in what is believed to happen to the individual after death. There is also variability in mortuary practices surrounding the disposal of the physical remains. Most common are cremation and burial.

In many cultures people of advanced age achieve their highest social status.

## Are We Still Evolving?

In Chapter 4 we noted that culture has enabled us to transcend many of the limitations imposed upon us by our biology. But, as we have frequently noted, that biology was shaped during millions of years of evolution in environments very different from those in which most of us live today. There is, to a great extent, a lack of fit between our biology and our twentieth-century cultural environment. Our expectations that scientists can easily and quickly discover a "magic bullet" to enable us to resist any disease that arises have been painfully dashed with rising death tolls from AIDS in all parts of the world. Drug-resistant strains of diseases we once controlled, such as tuberculosis, pneumonia, shigella, salmonella, gonorrhea and syphilis, are having significant impact on the health of people all over the world. These "new" diseases have themselves evolved in response to antibiotics, a human-induced agent of selection. Scientists believe that the crisis in antibiotic-resistant diseases will get even worse, before it gets better (Neu, 1992). Thus, human innovations are now the major agents of selection operating on our species (and most others) today.

Socioeconomic and political concerns have powerful effects on our species today. Whether you die of starvation or succumb to disorders associated with overconsumption depends a great deal on where you live, what your socioeconomic status is, and how much power and control you have over your life, factors not likely to be related to biology. This also has an effect on whether or not you are killed in a war or spend most of your life in a safe, comfortable community. Whether or not you are exposed to one of the "new" pathogens such as HIV or tuberculosis has a lot to do with your life-style and other cultural factors, but whether or not you die from it or fail to reproduce because of it still has a lot to do with your biology. The 4.3 million children dying annually from respiratory infections are primarily those in the developing world, with limited access to adequate medical care, clearly a cultural factor. But, in those same areas, lacking that same medical care, are millions of other children who are not getting the infections or are not dying from them. Presumably, among the factors affecting this difference is resistance afforded by genes. By considering this simple example, we can see that gene frequencies are still changing from one generation to the next in response to selective agents such as disease; thus, our species is still evolving.

Whether we will become a different species or become extinct as a species (remember, that is the fate of almost everything that has ever lived on earth) is not something we can answer. Whether our brains will get larger, our hands will evolve solely to push buttons, or we will change genetically so we no longer have to eat food is the stuff of science fiction, not anthropology. But as long as new pathogens appear, or new environments are introduced by technology, there is little doubt that the human species will continue to evolve or will become extinct, just as every other species on earth has done.

Culture has enabled us to transcend many limits imposed by our biology, and today people who never would have been able to do so in the past are surviving and having children. This, in itself, means we are evolving. How many of you would be reading this text if you had been born 500 years ago?

## ◆ Summary

1. The environment in which human biological characteristics evolved is very different from the environments in which most of us live today. Because of this, many characteristics that may have been advantageous in the past often have negative consequences for human health in today's world. Examples are the so-called diseases of civilization such as heart disease, cancer, stroke, and emphysema, which occur in part because of the incompatibility of our current life-styles with the environments in which we evolved.

2. Diseases that affect human beings have co-evolved with human biology and culture. Most of the infectious diseases that affect us today (e.g., influenza, measles, tuberculosis, plague) have evolved in the last 10,000 years, since the beginnings of agriculture. Today, cultural practices may be more important in determining who gets sick and who stays healthy than the disease-causing organisms themselves.

3. Human nutritional needs have also co-evolved with the types of foods that were consumed by our ancestors. For example, the human dependency on external sources of vitamin C is related to ancestral diets being high in this important nutrient. The essential amino acids needed in our diets are similar to those found in animal protein. Important vegetable sources of these amino acids could not be consumed by humans until fire was used for preparing food.

4. Virtually all of the major stages of the life cycle are given meaning and significance in cultures of the modern

world. These include conception, pregnancy, childbirth, puberty, and death. Although we can define most of these biologically for the human species as a whole, the cultural interpretations of these events or stages are highly variable.

5. Childbirth is an event in the life cycle that is celebrated with ritual in almost every known culture. Only rarely does birth routinely occur without assistance, in contrast to other primates for whom birth is a solitary event. The human need for assistance at birth is probably associated with the reorientation of the pelvis because of bipedalism.

6. Human infants in the evolutionary past were probably nursed for as long as three or four years, a length of time typical for great apes today. But unlike other mammals, human children continue to receive food from their parents until they are mature. As a result of this practice, far more human children survive than do the young of other species.

7. For girls, puberty is well marked by the physiological event of menstruation. It is also typically marked with ritual in most cultures of the world. For both boys and girls in most cultures, puberty signals the end of childhood and the beginning of adult roles and responsibilities.

8. The human species, like all other species, is constantly exposed to new disease-causing organisms such as that which causes AIDS. Some of the more dangerous pathogens are those that have evolved in response to antibiotics, a human-made agent of natural selection. These diseases, in turn, are agents of natural selection that operate on the current human gene pool. The result is continuing evolution of our species.

## ◆ Key Terms

| | |
|---|---|
| ascorbic acid | menopause |
| beriberi | metabolize |
| cretinism | osteoporosis |
| goiter | scurvy |
| Harris lines | synthesize |
| menarche | |

## ◆ Suggested Readings

Cohen, Mark Nathan. *Health and the Rise of Civilization,* New Haven: Yale University Press, 1989. Cohen argues, as we do in this text, that the shift from hunting and gathering to agriculture did not, in most instances, bring about an improvement in human health. One of the major consequences of the shift to agriculture was in increase in fertility and thus, an increase in world population. The book is written as an essay but has extensive documentation for those who want to consult the primary references used.

Diamond, Jared. *The Third Chimpanzee: The Evolution and Future of the Human Animal,* New York: Harper Collins, 1992. Diamond writes frequently about human evolution for magazines like *Natural History* and *Discover*. His style is very readable and his ideas somewhat controversial. In this book he discusses an array of current topics such as menopause, sex, human longevity, language, and environmental degradation. He also offers his proposed solutions to many contemporary problems.

Eaton, S. Boyd, Marjorie Shostak, and Melvin Konner. *The Paleolithic Prescription,* New York: Harper and Row, 1988. This is a very readable book that cogently argues that adopting a lifestyle more reminiscent of our Upper Paleolithic ancestors may lead to improved health and happiness. Two of the authors (Shostak and Konner) have lived among the !Kung San, a group of hunter-gatherers who often serve as models for ancestral hunter-gatherers. Two (Eaton and Konner) are physicians. Combining their various perspectives has led them to develop a prescription for better diets, activity levels, and child-rearing practices.

Sinclair, D. *Human Growth after Birth,* Oxford: Oxford University Press, 1989. A thorough introduction to growth of tissues, systems, and whole bodies. Includes a review of various factors such as genetic, nutritional, and environmental, which influence human growth and development.

Tanner, J. M. Foetus into Man: *Physical Growth from Conception to Maturity, Second Edition,* Cambridge, MA: Harvard University Press, 1990. Tanner's name is almost synonymous with studies of human growth. This text provides a basic introduction to growth and development in the human life cycle, from conception to death.

## Ancient Keys to Understanding Modern Health

### ◆ Moderate weight loss and exercise affect reproductive function in women

From observations of menstrual cycles of women athletes and ballet dancers, it has been concluded that the training regimen these women are subjected to contributes to suppression of ovulation. It has also been found that women who engage in vigorous exercise (one hour or more every day) are more likely to seek treatment for infertility than women who do not engage in such heavy exercise. Recently, Peter Ellison and Catherine Lager have found that even moderate exercise such as that engaged in by many American women as a result of our "fitness craze" can have a negative effect on fertility. They studied the reproductive hormone progesterone in recreational women runners who averaged about 12 miles (20 kilometers) per week. Even though their menstrual cycles appeared to be normal in length, they were producing less progesterone and for a shorter period of time than is optimal for pregnancy (Ellison, 1991).

Ellison and Lager also found that even a slight weight loss can lead to diminished fertility. They studied the reproductive hormones of dieting women who were losing about five pounds per month and found that they had much lower levels of the hormones necessary for pregnancy. In addition, only 62 percent of the menstrual cycles of the dieters were judged to be normal, ovulatory cycles. The effects continued for a few months, even after dieting and weight loss ceased (Ellison, 1991).

Certainly infertility is not as great a problem for the world as is overpopulation, but to individuals who find themselves to be inexplicably infertile, it can cause great anguish. These anthropological studies confirm that life-style factors may be contributing to infertility in some cases, and that changing behavior may enhance a woman's chances of becoming pregnant. They also confirm that diminished fecundity is adaptive under conditions of stress as indicated by weight loss. In the past, it was adaptive for women to be unable to conceive when conditions were deteriorating. Gradual weight loss is the body's signal that such conditions exist. Thus, anovulatory cycles in association with weight loss and heavy exercise can be seen as normal responses to certain environmental conditions rather than as a pathological state.

### ◆ Can an evolutionary perspective inform modern medical practice?

At a recent scientific conference, several anthropologists proposed that some of the current challenges to human physical and psychological health can be accounted for by the inconsistencies between the environments in which we live today and those in which we evolved. They call their relatively new field "evolutionary medicine" and suggest that by considering the evolutionary history of our species, we may be able to better serve our current health needs.

As one example, consider the mechanisms that the human body has evolved to help fight infection: elevated body temperature and withdrawal of iron. An elevated body temperature inhibits bacterial growth and stimulates white blood cells to act against microbes that cause infection. In some serious illnesses, the body withdraws from the bloodstream iron that infectious agents need to survive. Thus, both higher-than-normal temperature and lower-than-normal hemoglobin (the medical test that indicates the amount of iron in the bloodstream) represent the normal response to invasion of infectious organisms. Clinicians often treat both as pathologies, however, prescribing aspirin to lower temperature and iron supplements to raise hemoglobin. Both interventions may, in some instances, serve to increase the severity of the disease or prolong its duration. The evolutionary perspective asks about the adaptive significance of elevated temperature and decreased iron, leading in some cases to different treatments.

Anthropologist/physicians Melvin Konner and Boyd Eaton suggest that the high incidence of endometrial, breast, and ovarian cancers in Western women might be explained in part by the fact that these women experience frequent menstrual cycling, in contrast to the low numbers of menstrual cycles experienced by our ancestors. Frequent menstrual cycling means high levels of estrogen. In the evolutionary past, the most typical state for a woman was low estrogen—high progesterone due to frequent pregnancies and long periods of nursing. It has been estimated that women in noncontracepting cultures have an average of twelve to sixty menstrual cycles in their lifetimes. This is in obvious contrast to the 360 to 400 cycles that a woman in the United States or Canada might experience if she is practicing birth control. Perhaps women's bodies are simply not adapted to these frequent high doses of estrogen, with the result of increased pathologies as manifested in these cancers. The early developers of oral contraceptives, using observations of Western women, assumed that the "normal" state for a woman was cycling. Thus, they designed the first oral contraceptive to mimic the menstrual cycle with its high estrogen content. Had they recognized that the biologically normal state was noncycling, they may have avoided the early mistakes by designing the contraceptives to mimic pregnancy and lactation, with high progesterone content.

## CHAPTER 9

# Anthropological Archaeology

What do archaeologists contribute to anthropology?

What methods do archaeologists use to study past human cultures?

How are archaeologists trying to protect archaeological sites from destruction?

Archaeologists study human cultures and behavior through material remains. The largest number of archaeologists are interested in past cultures; these include **prehistoric** archaeologists, who study cultures that precede any written records, and **historical** archaeologists, who study cultures for which there are written records. Another group, **classical** archaeologists, study the civilizations of the Mediterranean area. In American universities, classical archaeologists most often work in departments of history or classics rather than in anthropology programs. However, anthropological and classical archaeologists share many methods and approaches to research. Recently, some anthropological archaeologists have applied archaeological methods to the study of modern societies; the best-known example is the Garbage Project, a long-term research project about consumption and disposal of material goods in modern Tucson, Arizona (see Applied Perspective in Chapter 10).

Like all anthropologists, archaeologists are interested in how people live their daily lives, how people understand the world around them, how they adapt to the surrounding environment, and how and why cultures change. For most of the thousands of years of past human cultures, the only way we can learn about these things is from the material remains that people left behind. Although archaeological data often are incomplete and fragmented, they are critical to our understanding of the development of human cultures and to expanding our comparative understanding of human cultures from all times and all places. In order to avoid ethnocentric generalizations about "human nature," it is very useful to have information about past human cultures as well as living ones.

As we saw in Chapters 6 and 7, many archaeological methods are also important to physical anthropologists who study early human evolution through fossilized human bones and associated tools and environmental evidence. Archaeology is one part of anthropology that spans the natural sciences, social sciences, and humanities, because archaeologists share research techniques with geologists, biologists, chemists, historians, economists, and cultural anthropologists.

The circumstances of each archaeological "dig" are unique, but archaeologists share a number of research techniques. In fact, probably the first thing to understand about archaeology is that it includes a great deal more than just digging; much of the important work is done in the laboratory and the library, or just walking over the surface of the ground.

## Archaeological Data

Archaeologists study three major kinds of material remains: **artifacts**, **features**, and **ecofacts**. Artifacts are probably the most familiar: these are objects made or modified by humans that you can pick up and take back to the laboratory. Artifacts include arrowheads, fragments of pottery, bone tools, grinding stones, and so forth. Features are also objects made or modified by humans, but you cannot pick them up and carry them away; they include fireplaces, walls, sunken house floors, or dark stains in the soil where once a wooden post held up a roof. The line between artifacts and features is not absolute, and archaeologists now employ some techniques by which a feature can be taken to a laboratory for further study (for example, by encasing the entire thing in plaster and lifting it out of the ground). But because of their size and condition, features must be thoroughly recorded in the ground through maps, drawings, photos, and notes.

Ecofacts are remains of natural things, such as bones, seeds, and wood, that humans have not made but have used, or that have become associated with artifacts and features. Ecofacts provide essential information about the environment and human use of natural resources. Some ecofacts, such as the bones of a deer, can be seen with the naked eye; others, such as pollen grains that provide climatic information, must be extracted from soil samples and studied with a microscope. In fact, even the soil is an ecofact, studied by specialists called **geoarchaeologists**, that provides information about past environmental conditions. The skeletal remains of humans themselves are also of interest to archaeologists who collaborate with physical anthropologists to study them.

Archaeologists usually study artifacts, features, and ecofacts from **sites**. There is a lot of debate among archaeologists about how to define a site, but in general it is a cluster of archaeological data. Archaeological sites range in size and complexity from scatters of stone tools only 10 meters by 10 meters to whole cities. Naturally, there is a lot of variability in the research methods to match the variability in sites.

The most important thing to understand about archaeology is that the artifacts, features, and ecofacts alone are not the essential sources of information. The key is their **context**, the patterns of association between and among these different material remains. Archaeologists may use the term **provenience** to mean the exact location and context of some piece of archaeological

Although beautifully made, this artifact cannot tell archaeologists much without knowledge of its context or provenience.

data. All archaeologists love to pick up a beautifully made ancient tool, but learning about past cultures requires not only having the object itself but knowing how deep it was, what kind of soil it lay in, what other artifacts were associated with it, what feature, if any, it came out of, and so on. In short, as archaeologist David Hurst Thomas says (1989:13), "This is all that matters in archaeology: objects and meaningful contexts."

## ◆  ◆  ◆
# Archaeological Research

To illustrate some important research methods, let us follow an idealized archaeological project. In real life, of course, very few archaeology projects follow these idealized stages in this order, but most archaeologists strive to accomplish as many of these steps as possible.

## RESEARCH PLAN

The first step is to define the goals of the project. Sometimes the research goals are imposed by the practical situation. For example, the local historical society may hire an archaeologist to discover the separate kitchen building associated with an eighteenth-century plantation; or the goal may be to acquire information from a site before it is bulldozed to build a shopping center. (Later in the chapter we will discuss some of the preservation laws that have been passed to make sure that archaeological information is saved in such situations.) But most archaeologists hope to focus on a set of specific research questions about human cultures in the past, especially about change in human cultures in the past. For example, Kathleen Deagan conducted a multiyear project in Haiti to investigate the process of culture contact between Spaniards and American Indians at the location of Columbus's first settlement and the resulting culture change in both communities. Thomas Jacobson led a long-term project at Franchthi Cave in southwestern Greece to learn about human adaptation to changing environments at the end of the glacial periods. Susan and Roderick McIntosh began excavations at Jenne-Jeno, Mali, to study the beginnings of agriculture and urbanism in sub-Saharan Africa.

Next, these broad questions are broken into more focused questions about such things as the location of sites of the relevant time period, the evidence for architectural style, the evidence for diet and health, and so forth. Each set of questions requires different research methods to recover and analyze the relevant data. Modern archaeology is frequently multidisciplinary with collaboration of numerous specialists. These include geoarchaeologists, **archaeobotanists** (who study plant remains from archaeological sites), **zooarchaeologists** (who study animal bones), **palynologists** (who study microscopic pollen), **lithic specialists** (who study the raw material, manufacture, and use of stone tools), and many others. Classical and historical archaeologists (and, occasionally, prehistorians) will also often collaborate with architects, historians, and art historians.

Archaeological research plans may take several years to accomplish in full, and sometimes they are sidetracked by unforeseen political or practical problems; flexibility is a very useful personality characteristic for an archaeologist. But the purpose of establishing the plan first is to organize the methods and specialists best suited to help answer the research questions.

## RECONNAISSANCE AND SURVEY

Many archaeological sites are located accidentally in the course of farming or construction activities, but for a focused research project, archaeologists will conduct a survey to locate and identify sites in the region they are interested in. The most common survey method is a **walking survey**, actually walking systematically over the landscape looking for signs of past human activity. These may include broken pieces of prehistoric pottery and stone tools, remnants of architecture, ditches, or earthen mounds. The ease and success of walking survey will be strongly influenced by regional vegetation. For example, in heavily wooded parts of the eastern United States, walking survey will often include raking or excavating small test pits (called shovel tests) in order to see beneath the underbrush and leaf litter; archaeologists will often be forced to focus much of their survey on plowed fields where ground visibility is improved.

Survey should always be conducted with good maps. When evidence of a site is located, the surveyors will stop and note their location on the map and evaluate and make notes about the size of the site, its environmental setting, and condition. They may make a **surface collection** of the visible artifacts, which will give a preliminary indication of the contents of the site. All the notes will be labeled in some way to key them into the map and to keep information from different sites separate. At a later stage of survey, larger and more complex sites will be surface collected and mapped in more detail, especially if there is standing architecture.

All archaeologists must grapple with the problem of **sampling** in their surveys. It is rarely possible to walk over the entire region of interest, so they must choose some portion of the landscape to survey and hope that the information from that portion is representative of the entire region. It is basically the same sampling problem that pollsters have during presidential campaigns; they cannot possibly talk to all voters, so they choose a sample from which to generalize. The trick is to choose a representative sample, and archaeologists use a number of mathematical random sampling procedures to do this. It is also true that, in many cases, the sample is constrained by environmental conditions of the region.

Archaeologists also have begun utilizing a number of **remote sensing** techniques to help them locate and evaluate sites. Remote sensing includes methods that give information about subsurface remains without digging. One technique, pioneered in Europe around World War I, is **aerial photography**. Buried remains of architecture that are invisible to viewers on the ground are often visible in **crop marks** (variations in density and color of crops) from the air; sometimes aerial photos reveal shadows of mounds and embankments so eroded that

These prehistoric burial mounds in southern England are clearly revealed in an aerial photo.

they are invisible from the surface. In recent years, conventional aerial photography has been supplemented with various newly developed techniques such as infrared film and radar. These have proved useful in such areas as the Maya region of Mesoamerica, where heavy vegetation obscures the surface of the ground. Pictures from space satellites have also been useful; physical anthropologists often use these newer technologies to identify areas that are geologically appropriate for searching for human fossil remains.

In addition, archaeologists use **magnetometry** and **resistivity** on the ground to discover a site's buried features. The first method uses special probes to measure the amount of magnetism at mapped points on a site; the second method measures resistance to an electrical current in the soil at different points on a site. Both magnetism and electrical resistivity will vary depending on soil moisture, the presence of rocks, the presence of clay walls or floors, and other archaeological features, and can provide a very useful guide to what is under the ground before excavation begins.

The goal of reconnaissance and survey is to gain a general picture of the nature and location of past human activity across the landscape. After a survey, archaeologists hope to have at least a starting idea of where people lived at different times, the size and function of different sites, and the relationship of sites to the regional environment.

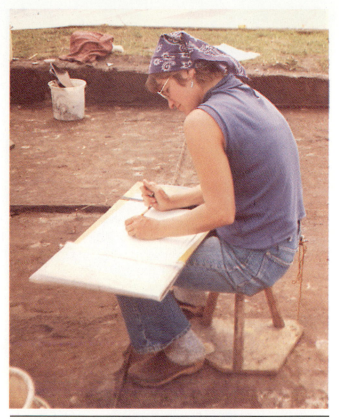

Record-keeping is an essential part of excavation.

## EXCAVATION

After gaining a regional overview, one or more archaeological sites will be chosen for excavation based on the research questions. (In real life, archaeologists often start with a particular site and conduct a regional survey after or at the same time as excavation.) The actual digging can be done with tools as diverse as shovels, trowels, spoons, paintbrushes, and backhoes, depending on the depth and nature of the sediments in the site. But no matter how an archaeologist actually removes the dirt to reveal artifacts, features, and ecofacts, all archaeologists face the same fundamental dilemma: to excavate a site is to destroy it. Excavations are something like experiments, but unlike laboratory experiments, they can never be repeated in the same place.

Therefore, the most important part of any excavation is not moving the dirt but observing and recording the context of archaeological remains. The most important archaeological tool is the pencil! Excavation is accompanied by extensive drawing, mapping, photographing,

and taking notes about everything that is seen in the ground. Today, some archaeologists are using battery-operated, laptop computers to keep excavation records right at the site.

In order to keep accurate records, archaeologists must know where artifacts, ecofacts, and features come from. The most common way to do this is to work within a **grid**. A grid is a miniature version of latitude and longitude, set out with a surveying instrument such as a transit, which divides the site into squares. The material from each square is excavated separately, labeled carefully, and kept separate. The size of the squares will depend on specific conditions at the site. Sometimes, artifacts are individually mapped exactly within each square; this is known as **piece plotting** and is used with special artifacts or in situations where artifacts are infrequent.

The grid provides horizontal control while digging. To maintain vertical control, archaeologists dig in layers, keeping material from each layer in each square separate. Some sites, such as plowed sites in the eastern

An archaeologist studies the layering of a site.

top and are caught in fine screens. Later they will be given to specialists to analyze. Underwater archaeologists have a whole range of special techniques to cope with their excavations; even so, they often do most of the actual digging with their hands. Archaeologists who work in caves have to consider lighting and ventilation. Physical anthropologists excavating human fossils will use detailed knowledge of the geological stratigraphy in their region. They may have to excavate with pick and hammer. Historical archaeologists must often deal with standing architecture that cannot be removed. Each excavation has its own special conditions, but for all of them, record keeping is paramount. Each excavator must also deal with sampling problems that are similar

◆   ◆   ◆

EXHIBIT 9-1
**An Example of Stratigraphy from a cave site (adapted from Thomas, 1989).**

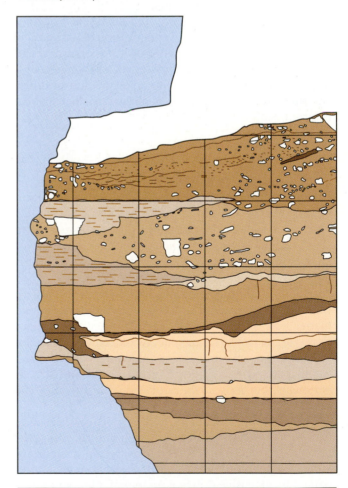

United States, are very shallow and have only one or two layers; others, such as the ancient city of Jenne-Jeno in Mali, may be 5 meters deep and consist of dozens of layers. Where soil layers can be differentiated by color and texture, archaeologists use these natural layers to guide excavation. Where the site does not have visible layers, archaeologists will use "arbitrary layers," often 10 centimeters or 20 centimeters deep. The study of the layering in an archaeological site is called **stratigraphy**, and it is an important key to understanding the dating of any site.

Different archaeological situations call for different excavation techniques. A water separation method, called **flotation**, is used to recover small bones and charred seeds and nuts that provide evidence of diet. In flotation, a soil sample is poured gently into a tub of water, which may be agitated by a sprayer or by hand; the dirt and rocks sink to the bottom and lighter materials such as fish bones and charred seeds float up to the to the ones encountered during survey. Except in rare cases, only a part of a site can be excavated, and a great deal of thought must go into deciding which part.

## ANALYSIS

Although the popular view of archaeology focuses on the "dig," in fact, far more time goes into cleaning, cataloging, and analyzing archaeological remains than actually removing them from the dirt. The analysis stage often involves many of the specialists mentioned above and may take several years. In many archaeological sites, only nonorganic artifacts, such as stone tools and pottery, are preserved. In special preservation situations, such as bogs or dry caves, more diverse organic artifacts may be found. For example, in Mammoth Cave, Kentucky, archaeologists have discovered woven sandals, wooden bowls, and gourds used as food containers (Watson, 1974). Entire sets of prehistoric woolen clothing have been discovered in Danish bogs, to say nothing of actual bodies of the famous "bog people" (Glob, 1969).

**Dating.** No matter what questions are being investigated, one of the first things researchers need is a chronology of the site or sites being studied. As we discussed in Chapter 6 for human fossils, the first evidence for dating comes from the stratigraphy of the site; this is "relative" dating because it can tell investigators which layers or associated artifacts and features are older and which are younger, but it does not provide calendar dates. What is lower down in a stratigraphic sequence is older than what is above it, assuming there have been no disturbances. Based on this principle, Joffre Coe determined in the late 1940s, at excavations at sites in central North Carolina, that notched and stemmed projectile points preceded triangular ones in time (Coe, 1964). This allowed him to put surface collections from other sites in basic chronological order and, therefore, begin to study changes in stone tool technology through time.

Although relative dating through stratigraphy is a useful start, for most problems archaeologists need what are called chronometric dates, or dates in calendar years. There are many dating techniques, most of which require collaboration with specialists in chemistry and physics. Potassium-argon dating, most important for studying the earliest hominid evolution, was discussed in Chapter 6. More archaeologists rely on **radiocarbon dating**, also known as C-14 dating, which is useful for dating material less than 50,000 years old.

Samples for radiocarbon dating must be remains of something organic, something that was once alive. Bones, leather, and wood are all possibilities, but in

Organic artifacts are preserved in rare situations. This wooden box, from the Ozette site in the state of Washington, was preserved in a mud slide.

practice the most common archaeological sample is charcoal. A small proportion of the carbon in all living things is radioactive; after death, the radioactivity decays in a systematic fashion. The radiocarbon laboratory measures the amount of radioactivity in the sample and is able to calculate how long ago this item died. For example, if it is charcoal from a fireplace, the date will give an indication of when people cut down the tree for that fire.

Archaeologists can combine the principles of stratigraphy and radiocarbon dating to illuminate the dating of a site. For example, an archaeologist may find a distinctive kind of pottery in one layer of a site, with a hearth in the layer above and a burned basket in the layer below. By determining radiocarbon dates on samples from the two burned features, the archaeologist is able to establish a date range for the pottery. Then, the date of a second site where this pottery is found can be established even if the second site has nothing organic preserved.

Radiocarbon dating provides a date range, not an exact year; another common dating technique, **dendrochronology** or tree-ring dating, can potentially provide a date to the exact year. Tree-ring dating was developed in the southwestern United States where prehistoric roof beams and wall posts are often preserved. A cross-section of a wooden post reveals annual rings that differ in width depending on the temperature and rainfall in each year that the tree was growing. A master sequence of ring widths has been established for the southwestern United States reaching back to about 100 B.C.; a new sample can be dated by comparing its pattern of thick and thin rings to this master chronology. We know that the four-story Pueblo Bonito in Chaco Canyon, New Mexico (see Chapter 11), was built in several stages during the tenth century from analysis of hundreds of tree-ring samples from preserved roof beams.

There are many other dating methods, including those discussed in Chapter 6. None of them are foolproof, but they are an essential step in archaeological analysis. All of them depend on careful excavation and record keeping. Rarely is the sample the object for which a date is wanted; usually, archaeologists wish to extrapolate the date to associated artifacts or features. Therefore, the exact context of the sample and associated artifacts must be observed and recorded at the time of excavation. Even the most high-tech laboratory cannot give a useful date if the excavation was sloppy.

EXHIBIT 9-2

**Dendrochronology is based on trees' annual growth rings**

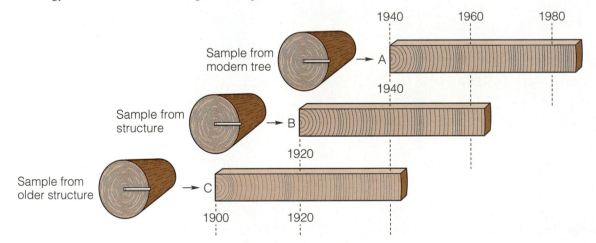

Timber samples from increasingly older sites are matched to create a master tree-ring sequence back into prehistory.

**Classification.** The first step in analyzing artifacts is sorting and classifying them based on shared characteristics or **attributes**. In archaeology, this is called **typology**. Attributes may include length, width, color, weight, thickness, raw material, or any other observable characteristics. Sorted artifacts can then be compared to finds from other sites or other regions or other time periods to begin to understand variations in tools and activities over time and from place to place. Typology is the archaeological equivalent of defining species in zoology and botany (see Chapter 5) and is essential for putting order into the mass of archaeological data.

**Environmental Reconstruction.** In modern archaeology, an important research concern is the relations between people and the natural environment. Therefore, archaeobotany, zooarchaeology, geoarchaeology, and palynology are important parts of research. Together, these specialists study the various ecofacts recovered and try to work out the past environment and the use people made of the environment. They study such things as ancient vegetation patterns based on microscopic pollen, hunting patterns from recovered animal bones, and patterns of crop cultivation from seeds.

**Chemical and Physical Analysis.** A number of chemical and physical techniques are used to determine what raw materials were used to make pottery, stone tools, metal artifacts, and so forth. Some of these techniques provide information about **trace elements**, chemical elements found in tiny amounts in the clay or flint or copper that help identify the quarry or mine where the material originated. This information has proved very useful in investigating trade routes in prehistory. Other kinds of specialized analyses can provide information about ancient manufacturing methods. For example, **metallography** is the specialized microscopic study of metal artifacts that tells about different stages of manufacture such as casting, hammering, quenching, and so forth. **Use-wear analysis** also employs a microscope to study the microscopic scratches, pits, and wear marks on the edges of stone tools, which provide information about the function of the tools.

**Ethnoarchaeology and Ethnohistory.** Historical archaeologists must utilize written documents in their research; these may include old maps, newspapers, or diaries. Ethnohistory is the use of historical sources from the periods of earliest writing or from cases where

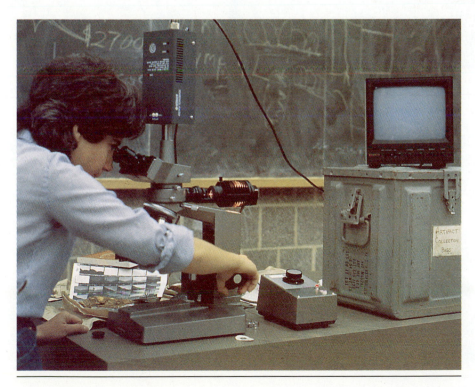

Archaeologists use various microscopic techniques to study the materials, manufacture, and use of artifacts.

people from a literate culture are writing about another, nonliterate culture. For example, archaeologists who research the period of contact between natives and Europeans in North America must integrate archaeological and ethnohistorical information. Ethnoarchaeology covers a wide variety of analytical techniques by which archaeologists study material culture in the present to understand more about the past. One kind of ethnoarchaeology is **experimental archaeology**, where modern investigators try to replicate the manufacture of use of prehistoric tools to get insights into past technology. Other ethnoarchaeologists study living peoples who maintain aspects of traditional life-styles, such as Hopi pottery making in Arizona, to gain insights into ancient cultures. For example, even though Inuit use snowmobiles and guns for hunting today, archaeologist Lewis Binford (1978) learned a great deal about migratory hunting patterns in Arctic environments from them, which he applied to his study of human life-styles in ancient glacial periods.

Other ethnoarchaeologists are interested in the processes by which archaeological sites are formed and modified. They may study trash disposal practices in different living cultures, or the way that flooding affects clay architecture, or other so-called **site formation processes**. Physical anthropologists are also interested in site formation processes. For example, C. K. Brain (1981) has studied how modern African carnivores, such as leopards, collect, crack, and gnaw on animal bones. This helps him understand some of the ways that bones of primates and early human ancestors came to be deposited in South African caves.

Drawings such as these from the 16th century provide ethnohistorical evidence.

## SETTING THE RECORD STRAIGHT

Archaeology can help us avoid preconceptions of our own culture. For example, many people have read Erich von Danikin's books about "ancient astronauts" who allegedly landed on earth in times past and, by advanced and mysterious technology, built the pyramids of Egypt, temple mounds in Mexico, and other great prehistoric monuments. It seems that people believe these fictions, among other reasons, because they do not understand how great blocks of stone or mounds of earth can be moved without modern machinery. This is a kind of ethnocentrism. Several ethnoarchaeology projects show how coordinated groups of people using only wooden tools and ropes can accomplish these building feats. Archaeologist Robert Heizer (Coles, 1973:88) observed 552 men in Sumba, Indonesia, move an 11,000-kilogram (about 24,200-pound) stone block over 3 kilometers (about 2 miles) and raise it with a ramp to form the capstone for a tomb. Experiments were also conducted on Easter Island in moving some of the famous large carved heads (Coles, 1973:94). One head, of approximately 25,000 kilograms (about 55,000 pounds), had fallen off its ceremonial platform. Twelve men, working eighteen days with wooden levers, stone wedges, and ropes, were able to raise the statue onto a stone heap 3 meters (about 10 feet) high and slide it gently back onto its platform.

In another experiment, Mesoamerican men tried digging and moving baskets of earth and blocks of stone similar to the ones in Mexican temple pyramids (Erasmus, 1965). One person, working for six hours in temperatures up to 110 degrees Fahrenheit, was able to carry over 2,500 kilograms (over 5,500 pounds) of earth over a 100-meter (about 330-feet) course. Another person, in a five-hour workday, carried 250 kilograms (about 550 pounds) of stone over a 1-kilometer (about .6-mile) course.

We have lost sight of the strength and skill of coordinated groups of humans working without machinery, but experimental archaeology shows that the great prehistoric monuments were distinctly *human* accomplishments without the involvement of fantastical ancient astronauts.

---

**Synthesis and Theoretical Developments.** Many other analytical techniques could be included here. In the ideal situation, the archaeologist will collate all this information and propose answers to his or her original research questions. Along the way, it may turn out that the research questions have changed as the sites have revealed their evidence of the past. How the evidence is interpreted depends not only on the analytical techniques but on the theoretical perspective of the archaeologist. Some archaeologists focus on the ecology of past human societies and believe that environmental conditions were the most important factor in influencing culture change. Other archaeologists emphasize social or ideological factors over environmental ones. General archaeological theory has been changing rapidly in the past thirty years, although most archaeologists share the goal of explaining how human cultures have changed through time. Archaeological theory has been strongly influenced by theoretical developments in cultural anthropology and in biology, so that evolutionism, diffusionism, functionalism, and structuralism (see Chapters 4 and 12), as well as other schools of thought, have been important intellectual influences at different times in the history of archaeology. Today, evolutionary theory continues to be a strong influence on many archaeologists (Dunnell, 1980), while others are investigating the applicability of

A lithic specialist experiments with manufacturing stone tools.

feminist theory (Conkey and Gero, 1991) and certain literary theories such as deconstructionism (Shanks and Tilley, 1987).

In addition to publishing their findings, archaeologists have the obligation to provide **curation** for the material and the documentation from their research. This means they must provide safe, accessible storage, because the objects and the information may be important sources of information for research projects in the future.

## ◆ ◆ ◆
## Preservation and Legislation

The greatest challenge to modern archaeologists is not the heat of tropical climates, the stratigraphy, or the sometimes bitter theoretical debates, but the increasing destruction of archaeological sites. Throughout the world, archaeological sites—a nonrenewable resource—are disappearing at a frightening rate. Sometimes modern politics takes its toll; the great temple pyramid at Ur in southern Iraq (see Chapter 10) was damaged by aerial bombing during Desert Storm in 1990. In many parts of the world, looting and illicit excavation are destroying sites. Pottery, jades, jewelry, and sculpture from all over

Latin America are being torn out of archaeological context to feed an international art market. The archaeological heritage of many countries in Africa is also being destroyed, and sites and museums in Greece are being looted (Meyer, 1973).

Many countries have laws forbidding uncontrolled and unprofessional excavation of archaeological sites. The most important antilooting law in the United States is the 1979 **Archaeological Resources Protection Act,** which applies to all federal lands including national parks, army bases, and national forests. Several states have similar laws that apply to state-owned lands. In other nations, such laws may apply to all archaeological sites, including those on private land. However, enforcement of these laws may be difficult, especially in impoverished countries of the Third World. The **UNESCO Convention on the Means of Prohibiting and Preventing the Illicit Import, Export, and Transfer of Cultural Properties** is an international treaty meant to prevent destruction of archaeological and historic sites around the world. Although there have been some successes in punishing looters and returning looted material to its country of origin, enforcement of the Convention is expensive and difficult. Furthermore, the United States is one of only a few developed nations that have ratified the treaty. Other developed nations have very active markets for antiquities but have not ratified the treaty.

Archaeological sites are also being destroyed by development and construction of roads, reservoirs, industrial parks, airports, and so forth. As do several other nations, the United States requires archaeological survey and excavation in advance of construction. In the U.S., these laws have opened up a growing area of archaeological research called **cultural resources management** (CRM). A large number of archaeologists are now employed in CRM, and there has been reasonable success in recovering information from archaeological sites before construction destroys them (see Applied Perspective).

There has been less success in saving sites from looting both in the United States and elsewhere in the world. A particularly notorious case occurred in western Kentucky in 1988 where a large cemetery site from the late prehistoric period, about 300–500 years ago, was pillaged for the finely decorated pots in the graves: "Today, Slack Farm looks like a battlefield—a morass of crude shovel holes and gaping trenches. Broken human bones litter the ground, and fractured artifacts crunch under foot" (Fagan 1988:15). Ten men were indicted for desecrating the burials, but the county attorney was unwill-

Looters in Arkansas destroy an archaeological site through uncontrolled and unprofessional excavation.

ing to prosecute; the men were put on one year's probation but paid no other penalty. Archaeologists and Native Americans were outraged; the one encouraging development to come out of this episode is that the Kentucky legislature began considering stricter preservation laws.

Most archaeologists believe that only education will ultimately stop looting of archaeological sites. For those who are fascinated by archaeology, there are opportunities to work responsibly with professional archaeologists in local surveys and excavations. The Arkansas Archaeological Survey, with branches at most universities in Arkansas, has probably the best-known training program for **avocational archaeologists**, members of the public with a strong interest in archaeological research who are willing to work with professionals. Many states have informal programs that are similar. A good place to get information is the anthropology department at a college or university or the State Historic Preservation Office in your state's capitol.

## ◆ Summary

1. Archaeology is the study of material remains to illuminate past human lifeways and contribute to comparative information about human culture.
2. Archaeological data include artifacts, features, and ecofacts.
3. Archaeological research includes developing a research plan, survey and reconnaissance, excavation, analysis, laboratory work, and writing.
4. Archaeologists have a unique dilemma: their major research method, excavation, inevitably destroys their data base. Therefore, meticulous observation and recordkeeping are essential to archaeology. The pencil is the most important archaeological tool.
5. Archaeologists use techniques and theories from biology, chemistry, geology, history, and the social sciences, including cultural anthropology; therefore, archaeology strongly integrates the natural sciences, social sciences, and humanities.

**6.** Archaeological sites are nonrenewable resources, which are threatened by development and by looting. Preservation legislation has created some protection, but the threat to the world's archaeological heritage is still great.

**7.** Archaeology contributes to the general goals of anthropology by expanding our knowledge of human cultures far into the past and by emphasizing the processes of culture change in human societies.

## ◆ Key Terms

archaeobotonist
Archaeological Resources
    Protection Act
aerial photography
artifact
attribute
classical
context
cropmarks
cultural resources man-
    agement (CRM)
dendrochronology
ecofact
experimental archaeology
feature
flotation
geoarchaeologist
grid
historical
lithic specialist
magnetometry
metallography
palynologist

piece plotting
prehistoric
provenience
radiocarbon dating
remote sensing
resistivity
sampling
site formation processes
sites
stratigraphy
surface collection
trace elements
typology
UNESCO Convention on
    the Means of Prohibit-
    ing and Preventing the
    Illicit Import, Export,
    and Transfer of Cul-
    tural Properties
use-wear analysis
walking survey
zooarchaeologists

## ◆ Suggested Readings

*Archaeology.* New York: Archaeological Institute of America. A well-written and well-illustrated magazine that covers archaeology from all over the world; written for the interested nonarchaeologist. Send subscription requests to *Archaeology,* Subscription Service, P.O. Box 420423, Palm Coast, FL 32142-0423.

Feder, Kenneth L. *Frauds, Myths, and Mysteries: Science and Pseudoscience in Archaeology.* Mountain View, Calif.: Mayfield Publishing, 1990. A very readable review of "fringe archaeology," with a clear explanation of using the scientific method to debunk extreme theories.

Joukowsky, Martha. *A Complete Manual of Field Archaeology.* Englewood Cliffs, N.J.: Prentice-Hall, 1980. Covers an enormous range of tools and techniques of survey, excavation, and laboratory work; somewhat biased toward classical archaeology, but informative for all areas of the field.

Price, Doug, and Gitte Gebauer. *Adventures in Fugawiland: A Computer Simulation in Archaeology.* Mountain View, Calif.: Mayfield Publishing, 1990. A user-friendly simulation for DOS computers; provides practical experience with problems of sampling, excavation, and interpretation of data.

Smith, George S., and John E. Ehrenhard. *Protecting the Past.* Boca Raton, Fla.: CRC Press, 1991. A large collection of papers on problems of looting and vandalism of archaeological sites and various responses to these problems.

Thomas, David Hurst. *Archaeology: Down to Earth.* Fort Worth: Harcourt Brace Jovanovich, 1991. An excellent short introduction to theory and methods of archaeology written in a personal, witty style.

Although archaeologists study the past, their research techniques are used to help solve problems of our modern industrial economy. Archaeologists are involved in several kinds of environmental impact research.

◆ **Cultural resources management has helped preserve archaeological information.**

Before the 1960s, most American archaeologists were academics or museum researchers and curators; although the government had used archaeology projects to employ people during the Depression, by 1960 there were only a few government archaeologists. However, beginning in the 1960s, the United States passed several important pieces of preservation and environmental protection legislation that created a significant public need for archaeologists. The most important pieces of federal legislation were the 1966 National Historic Preservation Act, the 1969 National Environmental Policy Act, the 1971 Executive Order 11593, and the 1974 Archaeological and Historic Preservation Act (McGimsey and Davis, 1984). Together these acts mandate archaeological survey and data recovery in advance of land disturbance on federal lands or on projects involving federal permits or funding. The goals of the legislation were to identify and protect cultural and historical resources (such as archaeological sites, historic houses or forts, and cultural landmarks) from destruction by federal actions such as highway or dam construction, new military bases, federally subsidized housing, etc. If the sites themselves cannot be saved because of unavoidable needs of the construction project, then archaeological research should take place to save the information from the site.

To respond to this legislation, archaeologists developed cultural resources management (CRM; also known as public archaeology, conservation archaeology, or contract archaeology). This field has grown so rapidly that perhaps half of all archaeologists are now employed in CRM. Some of these archaeologists work for government agencies such as state highway departments or the U.S. Forest Service, some work for special units within universities or museums, and some work for private, commercial companies. Government archaeologists evaluate upcoming construction, administer research programs, and conduct some research themselves. Private or university CRM archaeologists are hired to do much of the fieldwork, laboratory work, and other research. CRM archaeologists share research techniques with other archaeologists and also a desire to expand our understanding of past cultures, but they work under some different conditions than non-CRM archaeologists.

CRM archaeologists usually cannot define the region in which they want to do research; rather, the area is defined by the land that will be impacted by construction. They often work under more rigorous time constraints than archaeologists in more traditional research settings. Those who work in private businesses must have many accounting and business skills in addition to archaeological knowledge (Pastron, 1989). Their field activities

# Archaeology and Development

187

may well take place in well-populated areas and attract public attention, so CRM archaeologists also need to have public relations skills to explain their goals to a curious audience.

Other countries have laws that mandate similar kinds of archaeological activities, although the laws may be organized differently from those in the United States. In Denmark, the decision to create a gas pipeline network all over the country led to archaeological investigation of several hundred kilometers of land prior to digging trenches for the pipeline; more than 1,700 sites were identified, and 250 of them were excavated in some detail. This was a massive undertaking for a country smaller than the state of Maine. Unlike other countries, the U.S. lacks legal protection for sites on private lands affected by private actions. This has led to the loss of some important archaeological sites that were destroyed by an individual landowner leveling land for agriculture or taking other private actions.

There are some problems in CRM research. These projects have become so numerous that curation of the recovered materials is a difficult problem. There have been debates about the qualifications of some CRM archaeologists and the time and budget constraints under which they work. Publication is often underfunded or downplayed in the interests of saving money; this means that the archaeological evidence is not available to other archaeologists or to the public. Some public agencies are trying to overcome this latter problem. For example, the Tennessee Valley Authority conducted over ten years of research in eastern Tennessee prior to building the Tellico Dam; the information was published in a series of technical reports for professionals and in a well-illustrated book for nonprofessionals (Chapman, 1985).

Despite these problems, CRM archaeology has been quite successful in accomplishing the public goal of saving knowledge about past cultures of the United States.

### ◆ Archaeologists recommend monumental markers for nuclear waste storage sites.

The disposal of nuclear waste from industry, hospitals, and the military is one of the most difficult technological problems facing modern society. We are slowly developing techniques of safe burial, using information from geologists and hydrologists, although there is considerable debate among geologists, environmentalists, and nuclear engineers about the efficacy of various techniques. There remains the need to communicate the dangerous function of these disposal areas to future generations. Even if safe means of burial can be developed, human digging or disturbance could cause catastrophe—and the buried materials will remain radioactive for thousands of years. In fact, the Environmental Protection Agency (EPA) has proposed regulations by which nuclear waste disposal areas must be effectively marked to show their danger for the next 10,000 years. The EPA turned to archaeology for insights about what kind of markers would be most effective for this essential communication.

Maureen Kaplan and Mel Adams (1986) reviewed several significant monuments from different ancient cultures in order to understand the factors of size, placement, materials, and inscriptions in creating markers that will be both preserved and understandable for 10,000 years. They considered the pyramids at Giza, Stonehenge in southern England, the Acropolis in Athens, the Great Wall of China, the Nazca lines from the desert of southern Peru, and Serpent Mound in Ohio. They learned, first, that any marking system must include symbols, pictures, and linguistic inscriptions if we are to have any hope of communicating a specific message for this long period of time. For example, the earthen Serpent Mound is quite well preserved, and we recognize it as some kind of powerful symbol—but we have no idea what it says. Languages and writing systems also may die out, but the combination of symbols, pictures, and linguistic inscriptions is the best hope for communicating a message far into the future.

They also learned that natural materials—earth and stone, particularly granite—last the longest. The buildings on the Acropolis are deteriorating far worse than the much older Stonehenge because Greek architecture incorporated marble, which is destroyed by modern acid rain, and metal, which is now corroding badly; furthermore, metal monuments or statues are very often removed for recycling, whereas earth and stone will be left alone.

The Nazca lines demonstrated the need to plan a monument that can be grasped from ground level, for the lines can really only be understood from the air. The overall review suggested that monumental markers should be at least twice human height in order to be effectively noticeable. Kaplan and Adams propose a set of stone monoliths, each inscribed with repeated symbols, pictures, and language, as the best marker. They also proposed subsurface markers of brightly colored, high-fired pottery impressed with the messages; we have archaeological evidence that pottery can last in the ground for at least 8,000 years, and it stands out from the soil better than stone.

No marking system has yet been instituted in part because the federal government has not yet solved all the technological and political problems of creating a nuclear waste disposal site. In 1990, another working group of anthropologists, archaeologists, and linguists was convened to consider the marking problem specifically for the Waste Isolation Pilot Plant (WIPP) now being excavated in the desert of southern New Mexico (Williams, 1992). This new task force is grappling with the same issues of durability and understandability over 10,000 years. One proposal suggests incorporating pictographs of stick figures, because simplified human stick figures have been used in human art for a very long time and remain understandable. But all of the participants worry that long-term culture changes will make any messages indecipherable, and an interesting monument might attract attention rather than repel it. Until the WIPP is declared safe and open for deliveries, archaeologists and others will be working on this problem.

## CHAPTER 10

# The Great Transformations of Prehistory

What is the archaeological evidence for the development of agriculture and urbanism in ancient human societies?

Why did human beings develop these new economic and social patterns?

What were the effects of the Neolithic and Urban Revolutions on daily life?

In the previous chapter, we noted that archaeologists are anthropologists especially interested in investigating how and why cultures change. We have already described some of the major changes in tool technology, life-style, and other cultural practices during the Paleolithic (Chapters 6 and 7). During those several thousand years, humans lived in small, mobile family groups that hunted, fished, gathered, and collected wild plants and animals for food. In some areas, including much of Europe, large game species were the major basis of subsistence; with the end of the glacial period between 12,000 and 10,000 years ago, climate change caused the extinction or migration of many of these species and people began hunting, gathering, and fishing smaller and more diverse animal and plant species. Elsewhere, diverse wild resources were exploited throughout the Paleolithic.

But today, very few humans (perhaps .0001 percent) live this **foraging** life-style (see Chapter 15). Most people rely on domesticated crops and animals and live in permanent villages, towns, and cities. Archaeologist V. Gordon Childe popularized the terms **Neolithic Revolution** and **Urban Revolution** to label the processes by which these major subsistence and life-style changes occurred. In this chapter, we review the archaeological evidence and hypotheses about these major transformations of human culture.

## The Neolithic Revolution

The transition from foraging to farming, or from relying on wild food resources to relying on domesticated food resources, occurred several times independently in human history: in the Near East, Mesoamerica, eastern North America, China, and the Andean area of South America. This important culture change may have also

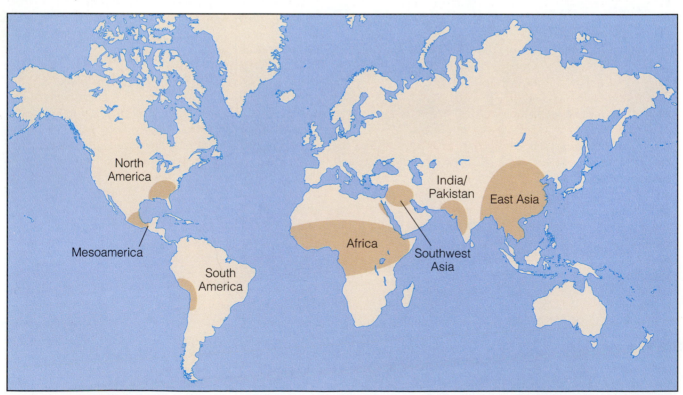

happened independently in the Indus Valley of Pakistan, parts of Southeast Asia, and parts of sub-Saharan Africa (see Exhibit 10-1), but the archaeological evidence is incomplete. Even in places where the Neolithic Revolution was partly initiated by contact with another culture, it is important to understand the local conditions that led to such a major cultural change. This transition involves more than simply changing foods; it is both a major ecological change and a major social change. That is, the Neolithic Revolution involves changes both in how humans perceive and interact with their surrounding environment (including plants, animals, parasites, climate, and land) and how humans interact with other humans. In this chapter, we will focus on the Neolithic Revolution in the Near East because the archaeological evidence is richest for this area. For purposes of comparison, we will briefly discuss Mesoamerica, but keep in mind that the Neolithic Revolution had different developmental patterns in different parts of the world.

## THE "NEOLITHIC PACKAGE"

In earlier analyses of the Neolithic Revolution, archaeologists, anthropologists, and historians focused on a set of material characteristics that were thought to be necessary to qualify a society as agricultural. These are (1) grinding stones, such as mortars and pestles, to process grains; (2) evidence, such as permanent architecture, of year-round occupation of villages; (3) the presence of domesticated food resources; and (4) pottery. This is the **Neolithic package,** the assumption being that these new material items developed together as a result of change in food resources. One implication of this idea was that if archaeologists found only one or two of these characteristics in an archaeological site, they could assume that the prehistoric people were living a Neolithic style of life. Given that plant remains are relatively more difficult to recover than grinding stones or pottery, the latter were often taken as markers of the Neolithic Revolution. However, intensive archaeological research in the Near East and Mesoamerica since World War II, accompanied by use of flotation for recovery of plant remains, shows that the Neolithic package is not a unitary package at all; indeed, in the Near East, there are perhaps 5000 years between the introduction of the first part of the package and the last part. Furthermore, the pattern is different in Mesoamerica than in the Near East. This reminds us that the Neolithic Revolution is a *process,* not an event, that led to major changes in all aspects of human life-style.

## THE NEOLITHIC REVOLUTION IN THE NEAR EAST—THE FERTILE CRESCENT

Humans have lived in the Near East since at least the time of *Homo erectus* (see Chapter 6). Much of the Near East is semiarid and was so in ancient times, although the exact climatic conditions were somewhat different at various past times than they are now. The changes we call the Neolithic Revolution particularly took place within a large arc-shaped area of land, including parts of what are now Israel, Jordan, Lebanon, Syria, southern Turkey, northern Iraq, and western Iran (see Exhibit 10-2). This area, called the Fertile Crescent, is comprised of moderately well-watered foothills between the high, cold mountains of the Taurus, Zagros, and other ranges and the harsh, dry central Arabian desert. Botanists and zoologists have demonstrated that this is also the area where several important wild species, including wheat, barley, legumes (peas and lentils), sheep, and goats, have their natural homeland; these are the species that became the basis of the new agricultural subsistence.

The first relevant sites are in the Levant (what is today Israel, Lebanon, Jordan, and parts of Syria) and date to about 14,500 to 13,000 years ago, which is called the Kebaran period or culture in this region. The sites are relatively small, open-air campsites, made by people who used microlithic flint tools set into bone or wood handles and hunted deer, gazelle, and wild boar. Although there is little direct evidence about the plant foods, people during this time probably gathered many different kinds of seeds and fruits. An important addition to material culture was made in the Kebaran: mortars and pestles, the first grinding stones for processing plant foods such as nuts and grains. This is the first part of the Neolithic package and suggests increased use of plant foods in the diet, possibly associated with increased rainfall in the region as indicated in the pollen and geological evidence from this time period (Bar Yosef and Belfer-Cohen, 1992).

The period of about 13,000 to 10,500 years ago is called the **Natufian** period or culture in this region. Various kinds of environmental evidence show that the wet and dry seasons became more sharply differentiated. Such a climate encourages *annual* plants such as wild grasses, weedy plants, and others; these are precisely the kinds of plants that became the major domesticated crops. During the Natufian, some caves were occupied, and people also lived in open-air sites. Some of these open-air sites have evidence of permanent occupation: (1) round houses with stone foundations and plaster

EXHIBIT 10-2
**The Fertile Crescent**

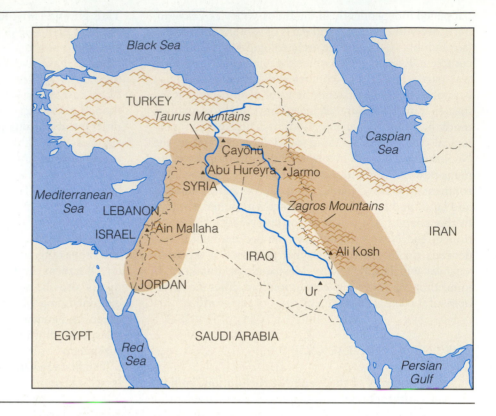

EXHIBIT 10-3
**Stone foundations of round houses at the Natufian site of Ain Mallaha**

(adapted from J. Perrot, *L'Anthropologie*, vol. 7, 1966)

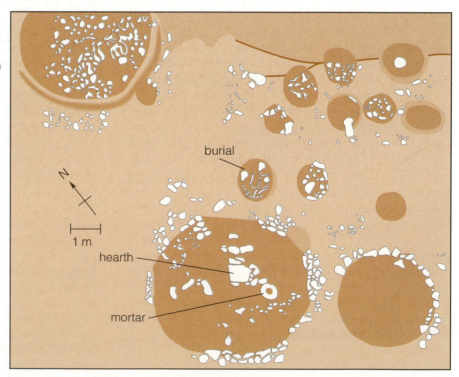

floors; (2) the first evidence of cemeteries (not the first burials, but the first repeated use of one locale for burials); (3) storage pits; and (4) the bones of mice and rats, pests that are found in permanent settlements. This evidence, suggesting **sedentism** (living year-round in one place) is the second part of the Neolithic package. The Natufian site of Ain Mallaha in southern Israel also contains interesting evidence of contacts between its community and distant places: small amounts of obsidian from volcanic areas of Turkey and shells from the Nile valley of Egypt are found there.

So far, there has been little successful use of flotation at Natufian sites, but we nevertheless can tell that grains were an important part of the diet. This is shown by the rich collection of grinding stones from Natufian sites, the frequent presence of stone blades used as sickles for harvesting, and the heavy wear on the skeletons' teeth, which comes from eating stone-ground grains. The existing evidence shows that all the grain was genetically wild and not domesticated, and analysis of the animal bones shows that gazelle was still the main source of meat. So, people in Natufian communities could technically be called "foragers" because they were living on gathered and hunted wild foods; however, the richness of wild resources in their habitat allowed at least some Natufian communities to become sedentary in permanent villages that resemble our idea of a Neolithic community. People of this time period were probably encouraging the stands of wild grains in various ways by watering, weeding, saving seed to plant from one year to the next, and so forth. However, human manipulation had not gone on long enough or intensively enough yet to lead to the genetic changes in crops that we call **domestication.**

Toward the end of the Natufian, developments similar to those in the Levant began to appear in other parts of the Near East. Two sites in northern Syria, Mureybit and Abu Hureyra, provide evidence of increasing use of wild wheat and barley around this time and permanent architecture somewhat later. Around 10,300 years ago, true domesticated grains appear in archaeological sites in the Levant for the first time; this may be associated with a short but severe dry period. Domesticated food resources are the third part of the Neolithic package. By 9,500 years ago, domesticated wheat, barley, peas, and lentils were cultivated in many parts of the Near East; around the same time, domesticated sheep and goats replaced gazelles and other wild game as the major source of meat. Later, pigs and cattle were added to the domesticated animals; after this time, animals gradually became as important for their wool, milk, manure, and ability to pull vehicles as for meat.

Sickles were made of microlithic blades set in bone or wood handles.

About 8,500 years ago, people in the Near East began using pottery vessels for storing, cooking, and serving food.

The final part of the Neolithic package, handmade pottery, was added to the material culture of the area about 8,500 years ago. Clay was certainly used earlier, both for building houses and making small figurines, but ceramic vessels appeared almost 6,000 years after the first signs of the Neolithic Revolution. The development of pottery probably marks changes in styles of cooking with more emphasis on stews and porridges and less on roasted meat. Pottery vessels probably also made carrying and storing water easier than before.

## A NEOLITHIC VILLAGE 8,000 YEARS AGO

The site of **Jarmo** in northern Iraq was excavated in the 1950s by a team led by Robert and Linda Braidwood. The excavations at Jarmo were important early contributions to multidisciplinary study of the Neolithic. Jarmo exemplifies a small Neolithic village in the Near East. People lived in permanent, clay-walled houses of square rooms clustered together to make an apartment-like dwelling. Numerous stone tools, including sickles, and plentiful bone tools were used for everyday tasks. Grinding stones and underground storage pits were used to process and store the grain harvest. Impressions of baskets found on clay floors or inside storage pits gave evidence of that technology, while the presence of loom and spindle weights tells us indirectly about production of cloth. The earlier occupants of Jarmo used polished stone bowls, but no pottery. Later, the pottery was mostly plain or decorated with simple geometric designs. Clay was also used to make small figurines of animals and humans. These may have had a ritual function, although this is difficult to tell. The plant and animal remains demonstrate a mixed farming and herding economy along with the hunting and gathering of a minor amount of wild foods. Although the people of Jarmo were probably mostly self-sufficient in their subsistence, they did have contacts with people in distant places as is shown by the presence of obsidian from sources in eastern Turkey.

While many people in the Near East lived in small, homogenous agricultural villages like Jarmo, other early Neolithic communities were more complex in architecture and material culture (Voigt, 1990). For example, at Çayönü in eastern Turkey there were large buildings with stone foundations that seem to have had special functions. One was decorated with an elaborate terrazzo (mosaic of polished pebbles and flagstones) floor and a large stone slab with a human head carved on it. Another contained piles of human bones. These buildings seem to have been communal ceremonial buildings of some kind, much more elaborate than architecture at Jarmo. Other early Neolithic sites show evidence of craft specialization, and some were considerably larger than Jarmo. So, while many Neolithic sites were small villages, others began developing social and economic complexity.

## THE NEOLITHIC REVOLUTION IN THE NEW WORLD

We have focused on the Near East where archaeological evidence about the Neolithic Revolution is rich. Agriculture and village life developed in the Americas independently from the Old World (the term "Neolithic Revolution" is not used frequently in American archaeology, but the process was similar). Our best evidence for this transition comes from the semiarid upland areas of central Mexico and from dry parts of coastal and highland Peru where preservation of plant and animal remains is much better than in the moist tropical areas of Latin America.

In Mesoamerica, the process seems to have begun around 9,000 years ago, and sedentary, pottery-using villages appeared by 4,300 years ago. As in the Near East, the staple domesticated crops included a grain and a legume; in Mesoamerica, the grain was maize (more familiarly called corn) and the legumes were beans of various kinds. Other early domesticated crops in Mesoamerica were gourds and squashes (including what we call pumpkin) as well as peppers, avocado trees, and, somewhat later, cotton.

Also as in the Near East, in Mesoamerica pottery was the last part of the Neolithic package, appearing only after many generations of experimentation with domesticated crops. However, there are two major differences in the process of the Neolithic Revolution between Mesoamerica and the Near East. First, there is little or no evidence from archaeological sites in Mexico that sedentism preceded the use of domesticated crops. There are no sites like the Natufian ones in the Levant that show a combination of genetically wild foods and permanent architecture and cemeteries. (The situation was different in coastal Peru where there is evidence of people in sedentary villages exploiting the rich marine foods, with little cultivation [Pearsall, 1992]). The archaeological evidence in Mexico is still incomplete enough that our understanding of the relationship between sedentism and domestication may change with future excavations.

The second contrast between Mesoamerica and the Near East is more significant: animals were not domesticated for food in Mesoamerica. Although there were domesticated dogs (and these were eaten in some periods), no sheep, goats, cattle, or pigs lived in the Americas until after contact with Europeans. So, hunting remained important for providing meat, and there was no development of wheeled vehicles or plows, which depend on draft animals. In Peru, llamas were domesticated and used sometimes for food; more often, they were used as pack animals or were sheared to supply

fiber for textiles. The lack of domesticated animals in many parts of the Americas probably had significant nutritional impact on populations at different times. Corn and beans together (as in refried beans wrapped in a tortilla) provide a complete protein, but lack of animal protein may have been a problem in some cultural periods.

By 3,500 years ago or earlier, in what is called the Formative Period in Mesoamerica, people lived in permanent villages, grew domesticated crops, worked with chipped stone and bone tools, prepared their corn with grinding stones called manos and metates, and made pottery that could be decorated with painted or incised designs. People were sometimes buried with food offerings, a few pots, and some jade beads. By this time in most parts of Mesoamerica, a few settlements were larger than their neighbors and may have included a public building built on a low mound in the center of the community; these are the first signs of increasing social complexity. Before we can go on to discuss the evolution of cities from these smaller communities, we need to consider some of the theoretical debate about the Neolithic Revolution.

## THEORIES AND EXPLANATIONS ABOUT THE NEOLITHIC REVOLUTION

The biggest question for anthropologists about the Neolithic Revolution is, why? Why did human populations in several different parts of the world gradually change

Llamas were domesticated in prehistory in the Andes. They were used more for transportation and wool than for meat.

their subsistence strategy from gathering, collecting, and hunting to cultivating domesticated crops and (in some places) herding domesticated animals? At one time, no one worried about this question; it was simply assumed that a sedentary, agricultural way of life was intrinsically better than a foraging life. Therefore, it was assumed that people made the change as soon as they had evolved enough intelligence to escape the hungry, wandering life of hunters and gatherers. However, our knowledge of human evolution (Chapter 7) tells us that fully modern human beings existed throughout the Old World by at least 40,000 years ago, if not sooner, yet the first steps toward the Neolithic Revolution did not occur until at least 25,000 years later; thus, it seems unlikely that biological evolution alone can explain the development of agriculture.

More importantly, we must also consider the ethnographic and historic evidence about foraging societies. These data tell us that foragers are not on the edge of starvation, always struggling for existence, as the older stereotypes lead us to believe; in fact, their diet is often nutritionally better and more varied than neighboring traditional agriculturalists. In modern American culture, we may find the prospect of moving every six or eight weeks disturbing, but many foragers put a positive cultural value on mobility and freedom from boundaries and possessions. And, ethnographic evidence tells us that, in temperate environments, leisure time is often greater in foraging societies than in traditional agricultural ones (this is probably not true of the Inuit in the Arctic). So, a farming style of life is not intrinsically better than foraging, and the question, why a Neolithic Revolution, becomes more difficult, but also more interesting, to answer.

V. Gordon Childe (1936), who coined the term Neolithic Revolution, believed that climatic change was the major cause of the development of agriculture in the Near East. He proposed that a worldwide period of drying and warming at the end of the Pleistocene forced humans in the Near East into smaller and smaller oases along the major rivers of the area, in close proximity with plants and animals. This proximity led to increased human understanding of the life cycles of plants and animals and, eventually, to increasingly intensive human manipulation of these species, ultimately leading to domestication. Childe thought the earliest agriculture occurred in the valleys of the great rivers of the Near East: the Nile, the Tigris, and the Euphrates. He did not con-

Early agriculture was based on human labor. In later prehistoric periods, plows were used in the Old World, but not in the Americas.

duct any field research himself, and it turns out that his understanding of climatic changes of the period was flawed. Nevertheless, his work is important because it brought archaeological attention to the problem. As described above, climatic factors do seem to have played a role in the Neolithic Revolution, although in a different way than Childe proposed.

The Braidwoods, in their excavation at Jarmo in northern Iraq, tried to determine whether Childe was correct about the location of the first agricultural communities. The Braidwoods suspected that the Neolithic Revolution did not occur first in the river valleys where rainfall is so low that farmers must use irrigation to grow crops, but in the foothills of the Fertile Crescent where the wild ancestors of wheat, barley, and legumes grew. Robert Braidwood (1960) thought that after several generations of experimenting with the various wild species, human inventiveness would eventually lead to domestication. However, this proposed explanation does not take into account the information about foragers' life-styles. Why should people give up a subsistence strategy that combines a well-balanced diet with relatively little work? Another way to put this question is to ask what would encourage people to obtain more food.

American archaeologist Lewis Binford (1968), incorporating ethnographic evidence about foragers into his hypothesis, proposed that the encouraging factor was population growth. He points out that the advantage of agriculture is that it feeds more people than does foraging in the same area. In Binford's opinion, human population slowly increased throughout the Pleistocene, and as the good hunting and gathering lands slowly filled up with people, small groups moved away to look for new resources. Eventually, all rich areas were occupied, and the slowly but continually increasing human population of the Near East had to occupy what Binford calls "edge zones," areas with less than ideal food sources. Here, people had to manipulate plant and animal species in order to intensify production, manipulation that ultimately led to genetic changes and domestication. Binford suggested that the earliest agricultural sites would be found not in the parts of the foothills with the richest wild resources but in drier environments at lower altitudes where the wild foods would be less adequate.

Some of Binford's ideas about population growth have been questioned, and sites with early domesticated plants have been found in a variety of environments. However, population pressure is still considered an important factor in many theories about the Neolithic Revolution in the Near East. The evidence of sedentary Natufian villages as early as 12,000 years ago fits in with this theory, because humans living in sedentary communities seem to have more babies that those living a mobile style of life.

The situation was apparently different in Mesoamerica where evidence of early sedentism is lacking. Kent Flannery (1968) suggests that in Mesoamerica the reason to develop agriculture was not to increase the amount of food but rather to increase its reliability. Controlling and manipulating certain plants would allow the human community to overcome problems with unpredictable harvests of wild foods. Reliability and predictability may also play an important role in the Near East; the evidence for population pressure is still incomplete and other factors probably were influential as well. The pattern of change from foraging to limited cultivation to full-time agriculture was probably different in different areas, in part due to differences in available plant resources. For example, wild wheat and barley in the Near East were much more productive than the wild grasses or the earliest maize available in Mesoamerica. So sedentism and full-time commitment to cultivation did not occur in Mesoamerica until the evolution of more productive forms of maize.

In recent years, some scholars (Bender, 1978; Hayden, 1992) have suggested that all these theories focus too much on ecological factors (such as environment and population size) and too little on social factors. They suggest that the first domesticated foods were not staples but special treats and condiments that might be considered feasting foods. For example, in various parts of the world, the earliest domesticates are chilies; gourds and squashes that can be used as decorated containers; dogs and avocados, which are both rich in fats, something that is particularly valued by many foragers; and barley, which can be brewed into beer. All of these could be high-prestige goods that ambitious individuals could use to attract followers by sponsoring feasts and ceremonies. Advocates of this perspective say that this process probably occurred in rich habitats that would eventually attract more and more people, leading to population pressure and the need to apply cultivation techniques to staple foods.

Debate continues about the beginnings of agriculture in different parts of the world. As new field research is conducted, explanatory hypotheses must be modified. For example, as noted above, recent research in the Levant shows that climatic change (which had been rather unpopular as an explanatory factor since Childe's day) probably played an important role, at least in the Near East. The evidence in Mesoamerica is not as clear. But however the transition occurred, it led to profound changes in prehistoric cultures and life-styles. Agriculture certainly allowed populations to increase. Although there is still debate about whether increased population caused the Neolithic Revolution, there is no doubt that dramatic population increases occurred after agriculture was established.

## THE CONSEQUENCES OF THE NEOLITHIC REVOLUTION

Because our own culture is based on agriculture, we ethnocentrically tend to consider the development of agriculture as "progress." Yet, there is archaeological evidence that the health of communities may actually have declined with the development of agriculture and settled villages (Cohen and Armelagos, 1984). One distinctive sign of sedentism in archaeological sites is the presence of bones of mice and rats, which have always been potential disease carriers. In addition, people in settled communities are more susceptible to epidemic and infectious diseases because of crowding and living constantly next to piles of garbage. Skeletons from agricultural sites almost always have more cavities in their teeth than those of foragers; skeletons of prehistoric agriculturalists are also frequently shorter than those of foragers and show higher incidences of anemia and malnutrition.

Thus, nutrition may be no better among agriculturalists than among foragers. However, agriculturalists do have an option that most hunters and gatherers do not: production and storage of surplus. Through manipulation, cultivation, and domestication of plants and animals, humans can produce more than they immediately need. And because they are sedentary, agriculturalists can develop a whole range of facilities in which to store this surplus; these include baskets, pots, bins, and granaries, all of which are found in archaeological sites. The combination of larger populations and ability to produce a surplus leads to a more complex division of labor than is found in most foraging societies. (There are some exceptions among foraging societies; for example, prehistoric villagers in coastal Peru relied on marine foods but were able to accumulate surplus and develop complex division of labor.) Some individuals become specialized craft workers or religious or political leaders. Attitudes toward land ownership also change with agriculture: people become more concerned with controlling land and passing it on to the next generation. The accumulation of surplus, tighter control of land, and more complex division of labor all create the potential for accumulation of wealth and more social stratification within the society. Together, these factors provide the fundamental background for the evolution of socially complex and politically hierarchical societies that Childe subsumed under the term Urban Revolution.

◆ ◆ ◆

# The Urban Revolution

Childe (1950) meant the term Urban Revolution to apply to the development of large, stratified, politically complex societies, which he also thought were always urban societies. We now realize that the development of such complex societies, known by anthropologists as **state-level societies,** may occur without the concurrent development of cities. This cultural development was extremely important in human history. Many Neolithic villages of the Near East, Mesoamerica, and elsewhere were relatively egalitarian communities, largely self-sufficient in their economies, with limited differentials of wealth and influence among families and few formal government institutions; the basis of social and political organization was kinship. Other Neolithic communities were larger and more socially complex, but no humans of that time lived in cities or in highly stratified societies. Yet, today, most people in the world live in nonegalitarian societies with dramatic differences in wealth and influence among individuals, centralized and bureaucratic governments, and economies that rely heavily on distant resources. How and why this transition occurred is one of the most significant anthropological research questions.

The independent development of state societies probably occurred six times in prehistory: in Mesopotamia (what is now parts of Iraq and Iran), in Egypt, in China, in Mesoamerica, in Peru, and in the Indus Valley of Pakistan and India. Again, we will focus on the archaeological research in the Near East.

## THE LAND OF SUMER

As noted above, by 8,000 years ago, agricultural villages were established throughout the Fertile Crescent, and some communities were increasing in size and social complexity. People began occupying the valleys of the Tigris and Euphrates rivers in what is now southern Iraq. In ancient times, this area was known as the land of **Sumer.** Over time, communities became larger, new crops and agricultural technologies were introduced, and elaborate crafts including metallurgy were developed. Stamp seals and clay tokens, used for administration and simple record keeping, are found in many of these sites. In addition to ordinary housing, some of these settlements had public buildings apparently for religious and administrative purposes. Some of these communities were probably **chiefdoms,** societies characterized by some social ranking and differences in prestige, but still fundamentally organized by kinship (See chapter 19). Because the land of Sumer has very low rainfall, irrigation was essential for agriculture to succeed; extensive systems of irrigation canals have been mapped through archaeological survey. Other than rich soil and rivers, Sumer lacks significant natural resources. Consequently, extensive trade routes gradually developed, providing metals, building stone, obsidian, semiprecious stones, and timber. By 5,000 years ago, people in Sumer had clustered into several walled, densely packed cities, including Uruk, Eridu, Kish, and Ur, the last of which is known in the Old Testament as the home of Abraham.

These cities were the first state-level societies in the world. By state-level society, we mean one with a hierarchical, centralized, bureaucratic government based on territorial loyalties, not on kinship. Similar processes were occurring about the same time in southwestern Iran and Egypt, but archaeological and historical evidence is richest for Sumer. It is difficult to tell from material evidence whether kinship formed the basis of political organization, so archaeologists look at other kinds of data to analyze early state societies. These data include settlement pattern, architecture, subsistence technology and economy, record keeping, and burials. Much of the evidence about the early cities of Sumer is archaeological, but some comes from the earliest written historical documents.

The Sumerian cities contained residential areas of densely packed mud-brick houses built around a central walled precinct that contained public buildings. The entire city was also walled, showing an emphasis on territoriality and defense that was missing from earlier settlements. Both archaeological and documentary evidence tell us that elaborate craft specialization in metallurgy, pottery, stone carving, and textiles existed. Farmers used complex irrigation systems to grow wheat, barley, legumes, vegetables, and date palms, which provided timber and thatch as well as the fruit, an important trade item. The irrigation canals also provided fish. Both cattle and sheep were kept, the latter supplying wool for the textile industry. Textiles were another important export.

State societies are intrinsically bureaucratic societies. This means that government is conducted by professional administrators. As we know from our own experience, bureaucrats need records and forms; archaeolog-

Cuneiform tablets such as this one recorded important economic transactions.

ically, this is revealed in the presence of the first written documents in the world. The writing system used in Sumer is called **cuneiform** and it was written by impressing a wedge-shaped stick into clay tablets; later, cuneiform was also carved on stone monuments. (Do not confuse the writing system with the language; cuneiform was used for several thousand years to write several different languages, including Sumerian, Akkadian, and Assyrian.) The cuneiform script, which was deciphered in the nineteenth century, was used by the early Sumerians mostly for economic records of taxes, trade, and other transactions. These are records of a complex, centrally controlled economy. Cuneiform tablets seem to have evolved out of the earlier system of clay tokens modeled into different shapes and often strung together for a simple record of economic transactions (Schmandt-Besserat, 1978).

In addition to writing, Sumerians used carved cylinder seals to label and sign documents, packages, and goods. The cylinder seals were often carved out of semiprecious stones that were imported from as far away as present-day Afghanistan. Seals are found in Sumerian sites a

Cylinder seals, such as this one from Syria, indicate a complex economy and long-distance trade.

more elaborately constructed than the homes of ordinary people. The most important public structure was the **ziggurat,** a stepped pyramid on top of which was the temple to the city's patron god or goddess. The written documents tell us that the temple was not only a significant religious institution but also an important economic institution that owned land, collected taxes, and stored surpluses for the government. Political leaders relied heavily on religious power to strengthen their secular influence. This was true not only in Sumer but apparently in all of the early state societies.

State societies are inherently nonegalitarian societies. This is shown both in architectural evidence of different sizes and qualities of residences, as well as in the early written documents, which tell us about individuals of such differing power as kings, priests, weavers, government officials, potters, farmers, and slaves. But the most striking archaeological evidence comes from burials, which reveal dramatically differing amounts of wealth in grave goods. Many individuals were buried with a few pots holding food offerings for the next life and some small personal ornaments. But the famous Royal Tombs of Ur revealed a small number of individuals buried with lavish wealth in gold, silver, bronze, carnelian, and lapis lazuli—and accompanied into the afterlife by their musicians, soldiers, wagonmasters (and wagons and oxen to pull them), and courtiers. This is powerful evidence that a small elite had rights of life and death over lower-class people.

Each of the Sumerian cities seems to have been an independent state, often competing and fighting with the

thousand years before the first cities and denote the early development of a complex economy. People who conduct trade through face-to-face barter do not need a means for signing or labeling their goods, but people who are involved in paying taxes, making and collecting loans, and trading their products at distant markets need more complex record keeping.

In Sumerian cities, the central precinct contained public buildings and elite residences that were larger and

The ziggurat at Ur, now reconstructed, marked both the political and religious center of the city.

others. Around 4,300 years ago, an effective general named Sargon unified the Sumerian city-states into a short-lived empire. Sargon built a new capital city, called Agade, which has never been identified archaeologically but probably was near the site of present-day Baghdad north of most of the Sumerian cities. Sargon's empire did not last beyond the life of his grandson, and later the Sumerian cities shrank in size and influence. In modern times, southernmost Iraq is settled only with small, dispersed villages rather than large, influential cities. Sir Leonard Woolley, who led excavations at Ur, described Sumer in the 1920s:

Standing on the summit of this mound [Ur] one can distinguish along the eastern skyline the dark tasselled fringe of the palm gardens on the river's bank, but to north and west and south as far as the eye can see stretches a waste of unprofitable sand. . . . It seems incredible that such a wilderness should ever have been habitable for man, and yet the weathered hillocks at one's feet cover the temples and houses of a very great city.

What happened to the great cities of Sumer? Although warfare and invasion played a role, one major factor in the decline of Sumer was an ecological crisis created by overuse of irrigation to feed rising population and support labor to build the great public monuments. This created a build-up of salts in the soil, leading to ever-decreasing yields of agricultural crops. At first, farmers grew less wheat and more barley, the latter of which is more salt-tolerant. Eventually the land could no longer support urban populations, and people and political power moved northward first to the land of Akkad near Baghdad and eventually to Assyria. The destruction of soil fertility was so severe that only after World War II was some of the land reclaimed for agriculture.

## STATE SOCIETIES IN MESOAMERICA

We have focused on early states in the Near East because the archaeological and historical evidence is so rich for that area, but as noted above, similar processes occurred in several parts of the world. In Mesoamerica, the earliest state societies reach a peak between 1,000 and 2,000 years ago, approximately the period known by archaeologists as the Classic Period. The great city of **Teotihuacan,** northeast of present-day Mexico City, reached a size of eight square miles, and numerous cities and ceremonial centers in the Maya area of southern Mexico, Guatemala, and Belize also flourished. These were the forerunners of the Aztec and Maya cultures met by the Spanish in the sixteenth century.

In Mesoamerica as in Sumer, there is archaeological evidence for great social stratification, centralized political systems, intensive agriculture, long-distance trade, and the interrelationship of religious and political power. Teotihuacan was designed on a grid system, and all buildings in the large city conformed to the grid; this was probably the result of both centralized political power and its related religious ideology. Ordinary people lived in close-packed stone and adobe apartment buildings while the center of the city was dominated by large stepped temple pyramids and other public build-

At the center of Teotihuacan were large stepped pyramids used for religious and, probably, political purposes.

## SETTING THE
## RECORD STRAIGHT

When archaeologists excavate the great urban centers of the ancient world, such as Ur, Teotihuacan, or Tikal, they find remains of elaborate architecture and lavish luxury items made of gold, bronze, jade, and other materials. Many people label these societies "civilization," implying that they represent a higher standard of living than do foragers or the earliest agriculturalists. But is this really the case? Other archaeological evidence suggests that many inhabitants of these societies suffered from health problems due to poor diet, crowding, and warfare.

Anthropologists analyze human skeletal remains for direct evidence of ancient health. Among the characteristics that are studied are patterns of adult height, changes in the bones of the skull and other parts of the body, and marks and flaws in tooth enamel. One of the striking patterns found in many parts of the world is a decline in adult height from earlier Paleolithic periods to later Neolithic periods. This may be partly due to changes in activity patterns but probably indicates a decline in quality of the diet. Among skeletons found in very early agricultural sites there is little evidence of increased disease and malnutrition, but skeletons from sites where intensive agriculture is well established often show dramatically higher levels of dental decay and markers of increased stress from infectious disease and anemia in teeth, leg and arm bones, and skulls (see papers in Cohen and Armelagos, 1984). It is frequently the case that the worst health and dietary stresses affect infants and children. Rachel Storey (1992) analyzed remains of 206 individuals from a lower-class residence area in Teotihuacan. She found evidence that their lives were short and stressful. Evidence of stunting and infectious disease was widespread in the skeletons, and the mean age at death was about 23.

---

ings, often decorated with elaborate wall paintings or stone carving. Different sections of the city were devoted to specialized workshops in obsidian, pottery, and leather.

**Tikal,** one of the largest Mayan sites, was not laid out on a grid like Teotihuacan, but it also contained architecture of different qualities for different classes of people. Most people lived in small pole-and-thatch houses that did not leave many archaeological traces. The elites lived in stone buildings clustered around elaborately decorated temple pyramids and other public buildings including ball courts. Wall paintings tell us that a ball game something like soccer, but with ritual implications, was played on these courts. The highest ranking people were buried in elaborately carved tombs with immense wealth in finely painted pottery, carved jade, shells, and obsidian. Many of these products were brought by trade from all over Mesoamerica. Analysis of skeletons from Tikal shows that people from wealthy tombs were taller than people from poorer tombs, suggesting that the wealthy had a better diet as well as more luxury goods.

At Tikal and the rest of the Mayan centers (but not at Teotihuacan) are also found many stone monuments carved with written inscriptions. The pictorial script, known as **glyphs,** has been partially deciphered. Unlike cuneiform in Sumer, glyphs were not used for economic records but for recording the rituals, genealogies, and accomplishments of the elite. The inscriptions record births, deaths, marriages, alliances, and warfare of the royal families from different Mayan centers, all linked to an elaborate calendar system that had religious as well as political significance. Among much other information, the inscriptions tell us that women of leading families often had significant political power in Maya society.

Like the cities of Sumer, many Mesoamerican cities of the Classic Period suffered destruction and depopulation. The reasons are complex and vigorously debated by anthropologists, but probably include some combination of invasion, ecological problems, and social unrest. Despite the collapse of individual cities, complex state societies were never absent from the Americas after this time.

## PROPOSED EXPLANATIONS FOR THE URBAN REVOLUTION

As with the Neolithic Revolution, the most interesting anthropological question is, why? Although we often talk of the "rise" of civilization, with implications of

Carved stone monuments, such as this stela, recorded the histories of members of the Maya ruling class.

progress and advancement, cities and state societies have some significant drawbacks for their members. Crowding, disease, poverty, and taxes all occur in cities. State societies are inherently nonegalitarian; this means that a small elite has wealth and power and dominates the majority of people. How could people be "conned" into developing a society in which most of them are at the mercy of a few powerful leaders?

As you might expect, this question has attracted as much theoretical attention as the question of the Neolithic Revolution. And, like that research problem, no one answer is accepted by all anthropologists. The proposed explanations can be generally divided into two categories—"**managerial**" (or "integrative") **explanations** and "**conflict**" (or "circumscription") **explanations.**

The general form of managerial explanations is that people allow a small group to gain wealth and power in return for managing a significant problem for the community. One of the most influential of these theories was proposed by historian Karl Wittfogel (1957), who suggested that irrigation was central to the development of state societies. Wittfogel drew attention to the environmental setting of the earliest states in Sumer, Egypt, and Peru; all of these are in areas with rich soils but very low rainfall, so that irrigation is essential for agricultural communities to survive. Wittfogel's **hydraulic theory** is that effective management of irrigation, so essential for survival, can be accomplished only by a small, efficient group. Thus, a community allows a small elite to gain power and influence because this elite manages this problem for the whole group. Gradually, the elite parlays the specialized power over irrigation into more general political power.

Other, similar arguments focus on the need for managing long-distance trade, defense, or internal exchange of specialized craft products. For example, long-distance trade was important for both Sumerian and Mayan societies because they lacked nearby sources of certain important natural resources, such as metals in Sumer or obsidian in the Mayan area. It has been proposed that elites gained power by efficiently managing long-distance trade for the larger community.

The archaeological evidence for all of these managerial theories is ambiguous. For example, there are certainly elaborate, centralized irrigation systems in Sumer, but they seem to have developed after the appearance of cities, not before. Before approximately 5,000 years ago, the archaeological evidence suggests that irrigation systems were small and localized and could be run communally by individual villages, as has been demonstrated ethnographically.

## SETTING THE RECORD STRAIGHT

We frequently talk of the "rise" of civilization and human "progress" since the Paleolithic. While the Neolithic and Urban Revolutions were certainly times of many useful innovations, they also introduced problems into human societies. One such problem was warfare. While some interpersonal violence occurs in all human societies, organized warfare is characteristic of larger and more socially stratified communities. Archaeologist Arthur Demarest has recently found evidence for expanding warfare at the end of the Classic Period in the Maya region. In 1991, he excavated the lavish tomb of a Maya king at the site of Dos Pilas in Guatemala (Folger, 1992). The inscriptions on the fine pottery found in the tomb showed that this king had greatly expanded his power by raising a large army and annexing nearby regions. This led to increasing warfare during the reigns of his successors and the need to build elaborate fortifications around certain major cities. Archaeologists at Dos Pilas found a deposit of numerous skeletons that were never buried; apparently the people were killed in battle (Carey, 1993). The land became so dangerous, Demarest thinks, that agriculture declined because people could not safely work in the fields. They tried to grow crops within the walls, but overuse of the soil led to a drastic decline in crop yields. This cycle of warfare and agricultural collapse may very well have contributed to the collapse of the major Maya cities.

Conflict or circumscription theories focus more on competition between groups of people. Scholars influenced by Marxist theory suggest that centralized state authority develops to control class conflict, which arises from increasing accumulation of wealth from intensive agriculture and craft specialization. Robert Carneiro (1970) suggests that state societies develop in environmentally limited locales (that is, blocked in by mountains or deserts) under conditions of population increase. As population grows, competition for arable land increases, leading to warfare. Eventually, there are winners and losers, but the losers cannot move away because of the environmental limits. Thus, they become a class subjected to the winners, forced to pay tribute or taxes or work for the benefit of others. The winning group then begins to accumulate wealth and power, leading eventually to the social stratification and centralized political systems characteristic of states. Such a scenario seems plausible in locales such as Sumer and Egypt, which are both hemmed in by deserts, but is less convincing in the tropical forest environment of the Maya.

In dry areas, such as Sumer, Egypt, and central Mexico where Teotihuacan is located, differential access to water would certainly lead to differences in agricultural success and, thus, differences in wealth. Poorer people might become indebted to wealthier ones and have to pay off their debts with labor for the benefit of others, leading eventually to complex stratification. So, although Wittfogel's original formulation is incorrect, his focus on irrigation and agricultural production is probably significant in several cases.

Of course, there is no reason to believe that exactly the same processes of state development occurred in all parts of the world. Most likely, several factors are important. There is ongoing field research and theoretical debate among anthropologists on this question; we can expect new ideas to be forthcoming. However, most anthropologists agree that state development is related in complex ways to growing population, growing economic surplus through agricultural intensification, and elaboration of craft specialization and trade. In addition, all early states seem to have a significant theocratic flavor. Rulers and other members of the elite laid claim to a special, powerful relationship with the supernatural world, thus legitimating their power in the living world. We find that elaborate religious structures were important public buildings in almost all early states.

The basic biology of modern human beings evolved during a time of a foraging, hunting, and gathering adaptation. Today, however, most people live in towns and cities and rely on agricultural products for food. The Neolithic and Urban Revolutions were the foundations of the cultures and adaptations of the modern world. In the coming chapters, we will discuss some of these cultural variations.

## ◆ Summary

1. V. Gordon Childe coined the terms Neolithic Revolution and Urban Revolution to label the two most important cultural transformations of prehistoric times. These transformations occurred independently in the Near East, Asia, and the Americas.

2. In the Near East, a "Neolithic package" of grinding stones, domesticated food resources, permanent architecture, and pottery developed gradually between about 14,500 and 8,500 years ago. In Mesoamerica, these archaeological traits appear between 9,000 and 4,500 years ago.

3. The most important difference between the Neolithic Revolution in the Old World and in the Americas was the lack of major domesticated animals in the latter. Hunting remained the major source of meat in the Americas (except Peru), and plows and wheeled vehicles were not developed.

4. The development of agriculture did not necessarily lead to better nutrition or health for foraging people, but it did provide a more predictable food source. Many proposed explanations for the Neolithic Revolution suggest that climate change or population growth or both were significant factors. However, some scholars think that the cause lies in social activities, not in ecological conditions.

5. The development of agriculture allowed the production and storage of surpluses, which allowed the accumulation of wealth. From an agricultural base, state societies developed, characterized by great inequalities in wealth and power. Many, but not all, early state societies were also characterized by the presence of cities. The earliest cities were those in Sumer, dating to about 5,000 years ago. In Mesoamerica, the first cities appeared around 2,000 years ago.

6. Early states are characterized by the presence of massive public buildings, record-keeping systems, lavish "royal" burials, long-distance trade, and intensification of agriculture. In almost all of the early states, political power seems to be associated with religious influence.

7. There is considerable debate about the causes of state societies. Some anthropologists believe they originate from conflicts over land and resources, while others believe that states begin as solutions to significant managerial problems within societies.

## ◆ Key Terms

| | |
|---|---|
| chiefdoms | Neolithic package |
| conflict explanation | Neolithic Revolution |
| cuneiform | sedentism |
| domestication | state-level societies |
| foraging | Sumer |
| glyphs | Teotihuacan |
| hydraulic theory | Tikal |
| Jarmo | Urban Revolution |
| managerial explanation | ziggurat |
| Natufian | |

## ◆ Suggested Readings

Braidwood, Linda. *Digging Beyond the Tigris*. New York: Henry Schuman, 1953. Autobiographical account of the excavations at Jarmo; amusing and enlightening information about doing archaeology in the Near East.

Cohen, Ronald, and Elman R. Service (Eds.). *Origins of the State: The Anthropology of Political Evolution*. Philadelphia: Institute for the Study of Human Issues, 1978. Collection of scholarly papers on important theoretical issues in the development of state societies; case studies from both Near East and Mesoamerica.

Cowan, C. Wesley, and Patty Jo Watson (Eds.). *The Origins of Agriculture: An International Perspective*. Washington, D.C.: Smithsonian Institution Press, 1992. The most up-to-date compilation of information on the Neolithic Revolution around the world. Provides detailed review of archaeobotanical and archaeological information and extensive bibliography.

Crawford, Harriet. *Sumer and the Sumerians*. Cambridge: Cambridge University Press, 1991. An up-to-date summary for the nonspecialist of archaeological and documentary evidence about Sumerian culture and history.

Weaver, Muriel Porter. *The Aztecs, Maya, and Their Predecessors* (3rd ed.). New York: Academic Press, 1993. Detailed and well-illustrated review of the prehistory of Mesoamerica, with extensive discussion of all major sites.

Wenke, Robert. *Humankind Emerging* (3rd ed.). New York: Oxford University Press, 1991. A thorough introduction to the prehistory of the world; contains good chapters and wide-ranging bibliography on the theoretical debates about the Neolithic Revolution and the Urban Revolution, as well as archaeological information from all parts of the world.

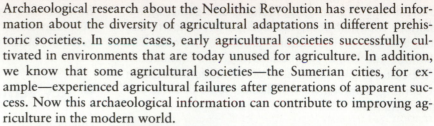
# Archaeology and Civilization

Archaeological research about the Neolithic Revolution has revealed information about the diversity of agricultural adaptations in different prehistoric societies. In some cases, early agricultural societies successfully cultivated in environments that are today unused for agriculture. In addition, we know that some agricultural societies—the Sumerian cities, for example—experienced agricultural failures after generations of apparent success. Now this archaeological information can contribute to improving agriculture in the modern world.

Research about both the Neolithic and Urban Revolutions has also revealed some of the drawbacks of what we frequently refer to as progress. One of these problems is garbage, an archaeologist's dream, but a city's dilemma. Recently, American archaeologists have applied their research methods to understanding the solid waste disposal problems of modern American cities.

### ◆ Garbalogists provide useful information about consumption and culture

In 1973, William Rathje began a research project with undergraduate and graduate students at the University of Arizona. Their goal was to study the garbage of modern Tucson with archaeological methods. This did not mean actually excavating modern garbage piles. Keep in mind, as noted in Chapter 9, that excavation is actually a small part of archaeological research. Rather, Rathje arranged for the Tucson Sanitation Department to deliver to his lab loads of household garbage from different Tucson neighborhoods. Then, students (appropriately gloved, dressed, and inoculated for safety) sorted, catalogued, and analyzed the material remains just as if they were 500 years old instead of five hours old. They identified and weighed food refuse and newspaper, sorted and counted bottles, cans, and packaging, and evaluated disposal patterns. As Rathje said many times in the 1970s, all archaeologists study garbage, this is just a bit fresher than usual.

The goals of the Garbage Project include training students in archaeological research and examining culture and life-style in modern America. The project is based on the essential archaeological assumption that we can learn about human behavior by studying material remains. The results of analysis of the garbage were compared with survey information from the same neighborhoods about purchase, consumption, and disposal of material goods. Both the archaeological and survey sets of data were controlled to protect the privacy of members of the community; all letters, envelopes, and other personal documents were discarded before students examined any garbage. In later years, the Garbage Project expanded to include study of garbage and disposal patterns in public parks, on college campuses, in communities outside of Arizona, and most recently in municipal landfills in several states. In public spaces, collection of data follows archaeological survey and surface collecting techniques. In the landfills, actual excavations were conducted by large machines under the supervision of archaeologists; thus, stratigraphic information is also available. This account is taken from numerous publications by Rathje and his collaborators (among many others, Rathje, 1978, 1989; Wilson and Rathje, 1990; Rathje et al., 1992).

The results of the twenty years of the Garbage Project are numerous and complex. Some of the results are of interest mainly to archaeologists, for example, information about how the size of a material item affects where it is disposed of. This has obvious implications for understanding site formation processes in prehistoric sites. However, a great deal of interesting information has been developed about modern consumption and waste disposal habits. This information is important for planning for future solid waste disposal, something that all American cities are grappling with.

In the early studies of household waste disposal, Garbage Project investigators first confirmed something that archaeologists have suspected for a long time: verbal testimony about human behavior is often inaccurate. In interviews, people consistently underestimated their consumption of alcoholic beverages, pastries, and fatty foods. These data are very useful for anyone, such as sociologists, medical anthropologists, and public health officials, collecting information about American dietary patterns and health. The obvious message is: direct, material evidence of consumption is more reliable than interview data, particularly with reference to foods that are widely publicized as poor dietary choices.

The Garbage Project also demonstrated that people do not give reliable information about the amount of material they recycle; level of income or education does not affect these results. In fact, the only reliable predictor of recycling behavior is the price paid for various materials at recycling centers. Rathje suggests this information has significant implications for developing successful municipal recycling programs; good will is probably not a sufficient motivator over the long term.

As you might expect, low-income households discard less waste than higher income households. What is less obvious, however, is how food habits affect disposal. Households with more repetitive diets have less food wastage than households with more variable diets. There is less wastage of familiar products, such as loaves of white bread, than of products used less regularly, such as bags of hotdog buns. And, surprisingly, the worst wastage occurs when food supplies appear short. For example, when beef prices went up in 1973, wastage of beef went up as well. Apparently, people bought unfamiliar, cheaper cuts and did not like them or hoarded supplies without adequate storage, so the meat spoiled.

Since 1987, the Garbage Project has focused on municipal landfills, using front-end loaders and large bucket augers to excavate samples from seven sites across the country. Again, direct material evidence contradicts a number of myths about solid waste disposal. First, despite public outcry about plastics and plastic foam containers, these make up less than 5 percent of landfill contents by weight and less than 12 percent by volume. In contrast, paper makes up 40 to 50 percent of all landfills, both by volume and by weight: "In all the handwringing over the garbage crisis, has a single voice been raised against the proliferation of telephone books? . . . Dig a trench through a landfill and you will see layers of phone books, like geological strata, or layers of cake" (Rathje, 1989:102). Second, the hoped-for biodegradation is much slower and more limited in landfills than usually as-

sumed; in 1989, Rathje found 1952 newspapers in almost fresh condition. This kind of direct, material information is useful for realistic planning of packaging, recycling, and solid waste disposal.

Rathje's goal is to clarify our knowledge of what is really in garbage, so we can deal with it realistically. He points out that, despite the media hype about fast-food packaging and disposable diapers, for example, the average modern American family disposes of less household waste than did its nineteenth-century ancestors and, in fact, less household waste than does an average family in Mexico City. (However, it is true that total amounts of garbage are going up because of rising population.) Improved packaging means, among other things, less spoilage—and thus less disposal—of food.

The research of the Garbage Project is ongoing. Currently, Rathje and colleagues are looking at what happens to heavy metals and other toxic chemicals in landfills. They have expanded collaboration with solid waste disposal professionals in several communities and have contributed to planning for the future. They emphasize that "garbalogy" is based on the same principles as traditional archaeology even if the material remains are fresh. Like archaeologists everywhere, members of the Garbage Project are concerned with human cultural behavior. In addition to practical results, they have gained unique insights into modern American cultural behavior. For example, household garbage collected immediately after Halloween contains mostly candy packaging, but household garbage collected after Valentine's Day contains both candy packaging *and* candy. The Garbage Project's conclusion: "On Halloween what's important is the candy; on Valentine's Day what's important is the gesture" (Rathje, 1986:15).

### ◆ Archaeological evidence helps restore agricultural productivity.

Both the Negev desert in Israel and the high Andes in South America are forbidding environments, and today they are occupied by small and dispersed communities. But archaeological evidence demonstrates that both were once home to complex state societies. How did these societies produce adequate food for their people? Although at first glance it might seem that adequate food supplies had to be carried into these areas, archaeological survey and aerial photographs show that parts of the Andes and parts of the Negev were once covered with complex agricultural fields. Archaeologists are now collaborating with agronomists and others to restore these agricultural systems for the benefit of modern people.

The Negev desert makes up about 60 percent of Israel's area. As population in Israel grows, the need for more food production intensifies. In 1954, botanist Michael Evenari, along with geologists, hydrologists, agronomists, and archaeologists, began a long-term, multidisciplinary study of the Negev (Evenari et al., 1971; Agarwal, 1977). Archaeological survey of the barren desert revealed not only the ruins of Nabatean, Roman, and Byzantine settlements that once housed up to 10,000 people but also extensive agricultural terracing, dams, and canals. Evidence showed that the Negev did not have greater rainfall in these periods but that the ancient people made efficient use of runoff. Ironically, today in the desert, erosion is a severe problem. When rain occurs, it often falls in harsh thunderstorms that wash out soils, flood the wadis (steep-walled valleys), and erode any fields. Yet, archaeological evidence shows that ancient people purposefully cleared the slopes of stones (which were piled up in long rows of stone heaps that show up very clearly in aerial photos) in order to *increase* runoff.

But this runoff was productive, not destructive, because the ancient people directed it into numerous small channels, often lined with stones, and led the water into small fields bordered by walls and terraces. The field walls were arranged with openings that led the water from one field to the next down the slope. These constructions had several productive results. First, runoff was channeled into numerous small streams instead of all rushing into the nearest wadi and eroding it further. Second, runoff from a large area could be led directly to a field, thus bringing far more water than would actually fall on the field as rain. Third, the walls and terraces held the water and the soil right where the farmers wanted them.

After mapping and studying these agricultural facilities, Evenari's team decided that the only way to convince others of the significance of their findings was to establish an experimental farm based on the archaeological and hydrological evidence. They chose to reconstruct an existing ancient set of fields, terraces, and canals. To start with, they grew crops mentioned in a Byzantine document, including wheat, barley, figs, grapes, and olives; they have also experimented with growing pasture as well as peach, apricot, almond, and pomegranate trees, and sunflowers, onions, peas, carrots, and cash crops such as asparagus and artichokes. Their first growing season was the extremely dry winter of 1960–61; yields were low, but most crops survived. By 1971, the orchards were established and beginning to bear fruit, and numerous other crops were successful. Because the project's goal was to improve modern agriculture rather than prove an archaeological point, they used modern tillers, fertilizers, and pest controls. But they used no modern irrigation at all. The techniques pioneered by Evenari and colleagues are now being tried in many arid lands in the Near East and Africa to improve food production in these areas of booming population.

In the high Andes, on the Peru–Bolivia border near Lake Titicaca, a similar pattern of archaeological evidence showed that extensive agricultural fields and terraces once covered what is now virtually barren land (Erickson, 1990). During the peak of the Tiawanaku civilization, between 1,000 and 1,500 years ago, the entire landscape was modified by human labor. Archaebotanical evidence showed that both potatoes and quinoa, a high-protein grain, were grown in raised fields all around the marshy edge of the lake. These were created by digging crisscrossing canals and piling the rich soil up. The canals acted as "heat sinks," with the water collecting warmth in the daytime and releasing it in the cold mountain nights to keep the crops from freezing. Rainfall was collected in canals and transported to various fields, thus lessening the problems of siltation and of salinization from ground water.

As in the Negev example, American and Bolivian archaeologists moved from studying and describing the ancient landscape to applying this information to modern agronomy (Bray, 1990; Painter, 1991). Experimental plots were built based on the archaeological evidence and produced at least double the yield of control plots. Furthermore, in years when frost destroyed almost all crops in the standard modern fields, the crops in the raised fields suffered little damage. Importantly, these techniques do not depend on heavy machinery, imported seed, or chemical fertilizers; local peasants using familiar tools can improve their own food supply without becoming dependent on outside supplies. Bolivian archaeologist Oswaldo Rivera notes: "Bolivia has imported many new technologies from abroad and many have been disasters. This system has come from the villagers' ancestors, and that's given them a belief in their own capacity—and a real source of national pride" (quoted in Painter, 1991:12).

## CHAPTER 11

# Prehistoric Cultures of North America

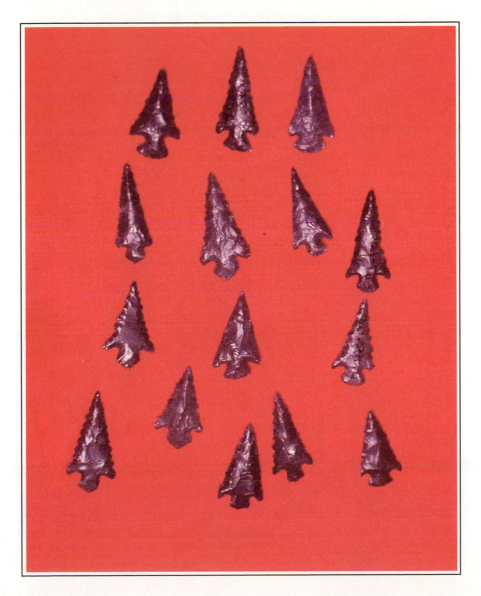

When and how did humans first occupy the Americas?

How have cultures changed in North America during the past 12,000 years?

How did prehistoric Americans adapt to their environments?

In this chapter, we review some of what anthropological archaeologists have learned about the native peoples of North America, who preceded Columbus by at least 12,000 years. For the purposes of this chapter, we are defining North America as the continent north of the modern nation of Mexico. Although one chapter can provide only a limited introduction to the subject, we will illustrate (a) archaeological techniques used to investigate North American prehistory; (b) the diversity of cultural adaptations found in North America; and (c) additional information on the major cultural transformations of the human species. In North America, as in other parts of the world described in Chapter 10, the beginnings of agriculture and the development of social complexity and stratification were two very important cultural changes.

## ◆ ◆ ◆ Peopling of the Americas

When the sixteenth-century European explorers eventually realized that the land mass they had happened upon was not Japan or elsewhere in Asia, they had a problem accounting for the origin of all the people they met. Were they the descendants of the Ten Lost Tribes of Israel or of the lost continent of Atlantis or of lost Phoenician sailors? In 1589, a Spanish missionary, José de Acosta, proposed that the American natives may have come from Asia by a land route in the far northwest of the continent. Although de Acosta had very little evidence to go on, this proposition turned out to be basically correct: the original inhabitants of the Americas migrated from Asia across the area that is now the Bering Sea between Siberia and Alaska, at some time probably between 15,000 and 40,000 years ago. The Americas, like the continent of Australia, have been occupied only by *Homo sapiens sapiens* and not by any other hominid type. In the thousands of years since this migration, the aboriginal peoples of the Americas increased dramatically in number, moved into virtually all the environments of both North and South America, and developed a broad diversity of cultures.

Virtually all anthropologists agree that indigenous Americans originated in Asia, based on much biological evidence including tooth form and blood groupings (Turner 1987; Zegura, 1987). The timing of the migration, however, is strongly debated, as is the kind of technology and life-style practiced by the earliest Americans. Archaeologists utilize two major lines of research in this debate: environmental evidence and archaeological evidence.

This distinctive form of tooth, called shovel-shaped incisors, indicates that American Indians are of Asian origin.

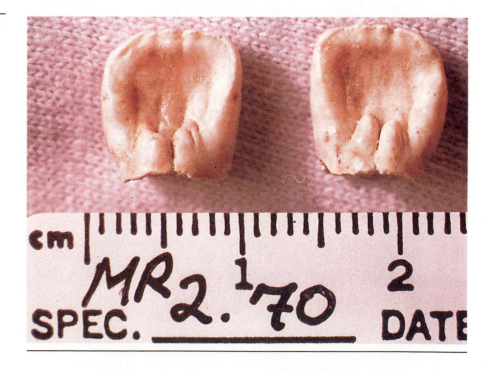

EXHIBIT 11-1

**Changes in glaciers and sea level in North America** (adapted from *Natural History,* Nov-1986)

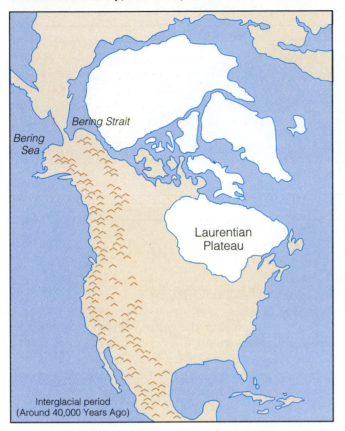

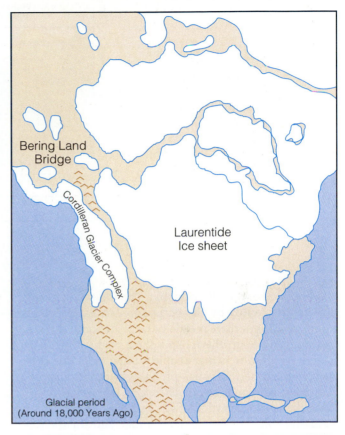

*Interglacial period (Around 40,000 Years Ago)*

*Glacial period (Around 18,000 Years Ago)*

## ENVIRONMENTAL EVIDENCE

For environmental evidence, archaeologists rely on palynologists, paleontologists, and geologists. The peopling of the Americas occurred during a time of recurring **glaciations,** periods of cooler-than-present earth temperature when ice sheets covered much of the northern hemisphere and high mountains in both hemispheres. Much of northern North America was covered by two ice sheets, the Laurentide to the east and the Cordilleran to the west. In very cold phases, these two ice sheets fused just east of the Rocky Mountains; in warmer phases, the ice sheets melted back, exposing an **ice-free corridor** (this "corridor" would have been dozens of miles wide). However, not all of the northern hemisphere was glaciated, even during very cold periods; parts of easternmost Siberia and western Alaska re-

mained unglaciated throughout the Pleistocene. At the same time, the formation of glaciers caused the lowering of sea levels worldwide. In the coldest periods, sea levels dropped sufficiently to create the **Bering land bridge,** (see Exhibit 11-1) dry land vegetated with tundra (cold-climate mosses, shrubs, and grasses but few or no trees) where the Bering Sea is today. The land bridge was continuous from what is now Siberia into what is now Alaska and was probably 1,000 miles from north to south. In warmer phases, the glaciers would melt and the sea would gradually encroach on the land bridge. At various times between 60,000 and 10,000 years ago, the land bridge was habitable by humans who hunted large Arctic grazing animals, including the now-extinct mammoth. We know from archaeological evidence from Siberia that humans were able to cope with Arctic tundra at least by 45,000 years ago.

EXHIBIT 11-2

**Changes in climate and sea level during the
Pleistocene (adapted from Fagan, 1991)**

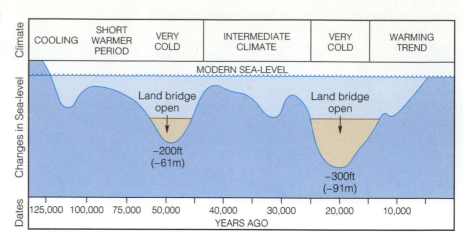

ARCHAEOLOGICAL EVIDENCE

Although some kind of human capability for using boats is attested to by the occupation of Australia by 40,000 years ago, there is little or no evidence that boats were used in the northern hemisphere at this time. The general assumption is that people walked from one continent to the other, although probably without purposefully planning a migration. Therefore, one strategy for dating the first occupation of the Americas is to evaluate the dating evidence for the land bridge and for the ice-free corridor and decide when humans *could* have occupied these areas. There are periods when the land bridge was available for human occupation east as far as the Alaskan border with the Yukon, but migration further south would have been blocked. There are also relatively brief (in geological terms) periods, such as around 45,000 years ago and 14,000 to 12,000 years ago, when both the land bridge and the ice-free corridor were available for human occupation. The problem for the anthropologist is to decide during which one or several of these possible periods humans *did* first migrate to the Americas. Keep in mind that prehistoric Asians did not know they were occupying a new continent, nor were they purposefully migrating. Rather, their gradual movements were a result of their subsistence strategies as they followed the migratory big game they hunted. As human population expanded in one area, groups of related families would break off and seek better hunting "down the road." Over time, humans spread throughout the new land.

Although it seems that the earliest evidence should be found in Alaska, actually it is not; this is due, in part, to the difficulties of doing research in Alaska and, in part, to lack of stratigraphy in the frozen soils. The most important archaeological evidence comes from further south in North America and from South America. It is widely agreed that humans occupied most of North America by or soon after 12,000 years ago. Thus, they may well have been in Alaska by 15,000 to 14,000 years ago. The earliest agreed upon occupation is attested to by finds of **Clovis** culture widely across the United States (more information will be given about Clovis later). The earliest widely accepted dates from South America are from about 11,000 years ago from caves in southernmost Argentina.

A relatively small but vocal group of archaeologists believe that humans were in what is now the United States before 12,000 years ago and certainly in North America before 15,000 years ago. Some, such as Knut Fladmark (1986), believe that prehistoric Siberian people were capable of boat travel or ice crossings and thus we do not have to concern ourselves with the dating of the land bridge. Fladmark suggests that humans may have migrated down the west coast of North America, bypassing the ice-free corridor altogether. A problem with testing this hypothesis is that sites of the relevant age are drowned by rising sea levels since the end of the glacial period. A number of others believe that several sites in both North and South America provide archaeological evidence for pre-Clovis occupation of North America prior to 12,000 years ago.

One of these sites is Meadowcroft Rock Shelter in western Pennsylvania where deeply stratified layers yield radiocarbon dates of approximately 14,500 years ago. These layers contain stone tools that are different from tools found at Clovis sites. Another widely discussed site is Monte Verde in southern Chile where accumulation of peat has led to extraordinary organic preservation. The excavator (Dillehay, 1989) believes that radiocarbon dates show human occupation as early as 13,000 years ago and possibly as much as 30,000 years ago; the implication is that humans must have been in North America long before this. A third intriguing site, Pendejo Cave in New Mexico, was excavated in the early 1990s; the excavator claims that it has yielded evidence of use by humans 30,000 or more years ago (McComb, 1993).

There have been other claims for evidence of human occupation as early as 30,000 years ago in both North and South America, but these are not widely accepted. In fact, the evidence from both Meadowcroft and Monte Verde has been criticized, while the data from Pendejo Cave are not yet fully analyzed. For example, at Meadowcroft, animal bones recovered from the oldest layers represent species adapted to modern climates; many archaeologists believe that if the radiocarbon dates are correct, then the animal species should be better adapted to cold climates. These critics suspect that the radiocarbon dates are wrong. Another major problem is that the artifacts from these sites do not look anything like the artifacts from the following Clovis sites; the excavators of Meadowcroft and Monte Verde (as well as others) claim there is no reason why there should be a connection, but many archaeologists believe there should be some stylistic similarity.

Those who support a "long chronology" (pre-15,000 years ago) argue that the conservative view of humans entering the Americas only shortly before 12,000 years ago does not give enough time for human population to expand and migrate to the tip of South America by 11,000 years ago. Recently, physical anthropologists have contributed to the debate with evidence from analysis of mitochondrial DNA (see Chapter 7) from modern American Indians (Gibbons, 1993). This evidence suggests that native American populations split from Asian populations at least 17,000 years ago and perhaps as much as 34,000 years ago.

This debate has been vigorous to say the least. Among archaeologists, all of the pre-12,000 years ago sites are controversial for one reason or another. David Meltzer (1989) has recently suggested that there may have been several small and ultimately unsuccessful early migrations that left skimpy and inconsistent archaeological evidence, but that the Clovis occupation is the best evidence of the first migration that was successful and led to widespread occupation of the Americas.

◆   ◆   ◆

## Paleoindian and Archaic Periods

By 11,500 years ago, people lived in small groups all over what is now the United States, while much of Canada was still covered with glaciers. The sites of the Clovis culture are part of the **Paleoindian** tradition, evidence of the first widespread successful occupation of North America. The best-known Clovis sites are found in the western United States. They are specialized hunting and butchering sites and they include Blackwater Draw near the town of Clovis, New Mexico, from which the name of the prehistoric culture is taken. Archaeologists have found stone tools for hunting, skinning, and butchering animals and the bones of many large grazing mammals, including the now-extinct mammoth, camel, horse, large forms of bison, and others. There are bone tools and scrapers and other tools made from chipped stone; the most distinctive is the **Clovis point,** a finely chipped, bifacial (chipped on both faces), parallel-sided spear point with a deep "flute" (grooved or thinned area) at the base to facilitate hafting to the shaft. These were spear points (and possibly knives) probably used with a spear thrower. One distinctive characteristic of Clovis stone tools is that they are made of high-quality raw materials, often from quarries many miles from where they are found. Clovis points made of Alibates flint from Texas are found up to 180 miles away from the source; a stone called Onondaga chert from New York is used over an equal distance. This evidence suggests that people of the time recognized and prized the best fine-grained stone materials for toolmaking and that they moved around enough in their hunting practices to acquire these distant resources.

Remains of vegetable foods have not been preserved in western Clovis sites, although the people must have gathered wild plant foods as well as hunted. In some of the earliest eastern Paleoindian sites we do have evidence of additions to big-game hunting. At the Shawnee-Minisink site in eastern Pennsylvania, archaeologists using flotation recovered tiny fish bones and remains of chenopodium (goosefoot), blackberry, and a

Fluted Clovis spear points are distinctive Paleoindian artifacts.

small fruit called hawthorn plum. The extraordinary underwater site of Little Salt Spring in Florida yielded evidence of hunting giant tortoises.

Between about 12,000 and 10,000 years ago, a number of changes in styles of making spear points occurred that allow us to date sites. Although there are regional and chronological variations, all over North America people in this period were probably migratory foragers, utilizing many wild foods but focusing on hunting large grazing animals. At this time, the climate was gradually warming and glaciers melting, leading to changes in rainfall and vegetation patterns across North America. Modern climatic conditions were reached by about 8,500 years ago, although there have been numerous fluctuations, including a warmer-than-modern period around 6,000 years ago.

In addition to changes in vegetation, there were changes in animal species. As in Europe, many of the large grazing animals called **megafauna** became extinct between 12,000 and 10,000 years ago. The extinctions include animals such as mammoth, camel, horse, and large bison that were hunted by humans, and mastodon and sloth that were not hunted by humans. There has long been a debate over the relative impact of climate change and overhunting by humans on these extinctions. It is likely that a combination of factors were at work. In any case, by 10,000 years ago, people throughout North America, like people in the Old World, had to adapt to different environmental condi-

tions than their ancestors experienced. The cultures dating to approximately 10,000 to 3,000 years ago are known as **Archaic** and represent human adaptations to basically modern climatic conditions.

There are hundreds of archaeological sites from the Archaic period and a great deal of regional variation, but there were a number of general trends during this period, some of which parallel changes that were occurring in Europe and the Near East during the Mesolithic period. First, people shifted from a focus on hunting big game to a more diversified foraging style of life, including gathering, hunting, and fishing. Nuts, berries, seeds, and other plant foods were more and more common. In the eastern U.S., shellfish became important in the diet, as shown by numerous coastal and riverine **shellmounds** dating from at least 6,500 years ago. New artifacts appeared, such as pounders and grinding stones used to process the wide range of vegetable foods; in the eastern U.S., finely polished stone axes were used to cope with the spreading forest.

Another trend during the Archaic period was growing regionalization. People shifted to using more local stone resources than they used in the Paleoindian period. The distribution of styles of spear points and knives became much more localized than with the widely used Clovis points. Evidence from the waterlogged Windover site in Florida and from dry caves in Nevada shows that basketry and twined textiles were used.

About 6,000 years ago in the eastern U.S., there is the first evidence of burial mounds and growing burial ceremonialism. Many archaeologists feel that the Archaic was a period of growing population and increasing sedentism. The use of burial mounds, which were a kind of cemetery, is one piece of evidence that people were becoming more sedentary (similar to the evidence of cemeteries in the Natufian sites of the Near East discussed in Chapter 10). By 4,500 years ago, the earliest pottery in North America was being used in parts of South Carolina, Georgia, and Florida. The large, mostly undecorated tubs and bowls were made of **fiber-tempered** pottery; grass or other plant fibers were ground up and mixed with the clay before firing. These relatively fragile containers are another sign of increasing sedentism.

◆  ◆  ◆

## Later Cultures

In the next sections, we will focus on the beginnings of agriculture in North America and on cultural developments in only two areas, the Southwest and the eastern woodlands, especially the Midwest and Southeast. Of course, human beings continued to occupy all of North America, including Canada, New England, the Great Lakes area, the west coast, and so forth, but space allows us to focus on only these two areas. These areas provide case studies of the major cultural transformations that took place during North American prehistory. In both areas, archaeological evidence is supplemented by ethnoarchaeological and ethnohistorical data. Accounts of early Spanish explorations of both areas provide some historic documentation, although it must be used with care. Descendants of these prehistoric people now live in the modern pueblos of the Southwest and in some Indian communities in the Southeast and Oklahoma, where many of the southeastern tribes were forced in the nineteenth century. Although their cultures have changed over the last 500 years, just as has any other culture, there are nevertheless continuities that illuminate the archaeological data.

## BEGINNINGS OF AGRICULTURE

Both in what is now the east and in the southwestern United States, Archaic peoples were, in a way, already adapted to beginnings of cultivation through their intensive gathering and processing of wild plant foods. In both areas, there was a well-established ground stone tool technology (for pounding and grinding nuts and other plant foods) that could be adapted to newly cultivated foods. By the end of the Archaic, people in eastern North America had domesticated certain native plants, including **sunflowers**; weeds called **goosefoot**, **sumpweed**, or marsh elder; and **squash** or gourds of some kind (see Exhibit 11-3). These provided seeds that were important sources of carbohydrates and fat in the diet. The earliest cultivation seems to have taken place along the river valleys of the Midwest and the Southeast, with experimentation beginning as early as 7,000 years ago and domestication beginning 4,000 to 2,000 years ago. Although the term "Neolithic" is not used in North American prehistory, these were the first steps toward the same major subsistence changes that took place during the Neolithic elsewhere in the world.

Archaeologists debate the reasons for beginning cultivation in the east. Although there was increasing population and sedentism at this time, there is little evidence that people lacked adequate wild food resources; the newly domesticated foods supplemented a continuing mixed subsistence of hunting, fishing, and gathering wild plants. Increasing predictability of food supplies may have been a motive. It has been suggested that some early cultivation was for medicinal and ceremo-

nial plants rather than for food (Prentice, 1986). Bruce Smith (1987) points out that the early domesticated plants were all weedy species that do well in open disturbed habitats, the kind that would form around human settlements where people cut down trees, trample the ground, deposit trash, dig holes, etc. Smith suggests that sunflower, sumpweed, and other plants almost "domesticated themselves"; that is, they thrived in human-disturbed habitats, so humans intensively collected them and began to control their distribution. Patty Jo Watson and Mary Kennedy (1991) point out that women in the Archaic communities were probably the main experimenters with cultivation, because ethnoarchaeological evidence tells us that women were the main collectors of plant food and had detailed knowledge of plants' habits.

In the southwestern United States, maize and squash were the first domesticates, dating to about 3,200 years ago. The cultivation of domesticated beans may have been a bit later. These crops were introduced, already domesticated, from Mexico (see Chapter 10), but they did not become the dominant part of the diet until about 1,700 years ago. People must have known about the Mexican crops for a long time before they began cultivating them. Contrary to earlier theories, it now appears

EXHIBIT 11-3

**Sunflower—an early domesticate in the eastern U.S.**

that the first experimentation with domesticated crops in the Southwest occurred during a period of relatively moist climate. Anthropologist W. H. Wills (1989) suggests that the first agriculture provided a small but unusually predictable food resource, which allowed the Archaic peoples to continue their traditional foraging with more confidence. As population increased, domesticated crops became more important because their yield could be increased by extra inputs of human labor.

Around 1,800 years ago, maize was first used in the eastern U.S., but it was a very small part of the diet until about 1,200 years ago. Around this time or shortly after, beans were introduced into this area and cultivated foods increased significantly in importance in the diet. Unlike in the Southwest, however, in the east maize and beans were added to an existing agricultural complex based on domestication of local native plants. We have evidence of the important cultivated crop, tobacco, from around 1,800 years ago, but pipes are found in archaeological sites much earlier than that, for people smoked a wide range of dried herbs and barks.

As in Mesoamerica, domesticated food animals were not significant in North America until after Europeans arrived. Domesticated dogs are known as early as Paleoindian times, and in the Southwest there is some evidence that people kept penned turkeys for food, but hunting continued to be the main source of meat throughout prehistory in North America. This lack of herds of domesticated animals did not prevent the development of large, dense populations and complex societies, but it may have contributed to nutritional deficiencies for some parts of the population at various times.

## LATER CULTURES OF THE MIDWEST AND SOUTHEAST

In these regions, archaeologists distinguish two major cultural periods following the Archaic: the **Woodland,** covering the period of about 3,000 to 1,000 years ago, and the **Mississippian,** covering the period from about 1,000 years ago until A.D. 1540. This last date, when the Spanish explorer Hernando de Soto crossed much of the area, is taken as an arbitrary ending point for prehistory, although, of course, the local cultures did not suddenly disappear in 1540. These chronological periods are further subdivided into numerous phases distinguished by changing styles of pottery, projectile points, burial practices, and architecture. Although there is a great deal of regional variation, the area is characterized throughout this time period by growing population, increasing sedentism, increasing reliance on cultivated plants, and periods of elaborate trade networks and ceremonial activity.

**Woodland Period.** It is important to keep in mind that the beginning of the Woodland period is a relatively arbitrary division created by archaeologists to bring order into their data. The actual changes from late Archaic to early Woodland were gradual and probably not explicitly recognized by the people living at the time. Although some pottery was used in limited areas of the Southeast in the Archaic, the widespread introduction of **grit-tempered pottery** around 3,000 years ago is taken as the start of the Woodland period. The clay was mixed with sand or crushed rock before being shaped and fired. The pots of the early Woodland were generally cylindrical, open-mouthed jars, often with a rounded or pointy bottom; they were clearly not designed to sit on a flat surface and were most likely cooking jars to be set into a ring of rocks or storage vessels to be set into a sandy floor.

The rest of the early Woodland material culture was not very different from the later Archaic and included chipped stone projectiles, knives, and scrapers; axes and grinding and pounding stones of various kinds; bone tools, including awls, needles, and fishhooks; and occasional shell ornaments. But the increased use of pottery

In the eastern United States, Woodland period pottery was decorated by incising, impressing, carving, or stamping.

suggests gradual changes in life-style. First, the early pottery was both heavy and fragile and therefore supports other evidence of increasing sedentism. Second, the presence of pottery suggests new means of cooking, particularly the capability to cook soups, stews, and porridges in a watertight container. Pottery allows better exploitation of both nuts (by boiling to extract the oil) and various gathered and cultivated seed plants. So, the development of pottery is associated with increasing dependence on cultivated crops. But pottery also provided a new medium for artistic and decorative ideas. Through the Woodland and Mississippian periods, stamping, impressing, incising, modeling, and painting were all used to decorate pottery and, in some cases, to present important symbolic motifs. Basketry almost certainly continued as an important craft, although it is much more difficult to track in the archaeological record. Because pottery making is also faster than basketry, pottery probably began to replace baskets for many storage purposes.

Several cultures of the Woodland period developed new and more elaborate styles of burying members of their communities. The best known of these is the **Hopewell** ceremonial complex (approximately 1,600 to 2,200 years ago). Hopewell-affiliated sites are found from northwest Florida to the Kansas City area. The most elaborate Hopewell sites are in southern Ohio, where complex mounds and large geometric earthworks were built by piling up baskets of soil (the result of this process, called **basket-loading,** can be seen when archaeologists make a stratigraphic excavation into the mounds). Under several of the Ohio mounds are found post hole patterns of large buildings in which ceremonial treatment of the dead took place. This may have included cremating or defleshing the bodies and conducting feasts of various kinds. After the ceremonies were complete, the buildings were destroyed and the mound raised over the space.

Throughout the Hopewell area, the dead were buried with elaborate artifacts including copper axes, beads, and **gorgets** (pendants worn around the neck or sewn to clothing at the chest); shell beads and cups; sheets of mica cut into pictorial or geometric designs; finely made pottery; carved bones including engraved human skull caps; polished lumps of galena (lead ore); sheets of silver or copper over wooden ear ornaments; stone pipes carved into animal forms; freshwater pearls; points and other artifacts chipped out of obsidian; and detailed human figurines. Animal symbols, especially the motif of the **raptorial bird,** a stylized bird of prey, were important in the Hopewell period.

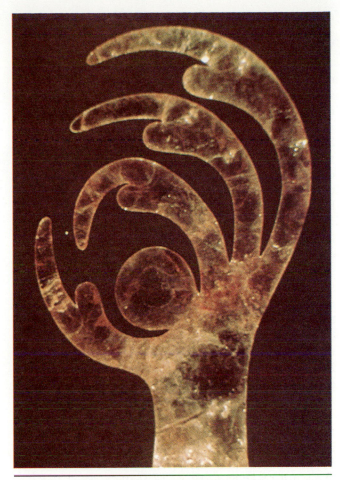

This mica cut-out of the claw of a raptorial bird was found in a Hopewell mound in Ohio.

The raw materials for the grave goods came from many places and provide archaeological evidence of a complex exchange system. The copper came from northern Michigan, many of the shells from the Gulf Coast, the mica from western North Carolina, the galena from western Illinois and Missouri, the silver from Ontario, and the obsidian has been shown by trace element analysis to come from the vicinity of Yellowstone National Park in Wyoming. At the same time that these special materials were moving around the eastern half of the continent, ideas about ritual and ideology must have also been circulating, creating what some archaeologists call the **Hopewell Interaction Sphere.**

The exchange networks had roots back into the late Archaic when Michigan copper and Gulf Coast shells were found in burials in Kentucky and elsewhere in the central Midwest, but the scale of exchange and the elaborateness of the artifacts greatly increased in the Woodland period.

At one time, it was believed that the large mounds and elaborate grave goods could not have been produced without intensive agriculture and a centralized government, but most archaeologists today disagree. For this period, we have more evidence from burials than from homes or villages. Although excavations in western Illinois suggest growing population and intensification of cultivation, hunting and gathering remained very important. Village sites in Ohio were small at this time. Some Hopewell groups may have resembled a modern "big man" society in New Guinea (see Chapter 16), where leadership is not inherited but acquired through an individual's skill and persuasiveness. Leadership in such societies is quite fluid and depends partly on perceived skills at manipulating the spirit world. Some of the elaborate burials in Hopewell mounds may have been of **shamans,** religious practitioners thought to be able to change themselves into animals to pass into the supernatural (see Chapter 21). The exchange network allowed different communities to establish alliances across a wide area.

About 1,600 years ago, the elaborate burial rituals went out of fashion. In the past, archaeologists often referred to this period as the Hopewell "decline," but that is an ethnocentric view. The fancy artifacts, sought after by modern museums, disappeared, but there is no evidence that everyday life was actually poorer. For the next 500 to 600 years, population increased throughout the eastern United States, and agriculture slowly intensified; village fortifications began to appear in the form of heavy wooden fences called palisades, suggesting increasing conflict, perhaps over good agricultural land. Although the elaborate Hopewell rituals disappeared, burials continued to be made in conical mounds, often with large numbers of shell beads.

**Mississippian Period.** Around 1,100 years ago (and perhaps earlier in parts of the Mississippi River valley), a new elaboration of culture occurred along the rivers of the central and southeastern part of the country. This was the Mississippian period, marked by new pottery styles, new traditions in mound building, and increased ceremonial activity. However, many of the distinctive Mississippian characteristics were elaborations of traits from earlier cultures, such as Hopewell.

Many Mississippian societies were **chiefdoms** (see Chapter 19), characterized by dense populations, inherited ranking, and complex economies. Prehistoric North American societies were following the same general path

Hoes are found at many Mississippian sites and emphasize the importance of agriculture in the economy.

of societies elsewhere in the world toward increasingly stratified communities, although, with the possible exception of the Cahokia site described below, urbanism did not develop in North America during this time. Most archaeologists would also argue that no state-level societies developed in prehistoric North America, although many of the chiefdoms had complex, stratified social systems.

The introduction of beans to the agricultural system at the beginning of the Mississippian period was important to the development of these societies. Maize and beans together form a complete protein that can be an effective substitute for meat, allowing for increased population. Intensive agriculture formed the economic base of the Mississippian economy as is shown by flotation evidence and by the recovery of numerous hoes and spades of shell, stone, and bone. In addition, the artifacts from Mississippian sites include **shell-tempered pottery;** small triangular points and other chipped stone tools; bone tools; and shell and copper ornaments. The dense population lived in communities of different sizes from small farmsteads to villages to large centers. Houses were square, built of large posts, with clay plastered over the walls of woven branches. Many settlements were fortified with palisades.

The large sites were characterized by a central plaza surrounded by flat-topped mounds and conical mounds. The flat-topped mounds, also called **temple mounds,** were bases for important buildings, while both kinds of mounds were used for burials. Many sites had just one or two mounds, but the largest Mississippian centers had thirty or more mounds around the plaza. The biggest prehistoric site in North America (north of Mexico) is the early Mississippian site of **Cahokia** in East St. Louis, Illinois, which reached its peak about 800 to 1,000 years ago. At one time it had at least 100 mounds (although only about twenty are still visible), including Monks Mound, which is the largest prehistoric structure in North America north of Mexico, at about 14 acres at its base and 100 feet high. Cahokia and other mound sites were regional centers where the rural population probably gathered for religious ceremonies and administrative and economic purposes. There is evidence of specialized shell-working and pottery-making neighborhoods within Cahokia. The burials show a strongly stratified society. Many people were buried in and around the houses, but the elite were buried in the mounds, often accompanied with lavish grave goods of copper, shell, polished stone, pottery, and textiles (the

The Etowah site in Georgia is a typical Mississippian site with flat-topped mounds arranged around a plaza.

latter preserved only in extraordinary circumstances). Some of the exchange routes and symbolic motifs first seen in Hopewell seem to have been revitalized at this time.

Perhaps the most striking evidence of ranking comes from Mound 72 at Cahokia. An adult male was buried on a platform of 20,000 shell beads and accompanied by at least nine other individuals who seem to have been his servants. Elsewhere in the mound are found four young men buried without heads or hands, as if they were sacrificed in some way, and a large pit holds the skeletons of fifty females between the ages of 18 and 23. Clearly, individuals of different status were treated very differently in death.

If any site in North America represents a state or proto-state society it would be Cahokia, but the lack of writing or other evidence of formal bureaucracy suggests to most archaeologists that Cahokia was a complex chiefdom. Cahokia at its peak may have had a population of 10,000, but it declined after about 700 years ago. In the later part of the Mississippian period, several southern sites were major centers, including Moundville in western Alabama, Etowah in northern Georgia, Fort Jackson in northwest Florida, and Spiro in eastern Oklahoma. Although these are all smaller than Cahokia, they are also characterized by flat-topped mounds, fortifications, intensive agriculture, craft specialization, and elaborate burials, suggesting that each was the center of a regional chiefdom. Although spread over at least 1,000 miles, these sites share symbolic motifs expressed in copper, shell, pottery, and polished stone. These motifs include raptorial birds, sun symbols, hand-and-eye symbols, spiders, woodpeckers, and snakes. Together, the motifs and elaborate craft items are called the **Southeastern Ceremonial Complex** (also known as the Southern Cult). This ceremonial complex is associated with elites at late Mississippian sites and seems to glorify both military accomplishments and some kind of ritual affiliation with a supernatural world that controls fertility. As is the case with ethnographically known chiefdoms and early states, political power of elites seems to have been bolstered by religious influence.

When the Spanish arrived in the Southeast at the beginning of the sixteenth century, they met societies that were basically Mississippian in culture. The chronicles of the de Soto and other expeditions tell us about chiefs receiving homage from their communities. For example, one chief, a woman known to the Spanish as the Lady of Cofitachequi (a site probably located near Camden, South Carolina), was brought to meet de Soto on a litter carried by six men. But archaeology has revealed that

This shell gorget shows several Southeastern Ceremonial Complex motifs.

many of the biggest Mississippian sites, including Cahokia, were in decline or even empty by the time of the Spanish exploration. These declines or collapses have attracted a great deal of archaeological attention. The strong palisades and the militaristic symbolism of the Southern Cult suggest that warfare was known in Mississippian cultures, although there is no evidence that Cahokia or other sites were actually conquered. It is possible that population outgrew the capabilities of the agricultural system, especially if chiefs demanded more and more surplus to support the building of lavish mounds, temples, and burials. As in the Near East and Mesoamerica, described in the preceding chapter, the intensification of agriculture and the growth of stratification are not necessarily "progress" if they lead to overexploitation of the environment and the community. However, the real disaster for Mississippian communities came after the arrival of the Spanish, as described below.

## LATER CULTURES OF THE SOUTHWEST

As noted above, southwestern communities began experimenting with cultivation of maize, beans, and squash during the late Archaic period. Large numbers of grinding stones from sites of this period suggest the importance of both gathered and cultivated plant foods. As cultivation intensified, all prehistoric southwestern communities had to cope with heat and dryness. The architecture and the agricultural practices differed from those of the eastern United States because of this environmental difference. The dry climate of the southwest has also preserved many more textiles than elsewhere in North America; we know that baskets, mats, bags, nets, and so forth were very important in the area throughout prehistory. Plant fibers such as reeds, bark, and yucca were used, as well as dog and mountain sheep hair; in later periods, cotton was cultivated for fiber.

From about 2,000 years ago, archaeologists distinguish at least three regional traditions in the southwest, differentiated by styles of pottery, architecture, and burials: **Mogollon** in east central Arizona and adjacent parts of southern New Mexico, **Hohokam** in southern Arizona, and **Anasazi** in northern New Mexico and Arizona and adjacent parts of Utah and Colorado (see Exhibit 11-4). At about this time, people became more sedentary than before. Communities from early phases of all these traditions are characterized by **pithouses,** round or squarish houses dug about 2 feet into the ground (probably for insulation), with large wooden posts holding up a thatched roof and with a central fireplace. Within a village of ten to fifteen pithouses, one might be larger than the others and have special architectural features such as a built-in bench around the edge. These were probably communal structures of some kind; archaeologists call them **kivas,** the word that modern Pueblo people use for specialized religious structures.

Pottery appears about 1,800 years ago in the Southwest. Much of it was painted in magnificent geometric designs. The Hohokam also used human and animal motifs, as did the people of a late phase of the Mogollon region called Mimbres culture. The stunning Mimbres bowls, with delicate paintings of people, fish, bears, birds, and many other animals, are widely sought by modern collectors. This has led, unfortunately, to disastrous looting of many Mimbres sites. The changes in pottery decoration provide one guide for dating southwestern sites. Dendrochronology was pioneered in the Southwest and is also very important for dating here.

**Hohokam.** The largest and best-known Hohokam site is **Snaketown,** occupied during 2,300 to 900 years ago. In addition to several hundred pithouses, Snaketown has several large trash mounds that in later periods were capped with clay, perhaps to form a ceremonial platform, and a structure that resembles Mesoamerican ball courts. The burials at Snaketown and other Hohokam sites are cremations. Some artifacts have affiliations with Mexico. These include mosaics of shell and stone inlaid onto wood, etched shell ornaments, carved stone plaques and vessels, feathers of tropical birds, and copper bells. There has long been a debate about the nature of contacts between Mexico and the Hohokam region. At one time, most archaeologists believed that there were one or more migrations from Mexico into the area. However, the excavator of Snaketown, Emil Haury (1976), now believes that the Mexican traits can be explained by trade and indirect contact rather than actual migrations.

From its start, Snaketown had an elaborate irrigation system of canals bringing water from the Gila River to the fields. Canal systems were important all over the very dry Hohokam area. An excavated Hohokam canal on the outskirts of Phoenix was at least five and a half feet deep and probably several miles long.

Around 900 years ago, Snaketown and many Hohokam pithouse towns were abandoned, and new sites were occupied with above-ground architecture. These multistoried buildings were made of thick adobe walls to keep out the cold of the desert in winter and the heat in summer. The "Great House" at Casa Grande between Phoenix and Tucson, which can be visited today, is three or four stories tall and definitely suggests some kind of

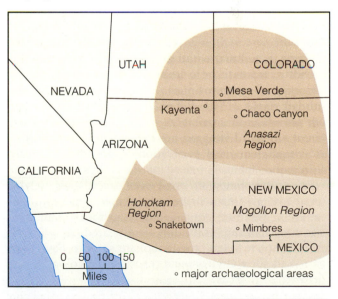

◆ ● ◆

EXHIBIT 11-4

**Major prehistoric traditions in the Southwest**

Mimbres pottery from southern New Mexico.

fortification. In some parts of the Hohokam region at this time, pottery similar to Anasazi styles became popular, and inhumation (burial in the flesh) replaced cremation. This may be evidence of people moving from the Anasazi region or local communities adopting new practices from that area. The irrigation systems were expanded, suggesting that agriculture intensified. Then, about 550 years ago, most of the known Hohokam sites were abandoned and population dropped precipitously. When the Spanish arrived in the 1500s, they found communities living in small pithouse villages, relying on many wild foods and very simple irrigation. The mounds, the ball courts, the multistoried buildings, and the elaborate crafts had disappeared. As with the Mississippian towns, the Hohokam seem to have overstretched their environment, causing an ecological and demographic crisis.

**Anasazi.** In the Anasazi region, pithouse villages were used until about 1,300 years ago. Then people began gradually building multistoried stone **pueblos.** Some of these were placed in rock overhangs and became the famous "cliff dwellings" of Mesa Verde and the Kayenta region. Within each pueblo, living and storage rooms were rectangular, while circular subterranean rooms were used as kivas. The climate, especially in protected rock shelters, has preserved many roof beams for dendrochronology. Burials were inhumations, and Mexican-style artifacts were rare.

Although the Anasazi region received more rainfall than the Hohokam region, precipitation could be erratic; in addition, much of the Anasazi region was located at an altitude where late frosts in the spring or early ones in the fall could destroy crops. The Anasazi did not have large rivers to use for irrigation; they

Anasazi people built pueblos, including so-called cliff dwellings, from about 1300 years ago onward.

focused efforts on controlling runoff from fierce summer thunderstorms through check dams, terracing, and stone grids to hold in soil and water. Modern Pueblo culture gives us some information about the importance of rain and fertility in religious rituals conducted both in kivas (which exist today at Zuni, Hopi, Acoma, and other pueblos) and in the central plazas of the pueblos. Most anthropologists think that somewhat similar rituals took place in the prehistoric pueblos.

One special region within the Anasazi area is **Chaco Canyon** in northern New Mexico. On the valley floor and on the tops of the mesas at Chaco are eleven large, multistoried pueblos and hundreds of small sites that were occupied during approximately 1,100 to 900 years ago. The largest is the four-story **Pueblo Bonito,** a D-shaped pueblo with numerous large kivas still preserved. At Pueblo Bonito were found the most Mexican artifacts of any Anasazi site. Today, Chaco Canyon is too dry for reliable agriculture, and palynology and geoarchaeology tell us that the same was probably true 1,000 years ago. The most elaborate water control systems of the Anasazi region, including canals and holding ponds, are found at Chaco. Aerial photography has revealed that Chaco was the center of a series of roads running out of the canyon and connecting with other pueblos up to 100 miles away. There are so many kivas at Chaco that it seems likely that people from a wide area came here for religious purposes; perhaps these roads were pilgrimage routes. The roads may also be the routes that human carriers followed to bring food into Chaco Canyon from more well-watered areas.

A pattern of growth and abandonment is characteristic of Anasazi settlement. One hundred and fifty years after Chaco Canyon reached its highest population, it

Pueblo Bonito is a large, D-shaped site in the dry Chaco Canyon of northern New Mexico.

was virtually empty, and a similar pattern occurred in other Anasazi regions. When the Spanish explorer Francisco Vásquez de Coronado arrived in 1540, most of the areas of major prehistoric population were almost empty, and pueblo people were clustered along the Rio Grande and in a few other places such as the Hopi mesas of northeast Arizona. Drought, warfare, and disease have all been suggested to explain these fluctuations in settlement, but archaeologists do not yet agree on a single answer. However, the Southwest is a very fragile environment, particularly in terms of adequate rainfall for agriculture. If populations grew beyond the limits of the environment, disease, conflict, and migration may have been the result.

## ◆ ◆ ◆
# Two Worlds Meet

We can try to imagine how news of strange, light-skinned men filtered through the Caribbean and into what is now the southern United States during the years after 1492. The Spanish explored the coasts of the southeastern U.S. in the 1520s, but the first concen-trated contact with Europeans occurred from 1535 to 1540 when Coronado explored the Southwest, de Soto explored the Southeast, and Jacques Cartier wintered on the banks of the St. Lawrence River.

By 1800, especially in the eastern U.S., the Native American population had dramatically declined and the native cultures were badly disturbed. Some of the death and destruction was due to purposeful European actions to force American Indians to change their cultures, though the Europeans were not better soldiers than the Indians, and the European guns of the early exploration period were not much more effective than bows and arrows in the hands of a skilled native warrior. But the Europeans had another weapon, one they may not have been aware of: disease. The native American population had never been exposed to measles, smallpox, influenza, and other diseases (possibly because native Americans had never lived in close contact with domesticated animals) and had no natural immunities to them. The death rate from disease was much higher among Indians than among Europeans.

After at least 12,000 years of cultural development and adaptation, aboriginal American cultures faced their most difficult experience of culture change.

## SETTING THE RECORD STRAIGHT

When you think of southern plantations, do you think of neat white frame cabins clustered around the gracious "Big House," like something out of *Gone with the Wind?* Do you think of the slaves as they were often described in writings by plantation owners, as childlike dependents who had to be fed, cared for, and told what to think? Historical archaeologists are joining with historians to reveal a much greater complexity in the lives of slaves and, in the process, restore the dignity of people who, although oppressed and exploited, struggled to maintain their own culture.

"Slave cabin archaeology" or "plantation archaeology" was pioneered by Charles Fairbanks of the University of Florida in the 1960s in response to a growing interest in black history inspired by the Civil Rights movement (Ferguson, 1992). Although excavation of slave houses is still infrequent compared to excavations in historic structures used by whites, archaeological evidence about slave life is growing. A picture is emerging of a culture maintaining significant ties to its African origins, particularly in the 1600s and 1700s. For example, archaeological evidence shows that prior to the nineteenth century, slaves (and ex-slaves) lived in houses—certainly built by themselves—with architectural parallels to West African structures. The walls were sticks and mud, not stone, logs, or boards, and the basic unit of construction was a twelve-foot by twelve-foot square (often two of these rooms side by side in each dwelling), not the sixteen-foot by sixteen-foot square typical of Anglo-American culture (Ferguson, 1992; Deetz, 1977). Some of the pottery that slaves used for cooking, eating, and storing food were commercial European ceramics issued by the slaveowners, but slaves also made their own pottery, called Colono Ware. They frequently incised the bottom of the vessels with geometric signs that resemble important symbolic motifs from West Africa. The slaves did not use all forms of European ceramics; excavation shows that they frequently prefered bowls for serving food and avoided plates and platters, even in the period when planters and slaveowners ate most of their food off of plates. This preference probably means that slaves held onto their traditional African cuisine, consisting of many small bowls of relishes eaten with a starch such as rice or porridge. Although some slave food was provided as rations from the planter, large amounts of excavated wild animal bone from slave cabin sites show that slaves controlled parts of their own diet through hunting and fishing. Slaves in the southeastern U.S. also decorated their pipes with African motifs.

In 1740, twice as many black people as white people lived in South Carolina, and these black people did much of the real work of the state, building plantation houses, creating elaborate rice fields, cooking, and caring for children. They or their ancestors had been brought forcibly to the New World. They may have been enslaved physically, but they maintained their own culture and expressed it where they could. That culture was ignored or denigrated by planters and so does not appear in written documents of the period. Archaeology allows us to understand better the true complexity and richness of slave life in the eighteenth century.

## HISTORICAL ARCHAEOLOGY

Although archaeology is most important for investigating prehistoric cultures, it is also useful in the investigation of periods for which there are historical documents, because such documents may give an incomplete or biased picture of the culture of the time. European accounts of the early explorations provide us with the European point of view. It is more difficult to figure out what the American Indians were thinking. They often greeted the explorers with both curiosity and hospitality but became wary and even violent after their hospitality was exploited by the Spanish.

Several early contact sites have been excavated, including **Anhaica,** the town of the Apalachee Indians where de Soto's expedition spent its first winter (Ewen, 1989). Most sixteenth-century sites show evidence that the Indians incorporated European goods into their existing culture; glass beads and silver ornaments were used along with aboriginal shell beads and gorgets in the burials of the elite. By the seventeenth century, more utilitarian trade goods, such as iron kettles and guns, were being used. Excavations near Chapel Hill, North Carolina (Dickens et al., 1987), show that by 1701 the native practice of digging round or oval burial pits had been replaced by the European practice of digging rectangular pits. Kathleen Deagan's excavations (1983) of sixteenth-century St. Augustine, Florida, revealed a distinctive *mestizo* material culture resulting from Spanish men and Indian women setting up households together: the cooking pottery and food preparation tools are completely Indian, but the "company dishes" were imported Spanish ceramics. A new cuisine quickly developed, joining American maize, beans, squashes, and peppers with European wheat, pork, peaches, and watermelon.

Historical archaeologists must have skills in using archives and frequently must map and excavate standing buildings. Many historical archaeologists focus their attention on the Euro-American cultures that were established following the exploration period. Long-term archaeological research projects at such sites as Williamsburg, Virginia, have yielded thousands of artifacts and architectural details that assist in the reconstruction of historic buildings. Anthropological archaeologists interested in the historic period also use archaeology to understand less material parts of the culture of the time. For example, James Deetz and colleagues (Deetz, 1977) have shown how changes in patterns of excavated ceramics and architectural remains in the Plymouth, Massachusetts, colony reflect changes in ideology and worldview from the sixteenth through the eighteenth century.

Excavations in historic period sites are also important because they reveal the lives of peoples who were cut off from education and access to written documents, such as Chinese immigrants in California and slaves on southern plantations. Excavations in several nineteenth-century sites in California reveal how important traditional Chinese food, cooking techniques, and medicines were to the immigrant community, about whom very few written records exist (Greenwood, 1978; Pastron, 1989). A growing number of excavations in the southern United States has revealed how complex the life of slaves was, a complexity that is often ignored in the writings of slave owners.

## ◆ Summary

1. The full range of archaeological techniques has been used to reveal the prehistory of North America. In addition, ethnographic, ethnohistorical, and historic evidence are also important to American archaeologists.

2. Humans entered North America from Asia at least 12,000 years ago. They probably arrived on foot in a gradual migration while hunting large game animals in the region of the Bering Land Bridge. Some archaeologists would argue for a much earlier arrival, but there is controversy about all sites identified as earlier than 12,000 years old.

3. Paleoindians all over North America lived a migratory hunting-and-gathering style of life, utilizing finely chipped, fluted points.

4. Between 10,000 and 3,000 years ago, during the Archaic period, people adapted to changing and generally warming climates. Among other things, subsistence became more diversified, ground stone tools became important, and the first burial mounds were used. In the Late Archaic, the first domesticated crops appeared. Pottery was introduced at this time in the eastern U.S. and about 1,800 years ago in the Southwest.

5. Later prehistory in both southwestern and eastern North America is characterized by growing populations, increasing sedentism, complex trade networks, increasing reliance on agriculture and, especially in the eastern U.S., growing stratification. In the Southwest, people developed sophisticated water control systems to support agriculture. In the Midwest and Southeast, burial mounds and temple mounds were important constructions.

6. The first significant contact between European adventurers and native North Americans occurred in the mid-sixteenth century. The contact included trade, warfare, missionization, and in some places, intermarriage. Introduced diseases, such as smallpox and influenza, were the Europeans' most effective weapons and led to the destruction of many, but not all, native cultures.

7. Historical archaeologists use both archaeological techniques and written records to investigate American cultures since the time of contact. Although much historical archaeology has focused on houses and towns of the Anglo-American elite, archaeologists have also made important contributions to our knowledge of minorities, who are often underrepresented in historical documents.

## ◆ Key Terms

Anasazi
Anhaica
Archaic
basket-loading
Bering land bridge
Cahokia
Chaco Canyon
chiefdoms
Clovis
Clovis point
fiber-tempered pottery
glaciations
goosefoot
grit-tempered pottery
gorget
Hohokam
Hopewell
Hopewell Interaction Sphere
ice-free corridor
kiva
megafauna
Mississippian
Mogollon
Native American Grave Protection and Repatriation Act
Paleoindian
pithouse
Pueblo Bonito
pueblo
raptorial bird
shaman
shellmound
shell-tempered pottery
Snaketown
Southeastern Ceremonial Complex
squash
sumpweed
sunflower
temple mound
Woodland

## ◆ Suggested Readings

Deetz, James. *In Small Things Forgotten: The Archeology of Early American Life*. New York: Anchor Press/Doubleday, 1977. A short, elegantly written introduction to historic archaeology, emphasizing Anglo-American sites.

Fagan, Brian M. *Ancient North America: The Archaeology of a Continent*. New York: Thames and Hudson, 1991. An excellently illustrated, comprehensive review of North American prehistory, with a large, useful bibliography.

*Natural History*. Vol. 95, no. 11 through Vol. 97, no. 2 (November 1986–February 1988). A series of fourteen articles about the controversies over the peopling of the Americas. Contributions by all the major players discussing all the major sets of data and points of view. Written for the interested layperson.

Thomas, David Hurst (Ed.). *Columbian Consequences*. Vols. 1–3. Washington, D.C.: Smithsonian Institution Press, 1989–1991. Three massive volumes about archaeological, ethnohistorical, and historical perspectives on the experience of contact between the Spanish and the American Indians. Volume 1 covers the Southwest, Volume 2 covers the Southeast and the Caribbean, and Volume 3 discusses general issues.

# Archaeology and Native Americans

Most archaeologists are fascinated by the skilled technology of American Indians before the time of Columbus. These peoples coped successfully with their world without the metal tools and machinery we tend to think of as essential. Unfortunately, despite the respect archaeologists feel for prehistoric Indian technology, conflicts have arisen between Native Americans and archaeologists and physical anthropologists (see also Applied Perspective, Chapter 6). In England or Greece, archaeologists study their own past, but in the United States, almost all archaeologists studying ancient Indian cultures are of European heritage, not Native American heritage. This is also true of museum curators. In recent years, tensions have grown between archaeologists and Indians. The debate has touched on excavation in general, but the most intensive focus is on excavation and curation of burials. The following case studies illustrate some of the practical ethical concerns of modern archaeology and the use of ancient technologies to solve modern problems.

## ◆ Archaeologists and Native Americans work out disagreements over burial excavations.

While many archaeologists and physical anthropologists feel that excavation and analysis of ancient American skeletal remains is essential for learning about the American past and for gaining information about human health and society in general, many Indians find the idea of such excavation repugnant. In the historical context of centuries of denigration and destruction of Indian cultures by the dominant white society, excavation is often seen by Indians as just one more imperialist act by Euro-Americans. Although there is not consensus among all Indians (nor among all archaeologists, for that matter), many Indian activists have protested excavations and lobbied for legislative protection for Indian burials.

From an anthropological perspective, this is a debate between competing value systems: one that emphasizes the positive value of scientific knowledge and one that emphasizes the positive value of traditional religious practices. The disagreements are exacerbated by a great deal of miscommunication. Archaeologists resent being lumped together with irresponsible pot hunters and being called vandals and racists. Indians resent the use of their ancestors for scientific analysis and museum displays. Similar debates are occurring in other countries, including Australia which has had a colonial history similar to that of the U.S. (McBryde, 1985). The outcome of these controversies has direct practical impact on archaeologists and museums. The debate raises the most important and difficult ethical and practical problems that archaeologists and curators currently face.

The debate consists of several questions. First, who, if anyone, should have the right to excavate and analyze human skeletal remains; and under what conditions? Some Indian activists propose that no excavation should be allowed under any circumstances, even if erosion or construction are destroying the burials. Others propose that excavation may occur in some situations but only after appropriate Indian groups have been consulted.

Some archaeologists think that limitations should apply only to historic-period burials where an actual genealogical link can be traced to living Indian people.

Second, should any curation of human skeletal remains be allowed, or should all skeletal remains, including those that have been stored for many years in museums, be reburied by Indian communities? Can very old prehistoric skeletons be curated but not more recent ones that are more closely related to living people?

Third, should artifacts accompanying burials also be protected from excavation, reclaimed from museums, and reburied with appropriate religious ceremonies? Should other artifacts that were never burial goods be returned from museums to Indian communities because of their traditional religious importance? An example of such artifacts is elaborately patterned wampum belts, made of shell beads, which are important ceremonial objects of the Onondaga Nation of New York. Twelve of these belts had been housed in the New York State Museum, some of them since 1898, but in 1989 the State Museum agreed to return the belts to the Onondaga.

One overarching question is: Who shall say? Or, as Australian archaeologist Isabel McBryde (1985) puts it: Who owns the past? Knowledge about the past can be a powerful ideological and political tool (consider how important black history became at the time of the Civil Rights movement), and control of access to that knowledge can be an important political issue. For Indian activists, this is an issue of fundamental human and civil rights.

Many states and the federal government have recently taken legislative steps to find a compromise among the many opinions on these issues. Numerous states now have laws that require consultation between archaeologists and Indian communities before the excavation of any burials; allow or encourage reburial of skeletal material after analysis; and forbid the public display of skeletal remains. Many of these state laws are recent and it is not yet clear how they will work in practice (Price, 1991). Extremists on both sides of the issue feel that any compromise is wrong, but these laws are a basis for respectful negotiation of the problems.

In 1990, the U.S. government passed the **Native American Grave Protection and Repatriation Act,** which applies both to burials discovered on federal land in the future and to existing museum collections of artifacts and skeletal remains from Native American burials. Representatives from the Society for American Archaeology and representatives from several Indian, Native Alaskan, and Native Hawaiian communities participated in writing this legislation. It mandates consultation with Native American groups before any excavation of burials on federal lands; gives complete authority over burials discovered on tribal lands to the tribal government; and mandates reburial of skeletal remains and return of sacred objects from existing museum collections upon the request of the appropriate group. As with many state laws, this legislation is so recent that actual implementation is still being worked out, but all the major anthropological museums in the country have begun responding to requests for return of skeletal and cultural material.

The controversy over excavation and study of prehistoric burials has been, at times, an angry and stressful one for all parties involved. However,

many hope that the ultimate solutions will include not only a recognition of Native American rights over their own past but new kinds of cooperation between archaeologists and Native Americans to preserve and learn about past American cultures.

The Zuni and Navaho tribes in New Mexico and Arizona and the Colville Confederated Tribes of the state of Washington provide examples of cooperation. Each tribe maintains tribal archaeological agencies that conduct cultural resource management and other archaeological research on tribal lands, provide education to tribal members and others in the area, and work as advocates for preservation (Klesert and Downer, 1990). These tribal agencies employ both Euro-American and, increasingly, Indian archaeologists. The Smithsonian is currently planning a new unit, the National Museum of the American Indian, whose staff will be largely Native American.

In the eastern United States, where Indian groups are often smaller in number and own less land than those in the west, the Mashantucket Pequots of Connecticut used archaeological evidence as an essential part of their application for federal recognition as an Indian tribe. Their application was approved in 1983 and immediately yielded practical benefits to the tribe through federally mandated social services and other grants for economic development (Silberman, 1991). Since 1983, the tribe has sponsored an intensive archaeological mapping project as part of its cultural heritage program. Originally, the tribe was completely opposed to excavation of burials, but the accidental disturbance of several historic Pequot burials during construction of a house in the region forced a reconsideration. The Euro-American archaeologists, supervised by tribal members, excavated the threatened burials and conducted a nondestructive analysis of bones and grave goods that revealed new information about Pequot history. Then the burials were reburied in a ceremony conducted by a traditional Indian medicine man. As archaeologist Neil Silberman (1991:39) says, this archaeological program "may well serve as a model for productive cooperation between archaeologists and indigenous peoples all over the world."

### ◆ Prehistoric obsidian tools provide improvements in modern-day surgery.

Modern Americans particularly take pride in the technological developments of our medical system. Recently, however, archaeologists have provided information about ancient tools that has helped improve chest and eye surgery. Don Crabtree of the Idaho State Museum first suggested the use of prehistoric obsidian tools to his surgeon. Obsidian is a natural glass available in areas of ancient volcanic activity. It can be chipped to make an extremely sharp edge and was widely sought after by prehistoric people of the Americas and elsewhere. Crabtree was one of the pioneers in experimentally replicating stone tools to study their manufacture, and he became familiar with the cutting qualities of both flints and obsidians found in the western United States. He examined some obsidian blades under an electron microscope and discovered that they were more than 200 times sharper than modern surgical scalpels (Sheets, 1993). He also discovered that when he cut himself with obsidian flakes during various experiments, the cuts healed rapidly.

In 1975, when Crabtree needed major lung surgery, he persuaded his doctor, Bruce A. Buck, to use obsidian blades instead of surgical scalpels. It turned out that healing with obsidian blades was faster than with standard equipment, and scarring was much reduced. Since 1980, archaeologists Payson Sheets, Jeff Flenniken, and others have all been experimenting with producing standardized obsidian blades for use by surgeons. Sheets did more systematic examination with an electron microscope to learn the details of the working edge of the blades and has been collaborating with eye surgeons. Eye surgery in particular requires accuracy and control of scarring. The extreme sharpness of obsidian blades gives the surgeon more control because there is less resistance and, therefore, the eye moves less. This particular experimental archaeology has some very personal aspects to it: Archaeologist William Clewlow produced the obsidian blades used in his kidney stone operation, and Errett Callahan produced the blades he used to cut his daughter's umbilical cord.

## CHAPTER 12

# The Growth of Ethnological Theory

Who have been the important theorists in cultural anthropology since the mid-nineteenth century?

What theories have been used by cultural anthropologists to explain cultural differences and similarities among the people of the world?

How can ethnological data be used to make large-scale comparisons between cultures?

Differences in the way people look, speak, think, and behave have been recognized throughout the course of human history. Even in the absence of any written records we can assume that early humans recognized differences in what we now refer to as the "culture" of foreign peoples. It is possible, for example, to trace the roots of ethnological thinking back to such early classical philosophers as Herodotus, Tacitus, and Strabo, all of whom had considerable curiosity about differences in the customs of those with whom they came into contact.

Our understanding of foreign populations took a quantum leap forward from the fifteenth century onward as a result of the worldwide explorations set into motion by Prince Henry the Navigator of Portugal. By the early nineteenth century, the Western scholarly community had accumulated sufficient "ethnographic" data to realize that there was enormous diversity in the world's populations.

As we accumulated more and more data on the uniqueness of life-styles of the world's population, a need arose to explain the cultural differences and similarities. This desire to account for the vast cultural variations found in the world gave rise to ethnological theories. A theory is a statement that suggests a relationship between phenomena. Theories enable us to reduce reality into an abstract set of principles, and these principles should then enable us to make sense out of a variety of ethnographic information from different parts of the world. A good theory is one that can both explain and predict. In other words, theories as models of reality enable us to bring some measure of order to a complex world.

Even when theories remain unproven, however, they are useful for research, for they can generate hypotheses to be tested in an empirical research investigation. In testing a hypothesis, it is possible to determine how close the *actual* findings are to the *expected* findings. If what is found is consistent with what was expected, the theory will be strengthened; if not, the theory will likely be revised or abandoned. Ethnological theory changes constantly in response to the scientific need to develop new theories in light of the new data being brought forth continuously.

Ethnological theories attempt to answer such questions as, Why do people behave as they do? and, How do we account for human diversity? These questions guided the early nineteenth-century attempts to theorize and continue to be relevant today. This chapter explores —roughly in chronological order—the major theoretical schools of cultural anthropology that have developed since the mid-nineteenth century. Some of the earlier

theoretical orientations (e.g., **diffusionism**) no longer attract much attention; others (e.g., **evolutionism**) have been refined and reworked into something new, while still others (e.g., **functionalism**) continue to command some popularity. It is easy, of course, to be a Monday morning quarterback by demonstrating the inherent flaws in some of the early theoretical orientations. We should keep in mind, however, that contemporary ethnological theories that may appear plausible today were in fact built on what we learned from those older theories. Table 12-1 is a summary of the theories discussed in this chapter. Table 12-2 is a time line that lists significant world events that occurred during various stages of anthropological development.

## Evolutionism

Trying to account for the vast diversity in human cultures, the first group of early ethnologists, writing during the mid-nineteenth century, suggested the theory of cultural evolution. The basic premise of these early anthropological theorists was that all societies pass through a series of distinct, sharply bounded evolutionary stages. We find differences in contemporary cultures because they are at different evolutionary stages of development. This theory, developed by **Edward Tylor** in England and **Louis Henry Morgan** in the United States, saw European culture at the top of the evolutionary ladder, while "less-developed" cultures occupied the lower stages. The evolutionary process was thought to progress from simpler (lower) forms to increasingly more complex (higher) forms of culture. Those "primitive" societies occupying the lower echelons of the evolutionary ladder need only to wait an indeterminable length of time before eventually (and inevitably) rising to the top. It was assumed that all cultures pass through the same set of preordained evolutionary stages. Although both Tylor and Morgan were familiar with the writings of Darwin, they were more heavily influenced by the notions of progress set forth by such social evolutionists as Comte and Spencer.

### EDWARD B. TYLOR

Edward B. Tylor (1832–1917) was an Englishman who took issue with earlier theories that contemporary pre-

**TABLE 12-1** ◆ **Some Ethnological Theories and Their Proponents**

| School | Major Assumption | Principal Advocates |
|---|---|---|
| Evolutionism | All societies pass through a series of stages. | Tylor, Morgan |
| Diffusionism | All societies change as a result of cultural borrowing from one another. | Smith, Perry, Graebner, Schmidt |
| American Historicism | The collection of ethnographic facts through direct fieldwork must precede the development of cultural theories. | Boas Kroeber |
| Functionalism | Through direct field research, early twentieth-century functionalists sought to understand how parts of contemporary cultures functioned for the well-being of the individual. | Malinowski |
| Structural Functionalism | Disregarding the search for origins, the task to the cultural anthropologist is to determine how cultural elements function for the well-being of the society. | Radcliffe-Brown |
| Psychological Anthropology | The central task of the cultural anthropologist is to show the relationship between psychological and cultural variables. | Benedict, Sapir, Mead |
| Neoevolutionism | Cultures evolve in direct proportion to their capacity to harness energy. | White |
| French Structuralism | Human cultures are shaped by certain preprogrammed codes of the human mind. | Lévi-Strauss |
| Ethnoscience | The ethnographer must describe a culture in terms of native categories (emic view) rather than in terms of his/her own categories. | Sturtevant Goodenough |

literate societies were examples of cultural degeneration. He posited that all cultures evolve from simple to more complex forms, passing through three basic stages (savagery, barbarism, and civilization). Even though this threefold evolutionary scheme appears terribly ethnocentric by today's standards, we must remember that it replaced the prevailing theory that explained the existence of small-scale, preliterate societies by claiming that they were people whose ancestors had fallen from grace. Hunters and gatherers, it had been argued previously, possessed simple levels of technology because their degeneration had made them intellectually inferior to those peoples with more technological sophistication.

To counter this theological/biological interpretation of human differences, Tylor suggested the notion of progressing through a series of different cultural stages. Yet despite his insistence upon the primacy of evolution, Tylor never discounted the notion of diffusion. For example, he was particularly struck by the incredible similarities between the Aztec game of *patolli* and the game of pachisi which originated in Asia and later became popular in Europe and the United States. Since he felt that a game so complicated could not be invented at two different times, he concluded that it must have been diffused.

## LOUIS HENRY MORGAN

While Tylor was writing in England, Louis Henry Morgan (1818–1881) was founding the evolutionary "school" in the United States. A lawyer in Rochester, New York, Morgan was hired to represent the neighboring Iroquois Indians in a land grant dispute. After the lawsuit was resolved, Morgan conducted an ethnographic study of the Seneca Indians (one of the Iroquois group). Fascinated by the Senecas' matrilineal kinship system, Morgan circulated questionnaires and traveled fairly extensively around the United States gathering information about kinship systems found among North American Indians and elsewhere in the world. This kinship research—which some have suggested may be Morgan's most enduring contribution to the comparative study of culture—was published in *Systems of Consanguinity and Affinity* in 1871.

In keeping with the general evolutionary tenor of his times, Morgan published his most famous book, entitled *Ancient Society*, in 1877. In it he developed a system of classifying cultures to determine their evolutionary niche. Morgan, like Tylor, used the categories of savagery, barbarism, and civilization but was more specific in defining them according to the presence or absence of

TABLE 12-2 ◆ Time Line

| Milestone Works in Anthropology | What Else Was Going On in the World? |
|---|---|
| Louis Henry Morgan, *Ancient Society* (1877) (example of 19th-century evolutionism) | —Rutherford B. Hayes elected U.S. president<br>—Edison invents phonograph<br>—Publication of Tolstoy's *Anna Karenina*<br>—First Wimbledon tennis championship<br>—Queen Victoria (England) proclaimed Empress of India |
| Fritz Graebner, "Kulturkreise und Kulturschichten in Ozeanien" (1903) (example of diffusionist school) | —First Tour de France bicycle race<br>—Ford Motor Company founded<br>—Alaskan frontier settled<br>—First powered aircraft flown by Wright Brothers<br>—Oscar Hammerstein builds Manhattan Opera House |
| Franz Boas, The Republic. *Mind of Primitive Man* (1911) (example of American historicism) | —Sun Yat-sen elected president of China<br>—Marie Curie wins Nobel Prize for Chemistry<br>—Ronald Reagan born<br>—Roald Amundsen reaches the South Pole<br>—Irving Berlin writes "Alexander's Ragtime Band"<br>—Golfing great Bobby Jones wins first tourney at age nine |
| B. Malinowski, *Argonauts of the Western Pacific* (1922) (example of British functionalism) | —Insulin first administered to diabetic patients<br>—Mussolini forms Fascist government in Italy<br>—King Tut's tomb discovered at Luxor<br>—Publication of James Joyce's *Ulysses*<br>—Prohibition against alcohol in effect in United States |
| Margaret Mead, *Coming of Age in Samoa* (1928) (example of psychological anthropology) | —Amelia Earhart flies across Atlantic Ocean<br>—Herbert Hoover elected U.S. president<br>—First Mickey Mouse animated cartoon released<br>—First scheduled TV broadcast in Schenectedy, New York<br>—Chiang Kai-shek elected president of China<br>—First color motion picture exhibited in Rochester, New York, by George Eastman |
| Leslie White, *The Evolution of Culture* (1959) (example of Neo-evolutionism) | —Charles De Gaulle becomes President of France<br>—Hawaii becomes fiftieth state in the Union<br>—Richard Rodgers writes *The Sound of Music*<br>—Zinjanthropus skull discovered at Olduvai Gorge<br>—Pope John XXIII calls first Ecumenical Council since 1870<br>—*The Twilight Zone* premieres on TV<br>—Vladimir Nabakov, *Lolita* (English translation) |
| Claude Levi-Strauss, *Structural Anthropology* (1963) (example of French structuralism) | —Assassination of John F. Kennedy<br>—Release of film *Tom Jones*<br>—Sonny Liston retains heavyweight boxing crown<br>—Jack Nicklaus wins his first Masters tournament<br>—United States post office introduces zip codes<br>—Joan Baez and Bob Dylan are most popular folk singers<br>—USSR puts first woman in space<br>—Marilyn Monroe dies of drug overdose<br>—Betty Friedan, *The Feminine Mystique* |

certain technological features. Moreover, Morgan divided the stages of savagery and barbarism into three distinct subcategories—lower, middle, and upper. Morgan defined these seven evolutionary stages—through which all societies allegedly passed—in the following way:

1. *Lower savagery*. From the earliest forms of humanity subsisting on fruits and nuts.
2. *Middle savagery*. Began with the discovery of fishing technology and the use of fire.
3. *Upper savagery*. Began with the invention of the bow and arrow.

TABLE 12-2 ◆ Time Line (continued)

| Milestone Works in Anthropology | What Else Was Going On in the World? |
| --- | --- |
| W. Sturtevant, "Studies in Ethnoscience" (1964) (example of ethnoscience) | —James Hoffa found guilty of jury tampering<br>—Lyndon Johnson elected U.S. president<br>—Poll tax abolished by Twenty-fourth Amendment<br>—United States Surgeon General declares cigarette smoking hazardous to health<br>—Martin Luther King wins Nobel Peace Prize<br>—Popular song: "I Want to Hold Your Hand" (Beatles)<br>—Jomo Kenyatta becomes president of Kenya<br>—North Americans dance the Watusi at discos<br>—Elizabeth Taylor divorces Eddie Fisher and marries Richard Burton ten days later<br>—796 arrested at Berkeley free speech movement protest |
| Derek Freeman, Margaret Mead and Samoa (1983) (stirred a controversy over the validity of ethnographic data) | —United States invades Grenada<br>—Sally Ride becomes first United States woman in space<br>—The biggest show on Broadway was *Cats*<br>—Korean airliner shot down after straying into Soviet air space<br>—Michael Jackson's *Thriller* becomes best-selling album of all time (more than $12 million in sales)<br>—Bombing of U.S. embassy in Beirut, Lebanon |

Lewis Henry Morgan, a 19th-century evolutionist, held that all societies pass through certain distinct evolutionary stages.

4. *Lower barbarism.* Began with the art of pottery making.
5. *Middle barbarism.* Began with the domestication of plants and animals in the Old World and irrigation cultivation in the New World.
6. *Upper barbarism.* Began with the smelting of iron and use of iron tools.
7. *Civilization.* Began with the invention of the phonetic alphabet and writing. (1877:12)

## DEFENSE OF EARLY THEORIES

The theories of the early evolutionists Tylor and Morgan have been criticized by succeeding generations of ethnologists. The nineteenth-century evolutionists have been charged with being ethnocentric, for they concluded that western societies represented the highest levels of human achievement. They have also been criticized for being armchair speculators, putting forth grand schemes to explain cultural diversity based on fragmentary data at best. While there is considerable substance to these criticisms, we must evaluate the nineteenth-century evolutionists with an eye toward the times in which they were writing. As Kaplan and Manners (1986:39—43) remind us, Tylor and Morgan may have overstated their case somewhat because they were trying to establish what Tylor referred to as "the science of culture"—whereby human behavior was explained in terms of a secular evolutionary progress rather than supernatural causes. Moreover, to fault Tylor and Morgan for not relying more heavily on empirical data overlooks two important points: (1) very little data existed in nineteenth-century libraries, and (2) both men made considerable efforts to obtain empirical data from fieldwork (at least in the case of Morgan), extensive travel, and correspondence with other scholars. Kaplan and Manners also point out:

Faced with this shortage of data, they attempted to bridge the gaps in their evolutionary schema with logical and frequently imaginative reconstructions, i.e., by engaging in "armchair speculation." Of course, this kind of speculation is perfectly acceptable scientific procedure. The mistake the speculators often made was to assume that the empirical world was under some obligation to conform to their logical reconstructions (1986:40).

Despite these very real methodological and theoretical shortcomings, the contributions of these early evolutionists should not be overlooked. For example, they firmly established the notion—upon which modern cultural anthropology now rests—that differences in human lifestyles are the result of certain identifiable cultural processes rather than biological processes or divine intervention. Moreover, Morgan's use of techno-economic factors to distinguish between fundamentally different types of cultures remains a viable concept. As Leacock reminds us:

In spite of the disfavor into which Morgan's work fell, his general sequence of stages has been written into our understanding of prehistory and interpretation of archeological remains, as a glance at any introductory anthropology text will indicate (1963:xi).

## ◆ ◆ ◆ Diffusionism

During the late nineteenth and early twentieth centuries, the diffusionists, like the evolutionists, addressed the question of cultural differences in the world. They came up with a radically different answer to that question. The evolutionists may have overestimated human inventiveness by claiming that cultural features have arisen in different parts of the world independently of one another, due in large measure to the **psychic unity** of humankind. At the other extreme, the diffusionists held that humans were essentially uninventive, claiming that certain cultural features were invented originally in one or several parts of the world and then spread, through the process of diffusion, to other cultures.

The diffusionists were divided essentially into two different groups—one from England and the other from Germany/Austria. The British group included, by all accounts, the most extreme proponents of the notion of diffusionism. The main proponents of this position, Sir **Grafton Elliot Smith** (1871–1937) and **W. J. Perry** (1887–1949), held that people were so incredibly uninventive that virtually all culture traits found anywhere in the world were first invented in Egypt and subsequently spread to other parts of the world. For Smith and Perry, the parallel evolution of a particular culture trait in two different parts of the world would be most unlikely, if not impossible. We must bear in mind that neither Smith nor Perry was a professional ethnologist. What Smith (an Australian anatomist and surgeon) and Perry (a school headmaster) had in common was that they both were uncritically enamored with early Egyptian civilization. According to their oversimplified (and inaccurate) scheme, the people of Egypt first developed agriculture and then shortly thereafter invented an elaborate complex of cultural features which then diffused to other parts of the world. Despite the fact that this theory was supported by no acceptable body of data, Smith and Perry's brand of diffusionism found a popular audience. This extreme diffusionist position was never widely accepted in cultural anthropology, its limited credibility was very short lived, and today it has been totally rejected.

**Fritz Graebner** (1877–1934) and Father **Wilhelm Schmidt** (1868–1954), the driving forces behind the German-Austrian group, had a far more scholarly approach to the subject of diffusion than Smith and Perry. The German-Austrians differed from their British counterparts in several important respects. First, whereas the British were concerned with the spread of individual culture traits, the German-Austrians concentrated on the diffusion of entire complexes of cultures. And second, unlike the British, who assumed that all culture traits were invented in one place (Egypt), Graebner and Schmidt suggested that there was a small number of different cultural complexes called culture circles (**kulturkreise**), which served as sources of cultural diffusion. This kulturkreise group devoted its energies to reconstructing these culture circles and demonstrating how they were responsible for worldwide patterns of cultural diffusion.

The diffusionists eventually ran their course after the first several decades of this century. To be certain, they started off with a particularly sound ethnological con-

Here in Calgary, Canada, is a meeting of two different cultural traditions. The diffusionist school of ethnology was based on the notion that borrowing of things, ideas, and behavior patterns will occur when two cultures come into contact with each other.

cept—i.e., cultural diffusion—and either took it to its illogical extreme or left too many questions unanswered. Few cultural anthropologists today would deny the central role that diffusion plays in the process of culture change, but some of the early diffusionists, particularly Smith and Perry, took this essentially valid concept *ad absurdum* by suggesting that everything found in the world could ultimately be traced back to the early Egyptians. Moreover, despite the collection of considerable quantities of historical data, the diffusionists were not able to prove primary centers of invention. Nor were the diffusionists able to answer a number of important questions concerning the process of cultural diffusion. For example, when cultures come into contact with one another, what accounts for the diffusion of some cultural items but not others? What are the conditions required to bring about diffusion of a cultural item? What determines the rate at which a cultural item spreads throughout a geographic region? Then there are some questions that the diffusionists failed to even raise, such as why certain traits arise in the first place. In spite of these limitations, however, the diffusionists did make a major contribution to the study of comparative cultures—that is, they were the first to point out the need to develop theories dealing with contact and interaction between cultures.

As we have seen, the nineteenth-century evolutionists and the diffusionists tried to explain why the world was inhabited by large numbers of highly diverse cultures. The evolutionists invoked the principle of evolution as the major explanatory variable. That is, the world's cultural diversity, according to Tylor and Morgan, resulted from different cultures being at different stages of evolutionary development. The diffusionists proposed a different causal variable to explain the diversity, namely, differential levels of cultural borrowing between societies. Even though both of these nineteenth-century "schools" offered different explanations for the diversity, what they had in common was their deductive approach to the discipline (reasoning from the general to the specific). They started off with a general principle (either evolution or diffusion) and then proceeded to use that principle to explain specific cases. The evolutionists and diffusionists based their theories on inadequate data at best. They seemed to be more interested in universal history than in discovering how different people of the world actually lived their lives. This type of genteel armchair speculation was poignantly illustrated by the evolutionist Sir James Frazer, who, when asked if he had ever seen any of the people about whom he had written, replied, "God forbid!" (Beattie, 1964:7).

## ◆ ◆ ◆ American Historicism

Around the turn of the century, a reaction to this deductive approach was being led primarily by Franz Boas (1858–1942). Coming from an academic background in physics and geography, Boas was appalled by what he saw as speculative theorizing masquerading as science. To Boas's way of thinking, ethnology was altogether on the wrong path. Rather than dreaming up large, all-encompassing theories to explain why particular societies are the way they are, Boas wanted to turn the discipline around 180 degrees by putting it on a sound inductive footing. At that time, the discipline of cultural anthropology simply did not have very much information about the various cultures of the world. According to Boas, any attempt to theorize on such a small and unreliable database was absolutely premature. Instead, the discipline needed to shift its attention away from theorizing to the careful collection of empirical data on as many specific cultures as possible. The development of theories must proceed from a strong empirical database. In other words, Boas argued that cultural anthropology as a discipline must become more inductive by proceeding from large numbers of specific (empirically based) cases to increasingly higher levels of theories and generalizations.

Franz Boas, born and educated in Germany, received a doctorate in physical geography from the University of Kiel. Following his own advice to collect precise and accurate ethnographic facts, Boas conducted extensive fieldwork among the Central Eskimos during the 1880s. Interested in exploring, among other topics, the effects of environment on Eskimo culture, Boas concluded that environment, rather than completely determining, only sets broad limits on the shape a culture will take. In contrast to the geographic determinism that was popular at the time, Boas took the position that cultures are shaped by a number of determinants, some historical, some environmental, and some resulting from the interaction with other cultures.

These early fieldwork experiences sensitized Boas to the complexities of human cultures. Boas felt that this enormous complexity of factors influencing the development of specific cultures rendered any type of sweeping generalization, such as those proposed by the evolutionists and diffusionists, totally inappropriate. Thus, Boas and his followers insisted upon the collection of detailed ethnographic information and at the same time called for a moratorium on theorizing. Boas devoted a considerable amount of his professional energy to uncovering specific cases that would refute the generalizations being set forth by the early evolutionists. As one ethnologist (Harris) put it, the strategy of Boas

... required an almost total suspension of the normal dialectic between fact and theory. The causal processes, the trends, the long range parallels were buried by an avalanche of negative cases (1968:251).

Indeed, some of Boas's more vociferous critics claimed that this antitheoretical stance was responsible for retarding ethnology as a science. Yet, in retrospect, most commentators would agree that his experience in the areas of physics and mathematics enabled Boas to bring to the young discipline of ethnology both methodological rigor and a sense of how to define problems in scientific terms. Even though Boas himself did little theorizing, he did leave the discipline on a sound empirical footing. Ruth Benedict perhaps said it best when she wrote:

Boas found anthropology a collection of wild guesses and a happy hunting ground for the romantic lover of primitive things; he left it a discipline in which theories could be tested (1943:61).

In addition to his insistence upon a rigorous type of empiricism, Boas also made significant contributions to the field of anthropological linguistics and took a strong stance against racism and genetic determinism.

The impact that Boas had on the discipline is perhaps most eloquently demonstrated by the long list of cultural anthropologists that he trained. As the first ethnological "guru" in the United States, Boas trained virtually the entire first generation of American ethnologists. The list of Boas's students reads like a *Who's Who in Twentieth-Century U.S. Cultural Anthropology*: Margaret Mead, Robert Lowie, Alfred Kroeber, Edward Sapir, Melville J. Herskovits, Ruth Benedict, Paul Radin, Jules Henry, E. Adamson Hoebel, and Ruth Bunzel.

Franz Boas, the teacher of the first generation of cultural anthropologists in the United States, put the discipline on a firm empirical basis.

In recruiting graduate students to study cultural anthropology with him at Columbia University, Boas from the beginning was very purposeful about attracting women into the discipline. Recognizing that male fieldworkers would be excluded from observing certain aspects of a culture by virtue of their gender, Boas felt that the discipline needed both male and female ethnographers if all of a culture was to be described. Today the discipline of cultural anthropology, as compared to other academic disciplines, has a relatively high number of women professionals, a legacy that can be traced back to Boas's methodological concerns when the discipline was in its formative period.

## Functionalism

While Franz Boas was putting cultural anthropology on a more empirical footing in the United States, Bronislav Malinowski (1884–1942) was proceeding inductively by establishing a tradition of firsthand data collection in the United Kingdom. Having completed a doctorate in physics and mathematics in his native Poland, Malinowski, after reading a copy of Frazer's *The Golden Bough,* became so fascinated with comparative cultures that he went to London in 1910 for postgraduate study in anthropology. When World War I broke out in 1914, Malinowski was traveling in the Pacific. Considered as one of the enemy by the British government (which was at war with Poland), Malinowski was forced to spend the duration of the war interned, doing fieldwork on the Trobriand Islands in the Pacific. During what was to become one of the longest uninterrupted fieldwork experiences on record, Malinowski not only set standards for the conduct of participant-observation research but also developed an important new way of looking at cultures, known as functionalism.

Like Boas, Malinowski was a strong advocate of fieldwork. Both men learned the local language and attempted to understand a culture from the perspective of the native. They differed, however, in that Malinowski had no interest in asking how a cultural item got to be the way it is. Believing that little could be learned about the origins of small-scale societies, Malinowski concentrated on how contemporary cultures operated, or functioned. This theoretical orientation assumed that cultures provided various means for satisfying both societal and individual needs. According to Malinowski, no matter how bizarre a cultural item might at first appear, it had a meaning and performed some useful function for the individual or the society. The job of the fieldworker is to become sufficiently immersed in the culture and language to be able to identify these functions. Malinowski's major disagreement with the early evolutionists revolved around Tylor's concept of survivals—those traits that have lost their functions. For Malinowski there were no functionless traits.

Not only do all aspects of a culture have a function, but, according to Malinowski, they are also interrelated. This functionalist tenet is no better illustrated than in Malinowski's own description of the kula ring found among the Trobriand Islanders. While performing the function of distributing goods within the society, the kula is related to many other areas of Trobriand culture, including, among others, political structure, magic, technology, kinship, social status, myth, and social control. To illustrate, the kula involves the exchange of both ceremonial necklaces and bracelets and everyday commodities between trading partners on a large number of islands. Even though the exchanges are based on the principle of reciprocity, there are usually long periods of time between repayments between trading partners. Gouldner (1960:174) has suggested that during these periods debtors are morally obligated to maintain peaceful relationships with their benefactors. If this is, in fact, the case, we can see how the kula ring maintains peace and thereby functions as a mechanism of social control as well as a mechanism of material exchange. Thus, as we examine a cultural feature (like the kula ring) in greater depth, the ethnographer, according to this functionalist perspective, will begin to see how it is related to many other aspects of the culture and what it contributes to both individuals and society as a whole.

Malinowski's theory of culture rested on three types of individual human needs: basic needs, such as food, protection, and sexual outlets; instrumental needs, such as the need for education, law, and social control; and integrative needs, such as the need for psychological security, social harmony, and a common world view. It is important to emphasize that Malinowski saw these as individual, not group, needs. Nevertheless, Malinowski held that every aspect of a culture functions in terms of one of these three types of needs. For Malinowski, then, culture was the instrument by which these basic human needs were met.

## STRUCTURAL FUNCTIONALISM

Another form of functionalism was developed by the British theoretician, **Alfred Reginald Radcliffe-Brown** (1881–1955). Like Malinowski, Radcliffe-Brown posited that the various aspects of a society should be studied in terms of the functions they perform. However, while Malinowski viewed functions mostly as meeting the needs of the individual, Radcliffe-Brown saw them in terms of how they contributed to the well-being of the society. Because of this emphasis on social functions rather than individual functions, Radcliffe-Brown's theory has taken the name of **structural functionalism**.

After studying anthropology at Cambridge University under W.H.R. Rivers, Radcliffe-Brown conducted fieldwork among the Andaman Islanders (a group of islands south of Burma) from 1906 to 1908 and again in Australia from 1910 to 1912. Nevertheless, being somewhat reserved and aloof, his temperament was not particularly well suited for being a fieldworker. Even though he expected extensive fieldwork from his students, he will not be remembered for his accomplishments as a brilliant participant-observer. Instead, his major contributions were more as a theorist and a teacher. During much of his career he was an "itinerant scholar," teach-

ing at universities in Chicago, Sydney, Cape Town, and Oxford.

Malinowski and Radcliffe-Brown were similar in some basic respects. For example, both men were strong advocates of direct fieldwork as the only legitimate way of obtaining ethnographic data. Moreover, both took a synchronic approach to the discipline, that is, looking at contemporary societies in terms of the relationship between customs and institutions rather than looking for historical origins. But there were also fundamental differences in the theoretical constructs each used. Malinowski drew heavily upon the concept of *culture*, a broadly defined abstraction used in much the same way as we defined it in Chapter 2. On the other hand, the unit of analysis for Radcliffe-Brown, which he called social structure, was more limited in scope than the concept of culture. Although not always precisely defined, social structure for Radcliffe-Brown referred to the network of social relations found among a group of people. More specifically, as one social theorist put it (Garbarino, 1977:58), social structure involves the "underlying principles of organization among persons and groups in society or the set of actual roles and relationships that could be observed." Since Radcliffe-Brown called for the comparative study of contemporary social structures, he viewed the discipline of anthropology largely as comparative sociology.

Radcliffe-Brown's analysis of **mother-in-law avoidance** serves as an excellent example of his structural-functional approach. Found in a number of different parts of the world, mother-in-law avoidance refers to a custom whereby the social interaction between a man and his wife's mother is either limited in some specific way or prohibited altogether. The nature of the avoidance takes a number of different forms: prohibitions against a man's having face-to-face interaction with his mother-in-law, mentioning her name in public, or eating her food. Radcliffe-Brown saw his task as one of explaining why this type of avoidance exists rather than seeking its historical origins. In other words, Radcliffe-Brown wanted to reveal what function the custom performs for the well-being of the social system.

If we were to view mother-in-law avoidance from the perspective of our own culture, we might conclude that it represents a form of hostility, for we tend to avoid people we dislike. However, based on research that he conducted among the Australian aborigines who practice an extreme form of mother-in-law avoidance, Radcliffe-Brown found that a man avoids contact with his wife's mother for exactly the opposite reason; that is, he has great respect and admiration for his mother-in-law

Sometimes our best intentions go unappreciated when trying to operate in a culturally different environment. While living in Ethiopia in 1964, one of the authors met two Peace Corps teachers assigned to a secondary school in Makele located in Tigre Provence. Even though both volunteers were well-trained, enthusiastic, and highly motivated teachers, they found themselves in the center of a controversy with their students. In fact, matters became so serious that the students went on strike, refusing to attend classes until certain changes were made in the classroom. The communication problems occurred because the teachers brought their own set of cultural assumptions about teaching into their classrooms in Ethiopia. Like any good educator in the United States, these two Peace Corps teachers wanted to go beyond their subject matter by teaching certain "carryover" skills such as critical thinking, debate skills, written forms of expression, and the capacity to see relationships between phenomena. In their own university training they had learned well the value of logic, the Socratic method of teaching, rational thought, the scientific method, and the need to seek reasons behind actions. Unfortunately, they assumed, quite uncritically, that these values were equally appropriate in northern Ethiopia. But the Ethiopian students came from a vastly different cultural tradition that does not necessarily value individual intellectual development. The students, confronted with highly competitive national exams for entrance into the university, wanted the teachers to stick as closely as possible to the set curriculum so as to maximize their chances of scoring well on these standardized exams.

because she was responsible for giving him his wife. The best way to ensure that nothing happens to jeopardize that relationship is to avoid, or seriously restrict, the amount of interaction that takes place. By minimizing potential conflict between family members, the custom of mother-in-law avoidance functions to ensure harmony and thus help to maintain the social structure.

## FUNCTIONAL ANALYSIS

The language of functional analysis can be very confusing. The term *function* is used in a number of different ways in the English language. For example, it is sometimes used to refer to a social gathering, such as a party or a wedding ("Wasn't it a lovely social function?"); economists use the term synonymously with *occupation;* political scientists speak of "political functionaries"; while mathematicians use the term to mean a relationship as in the statement "X is a function of Y." Cultural anthropologists have still another definition. For them, the function of any cultural item (i.e., thing, idea, or behavior pattern) is the *part it plays* either in satisfying individual needs or contributing to the cohesion and perpetuation of the society. To further complicate matters, cultural anthropologists sometimes use the term *function* synonymously with use, motive, purpose, aim, utility, and intention.

The functionalist approach, most closely associated with Malinowski and Radcliffe-Brown, is based on two fundamental principles. First, the notion of **universal functions** holds that every part of a culture has a function. For example, the function of a hammer is to drive nails into wood; the function of a belief in an omnipotent god is to control people's behavior; and the function of shaking hands in the United States is to communicate nonverbally one's intentions to be friendly. The second principle, known as **functional unity,** states that

As Robert Merton would suggest, the manifest function of the rain dance was to cause rain, while the latent function was to promote social cohesion.

a culture is an integrated whole comprising a number of interrelated parts. As a corollary to this second principle, it follows that if the parts of a culture are interconnected to one another, then a change in one part of the culture is likely to result in changes in other parts.

During the early twentieth century, when Malinowski and Radcliffe-Brown were first proposing their functionalist approach, they no doubt overstated the case for these two principles. They claimed, essentially, that *every* part of a culture had some function; there were, in other words, no functionless survivals. Moreover, in terms of the principle of functional unity, they claimed that *every* part of a culture was interconnected to every other part. Much of this exaggeration can be attributed to the exuberance of youth. Both Malinowski and Radcliffe-Brown were insistent upon these two principles because they were engaged in an ideological reaction against the deductive speculations of the evolutionists and the diffusionists that had dominated the ethnological imagination up until that time.

## MERTON'S VIEW OF FUNCTIONALISM

Once functionalism was accepted into the discipline of cultural anthropology, it appears that the functionalists were distracted from reevaluating and revising their theory by the overwhelming demands of ethnographic field research. Even though it was such anthropologists as Malinowski and Radcliffe-Brown who fought so rig-

orously for the acceptance of the functionalist approach, the most effective revisions of functionalist theory have come from sociologists, most notably Robert Merton. For example, in his influential book *Social Theory and Social Structure* (1957), Merton suggests that although every cultural item *may* have a function, it is premature to assume that every item *must* have a function. As a result, Merton proposed the notion of **dysfunction**, which tends to cause stress or imbalance within a cultural system. Whether a cultural trait is functional or dysfunctional, according to Merton, can be resolved only by empirical research.

In addition, Merton took issue with Malinowski and Radcliffe-Brown's notion of functional unity. While fully recognizing that all societies have some degree of functional integration, he could not accept the very high degree of interconnectedness suggested by the early British functionalists. Merton's more moderate views on the issue of functional unity are, at least in part, the result of his being a sociologist. Merton warns against applying these extreme functionalist assumptions (which may be more valid for small-scale, undifferentiated societies that cultural anthropologists tend to study) to those large, complex societies that are most often studied by sociologists.

A fundamental weakness of the early functionalist approach was its inability to distinguish between *functions* (the part something plays as perceived by the scientific observer) and *motives* (the actual intentions of members of the group). To suggest, for example, that a rain dance functions to build social cohesion among group members does not prove that this was in fact the intention of the people themselves. It may well be that the people themselves were conducting a rain dance for the rather straightforward purpose of causing rain. At the same time, it may also be true that one of the objective consequences of the rain dance is that it does in fact promote social cohesion. Again, Merton provides some needed clarification on this point with his distinction between *manifest* and *latent* functions. Manifest functions are those objective consequences that are intended and recognized by members of the society (i.e., the function of the rain dance is to produce rain). Latent functions, on the other hand, are considerably less obvious because they are neither intended nor recognized (i.e., the function of the rain dance is to promote social cohesion among group members).

# ◆ ◆ ◆ Psychological Anthropology

As early as the 1920s and 1930s, some American ethnologists became interested in the relationship between culture and the individual. Radcliffe-Brown, warning against what he called psychological reductionism, looked almost exclusively to social structure for his explanations of human behavior. A number of students of Boas, however, were asking some theoretically powerful questions: What part do personality variables play in human behavior? Should personality be viewed as a part of the cultural system? If personality variables are part of culture, how are they causally related to the rest of the system? Wanting to relate some of the insights of Gestalt and Freudian psychology to the study of culture, the early **psychological anthropologists** looked at child-rearing practices and personality from a cross-cultural perspective. They held that child-rearing practices (which are an integral part of a culture) help shape the personality structure of the individual, which in turn influences the culture. Thus, they saw an interactive relationship between child-rearing practices, personality structure, and culture.

## EDWARD SAPIR

Although best known for his linguistic research, **Edward Sapir** (1884–1934) was very interested in the area of culture and personality. Individuals learned their cultural patterns unconsciously, Sapir suggested, in much the same way that they learn their language. Rejecting the notion that culture existed above the individual, Sapir believed that the true locus of culture was in the interaction of individuals. Even though Sapir did no direct fieldwork himself in this area of culture and personality, his writings and lectures piqued the interest of others, most notably Ruth Benedict and Margaret Mead.

Psychological anthropologists, who look at the relationship between culture and personality, would be interested in the question, How do the TV-watching habits of U.S. children affect children's personality structure, and how do these personality structures, in turn, affect other parts of the culture?

## RUTH BENEDICT

One of the first to pick up on Sapir's notions was **Ruth Benedict** (1887–1948) who held that every society produces its own unique personality structure. At birth every individual is taught a limited number of traits (from a vast number of alternative traits) that the society deems important. By using a series of positive and negative sanctions, the society gradually molds the child into a certain personality type. Since all people in the society are coerced into conforming to the same set of limited traits, a group personality emerges. Thus, cultures are really individual personalities generalized to the whole culture.

Benedict presented her theory in 1934 in her widely read book *Patterns of Culture*, in which she attempted to describe cultures in terms of several major psychological traits. Drawing upon data from three different cultures, Benedict characterized the Kwakiutl as violent, warlike, aggressive, highly competitive, and excessive; the Zuni as restrained, unemotional, peaceful, serene, and moderate; and the Dobuans as paranoid, suspicious, and fearful. These characterizations were, according to Benedict, more than mere stereotyping but rather were patterned and integrated configurations that emerged after an in-depth study of the institutions and values of these three cultural groups. In another work, entitled the *Chrysanthemum and the Sword* (1946), Benedict again characterized cultural configurations in psychological terms by suggesting that the dual traits of aesthetic preoccupation and militarism dominated Japanese culture during the 1940s.

Despite its initial popularity, *Patterns of Culture* has been widely criticized. First, Benedict was more interested in artful description than in explanation, for she never offered a reason why each society selected a limited number of traits from a vast number of possibilities. Moreover, Benedict has been accused of being somewhat overzealous in her attempt to fit the ethnographic facts into her conceptual scheme. The beautiful symmetry of Benedict's descriptions, according to Marvin Harris (1968:405), rested upon "the omission or selective de-emphasis of nonconforming data."

## MARGARET MEAD

**Margaret Mead** (1901–1978), a student of both Benedict and Boas, was one of the earliest and most prolific writers in the field of culture and personality. After completing her graduate training under Boas at Columbia University, Mead became fascinated with the general topic of the emotional disruption that seemed to accompany adolescence in the United States. Certain scholars at the time (such as psychologist Stanley Hall) maintained that the stress and emotional problems found among American adolescents was a biological fact of life that occurs at puberty in all societies. But Mead wanted to know if this emotional turbulence was the result of being an adolescent or being an adolescent in the United States. In 1925 she left for Samoa to try to determine if the strains of adolescence were universal (i.e., biologically based) or if they varied from one culture to another. In her first book, *Coming of Age in Samoa* (1928), Mead reported that the permissive family structure and relaxed sexual patterns among Samoans were responsible for a relatively calm adolescence. Thus, she concluded that the emotional turbulence found among adolescents in the United States was culturally rather than biologically based.

Some fifty years after her original study, Mead's *Coming of Age in Samoa* was challenged on both methodological and factual grounds by Derek Freeman (1983), initiating a controversy of unprecedented proportions within the discipline (see, for example, Brady, 1983). Freeman strongly took issue with Mead on both the idyllic portrait she painted of Samoan adolescence and the theory of cultural relativity on which the description was based. Contrary to Mead's description, Freeman's research, conducted over a forty-year period, showed a good deal of tension, aggression, and hostility in Samoan society. Freeman also argued that Samoans are not relaxed, playful, and natural about their sexuality, as Mead had contended, but are prudish and even sexually aggressive. Moreover, Freeman presents his own findings that challenged Mead's description of Samoan families as informal, permissive, and having weak emotional bonds between parents and children, all traits that Mead claimed lead to a stress-free adolescence.

The Mead-Freeman controversy has not been resolved in any definitive way. While neither one has emerged a clear winner or loser, the discipline of cultural anthropology has been forced to do some soul-searching by reexamining a number of important issues, including the importance of ethnographic restudies, the effects of one's political or social ideology on the investigation, and the very nature of scientific ethnological inquiry.

From the turbulence of adolescence, Mead next turned to the question of male and female sex roles. Based on her research among the Arapesh, Tchambuli, and Mundugumor of New Guinea, she attempted to demonstrate that there were no universal temperaments that were ex-

Margaret Mead devoted the early years of her long and distinguished career in cultural anthropology to the study of cultural patterns in Samoa and New Guinea.

clusively masculine or feminine. More specifically, Mead reported that among the Arapesh, both men and women had what Westerners would consider "feminine" temperaments (i.e., nurturing, cooperative, nonaggressive, maternal); both Mundugumor men and women displayed exactly the opposite traits (i.e., ruthless, aggressive, violent demeanors), while among the Tchambuli there was a complete reversal of the male-female temperaments found in our own culture. Mead concluded in her *Sex and Temperament in Three Primitive Societies* (1935) that, based on these findings, our own Western conception of "masculine" and "feminine" are not sexlinked but are rather culturally determined.

Mead's formulations, like Benedict's, were criticized on the basis of both accuracy and methodology. Being more impressionistic art than objective social science, Mead's research paid little attention to issues of sampling, controls, or experimental design. Despite these and other criticisms leveled against her, Mead's major contribution to ethnological theory was her demonstration of the importance of cultural rather than biological conditioning.

# Neoevolution

As we have seen, Franz Boas and others were extremely critical of the nineteenth-century evolutionists, in part because they were accustomed to making sweeping generalizations based on little or inadequate data. Despite all of the criticisms, however, no one, including Boas himself, was able to demonstrate that cultures do not develop or evolve in certain ways over time.

### LESLIE WHITE

As early as the 1930s, **Leslie White** (1900–1975), a cultural anthropologist trained in the Boasian tradition, resurrected the theories of the nineteenth-century evolutionists. It was White's position that Tylor and Morgan had developed a useful theory. Their major shortcoming was only that they lacked the data to demonstrate it.

Like Tylor and Morgan, White believed that cultures evolve from simple to increasingly more complex forms and that cultural evolution is as real as biological evolution. White's unique contribution was to suggest the cause (or driving force) of evolution, which he called his Basic Law of Evolution.

According to White,

. . . culture evolves as the amount of energy harnessed per capita per year increases or as the efficiency of the means of putting energy to work is increased (1959:368–69).

Culture evolves, according to this theory, when people are able to increase the amount of energy under their control. For most of human prehistory, while people were hunters and gatherers, the major source of energy was human power. But with the inventions of agriculture, animal domestication, the steam engine, the internal combustion engine, and nuclear power, humans have dramatically increased, through technology, the

According to Steward's theory of multilineal evolution, these irrigated agricultural systems in present-day Israel were the result of the same set of developmental sequences experienced by ancient irrigation civilizations.

levels of energy at their disposal. To illustrate, the daily average energy output for a healthy man is a small fraction of a horsepower per day; the amount of energy produced from a kilo of uranium in a nuclear reactor is approximately thirty-three billion horsepower! For White, the significant equation was $C = E \times T$, where C is culture, E is energy, and T is technology. Cultural evolution, in other words, is caused by advancing levels of technology and a culture's increasing capacity to "capture energy."

## JULIAN STEWARD

Another ethnologist who rejected the particularist orientation of Franz Boas in the mid-twentieth century was Julian Steward. Like White, Steward was interested in the relationship between cultural evolution and adaptation to the environment. But White's approach —which focused on the whole of human culture—was far too general for Steward. Even though Steward rejected Boasian particularism, he was equally unaccepting of approaches that were overly abstract. The main problem with White's orientation is that it cannot explain why some cultures evolve by "capturing energy" while others do not. One way of characterizing the difference between these two prominent **neoevolutionists** is that White was interested in the broad concept of culture while Steward was more interested in developing propositions about specific cultures or groups of cultures.

Steward distinguished between three different types of evolutionary thought. First, there were **unilinear evolutionists** (Tylor and Morgan), who attempted to place particular cultures into certain evolutionary stages. Second, Steward referred to White's approach as **universal evolution**, since it is concerned with developing laws that apply to culture as a whole. In contrast to these two earlier forms of evolutionism, Steward referred to his own form as **multilinear evolution**, which focuses on the evolution of specific cultures without assuming that all cultures follow the same evolutionary process.

Steward held that by examining sequences of change in different parts of the world, it would be possible to identify paths of development and some limited causal principles that would hold true for a number of societies. To test out his formulation, Steward selected those areas of the world that produced complex societies (civilizations), such as Egypt and the Middle East in the Old World and Mexico and Peru in the New World. In all of these cases, Steward tried to show certain recurring developmental sequences from earliest agriculture up through large, complex urbanized social systems. For example, in all of these instances, people were faced with relatively dry environments which required the development of some methods of obtaining water for irrigation purposes.

Steward's approach was based on analysis of the interaction between culture and environment. That is, he argued that people who face similar environmental challenges (such as arid or semiarid conditions) are likely to develop similar technological solutions, which, in turn, lead to the parallel development of social and political institutions. Even though environment was a key variable in Steward's theory, he was not an environmental determinist, for he recognized the variety of human responses to similar environmental conditions. By focusing on the relationship between people, environment, and culture, Steward was the first and leading proponent of the study of cultural ecology.

# French Structuralism

No single theoretical orientation is as closely associated with a single person as **French structuralism** is associated with **Claude Lévi-Strauss** (1908– ). Despite the fact that both Radcliffe-Brown and Lévi-Strauss are called structuralists, their approaches to cultural analysis are vastly different. Whereas Radcliffe-Brown focused on identifying how the parts of a society function as a systematic whole, Lévi-Strauss concentrates on identifying those mental structures that undergird social behavior. For Lévi-Strauss, ethnology tends to be more psychological or cognitive than sociological.

The approach taken by Lévi-Strauss draws heavily from the science of linguistics. After assuming for decades that language is purely a learned response, many linguists in recent years have hypothesized that basic grammatical structures are preprogrammed in the human mind. Likewise, Lévi-Strauss argues that there are certain codes programmed into the human mind that are responsible for shaping cultures. Cultural differences occur, according to Lévi-Strauss, because these inherent mental codes are altered by environment and history. Yet, while recognizing these surface differences, Lévi-Strauss suggests that in the final analysis the mental structure of all humans is essentially the same. Although the *content* of a cultural element may vary from one society to another, the *structure* of these elements is limited by the very nature of the human mind. In essence, Levi-Strauss has reintroduced his own version of the psychic unity of humankind.

One of the basic tenets of the human mind for Lévi-Strauss is that it is programmed to think in binary oppositions—or opposites. All people have a tendency to think in terms of such opposites as male-female, hot-cold, old-young, night-day, right-left, and us-them. It is these dichotomies that give shape to culture. Consider, for example, Lévi-Strauss's interpretation of totemism—a belief system found in many parts of the world that states a relationship between social groupings (such as clans or lineages) and aspects of the natural world (such as plants or animals). Lévi-Strauss suggests that totemic beliefs are complex mental devices that enable people to classify the units of their culture and relate them to the natural world. How totemism serves as a dual system of classification for Levi-Strauss is described by Kaplan and Manners:

. . . when a native says he is a member of the Raccoon clan and his neighbor is a member of the Wild Cat clan, and that each of these clans is separately descended from these animals, his statement is not to be taken literally, as a biological theory of paternity. Rather he is employing a metaphor to characterize the differences and relationships between the two clans, to emphasize that these differences and relationships are similar to those that obtain in nature between the species. Totemism, then, is a kind of primitive science, an imaginative and aesthetic ordering of the world in terms of the perceived, sensible aspects of things (1986:175).

Lévi-Strauss's structuralism has been criticized for being overly abstract. Since his theories—while often brilliantly creative—are not susceptible to empirical testing, many ethnologists have rejected them. Even though French structuralism does not appeal to the more empirically oriented ethnologists, Lévi-Strauss has made a major contribution by directing our attention to the relationship between culture and cognition. In all likelihood, Lévi-Strauss will be remembered not for the development of theories that will help explain the real world but rather for his prodding of other researchers to generate more imaginative hypotheses which then can be tested through empirical research.

# Ethnoscience

The theoretical approach of Lévi-Strauss is similar in several significant respects to that of the **ethnoscientists**, a small but vocal group of American cultural anthropologists who gained considerable recognition during the 1950s and 1960s. For example, both approaches (1) draw on a linguistic model, (2) seek explanations in the human mind, and (3) view human behavior from a logical or rational perspective. The methods, however, are radically different. Whereas the French structuralists would infer mental structures or codes from cultural traits, the ethnoscientists (whose approach is also referred to as ethnosemantics, componential analysis, or the new ethnography) attempt to understand a culture from the point of view of the people themselves. Proponents of ethnoscience include Ward Goodenough (1956) and William Sturtevant (1964).

Aimed at making ethnographic description more accurate and replicable than in the past, ethnoscientists try to describe a culture in terms of how it is perceived, ordered, and categorized by the members of that culture rather than by imposing the categories of the ethnographer. To illustrate, traditionally Western ethnographers used categories from their own cultures for describing another culture. Whereas most middle-class North Americans would divide all of the items in the fresh produce department of a supermarket into either fruits or vegetables, people from some other cultures would not. While English speakers have different words for turquoise, aqua, and green, other cultures might include them all into a single color term, while still others would have thirty or more different words for various shades of blues and greens. Whereas some cultures have different linguistic categories for mother's brother's daughter and mother's sister's daughter, in the United States these two family members are lumped together under the single kinship category of *cousin*. Thus, the primary aim of ethnoscience is to identify the implicit rules, principles and codes that people use to classify the things and events in their world. The ethnoscientific approach assumes that if we can describe another culture by using native categories rather than our own, we will be able to both minimize investigator bias and get a more accurate picture of reality.

By using a linguistic model, the ethnoscientists treat cultures in much the same way that linguists treat language. That is, they assume that rules, principles, and codes can be derived for cultures just as linguists derive grammatical rules and codes for languages. In developing their theoretical positions, ethnoscientists have distinguished between the emic and the etic approaches to methodology. The emic approach—which they strongly advocate—attempts to understand a culture from the native's point of view. The etic approach, on the other hand, describes a culture in terms of the categories of the ethnographer.

Despite their somewhat idealistic claims for objectivity, the ethnoscientists have been criticized on several fronts. First, while admitting that it may be desirable to get the natives' viewpoint, some cultural anthropologists feel that because of one's own conditioning and preconceptions, it is impossible to get into the mind of someone from another culture. In other words, since they too have cultures, all ethnographers are conceptually muscle-bound well before they ever get into fieldwork. Second, even if it is possible to understand another culture from the natives' point of view (that is, by using native concepts and categories), how does one communicate one's findings to others in one's own linguistic/cultural group? Third, if every ethnographer describes specific cultures using native categories, there would be little or no basis for comparing different societies. And fourth, ethnoscience is extremely time-consuming. To date ethnoscientific studies have been completed on very specific domains of culture, such as kinship terms or color categories. The completion of an ethnoscientific study of a total culture would, no doubt, be beyond the time capabilities of a single ethnographer. Yet, while admitting the impracticality of the ethnoscientific approach, it has served as a useful reminder of a fundamentally sound ethnological principle: that people from different cultural and linguistic backgrounds organize and categorize their world in essentially different ways.

◆   ◆   ◆
## Statistical Cross-Cultural Comparisons

During the first half of the twentieth century, cultural anthropology, following the lead of Boas in the United States and Malinowski in Britain, had amassed considerable descriptive data on a wide variety of cultures throughout the world. Because of the many firsthand ethnographic field studies conducted by the students of Boas and Malinowski, there existed by the end of World War II sufficient data to begin testing hypotheses and building theory inductively.

The emergence of statistical, cross-cultural comparative studies was made possible in the 1940s by **George Peter Murdock** and his colleagues at Yale University who developed a coded data retrieval system known as the **Human Relations Area Files** (HRAF). The largest ethnographic data bank in the world, HRAF has vast amounts of information organized according to over 300 different cultures and over 700 different cultural subject headings. The use of the simple coding system enables the cross-cultural researcher to access large quantities of data within minutes for the purpose of testing hypotheses and drawing statistical correlations.

The creation of the HRAF has opened up the possibility for making statistical comparisons between large numbers of cultures. Murdock himself used the HRAF as versality of ethnological theories by using large numbers of ethnographic cases.

The HRAF data bank must be used carefully and in full recognition of some potential methodological pitfalls. For example, critics have noted the following:

1. Much of the data contained in HRAF varies considerably in terms of quality.
2. There is an unevenness of coverage, with a greater amount of material coming from non-Western cultures.
3. Since the data describe a wide range of types of social systems (such as tribes, clans, nations, ethnic groups), one can question if the units of analysis are in fact comparable.
4. There is a problem determining the independence of individual cases, for if a cultural institution that is found in ten different societies is traceable to a single source, should they all be considered independent units?
5. There is the problem of functional unity—that is, if, as the functionalists remind us, all parts of a culture are to some degree interconnected, how legitimate is it to pull a cultural trait from its original context and compare it to other cultural traits that have been similarly ripped from their contexts?

In the past several decades, however, largely through the efforts of Murdock and Raoul Naroll, most of these criticisms and objections to using HRAF for cross-cultural research have been adequately answered. Since many of these methodological shortcomings can now be overcome by thoughtful researchers, HRAF remains a powerful tool for testing universal theories and identifying causal relationships between cultural phenomena.

This student is using the world's largest ethnographic data bank, the Human Relations Area Files (HRAF), in its microfiche format. HRAF is now available in a CD ROM format as well.

## Some Concluding Thoughts on Ethnological Theory

This chapter has been written with distinct subheadings dividing the field of ethnological theory into neat, discrete schools. These divisions can serve as a useful device to help track, in general terms, the various emphases that ethnologists have taken since the mid-nineteenth century. However, these "schools" of ethnology are not particularly relevant categories for distinguishing between the different approaches used by contemporary ethnologists. Few ethnologists today would tie themselves to a single school or theoretical orientation such as neoevolutionist, structuralist, or functionalist.

the basis for his ground-breaking book, *Social Structure* (1949), in which he compiled correlations and generalizations on family and kinship organization. In the area of culture and personality, Whiting and Child (1953) used HRAF as the database for their cross-cultural study of the relationship between child-rearing practices and adult attitudes toward illness. More recently a host of studies using HRAF data have appeared in the literature, including studies on the adoption of agriculture (Pryor, 1986), sexual division of labor (White et al, 1981), female political participation (Ross, 1986), reproduction rituals (Paige and Paige, 1981), and magico-religious practitioners (Winkelman, 1987). Such cross-cultural studies are significant, for they allow us to test the uni-

Rather, contemporary ethnologists tend to be more eclectic and problem oriented, focusing on explaining cultural phenomena while drawing upon a wide variety of research methods and sources of data. Today it is generally recognized that many of these theoretical schools are not mutually exclusive. It is, no doubt, a sign that cultural anthropology as a discipline is becoming mature when its practitioners, by rejecting hard drawn lines between themselves, can enrich one another's thinking.

## ◆ Summary

1. Ethnological theory—which arose from the desire to explain the great cultural diversity in the world —enables us to reduce reality into an abstract yet manageable set of principles.

2. The first group of ethnologists used the notion of evolution to account for the vast diversity in human cultures. Such nineteenth-century evolutionists as Tylor and Morgan suggested that all societies pass through a series of distinct evolutionary stages. While criticized by their successors for being overly speculative and ethnocentric in their formulations, these early evolutionists fought and won the battle to establish that human behavior was the result of certain cultural processes rather than biological or supernatural processes.

3. The diffusionists explained cultural differences and similarities in terms of the extent of contact cultures had with one another. The British diffusionists, represented by Smith and Perry, held that all cultural features, wherever they may be found, had their origins in Egypt. The German-Austrian diffusionists, most notably Graebner and Schmidt, took a more methodologically sound approach by examining the diffusion of entire complexes of culture.

4. In contrast to the evolutionists and diffusionists, Franz Boas took a more inductive approach to cultural anthropology, insisting on the collection of firsthand empirical data on a wide range of cultures before developing ethnological theories. While criticized for not engaging in much theorizing himself, the meticulous attention Boas gave to the methodology put the young discipline of cultural anthropology on a solid scientific footing.

5. The British functionalists Malinowski and Radcliffe-Brown, who, like Boas, were strong advocates of fieldwork, concentrated on how contemporary cultures functioned to both meet the needs of the individual and perpetuate the society. Not only do all parts of a culture serve a function (universal functions), but they are interconnected to one another as well (functional unity) so that a change in one part of the culture is likely to bring about changes in other parts.

6. The early psychological anthropologists, most notably Ruth Benedict and Margaret Mead, were interested in exploring the relationships between culture and the individual. By examining the configuration of traits, Ruth Benedict described whole cultures in terms of individual personality characteristics. Margaret Mead's early research efforts brought her to Samoa to study the emotional problems associated with adolescence and later to New Guinea to study male and female sex roles.

7. The theory of evolution was brought back into fashion during the twentieth century by Leslie White and Julian Steward. White, like Tylor and Morgan before him, held that cultures evolve from simple to complex forms, but for White, the process of evolution was driven by his "basic law of evolution" ($C = E \times T$). Steward's major contribution was to introduce the concept of multilinear evolution, a form of evolution of specific cultures that did not assume that all cultures passed through the same stages.

8. Drawing heavily upon the models of linguistics and cognitive psychology, Claude Lévi-Strauss maintains that there are certain codes or mental structures preprogrammed in the human mind that are responsible for culture and social behavior. A fundamental tenet of Lévi-Strauss's theory is that the human mind thinks in binary oppositions—opposites that enable people to classify the units of their culture and relate them to the world around them.

9. Like the French structuralism of Lévi-Strauss, the theoretical approach known as ethnoscience is cognitive in that it seeks explanations in the human mind. By distinguishing between the emic and the etic approaches to research, the ethnoscientists attempt to describe a culture in terms of how it is perceived, ordered, and categorized by members of that culture rather than by the codes/categories of the ethnographer's culture.

10. Largely through the efforts of George Peter Murdock and his colleagues at Yale, the Human Relations Area Files (HRAF)—the world's largest ethnographic data retrieval system—was developed for the purpose of testing hypotheses and building theory. The files include easily retrievable ethnographic data on over 300 different cultures organized according to more than 700 different subject headings.

## Key Terms

barbarism
Benedict, Ruth
Boas, Franz
civilization
diffusionism
dysfunction
ethnoscientists
evolutionism
French structuralism
functional unity
functionalism
Graebner, Fritz
Human Relations Area
  Files (HRAF)
kulturkreise
Lévi-Strauss, Claude
Malinowski, Bronislav
Mead, Margaret
mother-in-law avoidance

Morgan, Louis Henry
multilinear evolution
Murdock, George Peter
neoevolution
Perry, W. J.
psychic unity
psychological
  anthropology
Radcliffe-Brown, A. R.
Sapir, Edward
savagery
Schmidt, Wilhelm
Smith, Grafton Elliot
structural functionalism
Tylor, Edward
unilinear evolutionists
universal evolution
universal functions
White, Leslie

## Suggested Readings

Bohannan, Paul, and Mark Glazer (Eds.). *High Points in Anthropology* (2nd ed.). New York: Alfred A. Knopf, 1988. A collection of writings dating back to Spencer, Morgan, and Tylor tracing the history and development of cultural anthropological thought up to the present time. Each selection is prefaced by editorial background notes on the theorists and their works.

Garbarino, Merwyn S. *Sociocultural Theory in Anthropology: A Short History*. New York: Holt, Rinehart and Winston, 1977. An overview of ethnological theory in historical perspective written for beginning undergraduates.

Harris, Marvin. *The Rise of Anthropological Theory: A History of Theories of Culture*. New York: Thomas Y. Crowell, 1968. A comprehensive and critical review of the history of ethnological theory over the course of the past 200 years. Writing from his own cultural materialist perspective, Harris is quite willing to point up the theoretical and methodological shortcomings of all theoretical orientations other than his own. Despite its very opinionated stance, or perhaps because of it, this spritely written book remains the best single history of ethnological theory.

Kaplan, David, and Robert A. Manners. *Culture Theory*. Prospect Heights, Ill.: Waveland Press, 1986. Discusses the major theoretical orientations of cultural anthropology and some of the major theoretical/methodological issues facing contemporary ethnologists. In terms of depth of coverage, this volume is a nice compromise between the very brief overview of Garbarino and the more encyclopedic work of Harris.

Kardiner, Abram, and Edward Preble. *They Studied Man*. New York: Mentor Books, 1961. The authors analyze the works of ten major scientists—Darwin, Spencer, Durkheim, Freud, Kroeber, Tylor, Boas, Frazer, Benedict, and Malinowski—and their contributions to our understanding of human behavior.

# Anthropological Theory

Applied anthropology, which is thought of as being immanently practical, has traditionally been contrasted to "pure" or "theoretical" ethnology, which, by implication, has often been characterized by being not practical. It is generally thought that ethnological theories, while serving to help us make sense of the vast array of ethnographic data, contribute little to the solution of everyday human problems. But as Van Willigen (1986:17) has pointed out, theoretical cultural anthropology and applied cultural anthropology developed together and are intimately interrelated. It should, therefore, come as no surprise that ethnological theories can make direct contributions to solving specific societal problems. This section examines several specific case studies that used ethnological theory in some very practical ways.

◆ **Evolution theory helps an applied cultural anthropologist solve the problem of deforestation in Haiti.**

The Agroforestry Outreach Project (AOP), a reforestation program in Haiti, is an excellent case in point of the role that ethnological *theory* can play in the design of a multimillion-dollar development project (see Murray, 1984, 1986, 1987). In recent decades, extreme population growth coupled with rapid urbanization has created high market demands in Haiti for both construction wood and charcoal. The cash-poor Haitian peasants have willingly attempted to meet this demand by cutting down large numbers of trees (estimated at approximately fifty million trees per year). The effect of this deforestation on the long-term health of the nation's economy can, of course, be devastating, for it not only denudes the country of trees but also significantly lowers agricultural productivity through soil erosion.

Faced with this rapid demise of trees in Haiti, the U.S. Agency for International Development (USAID) hired Gerald Murray, a cultural anthropologist who had conducted research on land tenure and population growth in Haiti, to conduct a study of the factors of success and failure on potential reforestation projects in Haiti. Based on his previous research, Murray outlined a set of determinants that would need to be designed into any reforestation project in Haiti if it was to be successful.

One design feature suggested by Murray seemed to fly in the face of most other government attempts at reforestation. Previous reforestation projects in Haiti (and in other parts of the world as well) took a conservationist approach, whereby peasants were rewarded for planting trees and penalized in certain ways for cutting them down. Moreover, whatever trees were planted were defined as belonging to the government or, at least, the general public. The peasants, in other words, had no particular ownership of the trees. Murray suggested, however, that peasant farmers should be given seedlings to plant on a cash-crop basis. Wood trees, in other words, were meant to be harvested and sold in much the same way as corn or beans. Murray based this radical (some might say heretical) assumption on the ethnographic reality that Haitian farmers are aggressive cashcroppers. Murray wanted to capitalize on this strong tradition of crop marketing by making wood trees just one more crop to be sold or traded.

Much to Murray's surprise, USAID not only accepted his recommendations but actually hired him to direct a four-million-dollar reforestation project that came to be known as the Agroforestry Outreach Project (AOP). To enlist the active participation of local farmers, three barriers had to be overcome. First, farmers had to be convinced that the new seedlings could in fact reach maturity in four years. This barrier was eliminated with relative ease by showing skeptical peasants existing four year stands of the types of tree under consideration. Second, the project had to persuade farmers that it was feasible to plant trees *along with* their food crops. By demonstrating border and row planting techniques, the AOP was able to show local farmers that they could plant 500 seedlings on only a small fraction of their land and in a way that would not interfere with their other crops. And, finally, the peasant farmers needed reassurance that whatever trees they planted on their own land did in fact belong to them (rather than to the government or the project) and that they had total rights to harvest the trees. The AOP gladly relinquished all tree rights to the farmers.

The AOP, funded by USAID from 1981 through 1985, met with enormous success. The project had set for itself the goal of having 6,000 peasants plant three million trees. When the project ended, some 20 million trees had been planted by 75,000 peasant farmers! This reforestation project in Haiti was significant in that it not only drew heavily on ethnological insights but also was implemented and directed by a cultural anthropologist. To be certain, ethnographic data played an important role in the success of the project. To illustrate, an understanding of the highly individualistic land tenure system of Haitian farmers led to the decision to design a program based on a more free-enterprise (cash-cropping) basis.

The project design was also directly affected by ethnological *theory*. Murray admits that his ideas about tree planting were heavily influenced by cultural evolutionary theories. Cultural evolutionists remind us that for the overwhelming majority of prehistory, humans, who were hunters and gatherers, faced food shortages. If hunters and gatherers became too efficient in exploiting these environments, they would eventually destroy their sources of food (i.e., wild plants and animals). The cultural evolutionists also remind us that this age-old problem of food shortages was not solved eventually by a conservationist's approach to the problem but rather by domesticating plants and animals. In other words, a quantum leap in the world's food supplies occurred when people began to *produce* food (around 10,000 years ago) rather than rely on what Mother Nature had to offer.

Murray saw the connections between tree planting in Haiti and the evolutionary theory of the origins of agriculture. He rejected the conservationist approach, which would have called for raising the consciousness of peasant farmers about the ecological need for conserving trees. Instead, he reasoned that trees will reemerge in Haiti when people start planting them as a harvestable crop, in much the same way that food supplies were dramatically increased when people started planting and harvesting food crops. Thus, the theory of plant domestication—arising from the anthropological study of the beginnings of agriculture—held the key to the solution of Haiti's tree problem.

◆ **The testing of traditional ethnological theories in Kenya provide new insights for the hiring practices of multinational corporations operating in Third World countries.**

Ethnological theories, when derived inductively, are generalizations based on large numbers of empirical observations. Such theories help us make sense out of the enormous range of human behaviors. One body of theory, developed largely by sociologists, relates to the nature of behavior in bureaucratic organizations. According to such theorists as Max Weber, people who operate in complex, bureaucratic organizations are expected to behave toward one another in a straightforward manner ". . . without regard to personal considerations" (1947:340). Relations in a bureaucratic situation are expected to be, in the words of sociologist Talcott Parsons, "universalistic" (1951:62). In other words, conduct is to be determined by a universally applicable set of rules rather than anyone's personal status. Based on these Western theories of complex organizations, strong kinship ties and obligations have no place within a bureaucracy. Such decisions as who gets hired are to be determined by some objective criteria (examination results, previous job experience, educational background) rather than on the basis of such particularistic considerations as how the applicant is related to the personnel director.

Cultural anthropologists have tended to describe behavior patterns in small-scale, non-Western societies as essentially the logical opposites of those found in complex, bureaucratic societies. In many traditional non-Western societies, people relate to one another in particularistic terms. That is, people emphasize personal status relationships with one another, such as kinship connections or common ethnic affiliation. In very practical terms, a person is expected to show particular loyalty to a kinsman *because* that person is a kinsman. Thus, in those societies that value loyalty between particular individuals, a person is likely to hire someone for a job because they have a special relationship (like being cousins) rather than because of any universally applicable set of criteria.

In the developing world, this basic value contrast between particularism and universalism can be seen most dramatically in urban areas. Rural migrants with their particularistic values come to cities seeking jobs in large corporations with their bureaucratic norms of universalism. It is generally held by Western bureaucrats that new members of the work force must shed their particularistic values, which they see as incompatible with bureaucratic structures. This notion, derived from the theories of Weber and Parsons, was the starting point of an applied cultural research project conducted by Peter Blunt on workers in the East African country of Kenya.

Kenya is an excellent example of a Third World country which, having experienced rapid urban growth during the twentieth century, has a work force recruited largely from rural areas. Like other developing nations, Kenya has massive unemployment, little affordable housing, and an urban population that is experiencing an increasing sense of powerlessness, exploitation, and alienation. Within this setting, Blunt wanted to test the relevance of Weber's and Parson's theories about organizational efficiency in

large, bureaucratic corporations. More specifically, he wanted to see if workers in this part of the world with a particularistic (kinship-ethnic) orientation are as incompatible with bureaucratic organizations as Weber and Parsons would have us believe.

Blunt conducted his research on two companies in Kenya which, contrary to conventional wisdom, recruited new workers on the basis of their kinship/ethnic relations with the present workers. In both situations, the overwhelming majority of employees were from the same ethnic group, and many of them were related to one another. In one of the two companies, the homogenization took place rather rapidly over the course of a single year. At the beginning of the twelve-month period, only a third of the employees were from the same ethnic group; a year later, 95 percent were.

Blunt was interested in measuring the organizational efficiency both before and after the homogenization of this particular work force. Contrary to traditional theories of bureaucracies, Blunt found that ethnic/kinship homogenization, rather than damaging the organization, actually improved organizational efficiency. For example, turnover rates fell from 105 percent to 40 percent; customer complaints declined, while the number of written commendations of workers by customers more than doubled; damage to company property was reduced 27 percent; and the number of poor performance warnings fell by 63 percent. Working with friends, relatives, or "people from home" enabled workers to cope more effectively with the alienation and loneliness so prevalent in cities. Moreover, the employee-recruiter felt a measure of satisfaction because of the ability to fulfill kinship obligations.

Blunt's findings are significant because they serve to remind us that theories that might be applicable in Chicago or Detroit are not necessarily relevant for other parts of the world. Multinational companies working in non-Western countries should take notice of the implications. Our Western notion of nepotism (allowing supervisors to hire kinfolk or fellow tribespeople) may actually maximize organizational efficiency in some situations despite the fact that the new recruit may have weaker skills than other candidates for the job. As one organizational theorist recently put it, "in one's group, the insider may be more effective than the outsider with superior ability" (Robinson, 1984:101). The lesson learned from Blunt's testing of these theories on bureaucracies is that corporate decision makers should not tie themselves to outdated notions of industrial organization. Instead, it would be beneficial to both the organization and its work force to experiment with different organizational structures that take into account the realities of the local cultures.

# Doing Cultural Anthropology

How do cultural anthropologists conduct fieldwork?

What types of data-gathering techniques do cultural anthropologists use?

What are some of the very real problems faced by cultural anthropologists that make fieldwork somewhat less than romantic?

A distinctive feature of twentieth-century cultural anthropology is the reliance on **fieldwork** as the primary context in which research is conducted. To be certain, cultural anthropologists carry out their research in other contexts as well—such as libraries and museums—but they rely most heavily upon experiential fieldwork. Like professionals from any other discipline, cultural anthropologists want to describe the basic subject matter of their discipline. They are interested in documenting the enormous variety of lifeways found among the contemporary peoples of the world. How do people feed themselves? What do they believe? How do they legitimize marriages? In addition to learning the what and the how of different cultures, cultural anthropologists are interested in answering why people in different parts of the world behave and think the way they do. To answer these questions of both description and explanation, cultural anthropologists collect their data and test their hypotheses by means of fieldwork.

As a research strategy, fieldwork is eminently experiential. That is, cultural anthropologists collect their primary data by literally throwing themselves into the cultures they are studying. This involves living with the people they study, asking them questions, surveying their environments and material possessions, and spending long periods of time observing their everyday behaviors and interactions in their natural setting. Doing firsthand fieldwork has become a necessary rite of passage for becoming a professional cultural anthropologist. In fact, it is very unusual to receive a Ph.D. in cultural anthropology in the United States without first having conducted fieldwork in some cultural milieu other than one's own.

The strong insistence on direct fieldwork has not always been an integral part of the discipline. As we saw in the previous chapter, most of the deductive theorizing of the nineteenth century was based on secondhand data at best and, frequently, on superficial and impressionistic writings of untrained observers. Morgan's classic work *Ancient Society* (1877), for example, was based largely on data collected by ships' captains, missionaries, explorers, and others who inadvertently came across cultures in some of the more exotic parts of the world. It wasn't until the turn of this century, largely at the insistence of Franz Boas, that fieldwork became the normative mode of collecting cultural data.

Even though cultural anthropologists have been routinely conducting fieldwork for most of the twentieth century, they have not been particularly explicit about discussing their field techniques until quite recently. Before the 1960s, it was usual for a cultural anthropologist to produce a book on "his" or "her" people several

"Anthropologists! Anthropologists!"

years after returning from a fieldwork experience. Nowhere in these books, however, was there much written about field methods or the fieldwork experience itself. The reader had no way of knowing, for instance, how long the investigator stayed in the field, how many people were interviewed and observed, how samples were selected, what data-gathering techniques were used, what problems were encountered, or how the data were analyzed. Since the credibility of any ethnographic study depends, at least in part, on its methodology, cultural anthropologists since the 1960s have been producing some excellent accounts of their own fieldwork experiences. Perhaps even more significantly, a number of books and articles have appeared in recent decades that explore the methodological issues involved in designing a fieldwork study, collecting the data, and analyzing the results.

Any general discussion of how to do fieldwork is difficult for the simple reason that no two fieldwork situations are ever the same. The problems encountered while studying the reindeer-herding Chukchee of Siberia would be quite different from those faced when studying hardcore unemployed street people in Philadelphia or rural peasant farmers in Southern Greece. Even studies of the same village by the same cultural anthropologist at two different times will involve different experiences, since in the intervening period between the two studies, both the anthropologist and the people under analysis will have changed. Despite these differences, there are a number of concerns, problems, and issues that all field-workers have in common. For example, everyone entering fieldwork must make many preparations before leaving home, gain acceptance into the community, select the most appropriate data-gathering techniques, understand how to operate within the local political structure, take precautions against investigator bias, choose knowledgeable **informants**, cope with **culture shock**, learn a new language, and be willing to reevaluate his or her findings in the light of new evidence. This chapter explores these and other common concerns of the field-worker, fully recognizing that every fieldwork situation has its own unique set of concerns, problems, and issues.

## Preparing for Fieldwork

The popular image of the cultural anthropologist in the field tends to be overly romanticized. Field anthropologists are frequently envisioned going about their data collection in an idyllic setting, reclining in their hammocks while being served noncarcinogenic foods by beautiful native people. In reality, conducting anthropological fieldwork is not a carefree vacation. Like any

scientific enterprise, it makes serious demands on one's time, patience, and sense of humor and requires a lot of hard work and thoughtful preparation. Although luck is a factor, the success of a fieldwork experience is usually directly proportional to the thoroughness of one's preparations.

It is not at all unlikely that a minimum of a year's lead time is required before embarking on any fieldwork project lasting more than a few months. During this period, to make a fieldwork project of a year or two a realistic possibility a number of essential matters must be attended to. First, since doing fieldwork is expensive, and unless the would-be fieldworker is independently wealthy, it is necessary to obtain funding from a source that supports anthropological research, such as the Social Science Research Council, the National Science Foundation, or the Wenner-Gren Foundation. Financial support (covering living expenses, transportation to and from the field, and various research-related costs) is awarded on a highly competitive basis to those proposals that have the greatest scientific merit. Even though a proposal may require months of preparation, there is no guarantee that it will result in funding.

A second area of prefieldwork preparation involves taking the proper health precautions. Before leaving home, it is imperative to obtain all relevant shots. Traveling to a malaria-infested area requires taking malarial suppressants before leaving home. In the event that the cultural anthropologist or a dependent becomes ill while in the field, it would be prudent to have information ahead of time about available health facilities.

No two anthropological field studies are ever the same. The study of contemporary Japanese culture presents different problems and challenges to the field anthropologist than does the study of village life in the Cameroons.

Third, if the field research is to be conducted in a foreign country (as most is), permission or clearance must be obtained from the host government. Since field projects usually last a year or longer, no foreign government will allow a cultural anthropologist to conduct research without prior approval. Some parts of the world are simply off-limits to U.S. citizens because of travel restrictions established by either U.S. officials or the governments of the particular countries. Even those countries that are hospitable to Westerners will require that the researcher spell out in considerable detail the nature of his or her research. These host governmental officials frequently want to make sure that the research will not be embarrassing or politically sensitive, that the findings will be useful, and that the researcher's presence in the host country will not jeopardize the safety, privacy, or jobs of any local citizens. Moreover, host governments often require cultural anthropologists to affiliate with local scholarly institutions to share their research experiences with local scholars and students. Sometimes, particularly in Third World countries, the approval process can be painstakingly slow.

A fourth concern that must be addressed before leaving for the field is proficiency in the local language. An important part of the tradition of fieldwork is that it must be conducted using the native language. If the fieldworker is not fluent in the language of the culture to be studied, it is advisable that he or she learn the language before leaving home. That may not always be possible, however, depending on the language. Dictionaries and grammar books may not even exist for some of the more esoteric languages, while the use of native speakers as tutors while still at home may not be possible. In such cases, the ethnographer will have to learn the language after arriving in the field.

Finally, the soon-to-be fieldworker must take care of a host of personal details before leaving home. Arrangements must be made for personal possessions such as houses, cars, and pets while out of the country; decisions have to be made about what to ship and what to purchase abroad; if families are involved, arrangements need to be made for children's education; equipment such as cameras and tape recorders needs to be purchased, insured, and protected against adverse environmental conditions; up-to-date passports need to be obtained; and a schedule for transferring money needs to be worked out between one's bank at home and a convenient bank in the host country. These and other pre-departure details should put an end to the illusion that fieldwork is a romantic holiday.

## Stages of Field Research

Even though no two fieldwork experiences are ever the same, every study should progress through the same basic stages:

1. Selecting a research problem
2. Formulating a **research design**
3. **Collecting** the **data**
4. **Analyzing** the **data**
5. **Interpreting** the **data**

Rather than discuss these five stages in abstract terms, it will perhaps be more meaningful to discuss them within the framework of an actual fieldwork project (the Kenya Kinship Study, a comparative analysis of rural and urban kinship interaction in Kenya) conducted by one of the authors during the 1970s.

### STAGE 1: SELECTING A RESEARCH PROBLEM

In the early part of this century, the major aim of fieldwork was to describe a culture in as much ethnographic detail as possible. In recent decades, however, fieldworkers have moved away from general ethnographies to research that is focused, more specific, and more problem oriented. That is, rather than study all of the parts of a culture equally, contemporary cultural anthropologists are more likely to examine more limited theoretical issues dealing with the relationship between various phenomena, such as the relationship between matrilineal kinship and high levels of divorce or the relationship between nutrition and food-getting strategies. This shift to a more problem-oriented approach has resulted in the formulation of hypotheses (stating the predicted relationship between two or more variables) that are then tested in a fieldwork setting.

The theoretical issue that gave rise to the Kenya Kinship Study (KKS) was the relationship between family interaction and urbanization. What happens to family patterns in the face of rapid urbanization? Throughout most of Western social thought there has been general agreement concerning the effects of urbanization on the family. The general proposition—which has been stated in one form or another since the mid-nineteenth century—sees a "nuclearization" of the family when confronted with urbanization. This relationship is perhaps best stated by Goode, who holds that urbanization brings with it ". . . fewer kinship ties with distant rela-

## CROSS-CULTURAL MISCUE

During the 1960s, a group of recent Cuban-American immigrants in New York City had applied for and received a permit to conduct a peaceful demonstration in front of the United Nations building. On the day of the demonstration, one of the leaders approached a New York City policeman to ask where the demonstrators needed to confine themselves. As the two men were talking, the police officer was becoming increasingly uncomfortable because the demonstrator kept getting too close to him. The officer told the demonstrator to "get out of my face," but owing to language differences, the demonstrator didn't understand what the policeman wanted. The Cuban-American just continued talking to the policeman while standing closer to the officer than the officer felt was appropriate. Within minutes, the Cuban-American was arrested for threatening the safety of a law enforcement officer.

This scenario, which ended unhappily, illustrates a cross-cultural misunderstanding of a very subtle aspect of culture. According to Edward T. Hall (1966), people adhere to predictable spacial distances when communicating. In other words, how close an individual will get to another while talking is, to a large extent, dictated by one's culture. To illustrate, Hall has found that most middle-class North Americans choose a normal conversational distance of no closer than twenty-two inches from each other's mouth. However, for certain South American and Caribbean cultures (such as Cubans), the distance is approximately fifteen inches, while still other cultures (in the Middle East) maintain a distance of nine to ten inches. These culturally produced spacial patterns are extremely important when communicating, or trying to communicate, with culturally different people because they are so subtle, and thus, so frequently overlooked.

The problem that occurred between the Cuban-American and the New York City policeman was that their respective cultures had different ideas about spacial distancing. The Cuban-American was attempting to establish what for him was a comfortable conversational distance of approximately fifteen inches. Unfortunately, the policeman felt threatened because his personal space, as defined by his culture, was being violated. Had either the patrolman or the Cuban-American demonstrator understood this aspect of cultural behavior, the breakdown in communication—and the arrest—could have been avoided.

---

tives and a greater emphasis on the 'nuclear' family unit of couple and children" (1963:1). The purpose of the KKS was to see if this alleged relationship between family interaction and urbanization held up in Kenya, a country that has been experiencing rapid urbanization since independence in the early 1960s. The general research problem thus generated the following hypothesis: As Kenya becomes more urbanized, extended-family interaction will be replaced by more nuclear-family interaction.

## STAGE 2: RESEARCH DESIGN

In this stage, the would-be fieldworker must decide how to measure the two major variables in the hypothesis:

urbanization and family interaction. In this hypothesis, urbanization is the **independent variable** (that is, the variable that is capable of affecting change in the other variable), while family interaction is the **dependent variable** (that is, the variable whose value is dependent on the other variable). In our research design, the dependent variable (family interaction) is the variable we wish to explain, while the independent variable (urbanization) is the hypothesized explanation.

Both the dependent and the independent variables in our hypothesis need to be made less abstract and more concrete and measurable so as to test the validity of the relationship. One way to do this with regard to the concept of urbanization is to design the study in a comparative fashion. This involves selecting two different populations in Kenya—one rural and one urban. The urban sample selected was from Nairobi, by far the largest city in Kenya and indeed in all of East Africa; the rural sample was selected from a small village very isolated from Nairobi and having none of the major features of a city, such as large populations, industrialization, or labor specialization. If we find that rural people interact with extended-family members to a greater extent than urban people, the hypothesis is supported. If we find no appreciable differences in patterns of family interaction between rural and urban populations, the hypothesis will be rejected.

The dependent variable in our hypothesis (family interaction) also needs to be defined more specifically so that it can be measured quantitatively. The task, in other words, is to identify certain concrete measures of family interaction. The KKS identified several such measures:

1. Residence patterns (Who lives with whom in the same house or compound? How close do people live to various types of family members?)
2. Visitation patterns (How frequently do people have face-to-face interaction with various types of family members?)
3. Mutual assistance (How frequently and to what extent do people exchange gifts or money with various types of family members?)
4. Formal family gatherings (How frequently and to what extent do people get together for formal family meetings or ceremonies?)

Whenever designing a research project, it is important to control for any extraneous factors that might interfere with the testing of the hypothesis. If we are examining differences in kinship interaction between rural and urban residents, it is important that we eliminate any variable (other than degree of urbanism) that might

explain the differences. For example, if we select the rural sample from among the Kikuyu and the urban sample from a neighborhood comprising Luo and Nandi, the differences in family interaction may be the result of tribal affiliation (ethnicity) rather than degree of urbanization. Consequently, to control for this ethnic variable, only one ethnic group (the Kikuyu) was used for both rural and urban samples.

## STAGE 3: COLLECTING THE DATA

Once the hypothesis has been made concrete, the next step involves selecting the appropriate data-gathering

Cultural anthropologists gather information by having direct contact with the people being studied. Here, anthropologist Ed Tronick makes direct observations of Efe children.

CHAPTER 13 ◆ DOING CULTURAL ANTHROPOLOGY

techniques for measuring the variables. The KKS used three principal data-gathering techniques: (1) participant-observation; (2) structured interviews; and (3) day histories, a highly specific type of biographical interview that focuses on what a person did and with whom he or she interacted during a twenty-four-hour period.

Participant-observation and interviewing—two primary field techniques used by cultural anthropologists—are discussed in the next section of this chapter. Since the day history technique was one that was developed (or at least modified) especially for this study, it is described here in some detail. Day histories were designed to answer such questions as Whom were you with? What relationship is this person to you? How much time did you spend with this person? How long have you known this person? How often do you see this person? What did you do while you were together?

Day histories were collected from fifty-three informants from the rural sample and eighty-six from the urban sample. Although there are obvious limitations to the usefulness of this technique, in the KKS, day histories generated specific and quantitative data on family interaction. Moreover, the day histories proved beneficial as an initial device for gathering general sociocultural data that was later helpful in the construction of the questionnaire used in the structured interviews.

## STAGE 4: ANALYZING THE DATA

Once the day histories had been collected, their content was analyzed and the various time segments categorized into one of nine types of social interaction (e.g., interaction with nonrelatives, interaction with nuclear-family members, interaction with extended-family members). Since every hour of the twenty-four-hour period was accounted for, it was a relatively straightforward matter to code the various time segments according to one of the nine categories. The next step in the analysis involved simply counting the number of minutes per twenty-four-hour period that each interviewee spent in nuclear-family interaction and the number of minutes spent in extended-family interaction. From there, it was a routine mathematical exercise to determine the mean number of minutes spent in each type of family interaction for both rural and urban samples.

When all of the data were coded and analyzed, no significant differences in family interaction emerged between urban and rural samples. In fact, part of the urban sample (those having resided in Nairobi for five years or longer) showed greater involvement with extended-family members than did those in the rural sample. These data generated from the day histories were supported by data collected from 298 structured interviews and thirteen months of participant-observation. The KKS concluded that living and working within the highly differentiated, industrial urban complex of Nairobi does not in itself lead to the truncation of extended kinship ties.

## STAGE 5: INTERPRETING THE DATA

Like any science, the discipline of cultural anthropology does more than simply describe cultures. The next step—and by far the most difficult to accomplish—involves explaining or interpreting the findings. Has the original hypothesis been confirmed or rejected? What factors can be identified that will help explain the findings? How do these findings compare with the findings of other similar studies? How generalizable are the findings to wider populations? Have these findings raised methodological or theoretical issues that have bearing on the discipline? These are the types of questions that the field anthropologist must wrestle with, usually after returning home from the fieldwork experience.

The significant lack of fit between the data and the so-called nuclearization hypothesis in the KKS requires an explanation. The key to understanding these data lies in the general socioeconomic status of the people under study. Kenya, like most other African nations in the 1970s, was a nation with a dual economy comprising two quite distinct categories of people. On the one hand was a small elite with secure, well-paying jobs and potential for further upward mobility; on the other hand was everyone else, with either poor-paying jobs or no jobs at all and little or no economic mobility. The critical dimension, then, is between the haves and the have-nots, and with but a few exceptions, all of the people in both rural and urban samples clearly qualify for have-not status.

The wide range of family interaction found among both rural and urban populations in Kenya can be understood largely in terms of lack of both money and economic security. For example, in the absence of a public welfare program protecting workers against accidents, illness, old age, and unemployment, it is reasonable to expect that welfare will continue to take place along already established lines of kinship. Moreover, family ties between rural and urban areas remain high in Kenya because of two important economic facts of life: (1) the

## CROSS-CULTURAL MISCUE

On a trip to the East African coastal city of Mombasa, an American college student, fascinated by all of the colorful sights, wanted to document on film his experiences to show the folks back home. While visiting the dock area, he decided to photograph some stevedores unloading one of the many sailing ships that travel between India and the East African coast. He became quite startled, however, when the stevedores began shaking their fists and shouting angrily at him. He made a hasty retreat back to his hotel room without ever finding out why these workers had become so enraged. The student had not realized that having one's picture taken has different meanings in different cultures. Even though cameras can be useful for documenting a foreign culture, they must be used with care. In addition to being an invasion of privacy—as it may be interpreted in our own society—there are cultural reasons that would make some East Africans reluctant to have their pictures taken. For example, since many people living in Mombasa are Islamic, they feel strongly about not wanting to violate the Koranic prohibition against making images of the human form. Moreover, people who do not understand the nature of photography may believe that having one's picture taken is tantamount to having their soul entrapped in the camera. In those societies where witchcraft is practiced, the prospect of having one's soul captured, particularly by a witch, can be terrifying.

instability of employment in Kenya and (2) the Kikuyu land tenure system whereby most land remains in the hands of the lineage (extended family). Urban migrants who neglect their rural kinship obligations are, in effect, relinquishing their rights to a portion of their lineage land, which in the case of most impoverished migrants remains their sole retreat from the insecurities of urban employment. Thus, given the national economy within which all Kikuyu are operating, the maintenance of strong kinship ties for both rural and urban residents is the most rational choice they can make.

## Data-Gathering Techniques

A central problem facing any fieldworker is determining the most appropriate methods for collecting data. Data-collection methods that might work in one culture might be totally inappropriate for a neighboring culture. Given the wide variety of cultures in the world, it is important that cultural anthropologists have a number of options so that they can match the appropriate set of data-gathering techniques to each fieldwork situation. There is a need to be flexible, however, for the techniques originally planned in the **research proposal** may prove to be inappropriate when actually used in the field. Whatever techniques are finally chosen, a variety of methods is needed so that the findings from one technique can be used to check the findings from others.

## PARTICIPANT-OBSERVATION

It seems only fitting to start a discussion of data-gathering techniques with **participant-observation** because cultural anthropologists use the technique more than any other single technique and more extensively than any other social science discipline. Participant-observation, as the name implies, involves participating in the culture under study while making systematic observations of what is going on. When fieldworkers participate, they become as immersed in the culture as the local people permit. They share activities, attend ceremonies, eat together, and generally become part of the rhythm of everyday life. Bernard captured the complexity of participant-observation when he said:

It involves establishing rapport in a new community; learning to act so that people go about their business as usual when you show up; and removing yourself every day from cultural immersion so you can intellectualize what you've learned, put it into perspective, and write about it convincingly. If you are a successful participant observer you will know when to laugh at what your informant thinks is funny; and when informants laugh at what you say, it will be because you *meant* it to be a joke (1988:148).

From the very first day of fieldwork, gaining entry into the community presents a major problem for the participant-observer. Cultural anthropologists in the field can hardly expect to be accepted as soon as they walk into the local community. Under the best of circumstances, the fieldworker, as an outsider, will be an object of curiosity. More frequently, however, the beginning fieldworker encounters a wide variety of fears, suspicions, and hostilities on the part of the local people that must be overcome. There is no reason whatsoever for traditional Samoan fishermen or Pygmy hunters to understand who the fieldworker is or what he or she is doing in their midst. In his classic study of the Nuer of the Sudan, Evans-Pritchard stated that the Nuer were so suspicious and reluctant to cooperate with him that after just several weeks of fieldwork ". . . one displays, if the pun be allowed, the most evident symptoms of Nuerosis" (1940:13).

**Guidelines for Participant-Observation Fieldwork.** By and large, the ethnologist conducting participant-observation fieldwork for the first time has probably received little instruction in how to cope with these initial problems of resistance. For most of the twentieth-century, cultural anthropology has been notorious for its sink-or-swim approach to preparing doctoral candidates for fieldwork. In a sense, it is not really possible to prepare the first-time fieldworker for every eventuality for the obvious reason that no two fieldwork situations, cultures, or ethnographers are ever the same. Nevertheless, it is possible to identify some general guidelines applicable to most fieldwork situations.

First, since the participant-observer is interested in studying people at the grass-roots level, it is always advisable to work one's way down the political hierarchy. Before entering a country on a long-term visa, the fieldworker must obtain **research clearance** from a high level of the national government. In the case of the KKS, research clearance came in the form of a brief letter from the office of the president of the country. Starting with this letter from the top of the political pyramid, courtesy calls were made on each descending rung of the ad-

ministrative ladder (from the provincial commissioner, through the district commissioner, location chief, sub-location chief, and finally to the local headman in the area where the study was to be conducted). Since the study had the approval of the president, it was not likely that any of the administrators down the line would oppose it.

Second, when introducing oneself, it is important to select one role and use it consistently. There are any number of ways that a field ethnologist could answer the question, Who are you? (a question, incidentally, that will be asked frequently and requires an honest and straightforward answer). In the case of the KKS, the author could have said, with total honesty, that he was a student (he was finishing his Ph.D.), an anthropologist (the research was funded by NIMH), Pam's husband, a visiting research associate at the University of Nairobi, Kathryn's father, a teacher, a former basketball player, Charles's son, a Catholic, and a member of the Democratic Party. Yet, many of these roles, while accurate, were not particularly understandable to the people asking the question. Even though the reason for his being there was that he was a cultural anthropologist, that particular role has little meaning to people with little or no education. So he selected a role that was comprehensible—the role of teacher, a role that was both well-known and, much to his advantage, well respected. While not teaching at the time, he had taught professionally prior to doing fieldwork, and had planned on a career in college teaching upon returning to the States. So, when asked who he was and what was he doing there, he *always* said that he was a teacher collecting information about Kikuyu culture so that he could teach his students about it. Had he not standardized his introductions, but instead told one person that he was an anthropologist, another that he was a student, and still another that he was a teacher, the local people would have thought either he was lying or, perhaps equally as bad, he didn't know who he was.

A third general piece of advice for most fieldworkers is to proceed slowly. Coming from a society that places such a high value on time, most U.S. cultural anthropologists do not take kindly to the suggestion to slow down. After all, since they will be in the field for a limited amount of time, most Western fieldworkers feel that they must make the best use of that time by collecting as much data as possible. The natural tendency for most Westerners is to want to "hit the ground running." There seems to be so much to learn and so little time.

Compelling reasons exist for not rushing into asking specific questions. First, since most fieldworkers have such an imperfect understanding of the culture during the initial weeks and months, they frequently do not know enough to even ask the right types of questions. And, second, the very quality of one's data will vary directly with the amount of social groundwork the fieldworker has been able to lay. In other words, ethnographers must invest a considerable amount of time and energy establishing their credibility by allowing the local people to get to know them. For example, in the KKS, the author spent the first three months engaging in a number of activities that didn't seem particularly scientific, including helping people with their tax forms, showing teenage boys how to shoot a fifteen-foot jump shot, taking people for rides in his car, sharing large quantities of food, and talking about life in the United States. None of these activities involved the gathering of cultural data about the Kikuyu, but they did help to demonstrate that the author was interested in them as people rather than merely as sources of information. Once the local people got to know and trust him, they were far more willing to give him the type of cultural information that he was looking for.

**Advantages of Participant-Observation.** The use of participant-observation has certain methodological advantages for enhancing the quality of the data obtained. For example, people in most cultures appreciate any attempt on the part of the anthropologist to live according to the rules of their culture. No matter how ridiculous one might appear at first, the very fact that the fieldworker is sufficiently interested in the local culture to struggle with it is likely to enhance rapport. And as trust levels increase, so too do the quantity and quality of the data.

Another major advantage of participant-observation is that it enables the fieldworker to distinguish between normative and real behavior—that is, between what people *should* do and what people *actually* do. When conducting an interview there is no way to know for certain if people behave as they say they do. The participant-observer, however, has the advantage of seeing actual behavior rather than relying on hearsay. To illustrate, as part of the KKS, urban informants were asked how frequently they traveled to their rural homelands to visit family. A number of male informants who lived up to ninety-five miles away said that they went home every weekend to visit family. However, through participant-observation it became apparent that many of the men remained in the city for a number of consecutive weekends. When confronted with this discrepancy between what they said they did and what they actually did, the

men claimed that their families wanted them to come home every weekend, but it was usually too costly and time-consuming. In actual fact, they traveled home on an average of about once a month. The difference between once a week and once a month constitutes a 400 percent error in the data. Thus, the participant-observer gains a more accurate picture by seeing both actual and expected behavior.

**Disadvantages of Participant-Observation.** On the other hand, participant-observation poses certain methodological problems that can diminish the quality of the data. For example, the very nature of participant-observation precludes a large sample size. Because participant-observation studies are both in-depth and time-consuming, fewer people are actually studied than in studies using questionnaires or surveys. A second problem with participant-observation is that the data are often hard to code or categorize, which makes synthesizing and comparing the data difficult. Third, participant-observers face special problems when recording their observations, since it may be difficult, if not impossible, to record notes while attending a circumcision ceremony, participating in a feast, or chasing through the forest after a wild pig. The more time that passes between the event and its recording, the more details that are forgotten. And, finally, a major methodological shortcoming of participant-observation is that it has an obtrusive effect on the very thing that is being studied. Inhibited by the fieldworker's presence, many people are likely to behave in a way they would not behave if he or she were not there.

Table 13-1 reviews the advantages and disadvantages of participant-observation.

TABLE 13-1 ◆ **Methodological Advantages and Disadvantages of Participant-Observation**

| Methodological Advantages | Methodological Disadvantages |
|---|---|
| Generally enhances rapport | Small sample size |
| Enables fieldworkers to distinguish actual from expected behavior | Difficult to obtain standardized comparable data |
| Permits observation of nonverbal behavior | Problems of recording |
| | Obtrusive effect on subject matter |

One disadvantage of participant-observation research is that the presence of the cultural anthropologist affects the very thing that is under study—i.e., people's normal way of life. Here, the arrival of the fieldworker at a small village causes a stir.

## INTERVIEWING

In addition to using participant-observation, cultural anthropologists in the field rely heavily upon ethnographic interviewing. This particular technique is used for obtaining information on what people think or feel (attitudinal data) as well as on what they do (behavioral data). Even though interviewing is used widely by a number of different disciplines to gather data (sociologists, economists, political scientists, psychologists, etc.), the ethnographic interview is unique in several important respects. First, in the ethnographic interview, the interviewer and the subject almost always speak different first languages. Second, the ethnographic interview is frequently much broader in scope because it elicits information on the entire culture. Third, the ethnographic interview cannot be used alone but rather is used in conjunction with other data-gathering techniques.

**Structured and Unstructured Interviews.** Ethnographic interviews are of two different types—unstructured or structured, depending on the level of control retained by the interviewer. Involving a minimum of control, **unstructured interviews** ask open-ended questions on a general topic and expect interviewees to respond at their own pace using their own words. At the other extreme, **structured interviews** ask all informants exactly the same set of questions, in the same sequence, and preferably under the same set of conditions. If we can use the analogy between interviews and school examinations, structured interviews would be comparable to short-answer questions, while unstructured interviews would be more like open-ended essay questions.

Ethnographers in the field are interested in studying all segments of a population—children as well as adults.

Structured and unstructured interviews have advantages that tend to complement each other. Unstructured interviews, which are usually used early in the data-gathering process, have the advantage of allowing informants to decide what is important to include in their information. In an unstructured interview, for example, an informant might be asked to describe all of the steps necessary for getting married in his or her culture. Structured interviews, on the other hand, have the advantage of producing relatively large quantities of data that are comparable and thus lend themselves well to statistical descriptions. Since structured interviews ask questions based on highly specific cultural information, they are used most commonly late in the fieldwork—only after the anthropologist knows enough about the culture to ask highly specific questions.

**Guidelines for Conducting Interviews.** In the past, some field anthropologists to one degree or another have made use of certain field guides that identify various aspects of culture about which questions can be asked.

The two most widely used field guides are *Notes and Queries on Anthropology*, published around the turn of the century by the Royal Anthropological Institute of Great Britain and Ireland, and the more recent *Outline of Cultural Materials*, published by George Peter Murdock as part of the Human Relations Area Files. The use of such field guides can be helpful in eliciting certain aspects of culture expected but not yet observed or aspects of culture that are not particularly obvious in people's behavior (such as values, attitudes, and beliefs). The danger in relying too heavily on such field guides for structuring ethnographic interviews is, of course, that they can force one's thinking into Western categories that have no relevance for the culture being studied.

Whenever using interviewing as a data-gathering technique, the fieldworker must take certain precautions to minimize distortions in the data. For example, it has been found that respondents are more likely to answer a question negatively when it is worded negatively. The fieldworker is less likely to bias the response by phrasing a question positively (e.g., Do you smoke cigarettes?) rather than negatively (You don't smoke, do you?).

Moreover, questions asked as part of a structured interview should be pretested—that is, given to a small number of people so as to eliminate ambiguous or misleading questions.

It is also important to be aware of the social situation in which the interview takes place. In other words, what effect does the presence of other people have on the validity of the data? In his field study of the Dusun, Williams explains how sex, age, or status influenced the way that his informants answered questions in front of others:

Women would not talk about childbirth before nonrelated males, adolescent boys did not want to talk about their games before young men for fear of being held childish, and most informants did not wish to appear to be questioning the status of a senior man or woman among the onlookers (1967:27).

**Validity of the Data Collected.** The cultural anthropologist in the field must devise ways of checking the validity of interview data. One way of accomplishing this is to ask the same question of a number of different people: if all people independent of one another answer the question in essentially the same way, it is safe to assume that the data are valid. Another method of checking the validity of interview data is to ask the same question of a person over a certain period of time. If the person answers the question differently, there is reason to believe that one of the responses might not be truthful. A third way of determining validity is to compare the responses with people's actual behavior. As we saw in the discussion on participant-observation, what people *do* is not always the same as what they *say they do*. And finally, since all people rationalize, project, or sublimate their fears and desires, the field anthropologist can learn something about the motives for distortions by studying the ego defense mechanisms of the informants.

## SOME ADDITIONAL DATA-GATHERING TECHNIQUES

Even though participant-observation and interviewing are the mainstays of anthropological fieldwork, cultural anthropologists use other techniques for the collection of cultural data at various stages of the field study, including **census taking**, mapping, **document analysis, genealogizing**, and photography. Although hardly exhaustive, the following list briefly examines these techniques:

**Census Taking.** Usually, early on in the fieldwork, cultural anthropologists will conduct a census of the area under investigation. Since this involves the collection of basic demographic data—such as age, occupation, marital status, and household composition—it is relatively nonthreatening to the local people. It is important for the fieldworker to update the census data continuously as he or she learns more about the people and their culture.

David Mayberry Lewis uses the interview technique of data gathering while working among the Xavante.

**Mapping.** Another data-gathering tool used in the early stages of fieldwork is **ethnographic mapping**—the attempt to locate people, material culture, and environmental features in space. To illustrate, ethnologists are interested in mapping where people live, where they pasture their livestock, where various public and private buildings are located, how people divide up their land, and how the people position themselves in relation to such environmental features as rivers, mountains, or oceans. While not advocating the notion of environmental determinism, we can learn a good deal about a culture by examining how people interact with their physical environment. Aerial and panoramic photography are particularly useful techniques for mapping a community's ecology.

**Document Analysis.** Sometimes cultural anthropologists use documentary data to supplement the information collected through interviewing and observation. Some examples of the types of documents used by cultural anthropologists in certain circumstances are personal diaries, colonial administrative records, newspapers, marriage registration data, census information, and various aspects of popular culture, such as song lyrics, TV programs, and children's nursery rhymes. To illustrate how cultural anthropologists can use already existing documents, we can cite how tax records in Swaziland from the 1920s and 1930s can shed light on the changing practice of polygyny (a man having more than one wife at a time). Let us suppose that a cultural anthropologist is interested in determining how the incidence of polygyny has changed over time. The present practice of polygyny can be assessed by using such direct methods as interviewing and participant-observation. To compare the present practice of polygyny with the practice in the 1930s, one needs only to consult the tax rolls, because during the decade of colonial rule (the 1930s), men were taxed according to the number of wives they had. A man with three wives paid three times as much tax as a man with one wife. The advantages of using this type of historical tax data are obvious: it provides large quantities of data, it is relatively inexpensive, and it is totally nonreactive or unobtrusive.

**Genealogizing.** Another technique used to collect cultural data is known as the genealogical method, whereby all of the relatives of a particular informant are written down. This is a particularly important type of information to collect in those societies that cultural anthropologists frequently study (i.e., small-scale, prelit-erate societies) where kinship relationships are the primary ones. Whereas in western societies, much of our lives are played out with nonfamily members such as teachers, employers, coworkers, and friends, in small-scale societies, people tend to interact primarily with their family. When using the genealogical method, each informant is asked to state the name and relationship of all family members and how they are referred to, addressed, and treated. From this information the cultural anthropologist can deduce how family members interact with one another and what behavioral expectations exist between different categories of kin.

**Photography.** A particularly important aid to the field-worker's collection of data is photography, both motion pictures and still photography. Recent decades have witnessed a proliferation of ethnographic films portraying a wide variety of cultures from all parts of the globe. To be certain, ethnographic films are valuable for introducing anthropology students to different cultures, but filmmaking can also have more specific uses for anthropological research. For example, motion pictures can be extremely helpful in **proxemic analysis** (i.e., how people in different cultures distance themselves from one another in normal interaction) or **event analysis** (i.e., documenting such events as circumcision ceremonies, marriages, or funerals). Owing to technological advances in recent years, video cameras (which are less expensive, more versatile, and easier to use) have largely replaced motion picture photography.

Still photography has become such an important part of research in cultural anthropology that it is hard to imagine anyone in the field without a 35-mm camera. As a research tool, the camera can be put to many uses. First, as mentioned above, the camera can produce a lasting record of land-use patterns and the general ecological arrangements in the community under study. Second, since a picture is, as the old adage suggests, worth a thousand words, still photography can document the technology of the culture (e.g., tools, weapons, machines, utensils), how these items are used (by whom, where, when, in what combinations, etc.), the sequences in a crafts process, and the sex roles associated with different items of technology. Third, photographs can be used as probes in the interview process. Since the photograph becomes the object of discussion, the informant feels less like a subject and more like an expert commentator. And finally, still photography can be used for "sociometric tracking." If a sufficient number of photos are taken of people interacting over a period of time, it is possible to quantify which members spend time with whom.

Photographs taken in the field can serve as probes during an interview as well as be useful sources of information.

Like any data-gathering technique, still photography has certain methodological advantages and disadvantages. Among its special assets, the camera allows us to see without fatigue; the last exposure is as clear as the first. Unlike the human eye, the camera is not selective; it captures everything in any particular frame. Photographs, which are a lasting record, can be used long after returning from the field. Photography also is often an easier and less time-consuming mode of data collection than written description.

The camera is not, however, without its liabilities. For example, some people object to being photographed, such as certain African peoples who believe that to be photographed is to have one's soul entrapped in the camera or the Amish whose religion forbids graven im-

ages. Moreover, photography can cause certain headaches for the fieldworker, such as in some societies where the person whose picture is taken asks for multiple copies of the photo to give to friends and relatives.

**Choosing a Technique.** Which of the variety of techniques available for collecting cultural data will in fact be employed will depend largely on the nature of the problem being investigated. Kinship studies are likely to draw heavily upon the genealogical method, studies of child-rearing practices will rely on observation of parent-child relationships, while studies of values will most likely use the interview (a technique particularly well-suited to generating attitudinal data).

Another significant factor influencing the choice of techniques is the receptivity of the people being studied. It is important that the fieldworker carefully plan ahead of time which techniques will be appropriate to use and determine the types of data to collect as well as the segments of the population to study. If, after entering the field, the cultural anthropologist finds that a technique is not working, he or she must be sufficiently flexible to revise the research design and sufficiently creative to come up with a workable alternative. In the final analysis, whatever technique is selected, it should be used in conjunction with other techniques. By using multiple techniques, the investigator is able to collect different types of data around the same set of issues which can be used to cross-check one another.

## The Pains and Gains of Fieldwork

It should be clear by now that the process of direct fieldwork is central to doing cultural anthropology. Unlike many other scientific endeavors, fieldwork inevitably has a powerful impact on the life of the practitioner. Spending a year or more at a time trying to live and work in an unfamiliar culture is bound to have, in some cases, life-altering consequences. The cultural anthropologist is never quite the same after completing a fieldwork project.

The fieldworker is faced with a number of anxiety-producing situations that can be both stressful and growth inducing. There are, in other words, both pains and gains associated with doing fieldwork. For example, cultural anthropologists in the field rarely, if ever, follow their research design step-by-step in cookbook fashion. Despite the most meticulous research design and predeparture preparations, doing fieldwork is fraught with

As Napoleon Chagnon reminds us, gaining the confidence of the Yanomamo (known as the Fierce People) was not a simple matter.

unanticipated difficulties. From day one in the field, the cultural anthropologist can expect to be surprised. Napoleon Chagnon's initial encounter with the Yanomamo Indians of Venezuela and Brazil was hardly what he had anticipated:

My heart began to pound as we approached the village and heard the buzz of activity within the circular compound . . . The entrance to the village was covered over with brush and dry palm leaves. We pushed them aside to expose the low opening to the village. The excitement of meeting my first Yanomamo was almost unbearable as I duck-waddled through the low passage into the village clearing.

I looked up and gasped when I saw a dozen burley, naked, sweaty, hideous men staring at us down the shafts of their drawn arrows! Immense wads of green tobacco were stuck between their lower teeth and lips making them look even more hideous, and strands of dark green slime dripped or hung from their nostrils—strands so long that they clung to their pectoral muscles or drizzled down their chins. We arrived at the village while the men were blowing a hallucinogenic drug up their noses. One of the side effects of the drug is a runny nose. The mucus is always saturated with the green powder and they usually let it run freely from their nostrils. My next discovery was that there were a dozen or so vicious, underfed dogs snapping at my legs, circling me as if I were to be their next meal. I just stood there holding my notebook, helpless and pathetic. Then the stench of the decaying vegetation and filth hit me and I almost got sick. I was horrified.

. . . I am not ashamed to admit that had there been a diplomatic way out, I would have ended my fieldwork then and there. I did not look forward to the next day—and months— when I would be left alone with the Indians; I did not speak a word of their language, and they were decidedly different from what I had imagined them to be. The whole situation was depressing, and I wondered why I ever decided to switch from physics and engineering in the first place (1983:10–11, reprinted by permission).

## CULTURE SHOCK

Not all introductions to fieldwork are as unsettling as this, of course. But even for those cultural anthropologists whose fieldwork experience is less traumatic, there will be some level of stress caused by culture shock, that psychological disorientation caused by trying to adjust to major differences in life-styles and living conditions. Culture shock, a term introduced by Kalervo Oberg (1960), ranges from mild irritation to out-and-out panic. This general psychological stress occurs when the anthropologist tries to play the game of life with little or no understanding of the basic rules. The fieldworker, struggling to learn what is meaningful in the new culture, never really knows when he or she may be committing a serious social indiscretion that might severely jeopardize the entire fieldwork project.

When culture shock sets in, everything seems to go wrong. You frequently become irritated over minor inconveniences. The food is strange; people don't keep their appointments; no one seems to like you; everything seems so unhygienic; people don't look you in the eye; and on and on. Even though culture shock manifests itself in a number of symptoms, it is usually characterized by the following:

◆ A sense of confusion over how to behave.
◆ A sense of surprise, even disgust, after realizing some of the features of the new culture.
◆ A sense of loss of the old familiar surroundings (e.g., friends, possessions, and ways of doing things).
◆ A sense of being rejected (or at least not accepted) by members of the new culture.
◆ A sense of loss of self-esteem because you don't seem to be functioning very effectively.
◆ A feeling of impotence at having so little control over the situation.
◆ A sense of doubt when your own cultural values are brought into question.

Table 13-2 lists sixteen symptoms of culture shock. One would hope that the training to become a cultural anthropologist and the specific preparations for entering the field would help to avoid extreme culture shock. Nevertheless, every fieldworker should expect to suffer, to some extent, from the discomfort of culture shock. Generally, the negative effects of culture shock subside as time passes, but it is likely that they will not go away completely. The very success or failure of a field project depends largely on how well the ethnographer can make the psychological adjustment to the new culture and

---

**T A B L E  13-2  ◆  Symptoms of Culture Shock**

◆ Homesickness
◆ Boredom
◆ Withdrawal (e.g., spending excessive amounts of time reading; only seeing other Americans; avoiding contact with host nationals)
◆ Need for excessive amounts of sleep
◆ Compulsive eating
◆ Compulsive drinking
◆ Irritability
◆ Exaggerated cleanliness
◆ Marital stress
◆ Family tension and conflict
◆ Chauvinistic excesses
◆ Stereotyping of host nationals
◆ Hostility toward host nationals
◆ Loss of ability to work effectively
◆ Unexplainable fits of weeping
◆ Physical ailments (psychosomatic illnesses)

SOURCE: L. Robert Kohls, *Survival Kit for Overseas Living* (Yarmouth, ME: Intercultural Press Inc., 1984), p. 65. Used with permission.

---

go beyond the frequently debilitating effects of culture shock.

## BICULTURALISM

Not all of the consequences of fieldwork, however, are negative. To be certain, culture shock is real and should not be taken lightly. Yet, despite the stress of culture shock—or perhaps because of it—the total immersion experience of fieldwork provides opportunities for personal growth and increased understanding. Spending weeks and months operating in a radically different culture can provide new insights into how the local people think, act, and feel. In the process of learning about another culture, however, we unavoidably learn a good deal about our own culture as well. When we become *bicultural*—which is an inevitable consequence of successful fieldwork—we develop a much broader view of human behavior. Richard Barrett captures the essence of this bicultural perspective which he claims enables cultural anthropologists

. . . to view the world through two or more cultural lenses at once. They can thus think and perceive in the categories of their own cultures, but are able to shift gears, so to speak, and view the same reality as it might be perceived by members of the societies they have studied. This intellectual biculturalism is extremely important to anthropologists. It makes them continually aware of alternative ways of doing things and prevents them from taking the customs of our own society too seriously (1984:20–21).

# ◆ Summary

1. Since the turn of the century cultural anthropologists have conducted their research in a firsthand manner by means of direct fieldwork. Explicit discussion of how practicing cultural anthropologists actually do their fieldwork is, however, a much more recent phenomenon.

2. A number of preparations must be made before any fieldwork experience is begun, including the securing of research funds, taking adequate health precautions such as immunizations, obtaining research clearance from the host government, gaining proficiency in the local language, and attending to a host of personal matters, such as making provisions for accompanying family members, securing passports and visas, purchasing equipment, and making sure that one's affairs at home are in order.

3. Although every fieldwork project in cultural anthropology has its own unique character, all projects go through the same basic stages: (a) selecting a research problem, (b) formulating a research design, (c) collecting the data, (d) analyzing the data, and (e) interpreting the data.

4. Since no two fieldwork experiences are ever identical, it is important that cultural anthropologists match the appropriate data-gathering techniques to their own fieldwork situations. Among the tools at the fieldworker's disposal are participant-observation, interviewing, ethnographic mapping, census taking, document analysis, the collection of genealogies, and photography.

5. Some general guidelines are applicable to most fieldwork situations. First, when attempting to work one's way into a small community, it is advisable to work one's way down, rather than up, the political hierarchy. Second, when introducing oneself to the local population, it is important to select a single role for oneself and use it consistently. And third, as a way of firmly establishing one's credibility with the local people, it is advisable to proceed slowly.

6. The use of the participant-observation technique has certain methodological advantages, including increasing rapport and being able to distinguish between real and normative behavior. Participant-observation is not, however, without its methodological shortcomings, such as (a) being time-consuming, (b) posing problems of data comparability, (c) presenting difficulties in recording data, and (d) interfering with the very thing that is being studied.

7. Ethnographic interviewing, particularly useful for collecting both attitudinal and behavioral data, is of two basic types: unstructured and structured interviews. Unstructured interviews, asking open-ended questions, permit interviewees to respond at their own pace. Structured interviews, by way of contrast, ask the same exact questions to all respondents, in the same order, and under the same set of social conditions.

8. Whenever cultural anthropologists conduct field research in cultures different from their own, they need to be personally flexible and should always expect the unexpected. Like anyone else trying to operate in an unfamiliar cultural setting, cultural anthropologists are susceptible to culture shock.

# ◆ Key Terms

| | |
|---|---|
| analyzing data | informant |
| census taking | interpreting data |
| collecting data | on-farm research |
| culture shock | participant-observation |
| dependent variable | proxemic analysis |
| document analysis | research clearance |
| ethnographic mapping | research design |
| event analysis | research proposal |
| fieldwork | *sondeo* |
| genealogizing | structured interview |
| independent variable | unstructured interview |

# ◆ Suggested Readings

Bernard, H. Russell. *Research Methods in Cultural Anthropology.* Newbury Park, Calif.: Sage Publications, 1988. The most complete and up-to-date discussion of how to do cultural anthropological fieldwork. Drawing upon a wide variety of examples from actual fieldwork situations, Bernard takes the student step-by-step through the procedures for preparing for the field, collecting data, and analyzing the findings.

Messerschmidt, Donald A. *Anthropologists at Home in North America: Methods and Issues in the Study of One's Own Society.* Cambridge: Cambridge University Press, 1981. A collection of seventeen essays expressly written for this volume on theories, methods, and styles of doing research in contemporary North America.

Pelto, P. J., and G. H. Pelto. *Anthropological Research: The Structure of Inquiry* (2nd ed.). New York: Cambridge University Press, 1978. An excellent introduction to the methods of collecting and analyzing cultural anthropological data.

Spradley, James P. *The Ethnographic Interview*. New York: Holt, Rinehart & Winston, 1979. A very readable discussion of the nature and value of ethnographic research. The author not only analyzes the uniqueness of the ethnographic interview process but also discusses it within the wider context of ethnographic fieldwork.

Stocking, George W. *Observers Observed: Essays on Ethnographic Fieldwork*. Madison, Wis.: University of Wisconsin Press, 1983. A volume comprising nine essays dealing with ethnographic fieldwork written by both anthropologists and historians. The essays by the historians offer a unique perspective on the participant-observation technique, which cultural anthropologists think of as distinctively their own.

# Methods in Cultural Anthropology

As this chapter has demonstrated, cultural anthropology has developed a set of methods and data-gathering strategies that set it apart from other social science disciplines. While drawing upon a wide number of techniques and strategies, the primary characteristic of ethnographic fieldwork is its experiential nature—that is, cultural anthropologists conduct their research in a firsthand manner through participant-observation by interacting with the people being studied. According to Edgerton and Langness, the ethnologist in the field "shares in the people's day-to-day activities, watches as they eat, fight, and dance, listens to their commonplace and exciting conversations, and slowly begins to live and understand life as they do" (1974:3). This section examines how the research methods of cultural anthropology have been used to aid in the solution of pressing social problems. Specifically, the first case study discusses how ethnographic data-gathering techniques can contribute to programs of agricultural reform in Ecuador; the second case study shows how ethnographic interviewing can be helpful in rehab programs for Skid Row alcoholics; and the final case study discusses how methods in cultural anthropology can contribute to a solution to our most serious health problem—the AIDS epidemic.

◆ **Ethnographic research on farming practices in Ecuador can contribute significantly to programs of agricultural reform.**

The use of participant-observation for the study of human behavior has relevance for and can be applied to a vast number of domains of human society. One such area is agricultural development in Third World countries. National and international foreign assistance organizations spend hundreds of millions of dollars each year on programs designed to improve levels of agricultural productivity among the developing nations of the world. Before positive (i.e., more productive) changes in traditional farming technologies can be made, research needs to be conducted on (a) the nature of the traditional farming practices; (b) certain technical issues of farming, such as soil composition and climatic conditions; and (c) the psychological, political, and social obstacles to change. In recent years, however, the effectiveness of farming research in developing countries has been called into question.

It has been suggested (Tripp, 1985) that cultural anthropologists—with their unique methods and perspective—can make significant contributions to strengthening farming research in the Third World that will eventually lead to more successful programs of agricultural reform. To be certain, this holistic approach to cultural analysis, which has been a hallmark of the anthropological perspective, can inform agricultural researchers by reminding them of "social context" and how farming is interrelated to other parts of the system. And, of course, there are many areas of anthropological expertise that impact the decision-making process of farmers and, consequently, the likelihood of their accepting or rejecting certain agricultural reforms. These include the division of household labor, land allocation, food preferences, crop marketing strategies, and the allocation of food supplies within the household, among other things. But, in addition to these substantive contributions, we are interested here in the methodological contributions that cultural anthropology can make to the process of farm research in the developing world.

In a recent article, Tripp (1985) showed how a type of agricultural research called **on-farm research** (OFR) has drawn heavily upon the use of ethnographic field methods. Although in past decades agricultural research was based largely on lengthy surveys and questionnaires, this approach has been criticized on the grounds that it is neither cost-effective nor particularly convenient for development planners to translate into practical terms. A new research strategy—designed to correct these two shortcomings—has recently emerged, called the *sondeo* (Hildebrande, 1981). The *sondeo* involves the use of informal interviews and participant-observation by teams of agricultural and social scientists. Over the course of several weeks, the research team is able to develop a composite picture of the local farming system. This relatively rapid and effective approach to the diagnosis phase of research is a direct application of the experiential and interactive methodology of the cultural anthropologist.

Tripp illustrated how a program of farming research in Northern Ecuador utilized a modified form of the *sondeo* for collecting diagnostic information. Owing to the scarcity of resources, the biological scientists (agronomists) were required to conduct all of the research themselves. The agronomists were schooled in a number of important analytical skills derived from ethnographic field methods. Among the methods were participant-observation, informal interviewing, and systematic note taking.

As part of the research process, the agricultural researchers learned how to visit with local farmers in their fields and homes and participate in local community events. They developed skills of recording the data they observed, which eventually led to unanticipated findings and which, in the final analysis, improved the quality of the research. By using these personal, interactive research methods, the agronomists learned to assume an attitude common in ethnographic fieldwork—that is, an attitude of honest curiosity rather than one of scientific or intellectual superiority. Thus, by using these methods, these agricultural researchers were able to overcome the costly survey methods of research and, in the process, derive data that were both relevant and ongoing throughout the duration of the project.

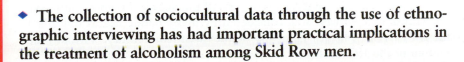

◆ **The collection of sociocultural data through the use of ethnographic interviewing has had important practical implications in the treatment of alcoholism among Skid Row men.**

In the social science literature, the term *Skid Row men* refers to indigents who regularly consume inexpensive alcoholic beverages as a way of life, are frequently picked up by the police for public drunkenness, and find themselves repeatedly in detox centers. According to most studies (Rooney,

283

1961:444; Spradley, 1970:225; Parsons, 1951:289), the Skid Row men have lost all significant involvement with their families. They are, in short, men without families and men who do not want families.

This general perception that Skid Row men do not maintain their family ties may be more the result of failing to investigate this aspect of their lives, rather than a true measure of reality. Prompted by such a possibility, Singer (1985) decided to conduct ethnographic interviews with twenty-eight Skid Row men who had been admitted to an Alcoholic Detoxification Center in Washington, D.C. The interview schedule, comprising 100 open-ended questions, was designed to collect information on family background, drinking history, current life-styles, and social networks. Singer reasoned that if, in fact, these Skid Row men do maintain kinship ties, it might be possible to use these kinship links as part of the strategy for therapeutic intervention.

Interestingly, the data revealed that this sample of Skid Row men maintained fairly regular contact with relatives. More specifically, 93 percent of the men both remained in regular contact with and felt emotionally close to at least one family member; 90 percent received nonmaterial aid from relatives; and 86 percent received material assistance from family. In spite of numerous disappointments caused by the alcoholics' inability to stay out of trouble, ties with certain kin (mostly female) were both persistent and emotionally laden. The Skid Row men were found to both respect and care for their supportive kin.

Based on these findings from the ethnographic interviews, Singer concluded that these female supportive kin may be an important link in the alcoholic rehabilitation programs for Skid Row men. Some of the men interviewed stated that some of their family had not given up on them and would be willing to participate in family therapy. Since there is general agreement among the therapeutic community that successful alcoholic rehabilitation requires the involvement of "significant others" who care, these findings can encourage the use of family therapy for the treatment of Skid Row alcoholics.

◆ **Ethnological research contributes to the ongoing search for a solution to the AIDS epidemic.**

In the early 1980s, very few Americans had ever heard of Acquired Immune Deficiency Syndrome (AIDS). By the end of the decade, however, this sexually transmitted disease was considered by many public health officials as the most serious health epidemic of the twentieth century. Virtually unknown in the 1970s, the AIDS epidemic has spread drastically from fewer than 200 reported cases in the United States in 1981 to about 31,000 cases in 1988 (Bureau of the Census, 1990:116).

As Gorman (1986:157) has suggested, the AIDS epidemic is particularly difficult to get under control for a number of reasons. First, the disease attacks the human immune system, one of the most complex and inadequately understood systems of the body. Second, the group of viruses thought to cause the disease are so poorly understood that a chemical cure is not likely to be found in the immediate future. Thus, the biological factors in solving the AIDS threat are highly complex. Efforts to stem the epidemic are further complicated by cultural factors. That is, the high-risk populations (gay males and intravenous drug users) are not very visible subcultural groups. This creates additional problems for programs of AIDS prevention.

Until a vaccine for AIDS is developed, education remains the best strategy for reducing the spread of the disease. Since AIDS is sexually transmitted, the world's populations must learn as much as possible about how to avoid contracting the disease. Yet, before public health officials can design effective educational programs, they need a good deal of cultural/behavioral information on high-risk populations. Cultural anthropologists can make significant contributions to programs of preventive education by conducting ethnographic research on the cultural patterns of sexual behavior among such high-risk groups as gay males in the United States.

One such applied anthropological study was conducted by Douglas Feldman (1985) among gay males in New York City. Owing to the relatively sensitive nature of the gay community, such a study was fraught with methodological difficulties. Since there are no census data on gay males, Feldman could not draw a random sample of gays in New York. Instead he utilized the *Gayellow Pages* (a national directory of gay businesses and organizations) from which he drew a varied sample of organizations. After explaining the purpose of the study, Feldman solicited active participation in the study by having each organization distribute copies of a prepared (two-page) questionnaire to its employees or members. In all, some 1,600 questionnaires were distributed and 403 returned, a response rate of 25 percent.

Feldman's study was designed to determine the concern about the AIDS epidemic of gay males in New York City and the extent to which that concern has affected gay men's sexual behavior. Respondents were asked the number of different sexual partners they had per month prior to their learning about AIDS compared to after learning about it. The study revealed a dramatic decrease of 47 percent in the number of sexual partners before and after. Moreover, the nature of the sexual activity also changed substantially away from those activities that are most likely to transmit the disease.

To be certain, applied studies such as Feldman's have their limitations. The collection of behavioral data on sexual practices among any group of people will always be difficult because of its highly personal nature. When seeking such sensitive information from a subgroup often stigmatized by the wider society, problems of data validity are greatly magnified. Moreover, our knowledge about the AIDS epidemic is growing so rapidly that data become obsolete very quickly. Nevertheless, cultural anthropology has an important role to play in the monumental effort it will take to eradicate this dread disease. Anthropologists such as Feldman—who are interested in both anthropology and epidemiology—can contribute to the design of successful prevention programs by providing both attitudinal and behavioral

285

data from the ethnographic study of gay communities in the United States. Gorman has effectively summarized the emerging role that applied anthropologists can play in the effort against AIDS:

The public health crisis that attended the AIDS epidemic represents unique opportunities for the application of social scientific perspectives in epidemiology. Due to the combination of biological, technological, social and behavioral phenomena encompassed by AIDS, rarely has a health crisis represented such a unique nexus of disease and culture. AIDS as yet remains a puzzle whose pieces are only slowly being identified and pieced together. Anthropology has contributed and will continue to assist in the assembling of these pieces (1986:169).

# Language

How does human language differ from forms of communication in other animals?

Are some languages superior to others?

What is the relationship between language and culture?

How do people communicate without using words?

# The Nature of Language

Perhaps the most distinctive feature of being human is the capacity to create and use language and other symbolic forms of communication. It is hard to imagine how culture could even exist without language. Such fundamental aspects of any culture as religion, family relationships, and the management of technology would be virtually impossible without a symbolic form of communication. Our very capacity to adapt to the physical environment—which involves identifying usable resources, developing ways of acquiring them, and finally forming groups to exploit them—is made possible by language. It is generally held that language is the major vehicle for human thought, since our linguistic categories provide the basis for perception and concept formation. Moreover, it is largely through language that we pass on our cultural heritage from one generation to the next. In short, language is such an integral part of the human condition that it permeates everything we do.

The term *language,* like so many others that we think we understand, is far more complex than we might imagine. Language, found in all cultures of the world, is a symbolic system of sounds that, when put together according to a certain set of rules, conveys meanings to its speakers. The meanings attached to any given word in all languages are totally arbitrary. That is, the word *cow* has no particular connection to that large bovine animal that the English language uses to refer to as a cow. The word *cow* is no more or less reasonable a word for that animal than would be *kaflumpha, sporge,* or *four-pronged squirter.* The word *cow* does not look like a cow, sound like a cow, or have any particular physical connection to a cow. The only explanation for the use of the word is that somewhere during the evolution of the English language someone decided that the word *cow* would be used to refer to a large domesticated animal that gives an abundant quantity of milk. Other languages use totally different, and equally arbitrary, words to describe the very same animal.

## DIVERSITY OF LANGUAGE

Given the very arbitrary nature of languages, it should come as no surprise that there is enormous linguistic diversity among human populations. Even though there is no precise agreement among linguists as to the number of discrete languages that exist, a reasonably conservative estimate would be several thousand. The criterion used to establish such estimates is mutual unintelligibility. That is, it is assumed by linguists that if people can understand one another, they speak the same language; if they are unable to understand one another, they speak different languages. The application of this criterion is not as straightforward as it might appear, however, owing to the fact that there are always differing degrees of intelligibility. Nevertheless, despite our inability to define with absolute precision the number of discrete languages found in the world today, the amount of linguistic diversity is vast. (Exhibit 14-1 on pages 290–291 illustrates the world's major language families.)

## COMMUNICATION—HUMAN VERSUS NONHUMAN

Communication is certainly not unique to humans, for most animals have ways of sending and receiving messages. Various bird species use certain calls to communicate a desire to mate; honeybees, through a series of body movements, communicate very accurately the distance and direction of sources of food; certain antelope species give off a cry that warns of impending danger; even amoebae seem to chemically send and receive crude messages by discharging small amounts of carbon dioxide.

Communication among primates, of course, is considerably more complex. Certain nonhuman primate species, such as gorillas and chimpanzees, draw on a relatively large number of modes of communication, including various calls as well as such nonverbal forms of communication as facial expressions, body movement, and gestures. Yet despite the relative complexity of communication patterns among nonhuman primates, these patterns differ from human patterns of communication in some significant ways. For example, since animal call systems are to a large extent genetically based, they are rigidly inflexible to the extent that each call always has the same form and conveys the same meaning.

**Open and Closed Communication Systems.** Chimpanzees make one sound when they have found a plentiful source of food, another when threatened, and a third when announcing their presence. Each of these three sounds is unique in both form and message. And each sound (call) is mutually exclusive. That is, the chimpanzee cannot combine elements of two or more calls in order to develop a new call. To this extent we speak of nonhuman forms of communication as being **closed systems of communication.** Humans, on the other hand, operate with languages that are **open systems of communication**, since they are capable of sending messages that have never been sent before.

Language enables humans to send literally an infinite array of messages, including abstract ideas, highly technical information, and subtle shades of meaning. Starting with a limited number of sounds, human languages are capable of producing an infinite number of meanings by combining sounds and words into meanings that may have never been sent before. To illustrate, by combining a series of words in a certain order, we can convey a unique message that has, in all likelihood, never been previously uttered: "I think that the woman named Clela with the bright orange hair left her leather handbag in the 1951 Studebaker that was involved in a hit-and-run accident later in the day." This productive capacity of human language illustrates how efficient and flexible human communication can be.

To suggest, as has been done in the past, that such nonhuman primates as chimps and gorillas have a closed communication system as compared to the open system used by humans is perhaps an oversimplification. Some linguistic scholars (e.g., Noam Chomsky, 1972) have posited that since human language is so radically different from other forms of animal communication, humans must be endowed with certain genetically based mental capacities found in no other species. However, as we have learned more about the communication systems of nonhuman primates, a growing number of scholars have questioned this theory by claiming that certain species like chimpanzees and gorillas have a latent capacity for language.

A major limitation to the development of language among gorillas and chimps is physical, for they do not possess the vocal equipment for speech. In an effort to circumvent this physical limitation, recent researchers have taught American Sign Language to chimpanzees and gorillas with some startling findings. In four years, a chimp named Washoe was taught by Allen and Beatrice Gardner (1969) to use 130 different signs. Of even greater significance is that Washoe was able to manipulate the signs in ways that previously had been thought possible only by humans. For example, Washoe was able to combine several signs to create a new word (having no sign for the word *duck,* she referred to it as *waterbird*), thereby "opening up" her system of communication.

In another important research effort in nonhuman communication, a gorilla named Koko was able by age four to use over 250 different signs within a single hour and, like Washoe, was able to name new objects by combining several different signs. In addition, Koko was able to express her feelings and actually scored between 80 and 90 on a nonverbal IQ test.

These recent developments in communication studies among nonhuman primates would suggest that chimps and gorillas do in fact have more advanced powers of reasoning than had been believed earlier. Some researchers have used this evidence to support the notion that chimpanzee and gorilla linguistic abilities differ from

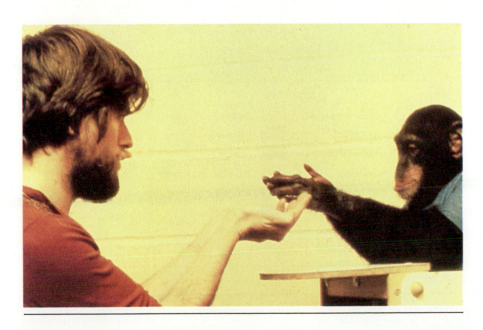

Even though this nonhuman primate can send and receive messages by using American Sign Language, the differences between this form of communication and human language are vast.

those of humans only in degree, not in kind. In other words, we should not think in terms of either closed or open systems of communication, but rather in terms of some systems being more open than others. If this is the case, however, it is important to bear in mind that the degree of the difference between human and nonhuman forms of communication remains immense.

**Displacement.** Human communication differs from other animal communication systems in at least two other important respects. One such feature of human language is its capacity to convey information about a thing or an event that is not present. This characteristic, known as **displacement**, enables humans to speak of purely hypothetical things, events that have happened in

E X H I B I T   14-1

**Major Language Families of the World**

Source: Reprinted by permission from pages 50–51 of *World Regional Geography: A Global Approach*, by George F. Hepner and Jesse O. McKee. Copyright © 1992 by West Publishing Company. All rights reserved.

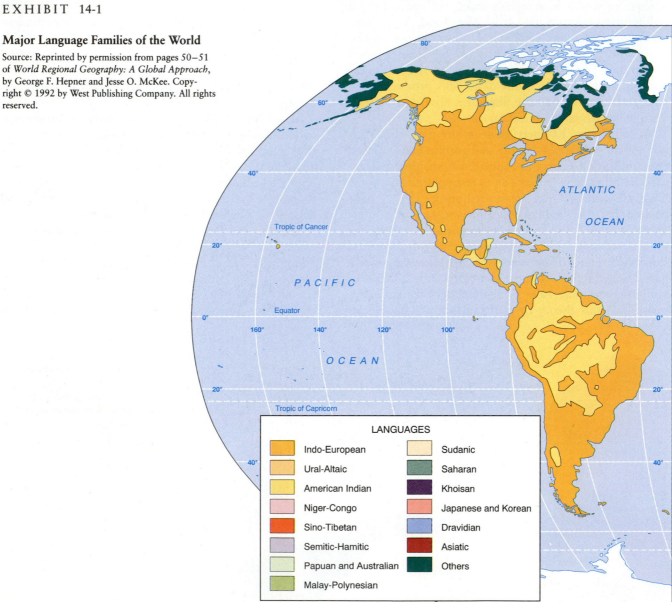

LANGUAGES

- Indo-European
- Ural-Altaic
- American Indian
- Niger-Congo
- Sino-Tibetan
- Semitic-Hamitic
- Papuan and Australian
- Malay-Polynesian
- Sudanic
- Saharan
- Khoisan
- Japanese and Korean
- Dravidian
- Asiatic
- Others

the past, and events that might happen in the future. In contrast to other animals, which communicate only about particular things that are in the present and the immediate environment, humans are able through language to think abstractly. Another feature of human communication that distinguishes it from nonhuman forms of communication is that it is transmitted largely through tradition rather than through experience alone. Even though our propensity (and our physical equipment) for language is biologically based, the specific language that any given person speaks is passed on from one generation to another through the process of learning. Adults in a linguistic community who already know the language teach the language to the children.

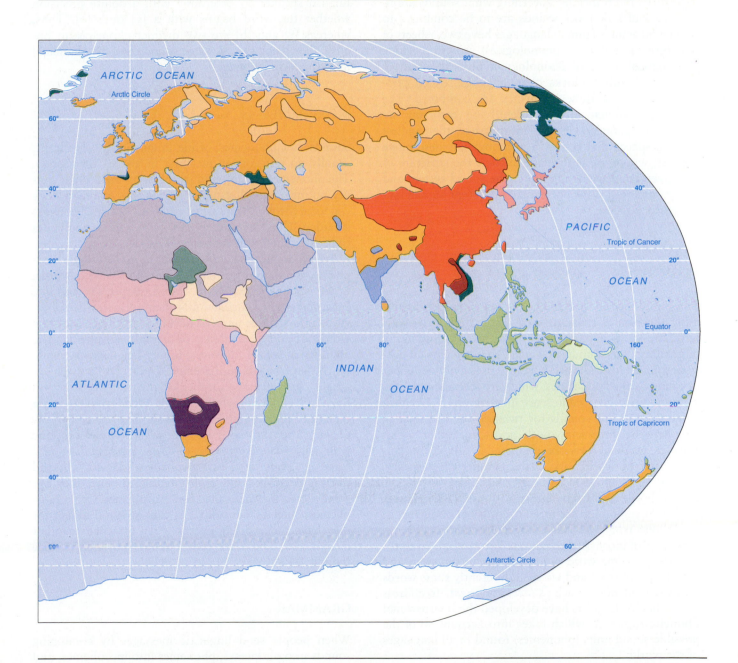

# The Structure of Language

Every language has a logical structure. Even though people are at first confused and disoriented when encountering an unfamiliar language, after becoming familiar with the language they eventually discover the rules of the language and how the various parts of the language are interrelated to one another. All languages have rules and principles governing what sounds are to be used and how those sounds are to be combined to convey meanings. Human languages have two aspects of structure: a sound (or phonological) structure and a grammatical structure. **Phonology** involves the study of the basic building blocks of a language, called phonemes, and how these phonemes are combined. The study of **grammar** involves identifying recurring sequences of phonemes, called **morphemes,** the smallest units of speech that convey a meaning. The descriptive linguist, whose job is to make explicit the structure of any given language, studies both the sound system and the grammatical system of as many different human languages as possible.

## PHONOLOGY

The initial step in describing any language is to determine the sounds that are used. Even though humans have the vocal apparatus to make an extraordinarily large number of sounds, no single language uses all possible sounds. Instead, each language uses a finite number of sounds, called phonemes, which are the minimal units of sound that signal a difference in meaning. The English language contains sounds for twenty-four consonants, nine vowels, three semivowels and some other sound features totaling forty-six phonemes. All of the languages of the world vary in the number of phonemes from a low of about 15 to a high of as many as 100.

Clearly the twenty-six letters of the English alphabet do not correspond to the total inventory of phonemes in the English language. This is largely because English has a number of inconsistent features. For example, we pronounce the same word differently (as in the noun and verb forms of *lead*) and we spell differently some words that sound identical, such as *meet* and *meat.* To address this difficulty, linguists have developed the International Phonetic Alphabet, which takes into account all of the possible sound units (phonemes) found in all languages of the world.

The manner in which sounds are grouped into phonemes varies from one language to another. In English, for example, the sounds represented by [b] and [v] comprise two separate phonemes. Such a distinction is absolutely necessary if an English speaker is to differentiate between such words as *ban* and *van* or *bent* and *vent.* The Spanish language, however, does not distinguish between these two sounds. When the Spanish word *ver* (to see) is pronounced, it would be impossible for the English speaker to determine with absolute precision whether the word begins with a [v] or a [b]. Thus, whereas [v] and [b] are two distinct phonemes in English, they belong to the same sound class (or phoneme) in the Spanish language.

## MORPHEMES

Sounds and phonemes, while linguistically significant, usually do not convey meaning in and of themselves. The phonemes [r], [a], and [t] taken by themselves convey no meaning whatsoever. But when combined, they can form the word *rat, tar* or *art,* each of which conveys meaning. Thus, it is possible for two or more phonemes to be combined to form a morpheme.

Even though some words are made up of a single morpheme, we should not equate morphemes with words. In the example cited above, the words *rat, tar,* and *art,* each made up of a single morpheme, cannot be subdivided into smaller units of meaning. In these cases, the words are in fact made up of a single morpheme. The majority of words, however, in any language are made up of two or more morphemes. The word *rats,* for example, contains two morphemes, the root word *rat* and the plural suffix [s], which conveys the meaning of more than one. Similarly, the word *artists* contains three morphemes: the root word *art;* the suffix *ist,* meaning one who engages in the process of doing art; and the plural suffix [s]. Some of these morphemes, like *art, tar,* and *rat,* can occur in a language unattached. Since they can stand alone, they are called **free morphemes.** Other morphemes, such as the suffix *ist,* cannot stand alone, for they have no meaning except when attached to other morphemes. These are called **bound morphemes.** (See Exhibit 14-2.)

## GRAMMAR

When people send linguistic messages by combining sounds into phonemes, phonemes into morphemes, and

**Morphemes Make Up Words**

The word *toasters* is made up of the morphemes *toast*, *er*, and *s*. Which morphemes are free and which are bound?

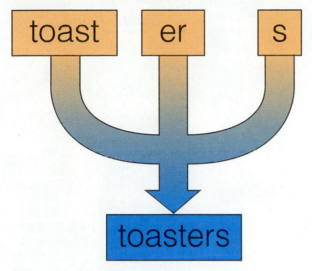

morphemes into words, they do so according to a highly complex set of rules. These rules, unique for each language, make up the grammar of the language and are well understood and followed by the speakers of the language. These grammatical systems, constituting the formal structure of the language, consist of two parts: (1) the rules governing how morphemes are formed into words (**morphology**) and (2) the principles guiding how words are arranged into phrases and sentences (**syntax**). In some languages, meanings are determined primarily by the way in which morphemes are combined to form words (morphological features), while in other languages meanings are determined primarily by the order of words in a sentence (syntactical features).

The distinction between morphology and syntax can be illustrated by looking at an example from the English language. From a grammatical point of view, the statement "Tom fix Mary phone" does not make much sense. The order of the words in the statement (i.e., the syntax) is correct, but clearly some revision in the way that the words themselves are formed (i.e., morphology) is required for the statement to make grammatical sense. For example, since the English language requires information about verb tense, we must specify whether Tom fixed, is fixing, or will fix the phone. The English grammar system also requires information about the number

of phones and the nature of the relationship between the phone and Mary. To make this statement grammatical, we can add an -ed to *fix,* an -s to *phone,* and an -'s to Mary. The revised statement ("Tom fixed Mary's phones"), which is now grammatically correct, tells us that Tom has already fixed two or more phones that belong to Mary.

Whereas the English grammar system requires that tense, number, and relationship be specified, other language systems require other types of information. For example, in Latin, a noun must have the proper case ending to indicate its role (i.e., subject, direct object, etc.) within the sentence. In some languages, such as Spanish, the ending on a noun determines the noun's gender (masculinity or femininity). In the Navajo language, certain verbs such as "to handle" will take different forms depending on the size and shape of the object being handled. Thus, we can see that every language has its own systematic way of ordering morphemes within a word to give linguistic meaning.

Syntax, on the other hand, refers to that part of grammar that has to do with the arrangement of words and phrases into sentences. In the original example above ("Tom fix Mary phone"), the syntax is correct because the order of the words is in proper sequence. The statement would be totally meaningless if the words were ordered "Fix Tom phone Mary," because the parts of speech are not in proper relationship to one another. Moreover, in English, adjectives generally precede the nouns they describe (such as "white horse"), while in Spanish adjectives generally follow the nouns they describe (such as "caballo blanco"). The order of the words, then, determines, at least in part, the meaning conveyed in any given language.

◆   ◆   ◆

## Are Some Languages Superior to Others?

Until the turn of the century, European linguists were convinced that Western languages were superior to all others in terms of elegance, efficiency, and beauty. It was generally assumed that small-scale, non-Western cultures characterized by simple technologies were equally simple in terms of their languages. In short, preliterate people were thought to have primitive languages with a diminished capacity for expressing abstract ideas. However, twentieth-century anthropological linguists, following the lead of Franz Boas, now hold such a view to be untenable. Based on studies of American Indian

While the Navajo and English languages have vastly different structures, these Navajo speakers can express abstract ideas every bit as effectively as native English speakers.

languages, linguists have demonstrated time and again that people from technologically simple societies are no less capable of expressing a wide variety of abstract ideas than are people living in high-technology societies.

To illustrate this point, we can compare the English language with that of a traditionally technologically simple society—the Navajo people of the American Southwest. It is true that Navajo speakers are unable to make certain grammatical distinctions commonly made in English. For example, in Navajo there are not separate noun forms for singular and plural (such as are found in English with the -s in *dogs* or the -ren in *children*); the third person pronoun is both singular and plural and gender nonspecific (it can be translated he, she, it, or they, depending on the context); and there are no adjectives, because the role of the adjective to describe nouns in English is played by the verb.

Despite the fact that the Navajo language does not make the same grammatical distinctions as does the English language, in other areas it can express certain in-

formation with considerably more precision and efficiency than English. According to Peter Farb (1968:56), using the Navajo language it is impossible to make a vague statement such as "I am going." Owing to the structure of this language, the verb stem would include additional information on whether the person is going on foot, by horseback, in a wagon, by boat, or in an airplane. If the selected verb form indicates that the person is going on horseback, it is necessary to further differentiate by verb form whether the horse is walking, trotting, galloping, or running. Thus, in the Navajo language a great deal of information is conveyed in the single verb form which is selected to express the concept of going. To be certain, the grammatical systems of the English and Navajo languages are very different. The English language can convey all of the same information, but it requires a far larger number of words. Nevertheless, it is hardly reasonable to conclude that one is more efficient at expressing abstract ideas than the other.

# Language and Culture

For the cultural anthropologist, the study of language is important not only for the practical purpose of communicating while doing fieldwork but also because a close relationship exists between language and culture. It is widely accepted today that it would be difficult, if not impossible, to understand a culture without first understanding its language, and it would be equally impossible to understand a language outside of its cultural context. It is for this reason that any effective language teacher will go beyond vocabulary and grammar by teaching students something about such topics as eating habits, values, and behavior patterns of native speakers. This important relationship between language and culture was recognized many decades ago by the father of modern American cultural anthropology, Franz Boas:

... the study of language must be considered as one of the most important branches of ethnological study, because, on the one hand, a thorough insight into ethnology cannot be gained without a practical knowledge of the language, and, on the other hand, the fundamental concepts illustrated by human languages are not distinct in kind from ethnological phenomena; and because, furthermore, the peculiar characteristics of language are clearly reflected in the views and customs of the peoples of the world (1911:73).

## HOW CULTURE INFLUENCES LANGUAGE

Although little research has been designed to explore how culture influences the grammatical system of a language, there is considerable evidence to demonstrate how culture affects vocabulary. As a general rule, the vocabulary found in any language will tend to emphasize those words that are considered to be adaptively important in that culture. This notion, known as **cultural emphasis,** is reflected in the size and specialization of vocabulary.

In Standard American English we find large numbers of words that refer to technological gadgetry (e.g., tractor, microchip, and intake valve) and occupational specialties (e.g., teacher, plumber, CPA, and pediatrician) for the simple reason that technology and occupation are points of cultural emphasis in our culture. Thus, the English language helps North Americans adapt effectively to their culture by providing a vocabulary best suited for that culture. Other cultures have other areas of emphasis. Based on field research conducted in the 1880s, Franz Boas noted that the Eskimos of Canada

had large numbers of words for snow, ice, and seals, all three of which played a vital role in Eskimo adaptation to the environment and, indeed, in their survival. To illustrate, Boas reports that in addition to a general term for seal, the Eskimo language contains specific words referring to a seal basking in the sun or a seal floating on a piece of ice, as well as a number of terms for seals of different age and gender.

**The Nuer.** A particularly good example of how culture influences language through the elaboration of vocabularies is provided by the Nuer, a pastoral people of the Sudan, whose daily preoccupation with cattle is reflected in their language (Evans-Pritchard, 1940). The Nuer have a vast vocabulary used to describe and identify their cattle according to certain physical features such as color, markings, and horn configuration. There are ten major color terms used to describe cattle among the Nuer: white (bor) black (car), brown (lual), chestnut (dol), tawny (yan), mouse-grey (lou), bay (thiang), sandy-gray (lith), blue and strawberry roan (yil), and chocolate (gwir). Whenever any of these colors are combined with white, there are no fewer than twenty-seven such color combinations. When these color possibilities are merged with the many different possibilities of marking patterns, there are more than several hundred combinations. And when these several hundred possibilities are combined with terminology based on horn configuration, there are potentially thousands of ways of describing cattle with considerable precision in the Nuer language.

This highly complex system of terminology is directly related to the prominence of cattle in Nuer society. Cattle, according to Evans-Pritchard (1940), are used in a number of important ways. First, they serve a vital economic function in Nuer society (as they do in most other pastoral societies) by providing the people with milk, blood, and meat on certain occasions. Second, cows are used to create and maintain social relationships between people. That is, for a Nuer marriage to be legitimate, cows must be transferred from the lineage of the groom to the lineage of the bride. Third, cows not only influence the relationship between people but also serve as a link with the people's dead ancestors. Cows are used as sacrificial animals for getting the attention of ancestor ghosts; in fact, it is impossible to communicate with the dead without frequent references to cattle. Fourth, every Nuer man takes as one of his names the name of an oxen given to him at birth or at his initiation. Men are frequently called by names that refer to the physical features of these oxen, and most age-mates prefer to be addressed by this oxname. (It is for this reason that Evans-Pritchard (1940:18) notes that a Nuer genealogy sounds very much like an inventory of a family's cattle.) And fifth, the names and traits of cows as well as the oxnames of men are frequently the subject of songs, poems, and stories. We could cite numerous other uses to which cattle are put, indicating their prominence within the Nuer culture. But suffice it to say that cattle are a dominant interest of the Nuer, or in Evans-Pritchard's own words:

They are always talking about their beasts. I used sometimes to despair that I never discussed anything with the young men but livestock and girls, and even the subject of girls led inevitably to that of cattle. Start on whatever subject I would, and approach it from whatever angle, we would soon be speaking of cows and oxen, heifers and steers, rams and sheep, he-goats and she-goats, calves, and lambs, and kids. . . . Consequently he who lives among the Nuer and wishes to understand their social life must first master a vocabulary referring to cattle and to the life of the herd (1940:18–19).

**Cultural Emphasis in the United States—One Example.**
In relatively small-scale cultures such as the Eskimos or the Nuer, where most people's lives revolve around hunting or herding, areas of cultural emphasis are quite obvious. In middle-class American culture, however, which tends to be more complex occupationally, it is not always easy to identify a single area of cultural emphasis. Nevertheless, sports tends to be one area of life in U.S. culture that can be shared by people from a wide variety of occupational or class backgrounds. Consequently, as Hickerson points out, we have many colloquialisms in American English that stem from the game of baseball, our "national pastime":

◆ He made a grandstand play.
◆ She threw me a curve.
◆ She fielded my questions well.
◆ You're way off base.
◆ You're batting 1000 (500, zero) so far.
◆ What are the ground rules?
◆ I want to touch all the bases.
◆ He went to bat for me.
◆ He has two strikes against him.
◆ That's way out in left field.
◆ He drives me up the wall.
◆ He's a team player (a clutch player).
◆ She's an oddball (screwball, foul ball).
◆ It's just a ballpark estimate (1980:118).

## HOW LANGUAGE INFLUENCES CULTURE

A major concern of linguistic anthropology since the 1930s has been the question of whether language influences or perhaps even determines culture. Despite the fact that there is no consensus among ethnolinguists, some have suggested that language is more than a symbolic inventory of experience and the physical world but indeed shapes our thoughts and perceptions. This notion was stated in its most explicit form by Edward Sapir:

The fact of the matter is that the real world is to a large extent unconsciously built up on the language habits of the group. No two languages are ever sufficiently similar to be considered as representing the same social reality. The worlds in which different societies live are distinct worlds, not merely the same world with different labels attached (1929:214).

**The Sapir-Whorf Hypothesis.** Drawing on Sapir's original formulation, Benjamin Lee Whorf, a student of Sapir's, conducted ethnolinguistic research among the Hopi Indians to determine if different linguistic structures produced different ways of viewing the world. Whorf's observations convinced him that linguistic structure was in fact the causal variable for different views of the world. This notion that different cultures see the world differently because of their different linguistic categories has come to be known as the **Sapir-Whorf Hypothesis.**

Both Sapir and Whorf were positing the notion that language does influence the way people see the world. That is, language is more than a vehicle for communication; it actually establishes mental categories that predispose people to see things in a certain way. If, for example, my language has a single word—aunt—that refers to my mother's sister, my father's sister, my mother's brother's wife, and my father's brother's wife, it is likely that I will perceive all of these family members as genealogically equivalent and consequently will behave toward them in essentially the same way. Thus, Sapir and Whorf would suggest that both perception and the resulting behavior will be determined by the linguistic categories we use to group some things under one heading and other things under another heading.

*Testing the Hypothesis.* Since Sapir and Whorf's original formulation, a number of ethnolinguists have attempted to test the hypothesis. One study (Ervin-Tripp, 1964) concluded that the very content of what is said by bilin-

In certain bilingual populations, such as Japanese-Americans, it has been shown that how a question is answered often will depend on the language in which the question is asked.

language that influences or channels perceptions as well as the content of verbal utterances.

One very creative attempt at testing the Sapir-Whorf Hypothesis was conducted by Casagrande (1960), using a matched sample of Navajo-speaking children. Half of the sample, which spoke only Navajo, was matched on all significant sociocultural variables (such as religion, parental education, family income), with the other half, which spoke both Navajo and English. Since both groups were identical on all important variables except language, it would be logical to conclude that whatever perceptual differences emerged between the two groups could be attributed to language.

Having a thorough knowledge of the Navajo language, Casagrande understood that Navajo people, when speaking about an object, are required to choose among a number of different verb forms depending on the shape of the object. When asking a Navajo speaker to hand you an object, you use one verb form if the object is long and rigid like a stick, and another verb form if it is long and flexible like a rope. Based on this Navajo linguistic feature, Casagrande hypothesized that children speaking only Navajo would be more likely to discriminate according to shape at an earlier age than those English-speaking children. English-speaking children would be more likely to discriminate according to other features such as size or color. This hypothesis was tested by having both groups of children participate in a number of tasks. The children were shown two objects (a yellow stick and a blue rope) and then asked to tell which of these two objects was most like a third object (a yellow rope). In other words, both groups of children were asked to categorize the yellow rope according to likeness with either the yellow stick or the blue rope. Casagrande found that the children who spoke only Navajo had a significantly greater tendency to categorize according to shape (yellow *rope* and blue *rope*) as compared to the bilingual children who were more likely to categorize according to color.

According to the Sapir-Whorf Hypothesis, then, language establishes in our minds categories that force us to distinguish those things we consider similar from those things we consider different. Language, in other words, is a coercive force that causes people to see the world in a certain way. If this is the case, the speakers of different languages will construct reality differently.

***Drawbacks to the Hypothesis.*** The problem with the Sapir-Whorf Hypothesis—and the reason that it remains a hypothesis rather than a widely accepted fact

gual people will vary according to which language is being spoken. Working with bilingual Japanese-American women in San Francisco, Ervin-Tripp (1964:96) found that the responses to the same question given at different times to the same women varied significantly depending on the language used. To illustrate, when asked in English to finish the statement "Real friends should . . . ," the respondent answered, "be very frank"; but when asked the same question in Japanese at a different time, she answered "help each other." Or, when asked, "When my wishes conflict with my family . . . ," the response in English was "I do what I want"; but in Japanese, the response was, "It is a time of great unhappiness." In other words, when the question was asked in Japanese, the bilingual respondent was more likely to give a "typical" Japanese response, and when questioned in English, she was more likely to give a "typical" American response. This is the type of evidence that has been presented to support the validity of the Sapir-Whorf Hypothesis, since it strongly suggests that it is the

## CROSS-CULTURAL MISCUE

For decades, a major focus of U.S. foreign policy has been on what we call the Middle East, an area that is largely Islamic in religion and Arabic in culture and language. In recent years, the U.S. government has sent Marines to Lebanon, had its embassy taken over in Tehran, engaged in retaliatory air strikes on Libya, and responded to the invasion of Kuwait by Iraq. Because of its close political, economic, and social ties to the state of Israel, the United States has been at loggerheads with most of the Arab world. All too often the American people—and far more seriously, our diplomatic community—seem to be reacting to events in the Middle East with only a minimal understanding of Arabic culture.

Linguistic style is one area of misinterpretation of Arabic cultures by Americans. Whereas some cultures (such as the Japanese) engage in linguistic understatement, Arabic speakers generally go to the opposite extreme through such linguistic conventions as exaggeration, overassertion, and repetition. For example, sometimes messages sent in Arabic are given more dramatic force by repeating certain pronouns; highly graphic metaphors and similes are commonly found in everyday speech; and Arabs frequently will string together—for the sake of dramatizing a point—a long litany of adjectives to modify a single noun. Because of differences in communication styles, what we would consider to be a strongly worded statement might seem weak and unassertive to an Arab. Or, a very strongly worded statement in Arabic would be viewed as absolutely fanatical to an American. It is important to bear in mind that in the Arabic world, very strongly worded statements—which have a psychologically cathartic function—should not be taken literally as an accurate description of the speaker's real thoughts or intentions. Understanding such a linguistic style is particularly relevant in the diplomatic/political realm, where an overreaction to a strongly worded threat could lead to armed conflict and the loss of lives.

---

—is one of causation. Whorf and Sapir were linguistic determinists who posited that language *determines* culture. In fact, Sapir suggested that people are virtual prisoners of their language when he stated that "human beings . . . are very much at the mercy of the particular language which has become the medium of expression for their society" (1929:209). Others, however, taking the opposite position, have suggested that language simply reflects, rather than determines, culture. To be certain, language and culture influence each other in a number of important ways. Yet problems arise when attempting to demonstrate that language determines culture, or vice versa, in any definitive way. What does seem obvious, however, is that all people, being constantly bombarded with sensory stimuli, have developed filtering systems to bring order to all of these incoming sen-

sations. Sapir and Whorf have suggested that the filtering system is language, which provides a set of lenses that highlight some perceptions and deemphasize others. Whatever may be the precise effect of language on culture, the Sapir-Whorf hypothesis has served to focus attention on this important relationship.

## Sociolinguistics

Anthropological linguistics has devoted much of its time and energy to the study of languages as logical systems of knowledge and communication. Recently, however, linguists have taken a keen interest in how people actually speak with one another in any given society.

CHAPTER 14 ◆ LANGUAGE

Whereas the earlier linguists tended to focus on uniform structures (morphology, phonology, and syntax), sociolinguists concentrate on variations in language use depending on the social situation or context in which the speaker may be operating.

In much the same way that whole speech communities adapt their language to changing situations, so too do the individuals in those speech communities. Bilingualism and multilingualism are obvious examples of the situational use of language. A Hispanic junior high school student in Miami, for example, may speak English in the classroom and Spanish at home. But frequently people who are monolingual will speak different forms of the same language depending on the social situation. To illustrate, the language that a college sophomore might use with a roommate would be appreciably different from that used when talking to his/her grandparents; or the choice of expressions heard in a football locker room would hardly be appropriate in a job interview. In short, what is said and how it is said is frequently influenced by such variables as the age, sex, and relative social status of the speakers.

The major focus of sociolinguistics is the relationship between language and social structure. What can we tell about the social relationships between two people from the language they use with each other? The analysis of terms of address can be particularly useful in this regard. Professor Green, for example, could be addressed as Dr. Green, Ma'am, Professor, Ms. Green, Elizabeth, Darling, Doc, Prof, or Beth, depending on who is doing the addressing. One would not expect that her mother or husband would refer to her as Ma'am or that her students would call her Beth. Instead we would expect that the term of address chosen would reflect appropriately the relative social status of the two parties. That is, in middle-class American society, the reciprocal use of first names indicates a friendly and informal relationship between equals; the reciprocal use of titles followed by last names indicates a more formal relationship between people of roughly the same status; and the nonreciprocal use of first names and titles is found among people of unequal social status. We would also expect that the same person might use different terms of address for Professor Green in different social situations.

The form of the English language that this U.S. teenager uses when speaking to her grandmother is quite different from the form she would use when talking to her peers.

Her husband, for example, might call her Beth at a cocktail party, Darling when they are making love, and Elizabeth when engaged in an argument.

## DIGLOSSIA

The situational use of language in complex speech communities has been studied by Charles Ferguson (1964) who coined the term **diglossia.** By this term, Ferguson was referring to a linguistic situation where two varieties of the same language (e.g., standard form, dialect, or pidgin) are spoken by the same person at different times and under different social circumstances.

Ferguson illustrates the concept of diglossia by citing examples from a number of linguistic communities throughout the world, including the use of classical or Koranic Arabic and local forms of Arabic found in North Africa and the Middle East, the coexistence of standard German and Swiss German in Switzerland, and the use of both French and Haitian Creole in Haiti. In all of these speech communities where diglossia is found there exists a long-standing connection between appreciably different linguistic varieties. Which form is used carries with it important cultural meanings. For example, in all cases of diglossia, one form of the language is considered to be "high" and the other "low." (See Table 14-1.) High forms of the language are associated with literacy, education, and, to some degree, religion. The high forms are usually found as part of religious services, political speeches in legislative bodies, in university lectures, in news broadcasts, and in newspapers. Low forms are likely to be found in the marketplace; when giving instructions to subordinates; in conversations with friends and relatives; and in various forms of pop culture, such as folk literature, television and radio programs, cartoons, and graffiti.

It is generally agreed that high forms of the language are superior to low forms, and frequently the use of the high form is associated with the elite and the upwardly mobile. This general superiority of the high form is at least partially the result of its association with religion and the fact that much of the literature of the language is written in the high form.

**Dialects.** It is not at all uncommon for certain dialects in complex speech communities to be considered substandard or inferior to others. Such claims are made on social or political rather than on linguistic grounds. That is, minority dialects are often assigned an inferior

### TABLE 14-1 ◆ Diglossia

| High Form | Low Form |
| --- | --- |
| Religious services | Marketplace |
| Political speeches | Instructions to subordinates |
| Legislative proceedings | Friendly conversations |
| University lectures | Folk literature |
| News broadcasts | Radio/TV programs |
| Newspapers | Cartoons |
| Poetry | Graffiti |

SOURCE: Charles A. Ferguson, "Diglossia," in *Language in Culture and Society: A Reader in Linguistics,* Dell Hynes (Ed.) (New York: Harper & Row, 1964), p. 429–439.

status by the majority for the purpose of maintaining the political, economic, and social subordination of the minority. Certain "Southernisms" such as "you'all" (as in the statement, "You'all come by and see us now") are considered by non-Southerners to be quaint or colorful regional expressions at best or inferior and inappropriate incursions into Standard American English at worst. A more obvious example would be majority attitudes toward the nonstandard English dialect used by Black Americans in Northern ghettos. Clearly, such usages as "You be going home" or "Don't nobody go nowhere" will never be used by major network newscasters. Despite the fact that such expressions are considered to be inferior by the speakers of Standard English, the use of these forms demonstrate logically consistent grammatical patterns and in no way prevent the expression of complex or abstract ideas. Nonstandard English should not be viewed as simply a series of haphazard mistakes in Standard English. Rather it is a fully efficient language with its own unique set of grammatical rules that are consistently applied. Thus, in linguistic terms, the grammar and phonology of ghetto English is no less efficient than the language of the rich and powerful.

◆ ◆ ◆

# Nonverbal Communication

To fully comprehend how people in any particular culture communicate, we must become familiar with their nonverbal forms of communication in addition to their language. **Nonverbal communication** is important because it both helps us interpret linguistic messages and frequently carries messages of its own. In fact, it has been suggested that as much as 70 percent of all messages sent and received by humans are nonverbal in nature.

Like language, nonverbal forms of communication are learned and as such, vary from one culture to another. Even though some nonverbal cues have the same meaning in different cultures, an enormous range of variation in nonverbal communication exists between cultures. In some cases, a certain message can be sent in a number of different ways by different cultures. For example, whereas in the United States we signify affirmation by nodding the head, the very same message is sent in Ethiopia by throwing the head back, by sharply thrusting the head forward among the Semang of Malaya, and by raising the eyebrows among the Dyaks of Borneo. Moreover, cross-cultural misunderstandings can occur when the same nonverbal cue has different meanings in different cultures. To illustrate, the hand gesture of making a circle with the thumb and forefinger, which means O.K. in the United States, signifies "money" in Japan, "worthlessness" or "zero" in France, and is a sexual insult in parts of South America.

Humans communicate without words in a number of important ways, including hand gestures, facial expressions, eye contact, touching, space usage, scents, gait, and posture. A thorough discussion based on the recent literature of these and other aspects of nonverbal communication would certainly take us beyond the scope of this textbook. Yet, to convey the importance of the nonverbal aspects of human communication, we will consider three of the more salient types of nonverbal communication: hand gestures, eye contact, and touching.

## HAND GESTURES

If we stop to consider it, we must realize that we use a number of hand gestures every day. We cup our hand behind the ear as a nonverbal way of communicating that we cannot hear. We thumb our noses at those we don't like. We can thumb a ride on the side of the highway. We can wave hello or goodbye. We tell people to be quiet by holding our forefinger vertically against our lips. We give the peace sign by holding up our forefinger and middle finger. And we send a very different message when we flash half of the peace sign. Some of these hand gestures used widely in the United States are also used and understood in Europe, which should come as no surprise, given our strong European heritage. Nevertheless, as Morris (1979) reminds us, there are a number of other nonverbal hand gestures used in Western Europe that have not been diffused across the Atlantic. For ex-

The same gesture often carries different meanings in different languages. Beware! Don't do this in parts of South America. It doesn't mean "O.K."

ample, stroking the face between the cheek bones and the chin with the thumb and forefinger is a nonverbal way of saying "You look ill or thin" in the southern Mediterranean; pulling down on the lower eyelid with the forefinger means "Be alert" in parts of Spain, Italy, France, and Greece; and in Italy, pulling or flicking one's own ear lobe is a way of calling into question a man's masculinity ("You are so effeminate that you should be wearing an earring.").

## EYE CONTACT

The use of eye contact also varies widely from one culture to another. In the United States, a certain degree

Most human messages are sent nonverbally—i.e., without using words. Here a San hunter from Southern Africa gives a nonverbal sign for the "secretary bird."

of eye contact is used to convey respect and attentiveness in normal conversation. In some cultures, however, people are taught from an early age that direct eye contact is threatening, disrespectful, or rude. According to Morsbach (1982:308), for example, Japanese avoid direct eye contact in normal conversation by focusing somewhat lower, around the region of the Adam's apple. Other cultures, on the other hand, insist on even more direct eye contact than might be expected in the United States. As Edward T. Hall reminds us, "Arabs look each other in the eye when talking with an intensity that makes most Americans highly uncomfortable" (1966: 161). In such cultures, the somewhat lower level of eye contact typically found in the United States could be viewed as inattentive, impolite, and aloof.

## TOUCHING

Touching is perhaps the most personal and intimate form of nonverbal communication. Humans communicate through touch in a variety of ways or for a variety of purposes, including patting a person on the head or back, slapping, kissing, punching, stroking, embracing, tickling, shaking hands, and laying-on hands. Every culture has a well-defined set of meanings connected with touching. That is, each culture defines who can touch whom, on what parts of the body, and under what circumstances.

Some cultures have been described as high-touch cultures, while others are low-touch. Some studies (Montagu, 1972; Sheflen, 1972; and Mehrabian, 1981) have suggested that Eastern Europeans, Jews, and Arabs tend to be high-touch cultures, while such Northern European cultures as Germans and Scandinavians tend to be low-touch cultures. The difference between high- and low-touch cultures can be observed in public places, such as subways or elevators. For example, Londoners (from a low-touch culture) traveling in a crowded subway are likely to assume a rigid posture, studiously avoid eye contact, and refuse to even acknowledge the presence of other passengers. The French (from a high-touch culture), on the other hand, have no difficulty leaning and pressing against one another in a crowded Parisian subway.

## CROSS-CULTURAL MISCUE

The scene is a classroom in an inner-city elementary school in Richmond, Virginia. Pedro, the nine-year-old son of a recent immigrant family from Puerto Rico, leaves his seat to sharpen his pencil. When the teacher, Ms. Harkins, asks Pedro where he is going, Pedro casts his eyes downward and tries to explain that he was going to the pencil sharpener. Ms. Harkins, thinking that Pedro has something to hide by not looking her in the eye, becomes so annoyed with him that she lifts up his chin and says, "Look at me when I'm talking to you!" Pedro cannot understand what he did wrong that made his teacher so angry.

This unfortunate scenario—played out all too often in our multicultural schools—is a classic example of how cross-cultural communication can be short-circuited. This needless escalation of ill will between student and teacher could have been avoided if Ms. Harkins had understood a fundamental feature of nonverbal communication in Pedro's Puerto Rican culture. In the teacher's mainstream U.S. culture, the student is expected to maintain a high level of eye contact with the teacher as a sign of respect. But in Puerto Rico, Pedro learned not only a different meaning of eye contact but also an opposite meaning. That is, in Puerto Rican culture, children are taught to *avoid* eye contact as a sign of respect for high-status people, such as teachers, priests, grandparents, and adults in general. Thus, while Pedro was trying to show the greatest respect for his teacher by avoiding eye contact, Ms. Harkins mistook his downcast eyes as a sign of disrespect or disinterest. This cross-cultural misunderstanding—stemming from a lack of knowledge about other cultures—hardly contributed to student-teacher rapport.

Without using words, these Eskimos communicate affection by a type of touching—rubbing noses.

## ◆ Summary

1. Language—and the capacity to use symbols—is perhaps the most distinctive hallmark of our humanity.
2. While nonhumans also engage in communication, human communication systems are unique in several important respects. First, human communication systems are open—that is, they are capable of sending an infinite number of messages. Second, humans are the only animals not confined to the present, for they can speak of events that have happened in the past or might happen in the future. And third, human communication is transmitted largely through tradition rather than experience alone.
3. All human languages are structured in two ways. First, each language has a phonological structure comprising rules governing how sounds are combined to convey meanings. Second, each language has its own grammatical structure comprising those principles governing how morphemes are formed into words (morphology) and

how words are arranged into phrases and sentences (syntax).

4. Despite considerable structural variations in the many languages of the world, there is no evidence to support the claim that some languages are less efficient at expressing abstract ideas than others.

5. Cultures can influence language to the extent that the vocabulary in any language tends to emphasize those words that are adaptively important in that culture. Thus, the highly specialized vocabulary in American English relating to the automobile is directly related to the cultural emphasis that North Americans give to that particular part of their technology.

6. According to the Sapir-Whorf Hypothesis, language is thought to influence perception. Language, according to Sapir and Whorf, not only is a system of communicating but also establishes mental categories that affect the way in which people conceptualize the real world.

7. Sociolinguists are interested in studying how people use language depending on the social situation or context in which they might be operating.

8. As important as language is in human communication, the majority of human messages are sent and received without using words. Human nonverbal communication—which, like language, is learned and culturally variable—can be made in such ways as facial expressions, gestures, eye contact, touching, and posture.

## ◆ Key Terms

| | |
|---|---|
| bound morpheme | diglossia |
| closed system of communication | displacement |
| | free morpheme |
| cultural emphasis of a language | grammar |
| | morphology |

nonverbal communication
open system of communication

phonology
Sapir-Whorf Hypothesis
syntax

## ◆ Suggested Readings

Farb, Peter. *Word Play: What Happens When People Talk*. New York: Knopf, 1974. A highly readable and spritely written account of linguistics for the nonspecialist.

Hickerson, Nancy P. *Linguistic Anthropology*. New York: Holt, Rinehart & Winston, 1980. A readable, nontechnical introduction to the field of anthropological linguistics, with chapters on historical linguistics, the classification of languages, descriptive linguistics, psycholinguistics, sociolinguistics, and language and culture.

Hymes, Dell. *Language in Culture and Society: A Reader in Linguistics and Anthropology*. New York: Harper & Row, 1964. A classic collection of sixty-nine articles in the general area of language and culture compiled for both scholars and serious students of anthropological linguistics.

Lehmann, Winifred P. *Historical Linguistics, An Introduction* (2nd Ed.). New York: Holt, Rinehart & Winston, 1973. An introduction to the general principles of historical linguistics, this small volume analyzes the classification of languages, methods used in gathering and analyzing historical linguistic data, and how languages change.

Trudgill, Peter (Ed.). *Applied Sociolinguistics*. London: Academic Press, 1984. A collection of nine essays by sociolinguists designed to demonstrate the range of real-world activities to which sociolinguistic data can be of interest, including education, psychology, the law, and the media.

Wardhaugh, Ronald. *An Introduction to Sociolinguistics*. Oxford: Basil Blackwell Ltd., 1986. Designed as a beginning text in sociolinguistics, this volume deals with such topics as dialects and regional variations, speech communities, language change, gender differences, the relationship between language and culture, and language policy.

Language is perhaps the most characteristic feature of *Homo sapiens*. Humans can send and receive a near infinite number of messages (both verbally and nonverbally) that convey meaning. Some of these meanings are abstract while others are concrete. To be certain, some other animal species have a limited capacity for symbolic communication. Humans, however, have developed this symbolizing capacity to such a degree that it serves as the single most distinctive hallmark of our humanity.

If, in fact, language is such a fundamental feature of our humanness, it should come as no surprise that it can have important implications for our everyday lives. This is particularly true when attempting to communicate across cultures. It is virtually impossible for anyone in the Western world today to avoid communicating—or attempting to communicate—with people from different cultural backgrounds. Whether we are a Peace Corps volunteer in Nigeria, a missionary in Samoa, or a machine salesman from Toledo trying to make a sale in Singapore, it is absolutely imperative that we have an understanding of the communication patterns of the people with whom we are interacting. Even if we never leave our home communities, it is becoming increasingly unlikely that we could avoid interacting with linguistically different people even if we wanted to.

◆ **A business corporation operating abroad can "shoot itself in the foot" when it fails to understand foreign languages.**

The success or failure of anyone working in a culturally different environment will depend largely on one's understanding of different languages. One of the most common causes of failure when working in cross-cultural situations is the erroneous assumption that a person who is successful in his or her home environment will be equally successful in a foreign culture. Yet the literature is filled with examples of experts in their field who run amuck when attempting to apply their expertise among linguistically different peoples. Some of these cross-cultural miscues can be mildly amusing. Others can be costly in terms of time, money, and reputation, while still others can be tragic. What they all have in common, however, is that they could have been avoided had the parties concerned understood the language of those with whom they were attempting to communicate.

To illustrate how well-intentioned but linguistically naive Westerners can miscommunicate, we can look at the area of international marketing. Frequently the words from one language do not always translate precisely into another language, as Paul Simon reminds us:

Body by Fisher, describing a General Motors product, came out "Corpse by Fisher" in Flemish, and that did not help sales . . . "Come Alive with Pepsi" almost appeared in the Chinese version of the *Reader's Digest* as "Pepsi brings your ancestors back from the grave" . . . An airline operating out of Brazil advertised that it had plush "rendezvous lounges" on its jets, unaware that in Portuguese, "rendezvous" implied a room for making love (1980:32).

# Language and Communication Systems

◆ **An anthropological linguist serves as an expert witness in a civil rights case heard by a federal district court.**

When language may have a bearing on the outcome of a court case, anthropologists (or more precisely, sociocultural linguists) may be brought in to give expert testimony. In 1979, a federal court in Ann Arbor, Michigan, concluded that black students from a public elementary school were being denied their civil rights because they were not being taught to read, write, and speak Standard English as an alternative to their dialect of Black English Vernacular (BEV). The presiding judge ruled that since the school system failed to recognize and use BEV as the basis for teaching Standard English, the black children were put at a disadvantage for succeeding in school and, consequently, in life as well (Chambers, 1983).

To a very large degree, this precedent-setting court decision rested on establishing the basic premise that BEV actually exists as a bona fide language. It was popularly held—and indeed implicitly built into the reading curriculum in the Ann Arbor schools—that the language of black students was nothing more than slang, street talk, or a pathological form of Standard English. But as William Labov, a sociolinguist from the University of Pennsylvania, was able to establish to the satisfaction of the court, BEV is a full-fledged linguistic system with its own grammatical rules, phonology, and semantics. In other words, Labov's testimony demonstrated that (a) the differences that exist between BEV and Standard English are governed by linguistic rules rather than being the result of errors in Standard English, (b) BEV is as capable of expressing a wide range of abstract and complex ideas as is Standard English, and (c) the BEV that is spoken by children in Ann Arbor is the same as the BEV spoken in New York, Washington, Chicago, and Los Angeles.

On the basis of Labov's testimony, the federal court concluded that language is a vital link between a child and the education the child receives. Children who speak the same language as the language of instruction learn more effectively than those who speak a nonstandard version of the language of instruction. It should be pointed out that the court did *not* rule that children had to be taught in BEV. Rather the court ordered that the local schools were to acknowledge the fact that language used at home and in the community can pose a barrier to student learning *when teachers fail to recognize it, understand it, and incorporate it into their instructional methods.*

Labov's contribution, however, went well beyond his testimony as an expert witness in federal court. Part of the judge's ruling ordered the Ann Arbor schools to develop strategies to inform its teachers of how best to teach Standard English to children who enter the schools speaking BEV. After spelling out in considerable detail the linguistic features of BEV, Labov (1983:29–55) went on to show how this linguistic system interferes with learning Standard English and how this can be taken into account when developing new methods for teaching reading. Here is a situation, then, in which the data and insights from linguistic anthropology can make practical contributions to both civil rights litigation and instructional programming.

CHAPTER 15

# Getting Food

What are the different ways by which societies get their food?

How do technology and environment influence food-getting strategies?

How have humans adapted to their environments over the ages?

For any culture to survive it needs to solve certain societal problems. As we pointed out in our discussion of cultural universals, all societies must develop systematic ways of controlling people's behavior, defending the group from outside forces, passing on the cultural traditions from generation to generation, mating, rearing children, and procuring food from the environment to meet their physical needs. Of all these basic societal needs, the need to secure food from one's surroundings is the most critical. The human body can survive for as long as a week or so without water and perhaps up to a month without food. Unless a society can develop a systematic and regular way of getting food for its members, the population will die off.

Like other aspects of culture, food-getting strategies vary widely from one society to another. Nevertheless, it is possible to identify five major food-procurement categories found among the world's populations:

*Hunting and Gathering*. The systematic collection of wild vegetation, the hunting of animals, and fishing.

*Horticulture*. A basic form of plant cultivation using simple tools and small plots of land and relying solely on human power.

*Pastoralism*. Keeping of domesticated animals (e.g., cows, goats, sheep) and using their products (e.g., milk, meat, blood) as a major food source.

*Agriculture*. A more productive form of cultivation than horticulture because of the use of animal power (e.g., horses, oxen) or mechanical power (tractors, reapers) and usually some form of irrigation.

*Industrialization*. The production of food through complex machinery.

## Environment and Technology

Which food-getting strategy is actually developed by any given culture will depend, in large measure, on the culture's environment and technology. When dealing with this relationship between physical environment and food-getting methods, it is not easy to categorize the earth into neat ecological zones, each with its own unique and mutually exclusive climate, soil composition, vegetation, and animal life. Nevertheless, geographers (e.g., James, 1966) frequently divide the world's land surface into a number of types, including grasslands, deserts, tropical forests, temperate forests, polar regions, and mountain habitats. Some of these environments are particularly hospitable to the extent that they support a number of modes of food acquisition. Others are more limiting in the types of adaptations they permit. Anthropologists generally agree that the environment does not determine food-getting patterns but rather sets broad limits on the possible alternatives. For example, subsisting on horticulture in the polar region is not an ecological possibility, but there are a number of other possible alternatives.

It is technology—a part of culture—that helps people adapt to their specific environment. In fact, the human species enjoys a tremendous adaptive advantage over all other species precisely because it has developed technological solutions to the problems of survival. Since some cultures have more complex technologies than others, they have gained greater control over their environments and their food supplies. For example, the complex farming technology used in the American Midwest produces more wheat than can be consumed domestically; at the other extreme, a small hunting-and-gathering society with a very simple level of technology has, at best, an imperfect and tenuous control over its environment and food supply. To suggest, however, that such variations in technological adaptations exist is not to imply that societies with simple technologies are either less intelligent or less able to cope with their environment. On the contrary, many societies with simple technologies adapt very ingeniously to their particular environment. As Collins reminds us:

Among some Eskimo groups, wolves are a menace—a dangerous environmental feature that must be dealt with. They could perhaps be hunted down and killed, but this involves danger as well as considerable expenditure of time and energy. So a simple yet ingenious device is employed. A sharp sliver of bone is curled into a springlike shape, and seal blubber is molded around it and permitted to freeze. This is then placed where it can be discovered by a hungry wolf, which, living up to its reputation, "wolfs it down." Later, as this "time bomb" is digested and the blubber disappears, the bone uncurls and its sharp ends pierce the stomach of the wolf, causing internal bleeding and death. The job gets done! It is a simple yet fairly secure technique that involves an appreciation of the environment as well as wolf psychology and habits (1975:235).

The specific mode of food getting, however, will be influenced by the interaction of a people's environment with its technology. To illustrate, the extent to which a foraging society is able to successfully procure food will depend on not only the sophistication of the society's tools but also the abundance of plant and animal life the environment provides. Similarly, the productivity of a

Most anthropologists agree that environment sets broad limits on the possible form that food-getting patterns might take. Cultures help people adapt to a number of generally inhospitable environments.

society based on irrigation agriculture will vary according to the society's technology as well as such environmental factors as the availability of the water supply and the natural nutrients in the water. These environmental factors set an upper limit on the ultimate productivity of any given food-getting system and the size of the population it can support. Cultural ecologists refer to this limit as the environment's **carrying capacity** (Glossow, 1978).

A natural consequence of exceeding the carrying capacity is damage to the environment, such as killing off too much game or depleting the soil. Because of this carrying capacity, societies cannot easily increase their food-getting productivity. Thus, if a society is to survive, it must meet the fundamental need of producing or procuring enough food and water to keep its population alive. But beyond satisfying this basic minimal need of survival, societies also satisfy their idiosyncratic and quite arbitrary *desires* for certain types of food. To a certain degree, people regularly consume those foods that are found naturally (or can be produced) in their immediate environment. But frequently people go out of their way to acquire some special foods while choosing not to use other foods that may be both plentiful and nutritious.

While early anthropologists wrote off such behavior as irrational and arbitrary, cultural ecologists in recent years, by examining these "peculiar" behaviors more carefully, have found that they often make sense in terms of the expenditure of energy versus the caloric value of the foods consumed. This theory—known as the **optimal foraging theory**—suggests that foragers will pursue those animals and plant species that tend to maximize their caloric return for the time they spend searching, killing, collecting, and preparing (see Smith, 1983). In other words, when specific foraging strategies are examined in ethnographic detail, decisions to seek out one food source and not others turns out to be quite rational, for they are based on a generally accurate assessment of whether or not it will be worth the effort.

## Major Food-Getting Strategies

The five forms of food procurement (**hunting and gathering**, **horticulture**, **pastoralism**, **agriculture**, and **industrialization**) are not mutually exclusive, for in most human societies we find more than one strategy. Where this is the case, however, one form will usually predominate. Moreover, within each category we can expect to find considerable variations largely because of differences in environment, technology, and historical experiences. These five categories of food getting are explored in more detail in the following sections.

### HUNTING AND GATHERING

Collecting food—as compared to producing food—involves the exploitation of wild plants and animals that already exist in the natural environment. People have been hunters and gatherers for the overwhelming majority of time that they have been on earth. It was not until the **Neolithic Revolution**—approximately 10,000 years ago—that humans for the first time produced their food by means of horticulture or animal husbandry. If we view the period of human prehistory as representing an hour in duration, then humans have been hunters and gatherers for all but the last ten seconds! With the rise of food production the incidence of hunting and gathering has steadily declined, as Murdock reminds us:

Ten thousand years ago the entire population of the earth subsisted by hunting and gathering, as their ancestors had done since the dawn of culture. By the time of Christ, eight thousand years later, tillers and herders had replaced them over at least half of the earth. At the time of the discovery of the New World, only perhaps 15 per cent of the earth's surface was still occupied by hunters and gatherers, and this area has continued to decline at a progressive rate until the present day, when only a few isolated pockets survive (1968:13).

Even though most societies have become food producers, there is still a handful of societies in the world today that remain hunters and gatherers. These few hunting-and-gathering societies vary widely in other cultural features and are to be found in a wide variety of environments (semideserts, tropical forests, polar region, etc.). For example, some hunting-and-gathering societies such as the !Kung of the Kalahari Desert, live in temporary encampments, have small-scale populations, do not store food, and are essentially egalitarian. At the other end of the spectrum are groups like the Kwakiutl, American Indians from the northwest coast, who live in permanent settlements, have relatively high-density populations, live on food reserves, and recognize marked distinctions in rank. Despite these considerable variations, however, it is possible to make the following generalizations about most or all of them:

1. *Hunting-and-gathering societies have very low densities of population.* The reason for this is that food collection has built-in checks upon its becoming a particularly efficient method for procuring large amounts of food. In other words, increased efficiency in the collection methods of these societies can ultimately destroy their source of food. To illustrate, if we were to give a small hunting-and-gathering society machine guns and four-wheeled vehicles, the people could become extremely efficient hunters. Armed with such modern technology, they could kill far more animals than they ever could using their bows and arrows. Their food supply would increase dramatically, and over the short run, the population would grow because they would be able to feed larger numbers of people. But since they would continue to draw their food supply from the natural environment without putting anything back, they would eventually kill off all the game. Thus, over the long run, mass starvation would occur and the population would return to its original small size.

2. *Food-gathering societies are usually nomadic or seminomadic rather than sedentary.* As a direct result of this continual geographic mobility, hunting-

## CROSS-CULTURAL MISCUE

In an attempt to locate an outlet for its products in Europe, a large U.S. manufacturer sent one of its promising young executives to Frankfurt to make a presentation to a reputable German distributor. The U.S. company had considerable confidence in the choice of this particular junior executive because the man not only spoke fluent German but also knew a good deal of German culture. When the American entered the conference room where he would be making his presentation, he did all the right things. He shook hands firmly, greeted everyone with a friendly *guten tag,* and bowed his head slightly as is customary in Germany. Drawing on his experience as a past president of the Toastmasters Club in his hometown, the U.S. executive prefaced his presentation with a few humorous anecdotes to set a relaxed mood. At the end of his presentation, however, he sensed that his talk had not gone well. In actual fact, the presentation was not well received, for the German company chose not to distribute the U.S. company's product line.

What went wrong? Despite careful preparation, the U.S. firm made two tactical miscues that conflicted with German business culture. First, despite the American executive's knowledge of his product line and his fluency in German, his age was one important factor working against him. Since executives in German corporations tend to be older than their U.S. counterparts, any young U.S. executive—no matter how competent—is not likely to be taken seriously because of his or her relative inexperience. The second factor contributing to the failure of the presentation was the American's attempt to set a relaxed tone by starting off with several jokes. While an effective public-speaking technique for a luncheon talk at the Kiwanis Club, it was considered too frivolous and informal for a German business meeting.

---

and-gathering peoples usually do not recognize individual land rights. By and large, food collectors move periodically from place to place in search of wild animals and vegetation. Since game frequently migrates during the yearly cycle, hunters need to be sufficiently mobile to follow the game. Conversely, food producers such as cultivators tend to be more sedentary owing to the large investment that farmers usually have in their land. There are notable exceptions to both of these generalizations, however. Some food collectors, such as certain northwest coast American Indian groups, live in particularly abundant environments that permit permanent settlements; and there are some horticultural societies (such as the Bemba of Zambia) that practice shifting cultivation and, for all practical purposes, are semi-nomadic.

3. *The basic social unit among hunting-and-gathering people is the family, or the band, a loose federation of families.* Consequently, social control revolves around family institutions rather than more formal political institutions.

4. *The contemporary hunting-and-gathering peoples occupy the remote and marginally useful areas of the earth.* These areas include such out-of-the-way places as the Alaskan tundra, the Kalahari Desert, the Australian outback, and the Ituru Forest of central Africa. It is reasonable to suggest that these food-gathering societies, with their relatively simple levels of technology, have been forced into these marginal habitats by the food producers with their more dominating technologies.

In most societies that rely on both hunting game and collecting wild vegetable matter, the latter activity provides the greatest amount of food. Despite the fact that hunting wild animals is both spectacular and highly prized, it has been suggested that the bulk of the diets of most hunters and gatherers consists of foods other than meat. For example, among the !Kung of the Kalahari Desert, Lee (1968:33) estimates that between 60 percent and 80 percent of the diet by weight is derived from vegetable sources. The notable exception to this generalization is the Eskimos, with the near total absence of vegetable matter from their diet.

Early anthropological accounts tended to portray hunters and gatherers as living precariously in a life-or-death struggle with the environment. More recently, however, some anthropologists (Sahlins, Lee) have suggested that certain hunting-and-gathering groups are relatively well off despite their inhabiting some very unproductive parts of the earth. The question of the relative abundance within hunting-and-gathering societies became a heated topic of debate in 1966 at a conference on food collectors. Although this issue was not resolved in any definitive way, there is considerable evidence to suggest that hunters and gatherers are capable of adapting to harsh environments with particular creativity and resourcefulness. Perhaps we can get a better idea of how hunters and gatherers procure their food by examining two very different contemporary groups—the !Kung of present-day Namibia and the Netsilik Eskimos of northern Canada—in greater detail.

**The !Kung of the Kalahari Region.** One of the best studied hunting-and-gathering societies, the !Kung inhabit the northwestern part of the Kalahari Desert, one of the least hospitable environments in the world. Inhabiting an area that is too dry to support either agriculture or the keeping of livestock, the !Kung are totally dependent upon hunting and gathering for their food. Food-procuring activities are fairly rigidly divided between men and women. Women collect roots, nuts, fruits, and other edible vegetables, while men hunt medium and large size animals. Although men and women spend roughly equivalent amounts of time on their food-procuring activities, women provide between two and three times as much food by weight as men.

Even though the term *affluence* or *abundance* tends to be relative, Lee (1968) presents convincing evidence to suggest that the !Kung are not teetering on the brink of starvation. In fact, there are reasons to believe that the !Kung food-gathering techniques are both productive and reliable. For example, the !Kung's most important single food item is the mongongo nut, which accounts for about half of the !Kung diet. Nutritionally,

the mongongo, which is found in abundance all year long, contains five times the calories and ten times the protein per cooked unit than cereal crops. Thus, quite apart from hunting, the !Kung have a highly nutritional food supply that is more reliable than cultivated foods. It is little wonder that the !Kung do not have a strong urge to take up agriculture when there are so many mongongo nuts around.

Another measure of the relative affluence of the !Kung is their selectivity in what foods they take from the environment. If they were indeed on the brink of starvation, they should be expected to exploit every conceivable source of food. But in actual fact, only about one-third of the edible plant foods are eaten, and only 17 of the 223 local species of animals known to the !Kung are hunted regularly (Lee: 1968:35).

Moreover, if the !Kung were in a life-or-death struggle with the natural environment, their survival rate and life expectancy would be low. Infant mortality would be high, malnutrition would be rampant, and the elderly and infirm would be abandoned. This is hardly the demographic picture for the !Kung. Based on fieldwork conducted in the 1960s, Lee (1968:36) found that approximately 10 percent of his sample population was sixty years of age or older, a percentage that was not substantially different from industrialized societies.

And finally, the !Kungs' relative abundance of resources can be judged from the amount of time they devote to procuring food. While it is true that food getting is the most important activity among the !Kung, it is no less true for cultivators and pastoralists. Although the amount of work hours varies from one hunting-and-gathering society to another, it appears that the !Kung, despite what might appear to be their harsh environment, are hardly overworked. Lee (1968:37) estimates that the average !Kung adult spends between twelve and nineteen hours per week in the pursuit of food. Usually women can gather enough food in one day to feed their families for three days, leaving a good deal of time for such leisure activities as resting, visiting, entertaining visitors, and embroidering. Even though men tend to work more hours per week than women, they still have considerable leisure time for visiting, entertaining, and dancing.

**The Netsilik Eskimos.** Inhabiting one of the most inhospitable regions of the world, the Netsilik Eskimos—in stark contrast to the !Kung—stand out as a society that is living in a very delicate balance with the environment. Living in a barren region northwest of Hudson Bay in

To survive in their harsh environment, the Netsilik Eskimos have had to develop a number of creative hunting strategies.

northern Canada, the Netsilik have had to adapt to an arctic climate of bitterly cold temperatures and short summers and a terrain almost totally devoid of edible plants. Under such conditions, the diet of these people is almost exclusively derived from animals (caribou, musk-ox, and seals) and fish. To adapt to such a harsh environment, the Netsilik have developed a number of very creative strategies for maximizing their survival chances.

Since food collecting is virtually nonexistent, the Netsilik have a number of different hunting strategies at their disposal. During the harsh winter months after the caribou have migrated, the Eskimos rely almost exclusively on seal hunting. Since seals need to get air periodically through numerous breathing holes in the ice, the most efficient form of seal hunting involves large hunting parties. Thus, to maximize their chances for catching seals, the Netsilik Eskimos organize themselves during the winter months into large igloo communities of up to sixty people from several distantly related extended families. It is during this time that social life is most intense and various ceremonies are most likely to occur.

During the summer months as game becomes more accessible, the extended igloo communities disperse into smaller social units. Hunting takes on a number of new forms. Seal continue to be hunted at the breathing holes but are also hunted on top of the ice; caribou are hunted with bows and arrows; salmon and trout running upstream are caught with pronged spears; large-scale co-operative caribou hunts, using beaters and spearers, are conducted at certain caribou crossing places; and toward the end of the summer months, these smaller hunting groups engage in spear fishing for salmon through the thin river ice. During these summer months social activities are considerably less intense. Thus, the Netsilik Eskimos have adapted by organizing their economic and social lives around the availability of various types of game and the strategies required for hunting them. That is, large social and hunting groups that are most functional for winter seal hunting split up during the summer into smaller groups that tend to maximize food-getting possibilities for caribou hunting and salmon fishing.

Despite their resourcefulness in getting food, the Netsilik Eskimos are under continuous ecological pressure. Unlike the !Kung, they are constantly searching for food, and consequently have precious little leisure time. Rasmussen (1931) reported that approximately 10 percent of the population died of starvation. Food getting in this extreme environment is highly stressful, as Balikci describes:

Traveling and moving camps was a very arduous task. Lack of dog feed severely limited the keeping of dogs to only one or two per family. The heavy sledges had to be pulled or pushed by both men and women. Only very small children were allowed to sit on the sledge. Old people had to drag themselves behind, and were often left behind to sleep out on the ice if they had not caught up with the others. Seal hunting involved a motionless watch on the flat ice under intense cold maintained for many hours. . . . Beating the fast running caribou over great distances in the tundra was an exhausting task. Stalking the caribou with the bow and arrow also involved endless pursuits across the tundra, the hunters lying on the wet grass and trying to approach the game while hiding behind tufts of moss. . . . Hunting was a never-ceasing pursuit, the game had to be brought to camp at all cost, and the hunter had to stay out until a successful kill (1968:81).

The two cases of hunting-and-gathering societies just cited—the !Kung and the Netsilik Eskimos—represent extremes in relative levels of abundance. The !Kung, with their year-round access to nutritional foods, are rarely in danger of starvation and appear to have considerable leisure time. The Eskimos, by contrast, must work long and arduously to acquire sufficient food to keep themselves alive. In terms of dietary abundance, the remaining hunting-and-gathering societies found in the world, no doubt, are somewhere between these two extremes.

## FOOD-PRODUCING SOCIETIES

Approximately 10,000 years ago, humans made a revolutionary transition from hunting and gathering to food production (the domestication of plants and animals). Before this time, humans had subsisted exclusively on hunting and gathering for hundreds of thousands of years. Then, for reasons that are still not altogether clear, humans began to cultivate crops and keep herds of animals as sources of food. For the first time, humans gained a measure of control over their food supply. That is, through tilling of the soil and animal husbandry, humans were now able to produce food rather than have to rely solely on what Mother Nature produced for the environment. This shift from collecting to producing food, known as the Neolithic Revolution, is discussed in greater detail in Chapter 10.

**Horticulture.** Horticulture refers to the simplest type of farming that uses basic hand tools such as the hoe or digging stick rather than plows or other implements driven by animals or machines. Since horticulturalists produce relatively low yields, they generally do not have sufficient surpluses to allow them to develop extensive market systems. The land, which is usually cleared by hand, is neither irrigated nor enriched by the use of fertilizers. A major technique of horticulturalists is the

A simple form of cultivation involves the technique known as slash and burn, as practiced here by the Yanomamo of Brazil and Venezuela.

**slash and burn method**, sometimes referred to as **swidden cultivation** or **shifting cultivation**. This technique involves clearing the land by manually cutting down the growth, burning it, and planting in the burned area. Even though the ash residue serves as a fertilizer, the land is usually depleted of its fertility within a year or two. The land is then allowed to fallow in order to restore its fertility, or it may be abandoned altogether. This technique of slash and burn cultivating can eventually destroy the environment, for if fields are not given sufficient time to fallow, the forests will be permanently replaced by grasslands.

At first glance it would appear that slash and burn agriculture makes very poor use of the land. Since most land must be left to fallow at any given time, the system

The use of draft animals involves a more complex form of crop production than slash and burn.

of slash and burn—when compared to intensive agriculture—cannot support high densities of population. While it is true that there are inherent limitations to food production in the slash and burn technique, it does not necessarily follow that the mere application of intensive agricultural methods (i.e., clearing the forests, tractor plowing, and the use of chemical fertilizers) would automatically produce larger yields. In those areas where the slash and burn method is most often found (i.e., the tropics), a conversion to intensive agriculture is not a viable alternative. For example, ecological studies of tropical areas have shown that most of the nutrients are located in the vegetation rather than in the soil itself. To clear the land of existing vegetation would leave nutrient poor soil. Moreover, the removal of the tree canopy would further deplete the nutrients from the soil through erosion and leaching from the direct contact with the sun. Given these ecological conditions found in many tropical areas, the slash and burn meth-

od of cultivation remains a rational food producing technique.

*Crops.* The crops grown by horticulturalists can be categorized into three types: tree crops, seed crops, and root crops. Tree crops include bananas or plantains, figs, dates, and coconuts; the major seed crops (which tend to be high in protein) are wheat, barley, corn, oats, sorghum, rice, and millet; the main root crops (which tend to be high in starch and carbohydrates) include yams, arrowroots, taro, maniac, and potatoes. Since seed crops require a greater quantity of nutrients than root crops, seed cultivators need longer periods of time to fallow their fields. In some cases, this can have consequences for settlement patterns. That is, if seed cultivators do in fact need a longer time to rejuvenate their fields, they may be less likely to live in permanent settlements than would root cultivators. However, even though swidden cultivation involves the shifting of fields, it does not necessarily follow that they also periodically shift their homes.

Many horticulturalists supplement their simple cultivation with other food-getting strategies. For example, some, such as the Yanomamo (Chagnon, 1983:56–68), may engage in hunting and gathering; others, such as the Swazi (Kuper, 1986: 79–80), keep a variety of domesticated animals, including cows, goats, sheep, horses, donkeys, and pigs; while still others (e.g., the Samoans) supplement their crops with protein derived from fishing.

*The Bemba.* One way of illustrating horticulture is by discussing a specific example in some detail. Audrey Richards (1960:96–109) provides a particularly good case study with her writings on the Bemba of present-day Zambia (formerly Northern Rhodesia). The Bemba, like a number of other peoples in South Central Africa, practice a type of shifting cultivation that involves clearing the land, burning the branches, and planting directly on the ash-fertilized soil without additional hoeing. Using the simplest technology (hoes and axes), the Bemba plant a fairly wide range of crops—including finger millet, bulrush millet, beans, cassava, and yams—but they rely most heavily on finger millet as their basic staple. Although predominantly horticultural, the Bemba do supplement their diet by some hunting, gathering, and fishing. The largest and most highly organized group politically in Zambia, the Bemba live in small, widely scattered, low-density communities comprising thirty to fifty huts.

Traditionally, Bemba society had a highly complex political system based on a set of chiefs whose authority rested on their alleged supernatural control over the land and the prosperity of the people. These supernatural powers were reinforced by the physical force that chiefs could exert over their subjects, whom they could kill, enslave, or sell. The power, status, and authority of the chiefs were based not on the accumulation of material wealth but rather on the amount of *service* they could extract from their subjects in terms of agricultural labor or military service. Interestingly, the marked status differences between chiefs (with their unchallenged authority) and commoners is not reflected in these people's diets. While chiefs and their families may have a somewhat more regular supply of food, both rich and poor people eat essentially the same types and quantities of food throughout the yearly cycle. Similarly, there are no appreciable differences in diet between Bemba men and Bemba women.

Since sparse rainfall at certain times of the year permits only one crop, a common feature of the Bemba diet is the alternation between scarcity and plenty. The harvest of finger millet, the mainstay of the Bemba diet, lasts no longer than nine months (roughly from April through December). During the lean months of January through March, dramatic changes take place in village life. Owing to the low energy levels, most activity—both leisure and work-related—is reduced to a minimum. Given these alternating periods of feast and famine, it is not surprising that food and diet occupy a prominent

This terraced form of farming as practiced in Indonesia involves a considerable investment of labor.

Pastoralists like the Bakarwal Dhera of Kashmir must move their herds periodically to ensure adequate pasturage.

place in Bemba culture. In much the same way that pastoralists frequently appear obsessed with their cattle, the Bemba tend to fixate on food. In fact, according to Richards, food and beer are the central topics of conversation among the Bemba:

Any one who can follow the ordinary gossip of a Bemba village will be struck at once by the endless talk shouted from hut to hut as to what is about to be eaten, what has already been eaten, and what lies in store for the future, and this with an animation and a wealth of detail which would be thought quite unusual in this country. . . . The giving or receipt of food is a part of most economic transactions, and many come to represent a number of human relationships whether between different kinsmen or between subject and chief. . . . To speak of a chief is to mention before the end of the conversation his reputation for generosity or meanness in the giving of porridge and beer. To describe an attitude of any particular kinsman leads almost invariably to a comment, for instance, on the food in his granary, the numbers of relatives he supports, the share of meat he has asked for, or the amount of beer he contributed at the marriage of his daughter or the visit of an elder. In daily life the women, whether at work in the kitchen or sitting gossiping on their verandas at night, exchange interminable criticisms as to the way in which some particular dish of food has been divided, or the distribution of the four or five gourds of beer made at a brew (1960:106).

**Pastoralism.** This form of food production, like horticulture's first appearing in the Neolithic period, involves the keeping of domesticated herd animals in those areas of the world that cannot support agriculture because of inadequate terrain, soils, or rainfall. These environments do, however, provide sufficient vegetation to support livestock, provided the animals are able to graze over a large enough area. Thus, pastoralism is associated with geographic mobility, for herds must be moved periodically to exploit seasonal pastures.

Some anthropologists have differentiated between two types of movement patterns: **transhumance** and **nomadism**. Transhumance involves some of the men in a pastoral society moving their livestock seasonally to different pastures while the women, children, and the other men remain in permanent settlements. Nomadism, on the other hand, with its absence of permanent villages, involves the whole social unit of men, women, and children moving their livestock to new pastures. But as the Dyson-Hudsons have pointed out (1980:18), the enormous variations even within societies render such a distinction somewhat sterile. For example, following seven Karamojong herds over a two-year period, anthropologists Rada and Neville Dyson-Hudson found that "each herd owner moved in a totally different orbit, with one remaining sedentary for a full year and one grazing his herd over 500 square miles."

Even though anthropologists tend to lump pastoralists into a single food-getting category, pastoralism is not a unified phenomenon. For example, there are wide variations in terms of the ways in which animals are herded. The principal herd animals are cattle in Eastern and Southern Africa, camels in North Africa and the Arabian Peninsula, reindeer in the subarctic areas of

Eastern Europe and Siberia, yaks in the Himalayan region, and various forms of mixed herding (goats, sheep, cattle, etc.) in a number of places in Europe and Asia. In addition to variations in type of animals herded, a number of other social and environmental factors can influence the cultural patterns of pastoral people, including, among others, the availability of water and pasturage, the presence of diseases, the location and timing of markets, governmental restrictions, and the demands of other food-getting strategies (e.g., cultivation) that the pastoralists may practice.

It is the general consensus among anthropologists that pure pastoralists—that is, those who get all of their food from livestock—are either extremely rare or nonexistent. Since livestock alone cannot meet all of the nutritional needs of a population, most pastoralists have a need for some grains to supplement their diets. Many pastoralists, therefore, either combine the keeping of livestock with some form of cultivation or maintain regular trade relations with neighboring agriculturalists.

It is clear that livestock in pastoral societies play a vital economic role not only as a food resource but also in terms of other uses to which their products can be put. In addition to the obvious economic importance of meat, milk, and blood as a food source, cattle provide dung (used for fertilizer, house building, and fuel), bone (used for tools and artifacts), skins (used for clothing), and urine (used as an antiseptic). But in addition to these important economic uses, livestock serve important noneconomic, or social, functions. Livestock frequently influence the social relationships among people in pastoral societies. To illustrate, the exchange of livestock between the families of the bride and the groom is required in many pastoral societies before a marriage can be legitimized. In the event of an assault or a homicide, livestock in some societies will be used to compensate the victim's family as a way of restoring normal social relations. The sacrifice of livestock at the grave site of ancestor gods is a way that people keep in touch with their gods. These and other social uses of livestock should re-

For the Masai of East Africa, cattle fulfill both economic and social functions.

mind us that domesticated animals in pastoral societies not only serve as the major food source but also are intimately connected to other parts of the culture, such as the systems of marriage, social control, and religion.

***Somali Pastoralism.*** The pastoral Somali of the East African Horn provide an excellent example of a pastoral society that engages in mixed herding. The Somali number over two million people in the Somali Republic itself, with an additional million presently living in southeastern Ethiopia and northern Kenya. As with other pastoral societies, not only do livestock supply the bulk of the Somali's subsistence, but in fact, household composition and nomadic movements are dictated largely by environmental conditions and the seasonal needs of the herds.

Somali pastoralism is based on the keeping of sheep, goats, camels, cattle, donkeys, and horses. Sheep and goats contribute most to the Somali diet in the form of milk and meat. Camels provide some milk, but their main role in the Somali economy is to transport the collapsible huts during periods of migration. Zebu cattle, relatively rare among the Somali, are used as a source of milk for domestic use and ultimately as an export commodity. Donkeys are used exclusively as beasts of burden, and horses, while scarce, serve as a means of rapid transportation and as a status symbol.

The physical environment of the Somali is anything but hospitable. Much of the terrain is semidesert, with sparse rainfall and intermittent vegetation. The Somali recognize three fairly distinct ecological zones which, depending on the season, provide differential quantities of the two resources absolutely essential to pastoralism—water and pasturage. Migration and temporary settlement take place in all three regions, depending on the four major seasons—two wet and two dry. Even under the best of conditions, these three ecological zones are so harsh that, as Lewis concluded, "the line between survival and disaster is precariously narrow" (1965:329).

To maximize their resources as well as their adaptation to an unforgiving environment, Somali herders divide into two distinct grazing units. One unit is the nomadic hamlet, comprising sheep and goats, that engages in migratory patterns designed to meet the regular watering needs of these important food-producing animals. Socially, these herding units consist of small groups of nuclear families related through the male line. Nomadic hamlets are not stable units, however, for frequently men periodically attach their nuclear or polygynous families to a number of different groups of kin dur-

ing any given season. On the average, nomadic hamlets contain three nuclear families but can involve more, particularly during times of warfare, when larger groups can provide greater security.

In contrast to the nomadic hamlet, the camel camp, containing only grazing camels, serves essentially as the training ground for boys to learn the skills of camel husbandry. Life in the camel camp is austere, especially during the dry season. The boys and men of the camel camp live predominantly on camel's milk, have no means of cooking, sleep out in the open, and spend large amounts of time driving their animals between water and pasturage. Unlike the hamlets, which may include a number of types of kin, the camel camps include only kin related through the male line, a distinction that reflects how the different types of livestock are viewed. Whereas sheep and goats are owned by individuals, camels are viewed as representing the wealth of the larger kin group—the lineage. While goats and sheep are used primarily to meet individual dietary needs, camels are the principle currency in such important lineage transactions as bridewealth and blood compensation. Owing to their different grazing requirements, the hamlets and the camel camps move independently of each other, being closer together during the wet seasons and more widely dispersed during the dry seasons.

## Agriculture.

Agriculture (intensive cultivation) differs from horticulture in that agriculture relies more on animal power and technology than on human power alone. Agriculture, a more recent phenomenon than horticulture, is characterized by the use of the plow, draft animals to pull the plow, fertilizers, irrigation, and other technological innovations that make intensive cultivation much more efficient than horticulture. A single cultivator using a horse-drawn plow, for example, not only can put a larger area of land under cultivation but also, since the plow digs deeper than the hoe or digging stick, unleashes more nutrients from the soil, thereby increasing the yield per acre. Animal fertilizers (from the excrement of the draft animals) permit the use of land year after year rather than having the land remain fallow to restore its fertility naturally. Irrigation of fields that do not receive sufficient or consistent rainfall is another innovation contributing to the increased efficiency of intensive agriculture. Moreover, the invention of the wheel has been a boon to the intensive farmer in transportation, the water-raising wheel, and pottery making (storage vessels for surplus crops). Thus, through the application of technology, the intensive cultivator has access to a much greater supply of energy than is available to the horticulturalist.

This greater use of technology enables the agriculturalist to support many times more people per unit of land than the horticulturalist. There is a price for this greater productivity, however, since intensive agriculture requires a greater investment of both labor and capital. First, in terms of labor, agriculturalists must put in vast numbers of hours of hard work to prepare the land. In hilly areas, the land must be terraced and maintained, while irrigation systems may involve drilling wells, digging trenches, and building dikes. All of these activities—which admittedly increase the land's productivity enormously—are extremely labor intensive. Second, intensive agriculture, as compared to horticulture, requires a much higher investment of capital in terms of plows (which need to be maintained), mechanical pumps (which can break down), and draft animals (which can become sick and die).

Agriculture, a more recent phenomenon than horticulture, is closely associated with both higher levels of productivity and more settled communities. In fact, not until early horticultural societies had developed into more intensive forms of agriculture could humankind develop civilizations (i.e., urban societies). In other words, a fully efficient system of food production, brought about by intensive agriculture, is a necessary, if not sufficient, condition for the rise of civilization.

As farming became more intensive, increasingly larger numbers of people were freed up to engage in occupations other than food production. The fact that a single farmer, under a system of intensive agriculture, can produce enough food for five people, enables four people to devote their time and energy to such activities as manufacturing, education, public administration, writing, or inventing rather than the pursuit of food. Thus, as intensive agriculture became more widespread, the division of labor became more complex; societies became more stratified (i.e., marked by greater class differences); political and religious hierarchies were established to manage the economic surpluses and mediate between the different socioeconomic classes; and eventually, state systems of government (complete with bureaucracies, written records, taxation, a military, and public works projects) were established.

*Peasantry.* With the intensification of agriculture and the rise of civilization came the development of the **peasantry**. Peasant farmers differ from American Indian horticulturalists, Polynesian fishing people, or East African herders in that they are not isolated or self-sufficient societies. Instead, peasants are tied to the larger unit (i.e., city or state) politically, religiously, and economically. More specifically, peasants are subject to the laws and controls of the state, are influenced by the urban-based religious hierarchies, and exchange their farm surpluses for goods produced in other parts of the state. Peasants usually make up a relatively large percentage of the total population and provide most of the dietary needs of the city dwellers.

The intimate relationship that peasants have with the cities and the state is succinctly stated by Foster, who refers to peasants as ". . . a peripheral but essential part of civilizations, producing the food that makes possible urban life, supporting the specialized classes of political and religious rulers and educated elite" (1967:7). Foster's statement is important because it reminds us that the relationship between the peasants and the state is hardly egalitarian. The peasants almost always occupy the lowest strata of society. Despite the fact that they supply the rest of the society with its food, peasants have low social status, little political power, and scanty material wealth. The more powerful urbanites, through the use of force or military power, frequently extract both labor and products from the peasants in the form of taxation, rent, or tribute.

The greater use of technology enables mechanized agriculturalists to support appreciably more people per unit of land than horticulturalists can.

## CROSS-CULTURAL MISCUE

The need for understanding other languages cannot be overemphasized. Slater reports on the problems that one U.S. company experienced because of a sloppy translation in an international advertising campaign:

. . . an American ink manufacturer attempted to sell bottled ink in Mexico while its metal outdoor signs told customers that they could "avoid embarrassment" (from leaks and stains) by using its brand of ink. The embarrassment, it seems, was all the ink company's. The Spanish word used to convey the meaning of "embarrassed" was "embarazar," which means "to become pregnant." Many people thought the company was selling a contraceptive device (1984:20).

**Industrialized Food Getting.** As mentioned earlier, the domestication of plants and animals around 8000 B.C. expanded people's food-getting capacity geometrically from what it had been when they relied on hunting and gathering alone. Similarly, the intensification of agriculture brought about by the invention of the plow, irrigation, and fertilizing techniques had revolutionary consequences for food production. A third major revolution in our capacity to feed ourselves occurred several hundred years ago with the coming of the Industrial Revolution. Industrialized food production relies on technological sources of energy rather than human or animal energy. While water and wind power (in the forms of waterwheels and windmills) were used in the early stages of the industrial period, today industrialized agriculture employs motorized equipment such as tractors and combines. The science of chemistry has been applied to modern agriculture to produce fertilizers, pesticides, and herbicides, all of which increase agricultural productivity. In addition to the quantum leaps in agricultural productivity in the past two hundred years, technology has been applied with equally dramatic results to other areas of food production. For example, ocean-going fishing vessels literally harvest enormous quantities of fish from the seas, scientific breakthroughs in genetics and animal husbandry now produce increasingly larger supplies of meat and poultry, and a certain amount of food in the modern person's diet is actually manufactured or reconstituted.

Food getting—and agriculture in particular—in contemporary industrialized societies has experienced some very noticeable changes since the late eighteenth century. Before the Industrial Revolution, agriculture was carried out primarily for subsistence: farmers produced crops for their own consumption rather than for sale. Today, however, agriculture is largely commercialized in that the overwhelming majority of food today is sold by food producers to nonproducers for some form of currency. Moreover, industrialized agriculture requires relatively complex systems of market exchange because of its highly specialized nature.

Within the past several decades in the Western world, the trend toward commercialization of agriculture has seen its most dramatic expression in the rise of agribusiness—large-scale agricultural enterprises involving the latest technology and a sizeable salaried work force. The appearance of large agribusiness in recent years has brought with it the decline of the mom-and-pop farms that drew mainly on family labor. As the number of family farms has declined and agriculture has become more highly mechanized, the developed world has witnessed a dramatic decline in the percentage of the world's population that is engaged in food production.

Even though the industrialization of agriculture has produced farms of enormous size and productivity, it has not been without a very high cost. The machinery and technology needed to run modern-day agribusiness is expensive. Fuel costs to run the machinery are high. With the vast diversification of foods found in modern diets (oranges from Florida, cheese from Wisconsin, corn from Iowa, avocados from California, and coffee from Colombia), additional expenses are incurred from processing, transporting, and marketing food products. Moreover, large-scale agriculture has been responsible for considerable environmental destruction. For example, large-scale agriculture in various parts of the world has led to (a) lowering of water tables, (b) changes in the ecology of nearby bodies of surface water, (c) the destruction of water fauna by pesticides, (d) the pollution of aquifers by pesticides, (e) salinization of soil from overirrigation, and (f) air pollution from crop spraying.

## ◆ Summary

1. If any culture is to survive, it must develop strategies and technologies for procuring or producing food from its environment. While not mutually exclusive, five major food procurement categories are recognized by cultural anthropologists: (a) hunting and gathering (foraging), (b) horticulture, (c) pastoralism, (d) agriculture, and (e) industrialization.

2. The relative success of various food-getting strategies will depend on the interaction between a society's technology and its environment. While different environments present different limitations and possibilities, it is generally recognized that environments influence rather than determine food-getting practices. The level of technology that any society has at its disposal is a critical factor in adapting to and utilizing the environment.

3. Carrying capacity is the limiting effect that an environment has on a culture's productivity. If a culture exceeds its carrying capacity, permanent damage to the environment usually results.

4. Hunting and gathering—the oldest form of food getting—relies on procuring foods that are naturally available in the environment. Approximately 10,000 years ago, people for the first time began to domesticate plants and animals. Since then the percentage of the world's population engaged in foraging has decreased from one hundred percent to a small fraction of one percent.

5. When compared to other food-getting practices, hunting and gathering societies, which tend to have low-density populations, are nomadic or seminomadic, live in small social groups, and occupy remote, marginally useful areas of the world.

6. Foraging societies tend to be selective in terms of the plant and animal species they exploit in their habitats. Which species are actually exploited for food can be explained by the optimal foraging theory, a theory developed by cultural ecologists that suggests that foragers select not arbitrarily but rather on the basis of maximizing their caloric intake for the amount of time and energy expended.

7. Horticulture, a form of small-scale plant cultivation relying on simple technology, produces low yields with little or no surpluses. Horticulture most often utilizes the slash and burn technique, a form of cultivation that involves clearing the land by burning it and then planting in the relatively fertile ash residue.

8. Pastoralism, the keeping of domesticated livestock as a source of food, is usually practiced in those areas of the world that are unable to support any type of cultivation. This food-getting strategy most frequently involves a nomadic or seminomadic way of life, small family-based communities, and regular contact with cultivators as a way of supplementing their diets.

9. Agriculture, a more recent phenomenon than horticulture, utilizes such technology as irrigation, fertilizers, and mechanized equipment to produce high yields and support large populations. Unlike horticulture, agriculture is usually associated with permanent settlements, cities, and high levels of labor specialization.

10. Industrialized food getting, beginning several centuries ago, uses vastly more powerful sources of energy than had ever been used previously. It relies on high levels of technology (tractors, combines, etc.), a mobile labor force, and a complex system of markets.

## ◆ Key Terms

agriculture
carrying capacity
horticulture
hunting and gathering
industrialization
Neolithic Revolution
nomadism

optimal foraging theory
pastoralism
peasantry
slash and burn method
  (shifting cultivation/
  swidden cultivation)
transhumance

## ◆ Suggested Readings

Barfield, Thomas J., *The Nomadic Alternative*. Englewood Cliffs, N.J.: Prentice-Hall, 1993. An historical and ethnographic discussion of pastoral societies in East Africa, the Middle East, and Central Eurasia focusing on such topics as comparative social organization, relations with nonpastoral peoples, and the ecology of nomadic pastoralism.

Bicchieri, M. G. *Hunters and Gatherers Today*. New York: Holt, Rinehart & Winston, 1972. A collection of eleven socioeconomic studies of hunting-and-gathering societies found throughout the world and the changes they have undergone during the present century.

Evans-Pritchard, E. E. *The Nuer*. Oxford: Oxford University Press, 1940. A classic ethnography about a pastoral society of the Sudan showing the central role that cattle play in the overall working of the society.

Harris, M., and E. B. Ross (Eds.). *Food and Evolution: Toward a Theory of Human Food Habits*. Philadelphia:

Temple University Press, 1987. A compendium of twenty-four essays by scholars from a number of disciplines explore why people in different parts of the world and at different periods of history eat the things they do. Perspectives from a wide range of academic disciplines are represented, including physical anthropology, psychology, archaeology, nutrition, and primatology.

Lee, Richard B. *The Dobe !Kung*. New York: Holt, Rinehart & Winston, 1984. The basic ethnographic case study of the !Kung, foragers living in Botswana and Namibia, by one of the leading contemporary authorities on hunting-and-gathering societies.

Schrire, C. (Ed.). *Past and Present in Hunter Gatherer Studies* Orlando, Fla.: Academic Press, 1984. A collection of ten thoughtful essays on hunting-and-gathering societies by anthropologists who have worked with groups from Southern Africa to Tasmania to the Philippines. The editor's aim in this work is to challenge the widely held notion that hunting-and-gathering societies have maintained their economic institutions through cultural isolation.

Service, Elman. *The Hunters* (2nd ed.). Englewood Cliffs, N.J.: Prentice-Hall, 1979. A slim volume designed to describe primitive band societies to beginning students of ethnology. The author attempts to present a well-balanced, integrated view of hunting-and-gathering societies by analyzing technologies, the economies, ideologies, political systems, and social relationships.

# Food Getting

In many developing countries, the process of national economic development almost always is interpreted as necessitating a change in traditional cultural patterns. Since these traditional cultural patterns are viewed by development officials as obstacles to necessary socioeconomic change, it is assumed that they need to be altered or obliterated as quickly as possible.

The process of economic development, however, involves more than the wholesale substitution of new ways of behaving for traditional ones. What is needed in the process of economic development in the Third World is not the elimination of traditional, long-standing cultural patterns but rather a thorough understanding of those patterns. If planners are to make rational decisions about what changes are even appropriate for achieving the goals of national economic development, they will need to know as much as possible about existing traditional economies. It may well be that in some situations, changing traditional economies will be contrary to the goals of economic development. Or, if it can be determined (and agreed upon) that certain changes in traditional economies would, in fact, contribute to national economic development, planners must have as much knowledge as possible about traditional cultures so as to be in the best position to affect changes with the least amount of disruption possible. In either case, the process of economic development must begin with a comprehensive understanding of traditional cultures—which cultural anthropologists are in the best position to provide.

◆ **Anthropological insights into traditional pastoral economies assist in the development of a beef ranching project in Tanzania.**

The Tanzanian Livestock Project serves as an excellent example of how the participation of a cultural anthropologist contributed to an economic development program in East Africa. The project, aimed at developing commercial beef ranching in Tanzania, involved a socioeconomic restructuring of pastoral economies. The objective of the program was to modify the largely subsistence nature of cattle keeping to one that was more income-producing and market oriented. This was to be accomplished by the creation of Ujamaa ("familyhood") ranches, whereby groups of local families from traditional pastoral societies would form cattle ranching partnerships under the skilled management of government husbandry experts. It was believed that if successful, such a commercialization of livestock would provide both needed capital to individual families and an increased food supply for domestic consumption and export.

Much to the credit of the project administrators, Priscilla Reining, a cultural anthropologist experienced with pastoral societies in northern Tanzania, was invited to participate in the appraisal of the project conducted by the World Bank. Reining was asked to assess a number of aspects of traditional culture that might have an impact on the formation of the proposed Ujamaa ranches, such as traditional sex roles, lines of authority, inheritance customs, value placed on age, and conceptions of property rights. Reining then had the difficult task of making recommendations on criteria for recruiting program participants, organizational features of the Ujamaa ranches, and incentives for participation.

Based on her understanding of the traditional cultures of these pastoral peoples, Reining made a number of recommendations designed to mesh the program goals with the traditional cultural features. In addition, Reining was able to point out to the program administrators the multiple uses of cattle for the local herding peoples. As mentioned earlier, cows have a different meaning for East African pastoralists than they do for Texas beef ranchers. To be certain, cattle are important economic commodities, but for the Tanzanian pastoralist, they are also important *socially* in terms of prestige, friendship bonds, and the legitimization of marriages. Armed with this understanding, the program administrators came to realize that the acceptance of commercial ranching would not be accomplished overnight. The success of the program depended on how well the social organization of the Ujamaa ranches provided appropriate alternatives for the many social uses of cattle found in the traditional cultures. Speaking of the anthropological contribution to the project, one administrator concluded the following:

It appears unlikely that the team, without an anthropologist, could have seen all of the ramifications of the changes the project was proposing. The anthropological input was significant; it added depth and understanding to our reasons for supporting ujamaa (Husain, 1976:78).

#### ◆ Knowledge of a traditional economy in Indonesia can be used to prevent counterproductive government decisions.

The Tanzanian Livestock Project illustrates how anthropological insights can be used to improve the design of an economic development project. Sometimes an understanding of the cultural realities of traditional peoples can lead to a decision to abandon a development scheme altogether because it is at odds with its own objectives. A case in point is a project involving the Punan society of Indonesia, a group of forest dwellers who collect, among other things, certain international trade items as rattan and resins (see Hoffman, 1988).

Unlike their settled agricultural neighbors, the Punan engage in no cultivation and have carved out for themselves a fairly specialized ecological niche as forest collectors. Although the Punan and their neighbors exploit different environments, they maintain extensive ties with each other. By exchanging forest products for food crops, the Punan and their neighbors are enriching each other's economies. Thus, the realities of Punan culture are that they contribute significantly to the modern export sector of the Indonesian economy and maintain very strong economic ties with their settled agricultural neighbors.

The Indonesian government holds a very different view of Punan culture. The official view is that the Punan society, an isolated group of hunters and gatherers, has an economy that contributes nothing to the national economy. Proceeding on this faulty perception, the government has embarked on a "development" program designed to make productive agriculturalists of the Punan. As Dove has commented:

... it is clear that this policy, if successful, will severely reduce or even terminate the role of the Punan in the collection of forest products, with a similar impact upon the not unimportant contribution of forest products to Indonesia's export sector. Such an impact would run directly counter to the government's all-out effort to find exportable commodities to replace the country's dwindling supplies of oil and gas (1988:11).

Here is an example, then, of an official development scheme based on erroneous cultural information that, if completed, will reduce the already appreciable contribution that the Punan are presently making to the export sector of the national economy. It is thus possible that the Indonesian government will complete a project that will be less advantageous economically than to have done nothing at all. If the government does choose to "shoot itself in the foot," it will not be because it lacked an accurate description of the cultural realities of the Punan culture.

### ◆ Understanding traditional values concerning work and productivity is an important factor in governmental planning efforts.

Third World countries, with their strong concern for economic development, are interested in determining how traditional economies, based on subsistence food getting, can be transformed into world market economies, thereby attracting foreign capital, providing jobs for local people, and dramatically raising the GNP and standard of living. In those developing countries with substantial numbers of slash and burn horticulturalists, the government's objective frequently has been to transform horticulture into more intensive forms of agriculture. By restricting or prohibiting slash and burn cultivation, the governments hope to increase agricultural productivity, thereby enabling local people to eat better as well as to contribute to the export economy.

A major problem in these efforts to transform traditional food-getting systems has been that the development planners frequently have a different set of values from those peoples whose economies they are attempting to change. In his study of small-scale horticulturalists from Indonesia, Brewer (1988) demonstrated that despite the government's attempt to actively discourage slash and burn cultivation, the practice has in fact increased over the years. The explanation for this apparent paradox is that the philosophical assumptions of the government planners/administrators are not shared by the horticulturalists.

In this particular case, the government of Indonesia has proposed wet rice agriculture as the alternative to slash and burn cultivation. The government starts from the value assumption that wet rice agriculture is preferable to slash and burn cultivation because of the high return *per unit of land*. The local horticulturalists, on the other hand, saw their slash and burn technique to be far preferable because of its relatively high return *per unit of labor*. Even though slash and burn cultivation produced relatively little per unit of land, it didn't require as much intensive labor as wet rice agriculture; consequently, local farmers preferred it because it made fewer demands on their time. In other words, local horticulturalists preferred to maintain their leisure time rather than produce larger crops. This is extremely important ethnographic information for government planners to have, for it will enable the government to either (a) scale down their (frequently costly) efforts to eliminate all slash and burn cultivation or (b) design alternative programs of planned change that will to a greater extent take the local values into account.

# Economics

How do anthropologists study economic systems cross-culturally?

How are resources such as land and property allocated in different cultures?

What are the different principles of distribution found in various parts of the world?

When we hear the word *economics,* a host of images comes to mind. We usually think of such things as money, supply and demand curves, lending and borrowing money at some agreed-upon interest rate, factories with production schedules, labor negotiations, buying stocks and bonds, foreign exchange, and gross national product. Although these are all topics that one might expect to find in an economics textbook, they are not integral parts of all economic systems. Many small-scale cultures exist in the world that have no standardized currencies, stock markets, or factories. Nevertheless, all societies (whether small-scale or highly industrialized) are faced with a common challenge—that is, they all have at their disposal a limited amount of vital resources, such as land, livestock, machines, food, and labor. This simple fact of life requires all societies to plan out carefully how to (a) allocate scarce resources, (b) produce needed commodities, (c) distribute their products to all people, and (d) develop efficient consumption patterns for their products so as to help people maximize their adaptation to the environment. In other words, every society, if it is to survive, must develop systems of production, distribution, and consumption.

The science of economics focuses on the three major areas of production, distribution, and consumption as observed in the industrialized world. The subdiscipline of economic anthropology, on the other hand, studies production, distribution, and consumption *comparatively* in all societies of the world—industrialized and nonindustrialized alike.

# Economics and Economic Anthropology

The relationship between the formal science of economics and the subspecialty of economic anthropology has not always been a harmonious one.

Formal economics has its philosophical roots in the study of Western, industrialized economies. As a result, much of formal economic theory is based on assumptions derived from observing Western, industrialized societies. For example, economic theory is predicated on the assumption that the value of a particular commodity will increase as it becomes more scarce (i.e., the notion of supply and demand) or on the assumption that when exchanging goods and services, people naturally strive to maximize their material well-being and their profits.

Economists use their theories (based on these assumptions) to predict how people will make certain types of choices when either producing or consuming commodities. Owners of a manufacturing plant, for example, are constantly faced with choices. Do they continue to manufacture only men's jockey shorts, or do they expand their product line to include underwear for women? Do they move some or all of their manufacturing facilities to Mexico, or do they keep them in North Carolina? Should they give their workers more benefits? Should they spend more of their profits on advertising? Should they invest more capital on machinery or on additional labor? Western economists assume that all of these questions will be answered in a rational way so as to maximize the company's profits. Similarly, Western economists assume that individuals as well as corporations are motivated by the desire to maximize their material well-being.

## SUBSTANTIVISTS

A long-standing debate between different schools of economics and anthropology has centered on the question of how universal are these and other assumptions that Western economists make about human behavior. How applicable are these economic theories to the understanding of small-scale, nonindustrialized societies? Are the differences between industrial and nonindustrial economies a matter of degree or a matter of kind? Some anthropologists—representing the **substantive approach**—hold the position that classical economic theories cannot be applied to the study of nonindustrialized societies. This "school" has argued that tribal or peasant societies, based as they are on subsistence, are different in kind than market economies found in the industrialized societies.

Whereas production and consumption choices are made in Western societies on the basis of maximization of profits, in nonindustrialized societies they frequently are based on other quite different principles, such as reciprocity or redistribution. The principle of reciprocity (based on the Biblical injunction of "Do unto others as you would have them do unto you") emphasizes the fair exchange of equivalent values and as such is in direct contrast to the principle of maximizing one's profits. Likewise, the principle of redistribution, found in many subsistence economies, discourages the accumulation of personal wealth by moving or redistributing goods from those who have to those who do not. Such principles as reciprocity and redistribution, emphasizing cooperation and generosity, are in stark contrast to the principle of maximization which fosters individual accumulation

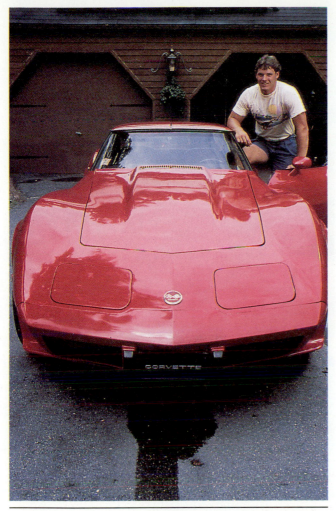

Formal economic theory—based primarily on observations of Western society—assumes that all people naturally seek to maximize their economic well-being. Some economic anthropologists, however, would argue that such an assumption does not hold true for all cultures of the world.

Western economies. For example, even though many nonindustrialized societies may not operate on a "profit motive" in our monetary sense of the term, we should not conclude that the concept of maximization is totally irrelevant. The formalists would argue that people operating in small-scale economies may be motivated by the desire to maximize their standing in the community, their physical security, or the breadth of their social networks rather than their material well-being. If that is indeed the case, then the traditional economic concept of maximization can be broadened to include all economies.

Formalists suggest, moreover, that the substantivists have overly romanticized the nature of nonindustrialized economies to the extent that they lose sight of their economic significance. To illustrate, while admitting that certain pastoralists may use cows for a number of noneconomic reasons (such as legitimizing marriages, establishing social hierarchies, and making religious sacrifices), the formalists would remind us that these same cows have very definite economic uses as well as social uses. As Schneider (1957) and Gray (1960) have pointed out, cows among East African pastoralists represent (a) **capital goods** (they produce milk, blood, and manure), (b) **consumer goods** (they produce meat for eating, hides for clothing, and bone for making artifacts), and (c) a form of *savings and investment* (they are a valuable reserve of economic resources on the hoof which, through animal husbandry, can be expanded). The difficulty, of course, lies in the fact that since the economic behavior of certain nonindustrialized peoples is an integral part of the social structure, it is frequently difficult to separate out what is economic and what is not.

## CROSS-CULTURAL EXAMINATION OF ECONOMIC SYSTEMS

A good deal of debate has taken place over the past half century between the formalists and the substantivists. The formalists hold the view that the principles of classical economics can be useful for the study of all societies, while the substantivists hold that they cannot. While it is true that these two "schools" start from two very different sets of philosophical assumptions, they may have more in common with each other than each is willing to admit. In spite of the substantial differences of economic systems found throughout the world—as well as the different theories used to analyze them—it is possible to examine economic systems cross-culturally along certain key dimensions:

and competition and consequently can lead to jealousy, hostility, and antagonism.

## FORMALISTS

In direct opposition to the substantive school are the **formalists**, who contend that the concepts of Western economics are appropriate for the study of *any* economic system provided they are broadened. While admitting that Western economic theory (as presently conceived) is too narrow, the formalists hold that it should be possible to broaden that theory to include non-

1. *The regulation of resources.* How land, water, and natural resources are controlled and allocated.
2. *Production.* How material resources are converted into usable commodities.
3. *Exchange.* How the commodities, once produced, are distributed among the people of the society.

## The Allocation of Natural Resources

Every society has access to certain natural resources in its territorial environment, including land, animals, water, minerals, and plants. Even though the nature and amount of these resources vary widely from one group to another, every society has developed a set of rules governing the **allocation of resources** and how they can be used. For example, all groups have determined systematic ways for allocating land among their members. Hunters and gatherers must determine who can hunt animals and collect plants from which areas. Pastoralists need to have some orderly pattern for deciding access to pasturage and watering places. Agriculturalists must work out ways of acquiring, maintaining, and passing on rights to their farmland.

In our own society, where things are bought and sold in markets, most of the natural resources are privately owned. Pieces of land are surveyed, precise maps are drawn, and title deeds are granted to those who purchase a piece of property. Individual property rights are so highly valued in the United States that under certain circumstances, a property owner is justified in killing someone who is attempting to violate those property rights. Relatively small pieces of land are usually held by individuals, while larger pieces of property are held collectively, either by governments (as in the case of roads, public buildings, parks, etc.) or by private corporations on behalf of their shareholders.

To be certain, there are limitations to the notion of private property ownership in the United States. To illustrate, certain vital resources such as public utilities are either strongly regulated or owned outright by some agency of government, rights of eminent domain enable the government to force owners to sell their land for essential public projects, and zoning laws serve to set certain limits on how a property owner will use his or her land. Nevertheless, the system of resource allocation found in the United States is based on the general principle of private ownership, whereby an individual or a

Individual property rights, while strongly valued and protected in the United States, are much more loosely defined in some other cultures of the world.

group of individuals have total or near total rights to a piece of property and consequently can dispose of it as they see fit.

Property rights are so strongly held in the United States (and other parts of the Western world) that some observers have suggested that humans have a genetically based territorial instinct that compels them to stake out and defend their turf (Ardrey, 1968). However, the degree to which humans are territorial varies widely throughout the world. By and large, the notion of personal land ownership is absent in most societies that base their livelihood on hunting and gathering, pasto-

332                                        CHAPTER 16    ◆    ECONOMICS

ralism, or horticulture. Let us examine how each of these types of societies deals with the question of access to land.

## HUNTERS AND GATHERERS

In most hunting-and-gathering societies, land is not owned, in the Western sense of the term, either individually or collectively. Hunters and gatherers have a number of compelling reasons to maintain flexible or open borders. First, since food collectors in most cases must follow the migratory patterns of animals, it makes little sense for people to tie themselves exclusively to a single piece of land. Second, claiming and defending a particular territory requires time, energy, and technology which many hunting-and-gathering peoples either do not have or choose not to expend. Third, territoriality can lead to conflict and warfare between those claiming property rights and those who would violate those rights. Thus, for hunting-and-gathering societies, having flexible territorial boundaries (or none at all) is the most adaptive strategy.

Even though hunters and gatherers rarely engage in private ownership of land, there is some variation in the amount of communal control. At one extreme are the Eskimos and the Hadza of Tanzania, two groups that have no concept of trespassing whatsoever. Anyone in these societies can collect food wherever he or she pleases. The !Kung of the Kalahari area do recognize, to some degree, the association of certain territories with particular tribal bands, but it is not rigorously maintained. For example, members of one !Kung band are allowed to track a wounded animal into a neighbor's territory with impunity. Moreover, any !Kung can use the watering holes of any neighboring territory provided he or she seeks permission, which is always granted. This type of reciprocity, cooperation, and permissive use rights is adaptive in that it serves to increase the chances of survival of all !Kung peoples. In a small number of hunting-and-gathering societies—most notably among certain native North American groups—local people live in permanent settlements and maintain strong control over land.

As a general rule, a hunting-and-gathering society will have open or flexible boundaries if animals are mobile and food and water supplies are relatively unpredictable. Conversely, food collectors are more likely to live in permanent settlements and maintain greater control over land in those areas where food and water supplies are more plentiful and predictable (Dyson-Hudson and Smith, 1978: 21–41).

## PASTORALISTS

Like hunters and gatherers, nomadic or seminomadic pastoralists require extensive territory. For pastoralists to maintain their way of life, it is imperative that they have access to two vital resources for their livestock—water and pasturage. Depending on the local environment, the availability of these two resources may vary widely. In marginal environments where grass and water are at a premium, pastoralists will need to range over wide territories and consequently will require relatively free access to land. In those more environmentally favorable regions of the world where grass and water are more abundant, one is likely to find greater control over land and its resources. In any event, pastoral groups must work out arrangements among themselves and with nonpastoralists to gain access to certain pasturage.

To avoid overgrazing and/or conflict, they may have to enter into agreements with other pastoralist families to share certain areas, or they may have to form contractual arrangements with sedentary cultivators to graze their animals on fallowing or recently harvested fields. The pastoral Fulani of northern Nigeria, for example, while remaining removed from village life on an everyday basis, nevertheless have had to maintain special contacts with sedentary horticulturalists for rights of access to water and pastures. According to Stenning, ". . . this has brought them into the orbit of the Muslim states of the western Sudan, in whose politics and wars they became involved principally to maintain or extend their pastoral opportunities" (1965:365).

## HORTICULTURALISTS

In contrast to hunters and gatherers and most pastoralists, horticulturalists tend to live on land that is communally controlled, usually by an extended kinship group. Individual nuclear or polygynous families may be granted the *use* of land by the extended family for growing crops, but the rights are limited. For example, the small family units usually retain their rights for as long as they work the land and for as long as they are in good standing with the larger family. Since they do not own the land, however, they are not able to dispose of it by selling it. They simply use it at the will of the larger group. Such a method of land allocation makes sense, given their farming technology. Since horticulturalists frequently are shifting cultivators, there would be no advantage to having claims of ownership over land that cannot be used permanently.

This communal type of land tenure is well illustrated by the Samoans of Polynesia. Under their traditional system, any piece of land belongs to the extended family that clears and plants it. Individual members of the extended family work the land under the authority of a *matai*, an elected family member who holds the title to the land on behalf of the entire group. The *matai's* authority over the land depends on his meeting his responsibility to care for his extended family. If he does not, the family can remove his title. Any individual of the extended family group has undisputed rights to use the land provided he or she (a) lives on the family land and (b) serves and pays allegiance to the *matai* (see O'Meara, 1990:128–39).

## INDIVIDUAL PROPERTY RIGHTS

As we have demonstrated, all societies have rules for determining how resources are used, by whom, and under what conditions. In the United States and in most other parts of the Western world, resources such as land, capital, livestock, and minerals are allocated according to the principle of private individual ownership. Most English-speaking people have no difficulty understanding the concept of private ownership. When we say we "own" a piece of property, such as an automobile, such ownership carries with it the implication that we have absolute and exclusive rights to the automobile. We are able to sell it, give it away, rent it, trade it for another piece of property, or drive it off a cliff, if we so choose. We have, in other words, one hundred percent rights to certain pieces of property.

This concept of individual **property rights** is so entrenched in our thinking and our culture that we sometimes fail to realize that many other cultures do not share that principle with us. This cultural myopia led some early anthropologists to ask the wrong types of questions when they first encountered certain non-Western peoples. To illustrate, when studying a small group of East African horticulturalists who also kept cattle, some early anthropologists—using their own set of linguistic categories—asked what to them seemed to be a perfectly logical question: Who owns that brown cow over there? In actual fact, no one owned the cow in our sense of the term, because no single individual had one hundred percent rights to the cow. Instead, a number of people may have had limited rights and obligations to the brown cow. The man we see with the cow at the moment may have rights to milk the cow on Tuesdays and Thursdays, but someone else has rights to milk it on Mondays and Wednesdays. The cows are actually controlled by the larger kinship group (the lineage or extended family), while the individual merely has limited rights to use the cow. This fundamental difference in property allocation is reflected in the local East African language of Swahili, which contains no word that would be comparable to the English word *own*. The closest Swahili speakers can come linguistically to conveying the notion of ownership is to use the word *nina*, which means literally "I am with . . . ."

◆　◆　◆

# Production

The initial step in meeting the material needs of any society is to establish a system of allocating the rights to resources to certain people. In very few situations, however, can resources be utilized by people in exactly the form they are found in nature. Animals must be butchered; grains must be ground and cooked; metal ores must be mined, smelted, combined with other chemical elements, and crafted before becoming tools; stones must be shaped before they can be put into the wall of a house. This process of obtaining goods from the natural environment and transforming them into usable objects is what economists refer to as ***production.***

Despite the fact that all humans must meet certain fundamental material needs (such as food, water, and shelter), *how* these needs are satisfied varies enormously from society to society. Some groups, like the Pygmies of Central Africa and the Siriono of Eastern Bolivia, have most of their material needs met by those goods procured from hunting and gathering. Others, like the Masai and Samburu of East Africa, live essentially from the products of their livestock. Still others, like people of the United States and certain Western European nations, go well beyond meeting their basic physical needs through a complex system of technology and industrialization. How do we explain such diversity? Why is there such a vast range of systems of production? Why do two cultures inhabiting apparently similar environments develop substantially different systems of production?

Part of the answer to these questions can be explained in economic terms. For example, why any society pro-

In some parts of the world—such as Hindu India—there is not much of a demand for the U.S. style hamburger. Each culture defines what is edible and what is not.

duces the things it does will be determined, to some extent, by such economic factors as the accessibility of certain resources, the technology available for processing the resources, and the abundance of energy supplies. This is only part of the explanation, however, since cultural values also play a role in determining production. To illustrate, the Hadza of Tanzania, while aware of the horticultural practices of their neighbors, choose not to practice it themselves for the simple reason that it involves too much effort for the anticipated yield. Also, in one form or another, most societies fail to exploit all of the resources at their disposal. Some societies living alongside bodies of water have strong prohibitions against eating fish. The Hindus in India, despite an abundance of cows, refuse to eat beef on religious grounds. The Eskimos, even though they frequently experience food shortages, practice a number of taboos against eating certain types of food. And, of course, people in the United States would never dream of routinely eating the flesh of dogs, cats, or rats, despite these animals being a rich source of protein.

The apparent failure by some societies to exploit all of the resources at their disposal may not stem from irrationality or arbitrariness. As some cultural ecologists have shown convincingly, often there are good reasons for certain types of economic behavior, which at first glance might appear irrational. The case of the sacred cow in Hindu India is a case in point. Despite the fact that the Indian population needs more protein in its diet, the Hindu religion prohibits the slaughter of cows and the eating of beef. This taboo has resulted in large numbers of half-starved cows cluttering the Indian landscape, disrupting traffic, and stealing food from marketplaces. But as Marvin Harris has demonstrated (1977:141–52; 1979:479–82), the taboo makes good economic sense because it prevents the use of cows for less cost-effective purposes. To raise cows as a source of food would be an expensive proposition, given the economic/ecological conditions found in India. Instead, cows are used as draft animals and for the products they provide, such as milk, fertilizer, and fuel (dung). The religious taboo, according to Harris, rather than being irrational, serves to regulate the system of production in a very effective way by having a positive effect on the carrying capacity of the land.

## UNITS OF PRODUCTION

Like other parts of culture, the way that people go about producing is not haphazard or random but rather is systematic, organized, and patterned. Every society breaks up its members into some type of productive unit comprising people with specific tasks to perform. In industrialized societies like our own, the productive unit is the private company that exists for the purpose of producing goods or services. These private firms range from small, individually owned retail operations on the one hand to gigantic multinational corporations on the other. Whatever the size and complexity, however, these private companies are made up of employees performing specific roles, all of which are needed to produce the goods and services, which are then sold for a profit. The employees do not consume the products of the firm, but instead receive salaries, which they use to purchase the goods and services they need.

**Production in the Household.** In most nonindustrialized societies, the basic unit of production is the household. In these small-scale societies most, if not all, of the goods and services consumed are produced by the members of the household. The household may be made up of a nuclear family (husband, wife, and children) or a more elaborate family structure containing married siblings, multiple wives, and more than two generations. In a typical horticultural society, household members produce most of what they consume, including planting, tending, and harvesting the crops; building houses; procuring firewood and other fuels from the environment; making their own tools; keeping some livestock; making their own clothes; and producing various containers for both storing and cooking foods. In the event that a particular task is too complex to be carried out by a single household, it is likely that larger groups of family members or neighbors will join together to complete the task.

Even though both the business firm and the household serve as units of production, there are significant structural differences between them. Whereas the business firm is primarily—if not exclusively—just a unit of production, the household performs a number of overlapping functions. When two male kinsmen who are part of the same household work side by side threshing wheat, it is very likely that they may play a number of other roles together. For example, one man, because of his advanced age, may be a religious specialist; the other man, owing to his particular leadership skills, may be called upon to play an important political role in the extended family; and both men may enjoy spending their leisure time together drinking beer and telling stories. Thus, this productive unit of the household is the very same group that shares certain religious, political, and social activities.

A second structural difference between the business firm and the household is that the household is far more self-sufficient. In most cases, the members of the household in small-scale societies can satisfy their own material needs without having to go outside the group. People employed in a business firm, on the other hand, rely on a large number of people for their material well-being, including the butcher, the TV repair person, the

barber, the schoolteacher, the auto mechanic, and all of those thousands of people who make all of the things with which people surround themselves.

A third difference is that a business firm, since it can concentrate on its exclusive economic function, is a more productive unit than the household. Since the family household is more than just a productive unit—and must be concerned with the emotional, social, psychological, and spiritual needs of its members—it is likely to use some of its resources in nonproductive ways. Consequently, the family-based household, when compared to the business firm, is less likely to be highly productive, progressive, or innovative in its methods.

## DIVISION OF LABOR

One very important aspect of the process of production is the allocation of tasks to be performed—that is, deciding which types of people are expected to perform which categories of work. Every society, whether large or small, distinguishes, to some degree, between the work appropriate for men and women and for adults and children. Even though many societies have considerably more complex divisions of labor, all societies do, in fact, make distinctions on the basis of sex and age.

**Sex or Gender Specialization.** Not only do all societies divide tasks according to sex, but the literature seems to suggest that there is a great deal of uniformity in the way that tasks are divided between the sexes. For example, in most cases men hunt, engage in warfare, trap small animals, fish, herd large animals, work with hard substances such as wood and stones, clear land, build houses, and serve as political functionaries. Women, on the other hand, tend crops, gather wild fruits and plants, prepare food, care for children, collect fuel, carry water, clean the house, and launder clothing. It is important to note that in many parts of the world today—because men are migrating to cities in search of wage employment—most agriculturally related tasks are being carried out by women.

A number of theories have been set forth to explain this very common, if not universal, division of labor by sex. One such explanation is that since men have greater body mass and strength, they are better equipped physically to engage in hunting, warfare, and land clearing. A second argument that often has been put forth is that women do the things they do because those tasks are compatible with child care. That is, unlike certain male

These women in Kashmir are engaging in activities that are compatible with looking after children.

tasks, such as hunting and warfare, women's tasks can be accomplished without jeopardizing the child's safety and without having to stray too far away from home. A third explanation is that, in terms of reproduction, men tend to be more expendable than women. In other words, because women have more limited (and therefore more valuable) reproductive capacities, they are less likely to be required to engage in dangerous activities. Although we can find exceptions to each of these explanations, all three theories, when taken together, go a long way in helping us understand this very commonly found sexual division of labor.

Despite these apparently rational theories designed to explain the sexual division of labor, many roles are allocated to men and women because of many different social, political, and historical forces operating in individual societies. When these forces are inadequately understood they can appear to be quite arbitrary. For example, although sewing clothes in the United States is thought of as women's work (most North American men have neither operated a sewing machine nor made

a purchase in a fabric store), among the traditional Hopi of Arizona, it is the men who are the spinners, weavers, and tailors. Moreover, in our own society, women have been virtually excluded from a number of different occupations (such as jockey, race car driver, and major league baseball umpire), even though men have no particular physiological advantage over women in performing these jobs.

Sometimes the division of labor by sex is so rigidly followed that both men and women remain ignorant of the occupational skills of the opposite sex. This point is well illustrated by the Mixe Indians of Mexico where men traditionally grew corn while women processed it for eating. According to Beals, Hoijer, and Beals:

Men received no training in the processing of maize and were incapable of surviving unless a woman was available to process the maize that the man produced. Although man's work involving the planting and raising of maize constituted a complicated technological process, it only represented one half of the food producing revolution. The other half, the processing of the crop, was equally complicated and time consuming. The

## CROSS-CULTURAL MISCUE

Since culture can influence the delivery of medical services, anthropologists in recent years have worked in hospital settings. Unless medical professionals understand the cultural "baggage" that patients bring with them into the hospital, decisions will be made that may not be in the best medical interest of the patient. This applies not only to doctors and nurses but also to such auxiliary staff as dieticians. It is important for those responsible for planning a patient's in-hospital meals to be aware of dietary restrictions. Let us suppose that following an appendectomy, the attending physician puts the recovering patient on a high-protein diet. In keeping with the doctor's prescribed diet, the patient is given a typical American breakfast consisting of two soft-boiled eggs, orange juice, toast, and hot tea. If the patient, however, is a Kikuyu woman from East Africa in her late twenties, it is highly unlikely that she will eat the eggs, for the Kikuyu believe that to eat chicken eggs causes women to become infertile. It is not very likely that during the several days of recuperation time in the hospital the staff will be able to talk the Kikuyu woman into abandoning her cultural prohibition against eating eggs. But by being aware of the prohibition from the outset, the dietician could plan to substitute cheese, meat, or some other high-protein food for the eggs so as to ensure that a rich source of protein will be eaten. Although not eating the two eggs for breakfast is hardly life-threatening, if the job of the hospital caregivers is in fact to help patients recover as quickly as possible, it is imperative that patients be given proper foods *that they are likely to eat*. Those decisions on the part of the dieticians can be made only if the dieticians first know something about the culturally formed eating practices that people bring with them into the hospital.

processing involved removing the maize from the cob; boiling it with the proper amount of lime for a sufficient time to remove the hard outer shell and soften the kernel; grinding it on a flat stone slab until it reached the proper texture; working water into the dough; and shaping it between the palms until a flat cake of uniform thickness was formed. The cake was then cooked at the correct heat on a flat griddle, properly treated to prevent sticking. A Mixe woman with a family of five would spend about six hours a day manufacturing tortillas. Under such circumstances it would be impossible for her to engage in the raising of the maize, just as it would be impossible for her husband to engage in the processing of the maize (1977:348–50).

**Allocation of Tasks by Age.** In much the same way that societies divide labor on the basis of sex, they allocate tasks according to age. Owing to the lack of knowledge and physical strength to perform certain jobs, children are frequently excluded from certain tasks. In our own

society, where formal education routinely lasts through the late teens (and frequently beyond), young people generally do not engage in much productive work. By way of contrast, children in less industrialized societies usually become involved in work activities at a considerably earlier age. At the other end of the age continuum, the elderly, because of their waning physical strength, are frequently prohibited from engaging in certain tasks or are expected to engage in different activities from those performed when they were younger. For example, according to Hart and Pilling (1960:46), old men among the Tiwi of North Australia give up the strenuous work of hunting in favor of staying at home to make hunting tools, such as spears and throwing sticks, for the younger men. In the United States, the transition from being employed to being retired is considerably more abrupt. Usually when most workers reach the age of 65, they receive a gold watch and cease their productive activity. Unlike the situation among the

Tiwi, when workers in the United States retire, they usually suffer a noticeable loss of prestige.

**Labor Specialization.** Labor specialization—another term for **division of labor**—is an important descriptive characteristic of any society. At one extreme, subsistence societies with low population densities and simple technologies are likely to have a division of labor based on little more than sex and age. Most men in these societies engage in essentially the same activities, and the same holds true for most women. If specialists do exist, they are usually part-timers engaged in political leadership, ceremonial activities, or specialized toolmaking. At the other extreme are industrialized societies, where most people are engaged in very specialized occupations, such as stockbroker, TV repair person, kindergarten teacher, janitor, CPA, or thoracic surgeon. One need only to consult the yellow pages of the phone directory for any major city in the United States to get an idea of the vast diversity of specialized occupations in our own society. These two extremes should be viewed as the poles on a continuum of division of labor, between which all of the societies of the world could be placed relative to one another.

One of the major consequences of the transition from hunting and gathering to plant and animal domestication (the Neolithic Revolution) has been the increasing amount of labor specialization in the world. Since agriculture represents a far more efficient way of producing food than hunting and gathering, some people were freed up from the tasks of food production. Simple horticulture evolved into more complex forms of cultivation, which eventually led to the rise of civilizations (urban society).

With each advance in food-producing capacity came an increase in the complexity of labor specialization. This more complex division of labor is significant because of the increase in specialized tasks that provided a new basis for social solidarity. According to nineteenth-century French social philosopher Emile Durkheim, in highly specialized societies where people engage in complementary roles, social solidarity arises from their mutual interdependence upon one another. That is, the teacher needs to be on good terms with the butcher, the carpenter, and the auto mechanic because the teacher is so highly specialized that he or she cannot procure meat on his or her own, build a wood deck, or fix a faulty carburetor. Durkheim calls the social solidarity resulting from this labor specialization and mutual interdependence *organic solidarity*. By way of contrast, societies with minimal division of labor also possess a form of

solidarity, but of a different type. This type of solidarity, which Durkheim calls *mechanical solidarity*, is based on commonality of interests, social homogeneity, strict conformity, and mutual affection.

◆  ◆  ◆

# Distribution of Goods and Services

Once goods have been procured from the environment or produced, they need to get into the people's hands. People frequently consume some of the commodities that they produce, but surpluses will enter the society's system of exchange. Systems of exchange are essential for every economy, for they allow people to dispose of their surpluses and, at the same time, maximize the diversity of the goods and services consumed. As Polanyi (1957) reminds us, goods and services are allocated in all societies according to three different modes of distribution: *reciprocity, redistribution*, and *market exchange.*

In the United States, most commodities are distributed according to a free market exchange system based on the principle of "each according to his or her capacity to pay." People receive money for their labor which is then used to purchase the goods and services they need or want. In theory, at least, if people have the money, they can purchase a loaf of bread; if they don't, they can't. Even though this is the prevailing type, we can see examples of the other two modes operating in the United States. The principle of reciprocity operates, for example, when friends and relatives exchange gifts for birthdays, holidays, and other special occasions. We can see the principle of redistribution at work in the United States when people hand over a certain portion of their personal income to the government for taxes. Even though more than one mode of distribution can operate in any given society at a time, usually only one mode will predominate. Let us examine each of these three modes of distribution in greater detail.

## RECIPROCITY

Reciprocity refers to the exchange of goods and services of relatively equal value between two parties without the use of money. Three types of reciprocity are generally recognized by economic anthropologists, depending upon the degree of closeness of the parties involved in the exchange: **generalized reciprocity, balanced reciprocity,** and **negative reciprocity** (Sahlins, 1972: 191–196).

**Generalized Reciprocity.** Usually played out between family members or close friends, generalized reciprocity carries with it the highest level of moral obligation. This involves a form of gift giving without any expectation of immediate return. Generalized reciprocity is perhaps best illustrated by the type of giving that takes place between parents and children in our own society. Parents, by and large, give (or, at least, try to give) their children as much as they can while their children are growing up—food, toys, a set of encyclopedias, a room of their own, etc. In fact, this providing of goods and services for children frequently continues after the children become adults. Parents, in other words, may provide babysitting services, a down payment on a first home, or a subsidized vacation for their adult children.

In most cases, parents provide for their children materially without the expectation that their children will repay them at any time in the future. Because of the intimate bonds between parents and children, parents usually provide for their children out of a sense of love, obligation, and social responsibility. In reality, this sense of love and obligation usually becomes a two-way street, for children usually come to the assistance of their elderly parents when their parents become too old to care for themselves. Thus, even in this most generalized form of reciprocity, the exchange of goods and services frequently will be balanced out over the long run.

Even though generalized reciprocity is found in our own society, it is not the predominating form of exchange as it is in smaller-scale societies, where the primary unit of economic organization is the nuclear or extended family and where material resources may be unpredictable and uncertain. An exchange system based primarily on generalized reciprocity is common among hunters and gatherers and indeed contributes to their very survival.

In most hunting societies, when a large animal such as a bush buck is killed, the hunter will keep enough for his own immediate family and distribute the rest to his more distant relatives. Because of an absence of refrigeration or other ways of preserving meat, it would make little sense for the hunter to hoard all of the meat himself, for it would spoil before it could be eaten. Instead, sharing with others becomes the expected norm. And, of course, given the uncertainty of hunting, sharing your kill today would entitle you to share someone else's kill tomorrow. Such an economic strategy helps all family members sustain themselves by providing a fairly steady supply of meat despite the inconsistent success of most individual hunters. In such societies generosity is perhaps the highest ideal, while hoarding and stinginess are seen as being extremely antisocial.

We should not think of generalized reciprocity as being motivated totally by altruism. For all people who

In hunting-and-gathering societies, food is frequently distributed along kinship lines.

CHAPTER 16 ◆ ECONOMICS

live at a subsistence level, the maintenance of reciprocal exchange relationships is vital to one's very economic self-interest. At subsistence levels, a person is more dependent on others for his or her material security. In the absence of worker's compensation, unemployment insurance, and bank loans, people must rely on others in the event that their crops fail or they become too sick to hunt. Subsistence farmers, for example, might not survive without the occasional help from their relatives, friends, and neighbors. A farmer may need extra seeds for planting, help with fixing a roof, or extra cash to pay for a child's school fees. The best way of insuring that these needs will be met is to respond quickly and unselfishly to the requests of others for similar types of assistance.

**Balanced Reciprocity.** Balanced reciprocity is a form of exchange involving the expectation that goods and services of equivalent value will be returned within a specified period of time. In contrast to generalized reciprocity, balanced reciprocity involves more formal relationships, greater social distance, and a strong obligation to repay the original "gift." The repayment in balanced reciprocity does not have to be immediate, for, as Mauss (1954) has suggested, any attempt to repay the debt too quickly can be seen as an unwillingness to be obligated to one's trading partner.

A major economic motivation of balanced reciprocity is to exchange surplus goods and services for those that are in short supply. Shortfalls and surpluses can result from different levels of technology, environmental variations, or production capacities. But whatever the cause, balanced reciprocity enables both parties in the exchange to maximize their consumption. The Indians of Oaxaca, Mexico, exemplify balanced reciprocity in the exchange of both goods and services. According to social custom, a man is expected to sponsor at least one fiesta celebrating a major saint's day. Such events, involving an elaborate amount of food, beverages, and entertainment, almost always were beyond the capacity of a man to provide by himself. Consequently, the man would need to solicit the help of his relatives, friends, and neighbors, thereby mortgaging his future surpluses. Those who helped out expected to be repaid in equivalent amounts when they were sponsoring a similar fiesta.

**The Semang.** In some cases of balanced reciprocity, people will go to considerable lengths to maintain the relationship. For example, the Semang, a pygmoid people of the Malay Peninsula, engage in a form of "silent trade," whereby they studiously avoid any face-to-face contact with their trading partners. The Semang leave their products collected from the forest at an agreed-upon location near the village of their trading partners. They return at a later time to receive those commodities (usually salt, beads, and tools) left in exchange. By avoiding social contact, both the Semang and their exchange partners eliminate the risk of jeopardizing the relationship by haggling or arguing over equivalencies (Service, 1966:17–18, 107).

**The Kula Ring.** Perhaps the most widely analyzed case of balanced reciprocity is the **kula ring** found among the Trobriand Islanders off the coast of New Guinea. First described by Bronislav Malinowski (1922), the kula involves a highly ritualized exchange of shell bracelets and shell necklaces that pass (in opposite directions) between a ring of islands. The necklaces move in a clockwise direction while the bracelets move counter-clockwise. Many of these shell objects have become well-known for their beauty, the noble deeds of their former owners, and the great distances they have traveled. The major significance of these shell necklaces and bracelets is as symbols of the reciprocal relationships between trading partners. These partnerships are frequently maintained for long periods of time.

The Trobriand Islanders and their neighbors have fairly diversified systems of production with considerable labor specialization. They produce garden crops such as yams and taro; they are accomplished fishermen; they build oceanworthy boats; they raise pigs; and they produce a wide range of crafts, including dishes, pots, baskets, and jewelry. When trading partners meet, they would exchange shell necklaces for shell bracelets according to a well adhered-to set of ceremonial rituals. But, for the next several days, they would also exchange many of their everyday commodities, such as yams, boats, pigs, fish, and crafts items.

The shell necklaces and bracelets have no particular monetary value, yet they are indispensable, for they serve as gifts that symbolize each partner's good faith and willingness to maintain the longevity of the trading relationship. Trading partners must avoid at all costs any attempt to gain an advantage in the exchange. Generosity and honor are the order of the day. Whoever receives a generous gift is expected to reciprocate.

This very complex system of trade found among the Trobriand Islanders was ladened with ritual and ceremony. Individuals were under a strong obligation to pass on the shell objects they received to other partners in the chain. After a number of years, these bracelets and necklaces eventually returned to their island of origin and from there continued on the cycle once again. Thus, the continual exchange of bracelets and necklaces tied together a number of islands, some of which were great distances from one another.

Since the ceremonial exchange of shell objects was always accompanied by the exchange of everyday, practical commodities, the kula ring clearly functioned as an effective, albeit complicated, system of exchange of goods. And yet, the kula ring was more than just an economic institution. Since there were no all-encompassing political institutions to maintain peace among all of these islands, the maintenance of cordial relationships between trading partners no doubt served as a peacekeeping mechanism. Moreover, the kula ring also played an important sociocultural role by creating and maintaining long-term social relationships and by fostering the traditional myths, folklore, and history associated with the circulating shell bracelets and necklaces.

**Negative Reciprocity.** Negative reciprocity is a form of exchange between equals in which the parties attempt to take advantage of each other. It is based on the principle of trying to get something for nothing or to get the better of the deal. Involving the most impersonal (possibly even hostile) of social relations, negative reciprocity can take the form of hard bargaining, cheating, or out-and-out theft. In this form of reciprocity, the sense of altruism and social obligation is at its lowest, while the desire for personal gain is the greatest. Since negative reciprocity is incompatible with close, harmonious relations, it is most often practiced against strangers and enemies.

The concept of negative reciprocity is well illustrated by the relationship between the hunting-and-gathering Mbuti Pygmies of Central Africa and their horticultural neighbors. The Pygmies maintain a somewhat strained symbiotic relationship with their neighbors from whom they receive grains and metal in exchange for meat and their labor. Customarily, individual Pygmies will attach themselves for brief periods of time to certain villages. While there, the Pygmies will bring small gifts from the forest and will do some work while eating the food of the villagers. But, as Turnbull reports, this is an uneasy alliance:

In the village there is a constant battle between the villagers, who make every attempt to put the visiting Pygmies to work, and the Pygmies, who use all their guile to avoid being put to work. When their welcome is outstayed, and the villagers re-

fuse to give any more handouts, the Pygmies simply return to the forest (1965:294–95).

## REDISTRIBUTION

Another principle of exchange is redistribution, whereby goods are given to a central authority and then redistributed to the people in a new pattern. The process of redistribution involves two distinct stages: an inward flow of goods and services to a social center, followed by an outward dispersal of these goods and services back to society. Although redistribution is found in some form in all societies, it is most common in those societies that have political hierarchies.

**Tribute.** Redistribution can take a number of different forms. In its simplest form, we can see redistribution operating within large families, where family members give their agricultural surpluses to a family head, who in turn stores them and reallocates them back to the individual family members as needed. In complex societies with state systems of government, such as our own, taxation is a form of redistribution. That is, we give a certain percentage of our earnings to the government in exchange for certain goods and services, such as roads, education, and public health projects. The giving of gifts to charitable institutions (such as the Salvation Army or Goodwill) can also involve a form of redistribution, since the gifts are usually given to the poor or homeless. In some societies without standardized currency, tribal chiefs are given a portion of food and other material goods by their constituents. Once received, some of these food items are given back to the people in the form of a feast. Such a system of redistribution—known as tribute—serves several important social functions at once. In addition to serving as a mechanism for dispensing goods within a society, it is a way of affirming both the political power of the chief and the value of solidarity among the people.

A good illustration of tribute can be seen in traditional Nyoro, a society with a state system of government from Uganda (Taylor, 1962:33). Even though most goods and services are dispersed within the family or local village, some redistribution followed feudal lines. The rank and file frequently gave gifts of beer, grain, labor, and livestock to the king and to various levels of chiefs. The king and chiefs in return would give gifts to their trusted followers and servants. These gifts might involve head of livestock, slaves, or pieces of land.

In the United States, such organizations as the Salvation Army engage in redistributing goods from the "haves" to the "have-nots."

Among the Nyoro, the major criterion for redistribution was, by and large, loyalty to the political hierarchy. Consequently, there was no particular incentive on the part of the king or chiefs to make an equitable redistribution or to see to it that the commoners received in return something roughly equivalent to what they had donated.

**Big Men.** In less centralized societies which do not have formal chiefs, redistribution is carried out by economic entrepreneurs which anthropologists call *big men*. Unlike chiefs, who usually inherit their leadership roles, big men are self-made leaders who are able to convince their relatives and neighbors to contribute surplus goods for the sake of community-wide feasting. Through verbal coercion and setting an example of diligence, big men, found widely throughout Melanesia and New Guinea, exhort their followers to contribute excess food for the sake of providing lavish feasts for the followers of other big men. The status of a local big man—as well as his followers—is increased in direct proportion to the size of the feast, his generosity, and hospitality. Big men of the South Pacific distinguish themselves from ordinary men by their verbal persuasiveness, generosity, eloquence, diligence, and physical fitness. Unlike chiefs, who are usually not producers themselves, big men work hard to produce surpluses and encourage their followers to do so as well, all for the sake of giving it away. In fact, since generosity is the essence of being a big

man, many big men often consume fewer food stuffs than ordinary people in order to save it for the feasts.

**Bridewealth.** Social institutions exist in addition to tribute and big manship that function to allocate material goods according to the principles of both redistribution and reciprocity. Since some of these social institutions perform functions other than economic ones, we often overlook their economic or distributive functions. One such social institution (discussed in considerable detail in Chapter 18) is bridewealth, which involves the transfer of valuable commodities (frequently livestock) from the groom's lineage to the bride's lineage as a precondition for marriage.

Even though bridewealth performs a number of non-economic or social functions—such as legalizing marriages, legitimizing children, creating bonds between two groups of relatives, and reducing divorce—it also serves as a mechanism for the *relatively* equitable distribution of goods within a society. Since lineages are the giving and receiving groups, and since lineages are made up of a relatively equal number of men and women, the practice of bridewealth ensures that all people will have access to the valued commodities. That is, no lineage is likely to get a monopoly on the goods, because each group must pay out a certain number of cows when marrying off a son while receiving a roughly equivalent number of cows when marrying off a daughter. Even though there are often differences in amounts paid based on social status of the bride's lineage, all lineages will have access to some of the material goods of the society.

**Potlatch.** Still another customary practice that serves as a mechanism of redistribution is the **potlatch** found among certain northwest coast Indians of North America. Perhaps the best known example of the potlatch was found among the Kwakiutl Indians of British Columbia, for whom social ranking was of great importance (see Rohner and Rohner, 1970). Potlatches were ceremonies in which chiefs or prominent men publicly announced certain hereditary rights, privileges, and high social status within their communities. Such claims were always accompanied by elaborate feasting and gift giving provided by the person giving the potlatch. In fact, at a potlatch, the host would either give away or destroy all of his personal possessions, which could include such articles as food, boats, blankets, pots, fish oil, and various manufactured goods. The number of guests present and the magnitude of the personal property given away was a measure of the prestige of the host. The more the host could give away, the stronger would be his claim to high social status. In addition to serving as a way of allocating social status, the potlatch was an important mechanism for the dispersal of material goods, for each time a person is a guest at a potlatch, he or she returns home with varying degrees of material wealth. Moreover, the potlatch serves a leveling function, preventing some people from accumulating great surpluses at the expense of others.

## MARKET EXCHANGE

The third major form of distribution is one based on the principle of market exchange, whereby goods and services are bought and sold frequently through the use of a standardized currency. In market exchange systems, the value of any particular good or service is determined by the market principle of supply and demand. Market exchange tends to be somewhat less personal than exchanges based on reciprocity or redistribution which frequently involve ties of kinship, friendship, or political relationships. In this respect, market exchanges are predominantly economic in nature, since people are more interested in maximizing their profits than in maintaining a long-term relationship or demonstrating their political allegiance to a chief or leader.

Market exchange systems are most likely to be found in sedentary societies which produce appreciable surpluses and have a relatively complex division of labor. Societies with very simple technologies, such as hunters and gatherers, are likely to have no surpluses or such small ones that they can be disposed of quite simply by reciprocity or redistribution. The amount of labor specialization in a society also contributes to a market exchange system, for an increase in the division of labor brings with it a proliferation of specialized commodities and an increased dependency on market exchange.

**Standardized Currency.** A commonly found trait of market economies is the use of some type of standardized currency for the exchange of goods and services. Market economies do not always involve money, however. In some small-scale societies, for example, it is possible to find market exchanges based on barter—that is, the exchange of one good or service for another without using a standardized form of currency. In a bartering situation, a metal smith may exchange a plow blade for several bushels of wheat, or an artist and a migrant laborer may swap a piece of sculpture for three days of labor.

Even in the highly complex market economy found in the United States, we find bartering institutions that facilitate the wholesale bartering of goods and services between large corporations. By turning over part of its surplus to a bartering corporation, a company that manufactures office furniture can exchange its surplus furniture for items it may need (such as air conditioners, automobile tires, or computers). More and more, individuals are using bartering (e.g., artists, therapists, typists, and other free-lance suppliers).

The major prerequisite of a market exchange is not whether the exchange is based on currency or barter, but rather that the relative value (or price) of any good or service is determined by the market principle of supply and demand. That is, we can consider an exchange to be based on a market principle when a person can exchange his pig for ten bushels of corn when pigs are scarce but can expect to receive only four bushels of corn when pigs are plentiful.

**Variety of Markets.** The extent to which markets are responsible for the distribution of goods and services in any given society varies widely throughout the world. The market economy of the United States, comprising a vast network of commercial interests and consumer products, represents one extreme. There is virtually nothing that cannot be bought or sold in our highly complex markets. In some of our markets (such as su-

Some markets—such as this one in Bangkok, Thailand—play social as well as economic roles.

permarkets, shops, and retail stores), buyers and sellers interact with one another in close proximity to the goods. But other types of markets in the United States are highly impersonal because the buyers and sellers have no personal interaction. For example, stock markets, bond markets, and commodities markets are all conducted electronically (through brokers), without buyers and sellers having face-to-face contact with one another. Such markets, which exist for the sole purpose of buying and selling, serve exclusively an economic function rather than any social functions.

At the opposite extreme are certain small-scale economies that have little labor specialization, small surpluses, and a limited range of goods and services exchanged in markets. Many of the material needs of a household are met by the productive activities of its members. Whatever surpluses exist will be brought to market for sale or exchange, the profits from which will be used to purchase other goods or to pay taxes. In such societies, the actual location of the market is important because of the many *social* functions that are performed in addition to the economic exchange of goods and services. In traditional West Africa, for example, the market is the place where buyers and sellers meet to exchange their surplus goods. But it may also be the place where a man will go to meet his friend, settle a dispute, watch dancing, hear music, pay respects to an important chief, get caught up on the latest gossip, or see some distant relatives.

## ◆ Summary

1. The study of economic anthropology has involved a theoretical debate between the formalists and the substantivists. The formalists believe that the concepts of Western economics are appropriate for the study of all economic systems, while the substantivists do not.
2. Economic anthropology involves examining how resources are allocated, converted into usable commodities, and distributed.

3. While property rights to land are strongly held in the United States, in most hunting-and-gathering societies, land is not owned either individually or collectively. The extent to which people have free access to land in pastoral societies will depend largely on local environmental conditions, with relatively free access to land found in those environments where water and pasturage are scarce. In contrast to land rights among foragers and pastoralists, land rights are more rigidly controlled among horticulturalists and agriculturalists.

4. People in some parts of the world do not share with most North Americans the notion of property ownership. Instead of owning something in our sense of the word, people have limited rights and obligations to the particular object.

5. Every society—to one degree or another—allocates tasks according to gender. Since the same type of activity (e.g., weaving) may be associated with the opposite gender in different cultures, the division of labor by gender is sometimes seen as arbitrary.

6. The amount of specialization (division of labor) varies from society to society. Based on the extent of division of labor, the French sociologist Durkheim distinguished between two fundamentally different types of societies—those based on mechanical solidarity and those based on organic solidarity. Societies with a minimum of labor specialization, according to Durkheim, are held together by mechanical solidarity, which is based on a commonality of interests, while highly specialized societies are held together by organic solidarity, which is based on mutual interdependence.

7. Goods and services are distributed according to three different modes: reciprocity, redistribution, and market exchange. Reciprocity refers to the exchange of goods and services of roughly equal value between two trading partners; redistribution, found most commonly in societies with political bureaucracies, is that form of exchange whereby goods and services are given to a central authority and then reallocated to the people according to a new pattern; market exchange systems involve the use of standardized currencies to buy and sell goods and services.

8. Economic anthropologists generally recognize three types of reciprocity depending upon the degree of closeness of the parties: generalized reciprocity involves giving a gift without any expectation of immediate return; balanced reciprocity involves the exchange of goods and services with the expectation that equivalent value will be returned within a specific period of time; and negative reciprocity involves the exchange of goods and services between equals in which the parties try to gain an advantage.

9. Whereas reciprocity essentially involves the exchange of goods and services between two partners, redistribution involves a social center from which goods are distributed. The institutions of tribute paid to an African chief, bridewealth, and the potlatch found among the northwest coast American Indians are all examples of distribution.

10. Market exchange, based on standardized currencies, tends to be less personal than either reciprocity or redistribution because people in such an exchange are primarily interested in maximizing their profits. As a general rule, the more labor specialization in a society, the more complex the system of market exchange.

## ◆ Key Terms

| | |
|---|---|
| allocation of resources | mechanical solidarity |
| balanced reciprocity | negative reciprocity |
| capital goods | organic solidarity |
| consumer goods | potlatch |
| division of labor | production |
| formalists | property rights |
| generalized reciprocity | reciprocity |
| kula ring | redistribution |
| market exchange | substantive approach |

## ◆ Suggested Readings

Dalton, George (Ed.). *Tribal and Peasant Economies: Readings in Economic Anthropology.* Garden City, N.Y.: Natural History Press, 1967. An impressive collection of essays on economic systems from all over the world including Africa, Oceania, Asia, Europe, and the Americas.

Douglas, Mary, and Baron Isherwood. *The World of Goods: Toward an Anthropology of Consumption.* New York: W. W. Norton, 1979. A study of theories of consumption examined from a cross-cultural perspective.

Malinowski, Bronislav. *Argonauts of the Western Pacific.* New York: E.P. Dutton and Company, 1922. A classic ethnography based on four years of uninterrupted fieldwork in which Malinowski describes in detail the kula exchange system found among the Trobriand Islanders.

Pryor, F. L. *The Origins of the Economy: A Comparative Study of Distribution in Primitive and Peasant Economies.* New York: Academic Press, 1977. An empirical approach to the cross-cultural study of distribution systems in primitive and peasant economies.

Schneider, H. K. *Economic Man.* New York: The Free Press, 1974. A study of the potential applications of formal economic theory to the noncommercial, nonindustrialized economies of the developing world.

This chapter on economic systems from a cross-cultural perspective has examined how people control and allocate natural resources and produce and distribute essential commodities throughout the society. The three applied case studies that follow have been selected specifically for their relevance to economic issues. The first case illustrates how it is vital to know something about the system of production before introducing new technology designed to change that production system. The second case, from South Africa, demonstrates how the knowledge of local patterns of consumption and resource allocation enabled a health team to solve an important problem in community health. The third case, involving the Kikuyu of Kenya during the colonial period, serves as a negative lesson in how not to administer a colonialized people.

# Economics

◆ **An anthropological understanding of the local food production system in rural Mexico is applied to the area of new-product marketing.**

During the 1960s, anthropologist Hendrick Serrie was hired by the Rockefeller Foundation to field test a newly developed solar cooking stove in the Mexican village of Oaxaca. Foundation-supported researchers wanted to introduce the new stove (which was capable of producing the same heat as conventional wood fires) to Mexican villagers as a more energy efficient alternative to burning wood. As a way of introducing the cooker to the local people, a prototype was made on a limited scale using local materials, labor, and technology. The Rockefeller Foundation wanted to "test market" the solar cooker before going into mass production. Despite initial interest among the local people, Serrie, by conducting a field study of the local food production system, found several important cultural factors that strongly suggested that the cooker might not be widely used by the local population.

One cultural factor that militated against the adoption of the solar cooker was the existing cooking routine of local women. According to Serrie's findings, local women did most of their cooking either early in the morning or in the early evening, those parts of the day when the solar energy is at its lowest. As a general rule, women did no cooking during the middle part of the day when the sun is strongest, preferring instead to eat a cold lunch in the fields.

A second cultural problem involved the major type of food normally prepared in that part of the world—that is, the *tortilla.* Although a solar cooker works well for boiling beans or making a stew, it is quite inadequate for baking these cornmeal pancakes. The focal point of heat coming from the cooker's four-foot wide parabolic reflector is so concentrated that it tends to burn a hole in one part of the *tortilla* while leaving the rest uncooked.

Finally, Serrie found that the solar cooker was incompatible with the "complex of behaviors associated with cooking" (1986:xvii). Women in this part of Mexico are accustomed to cooking while sitting on their kitchen floors for relatively long periods of time. From a sitting position, a woman is able to tend to her fire, knead the dough, cook the *tortillas,* and serve members of the family, all without having to move around the kitchen.

347

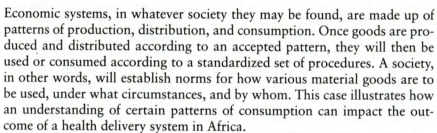

Thus, women who are used to doing all of the cooking from a seated position within their kitchens would have difficulty adjusting to a solar cooker, which must be attended to while standing and leaning over in the hot sun. Moreover, the parabolic reflector must be adjusted every fifteen minutes to compensate for the movement of the sun.

Owing to these cultural realities—which were revealed by direct participant-observation of an applied anthropologist—the decision was made not to mass-produce these solar cookers for local use, thereby avoiding a costly mistake. In all likelihood, the traditional patterns of food preparation were so well entrenched that local women would not have been willing to change them in exchange for a cooker that operated on a less expensive source of energy. Thus, in this situation the applied anthropologist played an important role as a marketing consultant.

♦ **A sensitivity to food consumption patterns in South Africa has a direct effect on the creation of a successful health delivery system.**

Economic systems, in whatever society they may be found, are made up of patterns of production, distribution, and consumption. Once goods are produced and distributed according to an accepted pattern, they will then be used or consumed according to a standardized set of procedures. A society, in other words, will establish norms for how various material goods are to be used, under what circumstances, and by whom. This case illustrates how an understanding of certain patterns of consumption can impact the outcome of a health delivery system in Africa.

During the 1940s the Polela Health Center served the medical needs of approximately 16,000 Zulu living in northern Natal Provence in South Africa. Health conditions among these people were exceedingly poor. Over 27 percent of Zulu infants didn't make it to their first birthday; various forms of malnutrition, particularly pellagra and kwashiorkor, were widespread; and people suffered from a rash of diseases, including typhoid, typhus, smallpox, tuberculosis, and venereal disease. One of the strategies adopted by the Polela Health Center for dealing with these poor health conditions was to reeducate people to eat more nutritional foods. In their efforts to initiate preventive health measures, the staff of the Polela Health Center found that some of the obstacles to change could be overcome with a little ingenuity, others could be circumvented, while some were insurmountable. In those situations where changes in dietary habits were possible, it was absolutely vital that the medical personnel understood the sociocultural system and how the local people utilized the resources at their disposal.

Perhaps the most serious nutritional problem facing the Zulu was the high incidence of kwashiorkor, a form of malnutrition caused by a lack of protein in the diet. Although the Zulus keep cattle, their overall supplies of milk, which might be used to offset the often deadly effects of kwashiorkor, are very limited. The relative scarcity of milk is further complicated by the deep-seated cultural belief that people are permitted to drink only the milk produced by the cows of their father's lineage.

While this dietary restriction applies to men, women, and children equally, the situation becomes particularly problematic for married women. Zulu society is patrilocal (that is, having a residence pattern in which a married couple lives with or near the husband's parents). When a woman marries, she moves away from her father's extended family and consequently no longer has access to the milk from that family's cows. The only way that a married woman could have access to milk is if her father presented her with a cow of her own when she married, but owing to the general poverty in the area, this would have been a very unlikely occurrence. Thus, milk as a source of protein was, for all practical purposes, unavailable to Zulu women.

Even though the reasons for this dietary restriction have long since been forgotten, the Zulu people had powerful feelings about maintaining it. Given such strong conviction, it would have served little purpose for the Polela Health Center staff to try to argue the Zulu out of their belief. This became a major problem facing the preventive health program, for it had severe health consequences for women in general but also—and even more importantly—for expectant and lactating mothers. Much to their credit, the Polela health team overcame the cultural obstacle to better nutrition for women by circumventing it. According to John Cassel:

Fortunately, it was possible to overcome this difficulty to a considerable extent by introducing powdered milk into the area. Even though people knew that this powder was in fact milk, it was not called milk in Zulu but was referred to as "powder" or "meal" and accepted by all families without protest. Even the most orthodox of husbands and mothers-in-law had no objection to their wives or daughters-in-law using this powder (1972:308).

Because the Polela health staff understood the essential features of Zulu culture, they were able to engage in some creative problem solving. All parties concerned were winners. The medical team was happy because it was able to improve the health of Zulu women. The Zulu themselves were pleased because they were healthier. And it was all accomplished without having to do battle with a part of Zulu traditional culture. Not all obstacles to initiating health programs are always resolved so easily. Nevertheless, this preventive health program would not have met with the success that it did without a thorough understanding and appreciation of traditional Zulu patterns of consumption and resource allocation.

◆ **A misinterpretation of the meaning of land tenure in traditional Kikuyu society by the British leads to decades of hostility and conflict.**

The history of Kenya for the first six decades of the twentieth century can best be characterized by increasing tensions between the British Colonial Office and Kenya's largest and most prominent ethnic group—the Kikuyu. The strained relations between the British government and the Kikuyu began with the alienation of Kikuyu land in the early 1900s and culminated in the Mau Mau Uprising of the 1950s. The tragedy of this long history of

◆　　◆　　◆　　◆　　◆

suffering and bitterness is that it was based on a British misinterpretation of the meaning of land in Kikuyu society. Applying their own Western notion of individual land ownership, the British colonial government misread the traditional Kikuyu system of land tenure.

Around the turn of the century, the British government undertook the building of the East African Railroad (from Mombasa to Lake Victoria) for the purpose of opening up the interior of Eastern Africa, stimulating legitimate commerce, thereby discouraging the last vestiges of the East African slave trade. The cost of constructing the railroad, however, was so high that there was a great need to develop the intervening territory (Kenya) so as to make the railroad pay for itself. As Sorrenson suggests: ". . . . a line with two ends and no middle—and thus no feeder traffic—can hardly pay" (1967:15). Since it was highly unlikely that the subsistence farmers in Kenya could produce marketable crops for transport to the coast, the most logical alternative for economic development, the government reasoned, was to encourage a European-based agricultural economy within the fertile Kenya highlands, much of which was located in Kikuyu country.

The fundamental issue that confronted the British Colonial Office in the early 1900s was to preserve Kikuyu land rights in the face of the pressing need for economic development. The government thought it was respecting native land rights by allocating only unused land to European immigrants. In practice, however, difficulties soon appeared arising from the government's misinterpretation of the Kikuyu land system. While it was true that the Kikuyu suffered a loss of population in the 1890s because of famine and a smallpox epidemic, these disasters caused government officials to overestimate their destructiveness and thus underestimate the existing Kikuyu population. It was convenient for the government—pressured by a small but vocal settler population—to assume that all land not under cultivation was unoccupied and thus available for alienation to European settlers. But in terms of the Kikuyu perception of the situation, this land, although temporarily unoccupied, was hardly ownerless. Rather, since the lineage (large extended family group) controlled land and its inheritance, the land reverted to the surviving members of the lineage.

The two laws passed in 1901 and 1902 enabling the government to alienate Kikuyu land remained the central source of conflict between the Kikuyu and the government throughout the colonial period. Both laws were predicated on the notion that the government could alienate any land that was not occupied or under cultivation. In effect, this was tantamount to acknowledging Kikuyu rights to land only if they were *using* it at the moment. According to these laws, as soon as the Kikuyu—who practiced shifting cultivation—moved to new plots, they forfeited their rights to their former holdings. It is true that the government did, in fact, compensate the Kikuyu for the land. However, the notion that there was such a thing as adequate compensation for the loss of lineage land illustrates how inadequately the government understood what land means to the Kikuyu. According to the Kikuyu perception, there can be no adequate compensation for a man evicted from the only spot on earth where he has the right to live.

The Kikuyu lineage was not merely a group of kin, but rather a corporate land-owning unit. Without lineage land, the lineage lost its sense of unity.

In other words, the land, which was the material symbol of lineage solidarity, was associated with an elaborate network of rights and obligations among kin. When a lineage lost control over its land, therefore, much more was at stake than the simple loss of a piece of property. Rather, it involved the suspension or alteration of an entire set of social relationships.

The history of Kikuyu land alienation during the early twentieth century provides us with an excellent example of how colonial governments can misunderstand the cultures of local people. The British officials viewed the land from their own Western perspective as simply an economic asset. If people were using the land, they reasoned, it was theirs; if they stopped using the land, it was up for grabs. The Kikuyu, on the other hand, saw the land as inalienable. Since they believed that the land was bequeathed to them by their ancestors, they assumed responsibility for keeping it safe and passing it on to their descendants. Had the British understood how the Kikuyu traditionally allocate their most valuable resource (i.e., land), much of the hostility arising from Kikuyu land alienation might have been avoided.

It is, of course, possible that the British Government was fully aware of the Kikuyu notion of land allocation but chose to ignore it because the political and economic stakes were so high. Nevertheless, a less cynical reading of history would suggest that the colonial officials failed to understand the meaning of land among the Kikuyu. If this was, in fact, the case then the British colonial government could have used the services of an applied anthropologist in the early 1900s.

# Kinship and Descent

Why have cultural anthropologists spent so much time studying kinship?

What are the various functions of descent groups?

What are the various ways by which cultures categorize kin?

It has been said on numerous occasions that humans are social animals. Even though other species display certain social features (such as baboons living in permanent troops), what sets humans apart from the rest of the animal world is the complexity of their social organization. People, to a much greater degree than any other species, live in groups. Individuals play specific social roles, have different statuses, and form patterned relationships with other group members.

Human social groups are formed on the basis of a number of factors, including occupation, kinship, social class, sex, age, ethnic affiliation, education, and religion. In most small-scale, nonindustrialized societies, social organization is based largely on kinship affiliation. That is, kinship is the basis for group membership, and most of an individual's social life is played out with other kin. By way of contrast, social relationships in industrialized societies are based on such other factors as profession, neighborhood, or common interests, and to a lesser degree on kinship. Although different societies give different weights to these different factors, kinship is without question the single most important factor contributing to social structure. In other words, how people interact with one another in all societies is influenced by how they are related to one another. Even in the United States, where kinship ties are sometimes overshadowed by nonkinship ties, relations between kin are usually more long-term, intense, and emotionally laden than are relations with nonkin.

## ◆ ◆ ◆ Kinship Defined

The term *kinship* refers to those relationships—found in all societies—that are based on blood or, somewhat more loosely, on marriage. Those people we are related to through birth or blood are referred to as **consanguineal relatives;** those people we are related to through marriage are **affinal relatives.** Each society has a well-understood system of defining relationships between these different types of relatives. Every society, in other words, defines the nature of kinship interaction by determining which kin are more socially important than others, the terms used to classify various types of kin, and the expected forms of behavior between them. Although the systems vary significantly from one society to another, one thing is certain—relationships based on blood and marriage are culturally recognized by all societies.

Even though kinship terms are used between people who are related by either blood or marriage, in some situations, kinship terms are applied to nonkin. This usage, known as *fictive kinship,* can take a number of different forms. For example, the process of adoption creates a set of relationships between the adoptive parents and child that have all of the expectations of those relationships that are in fact based on either descent or marriage. Not infrequently, close friends of the family will be referred to as "aunt" or "uncle," even though

Cultural anthropologists generally have studied societies in which kinship activities play a very important role. This Pakistani family includes three generations.

they have no biological or marital relationship. College fraternities and sororities and some churches use kinship terminology (i.e., brothers and sisters) to refer to their members. Members of the Black community in the United States will often refer to each other as "brother" or "sister." And, of course, the godparent-godchild relationship, which carries with it all sorts of kinship obligations, is frequently played out with non-kin. These examples should remind us that it is possible to have kinshiplike relationships (complete with well-understood rights and obligations) without having an actual biological or marital connection.

For much of the time that cultural anthropologists have been conducting fieldwork, they appear to have spent a disproportionate amount of time and energy describing kinship systems. That is, they have devoted more time to studying kinship systems than any other single topic; and they have spent more time than other social scientists have on kinship systems. The reason that cultural anthropologists spend so much time on what Malinowski called kinship algebra is related to the type of societies that they have studied traditionally. Cultural anthropology, while interested in all societies of the world, has in actual practice tended to concentrate on those small-scale societies in which kinship relations tend to be all-encompassing. In highly urbanized and technological societies, such as those studied most often by sociologists, relatively few social relationships are based on kinship. In the United States, for example, social relationships that are essentially political, economic, recreational, or religious are usually not played out with our kin. But in those societies that are small-scale, non-Western, preliterate, and technologically simple, kinship is at the heart of the social structure. Whom a person marries, where he or she lives, and from whom a person inherits property and status all depend on the person's place within the kinship system. In such societies, it might not be an exaggeration to say that kinship relations are tantamount to social relations.

## Cultural Rules Regarding Kinship

To be certain, all kinship systems are founded on biological connections. Family and kinship groups would not exist if men and women did not mate and have children. However, kinship systems involve more than biological relationships. Rather, each society classifies its kin according to a set of *cultural* rules that may or may not account for biological factors. For example, according to our own kinship system, we refer to both our father's brother and our father's sister's husband as uncles even though the former is a blood relative and the latter is not. In many societies, a man will refer to his father's brother and his mother's brother (both blood relatives) by different terms and will be expected to behave toward the two very differently. This distinction between the biological and cultural dimensions of kinship can be seen in U.S. society when we refer to our adopted children as sons and daughters (with all of the rights and obligations that biological children have), even though they have no genetic connection. Thus, as we can see, the way that different societies sort and categorize kinship relationships is as much a matter of culture as it is a matter of biology.

## Functions of Kinship Systems

All kinship systems, wherever they may be found, serve two important functions for the well-being of the total society. First, by its **vertical function**, a kinship system provides social continuity by binding together a number of successive generations. Kinship systems are most directly involved with the passing of education, tradition, property, and political office from one generation to the next. Second, kinship systems tend to solidify or tie together a society horizontally (that is, across a single generation) through the process of marriage. Since kinship systems define the local kin groups outside of which people must take a spouse, it forces groups to enter into alliances with other kinship groups, thereby creating solidarity within a much larger society. This **horizontal function** of kinship was perhaps best illustrated by the case of the late King Sobhuza II of Swaziland who solidified his entire kingdom by taking a wife from virtually every nonroyal lineage in the country.

## Using Kinship Diagrams

While kinship systems are found in every society, how any particular society defines the relationships between kin varies widely from one group to another. People in different societies with the same biological connection may be defined differently, labeled differently, and expected to behave toward each other differently. And, as we shall see, there is a vast array of possibilities from

One function of kinship systems is to bind together a number of successive generations, as with this child, mother, and grandmother in modern-day Japan.

which societies can choose. Before trying to sort out the complexities of different kinship systems, it would be helpful to introduce a form of shorthand used by cultural anthropologists in analyzing kinship systems.

As a way of simplifying kinship systems, anthropologists use kinship diagrams rather than relying on verbal explanations alone. In this standardized notational system, all kinship diagrams are viewed from a central point of reference (called **EGO**), that person from whose point of view we are tracing the relationship. All kinship diagrams use the symbols found in Exhibit 17-1.

Starting with our point of reference (EGO) and using the five symbols, it is possible to construct a hypothetical family diagram as in Exhibit 17-2 on page 357.

If we start with EGO (■) as our point of reference, we can refer to all of the people in the diagram (using our own U.S. terminology) in the following way:

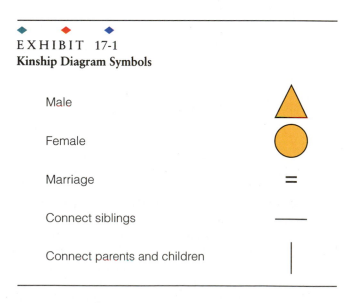

EXHIBIT 17-1
**Kinship Diagram Symbols**

| | |
|---|---|
| Male | △ |
| Female | ○ |
| Marriage | = |
| Connect siblings | —— |
| Connect parents and children | │ |

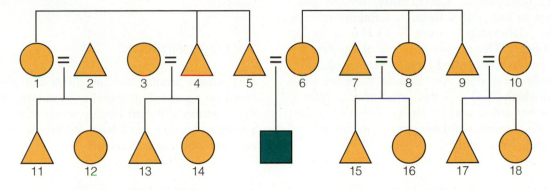

1. Father's sister (aunt)
2. Father's sister's husband (uncle)
3. Father's brother's wife (aunt)
4. Father's brother (uncle)
5. Father
6. Mother
7. Mother's sister's husband (uncle)
8. Mother's sister (aunt)
9. Mother's brother (uncle)
10. Mother's brother's wife (aunt)
11. Father's sister's son (cousin)
12. Father's sister's daughter (cousin)
13. Father's brother's son (cousin)
14. Father's brother's daughter (cousin)
15. Mother's sister's son (cousin)
16. Mother's sister's daughter (cousin)
17. Mother's brother's son (cousin)
18. Mother's brother's daughter (cousin)

◆      ◆      ◆

# Principles of Kinship Classification

There are no kinship systems in the world that use a different term of reference for every single relative. Instead, all kinship systems group relatives into certain categories, refer to them by the same term, and expect to behave toward them in a similar fashion. How a particular society categorizes relatives depends on which principles of classification are used. Various kinship systems use a number of principles to group certain relatives together while separating others, as discussed in the following subsections.

## GENERATION

In some kinship systems—our own being a good example—distinctions between kin depend upon generation. Mothers, fathers, aunts, and uncles are always found in the generation immediately above EGO; sons, daughters, nieces, and nephews are always one generation below EGO; grandmothers and grandfathers are always two generations above EGO, and so forth. Although this seems like the natural thing to do, there are kinship systems in some societies that do not confine a kin category to a single generation. It is possible, for example, to find the same kin category in three or four different generations.

## SEX OR GENDER

Some kinship systems group certain kin together because of common gender. In our English system, such kin categories as brother, father, uncle, nephew, son, and grandfather are always males, while sister, mother, aunt, niece, daughter, and grandmother are always females. The one area where we do not distinguish on the basis of gender is at the cousin level (but, then, the consistent application of a particular principle is not required). Even though this principle of gender operates at most levels of our own system, it is hardly universally applicable. There are, in other words, societies that allow for the possibility of both males and females occupying a single kin category.

## LINEALITY VS. COLLATERALITY

**Lineality** refers to kin related in a single line, such as son, father, grandfather. **Collaterality,** on the other hand, refers to kin related through a linking relative, such as the relationship between EGO and his or her parents' siblings. Whereas the principle of lineality distinguishes between father and father's brother, the principle of collaterality does not. That is, there are some societies in which EGO uses the term *father* to refer to both his or her father and his or her father's brother; similarly, EGO's mother and her sisters may be referred to by the single term *mother*.

## CONSANGUINEAL VS. AFFINAL KIN

Some societies make distinctions in kinship categories based on whether people are related by blood or through marriage. Our own kinship system uses this principle of classification at some levels but not at others. To illustrate, we distinguish between sons and sons-in-law and between sisters and sisters-in-law. But in EGO's parents' generation, we fail to distinguish between mother's brother (a blood relative) and mother's sister's husband (an affinal relative), both of whom we call uncle.

## RELATIVE AGE

In certain kinship systems relative age serves as a criterion for separating different types of relatives. In such societies, a man will have one kinship term for younger brother and another one for older brother. These different terms based on relative age carry with them different behavioral expectations, for frequently a man will be expected to act toward his older brother with deference and respect while behaving toward his younger brother in a much more informal way.

## SEX OF THE CONNECTING RELATIVE

While not a principle used in our own kinship system, some societies distinguish between different categories of kin based on the sex of the connecting (or intervening) relative. To illustrate, a mother's brother's daughter and a mother's sister's daughter (which in our system are called cousins) will be given two different kinship terms. One will be a cross cousin, while the other is called a parallel cousin. According to this principle, these two first cousins are considered to be different by virtue of the sex of their parents (mother's brother vs. mother's sister).

## SOCIAL CONDITION

Distinctions among kin categories can also be made based on a person's general life condition. According to this criterion, different kinship terms would be used for a married brother and a bachelor brother or for a living aunt and one that is deceased.

## SIDE OF THE FAMILY

A final principle has to do with using different kin terms for EGO's mother's side of the family and EGO's father's side of the family. The kinship system used in the United States makes no such distinction, for we have aunts, uncles, cousins, and grandparents on both sides of our family. In those societies that use this principle of classification, a mother's brother would be given a different term of reference than a father's brother.

# The Formation of Descent Groups

As we have seen, kinship systems play an important role in helping people sort out how they should behave toward various relatives. In anthropological terms, **kinship systems** refer to all of the blood and marriage relationships that help people distinguish between different categories of kin, create rights and obligations between kin, and serve as the basis for the formation of certain types of kin groups.

Anthropologists also use the term **descent**, a more narrowly defined term, to refer to the rules a culture uses to establish affiliations with one's parents. These rules of descent often provide the basis for the formation of social groups. These social groups, which are called descent groups, are collections of relatives (usually lineal descendants of a common ancestor) who live out their lives in close proximity to one another.

In those societies that have descent groups, the group plays a central role in the lives of its members. Descent group members have a strong sense of identity, frequently share communally held property, provide mutual economic assistance to one another, and engage in mutual civic and religious ceremonies. In addition, descent groups function in other ways as well by serving as a mechanism for inheriting property and political office, controlling behavior, regulating marriages, and structuring primary political units.

Rules of descent can be divided into two distinct types. The first is **unilineal descent,** whereby people trace their ancestry through either the mother's line or the father's line, but not both. Those unilineal groups that trace their descent through the mother's line are called **matrilineal descent** groups, while those tracing their descent through the father's line are called **patrilineal descent** groups. The second type of descent is known as **cognatic** (or nonunilineal) **descent,** which includes **double descent, ambilineal descent,** and **bilateral descent.** Since descent is traced in the United States according to the bilateral principle, many Westerners have difficulty understanding unilineal kinship systems.

## UNILINEAL DESCENT GROUPS

Approximately 60 percent of all kinship systems found in the world are based on the unilineal principle. Unilineal descent groups are particularly adaptive because they are clear-cut and unambiguous social units. Since a person becomes a member of a unilineal descent group by birth, there is absolutely no confusion as to who is a group member and who is not. For those societies that rely on kinship groups to perform most of their social functions (e.g., marriage, dispute settlement, religious ceremonies), unilineal descent groups, with their clear-cut membership, can provide a social organization with unambiguous roles and statuses. By knowing without question to which group one belongs, a person is clear about his or her rights of inheritance, prestige, and social roles.

**Patrilineal Descent Groups.** Of the two types of unilineal descent groups, patrilineal descent is by far the most common. Patrilineal descent groups are found on all of the major continents and in a wide range of societies, including certain hunting-and-gathering American Indian groups, some East African farmers and pastoralists, the Nagas of India, the Kapauku Papuans of the New Guinea Highlands, and the traditional Chinese. In societies with patrilineal descent groups, a person is

The Kikuyu of Kenya have patrilineal descent groups.

related through the father, father's father, and so forth. In other words, a man, his own children, his brother's children (but not his sister's children), his son's children (but not his daughter's children) are all members of the same descent group. Females must marry outside their own patrilineages and the children a woman bears belong to the husband's lineage rather than her own. The principle of patrilineal descent is illustrated in Exhibit 17-3.

**Matrilineal Descent Groups.** In a matrilineal kinship system, a person belongs to the mother's group. A matrilineal descent group comprises a woman, her siblings, her own children, her sisters' children, and her daughters' children. Matrilineal descent groups make up about 15 percent of the unilineal descent groups found among contemporary societies. They are found in a number of areas of the world, including some Native Americans (e.g., Navajo, Cherokee, and Iroquois), the Truk and Trobrianders of the Pacific, and the Bemba, Ashanti, and Yao of Africa.

It is important not to confuse matrilineal descent with matriarchy, whereby women have greater authority and decision-making prerogatives than men. In most cases where matrilineal descent is practiced, men retain the lion's share of power and authority. Political offices are held by men, and it is men, not women, that control property. In matrilineal societies, both property and political office pass from one man to another but *through* a woman. To illustrate, whereas in a patrilineal society a man passes his property and hereditary political office to his own son, in a matrilineal society property and office would pass from a man to his sister's son. In fact, the most important male relationship a man has in a matrilineal society is with his sister's son (or mother's brother). The principle of matrilineal descent is illustrated in Exhibit 17-4 on page 361.

**Types of Unilineal Descent Groups.** Cultural anthropologists recognize different types of kinship groups that are based on the unilineal principle. Categorized according to increasing levels of inclusiveness, the four major types of descent groups are (1) **lineages**, (2) **clans**,

EXHIBIT 17-3
**Patrilineal Descent**

In a patrilineal descent system, a person is connected to relatives of both sexes related through men only. Sons and

daughters belong to their father's descent group, as do the father's sons' children but not the father's daughters' children.

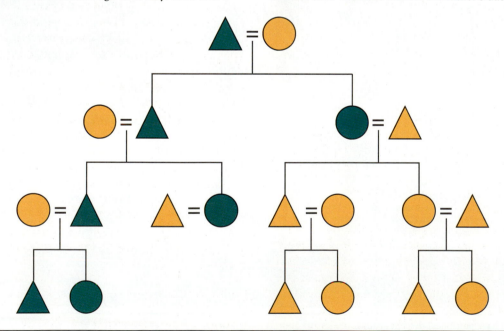

CHAPTER 17    ◆    KINSHIP AND DESCENT

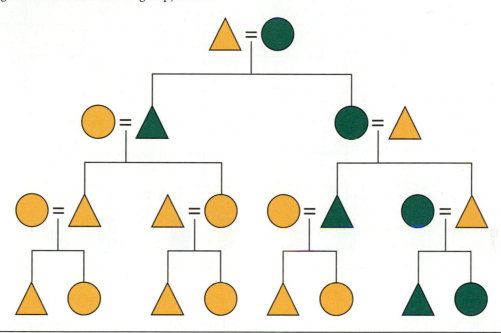

In a matrilineal descent system, a person is connected to kin of both sexes related through women only. Sons and daughters belong to their mother's descent group, as do the mother's daughters' children but not the mother's sons' children.

(3) **phratries,** and (4) **moieties.** These four types of unilineal descent groups can form an organizational hierarchy, with moieties comprising two or more phratries, phratries comprising two or more clans, and clans comprising two or more lineages. All societies may not have all four types of groups, but some can.

*Lineages.* A lineage is a unilineal descent group of up to approximately ten generations in depth, the members of which can trace their ancestry back (step-by-step) to a common founder. When descent is traced through the male line the groups are known as patrilineages; when traced through the female line, they are known as matrilineages.

Sometimes lineages undergo a process known as segmentation, a subdivision into smaller units depending on the social situation. This process can occur when antagonisms arise among lineage members. For example, a lineage can be divided into two secondary lineages, divided again into tertiary lineages, and further subdivided into minimal lineages. These minimal lineages

may be only three or four generations in depth. Such a segmentation process is diagrammed in Exhibit 17-5.

At certain times and under certain social situations, different segments will be competing with one another while at other times they will be allied. In the preceding diagram, since all of the minimal lineages are autonomous, normally (a) and (b) will not have a lot to do with each other. But, in the event that (d) should become involved in a dispute with (b), then (a) is likely to ally itself with (b) because of their common ancestry to (1). If, however, (d) was to have a conflict with (f), it is likely that (a), (b), and (c) would all come to the defense of (d), owing to their common genealogical connection to (A). It is also likely that (a) through (h) will all come together on certain ritual occasions to acknowledge their common relationship to (I). Thus, sublineages will be allied with one another at some times and in conflict with one another at other times.

*Clans.* Another type of unilineal descent group is the clan, a group of kin usually comprising ten or more generations whose members believe they are all related to a

EXHIBIT 17-5
**Lineage Segmentation**

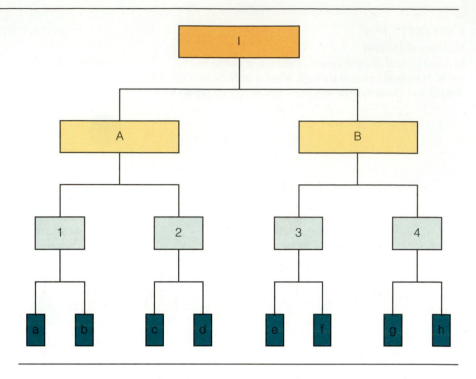

common ancestor but are unable to trace that genealogical connection step-by-step. When clans and lineages are found together, the clan will most likely be made up of a number of different lineages. Depending on which line is emphasized, there can be both matriclans or patriclans.

In some societies, clans can be close-knit groups, very much like lineages, in which members have a high degree of interaction with one another. It is more usually the case, however, that clan members are widely dispersed geographically and rarely get together for clanwide activities. Unlike lineages, which serve as corporate, functioning *groups*, clans tend to be larger and more loosely structured *categories* with which people identify. Frequently, clans are associated with animals or plants (i.e., totems) that provide a focal point for group identity.

*Phratries.* At the next order of magnitude are phratries, unilineal descent groups composed of two or more clans. In those societies in which phratries are found, the actual connection between the various clans usually are not recognized. Generally, phratries are rare and, when they are found, do not serve important social functions. Although it is true that in some cases, such as traditional Aztec society, phratries were significant social, political,

and religious groups, this is the exception rather than the rule.

*Moieties.* In some cases, societies are divided into two unilineal descent groups called moieties (a term derived from the French word for "half"). In those societies that have only two clans, the clans and the moieties are identical to each other. But when moieties are made up of more than two clans (as is usually the case), the moiety is the larger unit.

Moieties are an excellent example of social reciprocity. If, for example, a society is made up of these two large exogamous groups called moieties, each moiety provides the other group with its marriage partners. Moreover, moiety affiliation has been used for seating arrangements at ceremonial occasions or for sports competitions, or, as in the case of the Seneca Indians, one moiety performs mourning rituals for the other. Thus, although moieties can play important roles in the society, they are not a part of the political structure in the same way that lineages or clans are.

**The Corporate Nature of Lineages.** One feature of all unilineal descent groups—whether we are talking about lineages, clans, phratries, or moieties—is that they clearly define who is a member and who is not.

These collective kinship groups also last over time. Even though individual members are born into the group and leave it by dying, the unilineal descent group continues on. Owing to both their unambiguous membership and continuity, unilineal descent groups are good examples of corporate entities, which play a powerful role in the lives of the individual members.

We can cite a number of indicators of the corporate nature of unilineal descent groups. First, such unilineal groups as lineages frequently shape a person's identity in some significant ways. When asked by a stranger the simple question, "Who are you?," it is likely that some lineage members will respond, "I am a member of such and such a lineage," rather than "I am John Smith." Lineage members, in other words, see themselves first and foremost as members of the kinship group rather than as individuals. Second, unilineal descent groups regulate marriage to the extent that relatively large numbers of kin on both the bride's and the groom's side of the family must give their approval before the marriage can take place. Third, property (such as land and livestock), rather than being controlled by the individual, is usually regulated by the descent group. The group allocates to individual members specific pieces of property to use, but only because they are kin members in good standing. Fourth, even the criminal justice system in unilineal societies has a strong corporate focus. If, for example, a member of lineage (a) assaults a member of lineage (q), the entire lineage of (q) would seek compensation from or revenge upon the lineage of (a). The assaulter would not be held solely accountable for his or her individual actions, but rather the group (i.e., lineage or clan) would in the final analysis be culpable.

The corporate nature of unilineal descent groups is no better illustrated than in the strong bonds of obligations that exist between members. The kinship group provides a firm base of security and protection for its individual members. If crops fail, an individual can always turn to his or her unilineal descent group members for assistance; in the event of any threat from outsiders, a person should expect support and protection from members of his or her own descent group. The strength of these bonds of obligation depends on the closeness of the ties. Mutual assistance is likely to be taken very seriously among lineage members, less so among clan members, and very little at the phratry or moiety level.

## COGNATIC (NONUNILINEAL) DESCENT GROUPS

Approximately 40 percent of the world's societies have kinship systems that are not based on the unilineal principle. Cultural anthropologists refer to these nonunilineal kin groups as cognatic and classify them into three basic types: double descent, ambilineal descent, and bilateral descent.

**Double Descent.** Some societies practice a form of double descent (or double unilineal descent), whereby kinship is traced both matrilineally and patrilineally. In such societies, an individual belongs to both the mother's and the father's lineage. Descent under such a system is matrilineal for some purposes and patrilineal for others. For example, moveable property such as small livestock or agricultural produce may be inherited from the mother's side of the family, while immoveable property such as land may be inherited from the father's side.

Societies that practice double descent are relatively rare, with about 5 percent of the world's cultures practicing it. One such culture, the Yako of Nigeria, has been particularly well described by Daryll Forde (1967). For the Yako, both matrilineality and patrilineality are important principles of kinship. Among the traditional Yako, cooperation in everyday domestic life is strongest among members of the patriclan for the obvious reason that they live with or near one another. Patrilineal descent is also the line followed for the inheritance of such resources as land, forest products, and trees as well as the inheritance of membership into men's associations.

The mother's line is also important, even though matriclan members do not live in close proximity to one another. Since the Yako believe strongly that all life stems from the mother, the children of a mother are honor bound to help each other and maintain peaceful and harmonious relations between themselves. Certain moveable property, such as livestock and currency, passes from one matriclan member to another. Moreover, matriclans supervise funeral ceremonies and are responsible for providing part of the bridewealth payment. Thus, as the Yako well illustrate, in a double descent system the patrilineal groups and the matrilineal groups are active in different spheres of the culture.

**Ambilineal Descent.** In societies that practice ambilineal descent, parents have a choice of affiliating their children with either kinship group. Unlike unilineal systems, which restrict one's membership to either the mother's *or* the father's group, ambilineal systems are considerably more flexible because they allow for individual choice concerning group affiliation. The range of choice varies from one ambilineal system to another. In some cases, the parents are expected to choose the group with which their children eventually affiliate.

## CROSS-CULTURAL MISCUE

Understanding kinship systems in other cultures can have very practical repercussions on how effectively we do our jobs. Clyde Kluckhohn, who had spent much of his anthropological career studying the Navajo Indians of the American Southwest, tells of an intelligent and successful Chicago public schoolteacher he knew who was teaching in a Navajo reservation school. In answer to his question concerning how her Navajo students compared to her Chicago students, she responded that she was puzzled by the apparent bizarre behavior of several of her Navajo students. She told Kluckhohn:

The other night we had a dance in the high school. I saw a boy who is one of the best students in my English class standing off by himself. So I took him over to a pretty girl and told them to dance. But they just stood there with their heads down. They wouldn't even say anything (1949:19–20).

What appeared to the teacher to be strange behavior can make sense only if we first understand several features of Navajo culture—features that are radically different from the culture of a white middle-class schoolteacher from Chicago. First, the type of dancing that the teacher expected of these two Navajo teenagers is considered quite promiscuous by Navajo standards. Whereas middle-class North Americans attach little, if any, sexual meaning to the type of bodily contact involved in ballroom dancing, the Navajo think it highly inappropriate for adults of the opposite sex to move around the dance floor in a semi-embrace with the fronts of their bodies touching. Second, according to the Navajo kinship system, which is made up of exogamous clans, the incest taboo applies as strictly to all clan members as it does to members of one's own nuclear family. Unfortunately—and quite unbeknownst to the teacher—the Navajo boy and girl the teacher had chosen were members of the same clan and, as such, were strictly forbidden from having that type of public display of intimacy implied in Western-style dancing. As Kluckhohn suggested, the humiliation that these two Navajo youngsters must have experienced would have been roughly equivalent to the embarrassment the teacher would have felt had the manager of a crowded hotel asked her to share a bed with her adult brother. Here, then, was a needlessly tragic miscommunication which was the direct result of the teacher's not understanding the nature of the marriage and family system found among her culturally different students.

---

Other systems allow the individual to move continuously through life from one group to another, provided he or she affiliates with one descent group at a time. There are still other systems, which permit the overlapping of membership with a number of groups at the same time. This flexibility does not come without a price, however. As a general rule, the greater the flexibility concerning membership, the weaker the group's loyalties, cohesiveness, and impact on the lives of its members.

**Bilateral Descent.** In those societies that practice bilateral descent, such as our own, a person is related equally to both the mother's and the father's side of the family.

A bilateral system tends to be symmetrical to the extent that what happens on one side of the kinship diagram also happens on the other side. In other words, the grandparents, aunts, uncles, and cousins are treated equally on both sides of the family. In unilineal systems, a person is affiliated with a large number of kin over many generations but only on one side of the family. By way of contrast, bilateral systems create links from both sides of the family but usually include only relatively close kin from a small number of generations.

The kinship group recognized in a bilateral system is known as the **kindred**—a group of closely related relatives connected through both parents. Unlike unilineal descent, which forms discrete, mutually exclusive groups, bilateral systems give rise to the situation in which no two individuals (except siblings) have the same kindred. The kindred is not a group at all but rather should be thought of as a network of relatives.

Unlike the lineage or the clan, the kindred has no founding ancestor, precise boundaries, or continuity over time. In short, since kindreds are not corporate groups, they cannot perform the same types of functions—such as joint ownership of property, common economic activities, regulation of marriage, or mutual assistance—as unilineal groups. To be certain, an individual can mobilize some members of his or her kindred to perform some of these tasks, but the kindred does not function as a corporate entity. This type of loosely structured network of relatives works particularly well in a society like our own which highly values personal independence and geographic mobility.

## Six Basic Systems of Classification

Every society has a coherent system of labeling various types of kin. In any given system, certain categories of kin are grouped together under a single category, while others are separated into distinct categories. In our own society, we group together under the general heading of "aunt" our mother's sisters, father's sisters, mother's brothers' wives, and father's brothers' wives. Similarly, we lump together under the heading of "uncle" our father's brothers, mother's brothers, father's sisters' husbands and mother's sisters' husbands. By way of contrast, other societies might have separate terms for all eight of these categories of kin. Whatever system of classification is used, however, cultural anthropologists have found them to be both internally logical and consistently applied. Even though individual societies may

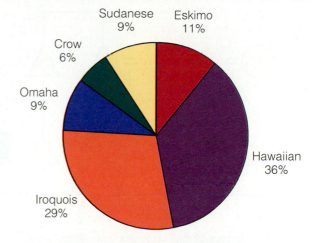

EXHIBIT 17-6
**World Distribution of Kinship Systems**

Murdock, George P., "Ethnographic Atlas: A Summary." *Ethnology* 6(2) (April 1967): 109–236.

have their own variations, six basic classification systems have been identified: Eskimo, Hawaiian, Iroquois, Omaha, Crow, and Sudanese (see Exhibit 17-6).

### ESKIMO SYSTEM

Found in approximately one-tenth of the world's societies, the **Eskimo system** of kinship classification (Exhibit 17-7) is associated with bilateral descent. The major feature of this system is that it emphasizes the nuclear family by using separate terms (e.g., mother, father, sister, brother) that are not used outside the nuclear family. Beyond the nuclear family, many other relatives (such as aunts, uncles, and cousins) are lumped together. This emphasis on the nuclear family is related to the fact that societies using the Eskimo system lack large descent groups such as lineages and clans. Moreover, the Eskimo system is most likely to be found in those societies (such as U.S. society and certain hunting-and-gathering societies) in which economic conditions favor a relatively independent nuclear family.

### HAWAIIAN SYSTEM

Found in approximately a third of the societies in the world, the **Hawaiian system** (Exhibit 17-8) uses a single

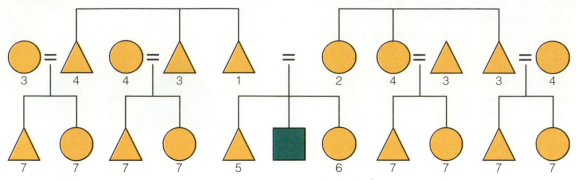

term for all relatives of the same sex and generation. To illustrate, a person's mother, mother's sister, and father's sister are all referred to by the single term *mother*. In EGO's own generation, the only distinction is one based on sex, so that male cousins are equated with brothers and female cousins are equated with sisters. The Hawaiian system, which uses the least number of terms, is frequently associated with ambilineal descent, which permits a person to affiliate with either the mother's or the father's kin. The Hawaiian system is found in those societies that submerge the nuclear family into a larger kin group to the extent that nuclear family members are roughly equivalent in importance to more distant kin.

## IROQUOIS SYSTEM

In the **Iroquois system** (Exhibit 17-9), EGO's father and father's brother are called by the same term, while EGO's father's sister is referred to by a different term. Likewise, EGO's mother and mother's sister are lumped together under one term, while a different term is used for EGO's mother's brother. Thus, a basic distinction of classification is made between the sex of one's parents' siblings (i.e., mother's brothers and sisters and father's brothers and sisters). At EGO's own generation, EGO's own siblings are given the same term as the parallel cousins (children of one's mother's sister or father's brother), while different terms are used for cross cousins (children of one's mother's brother or father's sister). Thus, the terminological distinction made between cross and parallel cousins is logical, given the distinction made between the siblings of EGO's parents. The Iroquois system emphasizes the importance of unilineal

descent groups by distinguishing between members of one's own lineage and those belonging to other lineages.

## OMAHA SYSTEM

Whereas the Iroquois system reflects the importance of unilineal descent groups, the **Omaha system** (Exhibit 17-10) is more specific in that it emphasizes patrilineal descent. Under this system, EGO's father and father's brother are referred to by the same term, and EGO's mother and mother's sister are also referred to by the same term. Equivalent terms are used for both parallel cousins and siblings, but separate terms are used for cross cousins. There is internal consistency in this pattern, because if EGO refers to some men and women as "father" and "mother," it follows logically that EGO should also refer to their children as "brothers" and "sisters."

On the mother's side of the family, there is a merging of generations. In other words, similar terms will be used for people in different generations. Since our own Eskimo system always uses separate terms for people in different generations, the type of generation merging found in the Omaha system seems somewhat strange to many Westerners. To illustrate this merging of generations, all men irrespective of age or generation who are part of EGO's mother's patrilineage will be called mother's brother. This can be seen in the following diagram with the cases of EGO's mother's brother (4) and EGO's mother's brother's son (4). In addition, similar kinship terms (2) are used for EGO's mother, mother's sister, and mother's brother's daughter.

EXHIBIT 17-8
**Hawaiian Kinship System**

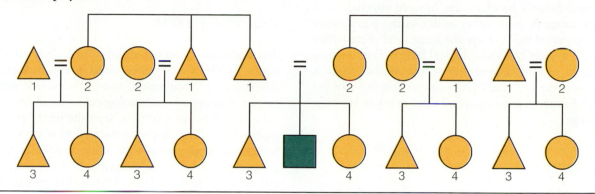

EXHIBIT 17-9
**Iroquois Kinship System**

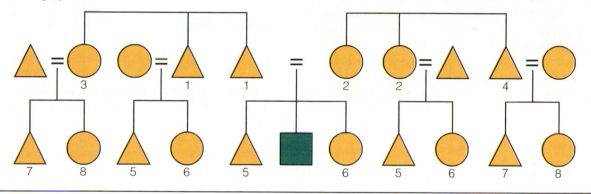

EXHIBIT 17-10
**Omaha Kinship System**

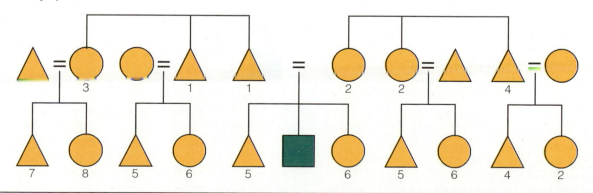

That merging of generations does not occur on EGO's father's side of the family is a reflection of the greater importance of the father's patrilineage. That is, EGO's father and father's brothers are lumped together as a *separate* category from other males in the patrilineage because paternal uncles have the same level of authority over EGO as does EGO's biological father. This lumping together of several generations on the mother's side is indicative of the fact that EGO's connection to his or her mother's lineage is less important than to his or her father's lineage.

## CROW SYSTEM

By concentrating on matrilineal rather than patrilineal descent, the **Crow system** of kinship classification (Exhibit 17-11) is the mirror image of the Omaha system. The Crow and Omaha systems are similar in that both use similar terms for (a) EGO's father and father's brother, (b) EGO's mother and mother's sister, and (c) EGO's sibings and parallel cousins. But owing to its less important nature, the father's side of the family merges generations. That is, all males in the father's line, irrespective of generation, are combined under a single term (1), as are all women in that line (3). However, on EGO's mother's side of the family, which is the

important descent group, generational distinctions are recognized.

## SUDANESE SYSTEM

The **Sudanese system** (Exhibit 17-12), named after the region in Africa where it is found, is the most extremely descriptive (particularistic) system because it makes the largest number of terminological distinctions. For instance, under such a system, separate terms are used for mother's brother, mother's sister, father's brother, and father's sister as well as their male and female children. As seen in the following diagram, EGO has eight different types of first cousins. This highly precise system, generally associated with patrilineal descent, is found in some societies that have considerable differences in wealth, occupation, and social status. A possible explanation of this is that the Sudanese system permits the recognition of socioeconomic differences.

## ◆ Summary

1. Although kinship relations are more important in some societies than others, kinship for all societies is the single most important aspect of social structure. Kinship

EXHIBIT 17-11
**Crow Kinship System**

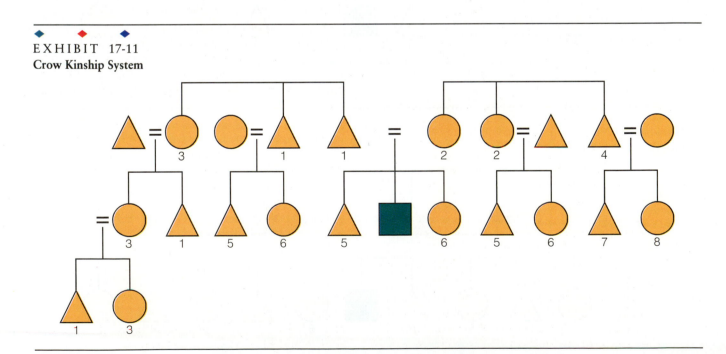

**EXHIBIT** 17-12
**Sudanese Kinship System**

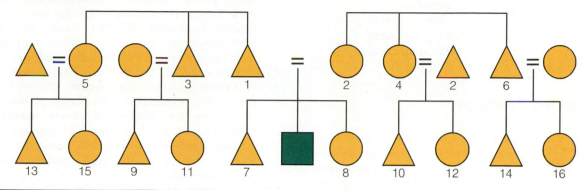

is based on both consanguineal (blood) relationships and affinal (marriage) relationships. Most societies recognize some type of fictive kinship, whereby kinship terms and obligations are applied to nonkin.

2. Kinship has both a biological and a cultural dimension. This accounts for the fact that some categories of relatives include some people that have biological connections and others that do not.

3. A fundamental feature of all kinship systems is that they group relatives into certain categories, refer to them by the same name, and expect to behave toward them in similar ways. How a particular culture categorizes its relatives varies according to different principles of classification. These principles are based on such criteria as generation, gender, lineality, consanguineality, relative age, sex of the connecting relative, social condition, and side of the family.

4. Many societies have sets of rules, called rules of descent, which affiliate people with different sets of kin. Patrilineal descent affiliates a person with the kin group of the father; matrilineal descent affiliates a person with the kin group of the mother; and ambilineal descent permits an individual to affiliate with either the mother's or the father's kin group.

5. Patrilineal descent groups, more common than matrilineal, are found in most areas of the world. A man's children, in a patrilineal system, belong to his lineage, as do the children of his son, but not the children of his daughter. Women marry outside their own lineage.

6. In matrilineal systems, a woman's children are affiliated with her lineage and not her husband's. Since the mother's brother is the social father of the woman's children, the relations between husband and wife in a matrilineal system tend to be more fragile than in patrilineal societies.

7. In those societies that trace their descent unilineally (through a single line), people recognize that they belong to a particular unilineal descent group or series of groups. These different levels of kinship organization include lineages (a set of kin who can trace their ancestry back through known links), clans (a unilineal group claiming descent but unable to trace all of the genealogical links), phratries (groups of related clans), and moieties (two halves of a society related by descent).

8. Bilateral descent, found predominantly among foraging and industrialized societies, traces one's important relatives on both the mother's and the father's side of the family. Bilateral systems, which are symmetrical, result in the formation of kindreds, which are more like loose kinship networks than permanent corporate functioning groups.

9. There are six primary types of kinship systems based on how the society distinguishes different categories of relatives: Eskimo, Hawaiian, Iroquois, Omaha, Crow, and Sudanese.

## ◆ Key Terms

| | |
|---|---|
| affinal relatives | Crow system |
| ambilineal descent | descent |
| bilateral descent | double descent |
| clan | EGO |
| cognatic descent | Eskimo system |
| collaterality | fictive kinship |
| consanguineal relatives | Hawaiian system |

horizontal function of
  kinship
Iroquois system
kindred
kinship system
lineage
lineality
matrilineal descent

moieties
Omaha system
patrilineal descent
phratries
Sudanese system
unilineal descent
vertical function of
  kinship

# ◆ Suggested Readings

Fox, Robin. *Kinship and Marriage*. Baltimore: Penguin Books, 1967. An excellent introduction to a broad and complex field of cultural anthropology written for serious students and laypersons alike. Fox not only brings together a number of different theories to explain the workings of different types of systems but also suggests some interesting theories of his own on the question of incest.

Keesing, Roger M. *Kin Groups and Social Structure*. New York: Holt, Rinehart & Winston, 1975. A discussion of the theories of kinship suitable for advanced students of social structure.

Murdock, George P. *Social Structure*. New York: Macmillan, 1949. A classic cross-cultural study of variations in such aspects of social structure as family, marriage, the incest taboo, and the regulation of sexual behavior.

Pasternak, Burton. *Introduction to Kinship and Social Organization*. Englewood Cliffs, N.J.: Prentice-Hall, 1976. A brief introduction to the cross-cultural study of family and kinship written for the beginning student.

Radcliffe-Brown, A. R., and D. Forde (Eds.). *African Systems of Kinship and Marriage*. London: Oxford University Press, 1950. A collection of nine essays by British social anthropologists on kinship and marriage systems in sub-Saharan Africa. Radcliffe-Brown's 85-page introduction, although somewhat dated, remains one of the best summaries of the literature on kinship and marriage in the non-Western world.

Schusky, Ernest L. *Manual for Kinship Analysis*. New York: Holt, Rinehart & Winston, 1965. A short text designed to give beginning anthropology students a clear statement of some of the essential features of kinship systems. By including a number of student activities, Schusky introduces the student to concepts of kinship logically and sequentially.

Kinship relations, based on both blood and marriage, provide a principle means for dealing with basic human problems. In small-scale societies, people live out their lives almost exclusively within family and kinship groups. As societies become more complex and differentiated, some of the functions traditionally performed by kinship groups are taken over by other educational, political, religious, and social institutions. Irrespective of level of social complexity, people from all societies play out at least part of their lives within the context of kinship groups. In fact, kinship ties, because they are so intense, intimate, and long-lasting, constitute our most important level of social organization. Consequently, kinship relations impact strongly on our lives, which make them vital to understand when attempting to solve human problems. The case studies presented here were selected with this in mind. The first case shows how an agricultural development program in West Africa was improved by conducting research on family and kinship patterns among the local population. The second case should serve to remind us that understanding our own kinship roles can be useful in making positive contributions to programs for mediating child custody disputes.

# Kinship

◆ **An applied anthropologist uses data on local family and kinship systems to help redesign an agricultural development program in the West African country of Guinea.**

In much the same way that salvage archaeologists excavate sites (frequently in rapid fashion) that are endangered by the construction of dams, roads, or buildings, cultural anthropologists have been called upon in recent decades to help reformulate international development projects that are not working. In those development programs that are foundering because they haven't adequately accounted for the sociocultural features of the target community, cultural anthropologists are being employed to salvage or correct the work of development specialists by analyzing the programs and recommending changes that will enable the program to meet its goals more effectively.

One such case of salvage anthropology was the redesign of an agricultural development project in the West African country of Guinea conducted by Robert Hecht (1986). Sponsored by USAID, the original project—called the Guinea Agricultural Capacity and Training Project—was a five-year, 4.9-million-dollar project designed to improve farm production by training agricultural researchers, extension workers, and administrators.

As originally conceived in the late 1970s, the project involved three main building activities: (1) an agricultural laboratory, (2) additional teaching facilities at the agricultural college, and (3) a research substation and demonstration farm. The project was directed at constructing these physical facilities and equipping them with American technology. The original program designers assumed that national agricultural productivity would be increased by improving the quality of research and the training of agricultural extension personnel. Since they assumed that modern technology from the United States would transform the rural areas, they did not think

371

it necessary to be acquainted with the sociocultural realities of the rural farmers.

By 1981 it was apparent that the project had some serious problems. First, the construction of the three facilities was running nearly two years behind schedule and the projected costs had escalated threefold to $15 million. Second, it became clear that plans for using these facilities were very inadequate. To address this problem of inadequate planning for using the facilities, USAID appointed a team comprising a cultural anthropologist (Hecht), an economist, and an agronomist to study the program and make recommendations for change.

The salvage team concluded that the most glaring weakness of the project was that it totally ignored the cultural realities of most of the small farmers in Guinea. Since the original planners expected agricultural productivity to follow from the importation of U.S. technology into Guinea, they saw no reason to focus on—or even understand—the rural cultural features. The original project planners neither consulted the farmers nor provided for their participation in the program. There were no mechanisms for obtaining feedback from the farmers or for enabling them to become auxiliary extension agents. In short, the original project did not include the peasant farmers (who produced the vast majority of crops) in designing, implementing, or evaluating the project.

To gain a better understanding of the problems facing the original project design, Hecht needed to gather data on the social and economic features of the Malinke peasants who made up the majority of the local population. On the basis of a number of village visits and ethnographic interviews, Hecht (1986:21–22) made some significant findings about the Malinke family and kinship system:

1. The average household is relatively large (approximately nine people), in part because of the high incidence of polygyny and in part because of the complex patrilineal kinship structure. These large kinship-based households have important implications for the project because of their potential for extended forms of economic cooperation among corporate lineage members (e.g., forming producer groups or building communal fertilizer storage facilities).

2. Since land in Malinke society is controlled by corporate lineages, a household had rights to land only by virtue of its membership in a patrilineal lineage. Rank among lineages in the village determined the allocation of land, with chiefly and higher status lineages controlling more land than commoner lineages. Even within lineages, elders have more and better land than heads of more junior households. Given this hierarchy within the land tenure system, Hecht recommended that the revised project should ". . . be sensitive to the needs of those at the bottom of the distribution hierarchy, who possessed the smallest plots and least fertile land" (1986:22).

3. Most farm labor (which was not based on wages) among the Malinke was supplied largely by household members and supplemented by other kin outside the household.

The basic picture that emerged from Hecht's research among the Malinke was one of a kinship-based production system based on land that was controlled by corporate lineages and a work force that was recruited along kinship lines. Only after this strong connection between the kinship and the agricultural systems had been revealed through anthropological research could adequate changes be made in this multimillion-dollar USAID project.

The traditional data-gathering techniques of household surveys, interviews, and participant-observation yielded the type of sociocultural data necessary for designing a workable program. As Hecht reminds us, ". . . the multidisciplinary or holistic approach usually associated with anthropology, and the emphasis placed by anthropologists on learning from the local population, may even make the anthropologist an appropriate person to serve as a team leader" (1986:25).

◆ **The collection of data on the U.S. kinship system, gender roles, and parenting helps one anthropologist develop a court-ordered custody mediation program for the State of Illinois.**

It has been estimated (Tischler, 1990:365) that approximately one of every two marriages contracted at the present time in the United States will eventually end in divorce. Frequently the breakup of a marriage can have devastating effects on the lives of children. This is particularly true in those divorces that involve bitter custody disputes. As a general rule, the more intransigent the disputants, the more harmful the effects on the children (as well as the parents' own adjustment process of restructuring their lives). The prevalence of divorce in the United States in recent decades and the custody disputes that frequently follow led one anthropologist, Linda Girdner, to focus her research efforts on the policies and practices relating to custody disputes among divorcing parents.

Girdner's original research examined the relationship between (1) legal customs in child custody cases and (2) the norms and symbols about gender and family in the United States. The research was designed to answer such questions as, What are the legal rules guiding decisions in custody cases? What does it mean to be a mother or a father in the United States? What codes of behavior are expected of "fit parents"? During the course of conducting this research, Girdner collected a good deal of descriptive data on the American kinship system, gender roles, and parenting as well as data on how this information relates to child custody policy and practices. The fieldwork took place during 1978–79 in the circuit and family courts in a large suburban county in the eastern part of the United States. Data-gathering techniques involved informal interviews with judges, attorneys, parents, and witnesses, systematic observations of "court culture," and the examination of court records.

Utilizing the results from eighteen months of anthropological research, Girdner took training as a family mediator, practiced family mediation for two years at a divorce clinic, and then participated in a number of ways in the development and implementation of a court-ordered custody mediation program in Illinois. Thus, over a several-year period, Girdner's initial role as a researcher became intertwined with the practitioner role. Based on her formal anthropological research and her experience as a custody mediator, Girdner put her knowledge and experience to use by helping to develop a custody mediation program with the local community and the state. Her utilization efforts, which lasted from 1981–87, involved three phases: (1) an *education phase,* comprising classroom teaching, presentations and workshops for professionals, and presentations to the lay public; (2) a *developmental phase,* consisting of serving as an advisor to the Family Law Section of the Illinois State Bar Association, which eventually formulated a statewide set of standards for custody mediation; and (3) an *implementation phase,* which involved training, developing public awareness, and program evaluation. Girdner's critical involvement in research and practice relating to child custody issues illustrates quite dramatically how anthropological methods and insights into the U.S. kinship system can be useful for the amelioration of social problems.

# Marriage and the Family

Is the family found universally in all cultures?

What functions do family and marriage systems perform?

How do we explain the fact that all societies have some notion of incest?

What are the different types of economic considerations of marriage found among the world's contemporary societies?

In what ways do societies regulate who a person can or cannot marry?

In all known societies, people recognize a certain number of relatives as making up that basic social group referred to generally as the family. This is not to imply, however, that all societies view the family in the same way. In fact, humans have developed a wide variety of types of families. To most middle-class North Americans, the family includes a husband and a wife and their children. To an East African herdsman, the term family might include several hundred kin related through both blood and marriage. Among the Hopi Indians, the family would be made up of a woman and her husband and their unmarried sons and married daughters, along with the daughters' husbands and children. This chapter examines the variety of family types found throughout the world's population and the process of marriage that is responsible for the formation of families.

◆　　◆　　◆

# Marriage and the Family: Some Definitions

The terms *family* and *marriage*—although everyday household words—are nevertheless ambiguous. Since both social scientists and laypersons alike use these terms indiscriminately, it would be helpful to define them in more detail. A family is a social unit characterized by economic cooperation, the management of reproduction and child rearing, and common residence. It includes both male and female adults who maintain a socially approved sexual relationship. Family members, both adults and children, recognize certain rights and obligations toward one another. The family is distinct from the institution of marriage, which is defined as a series of customs formalizing the relationship between male and female adults within the family. Marriage is a socially approved union between a man and a woman that regulates the sexual and economic rights and obligations between them. Marriage usually involves an explicit contract or understanding and is entered into with the assumption that it will be a permanent arrangement.

## SEXUAL UNION

As with any definition, marriage frequently has qualifications attached to its meaning. Marriage, according to our definition, is a socially legitimate sexual union. When a man and a woman are married, it is implied that they are having a sexual relationship—or that the society permits them to have one should they desire it. Al-

though this is generally true, we should bear in mind that this social legitimacy is not absolute, for there may be specified periods during which having sexual relations with one's spouse may be taboo. To illustrate, in many societies, sexual relations between spouses must be suspended during periods of menstruation and pregnancy. After a child is born, women in many societies are expected to observe a **post partum sex taboo,** lasting in some cases until the child is weaned, which can be as long as several years. As Stephens has suggested, ". . . there may be other sex taboos in honor of special occasions: before a hunting trip, before and after a war expedition, when the crops are harvested, or during various times of religious significance" (1963:10). Given this wide range of occasions where sex with one's spouse is illegitimate, it is possible that in some societies husbands and wives will be prevented from having sexual relations for a significant segment of their married lives.

## PERMANENCE

A second caveat to the definition above relates to the issue of permanence of the marital union. Frequently, as part of the marriage vows recited in Western weddings, spouses pledge to live together in matrimony "until death do us part." Even though it is difficult to precisely ascertain a person's intentions or expectations when entering a marriage, an abundance of data is available to suggest that the permanence of marriage varies widely, and in no societies do all marriages last until death. Recent statistics, for example, indicate that more than one of every two marriages in the United States ends in divorce. The relative impermanence of marriage can also be found among smaller scale societies. Leighton and Kluckhohn report that they frequently encountered Navajo men who had ". . . six or seven different wives in succession" (1948:83). In short, when dealing with the permanence of marriage, there will always be a discrepancy between ideal expectations and actual behavior.

## COMMON RESIDENCE

A qualifying statement must be made about the notion that family members share a common residence. Although, by and large, family members do live together, there are some obvious definitional problems. If we define "sharing a common residence" as living under the same roof, we will be able to cite a long list of exceptions. In Western society, dependent children sometimes live away from home at boarding schools and colleges. Additionally, in this age of high-speed transportation and communication, it is possible for a husband and wife to live and work in two different cities and see each other only on weekends. On a more global scale, 94 of the 240 African societies listed in Murdock's *Ethnographic Atlas* (1967) are characterized by wives and their children living in separate houses from the husband. In some non-Western societies, adolescent boys live with their peers apart from their families; and in some cases, such as the Nyakyusa (Wilson: 1960), adolescent boys have not only their own houses but indeed their own villages. In each of these examples cited, family membership and participation are not dependent upon living under the same roof.

The terms *marriage* and *family,* as we are beginning to see, are not easy terms to define. For years, anthropologists have attempted to define these terms in such a way as to cover all known societies. Frequently, anthropologists have debated whether or not families and the institution of marriage are universals. One interesting case is that of the Nayar of Southern India whom some claim (Gough, 1959) did not have marriage in the conventional sense of the term. Although pubescent Nayar girls took a ritual husband in a public ceremony, the husband took no responsibility for the woman after the ceremony, and frequently he never saw her again. Instead of cohabitating with her "husband," the Nayar bride continued to live with her parents while being vis-ited over the years by other "husbands." The bride's family retained full responsibility for the woman and whatever children she might bear during her lifetime. Thus, it would appear that the Nayar do not have marriage according to our definition in that there is no economic cooperation, regulation of sexual activity, cohabitation, or expectation of permanency.

♦  ♦  ♦

## Marriage and the Family: Functions

Whether or not marriage is a cultural universal found in all societies depends, of course, on the level of abstraction of our definitions. Without entering into that debate here, suffice it to say that the formation of families through marriage serves several important functions for the societies in which the families operate. One social benefit that marriage serves is the reduction of sexual competition. Since humans are always sexually receptive, there would be continual competition for mates unless somehow controlled by the culture. While recognizing that there are other ways to reduce sexual competition, the fact that marriage legitimizes sexual activity no doubt has the effect of reducing the rivalry for spouses and, consequently, reducing the chances of conflict.

A second social benefit of marriage is that it provides a mechanism for regulating the sexual division of labor

The family—such as this one in Ghana, West Africa—provides a structured environment in which to support and meet the needs of children.

that exists to some extent in all societies. For reasons that are both biological and cultural, men in all societies perform some tasks, while women perform others. To maximize the chances of survival, it is important for a society to arrange the exchange of goods and services of men and women. Marriage usually brings about the domestic relationships that facilitate the exchange of these goods and services.

Third, marriage functions to create a set of family relationships that can provide for the material, educational, and emotional needs of children for a relatively long period of time. Unlike most other animal species, human children are dependent on adults for the first decade or more of their lives for their nourishment, shelter, and protection. Moreover, human children require adults to provide the many years of cultural learning needed to develop into fully functioning members of the society. Even though it is possible for children to be reared largely outside of a family (such as is done on the Kibbutzim of Israel), marriage creates a set of family relationships in most societies that provide the material, educational, and emotional support children need for their eventual maturity.

## The Universal Incest Taboo

Every society known to anthropology has established for itself some type of rules regulating mating (sexual intercourse). The most common form of prohibition is mating with certain types of kin that are defined by the society as being inappropriate sexual partners. These prohibitions on mating with certain categories of relatives are known as **incest taboos**. Following the lead of Fox (1967:54–55), it is important to distinguish between sexual relations and marriage. Incest taboos refer to prohibitions against having sexual relations with certain categories of kin. This is not exactly the same thing as rules prohibiting marrying certain kin. Although incest taboos and rules prohibiting marrying certain kin often coincide with each other (that is, those who are forbidden to have sex are also forbidden to marry), it cannot be assumed that they do in fact coincide.

The most universal form of incest taboo involves mating between members of the immediate (nuclear) family —i.e., mothers-sons, fathers-daughters, and brothers-sisters, although there are several notable, yet limited, exceptions. For political, religious, or economic reasons, members of the royal families among the ancient Egyptians, Incas, and Hawaiians were permitted to mate with and marry their siblings, although this practice did not extend to the ordinary members of those societies. The incest taboo invariably extends beyond the scope of the immediate or nuclear family, however. In our own society, we are forbidden by law and custom from mating with the children of our parents' siblings (i.e., our first cousins). In some non-Western societies, the incest taboo may extend to large numbers of people on one side of the family but not on the other. And in still other societies, a man is permitted (even encouraged) to mate with and marry the daughter of his mother's brother (first cousin) but is strictly prohibited from doing so with the daughter of his mother's sister (also a first cousin). Thus, while it seems clear that every society has incest taboos, the relatives that the incestuous group comprises vary from one society to another. Given that incest taboos are universally found throughout the world, anthropologists have long been interested in explaining their origins and persistence. A number of possible explanations have been set forth.

## NATURAL AVERSION THEORY

One such theory, popular around the turn of this century, rests on the somewhat unsatisfying concept of human nature by suggesting that there is a natural aversion to sexual intercourse among those who have grown up together. Although any natural (or genetically produced) aversion to having sexual relations within the nuclear family is rejected today, there is some evidence to suggest that such an aversion may be developed. For example, according to Talmon (1964), sexual attraction between Israelis reared on the same **kibbutz** is extremely rare, a phenomenon attributed by the kibbutz members themselves to the fact that they had grown up together. Another study (Wolf, 1968) of an unusual marital practice in Taiwan, whereby infant girls are given to families with sons as their future brides, found that these marriages were characterized by higher rates of infidelity and sexual difficulties and fewer numbers of children. Thus, it would appear that in at least some situations, there may be little sexual interest among people who have grown up in homes that naturally breed high levels of familiarity. Nevertheless, this "familiarity theory" does not appear to be a particularly convincing explanation for the existence of the incest taboo.

If familiarity does lead to sexual aversion and avoidance, how do we explain the fact that incest does in fact occur with considerable regularity throughout the world? Indeed, in our own society, it has been estimated that between 10 percent and 14 percent of children under 18 years of age have been involved in incestuous relationships (Whelehan, 1985:678). In short, the familiarity theory does not answer the question of why we even need a strongly sanctioned incest taboo if people already have a natural aversion to incest.

## INBREEDING THEORY

Another theory that attempts to explain the existence of the incest taboo focuses on the potentially deleterious effects of inbreeding on the family. This inbreeding theory, proposed first in the late nineteenth century, holds that mating between close kin, who are likely to carry the same harmful recessive genes, tends to produce a higher incidence of genetic defects (which results in an increased susceptibility to disease and higher mortality rates). This theory was later discredited because it was argued that sharing the same recessive genes could produce adaptive advantages as well as disadvantages. Recent genetic studies, however, have given greater credence to the older theory that inbreeding does, in fact, lead to harmful consequences for human populations. Conversely, outbreeding, which occurs in human populations with strong incest taboos, has a number of positive genetic consequences which, according to Campbell (1979:74), include (a) increases in genetic variation, (b) a reduction in lethal recessive traits, (c) improved health, and (d) lower rates of mortality.

Even though it is generally agreed today that inbreeding is genetically harmful to human populations, the question still remains whether or not prehistoric people understood this fact when originally establishing the incest taboo. After all, the science of Mendelian genetics did not become established until the turn of this century. It is not necessary, however, for early people to have recognized the adaptive advantages of avoiding inbreeding through an incest taboo. Rather, the incest taboo could have persisted through time for the simple reason that it was adaptively advantageous. That is, groups that practiced the incest taboo would have more surviving children than those societies without the incest taboo. Thus, this greater reproductive success would explain, if not its origins, at least why the incest taboo has become a cultural universal.

## FAMILY DISRUPTION THEORY

Just as the inbreeding theory focuses on the biological consequences of incest, a third theory centers on its negative social consequences. This theory, most closely linked with Malinowski (1927), holds that mating between mother-son, father-daughter, or brother-sister would create such intense jealousies within the nuclear family that the family would not be able to function as a unit of economic cooperation and socialization. If, for example, adolescents were permitted to satisfy their sexual urges within the nuclear family unit, fathers and sons and mothers and daughters would be competing with one another, and consequently, normal family role relationships would be seriously disrupted. The incest taboo, according to this theory, originated as a mechanism to repress the desire to satisfy one's sexual urges within the family.

In addition to causing disruption among nuclear family members through sexual competition, incest creates the further problem of **role ambiguity.** If, for example, a child is born from the union of a mother and her son, the child's father will also be the child's half brother, the child's mother will also be the child's grandmother, and the child's father will be married to the child's grandmother. These are just some of the bizarre roles created by such an incestuous union. Since different family roles, such as brother and father, carry with them vastly different rights, obligations, and behavioral expectations, the child will have great difficulty deciding how to behave toward his or her immediate family members. Does the child treat the male who biologically fathered him or her as a father or as a brother? How does the child deal with the woman from whose womb he or she sprung—as a mother or a grandmother? Thus, the incest taboo can be viewed as a mechanism that prevents this type of role ambiguity or confusion from occurring.

## THEORY OF EXPANDING SOCIAL ALLIANCES

Incest avoidance can also be explained in terms of positive social advantages to those societies that practice it. By forcing people to "marry out" of their immediate family, the incest taboo functions to create a wider network of interfamily alliances, thereby enhancing cooperation, social cohesion, and survival. Each time one of your close relatives mates with a person from another family, it creates a new set of relationships with whom your family is less likely to become hostile. This theory, first set forth by Edward Tyler (1889) and later developed by Lévi-Strauss (1969), holds that it makes little sense to mate with someone from one's own group with whom one already has good relations. Instead there is more to be gained—both biologically and socially—by expanding one's networks outward. Not only does mating outside of one's own group create a more peaceful society by increasing the number of allies, but a larger

The marriage of this man and woman created a social alliance between their two lineages.

## Mate Selection: Whom Should You Marry?

As we have seen, every society has the notion of incest that defines a set of kin with whom a person is to avoid marriage and sexual intimacy. In no society is it permissible to mate with one's parents or siblings (i.e., within the nuclear family), and in most cases the restricted group of kin is considerably wider. Beyond this notion of incest, people in all societies are faced with rules either restricting one's choice of marriage partners or strongly encouraging the selection of other people as highly desirable mates. These are known as rules of **exogamy** (marrying outside of a certain group) and **endogamy** (marrying within a certain group).

### RULES OF EXOGAMY

Owing to the universality of the incest taboo, all societies to one degree or another have rules for marrying outside of a certain group of kin. These are known as rules of exogamy. In societies like the United States, which are not based on the principle of unilineal descent groups, the exogamous group extends only slightly beyond the nuclear family. It is considered either illegal or immoral to marry one's first cousin and, in some cases, one's second cousin, but beyond that one can marry other more distant relatives with only mild disapproval. In those societies that are based on unilineal descent groups, however, the exogamous group is usually the lineage, which can involve many hundreds of people, or even the clan, which can involve thousands of people who are unmarriageable. Thus, when viewed cross-culturally, rules of exogamy based on kinship do not appear to be based on genealogical proximity.

### RULES OF ENDOGAMY

In contrast to exogamy, which requires marriage *outside* one's own group, the rule of endogamy requires a person to select a mate from *within* one's own group. Hindu castes found in traditional India are strongly endogamous, believing that to marry below one's caste would result in serious ritual pollution. Caste endogamy is also found in a somewhat less rigid form among the Rwanda and Banyankole of eastern Central Africa. In addition to being applied to caste, endogamy can be applied to

gene pool is created, which gives a greater survival advantage over a smaller gene pool.

The extent to which wider social alliances are created by requiring people to "mate and marry out" is illustrated by a study of Rani Khera, a village in Northern India. In a survey of the village population, it was found (Lewis, 1955:163) that the 226 married women residing in the village had come from approximately 200 separate villages and that roughly the same number of village daughters married out. Thus, the village of Rani Khera was linked through marriage to hundreds of other northern Indian villages. In fact, this pattern of mating/marrying outside of one's own group (created out of a desire to avoid incest) is an important factor integrating Indian society.

other social units, such as the village or local community, as was the case among the Incas of Peru, or to racial groups, as is presently practiced in the Republic of South Africa.

Even though there are no strongly sanctioned rules of endogamy in the United States, there is a certain amount of marrying within one's own groups based on class, ethnicity, religion, and race. This general *de facto* endogamy found in the United States results from the fact that people do not have frequent social contacts with people from different backgrounds. Upper-middle-class children, for example, tend to grow up in the suburbs, take golf and tennis lessons at the country club, and attend schools designed to prepare students for college. By contrast, many lower class children grow up in urban housing projects, play basketball in public playgrounds, and attend schools with low expectations for college attendance. This general social segregation by class, coupled with parental and peer pressure to "marry your own kind," results in a relatively high level of endogamy in many complex Western societies such as our own.

## ARRANGED MARRIAGES

In Western societies, with their strong value on individualism, mate selection is largely a decision made jointly by the prospective bride and groom. Aimed at satisfying the emotional and sexual needs of the individual, the choice of mates in Western society is based on such factors as physical attractiveness, emotional compatibility, and romantic love. Even though absolute freedom of choice is constrained by such factors as social class, ethnicity, religion and race, individuals in most contemporary Western societies are relatively free to marry whomever they please.

In many societies, however, the interests of the families are so strong that marriages are arranged. Negotiations are handled by family members of the prospective bride and groom, and for all practical purposes, the decision of whom one will marry is made by one's parents or other influential family members. In certain cultures, such as parts of traditional Japan, India, and China, future marriage partners are betrothed while they are still children. In one extreme example—the Tiwi of North Australia—females are betrothed or promised as future wives *before* they are born (Hart and Pilling, 1960:14). Since the Tiwi believe that females are liable to become impregnated by spirits at any time, the only sensible precaution against unmarried mothers is to betroth female babies before birth or as soon as they are born.

All such cases of **arranged marriages**, wherever they may be found, are based on the cultural assumption that since marriage is a union of two kin groups rather than merely two individuals, it is far too significant an institution to be based on something as frivolous as physical attractiveness or romantic love.

Arranged marriages are found frequently in those societies with elaborate social hierarchies, perhaps the best example of which is Hindu India. Indeed, the maintenance of the caste system in India is dependent, by and large, upon a system of arranged marriages. As Goode reminds us:

Maintenance of caste was too important a matter to be left to the young, who might well fall prey to the temptations of love and thus ignore caste requirements. To prevent any serious opposition, youngsters were married early enough to ensure that they could not acquire any resources with which to oppose adult decisions. The joint family, in turn, offered an organization which could absorb a young couple who could not yet make their own living. . . . This pattern of marriage has always been common among the nobility, but in India it developed not only among the wealthy, who could afford early marriages and whose unions might mark an alliance between two families, but also among the poor, who had nothing to share but their debts (1963:208).

Arranged marriages in India are further reinforced by other traditional Indian values. Fathers, it was traditionally held, sinned by failing to marry off their daughters before puberty. Indeed, both parents in India shared the common belief that they were responsible for any sin the daughter might commit because of a late marriage. Hindu civilization, with its heritage of eroticism expressed in the sexual cult of Tantricism, has viewed women for centuries as lustful beings who tempt men with their sexual favors. Thus, a girl had to be married at an early age to protect both herself and those men who might become sinners. And, if females were to become brides before reaching adolescence, they could hardly be trusted to select their own husbands.

## PREFERENTIAL COUSIN MARRIAGE

A somewhat less coercive influence on mate selection than arranged marriages is found in societies that specify a preference for choosing certain categories of relatives as marriage partners. A common form of preferred marriage is called **preferential cousin marriage** and is practiced in one form or another in most of the major regions of the world. Unlike our own kinship system, kinship systems based on lineages distinguish between

In some parts of the world—such as in Agra, India—mate selection is often not a decision made by the bride and groom.

The most common form of preferential cousin marriage is between cross cousins because it functions to strengthen and maintain ties between kin groups established by the marriages that took place in the preceding generation. That is, under such a system of cross cousin marriage, a man originally would marry a woman from an unrelated family—and then their son would marry his mother's brother's daughter (cross cousin) in the next generation. Thus, since a man's wife and his son's wife come from the same family, it tends to solidify the ties between the two families. In this respect, cross cousin marriage functions to maintain ties between groups in much the same way that exogamy does. The major difference is that exogamy encourages the formation of ties with a large number of kinship groups, while preferential cross cousin marriage solidifies the relationship between a more limited number of kin groups over a number of generations.

A much less common form of cousin marriage is between parallel cousins, the child of one's mother's sister or father's brother (Murphy and Kasdan, 1959). Found among some Arabic societies in North Africa, it involves the marriage of a man to his father's brother's daughter. Since parallel cousins belong to the same family, such a practice can serve to prevent the fragmentation of family property.

## THE LEVIRATE AND SORORATE

Another form of mate selection that tends to limit individual choice are those that require a person to marry the husband or wife of deceased kin. The **levirate** is the custom whereby a widow is expected to marry the brother (or some close male relative) of her dead husband. Usually any children fathered by the woman's new husband are considered to belong legally to the dead brother rather than to the actual genitor. Such a custom both serves as a form of social security for the widow and her children and preserves the rights of the husband's family to her sexuality and future children. The **sororate**, which comes into play when a wife dies, is the practice of a widower's marrying the sister (or some close female relative) of his deceased wife. In the event that the deceased spouse has no sibling, the family of the deceased is under a general obligation to supply some equivalent relative as a substitute. For example, in some societies that practice the sororate, a widower may be given as a substitute wife the daughter of his deceased wife's brother.

two different types of first cousins—**cross cousins** and **parallel cousins**. This distinction rests on the gender of the parents of the cousin. Cross cousins are children of siblings of the opposite sex—that is, one's mother's brothers' children and one's father's sisters' children. Parallel cousins, on the other hand, are children of siblings of the same sex, namely the children of one's mother's sister and one's father's brother. In those societies that make such a distinction, parallel cousins, who are considered family members, will be referred to as "brother" and "sister" and thus be excluded as potential marriage partners. However, since one's cross cousins are not thought of as family members, they are considered by some societies as not just permissible marriage partners but actually preferred ones.

CHAPTER 18 ◆ MARRIAGE AND THE FAMILY

# Number of Spouses

In much the same way that societies have rules regulating whom one may or may not marry, they have rules specifying how many mates a person may or should have. Cultural anthropologists have identified three major types of marriage based on the number of spouses permitted: **monogamy** (the marriage of one man to one woman at a time) and two forms of plural marriage—**polygyny** (the marriage of a man to two or more women at a time) and **polyandry** (the marriage of a woman to two or more men at a time).

## MONOGAMY

The practice of having only one spouse at a time is so widespread and rigidly adhered to in the United States that most people would have great difficulty even imagining any other marital alternative. We are so accustomed to thinking of marriage as an exclusive relationship between husband and wife that for most North Americans, the notion of sharing a spouse is unthinkable. If a person should choose to take more than one marriage partner at a time, he or she will be in direct violation of conventional norms, religious standards, and the law and if caught will likely be fined or go to jail.

So ingrained is this concept of monogamy in Western society that we frequently associate it with the highest standards of civilization, while associating plural marriage with social backwardness and depravity. Interestingly, many societies that practice monogamy manage to circumvent the notion of lifelong partnerships by either permitting extramarital affairs (provided they are discretely conducted) or practicing serial monogamy, (taking a number of different spouses one after another rather than at the same time).

## POLYGYNY

Even though monogamy is widely practiced in the United States and generally in the western world, the overwhelming majority of world cultures do not share our values about the inherent virtue of monogamy. According to Murdock's *World Ethnographic Sample,* approximately seven out of every ten cultures of the world permit the practice of polygyny. In fact, in most of the major regions of the world, polygyny is the preferred form of marriage. It was practiced widely in traditional India and China and remains a preferred form of marriage throughout Asia, Africa, and the Middle East. There is even evidence to support the idea that polygyny played a significant role in our own Western background by virtue of the numerous references to polygyny in the Old Testament of the Bible.

To suggest that approximately 70 percent of the world's cultures practice polygyny is not tantamount to saying that 70 percent of the world's population practices polygyny. We must bear in mind that many of the cultures that practice polygyny are smaller scale societies with relatively small populations. Moreover, even in polygynous societies, the majority of men at any given time still have only one wife. In those societies where polygyny is the most intensively practiced, we would not expect to find more than 35 percent to 40 percent of the men actually having two or more wives. Polygyny in these societies is the preferred, not the usual, form of marriage. It is something for which men strive but only some attain. Just as the ideal of becoming a millionaire is more frequently not realized in the United States, so too in polygynous societies, only some men actually achieve the status of being polygynists.

Being the head of a polygynous household, which invariably carries with it high prestige, is hard work. For example, since marriage in polygynous societies frequently involves large numbers of kin, acquiring additional wives requires the lineage's economic and social support. In some polygynous societies, it was considered inappropriate for men of low rank to seek additional wives. And, once achieved, the management of two or more wives and their children within a household requires particularly strong administrative skills, particularly if the relations between co-wives are not congenial. In short, most men in polygynous societies, for a variety of reasons, have neither the inclination, family power base, nor social skills needed to achieve the relatively high status of being a polygynist.

### Economic Status of Women in Polygynous Societies

The rate of polygyny varies quite widely from one part of the world to another. A critical factor influencing the incidence of polygyny is the extent to which women are seen as economic assets (where they do the majority of labor) or liabilities (where men do the majority of work). To illustrate, in such areas of the world as sub-Saharan Africa where women are assets, it has been estimated (Dorjahn, 1959:102) that the mean rate of polygyny is approximately 35 percent, ranging from a low of 25 percent (Bushmen) to a high of 43 percent (Guinea Coast). Conversely, in those societies where women are an economic liability (such as among the Greenland Eskimos, where only about 5 percent of the men practice polygyny), few men can afford the luxury of additional wives (Linton, 1936:183).

**Sex Ratio in Polygynous Societies** For polygyny to work, a society must solve the very practical problem of the sex ratio. In most human populations, the number of men and women is roughly equal (in actual fact, there is a slight preponderance of male babies born in the world, with approximately 103 males born for every 100 females). The question therefore arises: Where do the excess women come from that are needed to support a system of polygyny? It is theoretically possible that the sex ratio could swing in favor of females if males were killed off in warfare, if women were captured from other societies, or if the society practiced male infanticide. All of these quite radical "solutions" may account for a small part of the excess of women needed for a polygynous marriage system in some societies.

More commonly, this numerical discrepancy is alleviated quite simply by postponing the age at which men can marry. That is, if females can marry from age 14 on and males are prohibited from marrying until age 26, a surplus of marriageable women always exists within the marriage pool. In some traditional societies, such as the Swazi of Southern Africa, young adult men were required by their regimental organizations (i.e., age groups) to remain unmarried until the inauguration of the next regiment. Generally, this meant that men were not free to marry until their mid to late twenties. Since women were able to marry in their teens, the Swazi society had solved the numerical dilemma presented by polygyny by simply requiring men to marry considerably later in life than females.

**Advantages of Polygyny** By and large, having two or more wives in a polygynous society is seen as a mark of prestige or high status. In highly stratified kingdoms, polygyny is one of the privileges of royalty and aristocrats, as was the case with the late King Sobhuza of Swaziland who, it was estimated, had well over a hundred wives. In societies that are stratified more on age than on political structure, such as the Azande of the Sudan and the Kikuyu of Kenya, polygyny is a symbol of prestige for older men. Whether aristocrat or commoner, however, having multiple wives means wealth, power, and high status for both the polygynous husband and the wives and children. That is, a man's status would increase as the man took additional wives *and* a woman's status would increase as the woman's husband took additional wives. It is for this reason that women in some African societies actually will badger their husbands to take more wives in much the same way that Western women will encourage their husbands to buy a house at the beach or a more luxurious station wagon. Clearly, these African women do not want to be married to a "nobody."

Sometimes multiple wives are taken because they are viewed by the society as economic and political assets. Each wife not only contributes to the household's goods and services but also produces more children, who are valuable future economic and political resources. The Siuai of the Solomon Islands provide an excellent example of how having multiple wives can be an economic advantage for the polygynous husband. Perhaps the most prized possession of Siuai adults is pigs. According to Oliver, "To shout at a person 'you have no pigs' is to offer him an insult . . ." (1955:348). Women are particularly valuable in the raising of pigs, for the more wives, the more hands to work in the garden, the more pig food, and, consequently, the more pigs. Oliver continues:

It is by no mere accident that polygynous households average more pigs than monogamous ones. Informants stated explicitly that some men married second and third wives in order to enlarge their gardens and increase their herds. . . . Opisa of Turunom did not even trouble to move his second wife from her village to his own. She, a woman twenty years his senior, simply remained at her own home and tended two of his pigs (1955:352–53).

**Competition Among Wives** Despite the advantages just discussed, living in a polygynous household is hardly without its drawbacks. Even though men desire multiple wives, they recognize the potential pitfalls. The major problem is jealousy among the co-wives, who frequently compete for the husband's attention, sexual favors, and household resources. In fact, in some African societies, the word *co-wife* is derived from the root word for jealousy. As LeVine relates, jealousy and dissension among co-wives is common among the Gusii of Western Kenya:

Each wife tends to be the husband's darling when she is the latest, and to maintain that position until he marries again. . . . This tendency in itself causes jealousy among the wives. In addition, any inequality in the distribution of gifts or money, or in the number of children born and died, or the amount of

The late King Sobhuza II of Swaziland was said to have had over 100 wives selected from all over the kingdom.

education received by the children, adds to the jealousy and hatred. A woman who becomes barren or whose children die almost always believes that her co-wife has achieved this through witchcraft or poisoning. She may then attempt retaliation (quoted in Stephens, 1963:57).

Even though competition among wives in polygynous societies can be a threat to domestic tranquility, there are several ways to minimize the friction. First, some societies practice a form of polygyny called sororal polygyny, where a man marries two or more sisters. It is possible that sisters, who have had to resolve issues of jealousy revolving around their parents' attention, are less likely to be jealous of one another when they become co-wives. Second, co-wives in many polygynist societies are given their own separate living quarters. As Bohannan and Curtin (1988:114) remind us, since woman may have more difficulty sharing their kitchens than their husbands, jealousy can be minimized by giving each co-wife her own personal space. Third, dissension will be lessened if the rights and obligations among the co-wives are clearly understood. Fourth, potential

conflict among co-wives can be reduced by establishing a hierarchy among the wives. Since the senior wife often will be able to exert considerable authority over more junior wives, she will be able to run a fairly smooth household by adjudicating the various complaints of the other co-wives.

Not only can the jealousies among co-wives be regulated, there are some ethnographic reports from polygynous societies indicating considerable harmony and cooperation among the wives. Elenore Smith Bowen (1964:127–28) relates the story of Ava, a Tiv woman who was the senior of five wives:

The women were fast friends. Indeed it was Ava who had picked out all the others. She saved up forty or fifty shillings every few years, searched out an industrious girl of congenial character, then brought her home and presented her to her husband: "Here is your new wife." Ava's husband always welcomed her additions to his household and he always set to work to pay the rest of the bridewealth, for he knew perfectly well that Ava always picked hard-working, healthy, handsome, steady women who wouldn't run away.

One way of reducing jealousy in polygynous households is to provide each co-wife her own physical space. Here in a Kikuyu compound, each co-wife has her own hut and granary for storing her food supplies.

## POLYANDRY

Polyandry involves the marriage of a woman to two or more men at a time. A much rarer form of plural marriage, polyandry is found in less than one percent of the societies of the world, most notably in Tibet, Nepal, and India. Polyandry can be fraternal (where the husbands are brothers) or nonfraternal.

Perhaps the best known case of polyandry is found among the Toda of Southern India, who practice the fraternal variety. When a woman marries a man, she also becomes the wife of all of his brothers, including even those that might not yet be born. Marriage privileges rotate among the brothers. Even though all of the brothers live together with the wife in a single household, there is little competition or sexual jealousy. Whenever a brother is with the wife, he places his cloak and staff at the door as a sign not to disturb him. When the wife becomes pregnant, paternity is not necessarily ascribed to the biological father (genitor) but is rather determined by a ceremony that establishes a social father (pater), usually the oldest brother. After the birth of two or three children, however, another brother is chosen as the social father for all children born to the woman thereafter.

Toda society is characterized by a shortage of females brought about by the traditional practice of female infanticide, and it has been suggested that one of the explanations of polyandry among the Toda is related to the shortage of women. Owing to the influence of both the Indian government and the Christian missionaries, however, female infanticide has largely disappeared today, the male-female sex ratio has become essentially balanced, and polyandry among the Toda is, for all practical purposes, a thing of the past.

In addition to explaining the existence of polyandry by the shortage of women, there are certain economic factors to consider. According to Stephens (1963:44), senior husbands among the wealthier families in Marquesans society recruited junior husbands as a way of augmenting the manpower of the household. It has also been suggested (Goldstein, 1987) that Tibetan serfs practice polyandry as a solution to the problem of land shortage. As a way of avoiding the division of small plots of land among their sons, brothers could keep the family land in tact by marrying one woman.

## Economic Considerations of Marriage

Most societies view marriage as a binding contract between at least the husband and wife and, in many cases, between their respective families as well. Such a contract includes the transfer of certain rights between the parties involved—rights of sexual access, legal rights to children, and rights of the spouses to each other's economic goods and services. Often the transfer of rights is accompanied by the transfer of some type of economic consideration. These transactions, which may take place either before or after the marriage, can be divided into five categories: **bride price, bride service, dowry, woman exchange,** and **reciprocal exchange**.

## BRIDE PRICE

Also known as bridewealth, bride price is the compensation given upon marriage by the family of the groom to the family of the bride. According to Murdock's *World Ethnographic Sample* (reported in Stephens, 1963:211), approximately 46 percent of all societies give substantial bride price payment as a normal part of the marriage process. Although bride price is practiced in most regions of the world, it is perhaps most widely found in Africa, where it is estimated (Murdock, 1967) that 82 percent of the societies require the payment of bride price, while most of the remaining 18 percent practice either token bride price or bride service (providing labor, rather than goods, to the bride's family).

Bride price is paid in a wide variety of currencies, but in almost all cases, the particular commodity used for payment is highly valued in the society. For example, reindeer are given as bride price by the reindeer-herding Chukchee; horses by the equestrian Cheyenne of the Central Plains; sheep by the sheep-herding Navajo; and cattle by the pastoral Masai, Samburu, and Nuer of Eastern Africa. In other societies, marriage payments take the form of blankets (Kwakuitl), pigs (Alor), mats (Fiji), shell money (Kurtachi), spears (Somali), loin cloths (Toda), and even the plumes of the bird of paradise (Siane).

Just as there are considerable variations in the commodities used in bridewealth transactions, there are differences in the amount of the transaction. To illustrate, an indigent Nandi of Kenya, under certain circumstances, can obtain a bride with no more than a promise to transfer one animal to the bride's father. A suitor from the Jie tribe of Uganda, on the other hand, normally transfers fifty head of cattle and one hundred head of small stock (sheep and goats) to the bride's family before the marriage becomes official. Such large amounts of bride price as found among the Jie are significant for several reasons. First, the economic stakes are so high that the bride and groom are under enormous pressure to make the marriage work. And second, large bride price payments tend to make the system of negotiations between the two families more flexible and, consequently, more cordial because when the bride price

is low, the addition or subtraction of one item becomes highly critical and is likely to create hard feelings between the two families.

The meaning of bride price has been widely debated by scholars and nonscholars alike for much of the twentieth century. Early Christian missionaries, viewing bride price as a form of wife purchase, argued that such a practice was denigrating to women and repugnant to the Christian ideal of marriage. Many colonial administrators, taking a more legalistic perspective, saw bride price as a symbol of the inferior legal status of women in traditional societies. Both of these negative interpretations of bride price led to a number of vigorous, yet unsuccessful, attempts to stamp out the practice of bride price payments.

Motivated less by moral or legal issues, cultural anthropologists saw the institution of bride price as a rational and comprehensible part of traditional systems of marriage. Rejecting the interpretation that bride price was equivalent to wife purchase, cultural anthropologists tended to concentrate on how the institution operated within the total cultural context of which it was a part. Given such a perspective, cultural anthropologists identified a number of important functions that the institution of bride price performed for the well-being of the society. For example, bride price was seen as security or insurance for the good treatment of the wife, as a mechanism to stabilize marriage by reducing the possibility of divorce, as a form of compensation to the bride's lineage for the loss of her economic potential and her childbearing capacity, as a symbol of the union between two large groups of kin, as a mechanism to legitimize traditional marriages in much the same way that a marriage license legitimizes Western marriages, as the transference of rights over children from the mother's family to the father's family, and as the acquisition by the husband of uxorial (wifely) rights over the bride.

To avoid the economic implications of "wife purchase," Evans-Pritchard (1940) suggested that the term *bridewealth* be substituted for the term *bride price*, while Radcliffe-Brown (1950:47) used the word *prestation*, a term with even fewer economic connotations. Although a much needed corrective to the earlier interpretations of bride price as wife purchase, much of the anthropological literature has overlooked the very real economic significance of bride price. It was not until near the end of the colonial period that Gray (1960) reminded social scientists that it was legitimate to view bride price as an integral part of the local exchange system and that in many traditional societies, wives are dealt with in much the same way as other commodities.

It is now generally held that a comprehensive understanding of the practice of bride price is impossible without recognizing its economic functions as well as its noneconomic functions.

## BRIDE SERVICE

In those societies with considerable material wealth, marriage considerations take the form of bride price and, as we have seen, are paid in various forms of commodities. But since many small-scale, particularly nomadic, societies, cannot accumulate capital goods, men will frequently give their labor to the bride's family instead of material goods in exchange for wives. This practice, known as bride service, is found in approximately 14 percent of the societies listed in Murdock's *World Ethnographic Sample.*

In some cases, bride service is practiced to the exclusion of property transfer; in other cases, it represents a temporary condition in which the transfer of some property is expected at a later date. When a man marries under a system of bride service, he often will move in with his bride's family, work or hunt for them, and serve a probationary period of several weeks to several years. This custom is similar to that practiced by Jacob of the Old Testament (Genesis, Chapter 29) who served his mother's brother (Laban) for his two wives Leah and her sister Rachel. In some cases where bride service is found, other members of the groom's family, in addition to the groom himself, may be expected to give service, and this work may be done not only for the bride's parents but also for her other close relatives, as is the case with the Taita of Kenya (Harris, 1972:63).

## DOWRY

In contrast to bridewealth, a dowry involves a transfer of goods or money in the opposite direction, from the bride's family to the groom or to the groom's family. While the dowry is always provided by the bride's family, the recipient of the goods varies from one culture to another. In certain Western societies, the dowry was given to the groom, who then had varying degrees of disposal to it. In rural Ireland, it was given to the father of the groom in compensation for land, which the groom's father subsequently bequeathed to the bride and groom. The dowry was then used, wholly or in part,

by the groom's father to pay the dowry of the groom's sister.

The dowry is not very widely practiced throughout the world. Less than three percent of the societies in Murdock's sample actually practice it. It is confined to Eurasia, most notably in medieval and Renaissance Europe and among the Rajputs of Khalapur in India.

In certain European countries—where it is still practiced to some extent today—substantial dowry payments have been used for the sake of upward mobility by marrying a daughter into a higher status family. Around the turn of the century, a number of daughters of wealthy U.S. industrialists entered into mutually beneficial marriage alliances with European nobles who were falling upon hard economic times. The U.S. heiresses brought to the marriage a substantial dowry in exchange for a title.

Even though bridewealth is the usual form of marriage payment in Africa, there are several instances where the payment is in the opposite direction. One such case is found among the Nilo-Hamitic Barabaig of Tanzania. Although a small number of goods are given to the bride's kin group, her family will confer upon her a dowry of from two to forty head of large stock depending on their means. This dowry cattle, which frequently outnumbers the cattle held originally by the groom, is kept in trust as inheritance cattle for the bride's sons and as dowry cattle for the bride's daughters. Since the Barabaig are patrilocal, the wife and her dowry cattle reside at the husband's homestead. Even though the husband has nominal control over the herd, he still must ask his wife's permission to dispose of any of the cattle, for technically the herd belongs to his wife's father. Until the herd is finally redistributed among their own children, it will remain a source of friction between the husband and wife because the very existence of such a dowry gives the wife considerable economic leverage in her marital relations.

## WOMAN EXCHANGE

Another variation of legitimizing marriage by means of economic considerations is the practice of woman exchange, whereby two men exchange sisters or daughters as wives for themselves, their sons, or their brothers. Such a practice, limited to a small number of societies in Africa and the Pacific, is found in less than three percent of the world's societies. According to Winter (1956:21),

Nairobi, like many African cities since the 1960s, has experienced enormous population growth. A major problem facing urban planners in Kenya over the past several decades has been that of providing adequate and affordable housing for the rapidly growing number of urban residents. During the 1970s, the city council of Nairobi attempted to address this problem by authorizing the construction of a low-cost housing project. The response of the African people to these new, clean, and spacious housing units was somewhat less than enthusiastic. The architectural design of these public housing units—comprising a living room, a dining room, a kitchen, a bathroom, and two bedrooms—was indistinguishable from the design of units one might find in Detroit, Boston, or Los Angeles. Like those built in the United States, the apartments built in Nairobi had the kitchen located next to the dining room, with no more than an open portal separating the two rooms. While this design feature works well in the United States, it violates a basic cultural value in East Africa—i.e., that the preparation of food is considered to be an unclean activity. The idea of serving food to one's guests in a room that has a full view of the kitchen is considered rude, offensive, and hardly conducive to commensality. To place a doorless kitchen adjacent to the dining room would be as inappropriate in East Africa as it would be to place a doorless bathroom next to the dining room in our society. Thus, it is important that architects, wherever they may practice, take into consideration the cultural features of the people for whom they are designing buildings.

woman exchange was the primary means by which marriages were legitimized among the traditional Bwamba of Uganda. Such a system, however, suffers from a considerable disadvantage—that is, the exchange of one woman for another allows little room for individual variation. Bwamba women differ, as they do elsewhere, in terms of age, beauty, and procreative powers. Bwamba men prefer young, attractive, industrious, and fertile women. The exchange system, however, cannot cope with variations in these qualities.

In a system using conventional material objects such as bridewealth cattle, a man's preference may be reflected to a certain degree by the quality and quantity of his gifts. We should also bear in mind that the system of woman exchange has different implications for the distribution of women (especially in polygynous societies) than does a system using more conventional objects of exchange. Under the latter system, it is the wealthy man in the society who is able to obtain a large number of wives, whereas under the exchange system the number

of wives a man can obtain is limited to the number of sisters and/or daughters at the man's disposal.

## RECIPROCAL EXCHANGE

This marital custom, found in approximately six percent of the societies listed in Murdock's *Ethnographic Atlas,* is most prominently found in the Pacific region and among traditional Native Americans. It involves the relatively equal exchange of gifts between the families of both the bride and the groom. Such a custom was practiced by the traditional Vugusu people of Western Kenya who exchanged a large variety of items between a sizeable number of people from both families. According to Wagner, the gifts made and the expenses incurred were basically reciprocal, with only "a slight preponderance on the bride's side" (1949:423). The variety of the reciprocal gift giving and the number of people involved in Vugusu society tends to emphasize the generally valid tenet that marriages in many parts of the world are conceived not simply as a union between a man and a woman but rather as an alliance between two families.

## ◆ ◆ ◆ Residence Patterns: Where Do Wives and Husbands Live?

In addition to establishing regulations for mate selection, the number of spouses one can have, and the types of economic considerations that must be attended to, societies set guidelines regarding where couples will live when they marry. When two people marry in our own society, it is customary for the couple to take up residence in a place of their own, apart from the relatives of either spouse. This residence pattern is known as *neolocal residence* (i.e., a new place). As natural as this may appear to us, it is, by global standards, a relatively rare type of residence pattern, practiced in only about five percent of the societies of the world. The remaining societies prescribe that newlyweds will live with or in close proximity to relatives of either the wife or the husband.

One question facing these societies is, which children stay at home when they marry, and which ones leave? Also, of those who leave, with which relative are they expected to reside? Although there are a number of ways of answering these questions, most residence patterns fall into one of five different patterns [percentages based on tabulations from Murdock's *Ethnographic Atlas* (1967)]:

*Patrilocal Residence.* The married couple lives with or near the relatives of the husband's father (69 percent of the societies).

*Matrilocal Residence.* The married couple lives with or near the relatives of the wife (13 percent of the societies).

*Avunculocal Residence.* The married couple lives with or near the husband's mother's brother (4 percent of the societies).

*Ambilocal (Bilocal) Residence.* The married couple has a choice of living with either the relatives of the wife or the relatives of the husband (9 percent of the societies.)

*Neolocal Residence.* The married couple forms an independent place of residence away from the relatives of either spouse (5 percent of the societies).

To a significant degree, residence patterns have an effect on the types of kinship systems (discussed in the

Typically, when two people marry in the United States, they live in a home of their own apart from the relatives of either spouse.

previous chapter) found in any society. There is, for example, a reasonably close correlation between patrilocal residence and patrilineal descent (tracing one's important relatives through the father's side) and between matrilocal residence and matrilineal descent (tracing one's important relatives through the mother's side). To be certain, residence patterns do not determine kinship ideology, but social interaction between certain categories of kin can be facilitated if those kin reside (and play out their lives) in close proximity to each other.

It should be kept in mind that these five residence patterns, like most other aspects of culture, are ideal types. Consequently, how people actually behave—that is, where they may reside—doesn't always conform precisely to these ideals. Sometimes, normative patterns of residence can be altered or interrupted by such factors as famine and epidemics, forcing newlyweds to reside in areas that would maximize either their chances for survival or their economic security. To illustrate, during the Depression years of the 1930s, the normal neolocal pattern of residence in the United States was disrupted when many young married adults moved in with one set of parents to save money.

# Family Structure

Cultural anthropologists have identified two fundamentally different types of family structure—the **nuclear family** and the **extended family**. The nuclear family is based on marital ties, while the extended family, a much larger social unit, is based on blood ties between three or more generations of kin.

### THE NUCLEAR FAMILY

Consisting of husband and wife and their children, the nuclear family is a two-generation family formed around the conjugal or marital union. Even though the nuclear family to some degree is part of a larger family structure, it remains a relatively autonomous and independent unit. That is, the everyday needs of economic support, childcare, and social interaction are met within the nuclear family itself rather than by a wider set of relatives. In those societies based on the nuclear family, it is customary for married couples to live apart from either set of parents (neolocal residence), nor is there any particular obligation or expectation for the married couple to care for their aging parents in their own homes. Generally, parents are not actively involved in mate selection for their children, in no way legitimize the marriages of their children, and have no control over whether or not their children remain married.

The nuclear family is most likely to be found in those societies with the greatest amount of geographic mobility. This certainly is the case in the United States, which presently has both considerable geographic mobility and the ideal of the nuclear family. During much of our nation's early history, the extended family—tied to the land and working on the family farm—was the rule rather than the exception. Today, however, the family farm housing parents, grandparents, aunts, uncles, cousins, and siblings is a thing of the past. Now, in response to the forces of industrialization, most adults move to wherever they can find suitable employment. Since one's profession largely determines where one will live, adults in the United States frequently live considerable distances from their parents or other non-nuclear family members.

In addition to being situated in such highly industrialized societies as our own, the nuclear family is found in certain societies located at the other end of the technological spectrum. In certain foraging societies residing in environments where resources are meager (such as the Inuit of Northern Canada and the Shoshone of Utah and Nevada), the nuclear family is the basic hunting-and-gathering unit. These nuclear families remain highly independent foraging groups that fend for themselves. Even though they cannot expect help from the outside in an emergency, they have developed a family structure that is well adapted to a highly mobile life. Thus, both U.S. society and some small-scale hunting-and-gathering societies have adopted the nuclear family pattern because of their need to maintain a high degree of geographic mobility.

Although the independent nuclear family has been the ideal in the United States for much of the present century, significant changes have occurred in recent years. According to the U.S. Census, only about one in three households consists of the nuclear family (parents and one or more children), a sharp decline from earlier decades. The other two thirds of the U.S. households are made up of married couples without children, single adults, single parents, unmarried couples, roommates, extended family members, or adult siblings. As Kottak (1987:310–11) has suggested, these changing patterns of family life have been reflected in a number of TV sitcoms. For example, during the 1950s the family was depicted by Ozzie and Harriet Nelson and their sons David and Ricky and by Ward and June Cleaver and their sons Wally and the Beaver. Even though the 1980s produced such nuclear family sitcoms as *Family Ties* and *The Cosby Show*, there has been an increasing number of TV shows featuring alternative living arrangements such as roommates (*Three's Company* and *Golden Girls*), single adults (*Perfect Strangers*), working mothers (*Kate and Allie*), and single parents (*One Day at a Time*). In fact, some of the most popular TV sitcoms of the 1980s featured characters who were neither related to nor living with one another (*Cheers, Taxi,* and *WKRP*).

There are several explanations for the decline of the nuclear family in the United States as we head into the twenty-first century. First, as more and more women complete higher education and enter the job market,

Many of the societies studied by anthropologists are based on extended families. This multigenerational family in North Syria is held together by ties of both blood and marriage.

they are more likely to delay marrying and having children. Second, the increasing cost of maintaining a middle-class household that includes not just the parents and children but also a three- or four-bedroom house, a cocker spaniel, and a car or two has caused some couples to opt for remaining childless altogether. Third, the ever-increasing divorce rate in the United States has contributed in recent decades to the increase in non-nuclear families.

## THE EXTENDED FAMILY

In societies based on extended families, blood ties are more important than ties of marriage. Extended families consist of two or more families that are linked by blood ties. Most commonly, this takes the form of a married

couple living with one or more of their married children in a single household or homestead and under the authority of a family head. Such extended families, which are based on parent-child linkages, can be either patrilineal (comprising a man, his sons, and the sons' wives and children) or matrilineal (comprising a woman, her daughters, and her daughters' husbands and children). It is also possible for extended families to be linked though sibling ties rather than parent-child ties, such as those extended families consisting of two or more married brothers and their wives and children. According to Murdock's *Ethnographic Atlas* (1967), approximately 46 percent of the 862 societies listed have some type of extended family organization.

When a couple marries in a society with extended families, there is little sense that the newlyweds are establishing a separate and distinct family unit. In the case of a patrilineal extended family, the young couple takes up residence in the homestead of the husband's father, and the husband continues to work for his father, who also runs the household. Moreover, most of the personal property in the household is not owned by the newlyweds, but is controlled by the husband's father. In the event that the extended family is large, it may be headed by two or more powerful male elders who run the family in much the same way that a board of directors runs a corporation. Eventually, the father (or other male elders) will die or retire, allowing younger men to assume positions of leadership and power within the extended family. Unlike the nuclear family, which lasts only one generation, the extended family is a continuous unit that can last an indefinite number of generations. As old people die off, they are replaced by the birth of new members.

It is important to point out that in extended family systems, marriage is viewed more as bringing a daughter into the family than acquiring a wife. In other words, a man's obligations of obedience to his father and loyalty to his brothers is far more important than his relationship to his wife. When a woman marries into an extended family, she most often comes under the control of her mother-in-law, who allocates chores and supervises her domestic activities.

In some extended family systems, the conjugal relationship is suppressed to such an extent that contact between husband and wife is kept to a minimum. Among the Rajputs of Northern India, for example, spouses are not allowed to talk to each other in the presence of family elders. Public displays of affection between spouses is considered reprehensible, and in fact, a husband is not permitted to show open concern for his wife's welfare. Some societies take such severe measures to subordinate the husband-wife relationship because it is feared that a man's feelings for his wife could interfere with his obligations to his own blood relatives.

Why do so many societies in the world have extended families? There is some indication that extended families are more likely to be found in certain types of economies than others. As previously mentioned, economies based on either foraging or wage employment (which require considerable geographic mobility) are more likely to be associated with nuclear than with extended families. In addition, a rough correlation exists between extended family systems and an agricultural way of life. Several logical explanations have been suggested for this correlation. First, extended families provide relatively large numbers of workers who are necessary for success in both farm production and the marketing of surpluses.

Second, in farm economics where cultivated land is valuable, an extended family system prevents the land from being continually subdivided into smaller and less productive plots. As an alternative explanation, Pasternak, Ember, and Ember (1976) have suggested that extended family systems develop in response to what they call "incompatible activity requirements." That is, extended families are likely to prevail in those societies where there is a lack of man and woman power to simultaneously carry out subsistence and domestic tasks.

## MODERN-DAY FAMILY STRUCTURE

Most Western social thinkers over the past century have been in general agreement concerning the long-term effects of urbanization and modernization on the family. In general they see a progressive nuclearization of the family in the face of modernization. This position is perhaps most eloquently presented by William Goode, who has stated that industrialization and urbanization have brought about ". . . fewer kinship ties with distant relatives and a greater emphasis on the 'nuclear' family unit of couple and children" (1963:1). Although in many parts of the world we can observe the association between modernization and fewer extended kinship ties, there are a number of exceptions, most notably in certain Third World areas. To illustrate, in the Kenya Kinship Study (KKS) discussed in Chapter 13, no significant differences were found in the extended family interaction between rural Kikuyu and Kikuyu living in Nairobi. This retention of extended family ties in this urban/industrialized setting could be explained by several relevant economic factors. First, the combination of a fiercely competitive job market and little or no employment benefits (e.g., workers' compensation, retirement, unemployment insurance) leads to little job security for the average urban worker. Second, despite the creation of freehold land tenure in Kenya in recent years, land inheritance still takes place, by and large, within the extended family. Urban workers who sever ties with their rural-based extended kin relinquish their rights to inherit land, which for many remains the only haven from the insecurities of urban employment.

Interestingly, we do not need to focus on Third World countries to find the retention of extended kin ties in urban, industrialized areas. For example, Carol Stack (1975) and J. W. Sharff (1981) have shown how extended kinship ties are used by urban Blacks in the United States as a strategy for coping with poverty. Moreover, at least one immigrant group in the United

The strong support of Vietnamese families in the United States has enabled their children to excel in all levels of U.S. education.

States—the Vietnamese—has used modern technology to help maintain and strengthen its traditional family values. Nash (1988) reports that immigrant Vietnamese families routinely rent Chinese-made films (dubbed in Vietnamese) for their VCRs. Whereas most films and TV programming in the United States tends to glorify the individual, Chinese films tend to emphasize the traditional Confucian value of family loyalty.

## ◆ Summary

1. Owing to the vast ethnographic variations found in the world, the terms *family* and *marriage* are not easy to define. Recognizing the difficulties inherent in such definitions, the family is a social unit, the members of which cooperate economically, manage reproduction and child rearing, and most often live together. Marriage—the process by which families are formed—refers to a socially approved union between male and female adults.

2. The formation of families through the process of marriage serves several important social functions by (a) reducing competition for spouses; (b) regulating the sexual division of labor; and (c) meeting the material, educational, and emotional needs of children.

3. Every culture has a set of rules (incest taboos) regulating which categories of kin are inappropriate partners for sexual intercourse. A number of explanations have been suggested for this universal incest taboo, including (a) the natural aversion theory, (b) the inbreeding theory, (c) the family disruption theory, and (d) the theory of expanding social alliances.

4. Cultures restrict the choice of marriage partners by such practices as exogamy, endogamy, arranged marriages, preferential cousin marriage, the levirate, and the sororate.

5. All societies have rules governing the number of spouses a person can have. Societies tend to emphasize either monogamy (one spouse at a time), polygyny (a man marrying more than one wife at a time), or polyandry (a woman marrying more than one husband at a time).

6. In many societies, marriages involve the transfer of some type of economic consideration in exchange for rights of sexual access, legal rights over children, and rights to each other's property. These economic considerations involve such practices as bride price, bride service, dowry, woman exchange, and reciprocal exchange.

7. All societies have guidelines regarding where a married couple should live after they marry. Residence patterns fall into five different categories. The couple can live with or near the relatives of the husband's father (patrilocal), the wife (matrilocal), or the husband's mother's brother (avunculocal) or the relatives of either the wife or the husband (ambilocal), or the husband and wife can form a completely new residence of their own.

8. Cultural anthropologists distinguish between two types of family structure: the nuclear family, comprising the wife, husband, and children; and the extended

family, a much larger social unit, comprising relatives from three or more generations.

# ◆ Key Terms

| | |
|---|---|
| ambilocal (bilocal) residence | monogamy |
| arranged marriage | neolocal residence |
| avunculocal residence | nuclear family |
| bride price (bridewealth) | parallel cousins |
| bride service | patrilocal residence |
| cross cousins | polyandry |
| dowry | polygyny |
| endogamy | post partum sex taboo |
| exogamy | preferential cousin marriage |
| extended family | reciprocal exchange |
| incest taboo | role ambiguity |
| kibbutz | sororate |
| levirate | woman exchange |
| matrilocal residence | |

# ◆ Suggested Readings

Fernea, Elizabeth. *Guests of the Sheik: An Ethnography of an Iraqi Village*. Garden City, N.Y.: Doubleday, 1965. While accompanying her anthropologist husband on a field trip to the Middle East, Fernea describes the sheltered world of women in a small desert town in Southern Iraq. Her very personal account of the difficulties she encountered in adapting to the culture of Iraqi women should be required reading for anyone interested in understanding the institution of marriage in the Islamic world.

Fox, Robin. *Kinship and Marriage: An Anthropological Perspective*. Baltimore: Penguin, 1968. An excellent introduction to the cross-cultural study of marriage, particularly exogamous systems.

Friedl, Ernestine. *Women and Men: An Anthropologist's View*. New York: Holt, Rinehart & Winston, 1975. Gender roles, a topic closely associated with marriage, is the subject of this volume, which draws on ethnographic data from a number of different societies to suggest a series of hypotheses about the determinants and expressions of sex roles.

Goody, Jack, and S. J. Tambiah. *Bridewealth and Dowry*. Cambridge: Cambridge University Press, 1973. These two forms of marriage transactions are analyzed in the context of Africa, where bridewealth predominates, and Asia, where dowry is the most common practice.

Hart, C. W. M., Arnold Pilling, and Jane C. Goodale. *The Tiwi of North Australia* (3rd ed.). New York: Holt, Rinehart & Winston, 1988. A fascinating ethnographic account of the Tiwi of Melville Island (off the northern coast of Australia), who practice an extreme form of polygyny, whereby all females are always married and males spend much of their lives competing for the society's major status symbol—i.e., wives.

Mair, Lucy. *Marriage*. Baltimore: Penguin, 1971. Drawing on data from a wide variety of non-Western societies, the author examines the functions, regulations, symbolic rituals, and economic considerations of marriage.

Stephens, William N. *The Family in Cross Cultural Perspective*. New York: Holt, Rinehart & Winston, 1963. Citing literature from all over the world, this cross-cultural study of marriage and the family examines such topics as the universality of the family, plural marriage, mate selection, sexual restrictions, divorce, and conjugal roles.

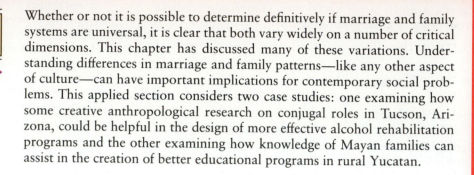

# APPLIED PERSPECTIVE

## Marriage and the Family

Whether or not it is possible to determine definitively if marriage and family systems are universal, it is clear that both vary widely on a number of critical dimensions. This chapter has discussed many of these variations. Understanding differences in marriage and family patterns—like any other aspect of culture—can have important implications for contemporary social problems. This applied section considers two case studies: one examining how some creative anthropological research on conjugal roles in Tucson, Arizona, could be helpful in the design of more effective alcohol rehabilitation programs and the other examining how knowledge of Mayan families can assist in the creation of better educational programs in rural Yucatan.

◆ **The anthropological study of the connection between alcoholism and conjugal relations can lead to the design of effective programs for alcohol rehabilitation.**

The understanding of such areas of concern as marriage patterns, family structures, conjugal roles, and parent-child relationships can be absolutely vital for the solution of certain pressing world problems. One such problem facing the world's population is alcoholism. Although alcoholic drinks have been used for thousands of years, the widespread abuse of alcohol is a relatively recent phenomenon. Cross-cultural studies of alcohol consumption (e.g., Marshall, 1979) have suggested, among other things, that alcohol consumption is affected by one's cultural background. If this is in fact the case, it seems logical that anthropologists, by examining the relationships between alcoholism and social structure, could contribute to the solution of this menacing social problem.

In a somewhat unorthodox approach to the study of alcohol use, Staski (1984) used the archaeological technique of "garbology" (i.e., counting the number of empty alcohol containers from people's garbage) to document alcohol consumption among contemporary residents of Tucson, Arizona. He found that the critical variable associated with alcohol consumption was household structure. More specifically, he found that alcohol use was highest in those households with the greatest differences in age, occupation, and education between the spouses. Conversely, little alcohol consumption was reported in those households where spouses were similar in these three social characteristics. Staski reasoned that greater differences between spouses lead to increased incompatibility, stress, potential conflict, marital instability, and, consequently, higher levels of alcohol consumption. Cultural anthropologists, using a wide variety of field techniques, including participant-observation, are in a particularly good position to analyze drinking behavior, relate it to other aspects of the culture (such as conjugal relationships), and design tailor-made strategies for reducing some of the more deleterious effects of alcoholism on the community.

◆ **The use of anthropological data on Mayan family life can increase the effectiveness of educational programs in rural Yucatan.**

Knowledge of family patterns can be vital to teachers, particularly those teaching students from culturally different backgrounds. It goes without saying that teachers must be aware of various aspects of the learning environments of their classrooms. Yet, the classroom does not exist in a vacuum. All too frequently, teachers do not consider their students' family interaction patterns, which influence the behavior and attitudes students bring with them into class. If teachers are to respond effectively to all of their students, they have to be aware of the home learning environment of their students and how the environment conforms to or conflicts with the learning environment of the classroom.

Stearns (1986) has shown how the ethnographic method can be used by anthropologists working with local teachers to make important linkages between the school and the families from which their students come. Working with students and teachers in rural Yucatan, Stearns described a school situation where the cultural backgrounds, values, and assumptions of the teachers were radically different from those of the students. Mayan students from traditional homes are faced with considerable cultural dissonance when they are faced with a school reflecting mainstream Mexican culture and a Spanish-speaking teacher whose teaching style is often incompatible with traditional Mayan learning styles.

Stearns attempted to bridge the gap between the cultural backgrounds of the Ladino teachers and their Mayan students by using an approach that he called directed ethnography. Working under the direction of anthropologist Stearns, the Ladino teachers, during their nonworking hours, collected sociocultural data from the families of their students, including data on (1) how parents organized their children's activities at home, (2) parental teaching styles, (3) learning styles of the children in the home, (4) certain nonverbal forms of communication (gestures, facial expressions, eye contact, etc.), (5) traditional Mayan perceptual models, and (6) traditional modes of verbal communication. The advantage to the teacher of the directed ethnographies, as Stearns put it, is that it is "a here and now mechanism to modify their teaching style and curriculum materials to better respond to the sociocultural norms of the indigenous community and to the learning style of their native students" (1986:8).

The findings from these directed ethnographies enabled the teachers to modify their teaching styles, classroom environments, and curricular materials to better reflect the cultural experiences of their third-grade Mayan students. Stearns, along with his team of teacher-ethnographers, reported a number of interesting findings. First, they found that the overwhelming majority of the more than 1,100 parent-child and child-child interactions observed in the homes were cooperative and reinforcing of family cohesiveness. Second, children, by and large, performed their household responsibilities without having to be reminded by their parents. Third, parents responded to their children's inappropriate behavior with a stern look of disapproval rather than having to resort to either verbal or corporal punishment. This nonverbal message usually resulted in the child's altering the inappropriate behavior.

Equipped with these insights, the teachers were able to make specific changes in their classrooms. To illustrate, one teacher who had often hit students' desks with his ruler in a threatening manner to emphasize a point, discontinued this practice because Mayan parents never threatened their children in such a way at home. Another teacher, noticing how slowly and deliberately Mayan parents speak to their children, found that he could communicate much more effectively to his Mayan students by slowing down his speech. A third teacher, having observed how attentive Mayan parents are when teaching their children, found that his students responded to his instruction more effectively when he showed them greater attention by standing closer to them. These, then, were just some of the educational improvements that the Ladino teachers were able to make in their classrooms after they had gathered valuable information on the interactional patterns found in the families of their students.

## CHAPTER 19

# Political Organization and Social Control

What are the different types of political organization?

What are the various theories concerning the origins of the state?

In the absence of kings, presidents, legislatures, and bureaucracies, how is social order maintained in stateless societies?

As mentioned in the discussion of cultural universals in Chapter 2, all societies—if they are to last as viable societies over time—must maintain social order. Every society must develop a set of customs and procedures for making and enforcing decisions, for resolving disputes, and for regulating the behavior of its members. Every society must make collective decisions about its environment and its relations with other societies and with the eventuality of disruptive or destructive behavior on the part of its members. These topics generally are discussed under such headings as political organization, law, power, authority, war, social control, and conflict resolution. While exploring all of these subjects, this chapter deals with those cultural arrangements by which societies maintain social order, minimize the chances of disruption, and cope with whatever disruptions do occur.

When most North Americans speak of politics or political structure, a number of familiar images come to mind. For example, one may think of any of the following:

1. Political leaders such as presidents, governors, mayors, or commissioners.
2. Complex bureaucracies employing thousands of civil servants.
3. Legislative bodies ranging from the smallest town council to the U. S. Congress.
4. Formal judicial institutions that comprise municipal, state, and federal law courts.
5. Such law enforcement bodies as police departments, national guard units, or the armed forces.
6. Political parties, nominating conventions, secret ballot voting, and the convening of the electoral college.

All of these, to be certain, are mechanisms in our own society for making and enforcing political decisions as well as coordinating and regulating people's behavior. Many societies in the world have none of these things—no elected officials, legislatures, formal elections, armies, or bureaucracies. We should not conclude from this, however, that such societies do not have some form of political organization, if by "political organization" we mean a set of customary procedures that accomplish decision making, conflict resolution, and social control.

◆　◆　◆
# Types of Political Organization

While political organization can be found in all societies, the degree of specialized and formal mechanisms varies considerably from one society to another. Societies differ in their political organization based on three important dimensions:

1. The extent to which political institutions are distinct from other aspects of the social structure; that is, in some societies, political structures are barely indistinguishable from economic, kinship, or religious structures.
2. The extent to which **authority** is concentrated into specific political roles.
3. The level of **political integration** (i.e., the size of the territorial group that comes under the control of the political structure).

These three dimensions are the basis for the classification of societies (following Service, 1978) into four fundamentally different types of political structure: **band societies, tribal societies, chiefdoms,** and **state societies.** Although societies do not all fit neatly into one or another of these categories, this fourfold scheme is useful to help us understand how different societies administer themselves and maintain social order.

## BAND SOCIETIES

The least complex form of political arrangement is the band, characterized by small and usually nomadic populations of hunters and gatherers. Although the size of a band can range anywhere from twenty to several hundred individuals, most bands number between thirty and fifty people. The actual size of particular bands is directly related to food-gathering methods; that is, the more food a band has at its disposal, the larger the number of people it can support. While bands may be loosely associated with a specific territory, they have little or no concept of individual property ownership and place a high value on sharing, cooperation, and reciprocity. Band societies have very little role specialization and are highly **egalitarian** in that few differences in status and wealth can be observed. Since this form of political organization is so closely associated with a hunting-and-gathering technology, it is generally held that it represents the oldest form of political organization.

Band societies have a number of traits in common with each other. First, band societies have the least amount of political integration; that is, the various bands (each comprising fifty or so people) are independent of one another and are not part of a larger political structure. What integration does exist is largely based on ties of kinship and marriage. All of the bands found in any particular culture are bound together by a com-

## CROSS-CULTURAL MISCUE

In some cases, a lack of understanding of different languages and ways of communicating can have life-or-death consequences. For example, in the late 1970s, Adolph Dubs, the U.S. ambassador to Afghanistan, was kidnapped and taken to the Kabul Hotel. The *Washington Star* reported that before the ambassador was slain, our "embassy officials had a brief chance to seize the initiative because they reached the hotel before the Afghan police. But no one in the American party spoke fluent Dari or Pushtu, the two most widely used Afghan languages. . . . " (Simon 1980:41–42) It is possible that the ambassador's life might have been spared had our embassy officials been able to talk to the kidnappers directly.

mon language and general cultural features. They do not, however, all pay political allegiance to any overall authority.

Second, in band societies political decisions are frequently embedded in the wider social structure. Since bands are composed of kin, it is difficult to distinguish between purely political decisions and those that we would recognize as family, economic, or religious decisions. Political life, in other words, is simply one part of social life.

Third, leadership roles in band societies tend to be very informal. In band societies, there are no specialized political roles or leaders with designated authority. Instead, leaders in foraging societies are frequently, but not always, older men respected for their experience, wisdom, good judgment, and knowledge of hunting. Most decisions are made through discussions by the adult men. The headman can persuade and give advice but has no power to impose his will on the group. The headman frequently gives advice on such matters as migratory movements, but he possesses no permanent authority. If his advice proves to be wrong or unpopular, the group members will look to another person to be headman. Band leadership, then, stems not so much from power but rather from the recognized personal traits admired by the others in the group.

The !Kung of the Kalahari exemplify a band society with a headman. Although the position of headman is hereditary, the actual authority of the headman is quite limited. The headman coordinates the movement of his people and usually walks at the head of the group. He chooses the sites of new encampments and has first pick of location for his own house site. But beyond these limited perks of office, the !Kung headman receives no other rewards. He is in no way responsible for organiz-

ing hunting parties, making artifacts, or negotiating marriage arrangements. These activities fall to the individual members of the band. The headman is not expected to be a judge of his people. Moreover, his material possessions are no greater than any other person's. As Marshall so aptly put it when referring to the !Kung headman, "He carries his own load and is as thin as the rest" (1965:267).

## TRIBAL SOCIETIES

Whereas band societies are usually associated with hunting and gathering, tribal societies are found most often among food producers (horticulturalists and pastoralists). Since plant and animal domestication is far more productive than foraging, tribal societies tend to have populations that are larger, more dense, and somewhat more sedentary in nature. Tribal societies are similar to band societies in several important respects. They are both egalitarian to the extent that there are no marked differences in status, rank, power, and wealth. In addition, tribal societies, like bands, have local leaders but do not have centralized leadership.

The major difference between tribes and bands is that tribal societies have certain **pan-tribal mechanisms** that cut across and integrate all of the local segments of the tribe into a larger whole. These mechanisms include such tribal associations as clans, age grades, or secret societies. Pan-tribal associations function to unite the tribe against external threats. These integrating forces are not permanent political fixtures, however. Most often the local units of a tribe operate autonomously, for the integrating mechanisms come into play only when an external threat arises. When the threat is eliminated,

Such tribal societies as the Masai of East Africa have certain pan-tribal mechanisms, such as clans and age organizations, that serve to integrate the tribe as a whole.

the local units return to their autonomous state. Even though these pan-tribal mechanisms may be transitory, they nevertheless provide wider political integration in certain situations than would ever be possible in band societies.

In many tribal societies, the kinship unit known as the clan serves as a pan-tribal mechanism of political integration. The clan is defined as a group of kin who consider themselves to be descended from a common ancestor, even though individual clan members cannot trace, step-by-step, their connection to the clan founder. Clan elders, while not holding formal political offices, usually manage the affairs of their clans (e.g., settle disputes between clan members) and represent their clans in dealings with other clans.

Another form of pan-tribal association based on kinship that is found in tribal societies is the **segmentary lineage system** (discussed in the chapter on kinship). While less common than tribal societies based on clans, those based on segmentary lineage systems are instructive because they demonstrate the shifting or ephemeral nature of the political structure in tribal societies. In a segmentary system, individuals belong to a series of different descent units (corresponding to different genealogical levels) that function in different social contexts.

The most basic or local unit is the minimal lineage, comprising three to five generations. Members of a minimal lineage usually live together, consider themselves to be the closest of kin, and generally engage in everyday activities together. Minimal lineages, which tend to be

politically independent, form a hierarchy of genealogical units. For example, minimal lineages make up minor lineages; minor lineages coalesce into major lineages; and major lineages form maximal lineages. When a dispute occurs between individuals of different segments, people are expected to side with that disputant to whom they are most closely related. Thus, people who act as a unit in one context merge into larger aggregates in other social situations. This process of lineage segmentation means that segments will unite when confronted by a wider group. In the words of Middleton and Tait:

. . . a segment that in one situation is independent finds that it and its former competitors are merged together as subordinate segments in the internal administrative organization of a wider overall segment that includes them both. This wider segment is in turn in external competitive relations with other similar segments, and there may be an entire series of such segments (1958:6–7).

It is important to keep in mind that these various segments—minimal, minor, major, and maximal lineages—are not groups but rather alliance networks that are activated only under certain circumstances. This process tends to deflect hostilities away from competing kin and toward an outside, or more distant, enemy. Such a level of political organization is effective for the mobilization of a military force either to defend the entire tribe from outside forces or for expanding into the territories of weaker societies.

The pastoral Nuer of the Southern Sudan serve as a good example of a tribal form of political organization (Evans-Pritchard, 1940). The Nuer, who number approximately 300,000 people, have no centralized government and no governmental functionaries with coercive authority. There are, of course, influential men, but their influence stems more from their personal traits than from the force of elected or inherited office. The Nuer, who are highly egalitarian, do not readily accept authority beyond the elders of the family. Social control among the Nuer is maintained by segmentary lineages in that close kin are expected to come to the assistance of one another against more distantly related people.

## CHIEFDOMS

As we have seen, in band and tribal societies, local groups are economically and politically autonomous, authority is uncentralized, and populations tend to be generally egalitarian. Moreover, roles are unspecialized, populations are small in size, and economies are largely subsistent in nature. But as societies become more complex—with larger and more specialized populations, more sophisticated technology, and growing surpluses—an increasing need for more formal and permanent political structures develops. In such societies, known as chiefdoms, political authority is likely to reside with a single individual, either acting alone or in conjunction with an advisory council.

The chiefdom differs from bands and tribes in that chiefdoms integrate a number of local communities in a more formal and permanent way. Unlike bands and tribes, chiefdoms are made up of local communities that are not equal, but rather differ from one another in terms of rank and status. Based on their genealogical proximity to the chiefs, nobles and commoners hold different levels of prestige and power. Chiefships are frequently hereditary, and the chief and his or her immediate kin constitute a social and political elite. Rarely are chiefdoms totally unified politically under a single chief; more frequently, they are composed of several political units, each headed by a chief.

Chiefdoms also differ from tribes and bands in that chiefs are centralized and permanent officials with higher rank, power, and authority than others in the society. Unlike bands or tribal headmen or headwomen, chiefs usually have considerable power, authority, and, in some cases, even wealth. Internal social disruptions are minimized in a chiefdom because the chief usually has authority to make judgments, punish wrongdoers, and settle disputes. Chiefs usually have the authority to distribute land to loyal subjects, recruit people into military service, and recruit laborers for public works projects. Chiefly authority is usually reinforced by certain alleged supernatural powers. Polynesian chiefs, for example, were believed to possess the supernatural power of *mana,* which lent a special type of credence to their authority.

Chiefs are also intimately related to the economic activities of their subjects through the redistributive system of economics (see the chapter on economics). Subjects will give food surpluses to the chief (not uncommonly at the chief's insistence) which are then redistributed by the chief through communal feasts and doles. This system of redistribution through a chief serves the obvious economic function of ensuring that no people in the society go hungry. It also serves the important political function of providing the people with a mechanism for expressing their loyalty and support for the chief.

Within the past hundred and fifty years, a number of societies with no former tradition of chiefs have had chiefships imposed on them by some of the European colonial powers. As the European colonial governments created their colonial empires during the nineteenth century, they created chiefs (or altered the nature of traditional chiefs) to facilitate administering local populations. For example, the British created chiefs for their own administrative convenience among chiefless societies in Nigeria, Kenya, and Australia. These new chiefs—who were given salaries and high-sounding titles such as paramount chief—were selected primarily on the basis of their willingness to work with the colonial administration rather than any particular popularity among their own people. In some cases, these new chiefs were held in contempt by their own people because they were seen to be collaborators with the colonial governments, which were often viewed as repressive and coercive.

The precolonial Hawaiian political system of the eighteenth century embodied the features of a typical chiefdom. According to Service (1975:152–54), Hawaiian society, covering eight islands, was layered into three basic social strata. At the apex of the threefold social hierarchy were the *ali'i,* major chiefs believed to be direct descendants of the gods and whose close relatives often served as advisers or bureaucrats under them. The second echelon, known as the *konohiki,* were less important chiefs who were frequently distant relatives of the *ali'i.* And finally, the great majority of people were commoners, known as *maka'ainana.* Since there was little or no intermarriage between these three strata, the society was, by and large, castelike. But since the *ali'i* had certain priestly functions by virtue of their connection with the gods, Hawaiian society was a theocracy as well.

The Hawaiian economy during the precolonial period was based on intensive agriculture (taro, breadfruit, yams, and coconuts) with extensive irrigation. Owing to their control over the allocation of water, the major chiefs and their subordinates wielded considerable power and authority over the general population. In addition, chiefs were in control of communal labor, craftspersons, and the drafting of people for warfare. In terms of the settlement of disputes, Hawaiian chiefs had considerable coercive power on the disputants, even though in actual practice most disputes were settled through collective action. In summary, the precolonial Hawaiian political system, according to Service,

. . . was a theocracy, held together by an ideology that justified and sanctified the rule of the hereditary aristocracy, buttressed by age-old custom and etiquette. Such a system is in some contrast to a primitive state, which, although it attempts to rule ideologically and customarily, has had to erect the additional support of a monopoly of force with a legal structure that administers the force (1975:154).

## STATE SYSTEMS

The state system of government is the most formal and the most complex form of political organization. A state can be defined as a hierarchical form of political organization that governs many communities within a relatively large geographic area. States possess the power to collect taxes, can recruit labor for armies and civilian public works projects, and have a monopoly on the right to use force. They are large bureaucratic organizations made up of permanent institutions with legislative, administrative, and judicial functions. Whereas bands and tribes have political structures based on kinship, state systems of government organize their power on a suprakinship basis. That is, one's membership in a state is based on his or her place of residence and citizenship rather than on kinship affiliation. Over the past several thousand years, the rise of state systems of government have taken a number of varied forms, including Greek city-states; the far-reaching Roman empire; certain traditional African states such as Bunyoro, Buganda, and the Swazi; theocratic states such as ancient Egypt; and such modern nation-states as Germany, Japan, and the United States.

State systems of government such as our own are characterized by a high degree of role specialization and a hierarchical organization.

The authority of the state rests on two important foundations. *First,* it is the state that holds the exclusive right to use force and physical coercion. Any act of violence not expressly permitted by the state is illegal and, consequently, punishable by the state. Thus, state governments make written laws, administer them through various levels of the bureaucracy, and enforce them through such mechanisms as police forces, armies, and national guards. The state needs to be continuously vigilant against threats both from within and from without to usurp its power through rebellions and revolutions. *Second,* the state maintains its authority by means of ideology. For the state to maintain its power over the long run, there must be a philosophical understanding among the citizenry that the state in fact has the legitimate right to govern. In the absence of such an ideology, it is frequently difficult for the state to maintain its authority by means of coercion alone.

State systems of government, first appearing about 3200 B.C., are associated with civilizations. As such, they are found in those societies with complex socioeconomic characteristics. For example, state systems of government are supported by intensive agriculture, required to support a large number of non-food producing bureaucrats. This fully efficient food production system gives rise to cities, considerable labor specialization, and a complex system of both internal distribution and foreign trade. Since the considerable surpluses produced by intensive agriculture are not distributed equally among all segments of the population, state societies are stratified. That is, such forms of wealth as land and capital tend to be concentrated in the hands of an elite who often use their superior wealth and power to control the rest of the population. Moreover, the fairly complex set of laws and regulations needed to control a large and heterogeneous population gave rise to the need for some type of writing, record keeping, and weights and measures.

State systems of government are characterized by a large number of **specialized political roles**. Large numbers of people are required to carry out very specific tasks such as law enforcement, tax collection, dispute settlement, recruitment of labor, and protection from outside invasions. These political/administrative functionaries are both highly specialized and full time to the extent that they do not engage in food-producing activities. This collection of permanent political functionaries, like the society itself, is highly stratified or hierarchical. At the apex of the administrative pyramid are those with the greatest power—e.g., kings, presidents, prime ministers, governors, legislators—who enact laws and establish policies. Below those at the top of the political hierarchies are descending echelons of bureaucrats responsible for the day-to-day administration of the state. As is the case in our own form of government, each level of the bureaucracy is responsible to the level immediately above it.

## VARIATIONS IN POLITICAL STRUCTURES: SOME GENERALIZATIONS

The preceding sections have looked at four fundamentally different types of political systems. Such a fourfold scheme, while recognized by other ethnologists, is not universally accepted. For example, in a classic study of political systems in Africa, Fortes and Evans-Pritchard (1940:5) distinguish between only two types of structures: state systems and **acephalous** (headless) **societies**. Others (Cohen and Eames, 1982:215) recognize three major forms of political structure: simple, intermediate, and complex. Such differences in the way that various ethnologists have conceptualized political structures should serve as a reminder that all of these schemes are ideal types. That is, all of the societies in the world cannot be fitted neatly into one box or another. Instead of seeing these categories as discrete, in reality there is continuous variation between bands (the simplest forms) at one extreme and states (the most complex forms) at the other. Thus, whether we use two, three, or four major categories of political organization, we should bear in mind that all political systems found in the world vary along a continuum on a number of important dimensions. To illustrate, as we move from bands through tribes and chiefdoms to states, gradations occur as in Exhibit 19-1.

◆  ◆  ◆

**EXHIBIT 19-1**
**Variations in Political Aspects of World Culture**

|  | Bands | Tribes | Chiefdoms | States |
|---|---|---|---|---|
| Degree to which political institutions are distinct from kinship | Indistinguishable | | | Distinct |
| Level of political integration | Local group | | | Many groups |
| Specialized political roles | Informal leadership | | | Highly special |
|  | Temporary | | | Permanent |
| Degree of political coerciveness | Little/none | | | Complete |

EXHIBIT 19-2

**Variations in Socioeconomic Aspects of World Cultures**

|  | Bands | Tribes | Chiefdoms | States |
|---|---|---|---|---|
| Major mode of subsistence | Foraging | Agricultural/herding | Intensive Agriculture | |
| Predominant mode of distribution | Reciprocity | Redistribution | | Market |
| Population size | Small, low density | | | Large, high density |
| Level of social differentiation | Egalitarian | | | Class/caste |

In addition to these variations in political structures, there are corresponding variations in other aspects of the cultures, as in Exhibit 19-2.

For the overwhelming majority of their existence humans have lived in small hunting-and-gathering bands characterized by little or no political integration and few, if any, specialized political roles. Not until the Neolithic Revolution (domestication of plants and animals) occurred approximately 10,000 years ago were socioeconomic forces unleashed that permitted the formation of larger, more complex sociopolitical systems. With the new food-producing technologies brought in with the Neolithic Revolution, populations have become larger and more heterogeneous, and as a result, political organizations have become increasingly complex and centralized. Today, state systems of government predominate in the world, while small-scale band societies account for a very small (and decreasing) percentage of the world's societies.

Despite the vast importance of the rise of state systems of government, there remains relatively little consensus on why these complex forms of government emerged. By examining both ancient and contemporary societies, anthropologists and social philosophers have developed a number of explanations as to why some societies have developed state systems while others have not. Explanations for the rise of the state hinge on the question of what induces people to surrender at least a portion of

their autonomy to the power and control of the state. Some theories suggest that people *purposefully* and *voluntarily* give up their sovereignty because of the perceived benefits. That is, these theorists reasoned that the limited loss of autonomy was outweighed by the benefits they would derive from their integration into a wider political structure. These benefits included (1) greater protection from hostile, outside forces, (2) more effective means of conflict resolution, and (3) the opportunity for increased food production. Others (e.g., Carneiro, 1970) have argued that state systems of government have been the direct result of conflict (warfare), not enlightened self interest. These various theories of state formation have been discussed in greater detail in Chapter 10.

◆ ◆ ◆
# Social Control

As seen in the previous section, political structures vary from very informal structures such as bands at one extreme to highly complex state systems of government at the other extreme. Whatever form of political organization may be found in a society, it must inevitably address the issue of **social control**. In other words, every society must ensure that most of the people behave themselves in appropriate ways most of the time. Statelike societies, such as our own, have a wide variety of formalized mechanisms that function to keep people's behavior in line, including written laws, judges, bureaucracies, prisons, electric chairs, and police forces. At the other extreme, small-scale band societies, such as the Eskimos or !Kung, while having no centralized political authority, nevertheless maintain social order among their members quite effectively through informal mechanisms of social control. In fact, in most band societies, the extent to which people deviate from acceptable behavior is considerably less than it is in societies with more elaborate and complex forms of political organization.

Every society has defined what are normal, proper, or expected ways of behaving. These expectations, known as **social norms**, serve as behavioral guidelines and help the society work smoothly. To be certain, social norms are not adhered to perfectly, but most people in any given society abide by them most of the time. Moreover, social norms take a number of different forms, ranging from etiquette to formal laws. Some norms are taken more seriously than others. On the one hand, all societies have certain social expectations of what is "proper," but such behavior is not rigidly enforced. To illustrate, although it is customary in the United States for people to shake hands when being introduced, the refusal of a person to shake hands would not constitute a serious violation of social norms. The person who does not follow this ritual might be considered rude but would not be arrested or executed for failing to observe the everyday rules of etiquette. At the other extreme, certain social norms (such as grand larceny or murder) are taken very seriously indeed because they are considered absolutely necessary for the survival of the society.

All social norms, whether trivial or serious, are sanctioned. That is, societies develop patterned or institutionalized ways of encouraging people to conform to the norms. These sanctions are both positive and negative, for people are rewarded for behaving in socially acceptable ways and punished for violating the norms. **Positive sanctions** range from a smile of approval to receiving the Congressional Medal of Honor. **Negative sanctions** include everything from a frown of disapproval to corporal punishment.

Social sanctions also vary in terms of their formality or informality, depending on whether or not a formal law (legal statute) has been violated. To illustrate, if a woman is having a dinner conversation in a restaurant that can be easily overheard by people at nearby tables, she will probably receive stares from the other diners. But if that woman starts yelling at the top of her lungs

Imprisonment serves as a negative sanction in those societies with state systems of government.

in the restaurant, she will probably be arrested for disturbing the peace or disorderly conduct. The difference, of course, is that in the first case the woman wasn't breaking the law, while in the second case she was.

Exhibit 19-3 illustrates a continuum of the formal-informal dimension of social norms and sanctions in U.S. society.

Just as there is considerable variation in the types of social norms found in any society, similar variations exist in the mechanisms used to encourage people to adhere to those norms. For most North Americans, the most obvious forms of social control are the formal or institutionalized ones. When we think of why it is that we tend to "behave ourselves," we frequently think of formal laws, police forces, courts, and prisons. We don't rob the local convenience store, in other words, because if caught, we are likely to go to prison.

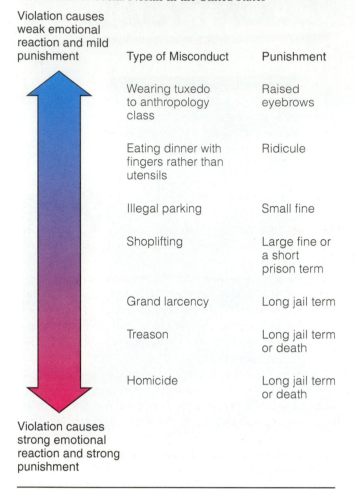

**Continuum of Social Norms in the United States**

Violation causes
weak emotional
reaction and mild
punishment

| Type of Misconduct | Punishment |
| --- | --- |
| Wearing tuxedo to anthropology class | Raised eyebrows |
| Eating dinner with fingers rather than utensils | Ridicule |
| Illegal parking | Small fine |
| Shoplifting | Large fine or a short prison term |
| Grand larceny | Long jail term |
| Treason | Long jail term or death |
| Homicide | Long jail term or death |

Violation causes
strong emotional
reaction and strong
punishment

Most of our "proper" behavior is probably due to less formal, and perhaps less obvious, mechanisms of social control. In those band and tribal societies that lack centralized authority, informal mechanisms of social control may be all that exists. The remainder of this chapter looks at those informal mechanisms of social control so characteristic of band and tribal societies and more formal institutions aimed primarily at social control, some of which involve laws and adjudicating bodies. It should be emphasized, however, that this distinction between formal and informal mechanisms of social control should in no way imply that informal means of social control exist only in band and tribal societies. Although societies with complex political organizations (state societies in particular) are best known for written

laws and courts, they also rely on an appreciable number of informal mechanisms of social control.

## INFORMAL MEANS OF SOCIAL CONTROL

When contrasted with complex state organizations, bands and tribes have little in the way that would appear to be governmental in the Western sense of the term. They include very low levels of political integration, have few, if any, specialized political roles, and little **political coerciveness**. These small-scale political systems have been referred to as acephalous (i.e., headless) or as "tribes without rulers" (Middleton and Tait, 1958). In the absence of formal governmental structures, how is it that these acephalous societies maintain some semblance of social order? The following subsections examine a number of informal mechanisms of social control that operate in acephalous societies but in many cases also operate in more complex societies.

**Socialization.** Every society, if it is to survive, must pass on its social norms from one generation to another. It seems blatantly obvious that people will not be able to conform to the social norms unless they are taught them. Thus, all societies have some system of **socialization**, and socialization in all societies involves teaching the young what the norms are as well as teaching that these norms—since they are inherently "proper"—should not be violated. People learn their social norms with a certain degree of moral compulsion. We learn, for example, that in the United States people wear clothes in public *and* that we should as well. Usually we internalize our social norms so effectively that we would never consider violating them. Some social norms—like not appearing nude in public—are so thoroughly ingrained in us through socialization that the thought of violating them would be distasteful and embarrassing. Other social norms do not have the same level of moral intensity, such as driving within the speed limit or maintaining good oral hygiene. But as a general rule when people learn their norms, they are at the same time internalizing the moral necessity to obey them.

**Public Opinion.** One of the most compelling reasons for not violating the social norms is **public opinion** or social pressure. It is generally true that people from all parts of the world wish to be accepted by the other members of their society. Most people fear being rejected or talked about by their fellows. This strong desire to win the approval of other members of one's society is summed up in such comments as, "Don't do that! What will the neighbors think?" It is, of course, impossible to determine how many people are deterred from violating the social norms because of fear of negative public opinion. At the same time, we can cite many incidents of how societies use social pressure very deliberately to keep people in line. Indeed, gossip, ostracism, rumor, sarcasm, and derision are all powerful corrective measures for reforming social behavior. To illustrate this appeal to public opinion, city and county governments in the United States will print the names of tax delinquents in the local newspaper in an attempt to embarrass them into paying their taxes. In colonial America, the stock and pillory was an excellent example of how the society used public opinion to control people's behavior. Someone who was caught breaking the social norms (e.g., committing adultery or stealing) was confined to the stock and pillory, which, not coincidentally, was always located right in the center of town. Even though long confinements in the stock and pillory were very physically uncomfortable, the thought that all of your friends, relatives, and neighbors saw you and knew of your crime was by far the greater punishment.

The deliberate use of social pressure to maintain social control is particularly important and, in some cases, quite dramatic in acephalous societies. A case in point is the custom of the duel found in Tiwi society of North Australia (Hart and Pilling, 1960). Men in traditional Tiwi society achieve power and status by amassing large numbers of wives. Under such conditions of intense polygyny, all females are married or betrothed before or at birth, while men do not take their first wives until their late thirties or early forties. Thus, at any given moment in time, all women are married to older men.

If a younger Tiwi male, say one in his twenties, is to have any intimate relations with a Tiwi woman, it must, by definition, be with an older man's wife. When this occurs, the older man challenges the young adulterer to a duel, which, like the use of the stock and pillory, is always public. Everyone in the community (men, women, and children) form a circle in an open field surrounding the older man and the accused adulterer. With the entire community watching, the older man throws spears at the younger man, along with a string of verbal insults. The younger man is expected to submit himself to this verbal harangue while sidestepping the spears. But before the event can end, the younger man must allow one of the spears to strike him, it is hoped in a nonvulnerable place.

The key to understanding the Tiwi duel is its public nature. Even though the alleged guilty party suffers some physical punishment (i.e., the superficial wound), the real punishment is the public disapproval of the younger man's behavior by all of the onlookers. The Tiwi duel, in other words, is an institutionalized form of public humiliation whereby public opinion is mobilized in an attempt to reform one's aberrant behavior. The Tiwi duel is a particularly effective mechanism of social control because it not only helps to reform the behavior of the accused but also serves as a reminder to all of the other members of the community who might be contemplating violating the social norms.

**Corporate Lineages. Corporate lineages** play a dominant role in most small-scale (acephalous) societies. Members of corporate lineages (which can number in the hundreds) frequently live, work, play, and pray together. Property is controlled by the lineage, people derive their primary identity from the group, and even religion (in the form of ancestor worship) is a lineage matter. Acting like a small corporation, the lineage has a powerful impact on the everyday lives of its members and can exert considerable pressure on people to conform to the social norms.

One means by which corporate lineages exert control over its members is economic. All important property, such as land and livestock, is controlled by the elders of the corporate lineage. Often property is allocated on the basis of conformity to societal norms. Those who behave as the society expects them to behave are likely to receive the best plots of land and use of the best livestock. Conversely, those who violate social norms are likely to be denied these valuable economic resources.

Corporate lineages, to some degree, also act as mechanisms of social control because of their scale. Corporate lineages serve as localized communities, numbering from several hundred to as many as several thousand relatives. Because members of the lineage have frequent and intense interaction with one another on a daily basis, it is virtually impossible for anyone to maintain his or her anonymity. People's lives are played out in such close proximity to one another that everyone knows what everyone else is doing. To illustrate, a man who wants to engage in socially inappropriate behavior (such as having an extramarital affair) would think twice because it would be difficult, if not impossible, to keep it a secret. By way of contrast, it is considerably easier in a large city to have an extramarital affair and remain undetected. Thus, the small-scale nature of corporate line-

Many people tend to conform to the social norms out of a strong belief in supernatural forces.

age communities tends to inhibit social deviance because it is much more difficult to "get away" with it.

The way by which roles are structured in corporate lineage societies also contributes to social control. In terms of role structure, corporate lineages have what Parsons and Shils (1952:83) refer to as diffuse roles. People play social roles in a number of different domains, such as kinship, economic, political, ritual/religious, and recreational roles. A role is diffuse when it ranges over two or more of these domains. For example, a diffuse role structure is illustrated by the man whose grandfather (kinship role) is also his teacher (educational role), his priest (religious role), the local chief (political role), and his hunting partner (economic role). The man, in other words, has a number of overlapping roles; he is playing roles from a number of different domains with the same person. By way of contrast, roles in large-scale, complex societies such as our own tend to be segmented or narrowly defined in that single roles are played out with one person at a time. People in corporate lineage societies (with diffuse or overlapping roles) have a built-in incentive *not* to violate the social norms, for to do so would have very serious consequences. The man in the preceding illustration who offends his grandfather not only is negatively affecting his kinship domain but is also affecting the educational, economic, political, and religious domains.

Marriage in corporate lineage societies tends to be highly collective. That is, marriage in such societies is regarded primarily as an alliance between two lineages—that of the bride and that of the groom—and only secondarily as a union between individuals. In many cases, the marriage is legitimized by bridewealth (the transfer of property—frequently livestock—from the kin group of the groom to the kin group of the bride). When a man wants to get married, he cannot pay the bridewealth himself, since he does not have personal control over property. He, like the rest of his relatives, have limited rights and obligations to such pieces of property as cattle. If marriage cattle are to be transferred from one's lineage to another, a group decision will need to be made. If, for example, eight cows must be given to the prospective bride's family before the marriage can be legitimate, the prospective groom must convince a number of his kin to give up their limited use of cows. In the event that the prospective groom has a reputation for violating the social norms, it is likely that the permission to transfer the cows will be withheld. Thus, the members of a corporate lineage, through their collective capacity to control marriage, possess considerable power to coerce people into appropriate behavior.

**Supernatural Belief Systems.** A powerful mechanism of social control in acephalous societies is the belief in supernatural forces such as gods, witches, and sorcerers. People will refrain from antisocial behavior if they believe that some supernatural (i.e., above-human) force will punish them for it. It is, of course, impossible to determine how many norms are *not* violated because people fear supernatural retribution, but we have to assume that the belief in supernatural sanctions acts as a deterrent to some degree. Nor is it necessary to prove that the gods, for example, will in fact punish the social deviants. If people believe that "god will get them" for doing something wrong, the belief itself is usually enough to discourage the deviant behavior.

*Ancestor worship.* **Ancestor worship** is a form of supernatural belief that serves as an effective means of social control in some acephalous societies. In such societies, dead ancestors are considered fully functioning members of the descent group. In fact, the death of a respected elder marks his or her elevation in status to that of supernatural being rather than the departure from the group. Respect for the ancestor-gods is frequently demonstrated by sacrifices and proper behavior, for which the living members, it is believed, are either rewarded or punished, depending on how well they meet these obligations.

The Lugbara society of Uganda provides a good example of ancestor worship. According to Middleton (1965:73–77), the well-being of the entire kinship group is insured only if people behave in socially appropriate ways. Personal and group tragedies are explained by the Lugbara as a direct result of the transgression of certain social norms, such as showing disrespect to both living and dead elders, adultery, incest, assault, or homicide.

The Lugbara generally believe that the ancestor-gods inflict with illness those living kin who endanger the well-being of the lineage by committing any of the above-mentioned offenses. Sickness of any type is explained in terms of ancestral displeasure with the conduct of the living. Thus, sickness (resulting from sin) is followed by either **ghost invocation** or **ghostly vengeance**. Ghost invocation is the practice of a living man—typically an elder—calling forth the wrath of the ancestor-gods against the alleged sinner. Ghostly vengeance is the belief that ancestor-gods inflict sickness on their own without having to be invoked.

Whether ancestral ghosts in traditional Lugbara society were directly responsible for sickness among the living is perhaps of greater interest to the theologian than to the anthropologist. What is of interest to the anthropologist, however, is the effects of the belief on the behavior of the living, for it is the *belief* that has implications for social control rather than its ability to undergo scientific verification. Such rites as ghostly invocation give regular expression to fears of supernatural retribution, which in turn control, or at least influence, a person's conduct.

**Witchcraft.** The existence of a belief in **witchcraft**—found often in acephalous societies—also functions to control people's behavior by discouraging socially deviant behavior. In those societies that believe in witchcraft, a deviant runs the risk of being labeled a witch, and fear of being accused a witch strongly encourages conformity. For example, in colonial America, those who were driven from their communities for allegedly being witches were the nonconformists, the freethinkers, or anyone who didn't conform to expected behavioral norms. The way by which witchcraft serves as a mechanism of social control is noted by Jean La Fontaine in her account of the Bantu-speaking Gisu of East Africa:

> . . . witchcraft beliefs act as a form of social control in discouraging behavior that is socially unacceptable. In Bagisu the eccentric is branded a witch. . . . Children grow up with the realization that the stigma of nonconformity is dangerous; too great a departure from the norms of everyday conduct will attract the suspicion of others and lead to isolation and eventual destruction (1963:217).

**Age Organizations.** In some acephalous societies, age organizations serve as effective means of social control. Those societies with age organizations have distinct groups of people passing periodically through distinct age categories. This involves the basic distinction that cultural anthropologists make between **age sets** and **age grades**. An age set is a group of people (usually men), initiated during a periodic ceremony and having a strong sense of group identity with one another. An age set lasts from its inception, usually when most members are late adolescents, until its last member has died. Age sets pass (as a group) through successive categories, called age grades, such as warriors, elders, or various subdivisions of these grades. Each age grade is associated with a well-understood set of social roles (i.e., they perform exclusive functions) and statuses (i.e., higher prestige is associated with increasing age). To illustrate this distinction further, an age set is analogous to a group of students who go through college together. The academic grades through which they pass—i.e., freshman through senior—are comparable to the age grades. Thus, we can speak of a particular age set occupying the senior warrior grade at a particular moment in time.

Age organizations function to control behavior in a number of significant ways. *First,* since age organizations establish a clear set of roles and statuses, they are particularly effective as channels for the distribution of authority. Since men of every age grade have well-defined and well-understood roles, there is little room for infringing on the authority or domain of others. There is little incentive, in other words, to try to usurp the authority of those above you for the simple reason that provided you lived long enough, you would eventually have that authority by virtue of your own advanced age.

*Second,* individuals enter the age set system at the lowest echelon through the process of initiation. These rites of passage are almost always preceded by intense periods of training in the norms and values of the society. These periods of intense socialization teach the soon-to-become adults not only the expected behaviors but also why the behaviors should be followed and the penalties for deviation.

*Third,* the bonds of camaraderie that exist between

members of the same age set are usually so strong that age sets tend to take on the characteristics of a corporate group. Age set members who have experienced their initiation ceremonies together support one another throughout the remainder of their lives in much the same way as do members of the same lineage.

Even though, unlike lineages, age sets are neither self-perpetuating nor property owning, they exert the same type of pressure to conform on their members as lineages do on theirs.

## FORMAL MEANS OF SOCIAL CONTROL

As previously noted, all societies use informal mechanisms of social control to some degree. Western cultures rely heavily on such mechanisms as socialization, public opinion, and supernatural sanctions to encourage people to maintain social order by behaving appropriately. Often these informal mechanisms of social control are not sufficient to maintain the desired level of conformity to the norms. Frequently, the violation of social norms results in disputes between people in the society. When such disputes become violent conflicts (such as theft, assault, or homicide), we refer to them as crimes. Since societies face the possibility of violent conflict erupting between its members, they need to develop explicit mechanisms to address and, it is hoped, resolve the conflicts.

Although no society in the world is immune from crime, there are considerable differences from society to society in the incidence of crime. It appears quite apparent that crime is more likely to occur in large, heterogeneous, and stratified societies than in small-scale societies. For example, it was found (USNCCPV, 1969) that in the United States the crime rate in cities with populations of over 50,000 people was eleven times as high as in rural areas. Several logical arguments support these findings. First, as mentioned in the discussion of corporate lineages, people in small-scale societies have little or no anonymity, which makes getting away with a crime more difficult. Second, since people in small-scale societies know most of the other people, they are more likely to be concerned with negative public opinion. Third, the heterogeneous character of populations found in large-scale, complex societies means that there will be a number of groups with different, and quite likely, conflicting interests. And finally, the fact that large-scale societies are almost always stratified into classes or castes creates certain segments (i.e., the lower strata) of the population that may feel blocked from upward mobility and conse-

The age organizations into which these Kayapo boys are being initiated can serve as effective mechanisms of social control.

## CROSS-CULTURAL MISCUE

Until recently, the importance of hand gestures has gone largely unnoticed. Hand gestures, however, can change the meaning of our words as well as carry meanings totally by themselves. We now know that unless we understand the meanings attached to certain hand gestures in different cultures, we are likely to send and receive unintended messages when dealing with people from different cultures. This was dramatically illustrated by the now famous clasped-hands-over-the-head gesture used by Soviet Premier Khrushchev when visiting the United States in the 1960s. This gesture, which for Russians is a sign of international brotherhood, was interpreted by most Americans as an arrogant gesture usually used by prizefighters after defeating an opponent. Needless to say, misreading this gesture did little to enhance U.S.-Soviet relations.

quently may be more likely to want to violate the rights of those in the more privileged strata.

**Song Duels.** Just as societies differ in terms of the incidence of crime, considerable differences exist in how disputes and crimes are handled. One example of a formal mechanism for resolving disputes was found among the Eskimos of Canada, Alaska, and Greenland. Since the Eskimos, because of their nomadic way of life, had relatively little property, conflicts rarely arose over violation of property rights. However, disputes did occur frequently between men over the issue of wife stealing. A man would attempt to steal the wife of a more prominent man as a way of elevating his own standing within the community.

A not uncommon way of resolving wife stealing among the Eskimos was to murder the wife stealer. In fact, Rasmussen (1927:250) had found that all of the men he studied had been a party to a murder, either as the murderer or as an accessory, and invariably these murders stemmed from allegations of wife stealing. There were, however, alternative resolutions to disputes over wife stealing. One such alternative was to challenge the alleged wife stealer to a derisive song contest, which was fought with song and lyrics rather than with weapons. The plaintiff and defendant, appearing in a public setting, would chide each other with abusive songs especially composed for the occasion. The contestant who received the loudest applause emerged the winner of this "curse by verse" **song duel.** Interestingly, the resolution of the conflict did not require the determination of guilt or innocence, only one's verbal dexterity.

**Intermediaries.** Some societies use **intermediaries** to help resolve serious conflicts. The Nuer of the African Sudan are a case in point (Evans-Pritchard, 1940:163–64). Even though the Nuer political system is informal and uncentralized, one role in the society—the **Leopard-skin Chief**—is, to a degree, institutionalized. In the absence of any formal system of law courts to punish serious crimes such as murder, the Leopard-skin Chief serves as a mediator between the victim's family and the family of the murderer. When a homicide occurs, the murderer, fearing the vengeance of the victim's family, will take sanctuary in the home of the Leopard-skin Chief. In an attempt to prevent an all-out feud, the Leopard-skin chief attempts to negotiate a settlement between the two families in order to avoid a feud. His role is to work out an equitable settlement between the two families whereby the murderer's family would compensate the victim's family with some form of property settlement (say ten head of cattle) for the loss of one of its members.

If either side becomes too unyielding, the Leopard-skin Chief can threaten to curse the offending party. The Leopard-skin Chief does not decide the case, however. Rather, he is only an intermediary, with no authority to determine guilt or force a settlement between the parties. Intervening on behalf of the public interest, he uses his personal and supernatural influence to bring the dis-

This traditional Kikuyu kiama (council of elders) still operates to settle disputes in Kenya.

puting parties to some type of agreed-upon settlement of their dispute.

**Council of Elders.** A somewhat more structured mechanism for conflict resolution, found among the Kikuyu of Kenya, is a **council of elders** called a *kiama* (Kenyatta, 1962; Middleton and Kershaw, 1965). Traditionally, the *kiama* adjudicated disputes between individuals and groups of individuals on a wide range of matters, including theft, paternity cases, and homicide. Although Kikuyu *kiamas* continue to operate on the local community level, they deal only with relatively minor civil and criminal cases because serious crimes are handled by the official state-run court system.

The elders question the parties to the case and render judgment on guilt or innocence. If guilt is established, the *kiama* sets an amount of compensation to which the injured party is entitled. Frequently, the relationship between the guilty party and the victim determines the amount of compensation. Whatever amount is set, however, the emphasis is on compensating the injured party.

Unlike our own court system, which usually separates the guilty party from the society by incarceration, the Kikuyu legal system stresses normalizing the relations in the community that have been disrupted by the conflict. Today the *kiamas* have no formal means of enforcing their decisions other than their own persuasiveness and stature within the local community. If the guilty party refuses to pay compensation, the case is referred to the official government court system, which usually accepts it.

**Oaths and Ordeals.** Another way of resolving conflicts—particularly when law enforcement agencies (such as governments) are not especially strong—is through such religiously sanctioned methods as oaths and ordeals. An **oath** is a formal declaration to some supernatural force that what you are saying is truthful or that you are innocent. While taking many different forms, oaths almost always are accompanied by a ritual act, such as smoking a peace pipe, signing a loyalty document, or swearing upon the Bible (as in our courts of law). Since some believe that to swear a false oath could lead to supernatural retribution, oaths can be effective in determining guilt or innocence.

An **ordeal** is a means of determining guilt by submitting the accused to a dangerous test. If the person passes the test, it is believed that a higher supernatural force has determined the party's innocence; if he or she fails, the gods will have signaled the party's guilt. Ordeal by drinking poison was found among the Ashanti in West Africa. If, after drinking a poison concoction, the accused vomited, the person was considered innocent; if the accused didn't vomit, he or she died and was therefore considered guilty.

It has been suggested (Roberts, 1967; Meek, 1972) that oaths and ordeals are most likely to be found in relatively complex societies in which the political leadership, lacking the power to enforce its judicial decisions, must rely on such supernaturally sanctioned mechanisms as oaths and ordeals to make certain that people will obey. Where political leaders wield greater power, oaths and ordeals are no longer needed.

**Courts and Codified Law.** A characteristic of state systems of government is that such systems possess a monopoly on the use of force. Through a system of codified laws, the state both forbids individuals from using force and determines how it will use force to require citizens to do some things and forbid them from doing others. These laws, which are usually in written form, are established by legislative bodies, interpreted by judicial bodies, and enforced by administrators. When legal prescriptions are violated, the state has the authority, through its courts and law enforcement agencies, to fine, imprison, or even execute the wrongdoer. To suggest that the state has a monopoly on the use of force should not imply that only the government uses force. State systems of government are constantly having to deal with unauthorized uses of force, such as **crime** (violent disputes between individuals or groups), **rebellions** (attempts to displace the people in power) , and **revolutions** (attempts to overthrow the entire system of government).

The system of codified laws used to resolve disputes and maintain social order in complex societies is distinct from other types of social norms. Legal anthropologist E. Adamson Hoebel (1972:504–506) has identified three basic features of **law**. While his definition of law goes beyond the type of law found in Western societies, it certainly holds true for that type of law as well. First, law involves the legitimate use of physical coercion. Law without the force to punish or deprive is no law at all, although in most cases, force is not necessary, because the very threat of force or compulsion acts as a sufficient deterrent to antisocial behavior. But when it is needed, a true legal system can draw upon the legitimate use of force. Second, legal systems allocate official authority to privileged people who are able to use coercion legitimately. Third, law is based on regularity and a certain amount of predictability. That is, since laws build on precedents, new laws are based upon old ones. It is this regularity and predictability that eliminates much of the whim and capriciousness from the law.

Legal systems in complex societies such as our own have different objectives than systems of conflict resolution found in other societies. The objective in the cases

By means of codified laws, state systems of government maintain a monopoly on the use of force.

of the Nuer Leopard-skin Chief and the Kikuyu council of elders, for example, was to compensate the victim and to reestablish harmony between the disputants and, consequently, peace within the community. Law enforcement and conflict resolution in complex societies, by way of contrast, tend to emphasize punishment of the wrongdoer which frequently takes the form of incarceration or, in some cases, death. It is not, in other words, aimed at either compensation or reintegrating the offender back into the community. This emphasis on punishment in complex societies is understandable in that lawbreakers pose a particular threat to the authority of the government officials. Unless serious offenders are punished or separated from the rest of society, they are likely to threaten the very legitimacy of political and legal authority.

## Summary

1. All societies have political systems that function to manage public affairs, maintain social order, and resolve conflict. The study of political organization involves such topics as the allocation of political roles, levels of political integration, concentrations of power and authority, mechanisms of social control, and means for resolving conflict.

2. Political anthropologists generally recognize four fundamentally different levels of political organization based on levels of political integration and the degree of specialized political roles: bands, tribes, chiefdoms, and states.

3. Societies based on bands have the least amount of political integration and role specialization. They are most often found in foraging societies and are associated with low population densities, distribution systems based on reciprocity, and egalitarian social relations.

4. Tribal organizations are most commonly found among horticulturalists and pastoralists. With larger and more sedentary populations than found in band societies, tribally based societies have certain pan-tribal mechanisms that cut across a number of local segments and integrate them into a larger whole.

5. At the next level of complexity are chiefdoms, which involve a more formal and permanent political structure than is found in tribal societies. Political authority in chiefdoms rests with a single individual, either acting alone or with the advice of a council. Most chiefdoms, which tend to have quite distinct social ranks, rely on feasting and tribute as a major way of distributing goods.

6. State systems—with the greatest amount of political integration and role specialization—are associated with intensive agriculture, market economies, urbanization, and complex social stratification. States, which first appeared about 3200 B.C., have a monopoly on the use of force and can make and enforce laws, collect taxes, and recruit labor for military service and public works projects.

7. Theories put forth to explain the rise of state systems of government have centered on the question of why people have surrendered at least some of their autonomy to the power and authority of the state. Some theories (such as those of Childe and Wittfogel) suggest that people voluntarily gave up their autonomy in exchange for certain perceived benefits such as protection, more effective means of conflict resolution, and greater food productivity. Other explanations, such as that offered by Carneiro, hold that states developed as a result of warfare and coercion rather than voluntary self-interest.

8. In the absence of formal mechanisms of government, many band and tribal societies maintain social control by means of a number of informal mechanisms such as socialization, public opinion, corporate lineages, supernatural sanctions, and age organizations.

9. In addition to using informal means of social control, societies control behavior by more formal mechanisms whose major function is maintaining social order and resolving conflicts. These mechanisms include verbal competition, intermediaries, councils of elders, oaths, ordeals, and formal court systems.

## Key Terms

acephalous society
age grade
age set
ancestor worship
authority
band society
chiefdom
coercive theory of state formation
corporate lineage
council of elders
crime
egalitarian
ghost invocation
ghostly vengeance
hydraulic theory of state formation
intermediary
law
Leopard-skin Chief
negative sanction

oath
ordeal
pan-tribal mechanism
political coerciveness
political integration
positive sanction
public opinion
rebellion
revolution
segmentary lineage system
song duel
social control
social norm
socialization
specialized political role
state society
tribal society
voluntaristic theory of state formation
witchcraft

## Suggested Readings

Cohen, Ronald, and Elman R. Service (Eds.). *Origins of the State: The Anthropology of Political Evolution.* Philadelphia: Institute for the Study of Human Issues, 1978. A collection of essays on how and why state systems of government have evolved, written by such noted political anthropologists as Morton Fried, Elman Service, and Robert Carneiro. An excellent introductory essay is written by one of the editors, Ronald Cohen.

Ferguson, R. B. (Ed.). *Warfare, Culture and Environment.* Orlando, Fla.: Academic Press, 1984. A compilation of eleven original essays on the anthropology of warfare, written from a materialist perspective. The editor's comprehensive introductory essay provides both a thorough discussion of many of the issues involved in the anthropology of warfare and a nineteen-page bibliography.

Fried, M. H. *The Evolution of Political Society: An Essay in Political Anthropology.* New York: Random House, 1967. A classic work in the field of political anthropology setting forth the fourfold typology of political organization—egalitarian societies, rank societies, stratified societies, and states—that has been widely used as a model for classifying different types of socio-political systems.

Kuper, Hilda. *The Swazi: A South African Kingdom* (2nd ed). New York: Holt, Rinehart & Winston, 1986. An excellent short monograph on the dual monarchy of the Swazis from traditional times up to the recent present.

Mair, Lucy. *Primitive Government.* Baltimore: Penguin, 1962. A regional study of traditional political systems in East Africa ranging from such minimal governments as the Nuer to the complex interlucustrine kingdoms, which include the Ganda, Soga, Nyoro, and Ankole.

Meggitt, Mervyn. *Blood Is Their Argument.* Palo Alto, Calif.: Mayfield, 1977. An ethnographic study of warfare among the Mae Enga tribesmen of New Guinea which explores the modes of clan warfare, the reasons for fighting, the outcomes of the conflicts, and methods for establishing peace.

# Political Organization

This chapter has examined political organization—how societies use legitimate power and authority to regulate behavior. In the process a number of different topics, including levels of political integration, specialization of political roles, degrees of political coerciveness, mechanisms of social control, concentrations of power and authority, and means of resolving conflicts, have been considered. As part of the political process, all of these topics are relevant to the applied anthropologist when working in programs of planned change. This final section looks at three specific examples of how an understanding of various aspects of political organization have contributed to the successful solution of societal problems. In the first case, the research of a legal anthropologist has assisted the new government of Papua New Guinea to integrate its many traditional legal systems with the Western legal system that it inherited from the colonial period. Closer to home, the second case study examines the role that an applied legal anthropologist played in reforming court procedure by studying the roles of deputy court clerks in the United States. The final case examines how an understanding of power and influence among traditional leaders in rural India spelled the difference between success and failure in an immunization project against smallpox.

♦ **An anthropologist's study of customary law in New Guinea leads to the creation of a new national legal system.**

As a general rule, when Western governments administered their colonies during the nineteenth and twentieth centuries, they invariably superimposed on local populations their own Western legal systems, which were often at odds with the local customary laws. As the colonial period came to an end during the 1960s and 1970s, many newly independent governments were faced with the need to develop a new national legal system that would be based on the customs and traditions of their own people rather than on those of the former colonial powers. For many newly independent governments, this was a formidable task, owing to the vast cultural diversity that existed within their geographic borders.

One such former colony—the country of Papua New Guinea, which won its independence in 1975—had a population of three and a half million people who spoke approximately 750 mutually unintelligible languages and had at least as many customary legal systems (see Scaglion, 1987:98). Thus, the Papuan New Guinea government was faced with the gargantuan two-fold task of (1) identifying the legal principles from these widely diverse customary legal systems and (2) reconciling them into a new statewide legal system. To accomplish these tasks, the parliament established a Law Reform Commission which, shortly after its own creation, sponsored the Customary Law Project. Headed by legal anthropologist Richard Scaglion, this project was designed to conduct research on local customary law so as to determine how and to what extent it might serve as the basis for a national legal system. (See Scaglion, 1987.)

As project director, Scaglion supervised a small cadre of local university students, fluent in the local languages and cultures, whose job it was to collect original conflict case studies from which principles of customary law could be extracted. The primary data-gathering technique used in this project was the case method of legal anthropology first made popular by Llewellyn and Hoebel (1941) and later refined by Laura Nader (Nader and Todd, 1978:5–8). These local student/researchers collected from all parts of the country approximately 600 detailed case studies which then constituted a legal database that the Law Reform Commission could use for its unification of customary law.

The collection of these detailed case studies made two very important practical contributions to the emerging (post-independence) legal system in Papua New Guinea. First, this legal data bank on customary law and legal principles was immediately useful to lawyers. The computerized retrieval system of case studies was a great help to lawyers in searching out legal precedents for their ongoing court cases.

The second major contribution of the Customary Law Project was that it helped to identify, and subsequently alleviate, certain problems arising from a conflict between customary law and the existing national legal system. Family law was one such area. To be specific, under customary marriage practices, polygyny was a perfectly permissible alternative, but it was strictly forbidden under existing statutory law. Drawing upon the legal data bank of case studies, the Law Reform Commission, in conjunction with the legislative and judicial branches of the government, drafted a family bill that formally recognized the legality of customary marriages and provided for polygyny under certain conditions. Thus, new legislation was introduced into the parliament that incorporated elements of customary law into the national system.

Although the implementation phase of the Customary Law Project has been completed (i.e., the creation of the original data bank of case studies), the research on additional case studies is ongoing. With an ever-increasing number of case studies from customary law, practicing lawyers will continue to have access to customary legal precedents relevant to those cases they are arguing in court. In terms of the more long-term process of national legal reform, those responsible for national legal reform will continue to draw upon the anthropological concepts, data, and methods established by the Customary Law Project under the direction of legal anthropologist Richard Scaglion.

◆ A study of deputy court clerks by a legal anthropologist leads to an improvement in the clerks' job performance and satisfaction.

While cultural anthropologists have conducted extensive research on law and dispute settlement in small-scale societies, they have devoted considerably less attention to those topics in our own society. In the same way that law, justice, and conflict resolution were studied among the Trobriand Islanders (Malinowski, 1926), the Tiv (Bohannan, 1957), and the Kapauku Papuans (Pospisil, 1958), it is possible to apply ethnological theory and

methods to the study of the judicial process in the United States. While some cultural anthropologists have conducted research on certain aspects of our own judicial system (see, for example, Hoane, 1978; Greenhouse, 1982; O'Barr, 1982; and Nader, 1980), legal anthropology in modern complex societies remains a rarity. One such study, however, which serves well as an example of how cultural anthropology can be applied to the study and improvement of our own judicial process is Purdum's (1985) study of the subculture of deputy court clerks in the southern region of the United States.

While deputy court clerks are low-level employees in the formal court system, they are nevertheless important because they are in the unique position of interacting, both formally and informally, with all of the courtroom players, including judges, attorneys, plaintiffs, and defendants as well as with their immediate supervisors, the clerks of court. Over the course of eighteen months, Purdum spent about 200 hours in the offices of the deputy clerks, reading court records, interviewing court clerks and their deputies, and observing the behavior of the deputy court clerks while performing their everyday duties. By using these traditional data-gathering strategies, the study demonstrated how the judicial system forces the deputy clerks into a no-win position, resulting in a high level of job frustration, tensions between the deputy clerks and the judges, and unfair obstacles and problems for unrepresented litigants.

According to the official job description, deputy clerks are expected to take people's claims, collect fees, keep their court files current, and set the docket. Deputy court clerks are reminded continuously by judges and the court clerks that when dealing with litigants they should give out no information that might be construed as legal advice. According to Purdum (1985:355), the deputy clerks were seen dispensing advice and information to litigants over the phone and in person on a number of occasions. Unfortunately, since the deputy clerks had not received adequate training, much of the advice and information was wrong or inadequate. Thus, the deputy clerks are in the untenable position of being expected to be polite and helpful to the litigants, yet if they are too helpful, they run the risk of dispensing inaccurate information *and* being accused by the judges of practicing law. The end result is that deputy clerks both resent the judges and create problems for the litigants by providing misinformation.

Based on her findings, Purdum was able to make some reasonable recommendations to improve the situation by enabling the deputy clerks to be more responsive and accessible to the people they serve while enhancing their own job satisfaction. Purdum suggested that the key to improving the situation was to provide adequate training for the deputy clerks to enable them to respond accurately and consistently to the many demands made on them by both the general public and the members of the court community. In the tradition of good applied anthropology, Purdum made the following practical recommendation based on her field observations:

The judges believe that for the deputy clerks to give any advice would constitute the "unauthorized practice of law." The judges, however, need to realize that the deputy clerks are forced through their interactions with people, both on the telephone and in person, to give advice every day. The judges should decide what in fact is "legal advice" and what is not. The deputy clerks could then be trained in certain areas and could perhaps distribute literature prepared by the judges or an attorney covering areas the judges consider to be legitimately reserved for attorneys (1985:358).

◆ **A public health project in rural India to vaccinate against smallpox is successful because health officials understood the power and influence of traditional leaders.**

Foreign aid programs designed to bring about beneficial changes in local populations will have a chance of succeeding only if they take into account local cultural patterns. Whether we are talking about programs of agricultural reform, curriculum change, or preventive health, any program of planned change is likely to fall short of its objectives unless the project administrators understand the local cultural realities. What follows is an example of how such cultural knowledge in rural India (specifically the influence of local leaders) was utilized to turn a potentially disastrous situation into a successful program of smallpox prevention.

According to Link and Mehta (1966), when smallpox broke out in a village in Orissa State (located in the eastern part of India), public health officials immediately dispatched a vaccinator to help prevent an epidemic. Upon arrival, the vaccinator went door-to-door asking mothers to allow him to vaccinate their children. He quickly met with near-complete resistance. Since the local villagers had no understanding of how a vaccination might prevent their children from dying, they were not about to turn their children over to the medical technician. The vaccinator's job was further complicated by the fact that since he had never been in this village before, he was a total stranger to the local people. Word spread quickly throughout the village that a stranger wanted to harm their children. Within hours, everyone shunned this medical technician, who was referred to as "the one who makes the babies cry." After several hours of being systematically rejected, the vaccinator left the village in desperation.

As was customary, the local people sought an explanation for the outbreak of the disease from the highly respected village priest, the *gurumai*. The priest declared that the disease was the direct result of the wrath of one of the local goddesses who would be pacified only if the villagers gave an elaborate feast. The lives of the children would be spared, according to the priest's explanation, only if the local villagers sacrificed a goat and organized a fancy feast in honor of the goddess. The priest volunteered to intercede with the enraged goddess on the people's behalf, provided, of course, he received a handsome fee.

Having made no progress in their efforts to vaccinate the villagers against smallpox, the public health officials, as a last-ditch effort, sought the help of the village priest. Since the people believed strongly in the priest's supernatural powers, the health officials asked the priest to convince the people to submit to the smallpox vaccine in addition to providing them with religious advice. At first the priest saw no reason to cooperate. After all, he reasoned, the disease would be controlled just as soon as the villagers placated the angry goddess with the elaborate feast. It appeared that the public health

421

personnel had once again failed to get their vaccination program off the ground. The following day, the priest learned that his own nephew had become ill. In an effort to save one of his own beloved kinsmen, the priest agreed to cooperate by helping to explain the vaccination program to the local villagers. That same day, a large crowd gathered in front of the priest's house to hear him explain that he had just talked to the angry goddess. She told him that she would save only those children who had been vaccinated. Word quickly spread throughout the village that all children, if they were to be spared, would need a vaccination. One by one, the parents brought their children to be vaccinated, and before long the threat of a smallpox epidemic had been averted.

The difference between success and failure in this example was the knowledge of local leadership in this rural Indian community. The Hindu priest, like any local leader, had a vested interest in his position. He was interested in using his "office" for his own personal benefit and enhancing the power and prestige of that office. By cooperating with the vaccination prevention program, the village priest benefited in at least two important ways. First, since the villagers were still planning to hold a ceremonial feast, the priest would receive his fee for serving as liaison between the villagers and the deity. Second, the priest could draw on the success of this medical program to bolster his own credibility among the villagers. Even though the village priest appeared to be acting in a very self-serving way, the medical team was willing to overlook it and enlist his active support. They realized that when local leaders see themselves benefiting from cooperating, they can be powerful allies. Conversely, if they are ignored or opposed, they can easily subvert the most enlightened programs.

## CHAPTER 20

# Social Stratification

What is the extent of variations found among the societies of the world in terms of the equitable distribution of power, prestige, and wealth?

How do class systems differ from caste systems?

What are the different ways of interpreting systems of social stratification?

One important difference between the societies of the world is the degree to which individuals in any given society have equal access to wealth, power, and prestige. To one degree or another, all people are socially differentiated on the basis of such criteria as physical appearance, ethnicity, profession, family background, sex, ideology, age, or skill in performing certain kinds of economic or political roles. Societies will confer a larger share of the rewards (i.e., wealth, power, and prestige) on those possessing the most admired characteristics. Scholars generally agree that all complex societies are stratified. That is, societies make distinctions between certain groups or categories of people that are hierarchically ranked relative to one another. When viewing the simpler societies of the world, however, many cultural anthropologists, while recognizing role and status differences, see no systems of social stratification in the sense of a clear-cut division of the society into hierarchically ranked strata.

## Dimensions of Social Inequality

Max Weber (1946) has delineated three basic criteria used for measuring levels of social inequality: wealth, power, and prestige. First, people are distinguished from one another by the extent to which they have accumulated economic resources or, in other words, their **wealth**. The forms that wealth may take vary from one society to the next. For the Mexican farmer, wealth resides in the land; for the Samburu of East Africa, a man's wealth is measured by the number of cows he has; and in the United States, most people equate their wealth with income earned in wages, property, stocks, bonds, equity in a home or other resources that have a cash value.

The extent of economic inequality found in any society varies from one society to the next. In some societies, such as the Pygmies, there are virtually no differences in wealth. By way of contrast, enormous differences in wealth exist in the United States. Economist Paul Samuelson described the magnitude of this economic inequality in the United States in graphic terms when he wrote: "If we made an income pyramid out of a child's blocks, with each layer portraying $1000 of income, the peak would be higher than the Eiffel Tower, but most of us would be within a yard of the ground" (1976:84).

A second dimension of social inequality, according to Weber, is **power**, which he defined as the ability to achieve one's goals and objectives even against the will of others. Power, to be certain, is often closely correlated with wealth, for economic success, particularly in Western societies, increases the chances of gaining power. Nevertheless, wealth and power do not always overlap. In certain parts of the world, power can be based on factors other than wealth, such as the possession of specialized knowledge or eloquence as a speaker. In such cases, it may be impossible to see any differences in wealth or material possessions between the powerful and the not so powerful.

The third dimension of social stratification, according to Weber's formulation, is **prestige**—that is, the social esteem, respect, or admiration that a society confers on people. Since favorable social evaluation is based on the norms and values of a particular group, sources of prestige vary from one culture to another. For example, among certain North American Plains Indians, warriors on horseback held high prestige; in certain age-graded societies, such as the Samburu of Kenya, old men were accorded the highest prestige; and in the United States, high prestige is closely associated with certain professions.

In terms of prestige in our own society, research indicates that occupations in U.S. society carry different levels of prestige and that these rankings have remained remarkably stable throughout much of the present century (Counts, 1925; National Opinion Research Center, 1947; Hodge et al., 1964; and Coleman and Rainwater, 1978). Not surprisingly, physicians, corporation presidents, scientists, and top-ranking governmental officials have high levels of occupational prestige, while garbage collectors, shoe shiners, and street sweepers are at the low end of the prestige scale.

It should be kept in mind that while these three dimensions of social inequality (wealth, power and prestige) often are interrelated, they can also operate independently of one another. To illustrate, it is possible to possess both power and wealth while having little prestige, as is the case with leaders of organized crime. Some people, such as classical pianists, may be highly esteemed for their musical virtuosity yet have modest wealth and little power or influence over people. And, odd as it may seem to Westerners, people in some societies (such as the Kwakiutl of British Columbia) acquire high prestige by actually destroying or giving away all of their personal possessions (refer to the discussion of the potlatch in chapter 16).

# Types of Societies

Following the lead of Morton Fried (1967), most anthropologists distinguish between three types of societies based on levels of social inequality: egalitarian, rank, and stratified societies. **Egalitarian societies** have few or no groups that have greater access to wealth, power or prestige; they are usually found among hunters and gatherers, have economies based on reciprocity, and have little or no political role specialization. In **rank societies**, certain groups enjoy higher prestige, even though power and wealth are equally distributed; they are usually found among chiefdoms, have economies based on redistribution, and illustrate limited political role specialization. **Stratified societies** illustrate the greatest degree of social inequality in terms of all three forms of social rewards—that is, wealth, power, and prestige. They are found in industrialized societies, have market economies, and are associated with state systems of government. Rather than thinking of these three types of societies as discrete and mutually exclusive, it would be more accurate to view them as points on a continuum, ranging from egalitarian societies (the least amount of social inequality) to stratified societies (the greatest degree of social inequality).

## EGALITARIAN SOCIETIES

In egalitarian societies, located at the low end of the inequality continuum, no individual or group has appreciably more wealth, power, or prestige than any other. Of course, even in the most egalitarian societies, personal differences in certain skills are acknowledged. Some people are more skilled than others at hunting, others may be recognized as particularly adept craftspersons, while still others may be well known and respected for their skills at settling disputes. Even though certain individuals in an egalitarian society may be highly esteemed, they are not able to transform their special skills into wealth or power. Irrespective of how much or how little respect an individual in an egalitarian society may have, he or she is neither denied the right to practice a certain profession nor subject to the control of others. Moreover, whatever esteem an individual manages to accrue is not transferable to his or her heirs.

In an egalitarian society, there is no fixed number of high-status positions for which people must compete. According to Fried, "there are as many positions of pres-

Band societies, such as the !Kung, tend to be highly egalitarian.

tige in any given age-sex grade as there are persons capable of filling them" (1967:33). The esteem gained by being a highly skilled dancer will be given to as many individuals in the society as there are good dancers. If fifteen people are highly skilled dancers this year, all fifteen will receive high status. If next year there are twenty-four skilled dancers, all twenty-four will be so recognized. Thus, the number of high-status positions in an egalitarian society is constantly changing to reflect the number of qualified candidates. In other words, everyone, depending on his or her personal skill level, has equal access to positions of esteem and respect.

Egalitarian societies are found most readily among geographically mobile hunters and gatherers such as the !Kung of the Kalahari region, the Eskimos, and the

Hadza of Tanzania. There are a number of logical reasons that unequal access to wealth, power, and prestige would be discouraged among nomadic foragers. First, the very nature of a nomadic existence inhibits the accumulation of large quantities of personal possessions. Second, since hunters and gatherers do not hold claims to territory, individuals can forage in whatever areas they please. In the event that someone might want to exercise control over others, any man or woman can choose to live in some other territory. Finally, hunters and gatherers tend to be egalitarian because sharing tends to maximize their chances for adaptation. When a large animal is killed, it would make no sense whatsoever, given the lack of refrigeration, for the hunter to keep the entire carcass for himself. Rather, it would make much more sense for the hunter to share the meat with the expectation that others would share their kill with him. In fact, foraging societies, with economies based on the principle of generalized reciprocity, place a high value on sharing. Generosity in such societies is expected, while attempts to accumulate possessions, power, or prestige are ridiculed.

Frequently, egalitarian societies are transformed considerably when they come into contact with highly stratified (statelike) societies. Sometimes this transformation from egalitarian to nonegalitarian society is the result of normal cultural diffusion. Often it occurs because such a change meets the needs of colonial governments. For example, during the early part of the twentieth century, the British colonial government in Kenya created, for its own administrative convenience, local chiefs among the Kikuyu, a traditionally egalitarian people with no history of any type of chief. Although the colonial government thought it was creating new high-status positions, the Kikuyu people themselves—adhering to their egalitarian ideals—failed to recognize the legitimacy of these new government-appointed chiefs.

## RANK SOCIETIES

Rank societies have unequal access to prestige or status but not unequal access to wealth or power. In rank societies, there is usually a fixed number of high-status positions, which only certain individuals are able to occupy. The others are systematically excluded irrespective of their personal skills, wisdom, industriousness, or any other personal traits. Such high-prestige positions as chief—which are largely hereditary in nature—establish a ranking system that distinguishes between various

levels of prestige and esteem. In fact, kinship plays an important role in rank societies. Since some clans or lineages may be considered aristocratic, their members will qualify for certain titles or high-status positions. Other kin groups will be rank-ordered according to their genealogical proximity to the aristocratic kin groups. Thus, the number of high-status positions in ranked societies is limited, and the major criterion for allocating such positions is genealogical.

Even though the chiefs in a rank society possess great prestige and privilege, they generally do not accumulate great wealth, for their basic standard of living is not noticeably different from the ordinary person. Chiefs usually receive gifts of tribute from members of other kin groups, but they never keep them for their personal use. Instead, they give them all away through the process of redistribution (refer to chapter 16). In many ranked societies, chiefs are considered to "own" the land, but not in the Western sense of the term. The chief certainly has no power to keep anyone from using the land. The chief may control land to the extent that he encourages people not to neglect either the land or their obligation to contribute to the chief's tribute. But the chief has no real power or control over the land. He maintains his privileged position as chief not by virtue of his capacity to impose his will on others but rather by virtue of his generosity.

Examples of rank societies are found in most areas of the world, but most prominently in Oceania and among the Northwest Coast Indians of North America. In fact, for reasons that are not fully understood, there are some strikingly similar cultural traits found between parts of Polynesia and the Northwest Coast Indians residing in a narrow coastal region between Northern California and Southern Alaska. These cultural similarities are particularly noticeable in the area of status ranking. One such group that exemplifies a rank society is the Nootka of British Columbia (Service, 1978). Like a number of ethnic groups in the American Northwest, the Nootka Indians, a hunting-and-fishing society, live in an area so abundant in food resources (e.g., big game, wild edible plants, waterfowl, and fish) that their standard of living is comparable to societies that practice horticulture and animal husbandry.

Social ranking among the Nootka Indians is closely related to the principle of kinship proximity. People are ranked within families according to the principle of primogeniture. Position, privileges, and titles pass from a man to his eldest son. All younger sons are of little social importance because they are not in direct line to inherit anything from the father. Furthermore, in much the

Stratified societies have different levels of power, prestige, and wealth, ranging from the homeless to the opulent.

same way that individuals are ranked within the family, so too are lineages graded according to the birth order (or genealogical proximity) of the founding ancestors of each lineage. Nootka society does not comprise clearly marked social strata but rather a large number of individual status positions ranked relative to one another. Thus, no two individuals have the exact same status.

Differential status takes a number of forms in Nootka society. First, the most visible symbol separating people of different rank is clothing. As a general rule, the higher the social position, the more ornate one's dress is. More specifically, wearing ornaments of teeth and shells or robes trimmed with the fur of sea otters is the exclusive privilege of chiefs. Second, an individual's status is directly linked to the bestowal of certain hereditary titles that are the names of important ancestors. Third, social position is expressed economically in terms of the amount of tribute (in surplus goods) a chief receives from those lower ranked individuals who acknowledge his higher status. The receipt of tribute in no way enhances the personal wealth of the chief, for he will redistribute the surplus goods back to the society in the form of elaborate feasts and ceremonies. Finally, social rank is determined by one's success in potlatch ceremonies, whereby prominent men compete with one another to see who can give away the largest quantities of material goods, such as food, blankets, and oil. Unlike in Western societies, which equate high status with the accumula-

tion of material wealth, the Nootka confer high status on those who can give away the greatest quantities of material goods. Even though potlatch ceremonies function to distribute needed material goods throughout the society, they also serve as a mechanism for validating rank.

## STRATIFIED SOCIETIES

Unlike rank societies, which are unequal only in terms of prestige, stratified societies are characterized by considerable inequality in all forms of social rewards—that is, power, wealth, and prestige. The political, economic, and social inequality in stratified societies is both permanent and formally recognized by the members of the society. Some people—and entire groups of people—have little or no access to the basic resources of the society, while others do. Various groups in stratified societies, then, are noticeably different in terms of their social position, wealth, life-styles, access to power, and standard of living. The unequal access to rewards found in stratified societies is, by and large, inheritable from one generation to the next.

Although distinctions in wealth, power, and prestige began to appear in the beginnings of the Neolithic Period (approximately 8000 B.C.), true stratified societies are closely associated with the rise of civilization which

## CROSS-CULTURAL MISCUE

Corporations operating abroad can experience serious problems if they ignore the cultural realities of their local workers. Lawrence Stessin (1979) tells of a U.S. manufacturing firm that bought a textile machine factory in Birmingham, England. In an attempt to make the workers in their new factory more productive, the U.S. managers wanted to shorten the time-consuming tea break to which all workers were entitled. According to Stessin:

In England, tea breaks can take a half-hour per man, as each worker brews his own leaves to his particular taste and sips out of a large, pint size vessel with the indulgence of a wine taster. . . . Management suggested to the union that perhaps it could use its good offices to speed up the "sipping time" to ten minutes a break. . . . The union agreed to try but failed. . . . Then one Monday morning the workers rioted. Windows were broken, epithets greeted the executives as they entered the plant and police had to be called to restore order. It seems the company went ahead and installed a tea-vending machine—just put a paper cup under the spigot and out pours a standard brew. The pint sized container was replaced by a five-ounce cup printed—as they are in America—with morale-building messages imploring greater dedication to the job and loyalty to the company. . . . The plant never did get back into production. Even after the tea-brewing machine was hauled out, workers boycotted the company and it finally closed down (1979:223).

began at approximately 3200 B.C. A basic prerequisite for civilization is a highly differentiated population in terms of role specialization. As societies become more specialized, there is a parallel growth in the complexity of the system of social stratification. Not all occupations or economic interest groups will have the same access to wealth, power, and prestige but rather will be ranked relative to one another. As a general rule, the greater the role specialization, the more complex the system of stratification.

**Class Versus Caste.** Social scientists generally recognize two different types of stratified societies: those based on **class** and those based on **caste**. The key to understanding this fundamental distinction is **social mobility**. In class systems, a certain amount of both upward and downward social mobility exists. It is, in other words, possible for an individual to change his or her social position dramatically within a lifetime. An individual, through diligence, intelligence, and good luck, could go from "rags to riches"; and conversely, a person born to millionaire parents could wind up as a homeless street person. Caste societies, on the other hand, have no so-

cial mobility. Membership in a caste is determined by birth and lasts throughout one's lifetime. Whereas members of a class society are able to elevate their social position by marrying into a higher class, caste systems are strictly endogamous (allowing marriages only within one's own caste).

Another important distinction associated with the difference between class and caste societies is how statuses (positions) within each type of society are allocated. Class systems are associated with an **achieved status** while caste systems are associated with an **ascribed status**. Achieved statuses are those that the individual chooses, or at least has some control over. An achieved status is one that a person has as a result of his or her personal effort, such as graduating from college, marrying someone, or taking a particular job. By way of contrast, an ascribed status, found largely in caste systems, is one into which a person is born and over which he or she has no control. Statuses based on such criteria as sex, race, or age are examples of ascribed statuses.

It is important to bear in mind that stratified societies cannot all be divided neatly into either class or caste systems. It is generally true that class systems are open to the extent that they are based on achieved statuses and permit considerable social mobility and caste systems tend to be closed in that they are based on ascribed statuses and allow little or no social mobility, either up or down. Having made these conceptual distinctions, however, we must also realize that in the real world, class and caste systems overlap each other. There are, in other words, elements of both class and caste in most stratified societies. Rather than think in either-or terms, we should think in terms of polarities on the ends of a continuum. There are no societies that have either absolute mobility (perfect class systems) or a total lack of mobility (perfect caste systems). Rather, all stratified societies found in the world fall somewhere between these two ideal polarities, depending on the relative amount of social mobility permitted in each.

*Class Societies.* Even though the boundaries between social strata in a class society are not rigidly drawn, social inequalities nevertheless exist. A social class is a segment of a population whose members share relatively similar life-styles and levels of wealth, power, and prestige. The United States is a good example of a class society. In some areas of the United States, such as coal-mining towns in Appalachia, there may be only two classes—the haves and the have-nots. More frequently, however, social scientists have identified five (or more) social classes: upper, upper middle, lower middle, working, and lower classes (Bensman and Vidich, 1987; Vanneman and Cannon, 1987; and Sullivan and Thompson, 1990).

The *upper class* in the United States, comprising approximately four percent of the population, consists of (a) old wealth (Carnegies, Rockefellers), (b) those who have recently made fortunes (**nouveau riche**), and (c) top government and judicial officials who, despite modest wealth, wield considerable power.

The *upper middle-class*, comprising about 12 percent to 15 percent of the U.S. population, is made up of business and professional people with relatively high incomes and modest amounts of overall wealth.

The *lower middle-class,* constituting approximately one-third of our population, is made up of hard-working people of modest income, such as petty entrepreneurs, teachers, civil servants, and lower level managers.

The largest segment of the U.S. population (approximately 45 percent) is the *working class*, comprised of such people as factory workers, construction workers, furniture movers, and appliance repair persons. While it is possible that these blue-collar workers may earn more income than some members of the lower middle class, their class carries with it considerably less prestige.

At the bottom of the status hierarchy is the *lower class*, comprising migrant workers, the unemployed, and certain marginal groups that are barely surviving in society, such as the homeless, the noninstitutionalized mentally ill, and derelicts with severe substance abuse problems.

It is generally believed—as part of our national mythology—that there exists a good deal of social mobility in the United States. After all, there are no formal or legal barriers to equality, and we all grow up believing that it is possible for anyone (or at least, any white male) to become president of the United States. Although it is possible to cite a number of contemporary

Although we like to think that there is a good deal of upward social mobility in the United States, how likely is it that this youngster growing up in the South Bronx, New York, will gain entry into the upper class?

Americans who, from modest beginnings, have attained great wealth, power, and prestige, studies of social class in the United States have shown that most people remain in the class into which they are born and marry within that class as well.

In many cases, a child's physical and social environment will greatly influence the child's life's chances and identification with a particular class. To illustrate, the son of a school janitor in Philadelphia living in a lower class neighborhood will spend his formative years playing in crowded public playgrounds, working at the grocery store after school, and generally hanging out with kids from the neighborhood. The son of the bank president, on the other hand, also living in Philadelphia, will attend a fashionable prep school, take tennis lessons at the country club, and drive his own car. By the time each boy finishes high school, it is likely that the janitor's son will not continue his education, while the banker's son will go off to a good college, perhaps follow that with law school, and then land a high-paying job. Even though it is possible that the janitor's son could go to Harvard Law School and become very upwardly mobile, such a scenario is not very likely.

Members of the same social class share not only similar economic levels but also similar experiences, educational backgrounds, political views, memberships in organizations, occupations, and values. In addition, studies of social class have shown, not surprisingly, that members of a social class tend to associate more frequently with one another than with people in other classes. In other words, a person's life chances, while not determined, are very much influenced by the person's social class.

***Caste Societies.*** In contrast to class societies, those based on caste rank their members according to birth. Membership in castes is unchangeable, people in different castes are segregated from one another, social mobility is virtually nonexistent, and marriage between castes is strictly prohibited. Castes, which are usually associated with specific occupations, are ranked hierarchically relative to one another.

Caste societies, wherever they may be found, have a number of characteristics in common. First, caste membership is directly related to such economic issues as occupation, workloads, and control of valuable resources. The higher castes have a monopoly on certain occupations, control the allocation of resources to favor themselves, and avoid engaging in difficult or low-status work. In short, the higher castes have more and do less.

Second, members of the same caste share the same social status, owing in large part to their strong sense of caste identity, residential and social segregation from other castes, and uniformity of life-styles. Third, caste exclusiveness is further enhanced since each caste has its own set of secret rituals, which tend to intensify group awareness. And fourth, the higher castes are generally most interested in maintaining the caste system for the obvious reason that they benefit from it the most.

***Hindu Caste System.*** While caste societies can be found in a number of regions of the world, such as among the Rwanda in Central Africa, the best known—and certainly the best described—example of the caste system is in Hindu India. Hinduism's sacred Sanskrit texts rank all people into one of four categories, called **varnas**, which are associated with certain occupations. Even though local villagers may not always agree as to who belongs to which *varna,* most people accept the *varna* categories as fundamentally essential elements of their society.

According to a Hindu myth of origin (see Mandelbaum, 1970:22–23), the four major *varnas* originated from the body of primeval man. The highest caste Brahmins (priests and scholars) came from his mouth; the Kshatriyas (warriors) emanated from his arms; the Vaishyas (tradesmen) came from his thighs; and the Shudras (cultivators and servants) sprang from his feet. Each of these four castes is hierarchically ranked according to its ritual purity. Below these four castes—and technically outside of the caste system—is still another category, called the Untouchables or, literally, outcastes. The Untouchables, confined to the lowest and most menial types of work, such as cleaning latrines or leatherworking, are considered so impure that members of the four legitimate castes must avoid all contact with them.

Ideally, all of Hindu India is hierarchically ranked according to these four basic castes. In actual practice, however, each of these four categories is further subdivided and stratified. To add to the complexity of the Indian caste system, the order in which these subcastes are ranked varies from one region to another. These local subgroups, known as **jati**, are local family groups that are strictly endogamous. All members of a *jati,* which share a common social status, are expected to behave in ways appropriate for that *jati.* A person's *jati* commands his or her strongest loyalties, serves as a source of social support, and provides the primary basis for personal identity. It is the *jati* that serves as the important social entity in traditional Hindu society. The corporateness of each *jati* is maintained in two ways: (1) through egali-

The Untouchables—who must refrain from having social contact with the four major castes—engage in a village celebration of their own in rural India.

tarian socializing with members of one's own jati and (2) by scrupulously avoiding any type of egalitarian socializing (e.g., marriage or sharing of food) with members of other *jati*. While originally the *jati* were linked to traditional occupations, that is no longer the case. For instance, today most members of the traditional leather-worker caste are landless laborers.

Even though the Indian government has attempted to discourage it legislatively, the caste system still plays an important role in the lives of most contemporary Indians. A major reason for the continued adherence to the principles of caste is that it is strongly sanctioned by the Hindu religion. According to Hindu religious teachings, members of higher castes must do everything possible to retain their ritual purity by avoiding any type of intimate interaction with members of lower castes; and correspondingly, members of lower castes must refrain from polluting higher castes.

An important tenet of Hindu religious teachings is reincarnation, the notion that at death a person's soul is reborn in an endless sequence of new forms. The caste into which a person is born is considered to be that person's duty and responsibility for that lifetime. Hindu scripture teaches that the good life involves living according to the prescriptions of the person's caste. It is taught that those who violate their caste prescription will come back in a lower caste position or, if the transgression is sufficiently serious, in a nonhuman form. Hindu scripture is very explicit about the consequences of violating prescribed caste behaviors. For example, the Brahmin who steals the gold of another Brahmin will be reincarnated in the next thousand lives as a snake, a spider, or a lizard. That's one powerful sanction! In other words, people's caste status, it is believed, is determined by how people behave in former lives, and their present behavior determines their caste status in future lives.

Even though the prohibitions against social intercourse between castes are as rigidly defined as anywhere in the world, the amount of interdependence among local castes should not be overlooked. This interdependence is largely economic in nature rather than social. Like any society with a complex economy, India has an elaborate division of labor. In fact, one of the basic features of caste in India is that each *jati* is associated with its own traditional occupation which provides goods or services for the rest of the society. Certain lower caste *jati* (such as barbers, potters, and leatherworkers) provide vital services for the upper echelon (landowning) castes from whom they receive food and animal products. For the economy to work, lower castes sell their services to the upper castes in exchange for goods. Thus, despite the very high level of social segregation between the castes in India, there is considerable economic interrelatedness, particularly at the village level.

## Sexual Stratification

It is generally recognized that the **status of women** varies from one society to another. In some societies, women tend to be in a clearly subordinate position in their social relationships with men. In other societies, the relationships between the genders are more egalitarian. While social scientists would agree generally that **sexual stratification** exists to some degree in all societies, there is considerably less agreement as to how one measures the status of men and women, since there are a number of different components of sexual stratification that may vary independently of one another. To illustrate, when considering the relative status of women in any society, one needs to look at the roles played by women, the value that society places on women's contributions, women's legal rights, whether and to what degree women are expected to be deferential to men, women's economic independence, and the degree to which women decide on the major events of their lives, such as marriage, professions, and conception. Women in certain West African societies, owing to their influence in the marketplace, may have gained an appreciable amount of economic independence, but they nevertheless remain relatively subordinate to their husbands in most other respects. The difficulty with determining the status of women, then, is that status is not a unidimensional phenomenon.

Another difficulty with ascertaining the status of women is that status is not a static phenomenon. In

In some societies, women are not allowed in certain areas that are "for men only," such as this coffee house in Cairo, Egypt.

some societies, the relative status of men and women will fluctuate along with political changes. To illustrate, during the reign of the Shah of Iran, changing women's roles kept pace with modernization. During the 1960s and 1970s increasingly large numbers of women abandoned the rules of **purdah** (domestic seclusion and veiling), received higher education, and gained entry to traditionally male professional roles. However, with the return of religious and cultural fundamentalism under the Ayatollah Khomeini, women have again taken to the veil and resumed more traditional female roles.

Muslim societies in the Middle East are among the most highly stratified along gender lines. As early as the seventeenth century B.C., the code of Hammurabi firmly established the legal subordination of women. While Mohammed in the seventh century A.D. set forth rules protecting the rights of women, women's rights were never intended to be equal to the rights of men. Moreover, as Mohammed's guidelines have come to be interpreted in recent centuries, women, confined to the domestic realm, are almost totally isolated from the public sphere of power.

Today in many of the small towns in Iraq, Iran, and Syria, women have very low status. Most adhere to the strict rules of *purdah* (domestic seclusion and veiling). If they must leave the seclusion of the family compound, they can do so only with the permission of their husbands and must be covered from head to toe in their black cloaklike garments. At mealtime, men are served first, while the women eat the leftovers from the men's plates. Women have essentially no economic autonomy, and legally they are viewed as being under the authority of their husbands and fathers. Given the seclusion expected of Arabic women and their strict insistence on virginity at marriage, women in the Muslim world have little or no control over their bodies or their sexuality, while no such restrictions apply to men.

In contrast to the marked status distinctions between the sexes found in traditional Middle Eastern cultures, the relationship between men and women in some foraging societies tends to be more egalitarian. For example, Turnbull (1982:153) reports a good deal of mutual respect between the sexes among the Mbuti Pygmies of Central Africa, while Leacock (1983:116) arrives at a similar conclusion about the Montagnais-Naskapi of Labrador. In such societies, the roles performed by men and women are very different, but their relative statuses are not. Such findings of relative sexual equality are not surprising, however, for marked status differences of any type are virtually nonexistent in the hunting-and-gathering societies. On the other hand, we cannot conclude from these findings that relatively equal status between the sexes is characteristic of all technologically simple peoples. One significant case in point is the Tiwi society of North Australia (Hart, Pilling, and Goodale, 1988), where women traditionally were the prizes in the endless male competition for wives.

## IS FEMALE SUBORDINATION UNIVERSAL?

It is possible to identify certain societies in which gender distinctions are kept to a minimum, but the overwhelming evidence suggests that in many critical areas of life, women in all societies tend to be subordinate to men. To be certain, from time to time in different cultures women have wielded considerable power, but there is no evidence to support the notion that **matriarchy**—rule or domination of women over men—exists anywhere in the world or, for that matter, has ever existed (Bamberger, 1974). Rather, what we find is that women, to one

degree or another, are excluded from the major centers of economic and political power and control. Moreover, the roles that women play as mothers and wives invariably carry with them fewer prerogatives and lower prestige than do male roles. Even in egalitarian societies, it is headmen—and not headwomen—who make such important decisions as how to allocate resources or whether or not war will be waged against a neighboring group.

While it is true that we do find reigning queens in the world today, they are usually temporary holders of regal power. The worldwide subordination of women in terms of political power can be seen in the single statistic that less than four percent of the independent nations of the world have women heads of state (*Information Please Almanac*, 1991). It is this type of data dealing with male dominance that has led Rosaldo and Lamphere to conclude that "sexual asymmetry is presently a universal fact of human social life" (1974:3).

Universal male dominance can be seen in a number of different cultural realms. In terms of religion, women are often excluded categorically from holding major religious leadership roles or participating in certain types of ceremonies. In some African societies, men's physical well-being is thought to be jeopardized by coming into contact with a woman's menstrual discharge. In Bangladesh and in other Muslim cultures, men are associated with the right side, while women are associated with the left side—a dichotomy that also denotes purity-pollution, good-bad, and authority-submission. Even in the area of food production, the foods procured by men (such as meat from the hunt) are frequently more highly valued than those gathered by women (roots or berries), even though the foods procured by women constitute the people's major source of nutrition. In many parts of the world women are treated legally as minors in that they are unable to obtain a driver's license, a bank account, a passport, or even a birth control device without the consent of their husbands or fathers.

This sexual subordination can also be revealed in the forms of language practiced by men and women. Among the Merina in Madagascar (Keenan, 1974), for example, speech patterns associated with men—which are indirect, allusive, and formal—are considered both respectable and sophisticated. Merina women, on the other hand, are thought to be ignorant of the subtleties of sophisticated speech and, consequently, are considered to be inferior. Moreover, submissiveness and a lack of social power can be observed in female speech patterns in the United States in terms of intonation, loudness, and assertiveness. To illustrate, women in the United States have a less forceful—and somewhat apologetic—style of speaking than men in that they use a greater number of qualifiers (e.g., "It's just my opinion but . . . "). Also, U.S. women frequently soften the impact of a declarative statement by ending it with a question such as ". . . wouldn't you agree?" (Kramer, 1974).

# ◆ ◆ ◆ Theories of Stratification

The inequitable distribution of wealth, power, and prestige appears to be a fundamental characteristic of most societies, particularly those with complex, highly differentiated economies. Some modern societies—such as the Soviet Union, The People's Republic of China, and Albania—have attempted to become classless by eliminating all vestiges of inequality. But even here it is clear that high-ranking government officials are far more generously rewarded than the rank and file.

The basic question is, Why is inequality a nearly universal trait of social life? The debate between social scientists, which at times has become heated, revolves around two conflicting positions, each based on different philosophical assumptions and each having distinct political implications. The more conservative position, the **functional theory**, holds that social inequality exists because it is necessary for the maintenance of society. The other position, the more liberal **conflict theory**, explains social inequality as the result of benefits derived by the upper classes who use their power and privilege to exploit those below them.

## THE FUNCTIONALIST INTERPRETATION

By stressing the integrative nature of social systems, functional anthropologists argue that stratification exists because it contributes to the overall well-being of the society. According to Davis and Moore (1945), complex societies, if they are to survive, depend on the performance of a wide variety of jobs, some of which are more important than others because they require specialized education, talent, and hard work. If people are to make the sacrifices necessary to perform these vital jobs, they must be adequately rewarded. For example, since the skills of a physician are in greater demand by our society than are those of a garbage collector, the rewards (money and prestige) are much greater for the physician. Functionalists argue that these differential rewards are necessary if societies are to recruit the best trained and

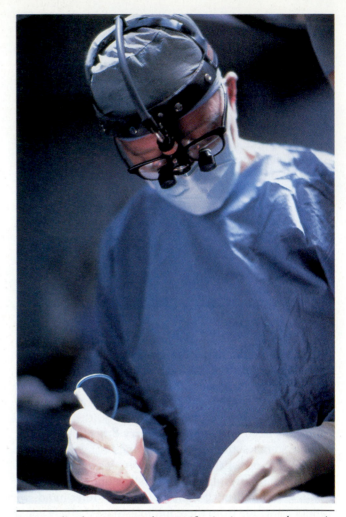

Functionalist theorists argue that stratification is necessary because it motivates the most highly skilled people to fill the important jobs in the society. They believe that if there were no status differences between physicians and garbage collectors, there would be no incentive to become a physician.

most highly skilled people for these highly valued positions. If physicians and garbage collectors received the same pay and social status, it is not likely that many people would opt to become physicians. Thus, social stratification, according to the functionalist interpretation, is necessary or functional for the society because it serves as a mechanism for allocating rewards and motivating the best people to fill the key jobs in the society.

While the functionalist view seems quite plausible, it is not without its weaknesses. First, some critics of the functionalist position point out that stratified societies do not always give the greatest rewards to those filling the most vital positions. There are many instances of rock singers, baseball players, and movie stars who make many times more money than teachers, pediatricians, or U.S. Supreme Court justices. Second, the functionalists do not recognize the barriers that stratification systems put in the way of certain segments of the society, namely members of low prestige and powerless groups. Ethnic and racial minorities, women, and the poor don't always have equal opportunities to compete because they are too poor or have the wrong accent, skin color, or gender. Third, the functionalist position can be called into question because it tends to make a fundamentally ethnocentric assumption. That is, the functionalists assume that people in all societies are motivated by the desire to maximize their wealth, power, and prestige. In actual fact, however, there are a number of societies that tend to emphasize the relatively equitable distribution of social rewards rather than reward individuals for amassing as much as possible for themselves.

## CONFLICT THEORY INTERPRETATION

Whereas the functionalist view starts with the assumption of social order, stability, and integration, the conflict theorists assume that the natural tendency of all societies is toward change and conflict. According to this theory, stratification exists because those people occupying the upper levels of the hierarchy are willing and able to use their wealth, power, and prestige to exploit those below them. The upper strata are able to dominate because of their use of force or the threat of force and by convincing those oppressed of the value of continuing the system. Thus, those at the top use their wealth, power, and prestige to maintain—perhaps even increase—their privileged position.

This conflict theory of social stratification is derived largely from the nineteenth-century writings of Karl Marx, who, unlike the functionalists, did not view stratification systems as either desirable or inevitable. Believing that economic forces are the main factors shaping a society, Marx (1909) viewed history as a constant class struggle between the haves and the have-nots. Writing during the late nineteenth-century Industrial Revolution in Europe, Marx saw the classic struggle occurring between the **bourgeoisie** (those who owned the means of production) and the **proletariat** (the working class who exchanged their labor for wages).

Owing to their control of the means of production, the relatively small bourgeoisie exerts significant influence over the larger working class. By controlling such institutions as schools, factories, government, and the media, the bourgeoisie can convince the workers that the existing distribution of power and wealth (i.e., the status quo) is preferable and that anyone can be successful if only he or she would work hard enough. Thus, according to the classical Marxist view, the bourgeoisie created a "false consciousness" among the workers who were led to believe that if they were not successful, it was attributable to their not working sufficiently hard rather than because their opportunities for advancement were blocked by the powerful upper class.

As long as the workers accepted this ideology legitimizing the status quo, the inequities of the stratification system would continue to exist. By believing that class conflict is inevitable, Marx predicted that eventually the proletariat would recognize both the extent of their own exploitation and their collective power to change it. When the workers developed a class consciousness, they would revolt against the existing social order, replace capitalism with communism, and eliminate scarcity, social classes, and inequality.

## FUNCTIONALISTS VERSUS CONFLICT THEORISTS

The functionalists and the conflict theorists—with their radically different interpretations of social inequality—have been locking horns for years. The functionalists hold that systems of stratification exist and are therefore necessary because they benefit the societies of which they are a part. The conflict theorists, on the other hand, claim that systems of stratification exist because they help those certain people at the top (i.e., the wealthy and powerful) maintain their privileged position. The functionalist position emphasizes the positive benefits of social stratification for the total society. The conflict theorists draw our attention to such negative aspects as the unjust nature of stratification systems and how that inherent unfairness can lead to rebellions, revolts, and high crime rates.

While there is truth in both of these interpretations, neither theory can be used exclusively to explain the existence of all types of stratification systems. The functionalists are correct to point out that open class systems, for example, are integrative to the extent that they promote constructive endeavor which is beneficial to the society as a whole. Yet, once established, these class systems often become self-perpetuating, with those at the top striving to maintain their superior positions at the expense of the lower classes. At the same time, the underclasses—through political mobilization, revitaliza-

## CROSS-CULTURAL MISCUE

The marketing manager of a U.S. knitwear firm was delighted with a multi-million-dollar order for men's underwear it received from a department store chain in Saudi Arabia. The jockey shorts were packaged in the usual way (three pair to a package, with a picture of a male modeling the briefs) and sent off to the customer in Saudi Arabia. However, Saudi customs officials were shocked to see a near totally nude man on packages that would be displayed in plain sight of Saudi women and children. In a country with very strict cultural taboos on nudity, such packaging was considered a form of obscenity, hardly acceptable for public display in department stores. Consequently, to satisfy Saudi customs officials, the entire shipment of mens' briefs had to be sent back to the United States for repackaging, costing the firm thousands of dollars. This was certainly a high price to pay for not understanding the culture of one's customers.

tion movements, and even violent revolutions—seek to free themselves from deprivation and exploitation. In short, functional integration is real, but then, so is conflict.

Not only do the functionalists and the conflict theorists represent two contrasting interpretations of social inequality, but they also have radically different policy implications for modern society. The functionalist view carries with it the implication that social stratification systems should be maintained because the best qualified people, through the competitive process, will be motivated to fill the top positions. By way of contrast, the view of the conflict theorists implies that social inequality should be minimized or eliminated altogether because many people at the lower strata never had a chance to develop their full potential. Thus, the functionalist position would want the government to take no action (e.g., welfare programs or a progressive income tax) that would redistribute wealth, power, or prestige. The conflict theorists would call for exactly the opposite governmental course of action, arguing that to eliminate barriers to social mobility would unleash the hidden brilliance of those presently living in the underclasses.

## ◆ Summary

1. Social ranking is an important feature found to one degree or another in all societies. The degree to which societies distribute wealth, power, and prestige on an equitable basis can be used to distinguish between three different types of societies. Egalitarian societies are unstratified in that they allocate wealth, power, and prestige relatively equally. Rank societies, which are partially stratified, have equal access to power and wealth but not to prestige. The most completely stratified societies are those based on class or caste which have unequal access to wealth, power, and prestige.

2. Stratified societies, which are associated with the rise of civilization, range from open class societies, permitting high social mobility, to more rigid caste societies, which allow for no social mobility. Class societies are associated with achieved status, those positions that the individual can choose or at least have some control over. Caste societies, on the other hand, are based on ascribed statuses into which one is born and cannot change.

3. The United States is often cited as a prime example of a class society with maximum mobility. Although part of our national credo involves the belief in the possibility of going from rags to riches, most people in the United States remain in the class into which they are born, because social environment has an appreciable effect on a person's life's chances.

4. Hindu India is most often cited as the most extreme form of caste found in the world. Social boundaries between castes are strictly maintained by caste endogamy and strongly held notions of ritual purity and pollution.

5. Sexual stratification varies widely throughout the world. Muslim societies make very strong distinctions between men's and women's behavior, while such foraging societies as the Pygmies of Central Africa make

few such status distinctions. Despite the wide range of variations, evidence from most societies suggests that women, by and large, tend to be subordinate to men.

6. There have been two conflicting interpretations of social stratification. The functionalist theory emphasizes the integrative nature of stratification systems by pointing out how class systems contribute to the overall well-being of a society by encouraging constructive endeavor. The conflict theorists believe that stratification systems exist because the upper classes strive to maintain their superior position at the expense of the lower classes.

## ◆ Key Terms

| | |
|---|---|
| achieved status | power |
| ascribed status | prestige |
| bourgeoisie | proletariat |
| caste | purdah |
| class | rank societies |
| conflict theory | sexual stratification |
| egalitarian societies | social mobility |
| functional theory | status of women |
| jati | stratified societies |
| matriarchy | varnas |
| nouveau riche | wealth |

## ◆ Suggested Reading

Bernardi, Bernardo. *Age Class Systems: Social Institutions and Policies Based on Age*. New York: Cambridge University Press, 1985. Drawing on ethnographic data largely from Africa, the author defines the characteristics of age class systems, their geographic distribution, and various anthropological approaches to their study.

Berreman, Gerald D., and Kathleen M. Zaretsky (Eds.). *Social Inequality: Comparative and Development Approaches*. New York: Academic Press, 1981. A collection of fifteen essays on the topic of social inequality that attempts to treat the subject (a) comparatively across a wide range of cultures, (b) comparatively over time, and (c) within the appropriate sociocultural context.

Fried, Morton. *The Evolution of Political Society*. New York: Random House, 1967. A widely quoted work that examines three fundamentally different types of societies (i.e., egalitarian, rank, and stratified) and how they relate to the political structure.

Jencks, Christopher. *Who Gets Ahead?: The Determinants of Economic Success in America*. New York: Basic Books, 1979. A descriptive study of individual success in the United States that looks at such variables as family background, cognitive skills, personality traits, years of schooling, and race.

Lenski, Gerhard E. *Power and Privilege: A Theory of Social Stratification*. New York: McGraw Hill, 1966. A broad-ranging analysis of human inequality that takes the reader through centuries and to all parts of the world. As the title of his first chapter indicates, Lenski asks the fundamental question of stratification studies: Who gets what and why? He then proceeds to answer the question by drawing liberally upon anthropological, historical, and sociological data.

Rosaldo, Michelle Zimbalist, and Louise Lamphere. *Woman, Culture, and Society*. Stanford, Calif.: Stanford University Press, 1977. A collection of essays written by female anthropologists that explore the role and status of women cross-culturally.

Schlegel, A. (Ed.). *Sexual Stratification: A Cross Cultural View*. New York: Columbia University Press, 1977. A series of essays on the status of women in different societies.

# Social Stratification

A main objective of this chapter has been to show variations in the extent to which people have access to wealth, power, and prestige. At one extreme, egalitarian societies make relatively few distinctions between people on these three dimensions, while at the other extreme, stratified societies recognize marked distinctions. People occupying different social strata within a society often have different levels of affluence, ways of behaving, and values. Sometimes when operating in an unfamiliar cultural setting, we fail to fully appreciate the fact that people occupying different social strata have quite different views of one another. These differential views of power and prestige often carry either negative or positive values about members of other strata or groups. To be certain, these different value perceptions can influence the way in which people interact with one another. The two applied cases that follow show how problems were either solved or avoided by understanding the values attached to different levels of occupational prestige.

◆ **A university mathematics professor draws upon knowledge of status systems in West Africa to avoid a potential misunderstanding between his students.**

A mathematics professor from a large university in North Carolina was walking to class with an armload of books when he met a group of five students from his class. Four of the students were native North Carolinians, while the fifth was an exchange student from Nigeria. As the professor and his students met, they greeted one another and proceeded to walk together to class. Almost immediately, the Nigerian student turned to the professor and asked if he could carry the professor's books. The professor declined the offer, but the Nigerian student insisted. As the professor finally relented and gave the books to the student, he noticed he was receiving some "funny looks" from his American students. It became immediately apparent to the professor that the American students thought that the Nigerian offered to carry the books as a type of bribe to get a higher grade in the course than he might deserve. The American students were clearly put off by what they considered to be the Nigerian's blatant attempt to better his own grade.

As the professor continued to walk to class with his students, he remembered a discussion he had had several weeks earlier with a colleague from the anthropology department. The anthropologist had mentioned that when he was a visiting professor at a Nigerian university, he was astounded at how much deference his students showed him. The recollection of the conversation raised an interesting question for the mathematics professor: Could this be a cross-cultural misunderstanding?

The professor decided to take the several remaining minutes before class to discuss the apparent bad feelings the U.S. students were having toward their classmate from Nigeria. He presented the students with his perception of what had occurred. The U.S. students admitted that they were feeling a good deal of resentment because they felt the Nigerian student was not "playing fairly" in the normal competition for good grades. Hearing this, the Nigerian student was shocked that his gesture to carry the professor's books had been so utterly misunderstood. He went on to explain that he had offered to carry the books out of a deep sense of respect for the professor's high status. University professors in Nigeria have a much higher social status among the general population than they have in the United States. It would be considered demeaning to a professor in Nigeria to engage in any type of manual labor, including carrying a heavy load of books. The Nigerian student went on to explain that he had offered to carry the books so that the professor would not "lose face" by engaging in physical labor.

This all made perfectly good sense to the American students once it was explained to them by their Nigerian classmate. The key, of course, to understanding the potential cross-cultural conflict was an understanding that the status system in Nigeria is appreciably different from that found in the United States. Much to his credit, the mathematics professor used his (albeit modest) knowledge of status systems in Nigeria to help diffuse some hard feelings among his students—and in the process taught them something about the need to understand cultural differences.

### ◆ Understanding the meaning of prestige in South America provides insights into an educational program for architects and city planners.

George Foster (1973:89–90), an anthropologist with extensive research experience in South America, provides us with a graphic illustration of how knowledge about prestige systems in South America can be applied to the solution of a practical educational problem. During the 1960s, the Organization of American States operated near Bogata, Colombia, the Inter-American Housing Center, a training center for architects and urban planners. As part of the curriculum, students were expected to learn about building materials and processes through the hands-on experience of mixing mortar, laying bricks, and engaging in other onsite manual tasks. Many of the Latin American students, however, felt that to engage in manual labor was an affront to their high status as architects. Professional (white-collar) architects, they believed, should have strong minds, not strong backs. The unskilled lower classes should do the manual tasks. Because of this reluctance to lose prestige, the experiential segment of this program was not at first very successful.

The problem facing the administrators of this educational program was to find a way to provide the young architectural students with the appropriate learning experiences without violating their perceived sense of high status. Finally, one of the program administrators came up with a creative solution to the problem—a solution that required an understanding of the local status system. As Foster (1973:90) reports, the administrators decided to provide the architectural students with official-looking white lab coats with their names over the pockets. In their new status as "lab technicians," the architectural students gladly performed their manual tasks because they were no longer in danger of being mistaken for common laborers.

439

# Religion

What is religion?

What functions does religion play for both the individual and the society as a whole?

What different forms does religion take among the societies of the world?

# Defining Religion

Modern anthropologists have devoted considerable attention to the analysis of religion since they began to make direct field observations of peoples of the world. While twentieth-century anthropologists have not always agreed on how to interpret different religious systems, there is one fact on which they can agree: that is, the many religious practices found throughout the world vary widely from one another as well as from our own. These religious systems might involve sacrificing animals to ancestor gods, using a form of divination called ordeals to determine a person's guilt or innocence, or submitting oneself to extraordinary levels of pain as a way of communicating directly with the deities.

While the forms of religion may vary enormously, they are all alike to the extent that they are founded on a belief in the supernatural. For our purposes in this chapter, we shall define religion as a set of beliefs and patterned behaviors concerned with supernatural beings and forces. Since human societies are faced with a series of important life problems that cannot all be resolved through the application of science and technology, they attempt to overcome these human limitations by manipulating certain supernatural forces.

Anthropologists have long observed that all societies have a recognizable set of beliefs and behaviors that can be called religious. According to George Peter Murdock's widely quoted list of cultural universals (1945: 124), all societies have religious rituals that propitiate supernatural forces, sets of beliefs concerning what we would call the soul, and notions about life after death. To be sure, certain nonreligious people can be found in all societies. But when we claim that religion (or a belief in the supernatural) is universal, we are referring to a cultural phenomenon rather than an individual one. For example, we can find individuals in the Western world who do not believe personally in such supernatural forces as deities, ghosts, demons, or spirits. Nevertheless, these people are part of a society that has a set of religious beliefs and practices adhered to by many (perhaps a majority) of the population.

Since religion, in whatever form it may be found, is often taken very seriously and passionately by its adherents, there is a natural tendency for people to see their own religion as the best while viewing all others as inferior. Westerners frequently use science, logic, and empirical evidence (for example, through the study of Biblical texts) to bolster and justify their own religious practices. Nevertheless, science and logic are not adequate to either establish the inherent validity of Western religious beliefs or demonstrate that non-Western religions are false. In other words, no religion is able to demonstrate conclusively that its deities can work more miracles per unit of time than those of other religions, although some certainly try. The central issue for anthropologists is not to determine which religion is better or more correct, but rather to identify the various religious beliefs in the world as well as how they function, to what extent they are held, and the degree to which they affect human behavior.

## PROBLEMS OF DEFINING RELIGION

Despite this rather facile definition of religion, we should hasten to point out that there is no universal agreement among anthropologists as to how to distinguish between religious and nonreligious phenomena. The problem lies in the fact that religion in some societies is so thoroughly embedded in the total social structure that often it is difficult to distinguish the religious from economic, political, or kinship behavior. To illustrate, when a Kikuyu elder sacrifices a goat at the grave of an ancestor god, is he engaging in **religious behavior** (he is calling for the ancestor god to intervene into the affairs of the living), **economic behavior** (the meat of the sacrificed animal will be distributed to and eaten by members of the kinship group), or **kinship behavior** (kin will have a chance to express their group solidarity at the ceremonial event)?

Such a ritual sacrifice is all of these at the same time. In highly specialized societies, such as our own, people tend to divide human behavior into what, at least for them, are logical categories—e.g., social, economic, political, religious, educational, recreational. Since many small-scale, less specialized societies do not divide human behavior into categories used in Western society, it is frequently difficult for Westerners to clearly recognize those aspects of human behavior that they think of as being religious.

Another difficulty in defining religion and the **supernatural** is that different societies have different ways of distinguishing between the natural world and the supernatural world. In our own society, we reserve the term *supernatural* for whatever phenomena we cannot explain through reason or science. Other societies, however, don't dichotomize the world into either natural or supernatural explanations. For example, the Nyoro of Uganda have a word for **"sorcery"** that means "to injure another person by the secret use of harmful medicines

## CROSS-CULTURAL MISCUE

Inattention to foreign cultures can result in some costly blunders when working in the international business arena. Alison Lanier, an international business consultant, tells of one U.S. executive who paid a very high price for ignoring the cultures of his international business partners:

A top-level, high-priced vice president had been in and out of Bahrain many times, where liquor is permitted. He finally was sent to neighboring Qatar (on the Arabian Gulf) to conclude a monumental negotiation that had taken endless months to work out. Confident of success, he slipped two miniatures of brandy in his briefcase, planning to celebrate quietly with his colleague after the ceremony. Result: not only was he deported immediately on arrival by a zealous customs man in that strictly Moslem country, but the firm was also "disinvited" and ordered never to return. The Qatari attitude was that this man had tried to flout a deeply held religious conviction; neither he nor his firm, therefore, was considered "suitable" for a major contract (1979:160–161).

or techniques" (Beattie, 1960:73). To be a sorcerer in Nyoro society can take a number of different forms. An act of sorcery could involve placing a person's body substances (such as pieces of hair or fingernail clippings) in an animal horn and putting the horn on the roof of the person's house with the intention of causing the person harm. But the Nyoro also consider it sorcery to put poison into an enemy's food or drink.

Given our own Western dichotomy between the natural and the supernatural, we would tend to interpret these two acts as substantially different in nature. We would interpret the first act as an attempt to harm another person by the use of magic. In the event that the intended victim should die, our own Western law courts would never hold the perpetrator culpable, for the simple reason that it could not be proven scientifically that placing the magical substances on the roof was, in fact, the cause of the death. Westerners would view the second situation, however (involving the sorcerer essentially poisoning his enemy) as premeditated murder because it could be determined scientifically (i.e., through an autopsy) that the poison did cause the person to die. This illustration should remind us that not all societies share our Western definition of *supernatural*. It is precisely because of this difference in viewing the natural and supernatural worlds that Westerners have so much difficulty understanding non-Western religions, which they usually label as irrational or contradictory.

## RELIGION AND MAGIC

Those anthropologists studying supernatural beliefs cross-culturally have had a long-term fascination with the relationship between religion and **magic**. While some anthropologists have emphasized the differences between these two phenomena, others have concentrated on the similarities. In actual fact, it is important to examine both the similarities and the differences between religion and magic because even though they can be found operating separately, most often they are found in some combined or compound form.

Both religion and magic share certain common features. Since both are systems of supernatural belief, they are nonrational—they are not susceptible to scientific verification. In other words, whether or not religious or magical practices actually work cannot be empirically demonstrated. Rather, such practices must be accepted as a matter of faith. Moreover, both religion and magic are practiced—at least in part—as a way of coping with the anxieties, ambiguities, and frustrations of everyday life.

On the other hand, magic and religion are different in a number of important respects. First, in terms of goals, religion deals with the major issues of human existence, such as the meaning of life, death, and one's spiritual relationship with deities. By way of contrast, magic is directed toward specific, immediate problems, such as curing an illness, bringing about rainfall, or ensuring

This voodoo ceremony being performed in Jacmel, Haiti, is an example of negative magic designed to harm people.

safety on a long journey. Second, religion uses prayer and sacrifices to appeal to or petition supernatural powers for assistance. Magical practitioners, on the other hand, believe they can control or manipulate nature or other people by their own efforts. Third, religion by and large tends to be a group activity while magic is more individually oriented. Fourth, whereas religion is usually practiced at a specified time, magic is practiced irregularly in response to specific and immediate problems. Fifth, religion usually involves officially recognized functionaries such as priests, while magic may be performed by a wide variety of practitioners who may or may not be recognized within the community as having supernatural powers.

Despite these five distinctions between religion and magic, we must realize that in actual practice, elements of both are frequently found together. In any religion, for example, there is a fine line—some would argue, no line at all—between praying for god's help and coercing or manipulating a situation to bring about a desired outcome. Also, it is not at all unusual for a person to simultaneously use elements of both religion and magic. To illustrate, a soldier about to enter combat may ask the god(s) for protection through prayer while carrying a lucky rabbit's foot (a magical charm).

Magic involves the manipulation of supernatural forces for the purpose of intervening in a wide range of human activities and natural events. The ritualistic use of magic can be found in some societies to ensure the presence of game animals, to bring about rainfall, to cure or prevent illness, or to protect oneself from misfortune. Magic, however, can also be (and frequently is) directed to cause evil. In some societies it is believed that certain people called witches or sorcerers use various supernatural powers to bring harm to people. Since these forms of "negative magic" hold such fascination for

CHAPTER 21   ◆   RELIGION

Westerners, it is instructive to examine them in greater detail.

## SORCERY AND WITCHCRAFT

While the terms **witchcraft** and sorcery are sometimes used synonymously, cultural anthropologists generally distinguish between them. As practiced in a wide variety of societies throughout the world, witchcraft is an inborn, involuntary, and often unconscious capacity to cause harm to other people. On the other hand, sorcery, which frequently involves the use of materials, potions, and medicines, is the deliberate use of supernatural powers to bring about harm. Some societies have specialized practitioners of sorcery, while in other societies, sorcery can be practiced by anyone. Since sorcery involves the use of certain physical substances, the evidence for the existence of sorcery is more easily found. Witchcraft, by contrast, is virtually impossible to prove or disprove, owing to the absence of any visible evidence of its existence.

Whereas sorcery involves the use of material substances to cause harm to people, witchcraft, it is thought, relies solely on psychic power (i.e., thoughts and emotions). In other words, witches can turn their anger and hatred into evil deeds simply by thinking evil thoughts. How witches are conceptualized varies widely from society to society, but in all cases, witches are viewed negatively. Witches, viewed universally as antisocial, are generally seen as being unable to control those human impulses that normal members of society are expected to keep in check. They have insatiable appetites for food, uncontrollable hatred, and perverted sexual desires. The Mandari believe that witches dance on their victims' graves. The Lugbara of Uganda speak of witches that dance naked, which for them is the ultimate social outrage. The Ganda and Nyoro of Uganda believe in witches that eat corpses. Among the Kaguru of Tanzania, witches are believed to walk upside-down, devour human flesh, commit incest, and in general fail to recognize the rules and constraints of normal society. In many parts of the world, witches are associated with the night, which separates them from normal people, who go about their business during the daytime. Moreover, witches are frequently associated with certain animals, such as bats, rats, snakes, lizards, or leopards, which may be black in color, dangerous, and nocturnal.

It is generally held that sorcerers, rather than acting randomly or capriciously, purposefully direct their ma-levolence against those they dislike, fear, or envy. In any given society, hostile relations can occur between people who have some relationship to one another—e.g., an outsider who married into a local village, rivals for a father's inheritance, co-wives in a polygynous household, men who are competing for a political office, or even rivals in competitive sports. People are therefore likely to explain their own personal misfortune by accusing of sorcery some rival who might gain from harming them. Thus, accusations of sorcery are patterned to the extent that they reflect the conflicts, rivalries, and antagonisms that already exist among the people in any given society.

While sorcery and evil forms of magic are usually associated with small-scale societies in the non-Western world, they are also practiced in the "civilized" world. Edward Moody (1974), for example, presents evidence of a group of Satanists from San Francisco who use sorcerylike techniques for cursing their enemies. Members of the cult are taught to "hate your enemies with a whole heart, and if a man smite you on one cheek, SMASH him on the other. . ." (Moody, 1974:334). If it is determined that a person has harmed or hurt a member of the cult, the perpetrator will be ritually cursed by the entire group. In one case, which Moody personally witnessed, a man who allegedly slandered the name of the cult was given the most serious form of magical curse, the ritualistic casting of the death rune, the sole purpose of which is death and total destruction. When the death rune is cast, the victim's name is written in blood on a special parchment and a lamb's-wool figurine is made to represent the victim. Then, according to Moody's account, in "an orgy of aggression. . . the lamb's-wool figure. . . was stabbed by all members of the congregation, hacked to pieces with a sword, shot with a small calibre pistol, and then burned."

After several weeks, the victim of the ritual entered the hospital with a bleeding ulcer and, when released, left the San Francisco area permanently. Did the curse result in the bleeding ulcer? To be certain, the Satanic cult claimed a resounding victory for black magic. Even though the victim was suffering from hypertension and had had problems with ulcers before, it is possible that his knowledge of the curse could have precipitated the bleeding ulcer and his hasty departure from the San Francisco area.

The anthropologist is not particularly interested in determining whether or not the Satanic curse actually had its intended outcome. What is important to the anthropologist is that this represents a dramatic case of how some people, even in industrialized societies, seek to explain events in their lives by a belief in sorcery or witchcraft.

## Functions of Religion

Anthropological studies of religion are no longer dominated by the search for origins. More recent studies have focused on how religious systems function for both the individual and the society as a whole. Since religious systems are so universal, it is generally held that they must fill a number of important needs at both personal and societal levels.

Anthropologists have always been fascinated by the origins of religion. For much of the nineteenth and

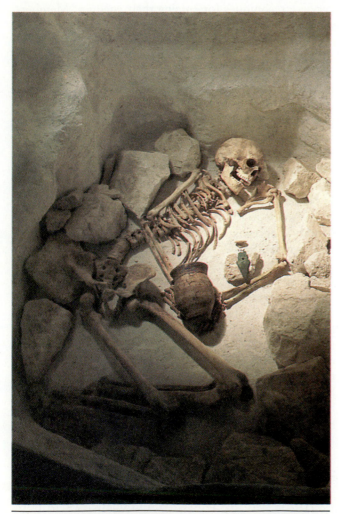

Anthropologists generally agree that the tools and artifacts found in prehistoric grave sites provide evidence of the belief in an afterlife.

twentieth centuries the lack of written records or archaeological evidence has made the subject highly speculative. More recently, however, archaeological evidence has given us a more complete picture of the early origins of religion. Lehmann and Myers (1985:2) remind us that the earliest archaeological evidence of religion dates back about 100,000 years to Neanderthal times. The tools, weapons, and artifacts found in Neanderthal graves have led anthropologists to conclude that these early people believed in an afterlife.

As anthropologists turned away from searching for the origins of religion, they became increasingly interested in a closely related question—that is, how can we explain the universal existence of religion? This question became all the more intriguing, particularly in light of the very elusive nature of religion. As far as we can tell, every society has some system of supernatural belief. Yet it is impossible to prove beyond a reasonable doubt that any supernatural powers (gods, witches, angels, devils, etc.) actually exist. Moreover, it should be obvious to most religious practitioners that supernatural powers don't always work as effectively as they think they should. For example, we pray to god for the recovery of a sick friend, but the friend dies nevertheless; a ritual specialist conducts a rain dance, but it still doesn't rain; or despite sacrificing a goat at the grave site of the ancestor god, the living relatives still are not spared the ravages of the drought. While supernatural beings and forces may not always perform their expected functions (i.e., to bring about supernatural events), they do perform less obvious functions for both the individual and the society as a whole. These latent functions, as they would be called by Robert Merton (1957), fall into two broad categories: (1) social and (2) psychological.

### SOCIAL FUNCTIONS OF RELIGION

One of the most popular explanations for the universality of religion is that it performs a number of important functions for the overall well-being of the society of which it is a part. Let's consider three such **social functions** in which religion plays a role: (1) social control, (2) conflict resolution, and (3) intensifying group solidarity.

**Social Control.** One very important social function of religion is that it serves as a mechanism of social control. Religion, through a series of both positive and negative sanctions, tends to maintain the social order by encouraging socially acceptable behavior and discouraging so-

Funeral ceremonies—such as this cremation in Bali, Indonesia—serve to intensify the group solidarity of all those community members in attendance.

cially inappropriate behavior. Every religion, irrespective of the form it might take, is an ethical system that prescribes proper ways of behaving. When social sanctions (rewards and punishments) are backed with supernatural authority, they are bound to become more compelling. Biblical texts, for example, are very explicit about the consequences of violating the Ten Commandments. Owing to a strong belief in ghostly vengeance, the Lugbara of Uganda scrupulously avoid engaging in any antisocial behavior that would provoke the wrath of the ancestral gods. As mentioned in the chapter on social stratification, Hindus in India believe that to violate prescribed caste expectations will jeopardize their position in future reincarnations.

From an anthropological perspective, it is quite irrelevant as to whether or not these supernatural forces really do reward good behavior and punish bad behavior. Rather than concern themselves with whether and to what extent supernatural forces work the way they are thought to, anthropologists are interested in whether and to what extent people actually *believe* in the power of the supernatural forces. It is, after all, the *belief* in the power of the supernatural sanctions that will determine the level of conformity to socially prescribed behavior.

**Conflict Resolution.** Another social function of religion is the role that it plays in reducing stress and frustrations that often lead to social conflict. In some societies, for example, natural calamities such as epidemics or famines are attributed to the evil deeds of people in other villages or regions. By concentrating on certain religious rituals designed to protect themselves against any more outside malevolence, people will avoid the potential disruptiveness to their own society that might occur should they take out their frustrations on the alleged evildoers. Moreover, disenfranchised or powerless people in stratified societies sometimes use religion as a way of diffusing their anger and hostility that might otherwise be directed against the total social system. To illustrate, in his study of **separatist Christian churches** in the Republic of South Africa, Sundkler (1961) showed how small groups of Black South Africans—who were systematically excluded from the power structure by apartheid—created the illusion of power by manipulating their own set of religious symbols and forming their own unique churches. By providing an alternative power structure, these breakaway Christian churches in South Africa served to reduce conflict by diverting resentment away from the wider power structure.

**Group Solidarity.** A third social function of religion is that in a number of important ways, it intensifies the group solidarity of those who practice it. Religion, for example, enables people to express their common identity in an emotionally charged environment. Powerful social bonds are often created between people who share the experiences of religious beliefs, practices, and rituals. Since every religion or supernatural belief system contains its own unique structural features, those who practice it will share in its mysteries, while those who do not will be excluded. In short, religion strengthens a person's sense of group identity and belonging. And, of course, as people come together for common religious experiences, they often engage in a number of other non-religious activities as well, which further strengthens the sense of social solidarity.

## PSYCHOLOGICAL FUNCTIONS OF RELIGION

In addition to serving the well-being of the society, religion functions psychologically for the benefit of the individual. Anthropologists have identified two fundamentally different types of **psychological functions** of religion: (1) a cognitive function, whereby religion provides an intellectual framework for explaining those parts of our world that we don't understand, and (2) an emotional function, whereby religion helps to reduce anxiety by prescribing some straightforward ways of coping with stress.

**Cognitive Function.** In terms of its cognitive/intellectual function, religion is psychologically comforting because it helps us explain the unexplainable. Every society is faced with a number of imponderable questions for which there are no definitive logical answers. When did life begin? Why do bad things happen to good people? What happens to us when we die? Even in societies like our own—where we have, or think we have, many scientific answers—there remain many unanswered questions. A medical pathologist may be able to explain to the parents of a child who has died of malaria that the cause of death was a bite by an infected anopheles mosquito. But that same pathologist cannot explain to the grieving parents why the mosquito bit their child and not the child next door. Religion can provide satisfying answers to such questions because the answers are based on supernatural authority.

Unlike any other life form, humans have a highly developed urge for understanding themselves and the world around them. But since human understanding of the universe is so imperfect, religion provides a framework for giving meaning to those events and experiences that cannot be explained in any other way. Religion assures its believers that the world is meaningful, that events happen for a reason, that there is order in the universe, and that apparent injustices will eventually be rectified. Humans have difficulty whenever unexplained phenomena contradict their cultural world view. One of the functions of religion, then, is to enable people to maintain their world view even when events occur that seem to contradict it.

**Emotional Function.** The emotional function of religion is to help individuals cope with the anxieties often accompanying illness, accidents, deaths, and other misfortunes. Since people never have complete control over the circumstances of their lives, they often turn to religious ritual in an attempt to maximize control through supernatural means. In fact, the less control people feel they have over their own lives, the more religion they are likely to practice. The fear of facing a frightening situation can be at least partially overcome by believing that supernatural beings will intervene on one's behalf; shame and guilt may be reduced by becoming pious in the face of the deities; and during times of bereavement, religion can provide a source of emotional strength.

People perform religious rituals as a way of invoking supernatural beings to control those forces over which they feel they have no control. This takes a number of different forms throughout the world. To illustrate, the Trobriand Islanders perform a series of magico-religious rituals for protection prior to a long voyage; some people in the United States still carry a St. Christopher medal in their car for protection while driving; and in Nairobi, Kenya, it has been reported that some professional football (i.e., soccer) teams hire their own ritual specialists to bewitch their opponents. In addition to providing greater peace of mind, such religious practices may actually have a positive indirect effect on those events they are intended to influence. For example, even if their witchcraft doesn't work, football players in Kenya are likely to play more confidently if they *believe* they have a supernatural advantage. This ability to act with confidence is a major psychological function of religion.

# Types of Religious Organization

Religion, like other aspects of culture, takes a wide variety of forms throughout the world. To bring some measure of order to this vast diversity, it would be helpful to develop a typology of religious systems based on certain elements of commonality. One such useful and commonly used system of classification, suggested by Anthony Wallace, is based on the level of specialization of the religious personnel who conduct the rituals and ceremonies. Wallace (1966) identified four principal patterns of religious organization based on what he refers to as cults: (1) **individualistic cults**, (2) **shamanistic cults**, (3) **communal cults**, and (4) **ecclesiastical cults**. These four major forms of religious organization, ac-

**TABLE 21-1** ◆ **Characteristics of Different Religious Organizations**

| | Role Specialization | Subsistence Pattern | Example |
|---|---|---|---|
| **Individualistic** | No role specialization | Hunter/gatherer | Crow vision quest |
| **Shamanistic** | Part-time specialization | Hunter/gatherer | Tungus shamanism |
| **Communal** | Groups perform rites for community | Horticulture/pastoralism | Totemistic rituals |
| **Ecclesiastical** | Full-time specialization in hierarchy | Industrialism | Christianity and Buddhism |

SOURCE: Adapted from Anthony F. C. Wallace, *Religion: An Anthropological View*. New York: Random House, 1966.

cording to Wallace's typology, form a scale. Those societies with ecclesiastical cults will also contain communal, shamanistic, and individualistic cults; those with a communalistic form will also contain shamanistic and individualistic cults; while those with shamanistic cults will also contain individualistic cults. Although it is possible that societies with only individualistic cults could have existed in earlier times, there are no contemporary examples of such religious systems.

Wallace's four types correspond roughly to different levels of socioeconomic organization. That is, in a very general way, individualistic and shamanistic cults are usually associated with hunting-and-gathering societies; communal cults are usually found in horticultural and pastoral societies; while ecclesiastical cults are characteristic of highly complex industrialized economies. We should bear in mind, however, that this association between forms of religious organization and socioeconomic types is only approximate at best, for there are some notable exceptions. For example, certain American Plains Indians and some aboriginal Australians had communal forms of religion even though they were hunters and gatherers and lived in bands. (See Table 21-1 for a summary of the characteristics of different religious organizations.)

## INDIVIDUALISTIC CULTS

Individualistic cults, in which there are no religious specialists, represent the most basic level of religious structure according to Wallace's typology. Each person has a relationship with one or more supernatural beings whenever he or she has a need for control or protection. Since individualistic cults do not make distinctions between specialists and laypersons, all people are their own specialists; or as Marvin Harris (1991:290) has put it, this represents a type of do-it-yourself religion. Even though there are no known societies that rely exclusively on this individualistic form of religion, some small-scale band societies do, in fact, practice it as a predominant mode.

The **vision quest**, a ritual found among a number of traditional Plains Indian cultures, provides an excellent example of an individualistic cult. During traditional times, it was expected that through visions, people would establish a special relationship with a spirit that would provide them with knowledge, power, and protection. Sometimes these visions came to people through dreams or when they were by themselves. More often, however, the individual had to purposefully seek out the visions through a series of means, including fasting, bodily mutilation, smoking hallucinogenic substances, and spending time alone in an isolated place.

A person would go on a vision quest if he or she wanted special power (e.g., to excel as a warrior) or knowledge (e.g., to gain insight into a future course of action). A Crow warrior, for example, would go to a place that was thought to be frequented by supernatural spirits. Here he would strip off his clothes, smoke, and abstain from drinking and eating. He might even chop off part of a finger or engage in other types of self-inflicted torture for the sake of getting the spirits' attention. In some cases the vision seekers never did receive a vision, but frequently, Crow vision seekers were successful.

While Crow visions took a variety of forms, they usually had several elements in common. First, the visions usually came in the form of a spirit animal, such as a bison, an eagle, or a snake. Second, some special knowledge or power was gained by the vision seeker. Third, the vision often appeared on the fourth day of the quest, four being a sacred number for the Crow. Finally, the animal spirit would adopt the quester by functioning as his or her own protector spirit.

It is important to bear in mind that the vision quest for the Crow was a normal way of dealing with the stresses and strains of everyday life. Robert Lowie reminds us of the wide range of problems that were addressed in Crow vision quests:

. . . the young man who has been jilted goes off at once to fast in loneliness, praying for supernatural succor. An elk spirit may come and teach him a tune on a flute, as a means of luring the maiden back. The young man plays his tune, ensnares the haughty girl, and turns her away in disgrace, thus regaining his self-respect. Similarly, a wretched orphan who has been mocked by a young man of family hastens to the mountains to be blessed by some being, through whose favor he gains glory and loot on a raid, and can then turn the tables on his tormentor. A woman big with child fasts and in a vision sees a weed which she subsequently harvests and through which she ensures a painless delivery. A gambler who has lost all his property retrieves his fortune through a revelation; and by the same technique a sorrowing kinsman identifies the slayers of his beloved relative and kills them. These are all typical instances, amply documented in personal recollections of informants and in traditional lore, showing the intrusion of religion into the frustrations of everyday living (1963:537).

## SHAMANISTIC CULTS

In addition to having individualistic cults, all contemporary societies operate at the shamanistic level. Shamans are part-time religious specialists who are thought to have supernatural powers by virtue of birth, training, or inspiration. These powers are used for healing, divining, and telling fortunes during times of stress, usually in exchange for gifts or fees. Shamanistic cults represent the simplest form of religious division of labor, for as Wallace reminds us, "the shaman in his religious role is a specialist; and his clients in their relation to him are laymen" (1966:86). The term **shaman**, derived from the Tungus-speaking peoples of Siberia (Service, 1978:127), encompasses a number of different types of specialists found throughout the world, including medicine men and women, diviners, spiritualists, palm readers, and magicians.

Shamans are generally believed to have access to supernatural spirits that they contact on behalf of their clients. The reputation of a particular shaman often rests on the power of the shaman's "spirit helpers" and the ability to contact them at will. Shamans contact their spirits while in an altered state of consciousness brought about by smoking, taking drugs, rhythmic drumming, chanting, or monotonous dancing. Once in a trance, the shaman, possessed with a spirit helper, becomes a me-

Two San hunters from southern Africa hold a shaman who is in an altered state of consciousness.

dium or spokesperson for that spirit. While possessed, the shaman may perspire, breathe heavily, take on a different voice, and generally lose control over his or her own body. In this respect, traditional shamans found in non-Western societies are not appreciably different from professional channelers in the United States who speak on behalf of spirits for their paid clients.

How an individual actually becomes a shaman varies from society to society. In some societies, it is possible to become a shaman by having a particularly vivid or powerful vision in which spirits enter the body. In other societies, one can become a shaman by serving as an apprentice under a practicing shaman. Among the Tungus of Siberia, mentally unstable people who often experience bouts of hysteria are the most likely candidates for shamanism because hysterical people are thought to be the closest to the spirit world (Service, 1978:127). In those societies that regularly use hallucinogenic drugs, almost any person can achieve that altered state of consciousness needed for the practice of shamanism. For example, Michael Harner (1973:17) reports that among the Jivaro Indians of the Ecuadorian Amazon who use hallucinogenics widely and have a strong desire to contact the supernatural world, about one in four men is a shaman.

As practiced by the Reindeer Tungus of Siberia, shamans are individuals who have the power to control various spirits, can prevent those spirits from causing harm, and, on occasions, can serve as a medium for those spirits (Service, 1978:127–128). Tungus shamans—who can be either men or women—use special paraphernalia, such as elaborate costumes, a brass mirror, and a tambourine. The rhythmic beating of the tambourine is used to induce a trance in the shaman and to produce a receptive state of consciousness on the part of the onlookers. The shaman, possessed by the rhythmic drumming, proceeds to journey into the spirit world to perform certain functions for individual clients or the group as a whole. These functions may include determining the cause of a person's illness, finding a lost object, conferring special powers in a conflict, or predicting future events. Shamanism among the Tungus does not involve the power to cure a particular illness, but rather only determines the cause of the malady. In this respect, the Tungusic shaman is a medical diagnostician rather than a healer or medicine man or woman.

## COMMUNAL CULTS

Communal cults—which involve a more elaborate set of beliefs and rituals—operate at a still higher level of organizational complexity. Groups of ordinary people (organized around clans, lineages, age groups, or secret societies) conduct religious rites and ceremonies for the larger community. These rites, performed only occasionally or periodically by nonspecialists, are considered to be absolutely vital to the well-being of both individuals and the society as a whole. Even though these ceremonies may include such specialists as shamans, orators, or magicians, the primary responsibility for the success of the ceremonies lies primarily with the nonspecialists, who at the conclusion of the ceremony, return to their everyday activities. Examples of communal cults are the ancestral ceremonies among the traditional Chinese, pu-

berty rites found in certain sub-Saharan African societies, and totemic rituals practiced by some aboriginal peoples of Australia.

Communal rituals fall into two broad categories: (1) rites of passage which celebrate the transition of a person from one social status to another; and (2) rites of solidarity, those public rituals serving to foster group identity and group goals and having very explicit and immediate objectives, such as calling upon the supernatural beings/forces to increase fertility or prevent misfortune. Let us look at these two types of communal cults in greater detail.

**Rites of Passage.** **Rites of passage** are ceremonies that mark a change in a person's social position. These ritualistic ceremonies—which have religious significance—help both individuals and the society deal with important life changes. Rites of passage—which take place for such occasions as birth, reaching puberty, marriage, and death—are, however, more than ways of merely recognizing certain transitions in a person's life. When a person marries, for example, he or she not only takes on a new status but also creates an entire complex of new relationships. These rites of passage, then, are important public rituals that recognize a wider set of altered social relationships.

According to Van Gennep (1960), all rites of passage, in whatever culture they may be found, tend to have three distinct ritual phases: separation, transition, and incorporation. The first phase—separation—is characterized by the stripping away of the old status. In cases of puberty rites, for example, childhood is ritually or symbolically "killed" by pricking the initiates' navels with a spear. In the second phase the individual is in an in-between stage, cut off from the old status but not yet integrated into the new status. Since this transition stage is associated with danger and ambiguity, it frequently involves the endurance of certain unpleasant ordeals as well as the removal of the individual from normal, everyday life for a certain period of time. The third and final phase involves the ritual incorporation of the individual into the new status. Ethnographic data from all over the world have supported Van Gennep's claim that all rites of passage contain these three discrete phases.

These three ritual phases are well demonstrated in the rites of adulthood practiced by the Kikuyu of Kenya, who initiate both girls and boys (Middleton and Kershaw, 1965). The Kikuyu, not unlike other traditional East African societies, practice initiation ceremonies as a way of ensuring that children will be converted into

These Masai warriors—attending an initiation ceremony—are participating in a rite of passage that marks the passage into adult status.

moral and socially responsible adults. Despite some regional variations, the Kikuyu initiation rite comprises certain rituals that conform to Van Gennep's threefold scheme.

Kikuyu initiation into adulthood involves a physical operation—circumcision for males and clitoridectomy for women. Days before the physical operation, the initiates go through a number of rituals designed to separate them from society and their old status as well as place them in close relationship to god. First, the initiates are adopted by an elder man and his wife, which event symbolically separates them from their own parents. Second, the initiates spend the night before the circumcision singing and dancing in an effort to solicit the guidance and protection of the ancestral gods. Third, the initiates have their heads shaved and anointed, symbolizing the loss of the old status. And finally, they are sprayed with a mixture of honey, milk, and medicine by their adoptive "parents" in another separation ritual, which Middleton and Kershaw (1965:58) refer to as "the ceremony of parting."

The second (transition) phase of the Kikuyu initiation ceremony, as Van Gennep's theory suggests, is a marginal phase filled with danger and ambiguity. The initiates undergo the dramatic and traumatic circumcision or clitoridectomy as a vivid symbolization of their soon-to-be assumed responsibility as adults. Both male and female initiates are physically and emotionally supported during the operation by their sponsors, who cover them with cloaks as soon as the operation is completed. Afterwards, the initiates spend a period of between four and nine days in seclusion in temporary huts (*kiganda*), where they are expected to recover from the operation and reflect upon their impending status as adults.

The third and final phase of Kikuyu initiation rituals involves the incorporation of the initiate (with his or her new status) back into the society as a whole. At the end of the seclusion period, the new male adults have certain ceremonial plants put into the large loops in their ear lobes (a form of body mutilation practiced during childhood) symbolizing their newly acquired status as adult men. This phase of incorporation (or reintegration) involves other rituals as well. The men symbolically put an end to their transition stage by burning their *kiganda*; their heads are again shaven; they return home to be anointed by their parents, who soon thereafter engage in ritual intercourse; they ritually discard their initiation clothing; and they are given warrior paraphernalia. Once these incorporation rituals have been completed, the young men become full adults with all of the rights and responsibilities that go along with their new status.

**Rites of Solidarity.** The other type of communal cult is directed toward the welfare of the community rather than the individual. These **rites of solidarity** permit a wider social participation in the shared concerns of the community than is found in those societies with predominantly shamanistic cults. A good example of cults that foster group solidarity is the ancestral cult, found widely throughout the world. Ancestral cults are based on the assumption that upon death, a person's soul continues to interact with and affect the lives of the living descendants. In other words, when people die, they are not buried and forgotten, but rather are elevated to the status of ancestor ghost or god. Since these ghosts, who are viewed as the official guardians of the social and moral order, have supernatural powers, the living descendants practice certain communal rituals designed to induce the ancestor ghosts to protect them, favor them, or at least not harm them.

Like many of their neighboring cultures in Northern Ghana, the Sisala believe that the ancestor ghosts are the guardians of the moral order. All members of Sisala lineages are subject to the authority of the lineage elders. Since the elders are the most important living members of the group, they are responsible for overseeing the interests and harmony of the entire group. While responsible for group morality, the elders have no direct authority to punish violators. The Sisala believe that the primary activity of the ancestor ghosts is to punish those living lineage members who violate behavioral norms. To be specific, ancestor ghosts are thought to take vengeance on any living members who steal from their lineage mates, fight with their kin, or generally fail to live up to their family duties and responsibilities. Mendonsa (1985:218–19) describes a specific case, which graphically illustrates the power of ancestral cults among the Sisala:

At Tuorojang in Tumu there was a young man named Cedu. He caught a goat that was for the ancestor of his house (*dia*), and killed it to sell the meat. When the day came for the sacrifice, the elders searched for the goat so they could kill it at the *lele* shrine. They could not find it, and asked to know who might have caught the goat. They could not decide who had taken the goat, so they caught another and used it for the sacrifice instead. During the sacrifice, the elders begged the ancestors to forgive them for not sacrificing the proper goat. The elders asked the ancestors to find and punish the thief. After the sacrifice, when all the elders had gone to their various houses, they heard that Cedu had died. They summoned a diviner to determine the cause of death, and found that Cedu had been the thief. He had been killed by the ancestors because he was the person who stole the goat which belonged to the ancestors.

This case illustrates the belief that the Sisala have concerning the power of the ancestor ghosts to protect the moral order. When a breach of the normative order occurs, the elders conduct a communal ritual petitioning the ghost to punish the wrongdoer. As with other aspects of religion, the anthropologist is not concerned with whether or not the diviner in the cited case was

This Asmat man from Irian Jaya is wearing around his neck the skull of a dead ancestor which, it is believed, has the supernatural power to protect the wearer.

correct in determining that Cedu died because he stole the goat. The anthropologist is concerned, however, with the communal ritual and its immediate social effects: namely, that it (1) served to restore social harmony within the lineage and (2) served as a warning to others who might be contemplating stealing from their lineage members.

## ECCLESIASTICAL CULTS

The most complex form of religious organization according to Wallace is the ecclesiastical cult, found in societies with state systems of government. Examples of ecclesiastical cults can be drawn from those societies with a pantheon of several high gods (e.g., traditional Aztec, Incas, Greeks, or Egyptians) or from those with essentially monotheistic religions, such as Hinduism, Buddhism, Christianity, Judaism, or Islam (see Exhibit 21-1). Ecclesiastical cults are characterized by full-time professional clergy, who are formally elected or appointed and devote all or most of their time performing priestly functions. Unlike shamans, these full-time priests conduct rituals that are calendrical (that is, oc-curring at regular intervals) as compared to shamans, who conduct rituals during times of crisis or when their services are needed.

Not only do ecclesiastical cults involve full-time ritual specialists, but these priests are organized into a hierar-chical or bureaucratic organization under the control of a centralized church or temple. Frequently, but not al-ways, these clerical bureaucracies are either controlled by the centralized governments or closely associated

EXHIBIT 21-1

**Major Religions of the World**

SOURCE: Reprinted by permission from pages 54–55 of *World Regional Geography: A Global Approach,* by George F. Hepner and Jesse O. McKee. Copyright © 1992 by West Publishing Company. All rights reserved.

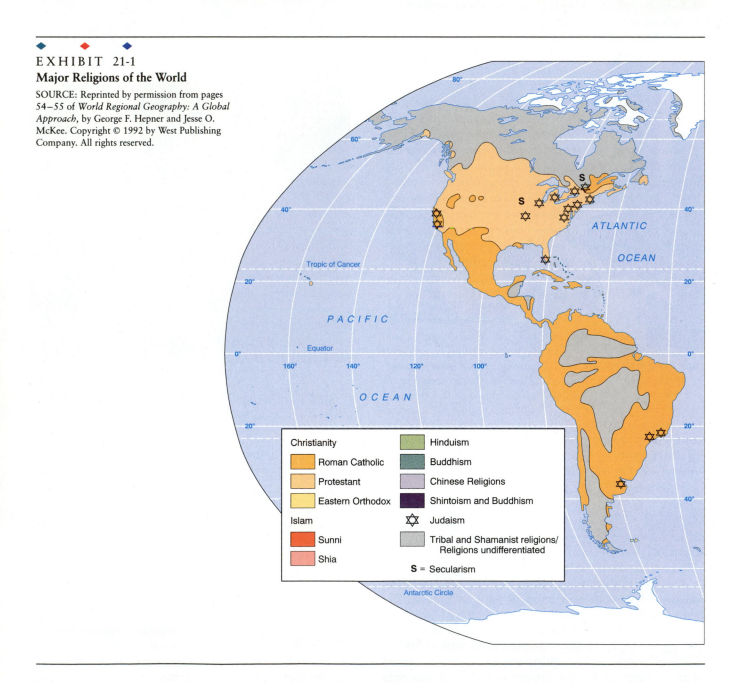

CHAPTER 21 ◆ RELIGION

with them. In many ecclesiastical cults, the prevailing myths and beliefs are used to support the supremacy of the ruling class. In fact, it is not unusual for the priests to be part of that ruling class. Because of this close association between the priesthood and the politicoeconomic institutions, women have not traditionally played very active roles as priests. This represents another important difference between priests and shamans, for there are at least as many women as men practicing shamanism throughout the world. Even in modern complex societies, women are particularly active as mystics, channelers, palm readers, astrologers, and clairvoyants.

In those societies with ecclesiastical cults, a clearly understood distinction exists between laypersons and priests. Laypersons are primarily responsible for supporting the church through their labor and their financial contributions. The priests, on the other hand, are responsible for conducting the religious rituals on behalf

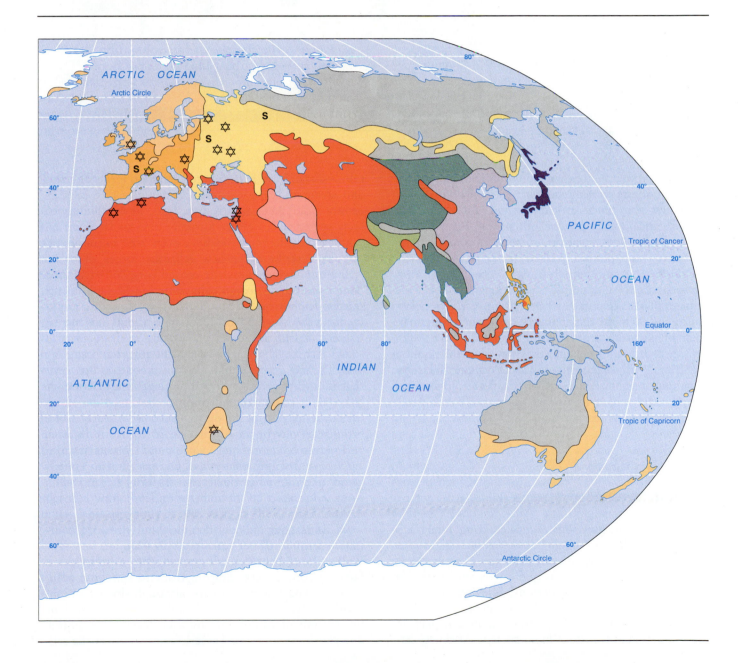

A Roman Catholic priest is a full-time religious specialist who works within a hierarchical organization.

of the lay population, either individually or in groups. While the priests serve as active ritual managers, the lay population participates in ritual in a generally passive fashion. Since the lay population has little control over religion, it becomes spiritually dependent on the priests for its ritual/supernatural well-being.

Ecclesiastical cults, while having enormous control over people's lives, certainly have not wiped out other forms of religion. Eskimos who have converted to Christianity, for example, may continue to consult a shaman when ill; Africans from Tanzania often still worship their ancestors while being practicing Roman Catholics; and in our own society, many people have no difficulty consulting a palmist, a psychic, or an astrologer even though they adhere to one of the large, worldwide, monotheistic religions.

## Religion and Change: Revitalization Movements

Reading about the functions of religion could likely lead one to conclude that religion is a highly conservative force within a society. After all, religion contributes to the maintenance of the status quo by keeping people in line through supernatural sanctions, relieving social conflict, and providing explanations for unfortunate events. But under certain circumstances, religion can play an important role in transforming a society. At times, cer-

tain societies have experienced such high levels of stress and strain that the conservative functions of religion cannot hold them together. Instead, new religions or sects spring up to create a totally new social order. A number of different terms have been used in the literature to describe these new religious forces of social change, including **nativistic movements**, found among American Indians; **cargo cults**, found in Melanesia; the **separatist churches** of Southern Africa; **mahdist movements** in the Muslim world; and **millenarian movements** found in Christian areas of the world.

All of these religious movements—aimed at breathing new life and purpose into the society—are called **revitalization movements** by Anthony Wallace (1966:30–34). The common thread running through them all is that they tend to occur during times of cultural stress brought about by rapid change, foreign domination, and perceived deprivation. Since these three conditions are frequently, but not always, associated with colonialism, many revitalization movements have appeared in those societies that have been under colonial domination.

While recognizing considerable differences in the details surrounding various revitalization movements, Wallace (1966:158–63) suggests that most follow a fairly uniform process. Starting from the state of equilibrium (in which change occurs, although slowly, and individual stress levels are tolerable), a society will be pushed out of equilibrium by such forces as conquest and social domination. These conditions lower the self-

**CROSS-CULTURAL MISCUE**

As McKenzie and Chrisman remind us, many Filipino-Americans believe at the same time in both Christianity and other supernatural forces (such as evil spirits and witches). It is generally held that a person can identify a witch by his or her reluctance to look a person in the eye. Given such a belief, it would behoove Western health practitioners to be sure to look their Filipino-American patients in the eye. For example, in the event that a nurse in a Philadelphia hospital failed to maintain eye contact with his or her Filipinio-American patient, the nurse "could be perceived as the instrument of illness and misfortune—a witch—rather than a health care provider" (McKenzie and Chrisman 1977:329).

esteem of an increasing number of individuals and place the individuals under intolerable stress. People become disillusioned, and the culture becomes disorganized (e.g., higher crime rates and a general increase in antisocial behavior). When the social fabric deteriorates sufficiently, revitalization movements are likely to appear in an effort to bring about a more satisfying society. Some movements call for a return to the better days of the past; others seek to establish a completely new social order.

## NATIVE AMERICAN REVITALIZATION MOVEMENTS

While revitalization movements have been found in many parts of the world, nowhere have they been more widespread and better documented than among Native American groups. The tragic suffering of American Indians since their earliest contact with Europeans has resulted in a number of revitalization movements, including the movement among the Seneca Indians in the late eighteenth century headed by Handsome Lake, several versions of the Ghost Dance, and the Peyote cults found among the Plains Indians. In recent decades, these religious revitalization movements have been replaced by more secular/political efforts to reclaim Indian land, resources, and dignity through the courts, political activism, and civil disobedience.

One of the earliest accounts of a Native American revitalization movement was that started by Handsome Lake (Deardorff, 1951; and Parker, 1913). By the year 1800, the Seneca Indians of New York State had fallen upon hard times. They had lost much of their land to the whites, who held them in contempt because they were on the losing side of the French and Indian War. They were confined to reservations, and their numbers had been severely reduced by such European diseases as measles and smallpox. Once a proud nation of warriors, hunters, and traders, the Seneca by the start of the nineteenth century were defeated, dehumanized, and demoralized. Alcoholism became rampant, while conflicts and accusations of witchcraft increased.

From this state of cultural disorganization came a prophet—Handsome Lake—who received a vision from god to stop drinking and start a new revitalizing religion. According to Handsome Lake's vision, the deity warned that the Seneca would suffer a great catastrophe (e.g., fire, destruction, and death) if they did not mend their ways. Most of the prescriptions set down by Handsome Lake constituted a new set of morality and behavior. Followers of the new religious movement were expected to stay sober, be peaceful, and lead pure and upright lives.

A number of other important cultural changes were instigated by Handsome Lake. For example, he urged his followers to adopt European agricultural practices involving both men and women working in the fields. In terms of the Seneca family, he emphasized the priority of the conjugal unit of man and wife over the matrilineage. Divorce, which had always been high in traditional Seneca society, was no longer permitted. This revitalization movement of Handsome Lake led to far-reaching cultural changes. The Seneca became models of sobriety, their family structure was altered, they initiated new farming practices, and they changed the traditional division of labor between men and women.

Since so many revitalization movements arise in opposition to powerful social, economic, and political forces, they frequently do not accomplish their avowed goals. Many of the Native American revitalization movements over the past several centuries have not ended the white domination. The black separatist churches in South Africa have hardly brought the apartheid system to its knees. The People's Temple movement, led by the Reverend Jim Jones, ended catastrophically when Jones and hundreds of his followers committed mass suicide.

At other times in recent history, certain revitalization movements have met with considerable, if not total, success. Examples of successful revitalization efforts include the Protestant Reformation of sixteenth-century Europe, the creation of Mormonism in Utah, and the Black Muslim movement in contemporary America. But even in those majority of situations where revitalization movements do not succeed in their objectives, such movements can serve useful purposes. That is, they can provide a renewed sense of both individual and group identity during times of suppression, frustration, and alienation. Equally important, they can stimulate changes in the existing social order in a more gradual fashion.

## ◆ Summary

1. While all cultures have supernatural beliefs, the forms the beliefs take vary widely from society to society. It is often difficult to define supernatural belief systems cross-culturally because different societies have different ways of distinguishing between the natural and the supernatural.

2. The anthropological study of religion does not attempt to determine which religions are better than others or which gods are able to work the most miracles per unit of time. Rather, cultural anthropologists concentrate on describing the various systems of religious belief, how they function, and the degree to which they influence human behavior.

3. Religion differs from magic in that religion deals with such big issues of life, death, and god, while magic deals with more immediate and specific problems. Whereas religion asks for help through prayer, magic is a direct attempt to control and manipulate supernatural forces.

4. Witchcraft and sorcery are two types of supernatural belief systems that cause harm to people. Whereas sorcery involves the deliberate attempt to cause people misfortune through the use of certain material substances, witchcraft is an inborn and generally involuntary capacity to work evil.

5. Religion performs certain social functions. It enhances the overall well-being of the society by (a) serving as a mechanism of social control, (b) helping to reduce the stress and frustrations that often lead to social conflict, and (c) intensifying group solidarity.

6. Religion also performs certain psychological functions by (a) providing emotional comfort by helping to explain the unexplainable and (b) helping a person cope with the stress and anxiety often accompanying illness or misfortune.

7. Following the scheme suggested by Wallace, there are four distinctive patterns of religious organization: (a) individualistic cults; (b) shamanistic cults; (c) communal cults; and (d) ecclesiastical cults. These four types of religion vary roughly with increasing levels of socioeconomic complexity, with individualistic cults associated with hunting-and-gathering societies while ecclesiastical cults are found in highly industrialized societies.

8. The most basic level of religious organization is the individualistic cult characterized by an absence of religious specialists. The vision quest practiced by certain North American Indian cultures is an example of an individualistic cult.

9. Shamanistic cults involve the least complex form of religious division of labor. Shamans are part-time religious specialists who, it is believed, help or cure their clients by intervening with the supernatural powers while in an altered state of consciousness.

10. Communal cults involve groups of ordinary people who conduct religious ceremonies for the well-being of the community. Examples of communal cults are the rites of passage (e.g., circumcision ceremonies) found widely throughout sub-Saharan Africa and the ancestral cults that function to foster group solidarity among members of a kinship group.

11. Ecclesiastical cults, found in societies with state systems of government, are characterized by full-time professional clergy who are usually organized into a hierarchy.

12. Revitalization movements—religious movements aimed at bringing new life and energy into a society—usually occur when societies are experiencing rapid culture change, foreign domination, or preceived deprivation. Revitalization movements have taken a number of different forms, including nativistic movements, cargo cults, and millenarian movements.

## ◆ Key Terms

cargo cults

communal cults

ecclesiastical cults

economic behavior

individualistic cults
kinship behavior
magic
mahdist movement
millenarian movement
nativistic movement
psychological functions
    of religion
religious behavior
revitalization movement
rite of passage
rite of solidarity

separatist Christian
    church
separatist church
shaman
shamanistic cults
social functions
    of religion
sorcery
supernatural
vision quest
witchcraft

## ◆ Suggested Readings

Douglas, Mary. *Purity and Danger*. Baltimore: Penguin, 1966. This provocative book is a systematic study of the rules of purity and pollution found in various societies which, the author claims, can be understood only within the context of a society's total set of values and ideas.

Mair, Lucy. *Witchcraft*. New York: McGraw Hill, 1969. A summary of the major anthropological thinking on the subject of witchcraft. The author looks at the nature of witchcraft, how witches are detected, the treatment of witches, and some varying theories on why witchcraft exists.

Norbeck, Edward. *Religion in Human Life: Anthropological Views*. New York: Holt, Rinehart & Winston, 1974. A slim but informative volume that covers the anthropology of religion by focusing on two main themes: (1) the description of religious events, functions, and rituals and (2) the nature of the anthropological study of religions worldwide.

Pandian, Jacob. *Culture, Religion, and the Sacred Self: A Critical Introduction to the Anthropological Study of Religion*. Englewood Cliffs, N.J.: Prentice-Hall, 1991. A relatively small but comprehensive discussion of the scope and objectives of the anthropological study of religion. Through the cross-cultural analysis of shamanism, myth, religious movements, and ritual, Pandian offers the reader an interpretation of the relationship between supernatural beliefs and the cultural formation of the self.

Swanson, Guy. *The Birth of the Gods: The Origin of Primitive Beliefs*. Ann Arbor: University of Michigan Press, 1960. Following the lead of Durkheim, Swanson discusses how the form of a number of non-Western religious practices are influenced by other parts of the social structure.

Wallace, Anthony F. C. *Religion: An Anthropological View*. New York: Random House, 1966. An old yet still valuable analysis of the anthropology of religion that discusses some general theories, the structure, goals, functions, and ritual processes of religion from a cross-cultural perspective.

## APPLIED PERSPECTIVE

◆　　◆　　◆　　◆　　◆

# Religion

◆ **Anthropological testimony serves as the basis for a Supreme Court ruling.**

Anyone traveling through the rural parts of Pennsylvania, Indiana, or Ohio is likely to see bearded men in black hats driving horse-drawn buggies and women wearing long dresses reminiscent of the nineteenth century. These people, seemingly so out of place in today's modern world, are the Old Order Amish, one of the oldest and most visible minorities in the United States. Amish society is characterized by several cultural themes to which they strongly adhere. First, they strive to separate themselves from the world to the extent that they avoid worldly goods, practice strict endogamy, and even refrain from entering into business partnerships with non-Amish. Second, they place high value on adult baptism and the acceptance of many social obligations that that baptism symbolizes. Third, the Amish maintain a highly disciplined church-community. Fourth, they maintain the purity of their church-community by excommunicating and/or shunning those erring members. Fifth, the Amish live their lives in harmony with the soil and nature.

In the early 1970s the Amish were involved in a legal battle with the State of Wisconsin that went all the way to the U.S. Supreme Court. The central issue revolved around whether the state's compulsory education law violated the free exercise of religion of the Amish. Holding the religious belief that their church-communities should be separate from the world, the Amish raise their children to be members of a self-sufficient community that rejects many of the values and physical trappings of mainstream U.S. society. The Amish argued that if they are required to send their children to public high schools, their self-sufficient church-communities would be destroyed in a generation or two.

In its landmark decision of *Wisconsin v. Yoder*, the U.S. Supreme Court ruled that for the state to require Amish parents to send their children to public school beyond the eighth grade was a violation of their constitutional rights. By agreeing with the Amish argument, the Court exempted the Amish from compliance with the state's compulsory education law on the grounds of their religious beliefs. In rendering its decision, the Court drew heavily upon the testimony of John Hostetler, an anthropologist who served as an expert witness at the lower level court proceedings. In fact, as one observer (Rosen) commented:

. . . a close reading of the Supreme Court opinion clearly demonstrates that the anthropological testimony in this case may well have been indispensable to the Court's assertion that enforcement of the school attendance law would have had an unusually harsh effect on the entire community of Amish people (nd:20).

Hostetler argued that to require Amish teenagers to attend high schools that fostered such radically different social and religious values would subject them to great psychological harm. That is, the conflicting values between mainstream schools and Amish church-communities would cause considerable alienation between Amish parents and their children. Central to Hostetler's argument is the anthropological theory of the integrated nature of a culture. Hostetler was able to convince the Court that Amish culture is an organic whole, the parts of which are intimately interconnected. More specifically, he pointed out the close interconnection between Amish religion and the Amish people's daily communal life.

Basing much of its decision on Hostetler's anthropological testimony, the Court concluded:

Aided by a history of three centuries as an identifiable religious sect and a long history as a successful and self-sufficient segment of American society, the Amish in this case have convincingly demonstrated the sincerity of their religious beliefs, the interrelationship of belief with their mode of life, the vital role that belief and daily conduct play in the continued survival of Old Order Amish communities and their religious organization, and the hazards presented by the State's enforcement of a statute generally valid to others.

Owing to the closeness of fit between Hostetler's testimony and the Court's decision, it seems safe to conclude that this landmark case might well have had a different outcome had John Hostetler not used his anthropological insights as an expert witness.

◆ **Medical caregivers in the United States need to be sensitive to the supernatural belief systems of their culturally different patients.**

Today it is generally understood by medical anthropologists that religion or supernatural beliefs play an important role in the delivery of health care services. In many cultures, the causes of certain illnesses are explained in supernatural terms rather than natural or scientific terms. These supernatural explanations can take a number of different forms, including attributing illness to witches, evil spirits, the wrath of god, voodooism, dead ancestors, and bad magic. How these folk beliefs and explanations are dealt with by members of the Western, scientifically based medical community will influence the effectiveness of the health systems they design for culturally distinct populations. It is the applied anthropologist who is in the best position to serve as a liaison between Western medical personnel and their traditional non-Western patients.

The collaborative work of Joan McKenzie, a nursing consultant, and Noel Chrisman, a medical anthropologist, illustrates how an understanding of religious explanations among Filipino-Americans can be helpful to the healing process. Filipino-Americans generally believe that illness is caused by such supernatural factors as sorcerers, witches, and ancestral spirits. It is believed that these dangerous supernatural forces can be neutralized through the use of talismans, prayers, and folk healers. While Filipino-Americans also use Western medicine, the services of these folk healers are frequently sought out when Western health practitioners fail to provide a cure.

Western medical personnel tend to dismiss, out of hand, explanations of illness and folk cures as mere superstition. But McKenzie and Chrisman argue that it is important for health practitioners to know about these folk

461

beliefs in order to develop effective therapeutic relationships with their patients. As has been demonstrated repeatedly by medical anthropology, some folk remedies can be clinically therapeutic, others therapeutically neutral, while still others can be clinically harmful.

McKenzie and Chrisman (1977:329) cite several cases of how some folk remedies can be clinically beneficial. For example, the Filipino-American folk cure for colic involving the mother's rubbing her hands together and placing them on the infant's abdomen is not substantially different from the remedy suggested by the public health nurse—that is, giving the infant warm water and placing the baby on its abdomen to create slight pressure. Other folk remedies—such as giving a patient with a cold a glass of vinegar to drink to flush impurities from the system—are therapeutically neutral, for it is neither beneficial nor harmful. It is advisable, according to McKenzie and Chrisman, for Western medical people to integrate these beneficial or neutral folk practices into their health care strategies in order to build rapport with their culturally distinct patients, thereby increasing the chances that other health measures will be followed. Moreover, as McKenzie and Chrisman have suggested:

The blending of folk remedies with scientific cures can help bridge the communication gap between nurse, client, and family, thereby increasing trust. Once trust is established, the individual and his family will be much more open to the replacement of a potentially harmful folk practice by a medically validated one (1977:329).

The role of applied anthropologists in this process of working with culturally different patients should be obvious. By studying the folk medical practices of different subcultural groups in the United States, applied anthropologists will be able to identify the nature of these practices and how and to what extent they are based on supernatural beliefs and, in cooperation with health professionals, indicate how they might be integrated into the overall health care systems.

# Art

How do anthropologists define the arts?

What are the various functions of art in society?

How do music and dance reflect other aspects of a culture?

Artistic expression is one of the most distinctive human characteristics. No group of people known to cultural anthropologists spend all of their time in the utilitarian pursuit of meeting their basic survival needs. In other words, people do not hunt, grow crops, make tools, and build houses purely for the sake of sustaining themselves and others. After the survival needs are met, all cultures, even technologically simple ones, decorate their storage containers, paint their houses, embroider their clothing, and create aesthetically pleasing designs on their tools. They compose songs, tell riddles, dance creatively, paint pictures, make films, and carve masks. All of these endeavors reflect the human urge to express oneself and take pleasure from aesthetics. It would be hard to imagine a society without art, music, dance, and poetry. As the study of cultural anthropology reminds us, however, artistic expression is found in every society, and aesthetic pleasure is felt by all members of humankind.

◆ ◆ ◆

# What Is Art?

For centuries, people from a wide range of perspectives—including philosophers, anthropologists, politicians, art historians, and professional artists themselves—have proposed definitions of art. As Mills has suggested, "definitions (of art) vary with the purposes of the definers. . ." (1957:77). To illustrate, the artist might tend to define art in terms of the creative process; the politician's definition would emphasize those communicative aspects of art that could mobilize public opinion; the art historian or knowledgeable collector would focus on the emotional response that art produces; and the cultural anthropologist might define art in terms of the role or function it plays in religious ceremonies. While recognizing the vast diversity in definitions of art, any definition, if it is to have any cross-cultural applicability, must include certain basic elements:

1. The artistic process should be creative, playful, and enjoyable and need not be concerned with the practicality or usefulness of the object being produced.
2. From the perspective of the consumer, art should produce some type of emotional response—either positive or negative.
3. Art should be **transformational**. An image from nature—such as a cheetah running at full speed—may be aesthetically pleasing in that it evokes a strong emotional response, but it is not art. It becomes art

only when someone transforms the image into a painting, dance, song, or poem.
4. Art should communicate information by being representational. In other words, once the object of art is transformed, it should make a symbolic statement about what is being portrayed.
5. Art implies that the artist has developed a certain level of technical skill not shared equally by all people in a society. Some people have more highly developed skills than others owing to the interplay of individual interests and opportunities with genetically based acuities.

Centuries of continual debate by reasonable people have failed to produce a universally agreed upon definition of art. While not presuming to propose a universal definition, it will be useful, for purposes of this chapter, to suggest a working definition of art based on the five elements just listed. Art, then, refers to both *the process and the products of applying certain skills to any activity that transforms matter, sound, or motion into a form that is deemed aesthetically pleasing to people in a society.*

By using these five features of art, we can include a wide variety of types of artistic activities in our definition of art. In all societies people apply imagination, creativity, and technical skills to transform matter, sound, and movement into works of art. The various types of artistic expression include (1) the graphic or plastic arts, such as painting, carving, weaving, sculpture, and basket making; (2) the creative manipulation of sounds and words in such artistic forms as music, poetry, and folklore; and (3) the application of skill and creativity to body movement that gives rise to dance. It should be pointed out that these three neatly defined categories of artistic expression will sometimes include forms that are not familiar to Westerners. Whereas the Westerner usually thinks of graphic and plastic arts as including such media as painting, sculpture, and ceramics, in the non-Western world people may also include the elaborate body decoration found among the Nubians (Faris, 1972), Navajo sand painting (Witherspoon, 1977), and body tattooing among the Eskimos (Birket-Smith, 1959). Moreover, sometimes activities that in our own society have no particular artistic content will be elevated to an art form in other societies. The Japanese tea ceremony is an excellent case in point.

Every society has a set of standards that distinguish between good art and bad art or between more and less satisfying aesthetic experiences. In some societies, such as our own, what constitutes good art is determined

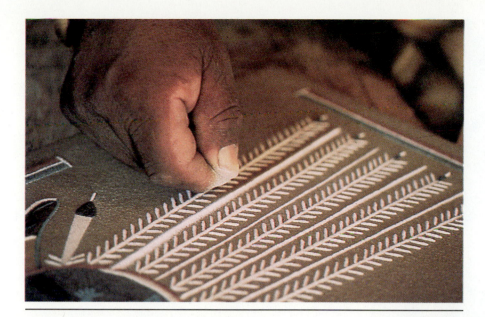

Navajo sand painting represents a somewhat unusual form of graphic art.

largely by a professional art establishment comprising art critics, museum and conservatory personnel, professors of art, and others who generally make their living in the arts. Although other societies might not have professional art establishments, their artistic standards tend to be more democratic in that they are maintained by the general public. That is, the decoration on a vase, the rhythm of a song, the communicative power of a dance, or the imagery of a painting will be subject to the evaluation of both artists and nonartists alike.

## Differences in Art Forms

As pointed out in Chapter 2, the term **primitive** has fallen out of fashion when referring to societies that are radically different from our own. The term, however, when associated with **art**, has had greater staying power. Despite numerous attempts by art historians and some anthropologists to disassociate themselves from the term, it still retains some legitimacy. This reluctance to eliminate the use of primitive was expressed in the newest edition of Janson's *History of Art*:

Primitive is a somewhat unfortunate word. . . . Still, no other single term will serve us better. Let us continue, then, to use primitive as a convenient label for a way of life that has passed through the Neolithic Revolution but shows no signs of evolving in the direction of "historic" civilizations (1986:35).

Despite such attempts by art historians to perpetuate the term primitive, the term will not be used in this text because of its misleading connotations of both inferiority and evolutionary sequencing. Instead, the term *small-scale* will be used to describe those relatively egalitarian societies with small populations, simple technologies, and little labor specialization.

Having disposed of the term *primitive,* we can now proceed to look at some of the major differences in art forms between small-scale and complex societies (this discussion of differences is developed in much fuller detail by Anderson, 1990:224–30). One such difference stems from the general life-styles and settlement patterns found in these logically opposite types of societies. Since small-scale societies tend to be foragers, pastoralists, or shifting cultivators with nomadic or semi-nomadic residence patterns, the art found in these societies must be highly portable. It is not reasonable to expect people who are frequently on the move to develop an art tradition comprising large works of art such as larger-than-life sculptures or large painted canvases. Instead, art in small-scale societies is limited to those forms that people can take with them relatively easily, such as (a) performing arts (song, dance, and story telling); (b) body decoration, such as jewelry, body painting, tattooing, and scarification; and (c) artistic decorations on such practical artifacts as weapons, clothing, or food containers.

Another significant difference between the art found in small-scale societies and that of complex societies

In complex societies, artistic standards are defined by full-time specialists such as philosophers, curators, professors of art, and art critics, many of whom are associated with such institutions as the Art Institute in Chicago.

stems from the societies' different levels of social differentiation (i.e., labor specialization). As societies began to develop increasingly more specialized roles following the Neolithic Revolution (c. 8000 B.C.), some segments of the population were freed up from the everyday pursuits of food getting. With the subsequent rise of civilizations there developed full-time specialists, such as philosophers, intellectuals, literati, and aesthetic critics, whose energies were directed, among other things, at distinguishing between good art and bad art. The standards of aesthetic judgment have become much more explicit and elaborately defined by specialists in more complex societies. To be certain, aesthetic standards exist in small-scale societies, but they are less elaborate, more implicit, and more widely diffused throughout the entire population.

A third major contrast arises from the differences in division of labor. As a general rule, as societies become increasingly more specialized, they also become more highly stratified into classes with differential levels of power, prestige, and wealth. Those aesthetic critics responsible for establishing artistic standards in complex societies are invariably members of the upper classes or are employed by them. Thus, art in complex societies becomes associated with the elite. Not only are the standard setters often members of the elite, but art in complex societies frequently is owned and controlled by the upper classes. Moreover, in some complex societies, art both glorifies and serves the interests of the upper classes. By way of contrast, since small-scale societies are egalitarian, art tends to be more democratic in that all people have relatively equal access to it.

## The Functions of Art

To gain a fuller understanding of art, we must move beyond our working definition to an examination of the roles art plays for both people and societies. The very fact that artistic expression is found in every known society would suggest that it functions in some important ways in human life. The two different approaches to functionalism taken by Malinowski and Radcliffe-Brown can be instructive for our analysis of the functions of art. As mentioned in Chapter 4, Malinowski tended to emphasize how various cultural elements functioned for the psychological well-being of the individual. Radcliffe-Brown, by way of contrast, stressed how a cultural element functioned to contribute to the well-being or continuity of the society. While we will examine the various functions of art for both the individual and society, it should be pointed out that in terms of the analysis of art, Radcliffe-Brown's more structural approach has been the more fruitful.

### EMOTIONAL GRATIFICATION FOR THE INDIVIDUAL

Quite apart from whatever positive benefits art may have for the total society, it is generally agreed that art is a source of personal gratification for both the artist and the viewer. It would be hard to imagine a world in which people engaged only in those pursuits that contributed to their basic survival needs. Although most people devote the lion's share of their time and energy to meeting those needs, it is equally true that all people derive some level of enjoyment from art because it provides at least a temporary break from those practical (and often stressful) pursuits. After the crops have been harvested, the African horticulturalist has time to dance, tell stories, and derive pleasure from either making or viewing pieces of art. Likewise, as a diversion from their workaday lives, many Westerners seek gratification by attending a play, a concert, or a museum. It was, no doubt, this personal gratification one derives from art that prompted Selzer to comment that "art . . . is necessary only in that without it life would be unbearable" (1979:196).

The psychologically beneficial functions of art can be looked at from two perspectives: that of the artist and that of the beholder. For the artist, the expression of art permits the release of emotional energy in a very concrete or visible way—i.e., by painting, sculpting, writing a play, or performing an interpretive dance. Artists, at least in the Western world, are viewed as living with a creative tension, which, when released, results in a work of art. This release of creative energy also brings pleasure to the artist to the extent that he or she derives satisfaction from both the mastery of techniques and the product itself.

From the perspective of the viewer, art can evoke pleasurable emotional responses in several important ways. For example, works of art can portray events, people, or deities that conjure up positive emotions. The symbols used in a work of art can arouse a positive emotional response. The viewer can receive pleasure by being dazzled by the artist's virtuosity. These pleasurable responses can contribute to the mental well-being of art viewers by providing a necessary balance with the stresses in their everyday lives.

It is possible, however, for art to also have the opposite effect by eliciting negative emotions. The artistic process, if not successful from the artist's point of view, can result in increased frustrations and tension. Moreover, any art form is capable of eliciting disturbing or even painful emotions that can lead to psychological discomfort for the viewer.

## ART AS A CONTRIBUTION TO SOCIAL INTEGRATION

In addition to whatever positive roles it may play for the individual, art functions to help sustain the longevity of the society in which it is found. Again, as the functionalist anthropologists remind us, art is intimately connected to other parts of the social system. One need only to walk into a church, a synagogue, or a temple (or any other place of worship) to see the interrelationship between art and religion. Moreover, art has been used in many societies to evoke positive sentiments for systems

This monumental piece of art—the Sphinx—was designed to evoke positive feelings about the ancient Egyptian government and the pharaohs responsible for its creation.

Much of the art found in Western churches—such as this one in Bayren, Germany—reflects the basic themes of Christianity.

religious themes central to Christianity. Thus, certain forms of graphic arts function to help integrate the society by making the dominant cultural themes, values, and beliefs more visible. By expressing these cultural themes in a very tangible way, art ultimately functions to strengthen the existing culture by reinforcing those cultural themes.

Other forms of art, such as music, also help to strengthen and reinforce both social bonds and cultural themes. Cultural values are, for example, passed on from generation to generation using the medium of song and dance. As part of the intense education found in African bush schools, various forms of dance are used to teach proper adult attitudes and behaviors to those preparing for initiation. The role of music as a mechanism of education is well illustrated by Bert, Ernie, Kermit, and the other characters of *Sesame Street* who sing about such values as cooperation, acceptable forms of conflict resolution, the fun of learning, and race relations. Music also can be used to solidify a group of people. Any history of warfare would be woefully incomplete without some mention of the role that martial music played to rally the people together against the common enemy.

## Graphic and Plastic Arts

The **graphic** and **plastic arts** include a number of forms of expression and a wide variety of skills. While the Western notion of graphic and plastic arts usually refers to painting, sculpture, printmaking, and architecture, the anthropological definition also includes such art forms as weaving, embroidery, tailoring, jewelry making, and tattooing and other forms of body decoration. While in some societies one form of art, such as woodcarving, may be highly developed, others, such as painting or metalworking, may be nonexistent. The analysis of these art forms is further complicated by the fact that different cultures use different materials and technologies depending, in part, on what materials are available locally. Whereas Native Americans of the Northwest Coast are well-known for their carvings of wood, other cultures may use horn, bone, ivory, or soapstone. In some small-scale societies, the nature of people's ceramic art will be determined by the availability of locally found clays. Often the level of technology will influence whether or not a culture uses metals such as gold, silver, and bronze in its art traditions.

of government and individual political leaders. This section explores some of the ways that art functions to contribute to the maintenance and longevity of a society.

Through various symbols, art, in whatever form it may take, communicates a good deal about the values, beliefs, and ideologies of the culture of which it is a part. The art forms found in any given society reflect the major cultural themes and concerns of the society. To illustrate, prominent breasts on female figures represent a major theme found in much of the wood sculpture from West Africa. This dominant theme reflects a very important social value in those West African societies— i.e., the social importance of having children. Somewhat closer to our own cultural traditions, much of the art in Renaissance Europe reflected many of the

## CROSS-CULTURAL VARIATIONS

Not only do different art traditions draw upon different materials, techniques, and media, but also the nature of the creative process can vary cross-culturally. To illustrate, in the Western tradition of art, the commissioning of a piece of art is quite widely practiced. For a fee, portrait artists use their creative talents to paint realistic (and usually flattering) likenesses of their prominent clients. However, it is not likely that a client could commission an Eskimo artist to carve a walrus from a piece of ivory. According to the Eskimo notion of the creative process, that would be much too willful, even heavy-handed. Whereas the Western artist, in a total act of will, is solely responsible for painting the canvas or molding the clay, the Eskimo carver will never force the ivory into any uncharacteristic shapes. The Eskimo artist does not create, but rather helps to liberate what is already in the piece of ivory. Carpenter describes the Eskimo's notion of the role of the artist:

As the carver holds the unworked ivory lightly in his hand, turning it this way and that, he whispers, "Who are you! Who hides there!" And then: "Ah, Seal!" He rarely sets out to carve, say, a seal, but picks up the ivory, examines it to find its hidden form and, if that's not immediately apparent, carves aimlessly until he sees it, humming or chanting as he works. Then he brings it out: Seal, hidden, emerges. It was always there: he did not create it, he released it; he helped it step forth (1973:59).

Of all of the various forms of art found in the world, the graphic and plastic arts have received the greatest amount of attention from cultural anthropologists. This is understandable because until recently, the plastic and graphic arts were the most manageable in terms of analysis. The analysis of music and dance, for example, have depended largely on the recent development of such data-gathering technology as sound recorders, motion pictures, and videotape recorders. The graphic and plastic arts, however, are very physical and can be removed from their cultural contexts, displayed in museums, and compared with relative ease. Moreover, a painting or a sculpture has a permanence of form not found in music, dance, or drama.

Art comes in many forms, some utilitarian, and others not. Here a man from Srinagar, Kashmir, weaves a rug.

## Art and the Status Quo

A popular perception of artists and their works in the Western world is that they are visionary, nonconformist, and often antiestablishment. While this is often the case in contemporary Western societies, much of the graphic and plastic arts found in other societies (and indeed in our own Western tradition in past centuries) functions to reinforce the existing sociocultural system. Art, for example, can help instill important cultural values in the younger generations, coerce people to behave in socially appropriate ways, and buttress the inequalities of the stratification system within a society. We will briefly examine several ways that the graphic and plastic arts can contribute to the status quo.

## SOCIAL CONTROL

First, art can serve as a mechanism of social control. While art historians generally recognize that art has a strong religious base, they have been less cognizant of the role art plays in other cultural domains. A notable exception has been Roy Sieber (1962), an art historian who has demonstrated how wooden masks serve as agents of social control in several tribal groups in Northeastern Liberia. It was generally believed by the Mano, for example, that the "god-spirit" mask embodied the spiritual forces that actually control human behavior. The death of a high-status man was marked by carving a wooden death mask in the man's honor. A crude portrait of the deceased, the death mask was thought to be the ultimate resting place of the man's spirit.

Through the medium of these pieces of art, the spirits were thought to be able to intervene into the affairs of the living. Specifically, the masks played an important role in the administration of justice. When a dispute arose or a crime was committed, the case was brought before a council of wise and influential men who reviewed the facts and arrived at a tentative decision. This decision was then confirmed (and given supernatural force) by one of the judges who wore the death mask while concealing his own identity. Thus, in addition to whatever other functions these artistically carved masks may play among the Mano, they definitely serve as mechanisms of social control and conflict resolution.

Art also plays an important role in controlling behavior in more complex societies. In highly stratified societies state governments sponsor art for the sake of instilling obedience and maintaining the status quo. In some of the early civilizations, for example, the state-sponsored monumental architecture, such as pyramids, ziggurats, and cathedrals, were visual representations of the astonishing power of both the gods and the rulers. Most people living in these state societies would think twice before breaking either secular or religious rules when faced with such awesome power and authority represented in these magnificent works of art.

## PRESERVATION OF THE STATUS QUO

By serving as a symbol for social status, art also contributes to the preservation of the status quo. To one degree or another, all societies make distinctions between different levels of power and prestige. As societies become more highly specialized, systems of stratification become more complex, and the gap between the haves and the have-nots becomes wider. Power is expressed in a number of different ways throughout the world, including the use of physical force, the control over political decisions, and the accumulation of valuable resources. One particularly convincing way to display one's power is symbolically through the control of valuable items in the society. The accumulation of practical objects such as tools would not be a particularly good symbol of high

Art auction at Christie's in London. Since many pieces of Western art bring high prices, they can serve as very visible symbols of social status for the upper classes.

prestige because (a) everyone has some and (b) one hardly needs an overabundance of everyday practical objects to meet one's own needs. The accumulation of art objects, however, is much more likely to serve as a symbol of high prestige because art objects are unique, not commonly found throughout the society, and frequently priceless. This association of art with status symbols is seen in many societies with ranked populations. For example, virtually all of the art in ancient Egyptian civilizations was the personal property of the pharaohs. The high status of the hereditary king of the Ashanti of present-day Ghana is symbolized by a wide variety of artistic objects, the most important of which is the Golden Stool. In the western world, many public art galleries are filled with impressive personal collections donated by powerful and high-status members of society (Getty, Hirschorn, Rockefeller, et al.).

## Music

We often hear the expression "music is the universal language." By this people mean that even if two people do not speak one another's language, they can at least appreciate **music** together. But like so many popular sayings, this one is only partially true. While it is true that all people have the same physiological mechanisms for hearing, what a person actually hears is influenced by his or her culture. Westerners tend to miss much of the richness of Javanese or Sri Lankan music because they have not been conditioned to hear it. Whenever we encounter a piece of non-Western music, we hear it (process it) in terms of our own culturally influenced set of musical categories dealing with scale, melody, pitch, harmony, and rhythm. And since those categories are defined differently from culture to culture, the appreciation of music across cultures is not always assured. To illustrate this point, Slobin and Titon tell a story about a famous Oriental musician who was brought to hear a symphonic concert in Europe during the mid-nineteenth century:

Although he was a virtuoso musician in his own country, he had never heard a performance of western music. The story goes that after the concert he was asked how he liked it. "Very well," he replied. Not satisfied with this answer, his host asked (through an interpreter) what part he liked best. "The first part," he said. "Oh, you enjoyed the first movement?" "No, before that!" To the stranger, the best part of the performance was the tuning-up period (1984:1).

## ETHNOMUSICOLOGY

The cross-cultural study of music is known as **ethnomusicology**, a relatively recent field involving the cooperative efforts of both anthropologists and musicologists. While still not a well-defined field of study, ethnomusicology has made rapid progress lately owing to the recent developments in high quality recording equipment needed for basic data gathering. Slobin and Titon (1984:2–8) have identified four major concerns of ethnomusicology:

1. *Ideas about music.* How does a culture distinguish between music and nonmusic? What functions does music play for the society? Is music viewed as beneficial or harmful to the society? What constitutes beautiful music? On what occasions should music be played?
2. *Social structure of music.* What are the social relationships between musicians? How does a society distinguish between various musicians on the basis of such criteria as age, gender, race, ethnicity, or education?
3. *Characteristics of the music itself.* How does the music in different cultures vary according to style (scale, melody, harmony, timing)? What different musical genres are found in a society (lullaby, sea chantey, hard rock, etc.)? What is the nature of musical texts (words)? How is music composed? How is music learned and transmitted?
4. *Material culture of music.* What is the nature of the musical instruments found in a culture? Who makes musical instruments and how are they distributed? How are the musical tastes reflected in the instruments used?

As we can see from these four components of the field, ethnomusicology is concerned with both the structure and techniques of music and the interconnections between music and other parts of the culture. Yet, during the course of cross-cultural studies of music, ethnomusicologists have been torn between two approaches. At one extreme, they have searched for musical universals—those elements found in all musical traditions. At the opposite extreme, they have been interested in demonstrating the considerable diversity found throughout the world. Nettl describes this tension:

. . . in the heart of the ethnomusicologist there are two strings: one that attests to the universal character of music, to the fact that music is indeed something that all cultures have or appear to have . . . and one responsive to the enormous variety of existing cultures (1980:3).

Ethnomusicologists would be interested in studying both the music of this folk orchestra in Tadzhik, USSR, and how it reflects the wider culture of which it is a part.

large-scale, stratified societies with complex systems of production (see Table 22-1).

These are just some of the dimensions of music that Lomax was able to relate to different types of subsistence. This monumental study, which required large samples and extensive coding of cultural material, was open to criticism on methodological grounds. The difficulties involved in such an approach help explain why ethnomusicology has made considerably greater gains in the analysis of musical sound than in the study of the cultural context of music. Nevertheless, the efforts of Lomax and his associates represent an important attempt to show how music is related to other parts of culture.

## Dance

**Dance** has been defined as purposeful and intentionally rhythmical nonverbal body movements that are culturally patterned and have aesthetic value (Hanna, 1979: 19). While dance is found in all known societies, the forms it takes and the meanings attached to it vary widely from society to society. Dance in some societies involves enormous energy and body movement, while in other societies, it is much more restrained and subtle. Since the variety of postures and movements the human body can make is vast, which body parts are active and which postures are assumed will differ from one dance tradition to another. In some African societies (e.g., Ubakala of Nigeria), drums are a necessary part of dance, while in others (e.g., Zulu) they are not. Dancing alone is the expected form in some societies, while in others it is customary for groups to dance in circles, lines, or other formations.

### FUNCTIONS OF DANCE

As with other forms of artistic expression, the functions of dance are culturally variable. Dance is likely to function in a number of different ways both between and within societies. While dance often performs several functions simultaneously within a society, some functions will be more prominent than others. To illustrate, dance can function *psychologically* by helping people cope more effectively with tensions and aggressive feelings; *politically* by expressing political values and attitudes, showing allegiance to political leaders, and controlling behavior; *religiously* by various methods of

All ethnomusicologists—whether they come from a background in music or cultural anthropology—are interested in the study of music in its cultural context. One of the most extensive studies of the relationship between music and other parts of culture was conducted by Alan Lomax and his colleagues (1968). Specifically, Lomax found some broad correlations between various aspects of music and a culture's level of subsistence. Foraging societies were found to have fundamentally different types of music, song, and dance than more complex producers. By dividing a worldwide sample of cultures into five different levels of subsistence complexity, Lomax found some significant correlations. To illustrate his findings, differences emerged between egalitarian small-scale societies with simple subsistence economies and

CHAPTER 22 ◆ ART

| Egalitarian Societies with Simple Economies | Stratified Societies with Complex Production Systems |
| --- | --- |
| Repetitious texts | Nonrepetitious texts |
| Slurred articulation | Precise articulation |
| Little solo singing | Solo singing |
| Wide melodic intervals | Narrow melodic intervals |
| Nonelaborate songs (no embellishments) | Elaborate songs (embellishments) |
| Relatively few instruments | Relatively large number of instruments |
| Singing in unison | Singing in simultaneously produced intervals |

communicating with supernatural forces; *socially* by articulating and reinforcing relationships between members of the society; and *educationally* by passing on the cultural traditions, values, and beliefs from one generation to the next.

## DANCE AND OTHER ASPECTS OF A CULTURE

Lomax and his colleagues (1968:224–26) have demonstrated quite graphically how dance is connected to other aspects of a culture. Specifically, their research showed how dance tends to reflect and reinforce work patterns. By examining over 200 films, they were able to find a number of similarities between work styles and dance styles. The Netsilik Eskimos provide an interesting—and not atypical—example. For the Netsilik, dancing, which consists of solo performances, takes place during the winter months in a large communal igloo. Lomax describes the dance in considerable detail:

One after another, the greatest hunters stand up before the group, a large flat drum covered with sealskin in the left hand, a short, club-like drumstick in the other. Over to the side sit a cluster of women chanting away as the hunter drums, sings, and dances. The performer remains in place holding the wide stance used by these Eskimos when they walk through ice and snow or stand in the icy waters fishing. Each stroke of the short drumstick goes diagonally down and across to hit the lower edge of the drum and turn the drumhead. On the backstroke it strikes the other edge, reversing the motion which is

Classical dancing in Thailand.

then carried through by a twist of the left forearm. The power and solidity of the action is emphasized by the downward drive of the body into slightly bent knees on the downstroke and the force of trunk rising as the knees straighten to give full support to the arm on the upstroke. The dance consists largely of these repeated swift and strong diagonal right arm movements down across the body. . . . (1968:226 Copyright by AAAS. Reprinted with permission of the publisher.)

Many of the same motions found in Netsilik dance are the very ones that are so necessary for successful hunting in an Arctic environment which Lomax describes:

A look at Eskimo seal hunting or salmon fishing shows this same posture and pattern of movement in use—a harpooning, hooking movement. The salmon-fisher stands hip deep in the clear waters of the weir, thrusting his spear down and across, lifting the speared fish clear of the water, twisting it off the barb, and threading it on the cord at his waist in a series of swift, strong, straight, angular movements tied together by powerful rotations of the forearm. At the seal hole on the ice pack, where the hunter may wait in complete stillness during the five frozen hours before the nose of the seal appears, there is a time for only one thrust of the spear: a miss spoils a day's hunting in subarctic temperature. His harpoon, then, flies in a lightning stroke, diagonally down across the chest (1968: 226–27).

We can see thus that the stylistic movements found in Netsilik dance are essentially identical to those found in their everyday hunting activities. Those qualities of a good Eskimo hunter—speed, strength, accuracy, and endurance—are portrayed and glorified in dance. In other words, as part of their leisure activity, Eskimo hunters, through the medium of dance, redramatize the essentials of their everyday subsistence activities so crucial for survival.

## ◆ ◆ ◆
# Verbal Arts

Creative forms of expression using words are found in all societies of the world. In Western societies—which place a great deal of emphasis on the written form—one might immediately think of the common literary genres of the novel, the short story, and poetry. Western societies also have a strong tradition of unwritten verbal arts, which are frequently subsumed under the general heading of **folklore**. In preliterate societies these unwritten forms are the only type of verbal art. Although the term *folklore* is a part of everyday vocabulary, it has eluded a precise definition. Alan Dundes has proposed a

definition of folklore by listing a considerable number of forms that it might take. While recognizing that this is only a partial listing, Dundes includes the following:

Myths, legends, folktales, jokes, proverbs, riddles, chants, charms, teases, toasts, tongue-twisters, and greeting and leave-taking formulas (e.g., see you later alligator). It also includes folk custom, folk dance, folk drama (and mime), folk art, folk belief (or superstition), folk medicine, folk instrumental music (e.g., fiddle tunes) folksongs (lullabies, ballads), folk speech (e.g., slang) folk similes (e.g., blind as a bat), folk metaphors (e.g., to paint the town red), and names (e.g., nicknames and place names). Folk poetry ranges from oral epics to autograph-book verse, epitaphs, latrinalia (writing on the walls of public bathrooms), limericks, ball-bouncing rhymes, finger and toe rhymes, dandling rhymes (to bounce the children on the knee), counting-out rhymes (to determine who will be "it" in games), and nursery rhymes. The list of folklore forms also contains games; gestures; symbols; prayers (e.g., graces); practical jokes; folk etymologies; food recipes; quilt and embroidery designs; . . . street vendors cries; and even the traditional conventional sounds used to summon animals or to give them commands. . . . (1965:2)

While this list is neither comprehensive nor exhaustive, it does give us some idea of the wide range of verbal arts that have been, or could be, studied by cultural anthropologists. Even though we could focus on any of the above forms of verbal art, our discussion concentrates on those forms that have received the greatest amount of attention—namely myths and folktales.

## MYTHS

**Myths** are specific types of narratives, involving supernatural beings, designed to explain some of the really big issues of human existence, such as where did we come from, why are we here, and how do we account for the things in our world? They are, in other words, stories of our search for significance, meaning, and truth. Not only do myths have an explanatory function, but they also validate some of the essential beliefs, values, and behavior patterns for a culture. That is, there exists a close connection between a culture's mythology and its moral and social order. It is important to point out that myth need not have any basis in historical fact. Although there may be elements of history in myth (and vice versa), the importance of myth from the perspective of the anthropologist is that the narrative reflects, supports, and legitimizes contemporary patterns of thought and behavior.

## CROSS-CULTURAL MISCUE

In recent decades, an increasing number of U.S. major league players have signed contracts to play in Japan. Many unsuspecting American ballplayers think that if they can pitch, field, or hit a baseball effectively at home, they will be equally successful playing in the Japanese league. Although America's pastime is played according to the same rules in Japan, the values, attitudes, and behaviors surrounding the game are worlds apart.

At the heart of the cultural differences between baseball in Japan and the United States is the concept of *wa,* translated as "group harmony" (Whiting, 1979). Baseball players in the United States—not unlike those in other sectors of American life—emphasize individual achievement. American ballplayers are constantly vying with one another for the most impressive set of statistics. Those with the best stats can demand the highest salaries. If management fails to meet their demands, the better players are likely to refuse to show up for spring training.

By way of contrast, Japanese ballplayers are expected to put the interest of their team above their own personal interests. Since it is assumed that the Japanese manager is always right, any disagreement with a manager's decision is a serious disruption of the team's *wa.* In the Japanese view, *wa* is the most important factor in having a winning team. As Whiting reminds us, "If you ask (a Japanese manager) how to know a team's *wa* is awry, he'd probably say, 'Hire an American'" (1979:61).

Whiting goes on to document a number of cases of U.S. ballplayers who had considerable difficulty adjusting to the radically different behavior expected on Japanese teams. Many American ballplayers—despite their own personal success on the field—frequently found themselves being traded because their very individualistic (and typically American) behavior was seen as damaging the team's *wa.* Those American players who have been successful in Japan have understood the importance of *wa.* Thus, even in the high-priced world of professional sports, it is imperative for athletes who want to be successful to understand cultural differences.

The relationship between the artistic expressions of myth and other aspects of a culture is well illustrated by the myths of creation found among the Yanomamo of Venezuela and Brazil. According to Chagnon (1983: 95), the Yanomamo have two separate creation myths, one for men and one for women. Both myths illustrate two fundamental themes of Yanomamo culture: fierceness and sexuality. According to the myth of male creation, one of the early ancestors shot the god of the Moon in the stomach with an arrow. The blood that dripped from the wound onto the ground turned into fierce men. The blood that was the thickest on the ground turned into the most ferocious men, while the blood that was more spread out turned into men who engaged in more controlled violence. Nevertheless, the fierceness of the Yanomamo people today is seen as a direct result of that early violence described in the male creation myth.

According to the other creation myth—which attempts to account for the beginning of Yanomamo women—the men created from the blood of the Moon god were without female mates. While collecting vines, one of the men noticed that the vine had a wabu fruit attached to it. Thinking that the fruit looked like what a woman should look like, he threw it to the ground and it immediately turned into a woman. The other men in the group, struck with intense feelings of lust, began copulating frantically with the woman. Afterwards the men brought the woman to the village, where she copulated with all of the other men of the village. Eventually she gave birth to a series of daughters, from whom descended all other Yanomamo women. This highly sexual account of the creation of women is certainly consistent with everyday Yanomamo life, for as Chagnon reminds us, " . . . much of their humor, insulting, fighting, storytelling, and conceptions about humans revolve around sexual themes" (1983 : 94).

It is generally thought in the Western world that myths, such as those described for the Yanomamo, are symptomatic of small-scale, non-Western, preliterate peoples. The entire history of Western civilization, particularly since the Enlightenment, has witnessed what Lane (1989) has described as a "demythologization"—a steady rejection of myth and illusion as we "progress" toward science, rationality, and critical insight.

Yet even the highly reason-oriented West is not without its mythology. How else can we account for the enormous popularity in recent years of the works of Joseph Campbell on mythology, the proliferation of seminars and books based on Jungian psychology, and such futuristic mythological figures as Luke Skywalker and Obi-Wan Kenobi? We continue to learn a great deal about living from myths, and indeed much of our scientific Western culture is molded by the power of myth, an art form that continues to have relevance for both Western and non-Western societies alike.

## FOLKTALES

In contrast to myths, **folktales** (or **legends**) are more secular in nature, have no particular basis in history, and exist largely for purposes of entertainment. While not having the same amount of sacred content as myths, folktales, like myths, nevertheless are instructive. Since most folktales have a moral, they play an important role in socialization. Particularly in those societies without writing, folktales can be significant in revealing socially appropriate behavior. Those heroes and heroines who triumph in folktales do so because of their admirable behavior and character traits. Conversely, those people who behave in socially inappropriate ways almost always get their comeuppance. To illustrate, tales with very strong social messages are told to Dahomean children in West Africa around a fire (Herskovits, 1967 : 275–76). Usually held at the compound of an elder, these storytelling sessions are designed to (1) entertain, (2) provide moral instruction for children, and (3) develop the children's storytelling skills by encouraging

them to tell tales of their own. Despite very different settings, the storytelling sessions among traditional Dahomeans is quite similar to parents reading their children "Jack and the Beanstalk" or "Cinderella" in front of the fireplace.

Folktales can be seen as an art form from two perspectives. Like written works of literature, folktales are creative expressions that can be analyzed in terms of plot, character development, and structure, even though the original author or authors may long have been forgotten. In much the same way that literary critics have analyzed the structure and meaning of Western literature (poetry, prose, etc.), it is also possible to analyze the literary and artistic structure of folklore in both complex and small-scale societies. For example, Hymes (1977) has demonstrated how the structure of folklore narratives of the Native American Chinooka people of Oregon and Washington was highly organized in terms of lines, verses, stanzas, scenes, and acts. According to Hymes:

A set of discourse features differentiates narratives into verses. Within these verses, lines are differentiated, commonly by distinct verbs. . . . The verses themselves are grouped, commonly in threes and fives. These groupings constitute "stanzas" and, where elaboration of stanzas is such as to require a distinction, "scenes." In extended narratives, scenes themselves are organized in terms of a series of "acts" (1977 : 431).

That such folk narratives as those of the Chinooka have such an elaborate structure allows us to regard such verbal texts as legitimate works of art.

But, in addition to the artistic features of the structure of folktales, there is also an artistry involved in telling and retelling the tales. Even though the basic elements of the original tale cannot be changed, the tale teller retains the right to embellish and dramatize the story as he or she sees fit. The rhythm of the storyteller's utterances, the dramatic emotions expressed, and the use of nonverbal gestures all possess an artistic content of their own. Chagnon reminds us that in reference to Yanomamo folklore a certain amount of artistry is in the telling:

Some of the characters in Yanomamo myths are downright hilarious, and some of the things they did are funny, ribald, and extremely entertaining to the Yanomamo, who listen to men telling mythical stories or chanting episodes of mythical sagas as they prance around the village, tripping out on hallucinogens, adding comical twists and nuances to the sidesplitting delight of their audiences. Everybody knows what Iwariwa did, and that part cannot be changed. But *how* he did it, what minor gestures and comments he made, or how much it hurt or pleased him as he did it is subject to some considerable poetic license, and it is this that is entertaining and amusing to the listener (1983:93 Copyright, reprinted by permission of the publisher).

## ◆ Summary

1. While there is no universal definition of art, for purposes of this chapter we have defined art as *the process and products of applying certain skills to any activity that transforms matter, sound, or motion into a form that is deemed aesthetically pleasing to people in a society.* The creative process of making art should be enjoyable, produce an emotional response, be transformational, convey a message, and involve a certain level of skill on the part of the artist.

2. The forms of artistic expression discussed in this chapter include (a) the graphic/plastic arts (painting, carving, weaving, etc.), (b) music, (c) dance, and (d) verbal art (myth, folklore, etc.).

3. Rather than using the term *primitive* to refer to certain types of art, instead we use the term *small-scale,* which refers to those essentially egalitarian societies with small populations, simple technology, no written language, and little labor specialization. In contrast to the art found in small-scale societies, the art of more complex societies is more permanent, has more elaborate and explicit standards of evaluation, and is associated with the elite.

4. Art contributes to the well-being of both the individual and the society. For the individual, art provides emotional gratification to both the artist and the beholder. From the social perspective, various forms of art strengthen and reinforce both social bonds and cultural themes, act as a mechanism of social control, and serve as a symbol of high status particularly in complex societies.

5. The study of ethnomusicologist Alan Lomax suggests that the music traditions found in small-scale societies differ from more complex societies in that the former are characterized by more repetitive texts, slurred articulation, little solo singing, nonembellished songs, relatively few instruments, and singing in unison.

6. Verbal art includes, among other forms, myths and folktales. Myths tend to involve supernatural beings while folktales are more secular in nature. Like other forms of art, the verbal arts are intimately connected to other aspects of a culture, as illustrated with the Yanomamo myth of creation.

## ◆ Key Terms

dance
ethnomusicology
folklore
folktales
graphic arts
*hija*

legends
music
myths
plastic arts
primitive art
transformational

## ◆ Suggested Readings

Anderson, Richard L. *Calliope's Sisters: A Comparative Study of Philosophies of Art.* Englewood Cliffs, N.J.: Prentice-Hall, Inc., 1990. This jargon-free study provides a unique look at the aesthetics in ten major culture areas of the world, including the San, the Eskimos, the Aztecs, the Japanese, and the Western world. The philosophies of art from the ten culture areas are used to make comparative statements about the nature of art, its origins, and its role in human affairs.

Dundes, Alan. *Folklore Matters.* Knoxville: University of Tennessee Press, 1989. A collection of essays written by one of the leading figures in the study of folklore. Of particular relevance are the essays on folklore and identity and how anthropologists use the comparative method in the study of folklore.

Hanna, Judith L. *To Dance Is Human: A Theory of Nonverbal Communication.* Austin: University of Texas Press, 1979. A comprehensive ethnological treatment of dance as a significant part of culture. It is particularly strong in drawing upon various forms of dance throughout the world to illustrate how this artistic form functions within religious, political, and social institutions.

Layton, Robert. *The Anthropology of Art.* New York: Columbia University Press, 1981. A scholarly introduction to the field of the anthropology of art with special attention given to art and social life, art and visual communication, stylistic variations, and the creative process.

Lomax, Alan. *Folk Song Style and Culture.* Washington, D.C.: American Association for the Advancement of Science, 1968. A classic study of musical styles around the world and how they relate to other aspects of culture.

Marriott, Alice. *Maria: The Potter of San Ildefonso.* Norman: University of Oklahoma Press, 1948. A very personal account of the life of one of the leading potters in the Tewa pueblo of New Mexico. The book, based on first-person observations, provides insights into the process of Tewa craft revitalization discussed in the applied perspective section of this chapter.

Titon, Jeff Todd, et al. *Worlds of Music: An Introduction to the Music of the World's Peoples.* New York: Schirmer Books, 1984. An introductory survey of music in various parts of the world including Native North American, African, Black North American, European, and Indian.

# Art

The very nature of art—functioning as it does to entertain and provide pleasure—is often seen as an aspect of culture that has little or no practical relevance. Such a view, however, is shortsighted and reveals a basic misunderstanding of the concept of culture. If we take seriously the idea that cultures are integrated wholes—with the various elements interrelated to one another—it would be unreasonable to consider any part of a culture irrelevant, because it is, at least potentially, connected to all other parts of the system. This segment of the chapter discusses two cases in which an understanding of artistic styles is useful for solving problems or meeting needs in other parts of the culture.

◆ **An understanding of an artistic form of Arabic rhetoric can be useful for interpreting diplomatic and political relations between contemporary Arab states.**

The Persian Gulf conflict, precipitated by the Iraqi invasion of Kuwait in August 1990, resulted in the most massive mobilization of military personnel and conventional weapons in history. High casualty rates and massive destruction of property were suffered by both Kuwait and Iraq. Moreover, massive divisions and realignments were made among the various states in the Arab world. While the Western press concentrated on the military and diplomatic maneuverings in the conflict, there was actually another war being waged—a propaganda war—between the principal Arabic players in the conflict: Iraq, Kuwait, and Saudi Arabia.

According to Ya'ari and Friedman (1991), for the months before the Allied bombing, the two sides in the conflict, using an archaic rhetorical art form, traded insults over the airwaves. This traditional genre, known as *hija*, has Biblical precedents in which warriors (e.g., Goliath) would loudly ridicule their adversaries while boasting of their own power. This ancient Semite tradition was founded on the assumption that there was supernatural power to be gained by insulting in rhyme one's opponent or, as Ya'ari and Friedman (1991:22) have put it, "cursing in verse." For centuries, the most highly esteemed poets in the Arabic literary tradition have been those with a flair for offensive and vitriolic insults. This *hija* rhetorical art form has its own format, meters, and rhyming patterns. Classical *hija* starts with boastful self-praise and then moves into a series of abusive insults.

Unbeknownst to most Westerners, there was a revival of *hija* rhetoric immediately after the Iraqi invasion of Kuwait in August of 1990. Without commercial interruption, Saudi, Iraqi, and Kuwaiti (in exile) television broadcast hours of *hija* poetry, praising the justness of their own cause and lambasting the opposition. Interestingly, many of the subtleties of this ancient artistic form of rhyming put-down are not widely understood by the viewing public. The poems are highly ambiguous—even to those well educated in classical Arabic—because one of the conventions of *hija* is to choose words, phrases, and metaphors that have been out of general use for centuries. Even though the use of such an archaic and esoteric art form would seem to dilute its effectiveness as a propaganda device, the messages were not lost on the general public. Although many of the subtleties escaped the average citizen, the general messages came through on a gut level. The verses, intoned with dramatic cadence, conjured up heroic images of one's own leaders and satanic images of the opposition's leaders.

The content of the *hija* poetry flowing over the airwaves was often vicious. With the buildup of Allied troops—some of whom were women—into Saudi Arabia prior to the outbreak of hostilities the Iraqi *hija* poets took the Saudis to task for "hiding behind the skirts of women," a scathing insult to Arab masculinity. Not to be outdone, Saudi *hija* poets constructed their own vitriolic verse berating Iraqi leader Saddam Hussein for attacking his enemies at night and for being a contemptible neighbor. More specifically, Hussein was portrayed as an ungrateful neighbor who repudiated the help he had received in his earlier struggles with Iran. Moreover, the Saudi *hija* poets delivered the ultimate put-down to Hussein by denouncing him as a Jew.

The significance of the recent revival of *hija* rhetoric goes beyond its serving as a patriotic mechanism or as a popular form of entertainment. As Ya'ari and Friedman have suggested, these *hija* recitations "provide channels for a kind of offbeat diplomacy by which more messages are transmitted across the lines than through conventional diplomatic means" (1991:24). In other words, the ebb and flow of the conflict can be assessed by analyzing the strength of the verbal venom coming from each camp. Provided one understands the art form, these quasi news programs may be an even more accurate barometer of contemporary political and diplomatic relations than official newscasts or press releases. Even though U.S. Intelligence may not have drawn upon this artistic form of poetry as a source of information, it has been reported that both Saddam Hussein and King Fahd of Saudi Arabia received daily intelligence summaries of what the opposition poets were saying.

◆ **The findings of anthropologists have served as the basis for a renaissance in traditional pottery making among the Tewa of New Mexico.**

A basic theme running through this textbook is that cultural anthropology is not just a discipline for those interested in curious and esoteric facts, but rather is eminently practical. When perusing museums exhibiting Native American arts and crafts, we frequently concentrate on one of two things: (1) certain artistic issues (e.g., design features, skills of the artist, use of colors) or (2) the cultural/historical significance of the objects. That such objects should be aesthetically appealing or educational is a good enough reason for anthropologists to collect them and display them in museums. Sometimes these traditional forms of art, such as pottery, can have far-reaching impacts on the lives of contemporary peoples. Such was the case at the Tewa pueblo of San Ildefonso in northern New Mexico.

According to Whitman (1963), in 1907 the School of American Research, under the direction of E. L. Hewett, initiated a series of archaeological excavations of the ancient ruins of the Pajarito Plateau. The workers employed for this archaeological dig were all local Tewa Indians from San Ildefonso.

479

The Tewa laborers—and particularly the women who periodically visited the site—took a keen interest in the pottery vessels that were being unearthed from the ruins. Some of the women, who were themselves local potters, held lively discussions of the ancient pottery styles and designs that had died out during the first century after the Spanish conquest. Within several years, it had become apparent that the contemporary potters were attempting to emulate the excellent quality of the ancient ceramic vessels. Gradually the local pottery makers began to improve the quality of their wares. Realizing the importance of this process, the staff at the School of American Research became directly involved by encouraging the women to incorporate the ancient artistic features into their own work. Pieces of ancient pottery (as well as photographs of other pieces in museums) were brought to the attention of the local Tewa potters by staff from the school.

In 1915, Dr. Hewett was put in charge of the displays of Indian culture at the Panama-California Exposition. As part of that exhibit, several women potters from San Ildefonso demonstrated their techniques before large audiences. Because of that experience and exposure, these local potters came to realize that their work—which by now had incorporated a number of traditional features and styles—could bring infinitely higher prices from tourists than they had ever imagined.

Over the course of the next several decades, the pottery industry at San Ildefonso—having been infused with the styles of the ancient pottery unearthed by the archaeologists—grew in quality. Equally as important, this revitalization of ancient ceramics had profound economic and social consequences for the Tewa pueblo as well. To illustrate, by the late 1930s, pottery had become the major source of income into the pueblo. Not only did it provide many people with a means of livelihood, but it also enabled people to purchase such commodities as radios and furniture and send their children to college. In other words, this example of a craft renaissance provided the people of San Ildefonso with a dramatic increase in economic independence. Moreover, this craft revitalization enabled the Tewa to rediscover and reassert its past cultural identity. Thus, in this particular case, the search to reconstruct a past culture through archaeology has had the additional consequences of breathing new life into the work of native artists, reviving native artistic styles, providing desirable economic development, and creating a resurgence of ethnic pride in the process.

## CHAPTER 23

# Culture Change

How do cultures change?

What are some obstacles to culture change?

What does it mean to be modern?

In a very real sense, any ethnographic description of a specific group of people is like a snapshot at one particular time. Should the ethnographer conduct a restudy of the same group five years later, it is likely that a number of cultural features will have changed. Some cultures (usually small-scale, preliterate, and technologically simple societies) tend to change slowly. Modern, complex, highly industrialized societies tend to change much more rapidly. Whatever the rate of change might be, however, there is one thing we can bank on when dealing with cultures: nothing is as constant as change.

If we require proof of this basic maxim, we need only turn to the republished (1969) volume of the 1902 edition of the Sears, Roebuck catalog. As one glances through the pages, one is struck by the enormity of the changes in our material culture that have taken place since the turn of the century. Because of its comprehensiveness, the catalog, in the words of Cleveland Amory " . . . mirrors the dreams and needs of Americans at a time when life was less complex than it is today" (1969: Introduction). In other words, it provides a near total inventory of our material culture at the turn of the century. Today many items in the 1902 catalog—such as horse-drawn plows, windmills, patent medicines, and hightop leather shoes—can be found only in museums. Other items appearing in the 1902 edition still exist as part of our material culture, but in drastically altered form, such as sewing machines, men's toupees, lawn mowers, and typewriters.

We can learn much about the attitudes and values of our turn-of-the-century ancestors from the material goods these people surrounded themselves with. For example, the section of the catalog advertising books included a substantial number of books on palmistry, astrology, and hypnotism. Many were "self-help" books that came in very handy in rural areas. Nearly a quarter of the book section was devoted to family Bibles. Another dramatic measure of the magnitude of changes that have occurred in U.S. culture is the three-page section devoted to the advertisement of corsets and bustles, designed to rearrange or accentuate certain features of the female anatomy. On nearly every page we are reminded of the vast cultural changes—both material and nonmaterial—that have occurred in U.S. society since the early 1900s.

As mentioned in Chapter 2, it is generally recognized that cultures change as a result of both internal and external forces. Internal mechanisms of change are known as inventions or innovations, while cultures change by external sources through the process of cultural diffusion or borrowing. Although diffusion is responsible for

An examination of a turn-of-the-century Sears catalogue reveals the vast changes that have occurred in U.S. culture during the present century.

the greatest amount of culture change, it is important to examine both processes of change in greater detail.

## Inventions

**Inventions** refer to any new thing, idea, or behavior pattern that emerges from within the society. Some inventions are very deliberate and purposeful while others are unconscious and unintentional. Ralph Linton (1936: 311), one of the most prominent scholars of culture change in the twentieth century, has suggested that over the long run, the unconscious inventor has had a greater impact on culture change than has the conscious inventor. The unconscious or accidental inventor contributes to culture change without being driven by an unmet societal need or even realizing that he or she is making a contribution. As Linton put it, "their inventions are, as a rule, of little individual importance, but they loom large in the aggregate" (1936:311).

These numerous unintentional inventors frequently go unnoticed and unrewarded, even though they may be making a very significant cumulative contribution to their cultures. Yet, it is the deliberate, intentional inventor who tends to receive the greatest rewards and recognition. From our own recent history, Eli Whitney was sufficiently motivated to invent the cotton gin by the need to produce more cotton; Jonas Salk discovered the polio vaccine to eradicate a crippling disease; and hundreds of other inventors have come up with new gadgets and ideas because they wanted to do something better or more efficiently.

There is a good deal of truth in the adage "Necessity is the mother of invention." Frequently an invention will develop because there is a pressing need for it. Linton (1936:313–15) relates a case of an invention that occurred around the turn of the century on the Island of Hiva Oa. A man from the neighboring Gilbert Islands took up residence on Hiva Oa, married a local woman, and became a fisherman. It soon became apparent to him, however, that theft of outrigger canoes was rampant on the island. Motivated by the desire to not have his own boat stolen, he invented a new type of outrigger canoe with a detachable outrigger. By removing the outrigger assemblage, he could leave the canoe on the beach unattended. Within a short period of time, this new detachable outrigger almost totally replaced the previous model because there was a felt need for this particular invention.

For years, social scientists have grappled with the question of who are the inventors and who are the innovators. (It should be pointed out that **innovation** and *invention* are not synonymous, for it is possible to be an innovator without being an inventor. Innovators are those people who are the first to adopt or use a new thing or idea.) Why do some people invent new things, ideas, and behavior patterns, while most do not? And once something is invented, who are the people who are most likely to adopt the invention? A number of interesting theories have been set forth. Some (Rogers, 1983; Tarde, 1903; Smith, 1976) have suggested that both inventors and innovators tend to be **marginal people** living on the fringes of society. Not bound by tradition or convention, these marginal people can see problems and their solutions with a fresh perspective. Spindler summed up this position when she noted that "Innovators are often 'marginal men', who are, for a variety of

reasons, somewhat divorced from the core of their culture and thus more free to create" (1984:15).

Rogers' (1983:263–65) research suggests that innovators and early adopters are most likely to come from the upper class, wealthy, and well-educated segments of society. He goes on to speak of a basic paradox whereby those people who most need the benefits of an innovation are generally the least likely to adopt it. Rogers illustrates this paradox by looking at the adoption of contraception in developing countries. Citing his own research, Rogers (1973:408) notes that elite families, which already had small numbers of children, were the most receptive to adopting contraceptives, while lower status (poorer) families, which averaged between five and six children, were the most resistant.

Others theorists tend to take a more psychological approach by looking at the effects of child rearing on innovative personalities. Hagen (1962:201), for example, holds that innovators are most likely to come from families with excessively demanding fathers or from families with weak fathers and nurturing mothers. In his classic studies on achievement, McClelland (1960) found that early training in the mastery of certain skills often leads to entrepreneurial success. As interesting as many of these theories are, we still do not have a very definitive understanding as to why some people are innovators and others are not. An idea may appear to be sound, a technological invention may appear to be efficient, or a new behavior may appear to make sense, and yet it will not be adopted by a particular group of people. The problem, of course, is that there are a multitude of variables—some social, some cultural, and others psychological—that are operating in some situations but not in others.

## Diffusion

In addition to changing through inventions and discoveries, cultures change through the process of cultural **diffusion**—the spreading of a thing, an idea, or a behavior pattern from one culture to another. As important as inventions and discoveries are to culture change, the total number of inventions in any given society is generally quite small. In fact, Linton (1936:325) estimates that no more than ten percent of all of the cultural items found in any culture—including our own—originated in that culture. If every culture had to rely solely on its own inventions, human progress over the centuries would indeed be slow. But as has been the case, cultures have developed as rapidly as they have precisely because the process of diffusion has enabled humans to pool their creative/inventive resources.

## GENERAL PATTERNS OF DIFFUSION

Since diffusion plays such a prominent role in culture change it is appropriate to examine this process in some detail. Even though cultural diffusion varies from situation to situation, a number of generalizations about the process are worth mentioning.

**Selectivity.** The process of diffusion is selective in nature. When two cultures come into contact, not every cultural item is exchanged with another. If that were the case, there would be no cultural differences in the world today. Rather, only a small number of cultural elements are ever diffused from one culture to another. Which cultural item will be accepted will depend largely on the item's utility and compatibility to already existing cultural traits. For example, it is not very likely that men's hair dyes designed to "get out the grey" will diffuse into parts of rural Africa where a person's status is elevated with advancing years. Similarly, most people in the United States have resisted adopting the metric system because they see no particular advantage to taking the time and effort to learn it. According to Rogers (1983:14–16), the speed with which an innovation is adopted—or whether it will be adopted at all—usually is affected by whether or not (1) it is seen to be superior to what already exists, (2) it is consistent with existing cultural patterns, (3) it is easily understood, (4) it is able to be tested on a trial basis, and (5) its benefits are clearly visible.

**Reciprocity.** Diffusion is a two-way process. We should not assume that cultural items diffuse only from technologically complex societies to simpler societies. The anthropological record from many parts of the world clearly shows that cultural traits are diffused in both directions. European contact with Native Americans is a case in point. Even though Europeans introduced much of their culture to Native Americans, they nevertheless received a number of cultural features in return, including such articles of clothing as ponchos, parkas, and moccasins; medicines such as quinine, anesthetics, and laxatives; and such food items as corn, beans, squash, yams, and even the so-called Irish potato.

**Modification.** Once a cultural element is accepted into a new culture, it may undergo changes in form or function. The pizza is a good example of how a cultural item can change form as it diffuses. The pizza, diffused from Italy to the United States in the late nineteenth century, has been modified in a number of significant ways to conform to American tastes. It is likely that the Italian originators of the pizza pie would hardly recognize a pizza made on French bread, English muffins, or pita bread and topped with pineapple, tuna fish, or jalapeño peppers.

Sometimes the reinterpretation process involves a change in the way an item is used. While living in Kenya one of the authors observed a stunning example of functional reinterpretation. The Masai of Kenya and Tanzania practice the custom of piercing their earlobes and enlarging the hole by inserting increasingly larger round pieces of wood until a loop of skin is formed. Rather than using pieces of round wood for this purpose, one group of Masai were observed using Eveready flashlight batteries obtained from the United States. In this case, the form of the batteries was the same, but the function was definitely reinterpreted.

**Likelihood.** Some parts of culture are more likely to be diffused than others. As a general rule, items of material culture are more likely candidates for diffusion than are ideas or behavior patterns. A traditional farmer in Senegal, for example, is more likely to be convinced of the advantages of a bulldozer over a shovel for moving dirt than he is of substituting Buddhism for his form of ancestor worship.

**Variables.** There is reason to believe that diffusion is also affected by a number of important variables: the duration and intensity of contact, degree of cultural integration, and the similarities between the donor and recipient cultures. Although we know a good deal about the process of diffusion, social scientists still are not able to predict with certainty when and where diffusion will take place.

◆ ◆ ◆

# Acculturation

While the concepts of diffusion and acculturation have some things in common, **acculturation** is, in fact, a special type of diffusion that takes place as a result of sustained contact between two societies, one of which is

Items of material culture are more likely to be diffused than are ideas or behavior patterns. Here one aspect of U.S. culture—Kentucky Fried Chicken—has been diffused to Seoul, Korea.

turation refers to the forced borrowing under conditions of external pressure.

The extent of the external pressure put upon a subordinate culture varies considerably from one acculturation situation to another. Some cultural anthropologists (e.g., Mead, 1956) have described situations of acculturation in which the less dominant culture "freely chooses" to emulate the culture of the more dominant society. At the other extreme we find examples of excessive coercion, such as the Spanish conquest of Mexico which involved the brutal exploitation of the local population by both the Spanish government and the Spanish church. (See Beals, Hoijer, and Beals, 1977:624–27 for more details.)

We should bear in mind that not all anthropologists agree on how to interpret the levels of coercion that subordinate peoples are subjected to. Some anthropologists (Bodley, 1982; Diamond, 1960) feel strongly that there is no such thing as volunteering for acculturation. They hold that there are simply different degrees of force and coercion. As Diamond has stated, " . . . acculturation has always been a matter of conquest . . . refugees from the foundering groups may adopt the standards of the more potent society in order to survive as individuals. But these are conscripts of civilization, not volunteers" (1960:vi).

At the "free choice" end of the spectrum are the Manus of the South Pacific as described by Margaret Mead (1956). When Mead first studied the Manus in the late 1920s, the people lived in stilt houses over the lagoons, had no writing, wore simple grass skirts, and lived in extended family groups. When she returned to restudy the Manus in the 1950s, Mead found a culture that was actively and intentionally seeking education and a place in the modern world. During that intervening quarter of a century, the Manus had been exposed to hundreds of thousands of American soldiers who passed through the Admiralty Islands during World War II. They had been exposed to large doses of American technology as well. The American armed forces built roads, houses, and runways with the help of Manus labor. Mead claims that the Americans in the Admiralty Islands were emulated by the Manus not only because the Americans had an impressive array of technology but also because they treated the Manus with greater respect than had earlier contacts. So complete was the transformation in a mere quarter of a century that Mead spoke of the Manus as having given up their old lives for new ones.

Whereas most previous studies of rapid culture change were quick to point up the deleterious effects on the affected culture, Mead's restudy of the Manus suggests

subordinate to the other. To be certain, both diffusion and acculturation involve culture change as a result of contact with another group. But the process of acculturation differs from the diffusion of a single trait or a complex of traits in that acculturation involves the widespread reorganization of one or both cultures over a short period of time. While both the dominant and subordinate culture may experience changes, the subordinate culture always changes most dramatically. The consequences of acculturation can take a variety of forms. The subordinate culture could become extinct, it could be incorporated as a distinct subculture of the dominant group, or it could be assimilated (blended) into the dominant group. But whatever form it may take, accul-

CROSS-CULTURAL
MISCUE

Sometimes well-intentioned but short-sighted environmental sanitation programs can go awry when the planners are not sufficiently aware of local cultural realities. Through various types of foreign aid programs, U.S. technicians have made major efforts to introduce sanitary latrines into many developing countries. While latrines, or outhouses, are not immediately thought of by most North Americans as the height of sanitation, they do represent a significant advance over some traditional ways of disposing of human waste. Latrines built by U.S. technicians are fashioned after outhouses—inexpensive wooden structures with a raised seat perforated by several holes—found in some rural parts of the United States. This latrine design, however, is not particularly well received in other parts of the world. George Foster relates an incident from El Salvador:

Several years ago a coffee planter, interested in the welfare of his employees, built a latrine for each house according to the standard American model. He was upset when his employees refused to use them. Finally an old man offered a suggestion. "Patron, don't you realize that here we are squatters?" . . . Latrines with raised seats seem to cause constipation among people who customarily defecate in a squatting position (1973:103).

that rapid culture change doesn't have to be disruptive. Mead claimed that if the local people are willful participants in the change, the disruptive effects of change, however rapidly the change may come, will be minimal. Even though Mead may have overestimated the Manus' willful participation in the acculturation process and underestimated the disruptive effects on their lives, this nevertheless serves as an excellent example of acculturation without much coercion.

Sometimes people will voluntarily become acculturated because they believe that the adoption of certain technologies or behaviors will increase their adaptation to the environment. A case in point is the extensive culture change that resulted from the rapid adoption of snowmobiles by the reindeer-herding Skolt Lapps of Finland. According to Pelto (1973:67–75), the first snowmobile was introduced into Finland in 1962, and nine years later fifty-eight of the seventy families under study owned at least one snowmobile.

Traditional Lapp culture had always placed considerable emphasis on transportation systems and mobility. The seminomadic Skolt Lapps had adapted to their environment by maintaining two separate households—their nucleated villages inhabited during the winter months and their calving and fishing ground which they inhabited during the spring. From these seasonal home-

steads, the Lapp herders would travel intensively rounding up their herds. The concern with transportation as a key to successful adaptation was expressed in songs and folklore, their recreational activities (i.e., reindeer races), and even their courting and marriage rituals. As Pelto reports, "personal mobility, it was told to me again and again, is a main characteristic of the successful reindeer man: 'You have to be able to get around'" (1973: 55). Thus, it is not difficult to understand the fascination that the Skolt Lapps had with the snowmobile: it provided them with a technological quantum leap in efficient mobility. In the process of adopting the snowmobile to reindeer herding, however, the Skolt Lapps experienced far-reaching changes in both their technology and their sociocultural patterns.

## Linked Changes

Chapter 2 introduced the concept that cultures are more than the sum of their parts. Rather, cultures are systematic wholes, the parts of which are interconnected. If, in fact, cultures are integrated wholes, it would follow that a change in one part of the culture is likely to bring about changes in other parts. In other words, most changes that occur in cultures are **linked changes**. The introduction of a single technological innovation, for example, may well set off a series of changes in other parts of the culture. This proposition can be illustrated by looking at one such innovation—television—which was introduced into U.S. society during the 1950s. When the TV set, part of our technological system, replaced the radio as the major form of electronic communication in U.S. households, it had far-reaching consequences for other nontechnological parts of the culture, such as the family system, the political process, and our religious institutions.

The advent of television has, without question, altered the nature of the American family. Before the widespread use of the TV, dinnertime provided an occasion for family members to have face-to-face interaction with one another. With the coming of the TV and the so-called TV dinner, however, parents and children began spending dinnertime interacting with the "electronic Cyclops" rather than with one another. Campaign politics has never been the same since the arrival of TV. Whereas Truman and Dewey conducted their presidential campaigns largely from the back end of a railroad car in 1948, subsequent candidates were brought into our homes via television advertisements and televised debates. Today's candidates for public office need to be as attentive to such variables as lighting, clothing, and makeup as they are to the substantive issues in the campaign. In the area of organized religion, the influence on evangelicalism has been greatly enhanced by television. One can legitimately question whether, if TV did not exist, Billy Graham would have such a lucrative ministry, Oral Roberts would have a university named after him, or Jim Bakker would be serving time in federal prison.

◆  ◆  ◆

# Obstacles to Culture Change

In every culture there are always two opposing sets of forces—those promoting the status quo and those promoting culture change. At certain times, the forces of conservatism are in control, while at other times, the forces of change are in ascendancy. These two sets of forces are really two sides of the same coin. People are motivated to change their culture by a host of factors, including the desire for prestige, economic gain, or a new, more efficient way of solving a problem. There are also certain barriers to culture change that are important to understand, particularly if one works as a change

agent. Some of the more prominent change-retarding factors are discussed in the following subsections.

## CULTURAL BOUNDARY MAINTENANCE

A very important mechanism for preventing culture change is the creation and **maintenance** of **cultural boundaries** that keep people separate from other groups. Sometimes these boundaries are physical to the extent that most or all of the people live in one geographic area while excluding those who are not in the group. The more physically isolated a group is, the less susceptible it is to cultural diffusion. A culture does not need to be physically remote from other cultures, however, to avoid, or at least retard, culture change. Rather a culture can maintain its distinctiveness by imposing certain *cultural* boundaries that strengthen and glorify its own cultural traditions and discourage cultural borrowing from other groups. Such aspects of culture as language, eating habits, clothing, folklore, and humor are all used by cultures in one way or another to both emphasize their uniqueness and exclude outsiders.

**Language.** Perhaps no other part of culture is more unique to a group than its language. As discussed in Chapter 6, language is more than merely a system for sending and receiving messages. It is also highly reflective of a people's ethos or world view. Language is, in other words, an embodiment of the people's values. If a group of people want to remain culturally separate, the way to do it is to (a) use their own language exclusively, (b) forbid the use of other languages, and (c) discourage outsiders from speaking their language. Perhaps the most dramatic expression of linguistic exclusiveness takes the form of battles revolving around national language policy. The selection as national languages of Hindi in India or Swahili in Tanzania can be seen as an example of an attempt to assert a particular cultural tradition while excluding others.

**Clothing.** In large part because of its high visibility, clothing is another important symbol of group identity used to distinguish "us" from "them." To maintain their own unique cultural identity, people (particularly when away from home) are likely to wear their own ethnic or national dress. Africans wearing brightly colored kenti cloth, Chinese wearing Mao jackets, or American bikers wearing black leather jackets are all examples of expressions of cultural uniqueness. Sometimes feelings run

The sharing of food and eating habits serves as a cultural barrier to contact with other cultural groups.

high about the meanings conveyed by ethnic dress. For example, a man from the Swiss-German section of Switzerland who was married to a German woman refused to allow his seven-year-old son (who was half German) to wear *lederhosen*, a distinctive type of leather pants from Southern Germany, because he wanted to make sure that everyone knew his son was Swiss and not German.

**Eating Styles.** Still another critical dimension of ethnicity that can serve as a cultural barrier to contact with other groups is eating customs. In most, if not all cultures, eating is a highly social activity. What foods are eaten, in what manner, how often, and particularly with whom are all factors that vary from one culture to another. The sharing of food is used by every culture in one way or another for maintaining social ties and group solidarity. This is no better illustrated than in Hindu India, where people are strictly forbidden from eating with members of other castes. In some societies, the communal aspects of eating are emphasized to a far greater degree than they are in the United States. For example, Amharic speakers from Ethiopia not only eat food from a common basket but on special social occasions will actually put the food into each other's mouths rather than in their own. Moreover, by creating and maintaining certain food taboos, cultures set themselves apart from other cultures that do not recognize such prohibitions.

## RELATIVE VALUES

Sometimes people resist changes in their culture because the proposed change is not compatible with the existing value system. Change agents (such as overseas development workers, Peace Corps volunteers, or missionaries) often fail to understand why some people are so resistent to certain changes and don't seem to comprehend the advantages of the change. If people from a particular culture refuse to participate in an agricultural improvement project, it may not be because of their lack of understanding of the likely outcome of the project. Instead, people may choose not to go along with a proposed change because the change would bring about a situation that would be less desirable (according to their values) than the status quo.

An illustration of resistance to change due to relative values occurred in Kenya in the early 1970s. Because of shortfalls in the maize production for several years running, the government, which controlled the sale of all maize meal in the country, decided to alleviate the shortage by mixing 10 percent wheat flour with 90 percent maize meal. Government officials reasoned that the ground wheat (obtained free from foreign assistance programs abroad) would make their dwindling maize supply last longer and avoid shortages in the retail stores. But the population reacted strongly against the government's attempt to "dilute" their basic staple (maize meal), which is used to make *ugali,* a porridge eaten at most meals. It seems that the maize meal mixed with 10 percent wheat had a somewhat different taste and consistency than 100 percent maize meal. As it turned out, according to the local value system, the *quality* of their maize meal was more important than the *quantity.* In other words, the people in Kenya were willing to put up with some degree of food shortages, provided the usual quality of their primary food source was not sacrificed.

Another example of relative values serving as a barrier to culture change comes from South America (Ferraro, 1990:138). A U.S. timber company harvesting wood from a remote area of the rain forest was experiencing difficulties recruiting labor from among the local Indian communities. In an attempt to attract laborers away from its main competitor (a German company), the U.S. firm invested heavily in housing for its employees, offered considerably higher wages than its competitor, and guaranteed the workers a forty-hour workweek (the Germans paid their workers by the hour). Yet despite these economic advantages, the majority of workers continued to work for the German firm. The explanation for this apparent "irrational" behavior on the part of the Indian work force is that what might be of value to workers in Detroit is not the same thing that appeals to Indian workers in the South American rain forest. For the Indian workers, flexibility of their time was more important than housing or high wages. Under the system used by the German firm—which paid an hourly wage rather than a forty-hour/week salary—the work-

ers were able to take time off work for their festivals and ceremonies without fear of losing their jobs.

## CULTURES AS ORGANIC WHOLES

The functional interrelatedness of the parts of culture—particularly among small-scale, technologically simple cultures—can serve as a conservative force discouraging people from culture change. After a number of generations of adapting to their environments, many small-scale societies are in a state of relative equilibrium. That is, solutions to most societal problems have been worked out (albeit imperfectly) and a balance of social relationships established between various members of the group. To change one part of such a culture is likely to threaten existing social and economic relationships. To illustrate, Alan Beals (1962) cites the case of Gopalpur, a village in South India, which for centuries has utilized farming techniques that do not produce great yields. The use of modern technology, pesticides, chemical fertilizers and more modern irrigation systems would, in all likelihood, result in increased agricultural productivity. But by adopting new farming techniques, the local farmer is jeopardizing some significant social and economic relationships. As Beals put it:

At every step, the farmer wishing to improve his agricultural practices must weigh the claims of the new method against the known economic and social benefits of the traditional method. To purchase improved agricultural equipment, the farmer must sever his traditional relationship with the Blacksmith and Carpenter. This is more than an economic relationship. Not only are the Carpenter and Blacksmith neighbors and friends, but they have religious functions that make their presence essential on such occasions as births, marriage, and death (1962:79).

As Beals demonstrates, to accept changes in one part of a culture (e.g., agricultural technology) is likely to bring about undesirable changes in other parts of the culture (e.g., social and religious relationships). By refusing to adopt new farming technology, the rural farmer is not necessarily reacting in an ultra-conservative way, but rather is responding very sensibly.

◆ ◆ ◆

# Modernization

Despite its many connotations in everyday usage, the term **modernization** in anthropological terms refers to the process by which traditional societies take on some of the sociocultural characteristics of industrialized societies. Most social scientists generally can agree on what have been the major sociocultural changes over the past several centuries. On most people's list would be such trends as advances in machine technology, industrialization, the growth of centralized political bureaucracies, urbanization, and the proliferation of nonkinship-based social groups, to mention just a few. There is considerably less consensus, however, on how to explain these major sociocultural trends.

A number of scholars have attempted to explain the process of modernization by proposing grand theories that frequently identify a single primary variable. Marx (orig. 1859) tended to focus on the centrality of modes of production and the resulting class structures. Max Weber (1930) singled out certain key values associated with the Protestant Reformation (hard work, diligence, thrift, and upward mobility) as the prime mover of modernization. Everett Hagen (1962) has suggested that modernization has its roots in certain sociopsychological processes revolving around personality development during childhood. While the debate over the causes of modernization has continued over the decades, the very processes of modernization which these grand theorists are attempting to explain not only have persisted but also have actually accelerated and intensified.

## MAIN FOCUSES OF MODERNIZATION

The study of modernization has essentially followed two broad approaches. The first, and by far the most common focus over the past century, has been on the *institutional* level. It focuses on how entire societies gain control over their environments by applying more and more technology to increasingly more complex levels of social organization. Social scientists studying the modernization of *political* institutions focus on increasing trends toward political centralization, the rise of bureaucracies, the broadening of political functions, and the proliferation of new social groups (i.e., interest groups) that participate in the political process. The study of the modernization of *economic* institutions has examined such trends as increased labor specialization, the intensification of technology and inanimate sources of energy, increasing interdependence of markets, and rising standards of living. Students of the modernization of *social* institutions have concentrated on the rise of voluntary social organizations, the shift from the extended to the nuclear family, and the increased complexity of systems of social stratification.

The other major approach to the study of modernization—which tends to be more psychological than sociocultural—focuses on the *individual's* change from traditional to modern. Rather than concentrating on institutional changes, this second approach concerns itself with the role of the individual in the process of modernization. Whereas the first approach stresses changing social and cultural structures, the second emphasizes ways of thinking, feeling, and valuing. Following the lead of Inkeles (1983), Kluckhohn and Strodtbeck (1961), and Berry (1980), the subsequent discussion of modernization takes the second approach, which essentially defines modernity as a state of mind. By looking at the individual in the process of modernization, we have identified a number of important dimensions of individual modernity—traits that make a person modern. Contrasting the traits of modern and traditional people should in no way imply that modern traits are better. Rather, when seen as ideal opposite types, these contrasts should be viewed as simply different responses to the world which may shed some light on the process of change. While not suggesting that such a list is exhaustive, these traits include those in the following subsections.

## RECEPTIVITY TO NEW EXPERIENCES

The modern person is more willing to accept new ways of thinking and behaving than is the traditional person. For the traditional person, novelty and change are viewed with skepticism and mistrust. Anything that disrupts traditional patterns is seen as potentially dangerous and should be avoided. This highly conservative orientation is embodied in a Spanish proverb heard widely throughout Latin America: "What is old and known is worth more than something new yet to be understood" (Foster, 1973:84). The modern person, on the other hand, welcomes change, or at least is willing to take the risks that often accompany change. For example, a modern man would choose to relocate himself and his family if he thought there was a good chance of improving the quality of life, even though he may be getting along reasonably well in his present situation.

Even though not all people in the United States have a readiness for change, the U.S. advertising industry certainly draws heavily upon this "love affair" with the new. We are told that since our toothpaste is "new and improved," it must be better than what existed before. Conversely, in the United States, one effective way of criticizing a thing—be it a camera, a dress, or an idea—is to call it old-fashioned.

## CROSS-CULTURAL MISCUE

In 1992, the twelve member nations of the European Community entered into a market arrangement with greatly reduced trade barriers. In preparation for this unified market, many companies are standardizing their brands for sale throughout Western Europe. For example, the U.S. candy manufacturer, Mars Inc., changed the name of the Marathon candy bar to Snickers for the sake of creating a more internationally recognized brand. Yet, despite the similarities that may be found in marketing and advertising throughout the nations of the European Community, there still remains a number of significant cultural differences that can affect the success of international marketing efforts. To illustrate, Prokesch reports that

. . . young, upwardly mobile professionals in France and Italy consider it classy to drink whisky, but those in Britain do not. English and French mothers have no qualms about feeding their babies prepared baby food, but most Spanish mothers do not think it nutritious. While the French and Italians tend to like creative, stylish advertisements, the Danes insist on factual, serious ones. The Germans and Spaniards want lots of product information, while the British like information presented in an entertaining way (1990).

Some European companies, however, have paid a high price for not being attentive to cross-cultural differences. Prokesch goes on to cite the case of Benetton, an Italian apparel company that had

. . . been running a "United Colors" campaign using what it deemed were universal images of friendship, peace and freedom. But at least one of the ads, showing a black man and a white man handcuffed together, was considered offensive to blacks in Britain. The London Regional Transport authority refused to use a poster of the ad in buses and subways and Benetton has severely curtailed its use in Britain (1990).

## EXPANDING OPINIONS

A person is more modern if she or he shows a disposition to form and express opinions on a wide range of issues, both within and outside one's immediate environment. Modern people are able to visualize themselves in positions of authority offering advice on how they might solve pressing societal problems. Inkeles and his colleagues (1983:37) have identified an additional dimension of this particular trait of modernity. Not only do modern people hold more opinions than their traditional counterparts, but they also have a greater awareness of and appreciation for the diversity of opinion.

This trait of modernity of expressing opinions is very closely associated with levels of education. That is, the more information a person gains through formal education on a wide range of contemporary topics, the more likely he or she will be to both develop an interest in a particular topic and form a personal opinion about it.

In fact, this trait of modernity presupposes the acquisition of information. Being modern, in other words, involves more than having opinions; it also involves possessing the factual data to support those opinions. It is one thing for a person to hold the opinion that Democrats are more interested in the average worker than are Republicans. It is something else to be able to cite specific pieces of legislation supported by each political party to buttress that opinion.

## THE PRECISE RECKONING OF TIME

A major component of being modern revolves around the definition of time. The modern person takes time very seriously and frequently makes minute distinctions between very small units of time such as seconds and minutes. The modern person treats time like a commodity which, like money, can be spent, saved, or wasted. To ensure that she uses her time prudently, the modern woman schedules appointments in advance, establishes timetables, and sets deadlines for herself. Since modern people are so conscious about dividing units of time so precisely, promptness, or being "on time," is highly valued.

This modern definition of time is perhaps nowhere more developed than it is in the United States, where time plays a central role in people's lives. To illustrate, we punch timeclocks to measure our work; we measure in hundredths of a second how long it takes to swim fifty meters; even our eating is usually done in response to the clock, for we often eat not when we are hungry but because it is lunchtime or dinnertime; and most adults in the United States have strapped to their wrists a small device that divides minutes into sixty equal parts so that we will never be caught without knowing, quite precisely, what time it is.

In modern societies, time—considered a vauable commodity—is taken very seriously.

## CONTROLLING ONE'S DESTINY

The modern person believes that he or she has control over his or her own destiny. In highly traditional societies, people tend to be very fatalistic—that is, they see their lives as being in the hands of other (external) forces such as gods, governmental officials, the church, wealthy landlords, or mother nature. In modern societies, however, it is believed that people not only can but should control their own destinies, their social and physical environments, and nature itself. If a river overflows its banks and destroys his house, the modern man will want to dam up the river and change its course. If the modern married couple wants to wait five years before having children, they will control the process of conception by using various contraceptive devices at their disposal. If gravity is a barrier to walking on the moon, the modern person will want to build a larger rocket engine to blast through the earth's gravitational pull. In other words, modern people believe that given sufficient time, energy, and money, there is little or nothing that can escape their control or few situations that cannot be changed. In short, modern people have confidence in their abilities, both individually and collectively, to master the challenges of their social and natural environments.

## PLANNING FOR THE FUTURE

The modern person is oriented toward long-term planning, both in public affairs as well as in his or her own private life. The modern person supports the notion that government should engage in long-term planning efforts. He or she agrees, for example, that the municipal government should be purchasing land today that will be used for new road construction two decades from now when automobile traffic will be greatly increased. Modern people are always focused toward the future. They pay life insurance premiums today to protect their families in the event that they should die prematurely some time in the future. They invest in stocks, IRAs, and long-term CD's to put away a nest egg for their retirement years. They are fascinated with futuristic books such as *Megatrends* (Naisbitt, 1982) and *The Third Wave* (Toffler, 1981), which make predictions about where the society, indeed the world, is heading. In short, the modern person places a high value on planning for the future and working in the here and now to make the future a better time in which to live.

The modern person is one who believes in controlling the forces of nature.

## APPLYING UNIVERSAL STANDARDS

Another important characteristic of modernity is the belief that rewards in the society should be based on a universally applicable set of standards, not on whim or any other type of irrational basis. The modern person would choose to hire employees based on some objective assessment of their skills to handle the job (grades in school, standardized tests, outside references) rather than the fact that they are related to the boss. Under a modern way of thinking, a worker would receive a promotion because of the efficiency of his or her performance on the job, not because the manager happens to like his or her hairstyle. This notion of rewarding people on the basis of some universally applied set of rules has been referred to as **universalism** (Parsons and Shils, 1952:81) and **distributive justice** (Inkeles, 1983:38–39). Whatever term we choose to use, we can recognize it as an ideal in the modern factory, office, or government bureaucracy.

## FORMAL EDUCATION FOR SCIENCE, TECHNOLOGY, AND NEW LEARNING

All societies, however traditional or modern, have systems of education, that is, ways of passing on the basics of the culture to the next generation. In traditional societies, education has as its main objective the preservation of traditional values. Koranic schools in Islamic cultures, for example, rely heavily on a rote method of learning to inculcate traditional religious wisdom. By way of contrast, modern people want to learn not only the three R's but also science, technology, and new ways of thinking and creating. Whereas traditional people think that science and modern learning are dangerous intrusions into the mysterious realm of religion, the modern person sees science and formal education as the best way of improving the quality of life. Modern people want to increase the rationality of their lives through education, while traditional people (who are more nonrational) want to preserve the mystery of the sacred realm.

This discussion of modernization—and particularly our neatly spelling out the differences between the traditional and the modern—will appear to some readers as being overly analytical. Such an approach might lead us to conclude that people are either traditional, modern, or somewhere in transition between these two types. People all over the world are, to one degree or another, feeling the effects of the process of modernization. The impact on people—which can be traumatic—is the most intense among peoples of the so-called Third World or developing countries. People in parts of Africa, Asia, and Latin America are experiencing massive changes in their cultures within a single generation or two. Simple, yet familiar, technologies have given way to the mysteries of the factory. The security of extended family patterns are giving way to more nuclear families or single-parent families. Traditional religions are being undermined by the proselytizing of outside religions.

Parents and children are separated from one another owing to the demands of migrant labor. Traditional systems of authority are breaking down. An enormous generation gap is developing between adjacent generations that have had radically different life experiences.

Adjustments to these rapidly changing sociocultural environments are exceedingly difficult if not impossible for most people. We must remember that in the United States and Europe, modernization occurred gradually over a number of generations. People of the developing world, however, are faced with monumental changes within the course of a single generation. This type of exposure to the forces of rapid modernization does not come without a high psychological cost. Many people find themselves caught between two different—and in some cases, diametrically opposed—systems of values. Sometimes the individual has given up his or her traditional life without fully embracing any new alternative. At other times, the individual is expected to behave according to different sets of cultural norms depending on the social situation. For example, a woman living in Mexico City is expected to behave according to one set of principles at the office but according to another set of principles when visiting with her grandmother. This living in two different worlds can be extremely anxiety producing.

To add to the confusion of trying to function in a rapidly changing world, many Third World peoples have in recent decades come to the sobering realization that much of the modern world that was so appealing initially is unattainable, at least in their lifetimes. Some Third World populations are growing more rapidly than their GNPs, which means that each year their material/economic well-being is worse than it was the year before. The gap between the haves and the have-nots is widening each year. People make enormous sacrifices to pay for their children's education only to find there are no jobs to absorb these well-educated young people into the economy. In short, many Third World people, moving to cities in search of a more modern way of life, have been frustrated by the lack of opportunities to fulfill their dreams.

## ◆ Summary

1. Although the rate of change varies from culture to culture, there are no cultures that remain unchanged. The two principal ways that cultures change are internally through the process of invention and externally through the process of diffusion.

2. Inventions can be either deliberate or unintentional. While the intentional inventor usually receives the greatest amount of recognition, it is thought that over the long run, unintentional inventors have had the greatest impact on culture change. Because they are not bound by conventional standards, many inventors and innovators tend to be marginal people living on the fringes of society.

3. It is generally recognized that the majority of cultural features (things, ideas, and behavior patterns) found in any society got there by diffusion rather than invention. The following generalizations can be made about the process of diffusion: (a) cultural diffusion is selective in nature, (b) it is a two-way process, (c) it is likely to involve changes in form and/or function, (d) some cultural items are more likely candidates for diffusion than are others, and (e) it is affected by a number of important variables.

4. Acculturation is a specialized form of cultural diffusion that refers to forced borrowing under conditions of external pressure. While some anthropologists have described situations of acculturation in which the nondominant culture has voluntarily chosen the changes, others claim that acculturation always involves some measure of coercion and force.

5. Since the parts of a culture are to some degree interrelated, a change in one part is likely to bring about changes in other parts. This insight from cultural anthropology should be of paramount importance to applied anthropologists, who are frequently involved directly or indirectly with planned programs of culture change.

6. Among the barriers to culture change are the following: (a) some societies can maintain their cultural boundaries through the exclusive use of language, food, and clothing; (b) some societies can resist change in their culture because the proposed change is not compatible with their existing value systems; and (c) sometimes people will resist change because they are unwilling to disrupt existing social and economic relationships.

7. Modernization refers to the process of traditional societies taking on some of the characteristics of industrialized societies. At the institutional level this involves trends toward political centralization, increased labor specialization, the nuclearization of the family, and the rise of voluntary social organizations.

8. When viewed from the perspective of the individual, modernization involves, among other things, an increase in one's receptivity to new experiences, a more precise reckoning of time, a greater sense of controlling one's destiny, and an orientation toward the future.

## ◆ Key Terms

acculturation
cultural boundary
  maintenance
diffusion
distributive justice
innovation

invention
linked change
marginal people
modernization
universalism

## ◆ Suggested Readings

Arensberg, Conrad M., and A. H. Niehoff. *Introducing Social Change: A Manual for Americans Overseas.* Chicago: Aldine, 1964. An old, yet important, book demonstrating the need for understanding other cultures when involved in programs of planned change abroad.

Bernard, H. R., and P. J. Pelto (Eds.). *Technology and Social Change* (2nd ed). Prospect Heights, Ill.: Waveland, 1987. A collection of thirteen essays discussing the effects of modern technology on non-Western cultures.

Bodley, John H. *Victims of Progress* (3rd ed). Mountain View, Calif.: Mayfield, 1990. An important book that examines the sometimes disastrous effects of Westernization and industrialization on tribal societies. Bodley discusses the high price small-scale societies pay for "progress" and the role that Western institutions play in this cultural devastation.

Inkeles, Alex. *Exploring Individual Modernity.* New York: Columbia University Press, 1983. A sequel to his earlier volume entitled *Becoming Modern* (1974), this long-term study examines the characteristics of the modern person and the forces of modernity in developing countries.

Kottak, Conrad P. *Assault on Paradise: Social Change in a Brazilian Village.* New York: Random House, 1983. A readable and highly personal account of changes occurring in Arembepe, a village in Brazil. An excellent book for introductory students because it not only documents important sociocultural trends but also highlights the changes that have taken place in the ethnographer over the span of two decades.

Pelto, P. J. *The Snowmobile Revolution: Technology and Social Change in the Arctic.* Menlo Park, Calif.: Benjamin Cummings, 1973. A study of sociocultural change documenting how a single technological device, the snowmobile, brought about vast economic and social changes among the reindeer-herding Skolt Lapps of Finland.

Rogers, Everett M. *Diffusion of Innovations* (3rd ed). New York: The Free Press, 1983. A quantitative, up-to-date, and richly documented study of the mechanism of cultural diffusion that discusses, among other topics, the history of diffusion research, how innovations are generated, rates of adoption of innovations, diffusion networks, and change agents.

Tonkinson, Robert. *The Jigalong Mob: Aboriginal Victors of the Desert Crusade.* Menlo Park, Calif.: Benjamin Cummings, 1974. In this study of sociocultural change among a group of Australian aborigines, the author provides a wealth of data on how one group was able to maintain its ethnic pride and traditional values in the face of Western colonialism.

Spindler, Louise S. *Culture Change and Modernization: Mini-Models and Case Studies.* Prospect Heights, Ill.: Waveland, 1984. A discussion of the process of culture change for introductory students, drawing liberally from many ethnographic studies for examples.

◆ ◆ ◆ ◆ ◆

# Culture Change

A major theme running through this chapter has been the concept of the interconnectedness of the parts of culture. That is, a change in one part of a cultural system causes changes in other parts. This notion is not just an interesting theory but has very practical implications for applied anthropologists who work in programs of planned change. When working to introduce change into another culture, either at home or abroad, it is imperative that applied anthropologists know how the part that is being changed is interconnected to other parts so as to avoid causing potentially harmful changes from taking place in other parts of the culture. The first case discusses how a cultural impact study conducted by an anthropologist revealed how a change in one part of the people's cultural environment was having harmful effects on other parts. The second case demonstrates how an anthropological study of changing attitudes and behaviors concerning marriage and family issues had important implications for a multimillion dollar USAID project on family planning in Swaziland.

◆ **Short-term anthropological research on the environmental impact of an interstate highway helps resolve a class action suit in federal district court.**

In the early 1970s, a group of urban residents in Charlotte, N.C., brought a class action suit against all those parties involved in building a highway through their neighborhood. Since the highway in question was part of the U.S. interstate highway system, the defendants in the case were the municipal government of Charlotte, the North Carolina Department of Transportation, and the U.S. Department of Transportation. Since much of the highway construction had already been completed at the time the lawsuit was filed, the plaintiffs were not asking the court to permanently stop the remainder of the construction. They did claim, however, that the construction of a major six-lane interstate highway through their neighborhood was having serious negative consequences. The legal grounds on which the suit was based was the fact that all three levels of government, in violation of federal law, had failed to conduct an environmental impact study on the neighborhood. Thus, on these grounds, the presiding judge ordered that all further construction on the highway be halted until an environmental impact study was conducted to (1) determine the negative effects the highway was having on the lives of local residents and (2) make recommendations for helping to alleviate some of the more serious consequences.

At the request of the attorneys for the plaintiffs and with the approval of the court, an urban anthropologist was hired to conduct a short-term environmental impact study on the project's effects on the community. Since work was totally halted (and people were temporarily out of work) until the study was completed, the court impressed upon this newly recruited applied anthropologist that time was of the essence. Unlike more conventional anthropological field studies, which can take a year or longer, this study was expected to take no longer than several weeks to complete.

Despite the very real time constraints, some traditional anthropological data-gathering methods were employed. By obtaining maps from the planning commission, it was possible to reconstruct a picture of the transportation flow between different parts of the neighborhood before the highway construction and how that flow had been disrupted. Extensive interviews were conducted with members of the community association, local entrepreneurs, and randomly selected neighborhood residents. And finally, the old anthropological standby—participant-observation—was used to actually observe the movement of people at certain key times, such as early-morning rush hour, late-afternoon rush hour, and Sunday mornings when people went to church.

Based on people's comments and personal observations, it became clear that the existence of a multilane highway constructed through the center of a neighborhood had significant disruptive effects on the lives of the residents. A change in the people's physical environment had affected other parts of their culture and life-styles.

The most damaging impact on the neighborhood had to do with the way people got around to take care of their everyday affairs, such as going to school, doing their grocery shopping, and attending their neighborhood churches. Since this was a low-income neighborhood (somehow planners never seem to build highways through the high-rent districts!), the majority of people did not own cars. They relied on public bus transportation to travel to other parts of the city, but since much of their lives was played out in the neighborhood itself, they had used a number of well-traveled pedestrian routes. With the coming of the highway, most of these routes were cut off. If a person lived on one side of the highway, he or she would have no way of walking to the other side to shop or attend church. For those with automobiles, the construction of the highway made car travel within the neighborhood somewhat less convenient. But the transportation patterns for the majority of people, who relied on walking, were disrupted almost completely.

Based on these findings, the following two recommendations were made to the court. First, since the one and only vehicular bridge spanning the highway had no provisions for pedestrian traffic, it was recommended that the builders add sidewalks, curb ramps for bicycles and baby carriages, traffic lights, and other amenities that would enable pedestrians to walk in safety. The second recommendation was to construct a separate pedestrian bridge over another part of the highway that would link part of the residential area with the neighborhood elementary school. This would add a second avenue for pedestrians to link up with both halves of the community as well as provide a traffic-free passageway for elementary schoolchildren. The court accepted both recommendations and required the defendants to carry them out as a precondition for the resumption of construction.

Here, then, is yet another example of how anthropological data and insights can be used to solve a particular societal problem. This short-term anthropological research project started with a fundamental idea about culture change. That is, a change in one part of the system is likely to bring about changes in other parts of the system. Through conventional field techniques (albeit for a short period of time), it was possible to document the degree to which a change in the people's material culture (i.e., system of roads and pathways) had affected their everyday patterns of transportation

and social interaction. Once the sociocultural problems were identified, it was then possible to make recommendations that would, while not eliminating, at least soften the negative impact of the highway construction on the lives of the local residents.

### ◆ A study of changing marriage patterns in Swaziland leads to policy recommendations for a program in population control.

Throughout much of the non-Western world, the issue of population control continues to be a major problem facing development planners. Even though population policy remains a sensitive issue in some Third World governments, most development strategists agree on the critical role that fertility plays in national development. High birthrates lead to a host of deleterious effects, including high levels of internal and external migration, unemployment and underemployment, a decline in standards of living, and a stagnation or decline in socioeconomic development. If development agencies are to make progress in improving health conditions, agricultural productivity, employment opportunities, and educational facilities, they need to make the issue of population control their top priority.

In the early 1980s, USAID, the foreign aid branch of the U.S. government, was keenly aware of how closely the question of fertility was connected to some of the other programs they were administering in Swaziland, a Southern African country with one of the highest birthrates in the world. To shed light on their population control efforts in Swaziland, USAID funded an anthropological research project designed to examine the implications of changing patterns of marriage on fertility (Ferraro, 1980). By drawing on a wide variety of both historical and contemporary research strategies, the study documented a number of changes in marital practices in Swaziland over this century. Major trends were examined in such areas as type of marriage contracted, the amounts of bridewealth transferred, age at marriage for men and women, the incidence of polygyny, divorce rates, and conjugal roles.

Trends that emerged from this study on the changing average age of marriage were particularly relevant to USAID's efforts in the area of population control. Based on information dating back to the 1920s, it was found that the average age at which women married in the early 1980s had increased by between six and seven years. Whereas Swazi women formerly married in their mid- to late teens, the evidence from several different sources indicated the average age at the time of the research was early to mid-twenties. Much of the change in the average age of women at marriage can be explained in terms of the greater educational opportunities for women. This more advanced age at which women were marrying tended to suppress the overall number of births, since it substantially reduced the number of childbearing years for the average married woman in Swaziland.

This 1980 study of changing patterns of marriage in Swaziland looked at attitudes toward marriage as well as actual behavior. The study found a generally strong inverse relationship between levels of education and traditional attitudes about marriage, conjugal relationships, and family size. That is, the greater the exposure to formal education, the less likely an individual will support such traditional practices as arranged marriages, polygyny, and unlimited family size.

These findings on the relationship between education and family size were supported by other studies as well. For example, Vilakazi's (1979:11–12) sample of educated women from urban Swaziland showed both a strong rejection of traditional family values and an equally strong affirmation of birth control values. Moreover, the 1976 census data (Blacker and Forsyth-Thompson, et al., 1979:166) revealed a reduction in family size among women with secondary or higher education. Thus, the findings from all three studies—along with the data on changing age at marriage—all tended to justify a fairly straightforward policy recommendation that was given to USAID for its program in population control. That is, one way of contributing to a decline in the birthrate in Swaziland is to support programs of secondary and higher education for women. Such a recommendation (which can contribute to the solution of the very serious social problem of runaway population rates) could have been made only after first studying the changing cultural patterns of the Swazis during the twentieth century.

# The Future of Anthropology

As the preceding chapters have shown, the scientific discipline of anthropology involves the study of humans in whatever place or time we might find them. Through the distinct, yet interrelated, subdisciplines of physical anthropology, archaeology, linguistics, and cultural anthropology, anthropologists have conducted research on both the biological and cultural aspects of the human condition through time. This book has explored a number of issues and concerns facing contemporary anthropologists. In all likelihood, the discipline of anthropology will continue to move in the direction it has set for itself in the past several decades. While a thorough discussion of all of these disciplinary issues would take us well beyond the scope of the book, it is possible to examine briefly some of the more important directions in which anthropology is heading.

## Responding to a Changing World

One need not be a scholar of culture change to notice that the pace at which cultures are changing is accelerating with every decade. Whereas the everyday lives of our grandparents seems simple and slow-moving, today people are overwhelmed with how quickly their cultures are changing. Alvin Toffler (1971) speaks of "future shock," which he defines as the psychological disorientation resulting from living in such a rapidly changing cultural environment that people constantly feel they are living in the future. Culture change is occurring at such an accelerated pace today that it is fre-

quently difficult to keep up with all of the new developments. Moreover, because of the recent revolution in transportation and electronic communications, the world seems smaller. Today it is possible to travel to the other side of the earth in about the same time it took our great-grandparents to travel fifty miles in a horse and carriage. And, we can see (via satellite) instant transmissions of live newscasts from anywhere in the world. Because of this vastly improved capacity to communicate with, and travel to, other parts of the world, the occurrence of cultural diffusion has increased dramatically in recent decades. Consequently, the differences between cultures have been diminishing.

If the cultural world is, in fact, shrinking, it has led some people to wonder whether the discipline of anthropology is losing its subject matter. They argue that it will be just a matter of years before all of the cultures of the world are homogenized into a single culture, leaving the discipline of anthropology without a field of study. If one takes a very traditional view of anthropology—the aim of which is to document the cultural and biological features of isolated indigenous peoples—then the future of the discipline is indeed bleak. It is certainly true that today exotic cultures (relatively untouched by the modern world) are few and far between. Today only a handful of anthropologists are studying the quickly diminishing number of pristine cultures. But the fact that former hunting-and-gathering societies are now involved in market economies and consumerism should not lead us to conclude that all cultural differences are disappearing. Though some of the obvious differences between cultures may be decreasing, there is little evidence to suggest that the world is becoming a cultural melting pot. Despite rapid culture change, there will, no doubt, be sufficient cultural diversity to keep anthropologists occupied well into the future.

## Preserving and Managing Archaeological Materials

Just as culture change and the disappearance of small-scale, isolated societies have influenced the recent development of other subfields of anthropology, the threat of a disappearing data base is a major influence on the future of archaeology. As noted earlier in this book, archaeological sites and resources are threatened both by vandalism and by land disturbance due to agriculture, construction, and other development. As human populations grow and require more food, housing, and transportation, these threats of destruction grow as well. Archaeological sites are disappearing in all parts of the world. Archaeologists of the present and the future must grapple with this serious problem.

Archaeologists in the future will increasingly rely on remote sensing and computerized data bases, building on the current explosion of electronic information technology. Remote sensing allows the acquisition of archaeological data with less excavation, which is inevitably destructive. Large, computerized data bases allow archaeologists to compare and analyze already excavated data more effectively than they could earlier, thus lessening the need for new excavation. Regional archaeological data bases provide essential information for planning future construction so it will impact archaeological sites in the least harmful way possible.

Archaeologists will continue and intensify efforts to preserve sites and cultural heritage. Public education, including outreach to community groups, museum exhibits, and writing for the general public, will become more important. In addition, archaeologists will have to develop new ways for members of the public to participate responsibly in survey, excavation, and analysis. Archaeologists must also help draft legislation at all levels of government and help law enforcement personnel enforce such legislation.

Not only are archaeologists grappling with the loss of parts of their data base, but they must also acknowledge and work with an intensified desire on the part of indigenous people to control their own past. Amer-

ican Indians, Native Australians, people living in African nations, and people in many other parts of the world no longer simply accept the presence of archaeologists and the removal of archaeological materials, even if it is for the purpose of legitimate research. People want to control research into their past and keep artifacts where they can be enjoyed by local citizens. In the future, archaeologists will probably have to cope with more and more restrictive regulation of archaeological research.

On a more positive side, archaeologists have an opportunity to provide public education and professional training in archaeological methods and preservation in communities where these have not been available. For example, the Society for American Archaeology has established a scholarship fund for American Indians who wish to train as professional archaeologists. The goal is increased and improved collaboration among professional archaeologists, avocational archaeologists, and indigenous communities in order to work together against the continuing loss of archaeological and cultural resources and to learn more about the human past in all parts of the world.

## The Study of Complex Societies

While Western anthropologists have traditionally tended to concentrate their research efforts on small-scale, "uncontaminated," non-Western societies, an increasing number in recent years have turned their attention to studying their own complex societies. A number of factors converged to set this trend in motion. First, a handful of anthropologists after World War II conducted some of the first urban anthropological studies in such places as Timbuktu, Mexico City, and Kampala because the so-called tribal peoples were migrating to cities in ever-increasing numbers during the postwar period. Second, the trend toward the study of urban, complex societies by anthropologists was stimulated, at least in the United States, by the growing interest in applied anthropology. After the affluent 1950s, the 1960s witnessed the rediscovery of ethnicity and poverty, both of which were defined as urban phenomena. U.S. policy makers in recent decades have used the findings of cultural anthropologists to help solve pressing social problems at home. And third, the study of various aspects of our own complex society has resulted from diminishing research opportunities in more traditional societies. Since gaining independence, many Third World countries have been reluctant to grant research permission to Western anthropologists. Moreover, shortages in research funding have prevented many Western scholars from conducting anthropological studies abroad.

The study by anthropologists of their own complex societies, however, is not without its own unique problems. One such problem is that cultural anthropologists run the risk of prejudice or distortion because they lack the perspective of an outsider. Another difficulty—and one that has not been adequately resolved—concerns just how well anthropologists studying complex societies are able to live up to their tradition of holism. A holistic approach—i.e., examining a culture within its total context—is much more manageable when studying a small-scale society comprised of several thousand people than it is when studying a "social system" comprised of 8 million people, such as New York City. Rather than writing holistic ethnographies of cities, anthropologists operating in urban or complex societies are studying small ethnic neighborhoods, specialized occupational groups, or other subcultural groups that operate within the more complex whole. Despite these problems, anthropology as a field of study has a good deal to offer the study of complex societies. For example, anthropologists bring to the study of cities and complex societies (1) a sensitivity to ethnic diversity, (2) a tradition of framing their research problems in broad, holistic terms, and (3) the research method of participant-observation, which provides an important supplement to the more quantitative methods of urban sociologists.

The topics covered by the anthropological study of U.S. society have been varied. For example, anthropologists in recent years have studied hippie life-styles, street gangs, retirement communities, adaptive strategies of urban tramps, and black urban families, to name a few. Within a more institutional framework, anthropologists have studied retirement communities, hospitals, classrooms, and volunteer fire departments. Certain occupations such as construction workers and railroad engineers have been treated as occupational subcultures by some anthropologists. And even certain aspects of popular culture in the United States—football, films, soap operas, and food—have been studied by anthropologists as symbols of our cultural values. Since anthropology involves the comparative study of culture in whatever form it may take—and since the United States provides one of many interesting cultural variations—

there is no reason to assume that this trend toward greater anthropological analysis of our own culture will not continue.

♦ ♦ ♦

## Survival of Indigenous People

In recent years anthropologists from all subfields have become increasingly concerned about the rapid disappearance of indigenous populations of the world. According to the World Council on Indigenous Peoples (quoted in Bodley, 1982: 166–67), an indigenous population is any "people living in countries which have populations composed of different ethnic or racial groups who are descendants of the earliest populations which survive in the area, and who do not, as a group, control the national government of the countries within which they live." Classic examples of "indigenous peoples" are small-scale cultures in Asia, Africa, and the Americas that came under the influence of the colonial powers during the past several centuries.

The concern that many anthropologists have is not that the disappearance of these indigenous peoples will eventually do away with the subject matter of their research. Rather, their concern centers on some basic human rights issues. A growing number of anthropologists feel strongly that indigenous populations over the past several centuries have been negatively affected by the onslaught of civilization. The cultural patterns, and in some cases the people themselves, have been eradicated as a direct result of civilizations' pursuit of "progress" and economic development. The industrial revolution in nineteenth-century Europe was "revolutionary" to the extent that it led to explosions in both population and consumerism, which in turn had drastically negative effects on indigenous peoples. The technological efficiency of the industrial revolution resulted in a quantum leap in population growth. To illustrate, prior to the industrial revolution it took 250 years for the world's population to double, whereas by the 1970s it took only thirty-three years (Bodley, 1982:3). At the same time that populations were exploding in the industrializing world, there was a concomitant growth in the notion of consumerism. If economies were to grow and prosper, production needed to be kept high, which could only be accomplished if people purchased and consumed the products of industry. In order to meet the needs of a growing population with ever-increasing desires to consume, industrialized nations needed to control and exploit natural resources wherever they could find them.

A major motivation for the colonization of the non-Western world was economic in that the natural resources found in Asia and Africa were needed to fuel European factories. The so-called scramble for Africa, initiated when the leaders of Europe set national boundaries in Africa at the Conference of Berlin in 1884, was a very "civilized" and "gentlemanly" way of dividing up the continent's natural resources for the industrializing nations of Europe. Unfortunately, the rights of indigenous populations were hardly protected. In many cases land and resources (needed by the indigenous peoples) were simply appropriated for use by the colonial powers. Landless populations were forced to become laborers, dependent on whatever wages the colonial governments and businesses wished to pay. Native resistance to this systematic exploitation was usually met with force. In some cases, large segments of the population were killed or died from European diseases. In other less severe situations, indigenous peoples were economically exploited, systematically kept at the lowest echelons of the society, and forced to give up their traditional identities.

Unfortunately, specific examples of the demise of indigenous populations are all too commonly found in the literature (see, for example, Bodley, 1982, and Burger, 1987). The tragic annihilation of the population of Tasmania in the nineteenth century is one of the more dramatic examples. Through the use of military force and heavy-handed missionary efforts, not only was the aboriginal culture of Tasmania eliminated, but the people themselves were literally exterminated, many by deliberate killings, because the white settlers wanted the land for sheep herding. Around the turn of the last century the Germans administered their "protectorate" in southwest Africa (presently Namibia) upon the principle that native populations should give up their land for European use. When the indigenous Herero people refused, the Germans made good on their threats to wage a war of extermination, justifying their military actions on the basis of social Darwinism and white supremacy. But we need not go to the far corners of the earth to find tragic examples of the exploitation of native peoples. The litany of atrocities committed against Native Americans in the name of progress and Manifest Destiny date back to the earliest European settlements. The massacre of the Pequot in Connecticut in 1637 and the massacre of the Sioux at Wounded Knee in 1890 are just two examples from our own history.

In recent years, the most dramatic examples of the degradation of indigenous peoples has come from Brazil, where Native Brazilians are being swept away by the relentless frontier of colonialism and economic development. To illustrate, during the 1960s an Indian village in Brazil was attacked by a gang of gunslingers allegedly hired by a large Brazilian corporation that wanted the Indians off the land. Davis (1977: 79–80) described the "Massacre at Parallel Eleven" in which the hired hit men attempted to wipe out the village and its inhabitants by throwing dynamite from a low-flying airplane. During the 1970s, the threats to indigenous peoples, while not quite so blatantly genocidal, were no less devastating. By building roads through the Amazonian frontier, the Brazilian government has introduced such diseases as influenza and the measles to the indigenous peoples of the region. By the 1990s, tens of thousands of gold prospectors had invaded the territory of the Yanomamo, extracted millions of dollars worth of gold from the land, and left the Yanomamo ravaged by disease. In a feeble attempt to protect the indigenous Yanomamo, the Brazilian government ordered the destruction of 110 airstrips build on Yanomamo land by the miners. The miners circumvented the government efforts to destroy their airstrips by using helicopters (Brooke, 1990), an indication of just how difficult it is to protect indigenous peoples from the onslaught of the industrial world.

Anthropologists have not only been documenting the demise of indigenous peoples, but many have also been using their specialized knowledge to help these endangered cultures survive. In one of the most urgent forms of applied anthropology, a number of anthropologists in recent years have contributed to the efforts of Cultural Survival, Inc., a nonprofit organization that supports projects on five continents designed to help indigenous peoples survive the changes brought about by contact with industrial societies. Founded in 1972, Cultural Survival works to guarantee the land and resource rights of tribal peoples while at the same time supporting economic development projects run by the people themselves. As part of their work with Cultural Survival, anthropologists have conducted research on vital cultural issues, served as cultural brokers between the indigenous people and government officials, and published literature informing the public about the urgency of these survival issues. Given the ever-increasing number of indigenous populations that are facing cultural extinction—including the San of Southern Africa, the Sherpas of Nepal, and the Kurds in the Middle East—it is likely that anthropologists will continue to apply their expertise to help these people avoid cultural genocide.

Concern over the demise of indigenous peoples goes beyond humanitarian concerns. We should also consider that these indigenous people have knowledge that may help the human species, as a whole, to survive. Ecological, biological, and cultural diversity have long been the keys to the success of our species. Biological anthropologists are concerned that if indigenous populations become extinct, the genetic variability of the human species will decrease, perhaps leaving us more vulnerable to the selective forces of new diseases and other factors of which we are not yet aware. As Barry Bogin noted in an article entitled "The Extinction of *Homos sapiens*," "Human biocultural diversity provides for genetic, technological, social, and ideological alternatives that may be used to solve small problems and avoid the large problems that threaten the life of our species." This reservoir becomes even more important as environmental degradation increases, rapidly changing the niche to which humans are now adapted. If we do not have variability in our gene and knowledge pools, we may not be able to respond (or adapt to) the changes our technology is now bringing about in this niche.

## Greater Utilization of Anthropological Knowledge

This text in anthropology has been written with an applied perspective. Since the overwhelming majority of introductory students will follow a variety of career patterns, this text has been designed to demonstrate how the insights from anthropology can be used by people from a number of professions. The text has illustrated how architects, law enforcement officials, businesspersons, medical personnel, educators, foreign aid personnel, court officials, family planners, and others can use anthropological knowledge to solve problems. For example, many deaths in today's world are the result of social and behavioral causes. These include dietary and other cancers linked to life-style, chronic degenerative diseases, and AIDS, all of which must be understood not only from biomedical perspectives but from socio-cultural perspectives as well. Biological anthropologists argue that most of our biochemical and physiological traits result from adaptation to life-styles and environments very different from the ones in which most people live today. Delineating the differences and understanding the environments for which we are best adapted can lead to suggested behavioral changes that may decrease mortality. The obvious link between sexual behavior and most cases of AIDS reminds us that there is a socio-cultural dimension to many of the diseases that affect us today. Without taking these factors into consideration, there is little hope for being able to control the transmission and incidence of AIDS and other as-yet-unknown diseases.

While this applied perspective has demonstrated how anthropology has contributed to the solution of societal problems, there remains a great deal to be done to increase the extent to which anthropological knowledge can actually be utilized by policy and decision makers. It is one thing to point out the potential uses of anthropological information, but it is quite another to actually use that information to make a difference in the quality of our lives.

As applied anthropology continues to become more prominent, more and more anthropologists, with an eye toward practical concerns, are seeking new strategies for ensuring that anthropological insights will have an impact on decision making into the twenty-first century. It is no longer enough for applied anthropologists to simply conduct their research and report their findings. According to Rylko-Bauer, van Willigen, and McElroy (1989), applied anthropologists also need to develop a comprehensive utilization strategy that will maximize the likelihood that the findings will be used by policymakers. Such a strategy, they suggest, should include the following elements:

1. Collaboration in the research process between applied anthropologists and potential users will increase the chances that findings will be used, because it "demystifies" the research, provides opportunities for valuable feedback, and increases their commitment to the research.
2. Applied anthropologists must become familiar with the organizations sponsoring their research. Specifically, they need to be clear about the organization's goals and philosophy, who are the relevant people in the decision-making chain of command, and what is the normal decision-making process.
3. Applied anthropologists must be sufficiently knowledgeable about the community under study to be able to identify possible sources of resistance to using the findings.
4. Since policy makers frequently need cultural infor-

mation quickly, applied anthropologists need to develop more time-efficient methods if they are to have their findings utilized.

Thus, applied anthropologists are becoming more astute in structuring their research with an eye toward utilization, a trend that will, no doubt, continue into the future.

In addition to developing societies for the utilization of applied research findings, there is an enormous potential for the use of already existing anthropological data. As we continue to experience a revolution in communication and transportation, all peoples of the world are being thrown together with increasing frequency. Businesspersons, diplomats, educators, technical assistance personnel, missionaries, scholars, and citizen-tourists are traveling throughout the world in greater numbers than ever before. Unhappily, advances in our understanding of other cultures has not kept pace with the advances in communications and transportation technology. Thus, a growing number of people are expected to perform their professional activities in an unfamiliar cultural environment. But, this need not be the case. For years cultural anthropologists have collected enormous quantities of data on the various cultures of the world. While cultural data exists on most peoples of the world, it is not always accessible or understandable by people who are not anthropologists. The great bulk of cultural data are hidden away in obscure anthropological journals and written in language that would require a Ph.D. in anthropology to comprehend. Perhaps one of the greatest challenges facing anthropologists as they approach the twenty-first century is to become involved in a process that will make their already existing data available and usable to nonanthropologists. In short, anthropologists must themselves become (or train others to become) cultural brokers who translate anthropological findings into terms that can be used by others to cope more effectively with the cultural environments in which they find themselves.

◆　◆　◆

## The Four-Field Approach Revisited

One issue that the discipline has wrestled with throughout the present century is the question of the four-field (or holistic) approach to the study of humans. From its nineteenth-century beginning as a scientific discipline, anthropology has defined itself by including the subspecialties of physical anthropology, archaeology,

linguistics, and cultural anthropology. In 1902, the founders of the American Anthropological Association (40 percent of whom were cultural anthropologists; the other 60 percent were equally divided among the other three subspecialties) were so committed to the four-field approach that subfields were not even mentioned in the bylaws. But, as anthropology matured during the present century, it also became increasingly more specialized, which has led many anthropologists to identify more closely with members of their own subspecialty (e.g., archaeologists) rather than as general anthropologists. This trend toward specialization and separatism has for years raised the question of the extent to which the four-field (holistic) approach to anthropology is myth or reality.

Despite the continuing debate, the AAA has reaffirmed the four-field perspective in each of its major reorganizations in 1946, 1968, 1983, and 1993. While there is certainly no consensus among today's anthropologists, it is safe to say that the majority of anthropologists continue to adhere to the principle of an integrated (four-field) approach to the study of humans. This is not to suggest that all four fields are equally represented in anthropology departments. At the present time—as well as for most of the century—cultural anthropology is the most widely represented subfield, while anthropological linguistics is the least represented. Nor do today's Ph.D. students in anthropology receive equal amounts of training in all four areas. Nevertheless, anthropology, among all academic disciplines, is the only one that "studies human beings simultaneously as biological species and cultural beings using a broadly comparative approach across species, across cultures, through history, through prehistory, and through paleohistory" (Sue Parker, *Anthropology Newsletter,* Jan. 1993:3). And while most anthropologists today are specialists in one area or another, they almost universally acknowledge the contributions made by researchers in the other three to their own research. In summarizing the debate on the utility of the four-field approach, Givens and Skomal (1992: 17) comment,

In 1992, the four field approach still keeps us honest. No matter what our research topic, colleagues in each of the other subdisciplines are never too shy to tell us, "There's a biological (or linguistic or archaeological or sociocultural) point you should consider."

If anthropology—at least as we now know it—is to have a future, it will need to continually reaffirm its holistic perspective. If, as some have predicted, the four subfields of anthropology were to split apart, anthropology would lose its reason for being. Without the unified discipline of anthropology, each of the subfields would have little support for maintaining its separate existence. In all likelihood, physical anthropology would become part of biology; cultural anthropology would merge with sociology; archaeology would link up with history and classical studies; while anthropological linguistics would become part of the wider discipline of linguistics. Moreover, the special contributions to the understanding of humans arising from the interaction of all four subfields would cease to exist.

# Glossary

**acclimatization** short-term physiological adjustments such as those which take place when a person goes temporarily to high altitudes.

**acculturation** a specific form of cultural diffusion which involves a subordinate culture adopting many of the culture traits of a more powerful culture.

**acephalous society** a society without a political head such as a president, chief, king, etc.

**achieved status** the status an individual acquires during the course of her/his lifetime.

**Adapidae** family of Eocene lemur-like primates.

**adaptive radiation** the process by which several species evolve from a single ancestral species in a relatively short period of time.

**affinal relatives** kinship ties formed through marriage (i.e., in-laws).

**age grade** permanent age categories in a society through which people pass during the course of a lifetime.

**age set** a group of people roughly the same age who pass through various age grade together.

**alleles** alternative forms of a gene; for example, the gene for ABO blood type has three alleles, A, B, and O.

**ambilineal descent** a form of descent that affiliates a person to a kin group through either the male or the female line.

**ambilocal residence** the practice of a newly married couple taking up residence with either the husband's or the wife's parents.

**amino acids** organic compounds which are the building blocks of proteins; there are 20 amino acids in living forms.

**anagenesis** evolution in an unbranching lineage; for example, the depiction of the evolution of *Homo sapiens* from *Homo erectus* is one of anagenesis.

**analogies** characteristics that are similar in function or structure, but are not the result of inheritance from a common ancestor; examples are bird wings and butterfly wings.

**Anasazi** prehistoric cultures of the Four Corners Region (northeast Arizona, northwest New Mexico, southwest Colorado, and southeast Utah); characterized by stone pueblos and cliff dwellings.

**anthropological linguistics** the scientific study of human communication within its socio-cultural context.

**apneas** interruptions of breathing.

**applied anthropology** the application of anthropological knowledge, theory, and methods to the solution of specific societal problems.

**arboreal** living in the trees.

**archaeobotany** study of plant remains from archaeological sites for information about diet and human use of the landscape.

**archaeology** the subfield of anthropology that focuses on the study of prehistoric and historic cultures through the excavation of material remains.

**Archaic** cultural period in North America between the end of the Paleoindian period and the beginning of sedentary, agricultural or part-agricultural societies, roughly 10,000 to 3,000 years ago; associated with the establishment of modern climates at the end of the Pleistocene.

**archaic primates** primates of the Paleocene whose relationship to modern primates is uncertain.

**arranged marriage** any marriage in which the selection of spouse is outside the control of the bride and groom.

**art** the process and products of applying skills to any activity which transforms matter, sound, and motion into forms that are considered aesthetically pleasing to people in a society.

**artifact** a portable object made by humans; one of the major categories of archaeological data.

**ascorbic acid** vitamin C; important in metabolism.

**ascribed status** the status a person has by virtue of birth.

**attribute** an observable characteristic such as the length, weight, or color of an artifact; used by archaeologists to sort and group artifacts.

**authority** the legitimate power exercised with the consent of the members of a society.

**avunculocal residence** the practice of a newly married couple taking up residence with or near the husband's mother's brother.

**balanced reciprocity** the practice of giving with the expectation that a similar gift will be given in the opposite direction either immediately or after a limited period of time.

**band** the basic unit of social organization found in foraging societies comprised of related nuclear families; particularly well suited for a nomadic way of life.

**beriberi** disease which results from deficiency of the B vitamin thiamine.

**Bering land bridge** the area of the present Bering Sea between Alaska and Siberia, revealed as dry land during the Pleistocene because of world-wide drop in sea levels; the major route of human migration into the Americas.

**binocular** the placement of the eyes on the front of the face so that the visual fields overlap.

**biostratigraphy** dating method which relies on cross-dating with animals found in other locations.

**bipedal** walking on two legs.

**bourgeoisie** a Marxian term referring to the middle class.

**brachiation** the mode of locomotion characterized by swinging arm over arm through the trees; gibbons are brachiators.

**bridewealth (bride price)** the transfer of goods from the groom's lineage to the bride's lineage to legitimize marriage.

**bride service** work or service performed for the bride's family by the groom for a specified period of time either before or after the marriage.

**Broca's area** part of the brain responsible for the motor actions of speech.

**burins** stone tools with chisel-like edges used for carving bone tools.

**cargo cult** a revitalization movement found in the southwestern Pacific that involves the idea that western goods are brought by supernatural powers.

**caste** a rigid form of social stratification in which membership is determined by birth and social mobility is nonexistent.

**chiefdom** an intermediate form of political organization in which integration is achieved through the office of chiefs.

**chromosomes** threadlike structures in the nucleus of the cell which contain the DNA sequences (genes).

**chronometric** dating methods which can be stated in years before the present; potassium-argon is a chronometric dating method.

**civilization** a term used by anthropologists to describe any society that has cities.

**cladogenesis** evolution by lineage branching; for example, the depiction of evolution of *Australopithecus robustus* and *Homo habilis* from *Australopithecus africanus* is one of cladogenesis.

**clan** a unilineal descent group comprised usually of more than ten generations consisting of members who claim a common ancestry even though they cannot trace step-by-step their exact connection to a common ancestor.

**class** a ranked group within a stratified society characterized by achieved status and considerable social mobility.

**Clovis** prehistoric culture dating to about 12,000 to 11,000 years ago, characterized by big game hunting with well-made fluted projectile points.

**codominant** when neither males nor females are dominant over the other sex; in genetics, when neither of two alleles is dominant and both are expressed in the phenotype (example is the genotype AB which is expressed as the AB blood type).

**communal cults** those societies with groups of ordinary people who conduct religious ceremonies for the wellbeing of the total community.

**conflict explanation** kind of theory explaining the development of state societies that emphasizes competition among different groups in the community as an important cause (see "managerial explanation").

**consanguineal relatives** one's biological or blood relatives.

**cretinism** mental retardation resulting from insufficient dietary intake of iodine during the mother's pregnancy.

**cropmarks** differences in growth of grain or other crops that reveal buried archaeological sites when viewed in aerial photographs.

**cross cousins** children of one's mother's brother or father's sister.

**cultural anthropology** the scientific study of cultural similarities and differences wherever and in whatever form they may be found.

**cultural diffusion** the spreading of a cultural trait (i.e., material object, idea, or behavior pattern) from one society to another.

**cultural relativism** the idea that cultural traits are best understood when viewed within the cultural context of which they are a part.

**cultural resources management (CRM)** archaeology done to identify, evaluate, and sometimes excavate sites before construction of roads, dams, etc.; a result of preservation and environmental protection legislation.

**cultural universal** those general cultural traits found in all societies of the world.

**culture shock** a psychological disorientation experienced when attempting to operate in a radically different cultural environment.

**cuneiform** the world's first writing system, used in southern Mesopotamia starting about 5000 years ago.

**dendrochronology** a dating method, based on counting annual growth rings in wood samples, that can potentially provide a date to a single year.

**deoxyribonucleic acid (DNA)** the nucleic acid which forms the genetic code and is responsible for the synthesis of proteins.

**dependent variable** a variable that is affected by the independent variable.

**descent** tracing one's kinship connections back through a number of generations.

**descriptive linguistics** that branch of anthropological linguistics that studies how languages are structured.

**diffusion** see cultural diffusion.

**diglossia** the situation in which two forms of the same language are spoken by people in the same language community depending on the social situation.

**diploid** the full chromosome complement in a cell (46 in humans).

**displacement** the ability that humans have to talk about things that are remote in time and space.

**division of labor** the set of rules found in all societies dictating how the day to day tasks are assigned to the various members of a society.

**domestication** the result of human manipulation of plant and animal species such that genetic changes occur in the species that improve human exploitation of the species; the basis for intensive agriculture.

**dominant** the genetic trait that is manifested in its physical form.

**double descent** a system of descent in which individuals receive some rights and obligations from the father's side of the family and others from the mother's side.

**dysfunction** the notion that some cultural traits can cause stress or imbalance within a cultural system.

**ecclesiastical cults** highly complex religious systems consisting of full time priest.

**ecofact** remains of natural things, such as bones, seeds, or wood, that have been used by humans in the past and become incorporated in an archaeological site; one of the major categories of archaeological data.

**egalitarian society** a society which recognizes few differences in status, wealth or power.

**emic** a perspective in ethnography that uses the concepts and categories that are relevant and meaningful to the culture under analysis.

**encephalization quotient** the ratio of brain size to body size; primates have high encephalization quotients relative to other mammals.

**enculturation** the process by which human infants learn their culture.

**endogamy** a rule requiring marriage within a specified social or kinship group.

**estrus** the period of time during which a female mammal is sexually receptive; corresponds with the period during which ovulation occurs.

**ethnocentrism** the practice of viewing the customs of other societies in terms of one's own; the opposite of cultural relativism.

**ethnography** the anthropological description of a particular contemporary culture by means of direct fieldwork.

**ethnolinguistics** that branch of anthropology that studies the relationship between language and culture.

**ethnology** the comparative study of cultural differences and similarities.

**ethnomusciology** the study of music in cross cultural perspective.

**ethnoscience** an approach to the study of culture that attempts to describe a culture in terms of how it is perceived, ordered and categoried by the members of that culture rather than by the anthropologist.

**etic** a perspective in ethnography that uses the concepts and categories of the anthropologist's culture to describe another culture.

**exogamy** a rule requiring the marriage outside of one's own social/kinship group.

**extended family** a family form which includes two or more related nuclear families.

**feature** object, such as a hearth or a pit, made by humans but not portable; one of the major categories of archaeological data.

**fictive kinship** relationships between individuals recognizing kinship obligations but which are not based on either consanguineal or affinal ties.

**fission tracks** lines left behind in rock when the radioactive element uranium 238 decays.

**fitness** in the evolutionary sense, reproductive success.

**folivores** species that obtain more than 50% of their food from leaves (foliage); colobus monkeys are folivores.

**folktales** traditional stories found in a culture, generally transmitted orally, which may or may not be based on fact.

**foraging** a subsistence adaptation in which humans hunt, fish, collect, and gather wild animals and plants for food.

**foramen magnum** the hole at the base of the skull through which the spinal cord passes.

**founder effect** occurs when one or more genes that were present in the original population may, by chance, not be present in a migrant population.

**frugivores** species that obtain more than 50% of their food from fruits; gibbons are frugivores.

**function** the contribution that a particular cultural trait makes to the longevity of the total culture.

**gametes** the sex cells, eggs and sperm.

**gene flow** movement of genes across populations due to migration.

**generalized** exhibiting traits which are adaptable in several environments; see specialized.

**generalized reciprocity** the practice of giving a gift with an expected return.

**genes** portions of DNA responsible for the synthesis of a sequence of amino acids which, in turn, determine a trait.

**genetic drift** changes in the gene pool of a population due to sampling error (chance) resulting from small population size.

**genotype** the genetic combination present in a living form.

**geoarchaeologist** a specialist who studies soils, sediments, and other geological features in and around archaeological sites.

**glyphs** the pictorial script used by the Maya for their writing and calendar system.

**goiter** swelling of the thyroid gland (located in the neck) resulting from insufficient intake of iodine.

**grammar** the systematic ways that sounds are combined in any given language to send and receive meaningful utterances.

**graphic art** those forms of art such as painting and drawing.

**grid** a system of squares laid out on an archaeological site to allow horizontal control and accurate record-keeping.

**gummivores** species that obtain more than 50% of their food from tree saps and gums; marmosets are gummivores.

**half life** the time period in which one half of a radioactive element will have decayed.

**haploid** half of the normal genetic complement of a species, located in the gametes (egg and sperm).

**Harris lines** growth interruption lines due to malnutrition or illness; seen in X-rays of arm and leg bones.

**heterodontism** having different kinds of teeth (incisors, canines, premolars and molars); a homologous characteristic shared by all members of the class Mammalia.

**heterozygous** inheritance of two different alleles for a gene.

**historical linguistics** the study of how languages change over time.

**Hohokam** prehistoric culture of southern Arizona, dating from about 2000 years ago until about 500 years ago; characterized by irrigation agriculture and important contacts with Mexico.

**holism** a perspective in anthropology which attempts to study a culture by looking at all parts of the system and how those parts are interrelated.

**homoiothermy** ability to maintain a constant body temperature; a homologous characteristic shared by all members of the class Mammalia.

**homologies** characteristics which are shared by species as a result of descent from a common ancestor; a bird's wing and a bat's wing are homologies.

**homozygous** inheritance of the same alleles for a gene.

**Hopewell** archaeological complex from Ohio and Illinois, dating to about 2000 years ago; characterized by burial mounds and graves accompanied by artifacts made of imported materials such as copper and marine shells.

**horticulture** a form of small scale crop cultivation characterized by the use of simple technology and the absence of irrigation.

**human relations area files (HRAF)** the world's largest anthropological data retrieval system used to test cross cultural hypotheses.

**hydraulic theory** Karl Wittfogel's theory that the needs of irrigation systems were the major cause of the development of state society in Sumer; a kind of managerial explanation.

**hyoid bone** bone at the base of the neck which supports the tongue muscles.

**ice-free corridor** the region just east of the Rocky Mountains in Canada which was periodically free of glaciers during the Pleistocene and is proposed as the route that migrating peoples took from the Bering land bridge region into the rest of the Americas.

**ilium** the blade of the hip bone.

**incest** the prohibition of sexual intimacy between people defined as close relatives.

**inclusive fitness** the fitness (reproductive success) measured by all of one's genes present in a population.

**independent variable** the variable that can cause change in other variables.

**individualistic cults** the least complex form of religious organization in which each person is his or her own religious specialist.

**informant** a person who provides information about his/her culture to the ethnographic fieldworker.

**innovation** the process of adopting a new thing, idea, or behavior pattern into a culture.

**insectivores** species that obtain more than 50% of their food from insects; tarsiers are insectivores.

**invention** any new thing, idea, or way of behaving that emerges from within a society.

**ischium** the bone humans sit on.

**jati** local sub-castes found in Hindu India.

**kindred** all of the relatives a person recognizes in a bilateral kinship system.

**kiva** subterranean rooms, often round, in Anasazi archaeological sites that were used for ritual purposes; kivas exist today in modern southwestern pueblos.

**kula ring** a form of reciprocal trading found among the Trobriand Islanders involving the use of white shell armbands and red shell bracelets.

**law of independent assortment** Mendel's law that genes responsible for one trait are passed down to the next generation independent of genes responsible for other traits.

**law of segregation** Mendel's law that genes are inherited in pairs, one from each parent.

**levirate** the practice of a man marrying the widow of a deceased brother.

**lineage** a unilineal descent group whose members can trace their line of descent to a common ancestor.

**linked changes** those changes brought about in a culture when other (interconnected) parts of that same culture undergo change.

**locomotion** the way in which an animal moves.

**managerial explanation** kind of theory explaining the development of state societies that emphasizes the organization needed to solve a community problem (such as defense or irrigation) as the major cause (see "conflict explanation").

**marginal people** those individuals who are not in the mainstream of their society.

**matriarchy** a society ruled by females.

**matrifocal** the female core of the social group.

**matrilineal descent** a form of descent whereby people trace their primary kin connections through their mothers.

**matrilocal residence** the practice of a newly married couple living with the wife's family.

**mechanical solidarity** a type of social integration based on mutuality of interests found in those societies with little division of labor.

**megafauna** large animals, including mammoth, mastodon, and large forms of bison, that were major prey of hunters during the Paleoindian period; they became extinct by 10,000 years ago.

**meiosis** the process by which sex cells reproduce themselves so that the chromosome complement is reduced by half.

**menarche** first menstruation.

**menopause** last menstruation.

**mesolithic** the period between the end of the Paleolithic and the Neolithic.

**microliths** small tools, characteristic of the mesolithic.

**Mississippian** cultural period in the valleys of the Mississippi River, its major tributaries, and the southeastern United States, beginning about 1000 years ago; characterized by the development of chiefdom societies in the area.

**mitosis** the process by which somatic (body) cells reproduce themselves with the exact same chromosome complement.

**mobiliary art** transportable art, such as figurines.

**modernization** the process of social change whereby traditional societies take on the characteristics of more industrialized societies.

**moiety** one of two complementary descent groups in a society.

**monogamy** the marital practice of having only one wife at a time.

**monomorphic** species in which the sexes are the same in most non-genital characteristics; gibbons are monomorphic in body size.

**myth** stories that are told about the deeds that supernatural beings played in the creation of human beings and the universe itself.

**natural selection** the process by which changes in gene frequencies occur as a result of differential reproduction and differential survival.

**Neolithic package** the presence of grinding stones, sedentary occupation, domesticated foods, and pottery which mark the full development of the Neolithic.

**neolithic period** that archaeological period, characterized by the domestication of plants and animals, beginning in the middle east approximately 10,000 years ago.

**Neolithic Revolution** term coined by V. Gordon Childe to label the major transformation of human culture from depending on foraging to depending on agriculture.

**neolocal residence** the practice of newlyweds taking up a new residence in a place independent from either the husband's or the wife's family.

**niche** the specific environment in which a species lives.

**nomadism** a lifestyle involving the periodic movement of human populations in search of either food or pasture for livestock.

**nonverbal communication** the various means by which humans send and receive messages without using words (e.g., gestures, facial expressions, touching, etc.).

**nouveau riche** people with newly acquired wealth.

**nuclear family** the most basic family unit composed of wife, husband, and children.

**nucleotides** organic compounds which are the building blocks of DNA (guanine, cytosine, adenine, thymine) and RNA (guanine, cytosine, adenine, uracil).

**oath** the practice of having a god bear witness to the truth of what a person says.

**olfaction** the sense of smell; chemical communication.

**omnivores** species that obtain their food from a variety of sources; no one source forms as much as 50% of the diet; humans are omnivores.

**Omomyidae** an Eocene primate family which may be ancestral to humans and other apes.

**ordeal** a painful, and possibly life-threatening, test inflicted on someone suspected of a wrong-doing.

**organic analogy** a way of describing the integrated nature of a culture by comparing the parts of a culture to the parts of a living organism such as a human body.

**organic solidarity** a type of social integration based on mutual interdependence found in those societies with relatively elaborate division of labor.

**osteoporosis** demineralization of bones which often occurs in women after menopause.

**oxytocin** a hormone, synthesized in the anterior pituitary, which is responsible for milk ejection, uterine contractions, and maternal behavior in mammals.

**paleoanthropology** the study of fossilized human ancestors.

**Paleoindian** the earliest well-documented prehistoric cultures in North America, dating from about 12,000 to 10,000 years ago. The best-known is the Clovis archaeological complex.

**paleomagnetism** a dating technique based on the reversals of the magnetic poles.

**paleontology** that specialized branch of physical anthropology that analyzes the emergence and subsequent evolution of human physiology.

**paleoprimatology** the study of fossilized primate ancestors.

**palynologist** a specialist who studies microscopic pollen to determine past vegetation and climate.

**parallel cousins** children of one's mother's sister or father's brother.

**Parapithecidae** an Oligocene family of monkey-like primates.

**participant observation** a fieldwork method in which the cultural anthropologist lives with the people under study and observes their everyday activities.

**particulate theory of inheritance** Mendel's theory that characteristics are passed from one generation to the next through discrete particles (genes) that retain their ability to be expressed, even though they may not appear in every generation.

**pastoralism** a food getting strategy based on animal husbandry found in those regions of the world which are generally unsuited for agriculture.

**patrilineal descent** a form of descent whereby people trace their primary kin relationships through their fathers.

**patrilocal residence** the practice of a newly married couple living with the husband's family.

**perineal** the area from the anus to the vagina; becomes swollen and red in baboon and chimpanzee females when they are in estrus.

**phenetic** classification system based on physical similarities among organisms.

**phenotype** the physical manifestation of the genotype.

**pheromones** chemical substances used for communication by some species of animals.

**phratry** a unilineal descent group comprised of a number of related clans.

**phyletic** classification system based on evolutionary relationships among organisms.

**phyletic gradualism** the process of evolution characterized by gradual gene substitutions through time.

**physical anthropology (biological anthropology)** that subfield of anthropology that studies both human biological evolution as well as contemporary racial variations among peoples of the world.

**plastic arts** those forms of art such as sculpture, carving, pottery and weaving.

**plesiadapiforms** archaic primates of the Paleocene; some say these are not primates but are related to bats.

**polyandry** the marriage of a woman to two or more men at the same time; in animals, the situation in which a female has two mates.

**polygenic** traits determined by several genes.

**polygyny** the marriage of a man to two or more women at the same time.

**post partum sex taboo** the prohibition of a woman from having sexual intercourse for a specified period of time following the birth of a child.

**potassium-argon** a dating method which relies on the rate of decay of the radioactive element potassium 40 to argon gas.

**potlatch** a form of competitive giveaway found among the Northwest Coast American Indians which serves as a mechanism for both achieving social status and distributing goods.

**power** the capacity to produce intended effects on oneself, other people, social situations, or the environment.

**prehensility** the ability to grasp with fingers, toes, or tail.

**prestige** social honor or respect within a society.

**primatology** the study of nonhuman primates in their natural environments.

**primitive** a derogatory term used to describe small-scale, preliterate, and technologically simple societies.

**Propliopithecidae** an Oligocene primate family.

**provenience** the exact location of an artifact, ecofact, or feature from an archaeological site.

**proxemic analysis** the study of how people in different cultures use space.

**psychic unity** a concept popular among some 19th century anthropologists that assumed that all people when operating under similar circumstances will think and behave in similar ways.

**pubic bone** the bone above the genitals.

**punctuated equilibrium** the process of evolution characterized by long periods of stability (equilibrium) punctuated by brief periods of rapid change.

**quadrupedal** walking on four limbs.

**race** a subgroup of human population that shares a greater number of physical traits with one another than they do with those of other subgroups.

**radiocarbon dating** widely used dating method based on the regular decay of radioactive carbon in all living things; provides a date range, not an exact date to the year.

**ranked society** those societies having unequal access to prestige and status but not unequal access to wealth and power.

**raptorial bird** symbolic motif of a bird of prey found on ceremonial items in Hopewell and Mississippian sites.

**rebellion** an attempt within a society to disrupt the status quo and redistribute the power and resources.

**recessive** the genetic trait that appears in its physical form only when two alleles for it are present.

**recombination** the reshuffling of chromosomes and genes which takes place during sexual reproduction (meiosis).

**redistribution** a form of economic exchange in which goods (and services) are given by members of a group to a central authority (such as a chief) and then distributed back to the donors, usually in the form of a feast.

**relative dating** age of an object; stated relative to another form; fluorine analysis is an example of a relative dating method.

**remote sensing** several techniques for discovering and evaluating buried archaeological sites without digging; includes aerial photography, resistivity, and magnetometry.

**revitalization movement** a religious movement designed to bring about a new way of life within a society.

**revolution** an attempt to overthrow the existing form of political organization, the principles of economic production and distribution, and the allocation of social status.

**rickets** bone deformation resulting from insufficient vitamin D.

**rite of passage** any ceremony celebrating the transition of a person from one social status to another.

**rite of solidarity** any ceremony performed for the sake of enhancing the level of social integration among a group of people.

**sacrum** the fused bones at the base of the spine.

**sanction** any means used to enforce compliance with the rules and norms of a society.

**Sapir-Whorf hypothesis** the notion that a person's language shapes her/his perceptions and view of the world.

**scurvy** disease resulting from a dietary deficiency of vitamin C.

**sedentism** living in one place all year round; usually found in agricultural or proto-agricultural societies.

**sexual dimorphism** non-genital physical differences between the sexes; for example, gorillas show extreme sexual dimorphism in size.

**sexual stratification** the ranking of people in a society according to sex.

**shaman** a religious practitioner who often utilizes trance and performs healing rituals; commonly found in foraging and horticultural societies.

**shamanistic cult** that form of religion in which part time religious specialists called shamans intervene with the deities on behalf of the clients.

**shifting cultivation (swidden, slash and burn)** a form of plant cultivation in which seeds are planted in the fertile soil prepared by cutting and burning the natural growth; relatively short periods of cultivation on the land are followed by longer periods of fallow.

**site formation processes** the different depositional and disturbance events that create archaeological sites; may include human deposit of trash, flooding, erosion, construction, animal burrowing, and many others.

**social control** mechanisms found in all societies which function to encourage people not to violate the social norms.

**social mobility** the ability of people to change their social position within the society.

**social norm** an expected form of behavior.

**social stratification** the ranking of subgroups in a society according to wealth, power, and prestige.

**sociolinguistics** a branch of anthropological linguistics which studies how language and culture are related and how language is used in different social contexts.

**sorcery** the performance of certain magical rites for the purpose of harming other people.

**sororate** the practice of a woman marrying the husband of her deceased sister.

**Southeastern Ceremonial Complex** a group of elaborate ceremonial artifacts from late Mississippian sites in the southern United States, decorated with motifs symbolic of fertility, warfare, and social status.

**specialized** exhibiting a close correspondence between a trait or a species and the environment to which it is adapted; problems may arise if the environment changes; see generalized.

**species** a population that is reproductively isolated from all other populations; members of a species can interbreed with each other and produce fertile offspring.

**state system of government** a bureaucratic, hierarchical form of government comprised of various echelons of political specialists.

**stereoscopic vision** in which the fibers from one eye are received and interpreted by both hemispheres of the brain; most primates have stereoscopic vision.

**stratigraphy** the interpretation of different layers from an archaeological site.

**structured interview** an ethnographic data gathering technique in which large numbers of respondents are asked a set of specific questions.

**Sumer** the area of southern Iraq where the world's first cities appeared about 5000 years ago.

**supernatural beliefs** a set of beliefs found in all societies that transcend the natural, observable world.

**taxonomy** a classification system.

**temple mound** rectangular, flat-topped earthen mounds found in Mississippian sites that held temples or chiefs' residences on top.

**tribal society** that type of small-scale society comprised of a number of autonomous political units sharing common linguistic and cultural features.

**typology** the process of sorting artifacts into different categories based on shared visible characteristics (see "attribute").

**unilineal descent** tracing descent through a single line (e.g., matrilineal, patrilineal) as compared to both sides (bilateral descent).

**unstructured interview** an ethnographic data gathering technique usually used in early stages of one's fieldwork in which interviewees are asked to respond to broad, open-ended questions.

**Urban Revolution** term coined by V. Gordon Childe to label the major transformation of human culture from small, relatively egalitarian villages to large, non-egalitarian social systems.

**use-wear analysis** the microscopic examination of the edges of stone tools to reveal scratches and marks left by different functions.

**varnas** caste groups in Hindu India which are associated with certain occupations.

**vertical clinging and leaping** the mode of locomotion used by tarsiers and some lemurs and lorises; the animals move by leaping from one upright branch to another.

**viviparity** giving birth to live young; a homologous characteristic shared by most members of the class Mammalia.

**wealth** the accumulation of material objects that have value within a society.

**Wernicke's area** the part of the brain responsible for comprehension of speech.

**witchcraft** an innate psychic ability to cause harm to another person.

**Woodland** cultural period in much of the eastern United States between approximately 3000 and 500 years ago; characterized by the extensive use of pottery, burial mounds in many places, and increasing reliance on agriculture.

**ziggurat** the stepped pyramid, found in early Sumerian cities, that was the foundation for the major temple.

**zooarchaeologist** a specialist who studies animal bones from archaeological sites for evidence of diet and human use of the environment.

**zygote** the result of the union of the sperm and egg; contains all the genetic material to develop into a new organism.

# Bibliography

Agarwal, Anil
  1977   Coaxing the Barren Deserts Back to Life. New Scientist 15:674–675.
Alexander, Richard. D. and Katharine M. Noonan
  1979   Concealment of Ovulation, Parental Care, and Human Social Evolution. *In* Evolutionary Biology and Human Social Behavior, Napoleon A. Chagnon and William Irons, eds. Pp. 436–453, Belmont, CA: Duxbury Press.
Amato, Ivan
  1992   From "Hunter Magic," a Pharmacopeia? Science 258:1306.
American Anthropological Association
  1942   Resolution. American Anthropologist 44:289.
Amory, Cleveland
  1969   Introduction: The 1902 Edition of the Sears, Roebuck Catalogue. New York: Bounty Books.
Anderson, David G. and J. W. Joseph
  1988   Prehistory and History Along the Upper Savannah River: Technical Synthesis of Cultural Resource Investigations, Richard B. Russell Multiple Resource Area. Atlanta, Georgia: Garrow and Associates, July.
Anderson, Richard L.
  1990   Calliope's Sisters: A Comparative Study of Philosophies of Art. Englewood Cliffs, NJ: Prentice-Hall.
Angrosino, Michael V.
  1976   The Evolution of the New Applied Anthropology. *In* Do Applied Anthropologists Apply Anthropology? Michael V. Angrosino, ed. Pp. 1–9. Athens, GA: Southern Anthropological Society.
Appell, G. N.
  1978   Ethical Dilemmas in Anthropological Inquiry: A Case Book. Waltham, MA: Crossroads Press.
Ardrey, Robert
  1968   The Territorial Imperative. New York: Atheneum.
Arensburg, B. L. Schepartz, A. Tillier, B. Vandermeersch, and Y. Rak
  1990   A Reappraisal of the Anatomical Basis for Speech in Middle Paleolithic Hominids. American Journal of Physical Anthropology 83:137–146.

Bagash, Henry H.
  1981   Confessions of a Former Cultural Relativist. Santa Barbara City College Publications. May.
Balikci, Asen
  1968   The Netsilik Eskimos: Adaptive Processes. *In* Man the Hunter. Richard B. Lee and Irven DeVore, eds. Pp. 78–82. Chicago: Aldine-Atherton.
Bamberger, Joan
  1974   The Myth of Matriarchy: Why Men Rule in Primitive Society. *In* Women, Culture and Society, Michelle Zimbalist Rosaldo and Louise Lamphere, eds. Pp. 263–280. Stanford, CA: Stanford University Press.
Bar-Yosef, Ofer and Anne Belfer-Cohen
  1992   From Foraging to Farming in the Mediterranean Levant. *In* Transitions to Agriculture in Prehistory. Anne Birgitte Gebauer and T. Douglas Price, eds. Pp. 21–48. Madison, WI: Prehistory Press.
Barinaga, M.
  1992   "African Eve" Backers Beat a Retreat. Science 255:686–687.
Barrett, Richard A.
  1984   Culture and Conduct: An Excursion in Anthropology. Belmont, CA: Wadsworth.
Beals, Alan
  1962   Gopalpur: A South Indian Village. New York: Holt, Rinehart and Winston.
Beals, Ralph L., Harry Hoijer, and Alan R. Beals
  1977   An Introduction to Anthropology. 5th edition. New York: Macmillan.
Bearder, S. K.
  1987   Lorises, Bushbabies, and Tarsiers: Diverse Societies in Solitary Foragers. *In* Primate Societies, Barbara B. Smuts, Dorothy L. Cheney, Robert M. Seyfarth, Richard W. Wrangham, and Thomas T. Struhsaker, eds. Pp. 11–24. Chicago: University of Chicago Press.
Beattie, John
  1960   Bunyoro: An African Kingdom. New York: Holt, Rinehart and Winston.
  1964   Other Cultures: Aims, Methods, and Achieve-

ments in Social Anthropology. New York: The Free Press.

Bender, Barbara
1978   Gatherer-hunter to Farmer: A Social Perspective. World Archaeology 10:204–222.

Benedict, Ruth
1934   Patterns of Culture. New York: Houghton Mifflin.
1943   Obituary of Franz Boas. Science 97:60–62.
1946   The Chrysanthemum and the Sword. Boston: Houghton Mifflin.

Bensman, Joseph, and Arthur Vidich.
1987   American Society: The Welfare State and Beyond. Rev. edition. South Hadley, MA: Bergin and Garvey.

Bernard, H. Russell
1988   Research Methods in Cultural Anthropology. Newbury Park, CA: Sage Publications.

Bentley, Gillian R.
1993   Ranging Hormones: Do Hormonal Contraceptives Ignore Human Biological Variation and Evolution? Presented at the New York Academy of Sciences Conference, Human Reproductive Ecology: Interactions of Environment, Fertility, and Behavior.

Berry, J. W.
1980   Social and Cultural Change. In Social Psychology. Handbook of Cross Cultural Psychology. Volume 5. H. C. Triandis and W. W. Lambert, eds. Boston: Allyn and Bacon.

Binford, Lewis
1968   Post-Pleistocene Adaptations. In New Perspectives in Archaeology. S. R. Binford and L. R. Binford, eds. Pp. 313–341. Chicago: Aldine.
1978   Nunamiut Ethnoarchaeology. New York: Academic Press.

Birket-Smith, K.
1959   The Eskimos. 2nd edition. London: Methuen.

Blacker, J.G.C., and P. R. Forsyth-Thompson et al.
1979   Report on the 1976 Swaziland Population Census. Volume 1. Unpublished manuscript.

Bloom, B. R. and C. J. L. Murray
1992   Tuberculosis: Commentary on a Reemergent Killer. Science 257:1055–1064.

Blunt, Peter
1980   Bureaucracy and Ethnicity in Kenya: Some Conjectures for the Eighties. Journal of Applied Behavioral Science 16(3):336–353.

Boas, Franz
1919   Correspondence: Scientists as Spies. The Nation. P. 797. December 20.
1911   Handbook of American Indian Languages. Bureau of American Ethnology. Bulletin 40.

Bodley, John
1982   Victims of Progress. 2nd edition. Palo Alto, CA: Mayfield.

Bogin, B.
1985   The Extinction of Homo sapiens. Michigan Quarterly Review, Spring.

Bohannan, Paul
1957   Justice and Judgment Among the Tiv. London: Oxford University Press.

Bohannan, Paul, and Philip Curtin
1988   Africa and Africans. Prospect Heights, IL: Waveland Press.

Bowen, Elenore Smith
1964   Return to Laughter. Garden City, NY: Doubleday.

Brady, Ivan, ed.
1983   Speaking in the Name of the Real: Freeman and Mead on Samoa (special section). American Anthropologist 85(4):908–947.

Braidwood, Robert J.
1960   The Agricultural Revolution. Scientific American 203(3):130–152.

Brain, C. K.
1981   The Hunters or the Hunted: An Introduction to African Cave Taphonomy. Chicago: Chicago University Press.

Bray, Warwick
1990   Agricultural Renascence in the High Andes. Nature 345:385.

Brewer, Jeffrey D.
1988   Traditional Land Use and Government Policy in Bima, East Sumbawa. In The Real and Imagined Role of Culture in Development: Case Studies from Indonesia. Michael R. Dove, ed. Pp. 119–135. Honolulu: Univ. of Hawaii Press.

Brooke, James
1990   Brazil Blows Up Miners' Airstrip, Pressing Its Drive to Save Indians. New York Times, May 23.

Brown, Donald E.
1991   Human Universals. New York: McGraw-Hill.

Brues, Alice M.
1977   People and Races. New York: Macmillan.

Burger, Julian
1987   Report from the Frontier: The State of the World's Indigenous Peoples. Zed Books/Cultural Survival Report 28.

Burley, Nancy
1979   The Evolution of Concealed Ovulation. The American Naturalist 114:835–858.

Burton, Michael L., and Douglas R. White
1987   Cross-Cultural Surveys Today. Annual Reviews of Anthropology (16):143–160.

Campbell, Bernard G.
1979   Mankind Emerging. 2nd edition. Boston: Little, Brown.

Cann, Rebecca, Mark Stoneking, and Alan Wilson
1987   Mitochondrial DNA and Human Evolution. Nature 325:32–36.

Carey, William
1993   Just Don't Call Him Indiana Jones. The Atlanta Constitution, January 24, 1993.
Carneiro, Robert
1970   A Theory of the Origin of the State. Science 169:733–738.
Carpenter, Edmund
1973   Eskimo Realities. New York: Holt, Rinehart and Winston.
Casagrande, Joseph B.
1960   The Southwest Project in Comparative Psycholinguistics: A Preliminary Report. In Men and Cultures: Selected Papers of the Fifth International Congress of Anthropological and Ethnological Sciences. Anthony F. C. Wallace, ed. Pp. 777–782. Philadelphia: University of Pennsylvania Press.
Cassel, John
1972   A South African Health Program. In Make Men of Them. Charles C. Hughes, ed. Pp. 302–314. Chicago: Rand McNally.
Chagnon, Napoleon A.
1983   Yanomamo: The Fierce People. 3rd edition. New York: Holt, Rinehart and Winston.
Chambers, John, ed.
1983   Black English: Educational Equity and the Law. Ann Arbor, MI: Karoma Publishers.
Chapman, Jefferson
1985   Tellico Archaeology: 12,000 Years of Native American History. Knoxville: University of Tennessee Press for the Tennessee Valley Authority.
Childe, V. Gordon
1936   Man Makes Himself. London: Watts.
1950   The Urban Revolution. Town Planning Review 21:3–17.
Chomsky, Noam
1972   Language and Mind. New York: Harcourt Brace Jovanovich.
Clark, George A., Nicholas R. Hall, George J. Armelagos, Gary A., Borkan, Manohar M. Panjabi, and F. Todd Wetzel
1986   Poor Growth Prior to Early Childhood: Decreased Health and Life-Span in the Adult. American Journal of Physical Anthropology 70:145–160.
Coe, Joffre L.
1964   The Formative Cultures of the Carolina Piedmont. Transactions, The American Philosophical Society, New Series, volume 54, part 5.
Cohen, Eugene N., and Edwin Eames
1982   Cultural Anthropology. Boston: Little, Brown.
Cohen, Mark N. and George J Armelagos, eds.
1984   Paleopathology at the Origins of Agriculture. Orlando, FL: Academic Press.
Coleman, Richard P., and Lee Rainwater
1978   Social Standing in America. New York: Basic Books.

Coles, John M.
1973   Archaeology by Experiment. New York: Scribner's.
Collins, John J.
1975   Anthropology: Culture, Society and Evolution. Englewood Cliffs, NJ: Prentice-Hall.
Condon, John, and Fathi Yousef
1975   An Introduction to Intercultural Communication. Indianapolis: Bobbs-Merrill.
Conroy, Glenn C.
1990   Primate Evolution. New York: W.W. Norton.
Council of the American Anthropological Association.
1971   Statement on Ethics: Principles of Professional Responsibility. May (as amended through November, 1976).
Counts, G. S.
1925   The Social Status of Occupations: A Problem in Vocational Guidance. School Review 33:16–27. January.
Cowan, J. Milton
1979   Linguistics at War. In The Uses of Anthropology. Walter Goldschmidt, ed. Pp. 158–168. Washington, DC: American Anthropological Association.
Crockett, Carolyn M.
1984   Family feuds. Natural History 93:30–34.
Crockett, Carolyn M. and John F. Eisenberg
1987   Howlers: Variations in Group Size and Demography. In Primate Societies, Barbara B. Smuts, Dorothy L. Cheney, Robert M. Seyfarth, Richard W. Wrangham, and Thomas T. Struhsaker, eds. Pp. 54–68. Chicago: University of Chicago Press.
Culotta, Elizabeth
1992   A New Take on Anthropoid Origins. Science 256:1516–1517.
Daniels, Denise
1983   The Evolution of Concealed Ovulation and Self-deception. Ethology and Sociobiology 4:69–87.
Davis, Kingsley, and Wilbert Moore
1945   Some Principles of Stratification. American Sociological Review 10:242–249. April.
Davis, Shelton H.
1977   Victims of the Miracle: Development and the Indians of Brazil. Cambridge: Cambridge University Press.
Day, M. H.
1986   Guide to Fossil Man. Chicago: University of Chicago Press.
Deagan, Kathleen
1983   Spanish St. Augustine. New York: Academic Press.
Deardorff, Merle
1951   The Religion of Handsome Lake. In Symposium on Local Diversity in Iroquois Culture, W.N. Fenton, ed. Washington D.C.: Bureau of American Ethnology, Bulletin 149.
Deetz, James
1977   In Small Things Forgotten. New York: Anchor Books.

Deutsch, Claudia H.
1991    Anthropologists Probe Company Cultures, The Charlotte Observer, February 24, P. 11-C.

Diamond, Stanley
1960    Introduction: The Uses of the Primitive. *In* Primitive Views of the World. Stanley Diamond, ed. Pp. v–xxix. New York: Columbia University Press.

Dickens, Roy S., Jr., H. Trawick Ward, and R. P. Stephen Davis, Jr., eds.
1987    The Siouan Project: Seasons I and II. Monograph Series No. 1. Chapel Hill, NC: Research Laboratories of Anthropology, University of North Carolina.

Dillehay, Thomas D.
1989    Monte Verde: A Late Pleistocene Settlement in Chile. Washington, D.C.: Smithsonian Institution Press.

Dorjahn, Vernon
1959    The Factor of Polygyny in African Demography. *In* Continuity and Change in African Cultures. William R. Bascom and M. J. Herskovits, eds. Chicago: University of Chicago Press.

Dove, Michael R.
1988    The Real and Imagined Role of Culture in Development: Case Studies from Indonesia. Honolulu: University of Hawaii Press.

Downs, James F.
1971    Cultures in Crisis. Beverly Hills, CA: Glenco Press.

Dundes, Alan
1965    What Is Folklore? *In* The Study of Folklore. Alan Dundes, ed. Englewood Cliffs, NJ: Prentice-Hall.

Dunnell, Robert C.
1980    Evolutionary Theory and Archaeology. *In* Advances in Archaeological Method and Theory, vol. 3. Michael B. Schiffer, ed. Pp. 35–99. New York: Academic Press.

Durkheim, Emile
1933    Division of Labor in Society (G. Simpson, trans.). New York: Macmillan.

Dyson-Hudson, Rada, and Neville Dyson-Hudson
1980    Nomadic Pastoralism. Annual Review of Anthropology 9:15–61.

Dyson-Hudson, Rada, and Eric A. Smith
1978    Human Territoriality: An Ecological Reassessment. American Anthropologist 80:21–41.

Eastman, Carol
1983    Language Planning: An Introduction. San Francisco: Chandler and Sharp.

Eaton, S. Boyd and Melvin J. Konner
1985    Paleolithic Nutrition: A Consideration of Its Nature and Current Implications. New England Journal of Mecicine 316:283–289.

Eaton, S. Boyd, Marjorie Shostak and Melvin Konner
1988    Paleolithic Prescription. Harper and Row, New York.

Edgerton, Robert B., and L. L. Langness
1974    Methods and Styles in the Study of Culture. San Francisco: Chandler.

Ellison, Peter T.
1991    Reproductive Ecology and Human Fertility. *In* Applications of Biological Anthropology to Human Affairs. C.G. N. Mascie-Taylor and G. W. Lacker, eds. Pp. 14–54. New York: Cambridge University Press.

Erasmus, Charles J.
1965    Monument Building: Some Field Experiments. Southwestern Journal of Anthropology 21:277–301.

Erickson, Clark
1990    Raised Field Archaeology in the Lake Titicaca Basin. Expedition 30, 3:8–16.

Ervin-Tripp, Susan
1964    An Analysis of the Interaction of Language, Topic, and Listener. American Anthropologist (special publication) 66:86–102.

Esber, George S.
1977    The Study of Space in Advocacy Planning with the Tonto Apaches in Payson, Arizona. Doctoral Dissertation, University of Arizona.
1987    Designing Apache Homes with Apaches. *In* Anthropological Praxis: Translating Knowledge into Action. Robert M. Wulff and Shirley J. Fiske. Pp. 187–196. Boulder, CO: Westview Press.

Essock-Vitale, Susan and Robert M. Seyfarth
1987    Intelligence and Social Cognition. *In* Primate Societies, Barbara B. Smuts, Dorothy L. Cheney, Robert M. Seyfarth, Richard W. Wrangham, and Thomas T. Struhsaker, eds. Pp. 452–461. Chicago: University of Chicago Press.

Evans-Pritchard, E. E.
1940    The Nuer. Oxford: Oxford University Press.

Evenari, Michael et al.
1971    The Negev: The Challenge of a Desert. Cambridge: Harvard University Press.

Ewen, Charles R.
1989    Apalachee Winter. Archaeology 42 (3):37–41.

Fagan, Brian
1988    Black Day at Slack Farm. Archaeology 41 (4):15–16.

Farb, Peter
1968    How Do I Know You Mean What You Mean? Horizon 10(4):52–57.

Faris, James C.
1972    Nuba Personal Art. Toronto: University of Toronto Press.

Feldman, Douglas A.
1985    AIDS and Social Change. Human Organization 44(4):343–347.

Ferguson, Charles A.
1964    Diglossia. *In* Language in Culture and Society: A Reader in Linguistics and Anthropology. Dell Hymes, ed. Pp. 429–439. New York: Harper & Row.

Ferguson, Leland
1992    Uncommon Ground: Archaeology and Early African America, 1650–1800. Washington, D.C.: Smithsonian Institution Press.

Ferraro, Gary

1973 Tradition or Transition?: Rural and Urban Kinsman in East Africa. Urban Anthropology 2(2):214–231.
1980 Swazi Marital Patterns and Conjugal Roles: An Analysis and Policy Implications. Unpublished report submitted to USAID, Mbabane, Swaziland. May.
1990 The Cultural Dimension of International Business. Englewood Cliffs, NJ: Prentice-Hall.

Fetterman, David M.

1987 A National Ethnographic Evaluation of the Career Intern Program. *In* Anthropological Praxis: Translating Knowledge into Action. Robert M. Wulff and Shirley J. Fiske, eds. Pp. 243–252. Boulder, CO: Westview Press.
1988 A National Ethnographic Evaluation: An Executive Summary of the Ethnographic Component of the Career Intern Program Study. *In* Qualitative Approaches to Evaluation in Education: The Silent Scientific Revolution, David Fetterman, ed. Pp. 262–273. New York: Praeger.

Fisher, Helen

1982 The Sex Contract. New York: Morrow.

Fitchen, Janet F.

1988 Anthropology and Environmental Problems in the United States: The Case of Groundwater Contamination. Practicing Anthropology 10(3–4): 5+.

Fladmark, Knut

1986 Getting One's Berings. Natural History 95, 11:8–19.

Flannery, Kent V.

1968 Archaeological Systems Theory and Early Mesoamerica. *In* Anthropological Archaeology in the Americas. Betty J. Meggers, ed., Pp. 67–87. Washington, D.C.: Anthropological Society of Washington.

Folger, Tim

1992 1991—Archeology. Discover 13 (1):59–60.

Forde, Daryll

1967 Double Descent Among the Yako. *In* African Systems of Kinship and Marriage. A. R. Radcliffe-Brown and Daryll Forde, eds. Pp. 285–332. London: Oxford University Press (orig. 1950).

Fortes, M. and E. E. Evans-Pritchard

1940 African Political Systems. London: Oxford University Press.

Foster, George M.

1967 Tzintzuntzan: Mexican Peasants in a Changing World. Boston: Little Brown.
1973 Traditional Societies and Technological Change. 2nd edition. New York: Harper & Row.

Fox, Robin

1967 Kinship and Marriage. Baltimore: Penguin.

Frayer, David W., Milford H. Wolpoff, Alan G. Thorne, Fred H. Smith, and Geoffrey G. Pope

1993 Theories of Modern Human Origins: The Paleontological Test. American Anthropologist 95:14–50.

Frazer, James

1958 The Golden Bough. New York: Macmillan.

Freeman, Derek

1983 Margaret Mead and Samoa: The Making and Unmaking of an Anthropological Myth. Cambridge: Harvard University Press.

Fried, Morton H.

1967 The Evolution of Political Society: An Essay in Political Anthropology. New York: Random House.

Friedl, John and John Pfeiffer

1977 Anthropology: The Study of People. New York: Harper and Row.

Frisancho, A. R.

1985 Human Adaptation: A Functional Interpretation. Ann Arbor: U. Michigan Press.

Frisch, Rose E.

1988 Fatness and Fertility. Scientific American 258:88–95.

Garbarino, Merwyn S.

1977 Sociocultural Theory in Anthropology: A Short History. New York: Holt, Rinehart and Winston.

Gardner, R. Allen, and Beatrice T. Gardner

1969 Teaching Sign Language to a Chimpanzee. Science. Pp. 664–672. August 15.

Gearing, Frederick O., Robert McNetting, and Lisa R. Peattie, eds.

1960 Documentary History of the Fox Project. Chicago: University of Chicago Department of Anthropology.

Geertz, Clifford

1984 Distinguished Lecture: Anti Anti-Relativism. American Anthropologist 86:263–278. June.

Gero, Joan M. and Margaret W. Conkey, eds.

1991 Engendering Archaeology: Women and Prehistory. Oxford: Basil Blackwell.

Gibbons, Ann

1993 Molecular Anthropology: Geneticists Trace the DNA Trail of the First Americans. Science 259:312–313.

Girdner, Linda

1989 Custody Mediation: Taking the Knowledge Act on the Policy Road. *In* Making Our Research Useful: Case Studies in the Utilization of Anthropological Knowledge. John Van Willigen, Barbara Rylko-Bauer, and Ann McElroy, eds. Pp. 55–70. Boulder, CO: Westview.

Givens, David B. and Susan N. Skomal

1992 "The Four Fields: Myth or Reality?" Anthropology Newsletter (American Anthropological Association) 33 (7), October, p1+.

Glasser, Irene

1989 Social Policy Implications of Soup Kitchen Research. Practicing Anthropology 11(1):17–18.

Glob, P. V.

1969 The Bog People. London: Faber and Faber.

Glossow, Michael

1978 The Concept of Carrying Capacity in the Study of Cultural Process. *In* Advances in Archaeological Theory and Method. Michael Schiffler, ed. Pp. 32–48. New York: Academic Press.

Goldizen, Anne Wilson
1987 Tamarins and Marmosets: Communal Care of Offspring. *In* Primate Societies, Barbara B. Smuts, Dorothy L. Cheney, Robert M. Seyfarth, Richard W. Wrangham, and Thomas T. Struhsaker, eds. Pp. 34–43. Chicago: University of Chicago Press.

Goldschmidt, Walter
1979 Introduction: On the Interdependence Between Utility and Theory. *In* The Uses of Anthropology. Walter Goldschmidt, ed. Washington, DC: American Anthropological Association.

Goldstein, Melvyn C.
1987 When Brothers Share a Wife. Natural History 96(3):39–48.

Goodall, Jane V-L.
1971 In the Shadow of Man. Boston: Houghton Mifflin.

Goode, William J.
1963 World Revolution and Family Patterns. New York: The Free Press of Glencoe.

Goodenough, Ward H.
1956 Componential Analysis and the Study of Meaning. Language 32:195–216.

Gorman, E. Michael
1986 The AIDS Epidemic in San Francisco: Epidemiological and Anthropological Perspectives. *In* Anthropology and Epidemiology. Craig R. Janes et al., eds. Pp. 157–172. Dordrecht, Holland: D. Reidel Publishing.

Gough, Kathleen
1959 The Nayars and the Definition of Marriage. Journal of the Royal Anthropological Institute 89:23–34.

Gould, Stephen J.
1977 Ontogeny and Phylogeny. Cambridge, MA: Harvard University Press.

Gould, Stephen J. and N. Eldredge
1977 Punctuated Equilibria: The Tempo and Mode of Evolution Reconsidered. Paleobiology 3:115–151.

Gouldner, Alvin
1960 The Norm of Reciprocity: A Preliminary Statement. American Sociological Review 25:161–178.

Gouzoules, Sarah and Harold Gouzoules
1987 Kinship. *In* Primate Societies, Barbara B. Smuts, Dorothy L. Cheney, Robert M. Seyfarth, Richard W. Wrangham, and Thomas T. Struhsaker, eds. Pp. 299–305. Chicago: University of Chicago Press.

Gray, Robert F.
1960 Sonjo Brideprice and the Question of African "Wife Purchase." American Anthropologist 62:34–57.

Green, Ernestine
1984 Ethics and Values in Archaeology. The Free Press.

Greenhouse, Carol
1982 Nature is to Culture as Praying is to Suing. Journal of Legal Pluralism 20:17–35.

Greenwood, Roberta A.
1978 The Overseas Chinese at Home. Archaeology 31, 5:42–49.

Gronseth, Evangeline
1988 Anthropology in Clinical Nursing on the San Carlos Reservation. Practicing Anthropology 10(2):10–12.

Hagan, E.
1962 On the Theory of Social Change. Homewood, IL: Dorsey Press.

Hall, Edward T.
1966 The Hidden Dimension. Garden City, NY: Doubleday.

Hamada, Tomoko
1988 Working with Japanese: U.S.-Japanese Joint Venture Contract. Practicing Anthropology 10(1):4–5.

Hanna, Judith Lynne
1979 To Dance Is Human: A Theory of Nonverbal Communication. Austin: University of Texas Press.

Harner, Michael J.
1973 "The Sound of Rushing Water." *In* Hallucinogens and Shamanism, Michael J. Harner, ed. Pp. 15–27. New York: Oxford University Press.

Harris, Grace
1972 Taita Bridewealth and Affinal Relations. *In* Marriage in Tribal Society. Meyer Fortes, ed. Pp. 55–87. Cambridge: Cambridge University Press.

Harris, Marvin
1968 The Rise of Anthropological Theory. New York: Thomas Y. Crowell.
1977 Cannibals and Kings: The Origins of Culture. New York: Random House.
1979 Comments on Simoons' Questions in the Sacred Cow Controversy. Current Anthropology 20:479–482.
1991 Cultural Anthropology. 3rd edition. New York: Harper-Collins.

Harrison, G. A.
1988 Human Genetics and Variation. Part II of Human Biology, Third Edition, G. A. Harrison, J. M. Tanner, D. R. Pilbeam, and P. T. Baker, eds. Pp. 147–332. Oxford: Oxford University Press.

Hart, C.W.M., and Arnold R. Pilling
1960 The Tiwi of North Australia. New York: Holt, Rinehart and Winston.

Hart, C.W.M., Arnold Pilling, and Jane Goodale
1988 The Tiwi of North Australia. 3rd edition. New York: Holt, Rinehart and Winston.

Harvey, Paul H. and T. H. Clutton-Brock
1985 Life History Variation in Primates. Evolution 39:559–581.

Hatch, Elvin
1985 Culture. *In* The Social Science Encyclopedia. Adam Kuper and Jessica Kuper, eds. P. 178. London: Routledge and Kegan Paul.

Haury, Emil
1976 The Hohokam, Desert Farmers and Craftsmen:

Excavations at Snaketown 1964–1965. Tucson: University of Arizona Press.

Hayden, Brian
1992 Contrasting Expectations in Theories of Domestication. *In* Transitions to Agriculture in Prehistory. Anne Birgitte Gebauer and T. Douglas Price, eds. Pp. 11–20. Madison, WI: Prehistory Press.

Hecht, Robert M.
1986 Salvage Anthropology: The Redesign of a Rural Development Project in Guinea. *In* Anthropology and Rural Development in West Africa. Michael M. Horowitz and Thomas M. Painter, eds. Pp. 13–26. Boulder, CO: Westview Press.

Heller, Scott
1988 From Selling Rambo to Supermarket Studies, Anthropologists Are Finding More Non-Academic Jobs. The Chronicle of Higher Education, June 1, 1988, P. A-24.

Herskovits, Melville
1967 Dahomey: An Ancient West African Kingdom. Volume 1. Evanston: Northwestern University Press (orig. 1938).
1972 Cultural Relativism: Perspectives in Cultural Pluralism. New York: Vintage Books.

Hertzberg, H. T. E.
1975 *"Albert Damon's Contributions to Engineering Anthropology."* American Journal of Physical Anthropology, 42:455–60.

Hewlett, Barry S.
1992 Father-Child Relations. New York: Aldine de Gruyter.

Hickerson, Nancy P.
1980 Linguistic Anthropology. New York: Holt, Rinehart and Winston.

Hildebrand, P.
1981 Combining Disciplines in Rapid Appraisal: The Sondeo Approach. Agricultural Administration 8:423–432.

Hill, Carole, and Roy S. Dickens
1978 Cultural Resources: Planning and Management. Boulder, CO: Westview Press.

Hoane, Arthur J.
1978 Strategems and Values: An Analysis of Plea Bargaining in an Urban Criminal Court. PhD Dissertaton, Anthropology Department, New York University.

Hoben, Alan
1986 Assessing the Social Feasibility of a Settlement Project in North Cameroon. *In* Anthropology and Rural Development in West Africa. Michael M. Horowitz and Thomas M. Painter, eds. Pp. 167–194. Boulder, CO: Westview Press.

Hockett, C. F.
1973 Man's Place in Nature. New York: McGraw Hill.

Hodge, Robert W., Paul M. Siegel, and Peter H. Rossi
1964 Occupational Prestige in the United States, 1925–1963. American Journal of Sociology 70:286–302. November.

Hoebel, E. A.
1972 Anthropology: The Study of Man. 4th edition. New York: McGraw-Hill.

Hoffman, Carl L.
1988 The "Wild Punan" of Borneo: A Matter of Economics. *In* The Real and Imagined Role of Culture in Development. Michael R. Dove, ed. Pp. 89–118. Honolulu: University of Hawaii Press.

Holmberg, Alan R.
1971 The Role of Power in Changing Values and Institutions of Vicos. *In* Peasants, Power, and Applied Social Change: Vicos as a Model. Henry F. Dobyns, Paul Doughty, and Harold D. Lasswell, eds. Beverly Hills, CA: Sage Publications.

Horowitz, Michael M.
1986 Ideology, Policy, and Praxis in Pastoral Livestock Development. *In* Anthropology and Rural Development in West Africa. Michael M. Horowitz and Thomas M. Painter, eds. Pp. 249–272. Boulder, CO: Westview Press.

Howard, Beth
1991 Ape Apothecary: Self-prescribing Chimps Lead Researchers to Nature's Medicine Cabinet. Omni 13:30.

Hrdy, S. B.
1981 The Woman That Never Evolved. Cambridge, MA: Harvard University Press.

Husain, Tariq
1976 Use of Anthropologists in Project Appraisal by the World Bank. *In* Development from Below: Anthropologists and Development Situations. David C. Pitt, ed. Pp. 71–81. The Hague: Mouton.

Hymes, Dell
1977 Discovering Oral Performance and Measured Verse in American Indian Narrative, New Literary History 8(3):431–457.

Information Please Almanac
1991 44th edition. Boston: Houghton Mifflin.

Inkeles, Alex
1983 Exploring Individual Modernity. New York: Columbia University Press.

James, Preston E.
1966 A Geography of Man. 3rd edition. Waltham, MA: Blaisdell.

Janson, H. W.
1986 History of Art. New York and Englewood Cliffs, NJ: Harry Abrams and Prentice-Hall. (Revised by Anthony F. Janson.)

Johanson, Donald, M. Taieb, and Y. Coppens
1982 Pliocene Hominids from the Hadar Formation, Ethiopia (1973–1977): Stratigraphic, Chronological, and Paleoenvironmental Contexts, with Notes on Hominid Morphology and Systematics. American Journal of Physical Anthropology 57:373–402.

Jolly, Clifford J.
1970 The Seed Eaters: A New Model of Hominid Differentiation Based on a Baboon Analogy. Man 5:5–26.

Kaplan, David, and Robert Manners
  1986   Culture Theory. Englewood Cliffs, NJ: Prentice-Hall.
Kaplan, Maureen F. and Mel Adams
  1986   Using the Past to Protect the Future: Marking Nuclear Waste Disposal Sites. Archaeology 39, 5:51–54.
Kasarda, John D.
  1971   Economic Structure and Fertility: A Comparative Analysis. Demography 8(3):307–318.
Keefe, Susan E.
  1988   The Myth of the Declining Family: Extended Family Ties Among Urban Mexican-Americans and Anglo-Americans. In Urban Life: Readings in Urban Anthropology. 2nd edition. George Gmelch and Walter Zenner, eds. Pp. 229–239. Prospect Heights, IL: Waveland Press.
Keenan, Elinor
  1974   Norm-makers, Norm-breakers: Uses of Speech by Men and Women in a Malagasy Community. In Explorations in the Ethnography of Speaking. Richard Bauman and Joel Sherzer, eds. Pp. 125–143 London: Cambridge University Press.
Kelso, A. J. and W. R. Trevathan
  1984   Physical Anthropology, Third Edition. Englewood Cliffs, NJ: Prentice-Hall, Inc.
Kenyatta, Jomo
  1962   Facing Mount Kenya. New York: Vintage Books.
Kerr, K. A.
  1992   Huge Impact Tied to Mass Extinctions. Science 257:878–880.
Kinzey, W. G.
  1987   Monogamous Primates: A Primate Model for Human Mating Systems. In The Evolution of Human Behavior: Primate Models, W. G. Kinzey, ed. Pp. 105–114. New York: SUNY Press.
Klesert, Anthony L. and Alan S. Downer, eds.
  1990   Preservation on the Reservation: Native Americans, Native American Lands, and Archaeology. Navajo Nation Papers in Anthropology #26. Flagstaff, NM: Navajo Nation Historic Preservation Department.
Kluckhohn, Clyde
  1949   Mirror for Man: Anthropology and Modern Life. New York: Wittlesey House (McGraw-Hill).
Kluckhohn, Florence, and Fred L. Strodtbeck
  1961   Variations in Value Orientations. Evanston: Row, Peterson.
Kohls, L. Robert
  1979   Survival Kit for Overseas Living. Chicago: Intercultural Press.
Konner, Melvin J. and Carol Worthman
  1980   Nursing Frequency, Gonadal Function, and Birth Spacing among !Kung Hunter-gatherers. Science 207:788–791.
Kottak, Conrad P.
  1987   Anthropology: The Exploration of Human Diversity. 4th edition. New York: Random House.

Kramer, Cheris
  1974   Folk Linguistics: Wishy-Washy Mommy Talk. Psychology Today 8(1):82–85.
Kroeber, A. L.
  1917   The Superorganic. American Anthropologist 19(2):163–213.
Kroeber, A. L., and C. Kluckhohn
  1952   Culture: A Critical Review of Concepts and Definitions. Papers of the Peabody Museum of American Archaeology and Ethnology 47(1).
Kuper, Hilda
  1986   The Swazi: A South African Kindom. 2nd edition. New York: Holt, Rinehart and Winston.
Labov, William
  1983   Recognizing Black English in the Classroom. In Black English: Educational Equity and the Law. John Chambers, ed. Pp. 29–55. Ann Arbor, MI: Karoma Publishers.
La Fontaine, Jean
  1963   Witchcraft in Bagisu. In Witchcraft and Sorcery in East Africa. J. Middleton and E. Winter, eds. Pp. 187–220. New York: Praeger.
Laitman, J. T.
  1984   Anatomy of Human Speech. Natural History 93:20–27.
Lancaster, Jane B. and Chet S. Lancaster
  1983   Parental Investment: The Hominid Adaptation. In How Humans Adapt: A Biocultural Odyssey, D. J. Ortner, ed. Pp. 33–66. Washington, DC: Smithsonian Institution Press.
Lane, Belden C.
  1989   The Power of Myth: Lessons from Joseph Campbell. The Christian Century 106:652–654. July 5.
Lanier, Alison
  1979   Selecting and Preparing Personnel for Overseas Transfers. Personnel Journal: 160–163. March.
Leacock, Eleanor
  1963   Introduction. Ancient Society. L. H. Morgan. Pp. i–xx. New York: Meridian Books.
  1983   Ideologies of Male Dominance as Divide and Rule Politics: An Anthropologist's View. In Women's Nature. Marian Lowe and Ruth Hubbard, eds. Pp. 111–121. New York: Pergamon Press.
Lee, Richard B.
  1968   What Hunters Do for a Living, or How to Make Out on Scarce Resources. In Man the Hunter. Richard B. Lee and Irven DeVore, eds. Pp. 30–48. Chicago: Aldine-Atherton.
Lehmann, Arthur C., and James E. Myers, eds.
  1985   Magic, Witchcraft, and Religion: An Anthropological Study of the Supernatural. Palo Alto, CA: Mayfield.
Leighton, Donna Robbins
  1987   Gibbons: Territoriality and Monogamy. In Primate Societies, Barbara B. Smuts, Dorothy L. Cheney,

Robert M. Seyfarth, Richard W. Wrangham, and Thomas T. Struhsaker, eds. Pp. 135–145. Chicago: University of Chicago Press.

Leighton, Dorothea, and Clyde Kluckhohn
1948   Children of the People. Cambridge: Cambridge University Press.

Levi-Strauss, Claude
1969   The Elementary Structures of Kinship. Boston: Beacon Press.

Lewin, Roger
1989   Human Evolution: An Illustrated Introduction. Boston: Blackwell Scientific Publications.

Lewis, I. M.
1965   The Northern Pastoral Somali of the Horn. *In* Peoples of Africa. James Gibbs, ed. Pp. 319–360. New York: Holt, Rinehart and Winston.

Lewis, Oscar
1952   Urbanization Without Breakdown. Scientific Monthly 75:31–41. July.
1955   Peasant Culture in India and Mexico: A Comparative Analysis. *In* Village India: Studies in the Little Community. McKim Marriott, ed. Pp. 145–170. Chicago: University of Chicago Press.

Lewontin, R. C. and D. L. Hartl
1991   Population Genetics in Forensic DNA Typing. Science 254:1745–1750.

Link, Eugene P. and Sushila Mehta
1966   A New Goddess for an Old. *In* A Casebook of Social Change. Arthur H. Niehoff, ed. Pp. 219–224. Chicago: Aldine Book Publishers.

Linton, Ralph
1936   The Study of Man. New York: Appleton-Century-Crofts.

Llewellyn, K., and E. Adamson Hoebel
1941   The Cheyenne Way: Conflict and Case Law in Primitive Jurisprudence. Norman: University of Oklahoma Press.

Lomax, Alan, et al.
1968   Folk Song Style and Culture. Washington, DC: American Association for the Advancement of Science.

Lovejoy, Owen
1981   The Origin of Man. Science 211:341–350.

Lowie, Robert
1963   Religion in Human Life. American Anthropologist 65:532–542.

Malinowski, Bronislaw
1922   Argonauts of the Western Pacific. New York: Dutton.
1926   Crime and Custom in Savage Society. London: Kegan Paul.
1927   Sex and Repression in Savage Society. London: Kegan Paul, Trench, Trubner and Company.

Mandelbaum, David G.
1970   Society in India, Volume 1. Berkeley: University of California Press.

Marshall, Lorna
1965   The !Kung Bushmen of the Kalahari Desert. *In* Peoples of Africa. James Gibbs, ed. Pp. 243–278. New York: Holt, Rinehart and Winston.

Marshall, Mac, ed.
1979   Beliefs, Behaviors, and Alcoholic Beverages. Ann Arbor: University of Michigan Press.

Marx, Karl
1904   The Critique of Political Economy. (I. N. Stone, trans.) Chicago: International Library Publication Company (orig. 1859).
1909   (orig. 1867) Capital. (E. Unterman, Trans.). Chicago: C. H. Kerr.

Mauss, M.
1954   The Gift. (I Cunnison, trans.) New York: The Free Press.

Mayer, Peter J.
1982   Evolutionary Advantages of Menopause. Human Ecology 10:477–494.

McBryde, Isabel
1985   Who Owns the Past? Melbourne: Oxford University Press.

McClelland, D. C.
1960   The Achieving Society. New York: Van Nostrand.

McCombs, Phil
1993   The Cave Bear. The Washington Post April 18, 1993: F1.

McGee, W. J.
1895   Some Principles of Nomenclature, American Anthropologist 8: 279–286.

McGimsey, Charles R., III, and Hester A. Davis
1984   United States of America. *In* Approaches to the Archaeological Heritage: A Comparative Study of World Cultural Resources management Systems. Henry Cleere, ed. Pp. 116–124. Cambridge: Cambridge University Press.

McKenna, James J.
1986   An Anthropological Perspective on the Sudden Infant Death Syndrome (SIDS): The Role of Parental Breathing Cues and Speech Breathing Adaptations. Medical Anthropology 10:9–92.
1990   Evolution and the Sudden Infant Death Syndrome (SIDS). Part III: Infant Arousal and Parent-Infant Co-Sleeping. Human Nature 1:291–330.

McKenzie, Joan L., and Noel J. Chrisman
1977   Healing Herbs, Gods, and Magic: Folk Health Beliefs Among Filipino-Americans. American Journal of Nursing 77(5):326–329.

Mead, Margaret
1928   Coming of Age in Samoa. New York: Morrow.
1935   Sex and Temperament in Three Primitive Societies. New York: Morrow.
1956   New Lives for Old. New York: Morrow.

Meek, Charles K.
1972   Ibo Law. *In* Readings in Anthropology. J. D. Jennings and E. A. Hoebel, eds. New York: McGraw-Hill.

Mehrabian, Albert
  1981  Silent Messages. 2nd edition. Belmont, CA: Wadsworth.
Meltzer, David
  1989  Why Don't We Know When The First People Came to North America? American Antiquity 54: 471–490.
Mendonsa, Eugene
  1985  Characteristics of Sisala Diviners. *In* Magic, Witchcraft, and Religion: An Anthropological Study of the Supernatural. Arthur C. Lehmann and James E. Myers, eds. Pp. 214–224. Palo Alto, CA: Mayfield.
Merton, Robert K.
  1957  Social Theory and Social Structure. Glencoe, IL: The Free Press.
Meyer, Karl
  1973  The Plundered Past. New York: Atheneum.
Middleton, John
  1965  The Lugbara of Uganda. New York: Holt, Rinehart and Winston.
Middleton, John, and Greet Kershaw
  1965  The Kikuyu and Kamba of Kenya. London: International African Institute.
Middleton, John, and David Tait, eds.
  1958  Tribes Without Rulers: Studies in African Segmentary Systems. London: Routledge and Kegan Paul.
Miller, Annetta, Bruce Shenitz, and Lourdes Rosado
  1990  You are What You Buy, Newsweek, June 4, 1990. Pp. 59–60.
Mills, George
  1957  Art: An Introduction to Qualitative Anthropology. Journal of Aesthetics and Art Criticism 16(1):1–17.
Miner, Horace
  1953  The Primitive City of Timbuctoo. Philadelphia: American Philosophical Society.
Molnar, Stephen
  1983  Human Variation: Races, Types, and Ethnic Groups. Englewood Cliffs, NJ: Prentice-Hall.
Montagu, Ashley
  1961  Neonatal and Infant Immaturity in Man. Journal of the American Medical Association 178:56–57.
  1972  Touching: The Human Significance of the Skin. New York: Harper & Row.
Moock, Joyce L.
  1978–1979  The Content and Maintenance of Social Ties Between Urban Migrants and Their Home-Based Support Groups: The Maragoli Case. African Urban Studies, No. 3 (Winter):15–32.
Moody, Edward J.
  1974  "Urban Witches" in Conformity and Conflict: Readings in Cultural Anthropology. James Spradley and David McCurdy, eds. Pp. 326–336. Boston: Little-Brown.
Moore, Lorna G. and Judith G. Regensteiner
  1983  Adaptation to High Altitude. Annual Reviews of Anthropology 12:285–304.

Morgan, L. H.
  1871  Systems of Consanguinity and Affinity of the Human Family. Washington, DC: Smithsonian Institution.
  1963  Ancient Society. New York: World (orig. 1877).
Morris, Desmond
  1988  Watch Your Body Language. The Charlotte Observer, P. 5. October 23.
Morris, Desmond, Peter Collett, Peter Marsh, and Marie O'Shaughnessy
  1979  Gestures: Their Origins and Distribution. New York: Stein and Day.
Morsbach, Helmut
  1982  Aspects of Nonverbal Communication in Japan. *In* Intercultural Communication: A Reader. 3rd edition. Larry Samovar and R. E. Porter, eds. Pp. 300–316. Belmont, CA: Wadsworth.
Murdock, George
  1945  The Common Denominator of Cultures. *In* The Science of Man in the World Crisis. Ralph Linton, ed. P. 123. New York: Columbia University Press.
  1949  Social Structure. New York: Macmillan.
  1967  Ethnographic Atlas: A Summary. Ethnology 6(2): 109–236.
  1968  The Current Status of the World's Hunting and Gathering Peoples. *In* Man the Hunter. Richard B. Lee and Irven DeVore, eds. Pp. 13–20. Chicago: Aldine-Atherton.
  1971  Outline of Cultural Materials. 4th edition. New Haven: Human Relations Area Files.
Murphy, R. F., and L. Kasdan
  1959  The Structure of Parallel Cousin Marriage. American Anthropologist 61:17–29.
Murray, Gerald F.
  1984  "The Wood Tree as a Peasant Cash-Crop: An Anthropological Strategy for the Domestication of Energy." *In* Haiti—Today and Tomorrow: An Interdisciplinary Study, Charles R. Foster and Albert Valdman, eds. Pp. 141–160. Latham, NY: University Press of America.
  1986  "Seeing the Forest While Planting the Trees: An Anthropological Approach to Agroforestry in Rural Haiti." *In* Politics, Projects, and People: Institutional Development in Haiti, Derick W. Brinkerhoff and J. Garcia-Zamor, eds. Pp. 193–226. New York: Praeger.
  1987  The Domestication of Wood in Haiti: A Case Study in Applied Evolution. *In* Anthropological Praxis. Robert Wulff and Shirley Fiske, eds. Pp. 223–240. Boulder, CO: Westview Press.
Nader, Laura (ed)
  1980  No Access to Law: Alternatives to the American Judicial System. New York: Academic Press.
Nader, Laura, and H. F. Todd, Jr.
  1978  The Disputing Process: Law in Ten Societies. New York: Columbia University Press.
Naisbitt, John
  1982  Megatrends: Ten New Directions Transforming Our Lives. New York: Warner Books.

Nash, Jesse W.
1988 Confucius and the VCR. Natural History. Pp. 28–31. May.

National Opinion Research Center
1947 Jobs and Occupations: A Popular Evaluation. Opinion News 9:3–13. September.

Nelson, H. and R. Jurmain
1991 Introduction to Physical Anthropology, Fifth Edition. St. Paul, MN: West Publishing Company.

Nettl, Bruno
1980 "Ethnomusicology: Definitions, Directions, and Problems." In Music of Many Cultures, Elizabeth May, ed. Pp. 1–9. Berkeley, CA: University of California Press.

Neu, H. C.
1992 The Crisis in Antibiotic Resistance. Science 257:1064–1073.

Nishida, Toshisada
1987 Local Traditions and Cultural Transmission. In Primate Societies, Barbara B. Smuts, Dorothy L. Cheney, Robert M. Seyfarth, Richard W. Wrangham, and Thomas T. Struhsaker, eds. Pp. 462–473. Chicago: University of Chicago Press.

Nolan, Riall W.
1986 Anthropology and the Peace Corps: Notes from a Training Program. In Anthropology and Rural Development in West Africa. Michael M. Horowitz and Thomas M. Painter, eds. Pp. 93–116. Boulder, CO: Westview Press.

O'Barr, William M.
1982 Linguistic Evidence: Language, Power, and Strategy in the Courtroom, New York: Academic Press.

Oberg, Kalervo
1960 Culture Shock: Adjustments to New Cultural Environments. Practical Anthropology. Pp. 177–182. July–August.

Oliver, Douglas
1955 A Solomon Island Society. Cambridge: Harvard University Press.

O'Meara, Tim
1990 Samoan Planters: Tradition and Economic Development in Polynesia. Fort Worth: Holt, Rinehart and Winston.

Ortner, D. J. and W. G. J. Putschar
1981 Identification of Pathological Conditions in Human Skeletal Remains. Washington, DC: Smithsonian.

Overfield, Theresa
1985 Biologic Variation in Health and Illness. Menlo Park, CA: Addison-Wesley.

Paige, K. E., and J. M. Paige
1981 The Politics of Reproductive Ritual. Berkeley/Los Angeles: University of California Press.

Painter, James
1991 Archaeology Makes Edible Impact. Christian Science Monitor October 9, 1991: 12.

Parker, Arthur C.
1913 The Code of Handsome Lake, The Seneca Prophet. Albany: New York State Museum Bulletin, No. 163.

Parker, Patricia L., and Thomas F. King
1987 Intercultural Mediation at Truk International Airport. In Anthropological Praxis. Robert Wulff and Shirley Fiske, eds. Pp. 160–173. Boulder, CO: Westview Press.

Parker, Sue
1993 "Why the Four Field Approach is Central to Our Identity." Anthropology Newsletter. (American Anthropological Association), 34 (1), January, p. 3.

Parsons, Talcott
1951 The Social System. New York: The Free Press.

Parsons, Talcott, and E. Shils
1952 Toward a General Theory of Action. Cambridge: Harvard University Press.

Partridge, William L., and Elizabeth M. Eddy
1978 The Development of Applied Anthropology in America. In Applied Anthropology in America. Elizabeth M. Eddy and William L. Partridge, eds. Pp. 3–45. New York: Columbia University Press.

Pasternak, Burton, Carol Ember, and Melvin Ember
1976 On the Conditions Favoring Extended Family Households. Journal of Anthropological Research 32(2): 109–123.

Pastron, Alan G.
1989 On Golden Mountain. Archaeology 42, 4:48–53.
1992 Opportunities in Cultural Resources Management. In Applying Anthropology: An Introductory Reader, 2nd edition. Aaron Podolefsky and Peter J. Brown, eds. Pp. 82–85. Mountain View, CA: Mayfield Publishing.

Pearsall, Deborah
1992 The Origins of Plant Cultivation in South America. In The Origins of Agriculture: An International Perspective. C. Wesley Cowan and Patty Jo Watson, eds. Pp. 173–206. Washington, D.C.: Smithsonian Institution Press.

Pelto, Pertti J.
1973 The Snowmobile Revolution: Technology and Social Change in the Arctic. Menlo Park, CA: Benjamin Cummings.

Pfeiffer, John E.
1978 The Emergence of Man. 3rd edition. New York: Harper & Row.

Polanyi, Karl
1957 The Economy as Instituted Process. In Trade and Market in the Early Empires. Karl Polanyi, Conrad Arensberg, and Harry Pearson, eds. Pp. 243–270. New York: The Free Press.

Posey, D. A.
1990 Intellectual Property Rights and Just Compensa-

tion for Indigenous Knowledge. Anthropology Today 6:13–16.

Pospisil, L.
1958 Kapauku Papuans and their Law. New Haven: Yale University Press.

Prentice, Guy
1986 Origins of Plant Domestication in the Eastern United States: Promoting the Individual in Archaeological Theory. Southeastern Archaeology 5:103–119.

Price, H. Marcus
1991 Disputing the Dead: U.S. Law on Aboriginal Remains and Grave Goods. Columbia, MO: University of Missouri Press.

Profet, Margie
1988 The Evolution of Pregnancy Sickness as Protection to the Embryo against Pleistocene Teratogens. Evolutionary Theory 8:177–190.

Prokesch, Steven
1990 Selling in Europe: Borders Fade. New York Times. May 31.

Pryor, F. L.
1986 The Adoption of Agriculture. American Anthropologist 88:879–897.

Purdum, Elizabeth D.
1985 Subculture of Deputy Court Clerks: Implications for Access and Reform. Human Organization, 44 (4): 353–359.

Queen, Stuart, R. W. Habenstein, and J. S. Quadagno
1985 The Family in Various Cultures. 5th edition. New York: Harper & Row.

Radcliffe-Brown, A. R.
1950 Introduction. *In* African Systems of Kinship and Marriage. A. R. Radcliffe-Brown and D. Forde, eds. Pp. 1–85. London: Oxford University Press.

Rasmussen, Knud
1927 Across Arctic America. New York:
1931 The Netsilik Eskimos: Social Life and Spiritual Culture. Report of the Fifth Thule Expedition, 1921–24, 8(1,2). Copenhagen: Glydendalske Boghandel.

Rathje, William L.
1978 Archaeological Ethnography . . . Because Sometimes It Is Better to Give Than to Receive. *In* Explorations in Ethnoarchaeology. Richard A. Gould, ed. Pp. 49–76. Albuquerque: University of New Mexico Press.
1989 Rubbish! The Atlantic Monthly 67 (6):99–109.

Rathje, William L., et al.
1992 The Archaeology of Contemporary Landfills. American Antiquity 57:437–447.

Raup, David M.
1986 Biological Extinction in Earth History. Science 281:1528–1533.

Richard, Alison F.
1985 Primates in Nature. New York: W. H. Freeman and Co.
1987 Malagasy Prosimians: Female Dominance. *In* Pri-

mate Societies, Barbara B. Smuts, Dorothy L. Cheney, Robert M. Seyfarth, Richard W. Wrangham, and Thomas T. Struhsaker, eds. Pp. 25–33. Chicago: University of Chicago Press.

Richards, Audry I.
1960 The Bemba—Their Country and Diet. *In* Cultures and Societies of Africa. Simon and Phoebe Ottenburg, eds. Pp. 96–109. New York: Random House.

Roberts, John M.
1967 Oaths, Autonomic Ordeals, and Power. *In* Cross Cultural Approaches: Readings in Comparative Research. Clellan S. Ford, ed. New Haven: HRAF Press.

Roberts, L.
1992 How to Sample the World's Genetic Diversity. Science 257:1204–1205.

Robinson, Richard D.
1984 Internationalization of Business: An Introduction. New York: Dryden Press.

Rodman, Peter S. and Henry M. McHenry
1980 Bioenergetics and the Origin of Human Bipedalism. American Journal of Physical Anthropology 52: 103–106.

Rodman, Peter S. and John C. Mitani
1987 Orangutans: Sexual Dimorphism in a Solitary Species. *In* Primate Societies, Barbara B. Smuts, Dorothy L. Cheney, Robert M. Seyfarth, Richard W. Wrangham, and Thomas T. Struhsaker, eds. Pp. 146–154. Chicago: University of Chicago Press.

Rogers, Everett M.
1973 Communication Strategies for Family Planning. New York: The Free Press.
1983 Diffusion of Innovations. 3rd edition. New York: The Free Press.

Rohner, Ronald P., and Evelyn C. Rohner
1970 The Kwakiutl: Indians of British Columbia. New York: Holt, Rinehart and Winston.

Rooney, James F.
1961 Group Processes Among Skid Row Winos. Quarterly Journal of Studies on Alcohol 22:444–460.

Rosaldo, Michelle Zimbalist and Louise Lamphere
1974 Introduction. *In* Women, Culture and Society. Michelle Zimbalist Rosaldo and Louise Lamphere, eds. Pp. 1–15. Stanford, CA: Stanford University Press.

Rosen, Lawrence
no date The Anthropologist as Expert Witness. Mimeographed paper on file with the Applied Anthropology Documentation Project at the University of Kentucky.

Ross, M. H.
1986 Female Political Participation. American Anthropologist 88:843–858.

Rylko-Bauer, Barbara, John Van Willigen, and Ann McElroy
1989 Strategies for Increasing the Use of Anthropological Research in the Policy Process: A Cross-Disciplinary Analysis. *In* Making Our Research Useful. John Van Wil-

ligen, Barbara Rylko-Bauer, and Ann McElroy, eds. Boulder, CO: Westview Press.

Sahlins, Marshall
1972   Stone Age Economics. Chicago: Aldine-Atherton.

Salisbury, Richard F.
1976   The Anthropologist as Societal Ombudsman. *In* Development from Below: Anthropologists and Development Situations. David C. Pitt, ed. Pp. 255–265. The Hague: Mouton.

Samovar, Larry A., and Richard E. Porter, eds.
1991   Communication Between Cultures. Belmont, CA: Wadsworth.

Samuelson, Paul A.
1976   Economics. 10th edition. New York: McGraw-Hill.

Sapir, Edward
1929   The Status of Linguistics as a Science. Language 5:207–214.

Sauer, Norman J.
1992   Forensic Anthropology and the Concept of Race: If Races Don't Exist, Why are Forensic Anthropologists So Good at Identifying Them? Social Science and Medicine 34:107–111.

Scaglion, Richard
1987   Customary Law Development in Papua New Guinea. *In* Anthropological Praxis. Robert Wulff and Shirley Fiske, eds. Pp. 98–107. Boulder, CO: Westview Press.

Schmandt-Besserat, Denise
1978   The Earliest Precursor of Writing. Scientific American 238, 6:50–59.

Schneider, Harold K.
1957   The Subsistence Role of Cattle Among the Pokot in East Africa. American Anthropologist 59:278–300.

Scrimshaw, Susan C. M.
1976   Women's Modesty: One Barrier to the Use of Family Planning Clinics in Ecuador. Monographs of the Carolina Population Center. Pp., 167–183.

Selzer, Richard
1979   Confessions of a Knife. New York: Simon and Schuster.

Serrie, Hendrick
1986   Anthropological Contributions to Business in Multicultural Contexts. In Anthropology and International Business, Henrick Serrie, ed. Pp. ix-xxx. Williamsburg, VA: Dept. of Anthropology at William and Mary.

Service, Elman R.
1966   The Hunters. Englewood Cliffs, NJ: Prentice-Hall.
1975   Origins of the State and Civilization. New York: Norton.
1978   Profiles in Ethnology. 3rd edition. New York: Harper & Row.

Shanks, Michael and Christopher Tilley
1987   Reconstructing Archaeology. Cambridge: Cambridge University Press.

Sharff, Jagna W.
1981   Free Enterprise and the Ghetto Family. Psychology Today. March.

Sheets, Payson D.
1993   Dawn of a New Stone Age in Eye Surgery. *In* Archaeology: Discovering Our Past, 2nd ed. Robert J. Sharer and Wendy Ashmore. Pp. 470–472. Mountain View, CA: Mayfield Publishing Company.

Sheflen, Albert E.
1972   Body Language and the Social Order. Englewood Cliffs, NJ: Prentice-Hall.

Shipman, Pat
1986   Scavenging or hunting in early hominids. American Anthropologist 88:27–43.

Sieber, Roy
1962   Masks as Agents of Social Control. African Studies Bulletin 5(11):8–13.

Silberman, Neil A.
1991   Pequot Country. Archaeology 44, 4:34–39.

Simon, Paul
1980   The Tongue Tied American. New York: Continuum Press.

Singer, Merrill
1985   Family Comes First: An Examination of the Social Networks of Skid Row Men. Human Organization 44(2):137–142.

Slater, Jonathan R.
1984   The Hazards of Cross-Cultural Advertising. Business America. Pp. 20–23. April 2.

Slobin, Mark and Jeff T. Titon
1984   "The Music Culture as a World of Music" *In* Worlds of Music: An Introduction to the Music of the World's Peoples, Jeff T. Titon et al, eds. Pp. 1–11. London: Collier Macmillan Publishers.

Smith, Anthony D.
1976   Social Change: Social Theory and Historical Processes. London: Longman.

Smith, Bruce D.
1987   The Independent Domestication of Indigenous Seed-Bearing Plants in Eastern North America. *In* Emergent Horticultural Economies of the Eastern Woodlands. William F. Keagan, ed. Pp. 3–48. Carbondale, IL: Southern Illinois University Press.

Smith, E. A.
1983   Anthropological Applications of Optimal Foraging Theory: A Critical Review. Current Anthropology 24:625–651.

Smuts, Barbara B.
1985   Sex and Friendship in Baboons. Hawthorne, NY: Aldine.
1987   What Are Friends for? Natural History 96:36–44.

Snow, Clyde C. and James L. Luke
1989   "The Oklahoma City Child Disappearances: Forensic Anthropology in the Identification of Skeletal Re-

mains." In Aaron Podelefsky and Peter Brown, Applying Anthropology: An Introductory Reader. Mountain View, CA: Mayfield, pp. 57–63.

Sorrenson, M.P.K.
1967   Land Reform in the Kikuyu Country. Nairobi: Oxford University Press.

Spindler, Louise S.
1984   Culture Change and Modernization. Prospect Heights, IL: Waveland Press.

Spradley, James
1970   You Owe Yourself a Drunk. Boston: Little, Brown.

Stack, Carol
1975   All Our Kin: Strategies for Survival in a Black Community. New York: Harper & Row.

Stahl, A. B.
1984   Hominid Dietary Selection before Fire. Current Anthropology 25:151–161.

Staski, Edward
1984   Just What Can a 19th Century Bottle Tell Us? Historical Archaeology 18:38–51.

Stearns, Robert D.
1986   Using Ethnography to Link School and Community in Rural Yucatan. Anthropology and Education Quarterly 17(1):6–24.

Stenning, Derrick J.
1965   The Pastoral Fulani of Northern Nigeria. In Peoples of Africa. James Gibbs, ed. Pp. 363–401. New York: Holt, Rinehart and Winston.

Stephens, William N.
1963   The Family in Cross Cultural Perspective. New York: Holt, Rinehart and Winston.

Stessin, Lawrence
1979   Culture Shock and the American Businessman Overseas. In Toward Internationalism: Readings in Cross Cultural Communication. E. C. Smith and L. F. Luce, eds. Pp. 214–225. Rowley, MA: Newbury House.

Stewart, T. D.
1979   Forensic Anthropology. In The Uses of Anthropology. Walter Goldschmidt, ed. Pp. 169–183. Washington, DC: American Anthropological Association.

Storey, Rebecca
1992   Life and Death in the Ancient City of Teotihuacan: A Modern Paleodemographic Synthesis. Tuscaloosa: University of Alabama Press.

Strier, Karen B.
1993   Menu for a Monkey. Natural History 102:34–45.

Stringer, C. B. and P. Andrews
1988   Genetics and the Fossil Evidence for the Origin of Modern Humans. Science 23:1263–1268.

Sturtevant, William
1964   "Studies in Ethnoscience." American Anthropologist, 66(3) Part 2:99–131.

Sullivan, Thomas J., and Kenrick Thompson
1990   Sociology: Concepts, Issues, and Applications. New York: Macmillan.

Sundkler, Bengt
1961   Bantu Prophets of South Africa. 2nd edition. London: Oxford University Press.

Talmon, Yohina
1964   Mate Selection in Collective Settlements. American Sociological Review 29:491–508.

Tanner, Nancy and Adriane Zihlman
1976   Women in Evolution: Part I: Innovation and Selection in Human Origins. Signs 1:585–608.

Tarde, Gabriel
1903   The Laws of Imitation (trans. by Elsie Clews Parsons). New York: Holt.

Taylor, Brian K.
1962   The Western Lacustrine Bantu. London: International African Institute.

Templeton, Alan R.
1993   The "Eve" Hypothesis: A Genetic Critique and Reanalysis. American Anthropologist 95:51–72.

Thomas, David Hurst
1989   Archaeology. 2nd ed. Ft. Worth: Holt, Rinehart and Winston.

Tiger, Lionel and Robin Fox
1971   The Imperial Animal. New York: Holt, Rinehart, and Winston.

Tischler, Henry L.
1990   Introduction to Sociology. 3rd edition. Fort Worth: Holt, Rinehart and Winston.

Toffler, Alvin
1971   Future Shock. New York: Bantam Books.
1981   The Third Wave. Toronto: Bantam Books.

Toth, Nicholas
1987   The First Technology. Scientific American 112–121.

Trevathan, Wenda
1987   Human Birth: An Evolutionary Perspective. Hawthorne, NY: Aldine de Gruyter.

Tripp, Robert
1985   Anthropology and On-Farm Research. Human Organization 44(2):114–124.

Turnbull, Colin
1965   The Mbuti Pygmies of the Congo. In Peoples of Africa. James Gibbs, ed. Pp. 281–317. New York: Holt, Rinehart and Winston.
1982   The Ritualization of Potential Conflict Between the Sexes Among the Mbuti. In Politics and History in Band Societies. Eleanor Leacock and Richard Lee, eds. Cambridge: Cambridge University Press.

Turner, Christy
1987   Telltale Teeth. Natural History 96 (1):6–10.

Tylor, Edward B.
1871   Origins of Culture. New York: Harper & Row.
1889   On a Method of Investigating the Development

of Institutions: Applied to Laws of Marriage and Descent. Journal of Royal Anthropological Institute 18: 245–269.

Ubelaker, Douglas H.
1990 Positive Identification of American Indian Skeletal Remains from Radiograph Comparison. Journal of Forensic Sciences 35:466–472.

U.S. Bureau of the Census
1990 Statistical Abstract of the United States, 1990. 110th edition. Washington, DC: U.S. Government Printing Office.

U.S. National Commission on the Causes and Prevention of Violence
1969 Justice: To Establish Justice, To Ensure Domestic Tranquility. Washington, DC: U.S. Government Printing Office.

Van Gennep, Arnold
1960 The Rites of Passage. Chicago: University of Chicago Press (orig. 1908).

Vanneman, Reeve, and L. W. Cannon
1987 The American Perception of Class. Philadelphia: Temple University Press.

Van Willigen, John
1986 Applied Anthropology: An Introduction. South Hadley, MA: Bergin and Garvey.

Van Willigen, John, Barbara Rylko-Bauer, and Ann McElroy
1989 Making Our Research Useful. Boulder, CO: Westview Press.

Vilakazi, Absolon L.
1979 A Study of Population and Development. Mbabane: Ministry of Agriculture and Cooperatives.

Voigt, Mary M.
1990 Reconstructing Neolithic Societies and Economies in the Middle East. Archaeomaterials 4:1–14.

Wagner, Gunter
1949 The Bantu of North Kavirondo. London: Published for the International African Institute by Oxford University Press.

Wallace, Anthony F. C.
1966 Religion: An Anthropological View. New York: Random House.

Watson, Patty Jo, ed.
1974 Archaeology of the Mammoth Cave Area. New York: Academic Press.

Watson, Patty Jo and Mary Kennedy
1991 The Development of Horticulture in the Eastern Woodlands of North America: Women's Role. In Engendering Archaeology: Women and Prehistory. Joan M. Gero and Margaret W. Conkey, eds. Pp. 255–275. Oxford: Basil Blackwell.

Weber, Max
1930 The Protestant Ethic and the Spirit of Capitalism. London: Unwin University Books.
1946 From Max Weber: Essays in Sociology. (Hans Gerth and C. Wright Mills, trans. and eds.) New York: Oxford University Press.
1947 The Theory of Social and Economic Organization (translated by Talcott Parsons). New York: Oxford University Press.

Whelehan, Patricia
1985 Review of Incest: A Biosocial View by Joseph Shepher (New York: Academic Press, 1983). American Anthropologist 87:677.

White, Benjamin
1973 Demand for Labor and Population Growth in Colonial Java. Human Ecology 1(3):217–236.

White, D. R., M. L. Burton, and M. M. Dow
1981 Sexual Division of Labor in African Agriculture. American Anthropologist 83:824–849.

White, Leslie
1959 The Evolution of Culture. New York: McGraw-Hill.

Whiting, John W., and Irvin L. Child
1953 Child Training and Personality: A Cross Cultural Study. New Haven: Yale University Press.

Whiting, Robert
1979 You've Gotta Have "Wa." Sports Illustrated. Pp. 60–71. September 24.

Whitman, William
1963 The San Ildefonso of New Mexico. In Acculturation in Seven American Indian Tribes. Ralph Linton, ed. Gloucester, MA: Peter Smith (orig. 1940).

Williams, Florence
1991 Don't Even Think of Parking Here! High Country News, January 27, 1992: 16.

Williams, George C. and Randolph M. Neese
1991 The Dawn of Darwinian Medicine. Quarterly Review of Biology 66:1–22.

Williams, Thomas R.
1967 Field Methods in the Study of Culture. New York: Holt, Rinehart and Winston.

Wills, W. H.
1989 Early Prehistoric Agriculture in the American Southwest. Santa Fe, NM: School of American Research.

Wilson, Douglas C. and William L. Rathje
1990 Modern Middens. Natural History May 1990: 54–58.

Wilson, E. O.
1992 The Diversity of Life. Cambridge, MA: Harvard University Press.

Wilson, Monica
1960 Nyakyusa Age Villages. In Cultures and Societies of Africa. Simon and Phoebe Ottenberg, eds. Pp. 227–236. New York: Random House.

Winkelman, M. J.
1987 Magico-Religious Practitioner Types and Socioeconomic Conditions. Behavioral Science Research 22.

Winter, Edward H.
1956 Bwamba: A Structural Functional Analysis of a

Patrilineal Society. Cambridge: Published for the East African Institute of Social Research by W. Heffer.

Wissler, Clark
1917   The American Indian: An Introduction to the Anthropology of the New World. New York: D. C. McMurtie.

Witherspoon, Gary
1977   Language and Art in the Navajo Universe. Ann Arbor: University of Michigan Press.

Wittfogel, Karl
1957   Oriental Despotism: A Comparative Study of Total Power. New Haven: Yale University Press.

Wolf, Arthur
1968   Adopt a Daughter-in-Law, Marry a Sister: A Chinese Solution to the Incest Taboo. American Anthropologist 70:864–874.

Wolf, E.
1964   Anthropology. Englewood Cliffs, NJ: Prentice-Hall.

Ya'ari, Ehud, and Ina Friedman
1991   Curses in Verses. Atlantic 267(2):22–26.

Zegura, Stephen L.
1987   Blood Test. Natural History 96 (7):6–10.

# Index

Dubs, Adolph, 401
Dundes, Alan, 474
Durkheim, Emile, 339
Dyson-Hudson, Neville, 317
Dyson-Hudson, Rada, 317

# E

Eating customs and cultural identity, 488
Eaton, Boyd, 171
Ecclesiastical cults, 453–456
Ecofacts, 174
Ecology
  cultural, 253
  and demise of Sumer, 203
  and primate group sizes, 88
  *See also* Environment; Environmental
    impact studies
Economic anthropology, 330–332
  defined, 8
Economics, 330–351
  in a caste society, 432
  of marriage, 386–390
  and religion, 442
  role of livestock in, 318–319
  and social structure, 331
Economic systems, 26–27
  cross-cultural comparisons, 331–332
  and development of written communica-
    tion, 201–202
  factors in production, 335
  *See also* Trade system
Ecuador
  family planning study in, 52–54
  farming practices study in, 282–283
Education
  and cultural understanding, 396–397
  and family size, 498–499
  and language, 306
  study of drop-outs, 54–56
Educational anthropology, defined, 10
Educational systems, 27–28
Efficiency, and language/dialect, 300
Egalitarian societies, 425–426
  band, 400
  Neolithic, 200
  tribal, 401
EGO point of reference in kinship diagrams,
    356–357
Elders, council of, 414
Elites
  and art in complex societies, 466
  and power in ancient societies, 205
Ellison, Peter, 170
Emic approach, 40, 41
  versus an etic approach, 254
Emotional function of religion, 448
Emotional gratification as a function of art,
    466–467
Empiricism, 244

Employment
  cultural context of, 428
  recruitment, and cultural values, 261
Encephalization quotient, 81
Enculturation, 20
Endogamy
  in cast systems, 428
  rules of, 380–381
Energy, surplus, and culture, 251
Environment
  adaptation to, 252–253
  carrying capacity of, 309–310
  and culture, 253
    roles of food, 316–317
  and evidence for human migration to the
    Americas, 215–216
  and food-getting strategy, 308–310
  reconstruction of, research site, 181
  *See also* Climate
Environmental change
  and cultural perception, 486
  destruction caused by agriculture,
    321–322
  responses to, 66–70
Environmental impact studies
  cultural change as part of, 496–498
  mandated, 45
Environmental Protection Agency (EPA),
    188
Epidemiology, 5
Erosion, control of, historic techniques, 211
Esber, George, 34
Eskimos, 11–12, 29, 244, 366, 425–426
  artist's role among, 469
  art of, 464
  culturally adapted technology, 308
  economic behavior of, 335
  kinship system, 365
  language of, 295–296
  Netsilik, 312–314
    dance in culture of, 473–474
  and territoriality, 333
Estrus, primate, 92, 113
Ethics
  in applied anthropology, 46–48
  and excavation, 232–234
  of medical research using animals, 98
  professional, 46
  *See also* Values
Ethnicity, and diversity within a culture, 20
Ethnoarchaeology, 181–182
  information about cultivation, 219–220
Ethnobiology, 72
Ethnobotany, 72–73
Ethnocentrism, 24–25
*Ethnographic Atlas* (Murdoch), 377
*Ethnographic Sample* (Murdoch), 383
Ethnography
  defined, 8
  evaluation of a system, 55
  mapping, 276

and housing design, 34
Ethnohistory, 181–182
Ethnolinguistics, 7
  research in, 296
Ethnology
  applied theory of, 259
  defined, 8
Ethnomusicology, concerns of, 471–472
Ethnoscience, 253–254
Ethos, documentation of, 55
Etic approach versus an emic approach, 254
Etowah, 224
Evaluator, applied anthropologist as, 39
Evanari, Michael, 210
Evaporation, from human skin, 134–135
Event analysis, 276
Evolution, 65–66
  continuation of, 168
  cultural, 238
  parallel, 242
  of primates and hominids, 102–125
  theory of, 58–73
  *See also* Mitochondrial DNA
Evolutionism, 238–242
  cultural, 240–241
  and deforestation in Haiti, 258–259
  unilinear and multilinear, 252–253
  *See also* Evolution
Excavation, 177–179
Exchange system
  bridewealth in the, 387–388
  in marriage, 378
  principle of redistribution, 342–344
  *See also* Economic systems; Trade system
Executive Order 11593, cultural resources
    management, 187
Exercise, and fertility, 170
Exogamy, rules of, 380
Expanding social alliances theory, 379–380
Experimental archaeology, 182
  examples, 183
  irrigation of deserts, 211
Expert witness, 460–461
  anthropologist as, 40, 306
Extended family, 392–393
Exterogestation, 161
Extinction, 66–67, 72
Extraneous factors, control of, 268
Eye contact as communication, 301–302,
    303
Eyes, color of, 136–137

# F

Fairbanks, Charles, 229
Family
  defined, 376–398
  primate, 86
    small groups, 87–88
  side of, and kin category, 358

structure of, 391–394
   disruption theory, 379
Family planning, study in Ecuador, 52–54
Farb, Peter, 294
Fat
   from domesticated grains and seeds, 219
   insulating layers of, 137–138
   minimum requirement for ovulation, 165
   storage of, adaptive advantage, 153
Features (material remains), 174
Feet in bipeds, 108
Feldman, Douglas, 285
Females
   infanticide, 386
   legal subordination of, 433–434
   transfer among gorillas, 93
   universality of subordination of, 433–434
Ferguson, Charles, 300
Fertile Crescent, 193–196, 199
   Sumer, 200–203
Fetterman, David, 54–55
Fictive kinship, defined, 354–355
Field guides, 274
Fieldwork, 245, 264–286
   effects on the anthropologist, 277–280
   funding of, 265
   preparation for, 265–266
   stages of, 266–270
Fire, dating of use by hominids, 112
Fisher, Helen, 92
Fission tracks, for dating obsidian, 102
Fitness, evolutionary, 65–66
Fladmark, Knut, 216
Flannery, Kent, 199
Flenniken, Jeff, 235
Flotation, 178
Folivores, 91
Folklore, 474
Folktales, 476–477. *See also* Legends
Food-getting strategies, 308–327, 324–327
   industrialized, 321–322
   *See also* Hunters and gatherers
Food-producing societies, 314–322
Foraging, 192
   in the Americas, 218
   in Natufian communities, 195
   by nuclear family groups, 391
Foramen magnum, and bipedalism, 108
Force, use of, and state systems, 404
Forde, Daryll, 363
Ford Foundation, 38
Foreign Assistance Act (1973), 45
Forensic anthropology, 14, 36
   DNA fingerprinting, 73
   identification of a skeleton, 125
   and racial identification, 147–148
   specialist in, 40
Formal education, and modernity, 493
Formalism, 331
Formative Period, Mesoamerica, 197

Fortifications in Mississippian chiefdoms, 224
Fort Jackson, 224
Fossey, Dian, 2
Fossil record, 102, 105–122
   of Australopithecines, 115–118
   of birth canal changes in *Homo* species, 115
   of cultural evolution, 112
   of *Homo sapiens*, 128–130
Foster, George, 439, 486
Founder effect on distribution of ABO alleles, 139
Four-field approach, 502–503
Fox Indian project, 44
Franchthi Cave, 175
Frazer, Sir James, 244
Free choice
   and acculturation, 485
   free will, and conformity, 20
Freeman, Derek, 250
Fried, Morton, 425
Friedl, John, 12
Friendship, among primates, 94
Frugivores, 91
Fulani (Nigeria), 333
Functional analysis, 247–248
Functionalism, 238, 245–249
   versus conflict theory, 435–436
   and social stratification, 434–435
   structural, 246–247
Functional unity, 247–248
Functions
   of art, 466–468
   of bride price, 387
   latent, 249
   manifest, 249
   of marriage and the family, 377–378
   versus motives, 248–249
   social
      of dance, 472–473
      of religion, 446–448
Future shock, 497

# G

Gametes, chromosome complement of, 64
Ganda (Uganda), 445
Garbage Project, 174, 208–210
Garbology for study of alcohol consumption, 396
Gardner, Allen, 289
Gardner, Beatrice, 289
Gardner, Burleigh, 42
*Gayellow Pages*, 285
Geertz, Clifford, 13
Gender
   in kinship systems, 357
   specialization of labor and, 219

*See also* Females; Males; Matrilineal descent; Patrilineal descent; Women
Genealogy, 276
   in Mayan glyphs, 204
Gene flow, 65
Generalization, and evolutionary survival, 67
Generalized reciprocity, 339–341
Generation, in kinship systems, 357
Genes, 58–73
   for hemoglobin, 140–141
Genetic change
   adaptation through, 68
   and natural selection, 62
Genetic code, 63
Genetic drift, 65, 69–70
   and variation in blood types, 139
Genetics, 5
   Mendelian, 65
Genitor versus social father, 386
Genocide, prevention of, 500–501
Genotypes, 60
   and response to infectious diseases, 153
Geoarchaeology, 174, 175
Gestation, typical primate times for, 92–93
Ghost invocation, 411
Ghostly vengeance, 411
Gibbons, 87–88
Girdner, Linda, 373–374
Gisu (East Africa), 411
Glaciation, effects of, in North America, 215
Glyphs, 204
Goiter, 158
*Golden Bough, The* (Frazer), 245
Goodall, Jane, 91, 95
Goode, William, 393
Goodenough, Ward, 254
Gorer, Geoffrey, 42
Gorillas, 84
   gestation period, 92
   social system of, 89–90
Gould, Stephen Jay, 161
Governments, responsibility to, 47
Graebner, Fritz, 242–244
Grammar, and language, 292–293
Graphic and plastic arts, 468–469
Grave goods, 221
Grid for recording context of an excavation, 177
Grinding stones, inferences from presence of, 195
Group personality, 250
Group solidarity, as a function of religion, 447–448
Guanine, 62
Guidelines
   for conducting interviews, 274–275
   for participant-observation fieldwork, 271–272
Gummivores, 91

*Gurumai*, 421
Gusii (Kenya), 384

# H

Hadar (Ethiopia), *Homo erectus* fossils
    from, 121
Hadza (Tanzania), 21, 26–27, 426
    economic behavior of, 335
    and territoriality, 333
Hagen, Everett, 490
Hair, color of, 136–137
Haiti, reforestation in, 258–259
Half life, of radioisotopes, 102
Hall, Edward T., 267, 302
Hamadryas baboons, social system of, 89
Hammurabi Code, and legal subordination
    of women, 432
Hand gestures, as communication, 301
Handsome Lake (Seneca leader), 457
Haploid chromosome complement, 64
Harem
    of hamadryas baboons, 89
    primate social system, 88
Harner, Michael, 451
Harpoons, barbed, 132
Harris, Marvin, 335, 449
Harris lines, 159
Haury, Emil, 225
Hawaiian society
    as a chiefdom, 403–404
    kinship system, 365–366
        diagram, 367
Headman in band societies, 400
Health
    and agricultural development, 200
    in ancient cities, 204
    contribution of biological anthropology
        to, 501
    inferring for populations of the past,
        159
    precautions in fieldwork, 265
    prediction of, 124–125
    and religious beliefs, 461–462
    vaccination and cultural practices,
        421–422
    *See also* Genetics; Infectious diseases;
        Medical anthropology
Hecht, Robert, 371
Heizer, Robert, 182
Hemoglobin, point mutation in sickle-cell
    anemia, 64
Hereditary chiefships, 403
Herero people (Namibia), extermination
    of, 502
Herskovits, Melville, 11
Heterodontism of Mammalia, 78–79
Heterozygous characteristics, 60
Hewitt, E. L., 479–480

Hierarchy
    in chimpanzee groups, 91
    kinship based, 94
    in primate groups, 86
    in traditional Hawaiian society, 403
*Hija* (exchange of insults), 478–479
Hindus
    arranged marriage among, 381
    caste system, 430–432
    economics of customs, 335
Historical archaeology, 7, 174, 230
Historical linguistics, 7
History of applied anthropology, 42–46
*History of Art* (Janson), 465
Hoebel, E. Adamson, 415
Hohokam (Arizona), 225–226
Holism, 11, 13, 40, 502–503
    cultural, 489
    and study of complex societies, 499
Holmberg, Allan, 44
Hominidae, 78, 84
Hominids, origin of, 108–110
*Hominoidea*, 84
*Homo erectus*, 108, 193
    as ancestor to *Homo sapiens*, 128
    fossil record of, 120–122
    use of fire by, 112
*Homo habilis*, 108
    fossil record of, 118–120
Homoiothermy of Mammalia, 78–79
Homology, basis for phyletic taxonomy, 77
*Homo sapiens*, 86, 108, 128–149
*Homo sapiens sapiens*, 214
Homozygous characteristics, 60
Hooton, E. A., 52
Hopewell ceremonial complex, 221
Hopewell Interaction Sphere, 221–222
Hopi Indians, 337
    language of, 296
Horizontal function of kinship, 355
Horticulture, 308, 315–317
    and territoriality, 333–334
Hostetler, John, 460–461
Household as a production unit, 336
Housing
    and cultural patterns, 389
    design of, and culture, 33–34
Howler monkeys, social system of, 89
Human Genome Diversity Project, 144
Human Genome Project, 144
*Human Organization* (periodical), 42
Human Relations Area Files (HRAF),
    254–255, 274
Humans
    classification of, 78–79
    gestation period of, 92
    primate-like behaviors of, 91–96
    variation among, 3–6
    *See also* Populations; Primate
Hunters and gatherers, 308, 310–314

generalized reciprocity among, 340
and territoriality, 333
*See also* Food-getting strategies
Hunting strategies of Netsilik Eskimos,
    313
Hydraulic theory of state formation, 205
Hylobatidae, 84
Hyoid bone, and language, 112
Hypothesis, 238
    formulation of, 266–267
    and taxonomy, 76
Hypoxia, at high altitude, 138

# I

Identity in terms of lineage, 363
Ideology, and state systems, 404
Ilium, and bipedalism, 108
Immune function, and size of vertebral
    canal, 125
Impact assessor, applied anthropology, 39
Implementation, applied anthropology,
    42–46
Inbreeding theory, 379
Incest
    avoidance of, among primates, 94
    taboo against, 378–380
        application to clan members, 364
Inclusive fitness, 66
Incorporation, rites of passage for, 451, 452
Independent variable, 268
Indian Affairs, Bureau of, 38
Indian Reorganization Act (1934), 42
Indigenous peoples, endangered populations
    of, 499–501
Individualistic cults, 449–450
Individuals
    and culture, 31
    focus of modernity on, 490
    property rights of, 334
Indonesia, traditional economy in, 325
Inductive approach, defined, 244
Industrialization, 308
Industrial Revolution, and agriculture, 321
Infancy, 163–165
Infectious diseases
    increase in
        native Americans after colonization, 228
        with sedentism, 200
    response to
        and blood type, 139
        and evolution, 153
        and hemoglobin allele, 140–141
    in Teotihuacan, 204
    *See also* Health
Informants for fieldwork, 29
Informed consent of research subjects, 47
Inheritance
    particulate theory of, 60

Outline of Cultural Materials, 274
Overfield, Theresa, 148
Ovulation
    human and primate, 92, 113–114
    requirement of body fat for, 165–166
Oxytocin, 62–63

# P

Pace of fieldwork, 271–272
Paleoanthropology, 4, 102
    taxonomies established in, 76–77
Paleoindian period, 217–218
Paleomagnetism, 103
Paleoprimatology, 102
Palynology, 175
    of Chaco Canyon, 227
Pan-tribal mechanisms of political organiza-
        tion, 401–402
Parallel cousins, 358, 366
    and preferential cousin marriage, 382
Parapithecidae, 106
Parental care in primate populations, 93
Parker, Patricia, 50–51
Parsons, Talcott, 260
Participant-observation, 36, 40, 245, 269,
        270–272, 282–283, 348, 497
    advantages and disadvantages of, 272
Particularistic values, 260
Particulate theory of inheritance, 60
Pastoralism, 308, 317–319
    and territoriality, 333
Paternal care, among primates, 93
Patrilineal descent
    defined, 359–360
    in the Omaha kinship system, 366
Patrilineal family, extended, 392–393
Patrilocal residence, 390
Patterns of Culture (Benedict), 250
Payson Project, 34
Peasantry, 320–321
Pellagra, 156
Pelvis, reorientation of, and bipedalism, 163
Pendejo Cave (New Mexico), 217
People's Temple movement, 458
Pequots
    Mashantucket, 234
    massacre of, 500
Perception
    and culture, 22–23
    and language, 296–297
Perineal area, estrus-related changes in, 92
Permanence of marriage, 376
Perry, W. J., 242–244
Persistence hunting, 112–113
Personal gratification, and art, 466–467
Personality
    and culture, 250
    and friendship among primates, 94
Peruvian Institute of Indigenous Affairs, 44

Pfeiffer, John, 12
Phenetic system, 77
Phenotypes, 60
    ABO blood group, 139
Pheromones, 92
Philosophy, value-free, 43
Phonemes, 292
Phonology, 292
Photography
    ethnographic films, 276
    still, 276–277
Phratries, 362
Phyletic gradualism, 69–70
Phyletic system, 77
Phylogeny, 77
    of australopithecines, 118–122
Physical anthropology, 2, 3, 4–6
    application to gun turret design, 51–52
    evidence for date of migration to the
        Americas, 217
Physical variations, among humans, 5–6
Piece plotting, 177
Pithouses, 225
Planner, applied anthropologist as, 39
Play, 165
Plesiadapiforms, 105
Point mutations, 63–64
Polela Health Center (Zulu), 348
Policy research
    in applied anthropology, 39
    by cultural anthropologists, 45
    functionalist versus conflict theorists' view,
        436
Political systems, 400–422
    centralized, in state societies of Mesoamer-
        ica, 203–204
    coerciveness in, 408
    and religious forms, 454–455
    variations in, 405–407
Polyandry, 386
    among primates, 86
Polygenic traits, 138
Polygyny, 383–385
    and education, 499
    legal recognition of, 419
    among the Malinke, 372
    and sexual dimorphism, 114
Pongidae, 78, 84
Population biology, 5
Population control, 498–499
Population Council, 38
Population pressure, and the Neolithic Revo
        lution, 199
Populations
    of African origin, in the United States, 229
    as classification units, 144
    differences in responses to medication,
        148–149
Positive sanctions, 407
Potassium-argon dating, 102, 179
Potlatch, 344

as a mechanism for validating rank, 427
Pottery making, 195–196
    adaptation of ancient styles, 480
    fiber tempering, 218
    grit tempering, 220
    Hohokam, 226
    in Mesoamerica, 196
    shell tempering, 222–223
    by slaves in the United States, 229
    in the Southwestern U.S., 225
Power, and social inequality, 424
Practical anthropology. See Applied
        anthropology
Predictability of food supplies, and agricul-
        tural development, 199
Preferential cousin marriage, 381–382
Pregnancy, cultural responses to, 161
Prehensility, 80
Prehistoric archaeology, 7
Prehistory, 192–212
Prestige
    in rank societies, 426
    and social inequality, 424
Priests, in ecclesiastical cults, 454–456
Primates
    characteristics of, 76–86
    communication among, 288–290
    Eocene, 105
        diet of, 155
    Miocene, 107–108
        diet of, 155
    Oligocene, 105–107
    Paleocene, 105
    social systems of, 86–96
    suborders of, 81–86
Primatology, 4
Primitive art, 465
Processes
    of cultural change, 23–24
    of cultural diffusion, 242
    Neolithic Revolution, 193
Production, 330
    economics of, 334–339
    kinship-based, 373
    units of, 335–336
Productivity
    in agriculture, 320
    and food supply, 308
    traditional values concerning, 326–327
Professional code of ethics, 46
Profits, maximization of, 330
Progesterone, population differences in levels
        of, 149
Project Camelot, 46–47
Proletariat, 435
Property rights
    individual versus communal, 334
    regulation of, in terms of lineage, 363
    in the United States, 332
Propliopithecidae, 106
Protein

animal
consumption by humans, 112, 197
ability to metabolize, 155
complete, from maize and beans, 222
Protestant Reformation, as a revitalization
movement, 458
Proto-state society, Cahokia, 224
Provenience, 174–175
Proxemic analysis, 276
Psychic unity, 242, 253
Psychological anthropology, 249
defined, 8
Psychological functions of religion, 448
Psychological reductionism, 249
Puberty, factors affecting, 165
Pubic bone, and bipedalism, 108
Public archaeology, 36, 187
Public opinion, 408–409
Public responsibility of anthropologists, 47
Pueblo Bonito, 227
Pueblo people, 225
culture of, 227
Pueblos, 226–228
Punan (Indonesia), forest collectors,
325–326
Punctuated equilibrium, 69–70
Purdah, 432, 433
Pygmies (Central Africa)
Mbuti
negative reciprocity among, 342
sexual equality among, 433
production of, 334

## Q

Quadrupedal walking, 59

## R

Race, 5
concept of, 142–145
*See also* Populations
Radcliffe-Brown, Alfred Reginald, 246–247
Radiocarbon dating, 179–180
Rajputs (India), 393
Ramapithecines, 108
Rani Khera village, study of, 380
Rank societies, 426–427
defined, 425
Raptorial bird, 221, 224
Rathje, William, 208
Reality, construction from language, 297
Receptivity to new experiences, 490
Recessive traits, 59–62
Reciprocal exchange, in marriage observ-
ances, 389–390
Reciprocity, 245–246, 339–342
and allocation of resources, 333
in cultural diffusion, 484

defined, 330–331
among moieties, 362
Recombination, genetic, 64–65
Redistribution
in chiefdoms, 403
defined, 330–331
as an exchange principle, 342–344
in rank societies, 426
Regional expertise, 40, 41
Reincarnation, Hindu caste system, 431
Reindeer Tungus (Siberia), 451
Reining, Priscilla, 324–325
Relative age, 358
Relative dating
of fossils, 102–103
at a research site, 179
Relative values, and change, 488–489
Religion, 442–462
Anasazi, 227
and art, 467
early theocratic states, 206
versus other cultural behavior, 442
and political power, 224
in state societies of Mesoamerica,
203–204
in Sumer, 202
in traditional Hawaiian society, 404
types of organizations, 448–456
Religions of the world (map), 454–455
Remote sensing, 176
Replacement with interbreeding model for
the origin of *Homo sapiens*, 128
Replication, and research planning, 55–56
Reproduction
effect of high altitude on, 138
and evolutionary survival, 58–59
hominid, 113–114
and natural selection, 65
primate characteristics, 92–93
Research, 13–15
archaeological, 175–184
clearance for, 266
design of, 267–268
ethnolinguistic, 296
informed consent of subjects, 47
responsibility toward subjects, 47
selection of a topic for, 266–267
Research analyst, 39
Research clearance, 35
in field work, 271
Research proposal, 34
Residence patterns, in marriage, 390–391
Resistivity, ground, for surveying sites, 177
Resources
allocation of, 332–334
cultural management of, 14
Responsibility, ethical, 47
Revitalization movements (religious),
456–458
Richards, Audrey, 316
Rickets, 159

and exposure to sunlight, 136
Rites
of passage, 451–452
to adulthood, 166
for life-cycle events, 160
of solidarity, 452–453
Rituals, 55
burial, Hopewell, 222
calendrical, in ecclesiastical religions, 454
surrounding birth, 162–163
Ritual sacrifice, 442
Rivera, Oswaldo, 212
Rockefeller Foundation, 347
Rodriguez, Elroy, 98
Role ambiguity, created by incest, 379
Roles of anthropologists
applied, 39
in fieldwork, consistency of, 271
Royal Tombs of Ur, 202
Rules
cultural, of kinship systems, 355
of descent, 359

## S

Sacrum, and bipedalism, 108
Sagittal crest, 117
Salisbury, Richard, 50
Salvage archaeology, 36
Samburu (East Africa), 30, 424
integrated culture of, 30
production of, 334
Samoans (Polynesia), cummunal land tenure,
334
Sampling
an excavation, 178–179
for surveys, 176
Samuelson, Paul, 424
Sanctions, and social norms, 407–408
Sanitation, and disease, 154
Sapir, Edward, 249–250, 296
Sapir-Whorf Hypothesis, 296–298
Sargon, 203
Satanists, 445
Sauer, Norman, 147
Savagery stage of cultural evolution, 239
Savannah baboons, social system of, 91
Savings and investment, in pastoral society,
331
Scaglion, Richard, 418–419
Scavenging, and human adaptation, 113
Schmidt, Wilhelm, 242–244
School of American Research, 479–480
Science, and modernity, 493
Scientific classification, 77–78
Scrimshaw, Susan, 52–54
Scurvy, 155, 159
Sedentism, 195, 196, 199
evidence of
Southwestern U.S., 225

## U

Ubelaker, Douglas, 125
Ujamaa projects, Tanzania, 324–325
UNESCO, transfer of cultural properties, 184
Unilineal descent groups, 359–363
    as corporate entities, 362–363
    and the Iroquois kinship system, 366
Unilinear evolution, 252
Units of production, 335–336
Universal evolution, 252
Universal functions, 247–248
Universalism, 493
Universals, cultural, 29
Unstructured interviews, 273
Untouchables in the Hindu caste system, 430
Upper class, defined, 429
Upper middle-class, defined, 429
Upper Paleolithic, 130
    cultural advancement in, 132–134
Ur
    excavation of, 203
    Royal Tombs of, 202
Uranium 238, dating fossils with, 102
Urban anthropology, defined, 8
Urbanism, theory of, 13
Urbanization, and the extended family, 393
Urban Revolution, 192, 200–207
USAID, agricultural development, 371–373
Use-wear analysis, archaeological research, 181

## V

Validity, of data obtained by interviews, 275
Value-free philosophy, 43
Values
    and cultural change, 24, 488–489
    cultural definition of, 247
    and cultural relativism, 26, 40
    effect of, on nutrition, 158–159
    particularistic, 264
    and professional judgment, 43
    See also Ethics
Variables
    in cultural diffusion, 484

independent and dependent, 268
Variation, human, 144. See also Diversity
Varna, category in Hindu society, 430
Venuses, cave art, 133
Verbal arts, 474–477
Verguenza (embarrassment), 53
Vertebrata subphylum, human place in, 78
Vertical clinging and leaping, 82
Vertical function of kinship, 355
Vicos Project, 44–45
Vietnamese, extended families, 393–394
Vision quest, among Plains Indians, 449
Vitamin C, synthesis of, in animals, 155
Vitamin D, synthesis of, and skin pigmentation, 136
Viviparity of Mammalia, 78–79
Voluntaristic theory of state formation, 406
Vugusu (Kenya), 389

## W

Wa (Japanese concept of group harmony), 475
Walking survey, 176
Wallace, Anthony, 448–449, 456
Warfare
    and demise of Mayan urban centers, 206
    development of, 206
Warner, W. Lloyd, 42
Washington Area Association of Professional Anthropologists (WAPA), 46
Washoe, 289
Waste Isolation Pilot Plant (WIPP), 189
Water control systems
    Anasazi, 227
    See also Irrigation
Watson, Patty Jo, 219–220
Wealth
    in !Kung society, 312
    and polygyny, 384
    and social inequality, 424
Weber, Max, 260, 424, 490
Wernicke's area, 110–111
White, Leslie, 251–252
Whorf, Benjamin Lee, 296
Wills, W. H., 220

Wilson, Allan, 129
Wilson, E. O., 72
Windover site (Florida), 218
Wisconsin v. Yoder, 460–461
Witchcraft, 445–446
    and social control, 411
Wittfogel, Karl, 205
Woman exchange, 388–389
Women
    economic status in polygynous societies, 383–384
    in ethnology, 245
Woodland period, 220–221
Woolley, Sir Leonard, 203
Work, traditional values concerning, 326–327
Working class, defined, 429
World Ethnographic Sample (Murdoch), 387, 388, 389, 390, 392
World Health Organization (WHO), 38
World view (ethos), and language, 487
World War II, applied anthropology during, 42
Wrangham, Richard, 98–99
Written historical documents, 201
WT17000 fossil, 117

## Y

Yako (Nigeria), 363
Yanomamo (Venezuela, Brazil), 278, 475–476

## Z

Ziggurat, 202
Zihlman, Adrianne, 109
Zinjanthropus, 117
Zooarchaeology, 175
Zoos, social groups in, 87
Zulu (South Africa), health center, 348–349
Zuni, 250
    archaeological agency of, 234
Zygotes, 62

## Chapter 6

101 Gary Ferraro; 103 Precision Graphics, Inc.; 104 Reprinted by permission from p. 395 of *Introduction to Physical Anthropology* 5/e by Harry Nelson and Robert Jurmain. © 1991 West Publishing Company. All Rights Reserved; 107 Precision Graphics, Inc.; 109 Precision Graphics, Inc.; 111 Reprinted by permission from p. 425 of *Introduction to Physical Anthropology* 5/e by Harry Nelson and Robert Jurmain. © 1991 West Publishing Company. All Rights Reserved; 113 Reprinted by permission from p. 245 of *Introduction to Physical Anthropology* 5/e by Harry Nelson and Robert Jurmain. © 1991 West Publishing Company. All Rights Reserved; 114 Precision Graphics, Inc.; 116 top © Tom McHugh/Photo Researchers, Inc., bottom United Press International/Bettmann; 117 © Janathan Blair All Rights Reserved/Woodfin Camp and Associates; 118 top © Cannon-Bonaventure/Anthro-Photo File, bottom Harry Nelson/Reprinted by permission from p. 392 of *Introduction to Physical Anthropology* 5/e by Harry Nelson and Robert Jurmain. © 1991 West Publishing Company. All Rights Reserved; 119 Precision Graphics, Inc.; 120 top Reproduced with the permission of the National Museums of Kenya. Copyright reserved; courtesy of Alan Walker, bottom © Tom McHugh/Field Museum of Chicago/Photo Researchers, Inc.; 121 Reprinted by permission form p. 403 of *Introduction to Physical Anthropology* 5/e by Harry Nelson and Robert Jurmain. © 1991 West Publishing Company. All Rights Reserved; 122 top Reproduced with the permission of the National Museums of Kenya. Copyright reserved; courtesy of Alan Walker, bottom Reprinted by permission from p. 491 of *Introduction to Physical Anthropology* 5/e by Harry Nelson and Robert Jurmain. © 1991 West Publishing Company. All Rights Reserved

## Chapter 7

127 © George Holton/Photo Researchers, Inc.; 128 Precision Graphics, Inc.; 131 left Reprinted by permission from p. 527 of *Introduction to Physical Anthropology* 5/e by Harry Nelson and Robert Jurmain. © 1991 West Publishing Company. All Rights Reserved; 131 right © Fred Smith/Musée de L'homme;133 © 1972 Tom McHugh/Photo Researchers, Inc.; 135 From C. S. Coon and E. E. Hunt, *The Living Races of Man* © Copyright 1965 Alfred A. Knopf, Inc. and reprinted by permission from p. 157 of *Introduction to Physical Anthropology* 5/e by Harry Nelson and Robert Jurmain, © 1991 West Publishing Company. All Rights Reserved; 136 Precision Graphics, Inc.; 137 © George Holton/Photo Researchers, Inc.; 141 top Courtesy of D. E. Schreiber, IBM Research Laboratory, San Jose/Reprinted by permission from p. 128 of *Introduction to Physical Anthropology* 5/e by Harry Nelson and Robert Jurmain. © 1991 West Publishing Company. All Rights Reserved, bottom Reprinted by permission from p. 129 of *Introduction to Physical Anthropology* 5/e by Harry Nelson and Robert Jurmain. © 1991 West Publishing Company. All Rights Reserved; 142 © David Austen 1985 All Rights Reserved/Woodfin Camp and Associates; 143 left © Labat-Y. A. Bertrand, Agence Vandystadt/Photo Researchers, Inc., right © Jose Azel/ Contact, All Rights Reserved/Woodfin Camp and Associates

## Chapter 8

151 © Snowdon/Hoyer Focus/Woodfin Camp and Associates; 152 © Cyril Toker/Photo Researchers, Inc.; 154 © Jeffrey D. Smith, All Rights Reserved/Woodfin Camp and Associates, Inc.; 156 Precision Graphics, Inc.; 159 both Precision Graphics, Inc.; 160 Precision Graphics, Inc.; 162 Precision Graphics, Inc.; 163 Precision Graphics, Inc.; 164 Precision Graphics, Inc.; 166 © Jose Azel/Contact Press 1989/Woodfin Camp and Associates, Inc.; 167 Bettmann

## Chapter 9

173 © Cannon/Anthro Photo; 175 Bettmann; 176 © 1989 Georg Gerster/Comstock; 177 Janet Levy; 178 left Modely/Anthro Photo, right Precision Graphics, Inc.; 179 Pictures of Record, Inc.; 180 Precision Graphics, Inc.; 181 Gibson/Anthro Photo; 182 Stock Montage, Inc.; 184 Laden/Anthro-Photo File; 185 Arkansas Archaeological Survey

## Chapter 10

191 © Kal Muller All Rights Reserved/Woodfin Camp and Associates; 192 Precision Graphics, Inc.; 194 both Precision Graphics, Inc.; 195 top © F. Burian and E. Friednan/Anthro Photo, bottom © 1988 Pictures of Record, Inc.; 197 top Precision Graphics, Inc., bottom © Teas/Anthro Photo; 198 © Nichter/Anthro Photo; 201 © 1976 Photo Researchers, Inc.; 202 top © William Curtsinger/National Geographic Society/Photo Researchers, Inc., bottom © 1991 Georg Gerster/Comstock; 203 © Richard Reed/Anthro Photo; 205 © Robert Feldman All Rights Reserved/Antho Photo

## Chapter 11

213 © 1980 Pictures of Record, Inc.; 214 © 1993 Pictures of Record, Inc.; 215 Precision Graphics, Inc.; 216 Precision Graphics, Inc.; 218 Brain/AnthroPhoto; 219 Precision Graphics, Inc.; 220 © 1982 Pictures of Record, Inc.; 221 © Pictures of Record, Inc.; 222 © 1980 Pictures of Record, Inc.; 223 Aerial Photography, Ltd.; 224 © William H. Allen, Jr.; 225 Precision Graphics, Inc.; 226 Mimbres bowls, ca. A.D. 1050–1140, Douglas Kahn, Photographer, Courtesy Museum of Indian Arts and Culture/Laboratory of Anthropology, Santa Fe, NM; 227 © Myron Wood/Photo Researchers, Inc.; 228 Janet Levy

## Chapter 12

237 Zefa-U.K./H. Armstrong Roberts; 241 © Brown Brothers; 243 Blumebild/H. Armstrong Roberts; 245 UPI/Bettmann Archives; 248 Bill Gillette/Stock Boston; 249 John Coletti/Stock Boston; 251 Bettmann Archives; 252 H. Armstrong Roberts; 255 Gary Ferraro

## Chapter 13

259 Edward Tronick/Anthro-Photo #4058; 261 left M. Spector/H. Armstrong Roberts; right © P. Maitre/Viesti Associates; 264 Edward Tronick/Anthro-Photo #5929; 269 Cannon/Anthro-Photo #0046; 270 K. Scholz/H. Armstrong Roberts; 271 Crawford/Anthro-Photo #6037; 273 George Riley/Stock Boston; 274 Napoleon Chagnon/Anthro-Photo #6281

## Chapter 14

283 © M. Renaudeau/Viesti Associates; 285 H. S. Terrace/Anthro-Photo; 290 Lionel Delevingne/Stock Boston; 293 Russell T. Loesch/Stock Boston; 295 Camerique/H. Armstrong Roberts; 297 Gary Ferraro; 298 Irven DeVore/Anthro-Photo #6272; 299 © Henry Larsen, Public Archives, Canada

## Chapter 15

303 Zefa/H. Armstrong Roberts; 305 top Bob Daemmrich/Stock Boston, bottom J. Morgan/Anthro-Photo; 309 Tom Walker/Stock Boston; 310 Tim Ashe/Anthro-Photo #0356; 311 Charles Gupton/Stock Boston; 312 David Austen/Stock Boston; 313 Kamal Sahai from *Crafts of Jammu, Kashmir, and Ladakh* published by Grantha Corporation,

80 Cliffedgeway, Middletown, NJ 07701, USA in association with Mapin Publishing Pvt.Ltd., Ahmedabad. Copyright © Grantha Corporation; **314** Ferraro; **316** Scherer/Miller/H. Armstrong Roberts

## Chapter 16

**325** K. Reno/H. Armstrong Roberts; **327** Michael Grecco/Stock Boston; **328** Fredrik Bodin/Stock Boston; **331** Charles Gupton/Stock Boston; **333** Kamal Sahai from *Crafts of Jammu, Kashmir, and Ladakh* published by Grantha Corporation, 80 Cliffedgeway, Middletown, NJ 07701, USA in association with Mapin Publishing Pvt.Ltd., Ahmedabad. Copyright © Grantha Corporation; **336** Stan Washburn/Anthro-Photo #5693; **339** © 1989, Paula Keller, The Salvation Army; **341** H. Armstrong Roberts

## Chapter 17

**349** James Holland/Stock Boston; **350** Schuler/Anthro-Photo #4101; **352** R. Rober/H. Armstrong Roberts; **355** Irven DeVore/Anthro-Photo #2165

## Chapter 18

**371** H. Armstrong Roberts; **373** H. Armstrong Roberts; **376** H. Armstrong Roberts; **378** John Elk/Stock Boston; **381** UPI/Bettmann Archives; **382** Ferraro; **386** D. Degnan/H. Armstrong Roberts; **388** G. Tortoli/H. Armstrong Roberts; **390** Frank Siteman/Stock Boston

## Chapter 19

**395** H. Armstrong Roberts; **398** Dolder/Huber/H. Armstrong Roberts; **400** R. Kord/H. Armstrong Roberts; **403** Camerique; **406** David Woo/Stock Boston; **408** Joan Bamberger/Anthro-Photo #5188; **410** Gary Ferraro; **411** H. Armstrong Roberts

## Chapter 20

**419** © D. Laine/Viesti Associates; **421** © Stan Washburn/Anthro-Photo; **423 left** H. Armstrong Roberts, **right** David Woo/Stock Boston; **425** Chromosohm Media/Stock Boston; **427** Cary Wolinsky/Stock Boston; **428** K. Scholz/H. Armstrong Roberts; **430** © Joe Viesti/Viesti Associates

## Chapter 21

**437** David Austen/Stock Boston; **440** J. Farber/H. Armstrong Roberts; **442** Patrick Ward/Stock Boston; **443** A. Foley/H. Armstrong Roberts; **446** Irven DeVore/Anthro-Photo #4119; **448** Stuart Smucker/Anthro-Photo #6189; **449** Tobias Schneebaum; **452** Miro Vintoniv/Stock Boston

## Chapter 22

**459** Boutin/Zefa/H. Armstrong Roberts; **461** Terry Eiler/Stock Boston; **462** Camerique; **463** Ferraro; **464** H. Armstrong Roberts; **465** Kamal Sahai from *Crafts of Jammu, Kashmir, and Ladakh* published by Grantha Corporation, 80 Cliffedgeway, Middletown, NJ 07701, USA in association with Mapin Publishing Pvt.Ltd., Ahmedabad. Copyright © Grantha Corporation; **466** Steve Benbow/Stock Boston; **468** M. Koene/H. Armstrong Roberts; **469** Huber/H. Armstrong Roberts

## Chapter 23

**477** Adam Koons/Anthro-Photo #5124; **478** Courtesy of Sears, Roebuck, and Co.; **481** © Mary Altier, 1990; **484** J. Boisberranger/Viesti Associates; **488** © Dario Perla/International Stock Photography Ltd.; **489** Courtesy of NASA